Configuring SAP Financial Accounting

SAP S/4HANA Finance

Narayanan Veeriah

Configuring SAP Financial Accounting

SAP S/4HANA Finance

© Narayanan Veeriah
1st Edition, 2020

Acknowledgements

I acknowledge the understanding and adjustments made by my family, especially my wife, for all the encouragement and letting me concentrate working on this book, as with previous other books. I thank Narayanan Krishnan, who helps in checking out the content for its correctness.

Preface

This book on *'Configuring SAP Financial Accounting'* in *SAP S/4HANA Finance*, has been published in two volumes: Volume I and Volume II.

The Volume I (this book) covers:

- Case Study
- Enterprise Structure
- FI Global Settings I (Fields, Ledgers, Fiscal Year, Posting Period, Parallel Accounting, Integration of SAP CO with SAP FI, and Company Code Global Parameters)
- FI Global Settings II (Documents, Inflation Accounting and Correspondence)
- FI Global Settings III (Taxes including Extended Withholding Tax)
- G/L Accounting

The Volume II covers:

- Case Study
- Accounts Receivable and Accounts Payable
- Contract Accounts Receivable and Payable
- Bank Accounting
- Asset Accounting

(You can see the detailed coverage at the end of this book)

Here, in Volume I, you will see that an effort has been made to bring in the necessary context and relevance in the form of explanation on SAP HANA, SAP S/4HANA and SAP S/4HANA Finance, before actually discussing the configuration of SAP Financial Accounting.

The **Chapter 1** discusses on SAP HANA, bringing out the evolution of SAP application from SAP R/1, to SAP ERP, to the current form of SAP HANA 2.0. It helps you to trace the history of SAP HANA with its first introduction in 2008. It makes you to understand the HANA architecture and gives you a brief view of the options that are available for its deployment.

In **Chapter 2**, you are provided with an overview of SAP S/4HANA. You will understand why SAP S/4HANA is termed as the digital core of modern business. You will learn about the key benefits, the capabilities and the deployment options. You will also understand SAP's release and maintenance strategy with regard to SAP S/4HANA.

We shall be discussing SAP S/4HANA Finance in **Chapter 3**. You will learn about the overview, the primary capabilities and the key benefits of going in for SAP S/4HANA Finance. You will understand how SAP S/4HANA Finance can overcome the pain points, that were there in the traditional ERPs, in various application area of SAP FI.

As mentioned already, this book follows a case-study approach with a story-board technique, that provides you with the required business background for a given configuration activity. The **Chapter 4** discusses two case-studies (*Project Dolphin and Project Oyster*) in its entirety, setting up the tone for further discussions, in the remaining Chapters. You will, of course, come across the case study briefs, in each of the remaining Chapters, for each of the configuration activity, to provide the required context for that activity.

The **Chapter 5** deals with SAP enterprise structure. The Chapter focusses on SAP FI/CO organizational units, their definition and assignment.

The Chapters 6, 7 and 8 deal with FI global settings:

- The **Chapter 6** discusses fields, ledgers, field status variants, fiscal year and posting periods. It also discusses parallel accounting, integration of SAP Controlling with SAP FI. It deals extensively on configuring company code global parameters.
- In **Chapter 7**, you shall be primarily learning about documents. You shall learn about document structure, document types, posting keys, screen variants for document entry, rules for document change, bar code entry, tolerance groups, text IDs, summarization, default values, business transaction types, recurring entries, document parking and document archiving. You shall, also, learn about inflation accounting and correspondence.
- The **Chapter 8**, deals with taxes. It covers, in detail, the tax on sales and purchases; the settings required for calculation and posting. It deals with how to interface your SAP system with external tax application, Vertex, for managing tax on sales and purchases in USA. It also deals with withholding tax, including extended withholding tax: the settings and how to manage withholding tax changeover.

The last one (**Chapter 9**), covers SAP G/L Accounting in great detail. It covers the preparations required for creating the master data in the system including chart of accounts, account groups, sample accounts etc. It covers how to create and process G/L accounts. It, also, covers the configuration towards business transactions like document splitting, cross-company code transactions, open item clearing, balance interest calculation etc. It provides an insight into the various closing operations, and their settings in the system, as a part of periodic processing, besides helping you to prepare for 'going live'. It discusses the SAP G/L Information System, towards the end of the Chapter.

As with my other books on SAP, this book also follows a case-study approach to make your learning easy. Efforts have been taken, throughout the book, to guide you step-by-step in understanding how to configure your SAP system, to meet your exact business needs. Each configuration activity has been discussed with appropriate screen shots (from an SAP system) and illustrations to help you 'see' what is being discussed in that activity / step. You will see a lot of additional information, provided across the Chapters and the Sections, to help you understand a topic or a configuration setting or a concept better. The entire content of the book, vide various Chapters, has been presented as in SAP IMG (Implementation Guide), for easy comprehension. You will come across with appropriate menu paths and Transactions, to help you to navigate the various activities.

In all, you can use this book as a desktop-reference for configuring SAP FI. As the Chapters have been progressively elaborated, you will certainly find this as informative and easy to comprehend. The screenshots, in each of the Chapters, will help you understand the settings better and will lead to a happy learning.

Hope you will enjoy learning SAP Financial Accounting, through this book!

Contents at a Glance

Contents

1 SAP HANA

S AP, the world's leading *enterprise resource planning* (ERP) application, has been through several changes in its design and functionalities since its launch in 1972: from SAP R/1 to SAP R/2, SAP R/3, SAP HANA, SAP S/4HANA and very recently SAP HANA 2.0. In this Chapter, we will take you through the evolution of SAP application first, before getting to the details of SAP HANA. While dealing with SAP HANA, we will help you to understand the inception, the evolution (design and deployment), the architecture, the benefits & advantages, the various editions etc. At the end, we will also discuss SAP S/4 HANA 2.0.

Let us start with the evolution of the SAP application.

1.1 Evolution of SAP

Started by a group of five former employees of IBM, it was called *Systemanalyse und Programmentwicklung* in German, which translates into 'System Analysis and Program Development', popularly known as "SAP". The SAP R/1 was the initial release (1973) and was more of a financial accounting application, with the 'R' standing for 'real-time' data processing. The first technological improvement happened in 1979 leading to the release of SAP R/2 with the packaging of mainframe software application that processed and integrated all the functions of a business enterprise in real-time. In 1993, SAP brought out the client-server version of the software, SAP R/3, enabling businesses to run their operations more efficiently. Until 2001, there were several releases (like 4.0B, 4.0C, 4.5B etc.) to SAP R/3, with SAP R/3 4.6C being the final one released in 2001. SAP called the 4.70 release of the application as SAP R/3 Enterprise Release in 2003, SAP ECC 5.0 ERP (also called as mySAP ERP) in 2004 and SAP ECC 6.0 ERP in 2005. SAP then released the SAP Business Suite 7 (also known as SAP ERP 6) in 2009.

SAP came out with SAP HANA in 2010, offering the in-memory processing platform enabling customers to analyze data in seconds, which would otherwise take days or even weeks. The SAP HANA combines a robust database with services, enabling real-time business by bringing together the transactions and analytics into one, on an in-memory platform. You can run SAP HANA either 'on premise' or 'in the cloud'.

Let us now move on to understand more about SAP HANA in the next section.

1.2   SAP HANA

Historically, the transactional data and analytical data were stored separately in two different databases. Often, data needs to be moved from operational systems to data warehouses and retrieved later for data analysis resulting in considerable delay in the availability of processed data. To address this issue, SAP developed SAP HANA which is an in-memory, column-oriented, *relational database management system* (RDBMS) with its primary function (as a database server) of storing/retrieving data as requested by the applications and performing analytics as an application server.

Let us understand the evolution of SAP HANA, in the next Section.

1.3   History of SAP HANA

SAP, along with Hasso Plattner Institute and Stanford University, demonstrated in 2008, an application architecture for real-time analytics & aggregation, and called the same as 'HANA' (Hasso's New Architecture). For some time, before the name HANA became popular, the database associated with this architecture was known as 'new database', and the software was called as 'SAP High-Performance Analytic Appliance'.

The Table 1.1 provides you with the chronology of SAP HANA since its inception in 2008:

Year	Details
2008	SAP demonstrated the SAP HANA architecture
2010	1st product of SAP HANA
2011	SAP HANA support of SAP NetWeaver Business Warehouse
2012	(1) SAP HANA Cloud Platform as 'Platform as a Service' (2) SAP HANA One (with smaller memory)
2013	(1) SAP HANA Enterprise Cloud (a managed private cloud offering) (2) SAP Business Suite on SAP HANA (to run SAP ERP on SAP HANA platform
2015	SAP S/4HANA (a simplified business suite, combining the functionalities of ERP, CRM, SRM and others, into a single HANA system)
2016	SAP HANA 2.0 (enhanced database management & application management, besides including two new cloud services: Text Analysis & Earth Observation Analysis)
2018	SAP C/4HANA (integrated offering to modernize the sales-only focus of legacy CRM)

Table 1:1 History of SAP HANA

With this, let us understand the architecture of SAP HANA, in brief, next.

1.4   Architecture

The SAP HANA system, in a classical application context, consists of multiple components, including the index server, the name server and the preprocessor server (Figure 1.1).

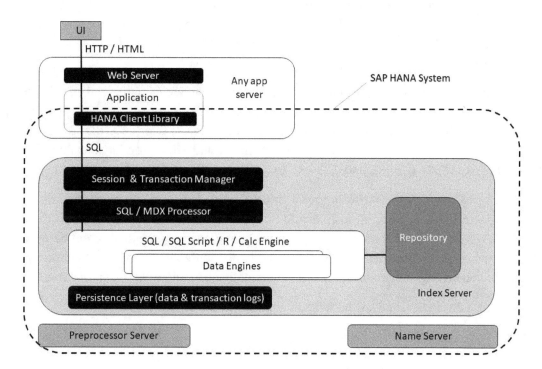

Figure 1.1: SAP HANA Architecture

1.   Index Server

The *'index server'* is the main SAP HANA database management component that contains the actual data stores and the engines for data processing. It processes (using SQL/MDX processor) incoming SQL or MDX statements in the context of authenticated sessions and transactions. Besides the data engines that handle all the SQL/MDX queries, the index server also contains a *'persistence layer'* responsible for durability and atomicity of transactions. It ensures that the SAP HANA system is restored back to the most recently saved state when there is restart, because of a system failure, with the transactions that are either completely executed or completely undone. It also contains the *'session & transaction manager'* that manages the transactions, besides keeping track of all running and closed transactions.

2.   Preprocessor Server

The index server uses the *'preprocessor server'* for analysing text data and extracting the information on which the text search capabilities are based.

3.   Name Server

The *'name server'* contains the system landscape information of the HANA system. In a distributed system, the name server knows where the components are running and which data is located on which server. It helps to minimize the time required for re-indexing.

The SAP HANA database has its own scripting language named *SQLScript*, which embeds data-intensive application logic into the database. The classical applications tend to offload only very limited functionality into the database using SQL. This results in extensive copying of data from and to the database, and in programs that slowly iterate over huge data loops and are hard to optimize and parallelize. SQLScript is based on side-effect free functions that operate on tables using SQL queries, and is therefore parallelizable over multiple processors.

Besides SQLScript, SAP HANA supports a framework for installation of specialized and optimized functional libraries, including SAP HANA *Business Function Library* (BFL) and SAP HANA *Predictive Analytics Library* (PAL), that are tightly integrated with different data engines of the index server. Both SQL and SQLScript are implemented using a common infrastructure of built-in data engine functions accessing meta definitions and SQLScript procedures.

With this let us look at the key benefits of going in for SAP HANA.

1.5   Key Benefits

The SAP HANA will be help you to:

- Accelerate response & analysis with in-memory processing, eliminating latency.
- Acquire & integrate data from various sources to boost visibility, besides increasing scalability and lowering complexity.
- Enable stakeholders work smarter, drawing insight from complex data sets and ongoing transactions without compromising data privacy.
- Usher in next wave of change with innovative new applications, supporting geospatial and streaming data.
- Maintain security and business continuity to keep business secure, minimize downtime, and support compliance with security standards.

The three major benefits that will accrue from SAP HANA are:

1. Reduced Complexity
SAP HANA will let you reduce & simplify IT landscape with just ONE platform, combining both transactional & analytical applications. It will bring in 'live data analysis' through its in-memory computing supporting business in real-time, reducing data redundancy, duplication, time lag, multiple hardware etc. The SAP HANA's revolutionary *in-memory database* will deliver required performance to run analytics without slowing down transactions, as it combines memory optimization with unified data.

2. Flexible Deployment
You can be as flexible as you want with SAP HANA deployment, and select the best option:

- If you want maximum control, then, you should opt for 'on-premise' deployment. Select either (a) *'on-premise: appliance'* option of a pre-configured solution of hardware & software for quick 'go-live' or (b) *'on-premise: tailored data center integration'* option to leverage existing IT infrastructure & reduce cost.
- To get the deployment faster, opt for 'cloud' deployment (public or private cloud). You may either (a) bring in your own license to run SAP HANA on the cloud platform of your choice via SAP HANA Infrastructure Services, or (b) go for a fully managed SAP HANA instances on the cloud (private or public).
- A 'hybrid' option combining best of 'on-premise' and 'in-cloud' deployments.

3. Better Business Outcomes
SAP HANA platform can help in creating significant value for your business, through real-time analytical insights. It can deliver applications and services by (a) simplifying operations using a single copy of enterprise data and a secured data platform, (b) processing transactions and analytics data using data virtualisation, integration or replication, and (c) leveraging advanced data processing engines.

Let us now discuss the details of various editions of SAP HANA

1.6   SAP HANA Editions

You will come across several editions (=options) with regard to the licensing and memory, while deploying SAP HANA.

In the case of 'on-premise', you have four editions:

- *SAP HANA Standard Edition*: a database for innovative use cases with the flexibility to go for advanced features as and when needed.
- *SAP HANA Express Edition*: free streamlined application package with up to 32GB of memory, with the provision for additional memory on payment of a licence fee

- *SAP HANA Runtime Edition*: a restricted platform designed exclusively to run SAP applications with limited use of advanced features
- *SAP HANA Enterprise Edition*: unrestricted platform for supporting innovation efforts and the use of SAP applications in modern hybrid environments

If you want to deploy your system 'in the cloud', then, you can try any of the following editions:

- *SAP HANA as a Service (Public Cloud):* this provides you with the on-demand access to the SAP HANA business platform with the latest capabilities for configuring an SAP HANA instance online and expanding the memory size seamlessly without interruption.
- *SAP HANA Enterprise Cloud (Private Cloud):* use this edition to deploy and manage an SAP HANA instance on an enterprise cloud managed by SAP, with the option to bring in your own on-premise licence or purchase subscription based licences.

With this, let us next understand the latest in SAP HANA namely SAP HANA 2.0.

1.7   SAP HANA 2.0

SAP released SAP HANA 2.0, in 2018. It was made up a mix of new and continuous innovations in the areas of data/database management, analytical and application fronts:

- The database enhancements bring in advanced data/privacy protection with additional algorithms, for better and configurable retention policies to enable improved audit functionalities. Some of the major enhancements include:
    - An increased system availability for business-critical applications.
    - A 'follow-the-sun' option with optimized latency for 'write' transactions. This can be achieved by rotating the primary system across the globe.
    - A fast-restart functionality using TMPFS (temporary file storage) at the OS Level that will reduce the restart times to a greater extent.
    - A new Native Storage Extension (NSE) that can enable denoting tables, columns or partitions as warm data.

> **i** The 'warm data' is loaded to an in-memory buffer cache as and when required for query processing.

- The data management enhancement includes high-availability *Hadoop* clusters and a general framework for *Smart Data Access*. The *Smart Data Integration* (SDI) now allows to group multiple agents, besides providing for real-time support for Mainframe DB2 and integration into *Web IDE*. SAP HANA 2.0 provides geocoding support for India addresses and FIAS compliant address assignments in Russia, to enhance data quality. For better data modeling, the *Enterprise Architecture Designer* (EAD) now supports SAP *Big Data Services, Hadoop Hive* 2.0 data lakes and HANA versioned tables. The *Calculation View* modeling (via Web IDE) now enables integrating data sources more easily than before.

- On the analytical front, the enhancements help increasing the execution performance and productivity for data analysis, by providing additional API's for *Python* and *R*. There is also a new *Gradient Boosting Tree* (GBT) algorithm. The new linear referencing methods, hexagonal grid-based aggregation and the labelling tools together with the new APIs, will allow more insight from geocoding. With SAP HANA 2.0, you can do more complex analysis and build scenarios with more flexibility, improved debugging and so on.

- The application development enhancements, in SAP HANA 2.0, include new functions for *SQLScript, SQL, SQLScript Debugger* and *Code Analy*zer enhancements, besides a vastly improved unit test framework. Now, the Web IDE with its improved editors, Python support, wizards etc, allows several workspaces and single import of synonyms. The *HANA Run Time Tools*, now, with its enhanced SQL console, enables more flexibility through session recovery, and performance improvements.

This completes our discussion on SAP HANA

1.8   Conclusion

You learned about the evolution of SAP, from SAP R/1 to the latest, the SAP HANA. You, then, went on to learn, in detail, about SAP HANA which is an in-memory, column-oriented, relational database management system with its primary function of storing / retrieving data, as requested by the applications and performing analytics as an application server. You, also, learned about SAP HANA's history and architecture, before moving on to learn about its benefits and editions ('on-premise' and 'in-cloud'). While learning about the 'on-premise' editions, you understood that there are four variants namely standard, express, runtime and enterprise editions. In addition, you understood that you could go in either for a public cloud (SAP HANA as a Service) or private cloud (SAP HANA Enterprise Cloud) in the case of 'in-cloud' editions. Finally, you learned about the latest in SAP HANA, the SAP HANA 2.0 and its innovations and improvements.

You will learn about SAP S/4HANA, in the next Chapter.

2 SAP S/4HANA

Launched in 2015, SAP S/4HANA is the short name for *'SAP Business Suite 4 SAP HANA'*, meaning that it is the fourth version of SAP Business Suite, designed to run only on SAP HANA. It is a simplified business suite, combining the functionalities of ERP, CRM, SRM and others into a single HANA system.

SAP S/4HANA is the nerve center (=the digital core) of your entire business, consolidating internal and external elements into a single, living structure that goes beyond traditional ERP. It connects all of your processes, provides you with live information and insights, and seamlessly integrates your enterprise with the digital world. Combining the core capabilities with the solutions in SAP portfolio for each line of business (LoB), SAP S/4HANA LoB solutions allow you to go beyond traditional transactions and drive digitized operations across all LoBs, based on a single source of information from planning, execution, prediction, simulation to analysis, all in real-time with one system. In short, it enables you to leverage today's digital world, by removing common obstacles associated with legacy ERP applications (like, batch latency, complex and/or multiple landscapes, and manual processes).

We shall discuss, in this Chapter, the benefits you will reap by going in for SAP S/4HANA, the key capabilities, the various deployment options, the release strategy, the implementation options and its integration with SAP solutions.

Let us start with the major benefits of going in for SAP S/4HANA.

2.1 Major Benefits

The major benefits include:

- Improved user experience across the entire organisation, including a context-aware, business-savvy digital assistant.
- Automating, through intelligent functionality and learning capabilities, key functions and signalling users when input is required.
- Empowering users to make better and faster decisions by unlocking new business value with the latest innovations

Let us move on to understand the major capabilities of SAP S/4HANA.

2.2   Capabilities

The important capabilities of SAP S/4HANA, as depicted in Figure 2.1, include:

Figure 2.1: SAP S/4HANA Capabilities

- *SAP S/4HANA for Finance*: helps you to understand financial performance in real time, to optimise finance processes (from planning & analysis to period end close, and treasury management) and ensures one source of the truth for finance and operational. We will discuss more about this in Chapter 3.
- *SAP S/4HANA Human Resources*: brings in operational alignment between HR and finance to optimize capabilities and align with the business, enables consolidated access to real-time data to provide insights and measures the business impact of HR and integrates end-to-end processes across financials and HR.
- *SAP S/4HANA for Supply Chain*: helps you to control of your supply chain for increased visibility and agility across the digital supply chain by leveraging machine learning for logistics, manufacturing, and asset management.
- *SAP S/4HANA for Sourcing and Procurement*: using intelligent applications with machine learning, it enables improved supplier management, streamlined purchasing, besides helping in deploying collaborative sourcing and contract

management. Coupled with SAP Ariba and SAP Fieldglass solutions, it enables companies to manage spend across every major category while reducing direct costs.

- *SAP S/4HANA Manufacturing*: enables to integrate and embed intelligence in manufacturing processes with one single source of live information, by providing an optimal coordination of planning and execution processes, covering all aspects of the manufacturing cycle from planning to shop floor.
- *SAP S/4HANA for Sales*: provides you with a complete picture of operations and enables using customer insights to help marketing, sales, and service teams to work more productively besides accelerating opportunities to grow revenue.
- *SAP S/4HANA Marketing*: helps in consolidating customer information into one enriched view, and leverages advanced analytics to gain insights. The high performance discovery and targeting tools enables to generate microsegments and group.
- *SAP S/4HANA Asset Management*: enables to manage the entire asset lifecycle, with real-time visibility into asset performance using powerful analytics. It makes it easier to optimize asset usage, lower risks and manage capital expenditures better.
- *SAP S/4HANA for Research and Development*: enables effectively managing product lifecycles through a fully aligned product portfolio thereby controlling costs.
- *SAP S/4HANA Service*: enables seamless transition between communication channels, without losing context by leveraging on-premise systems of record to resolve customer issues or execute service orders.

In the next Section, let us discuss about the deployment options for SAP S/4HANA.

2.3   Deployment Options

As already discussed in Chapter 1, you can deploy SAP S/4HANA 'on-premise' or 'in-cloud' (public or private) option:

- *On-premise*
  You can use your own infrastructure or an infrastructure-as-a-service (IaaS) provider. You will be able to customise and extend SAP S/4HANA with complete control of your environment when deployed on-premise.
- *In-cloud*
  You can leverage the advantages offered by the public cloud to meet your industry-specific needs or you can opt for custom requirements in a dedicated, private cloud (*SAP HANA Enterprise Cloud*) environment.

By going in for SAP HANA Enterprise Cloud, which is a fully scalable and secure service, you can accelerate the path to cloud readiness and transform into an intelligent enterprise. This private cloud offering from SAP provides you with the production availability spanning across your entire application and infrastructure stack. It comes with a full menu of functional and technical services (including guaranteed service levels and availability of IT stack), with the control you will otherwise expect on deploying the solution on-premise.

Now, we can move on to discuss about release and maintenance strategy for SAP S/4HANA.

2.4 Release and Maintenance Strategy

The release and maintenance strategy includes (i) how and when SAP S/4HANA releases are planned, (ii) how long these releases will be in mainstream maintenance, and (iii) what will happen thereafter. This will allow customers using the on-premise edition to benefit from the short innovation cycles of typical cloud deployments, while at the same time providing for long-term stability and investment protection. The strategy follows the principle of 'one innovation codeline': series of releases coming over time combine to form a continued innovation delivery based on an evolving codeline.

SAP delivers innovation through new releases and feature packages: while the annual new releases (also known as *'key releases'*) contain larger innovations, the feature packages (through FPS or *Feature Pack Stack*) are intended to include additional smaller functional enhancements.

Since its first release in 2015, SAP has been offering improvements and innovations in SAP S/4HANA through periodic releases. Instead of the traditional way of numbering the releases (say, ERP 6.0), the releases of SAP S/4HANA are now versioned according to the year and month with a four-digit number (YYMM) with the first two digits indicating the year (like, 17,18 etc) and the last two indicating the month of release (say,11,10,09 etc). So, for SAP S/4HANA 1909, the 1909 stands for September 2019.

> **i** For SAP S/4HANA on premise edition, SAP is currently delivering one new key release per year (say, 1809) and some successive FPS. Then, comes the next key release (say, 1909), followed by several FPS. While the FPS includes non-disruptive and optional innovations in addition to corrections and legal changes, the *Support Pack Stacks* (SPS) are shipped for a given release, once the N+1 release is made available, until the end of the mainstream maintenance. The first SPS of a new release may contain selected features and is labelled as FPS (Figure 2.2). SPS are compiled periodically and made available in the SAP *Service Marketplace*.

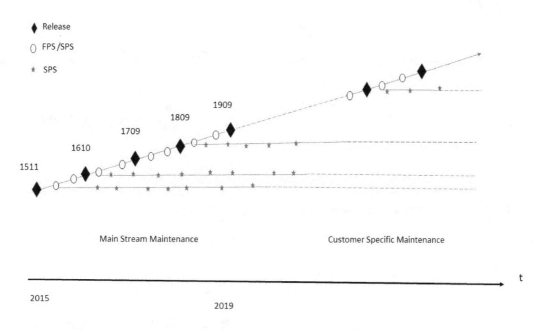

Figure 2.2: Releases, Future Pack Stacks (FPS) and Support Pack Stacks (SPS) in SAP

SAP currently intends to make available:

- One major delivery (release) a year
- Mainstream maintenance (of about five years) for each release
- Ongoing shipment of innovations (releases and feature packs)
- Support packages (SPS) during mainstream maintenance
- Customer-specific maintenance after mainstream maintenance

In SAP S/4HANA, there has been seven on-premise releases and 15 in-cloud release until now. As of September 2019, there were around 2300+ innovations related to SAP S/4HANA, 1000+ user experience innovations, and approximately 500+ innovations in digital transformation.

> **i** While SAP S/4HANA on-premise releases are once per year, SAP S/4HANA in-cloud releases are quarterly.

Let us now understand the release strategy for 2019/2020.

2.4.1   Release Strategy for 2019/2020

The Figure 2.3 displays the release strategy for SAP S/4HANA (on-premise) for year 2019 and beyond.

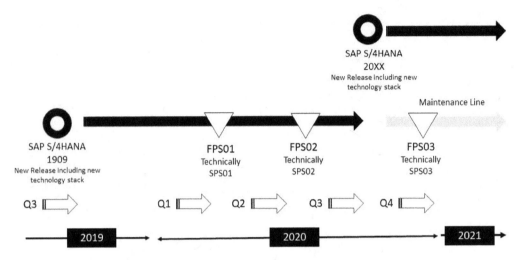

Figure 2.3: SAP S/4HANA Release Strategy for 2019 and beyond

With this, let us see the key innovations in Release 1909

2.4.2   Key Innovations in Release 1909 (SAP FI)

With SAP S/4HANA 1909 release, SAP's innovations are in the 5th wave. It has expanded the ERP core and re-architected the data model enabling customers to benefit from the latest innovations. The list of new capabilities / innovations in SAP S/4HANA 1909 has been extensive: in 2017, the number of SAP S/4HANA innovations was 966, in 2018 it was 2,389, and now, in 2019, it stands at a whopping 3,312. Parallelly, the user experience (UX) innovations have gone from 646 to 1,048, and to now 1,496.

Though the innovations in Release 1909 spans across several application areas like finance, manufacturing, sales & distribution, inventory management etc, we shall restrict our discussion only to finance (SAP /4HANA Finance):

- *The Financial Closing Processes*: Companies typically face a number of bottlenecks in the group close process which delay the time to close the books and report the financial results. SAP has brought in increased process efficiency both on entity and group level, for fast close. The *Group Reporting* in SAP S/4HANA, now, supports intercompany reconciliation and matrix consolidation.

- *Receivables Management*: In this area, the added value of specific cloud applications like *Cloud for Credit Integration, Cloud for Customer Payments* and *Cloud for Digital Payments* not only decrease the cost of the invoice to cash process through the support of self-service scenarios and new payment methods, but also have a risk limiting aspect, ensuring organizations get better forward looking insights.
- *Treasury Management*: SAP has brought in several enhancements in the area of SAP *Treasury and Risk Management*, for example, highlighting the evolution regarding trading platform integration – but also the evolution on the level of treasury reporting and planning.
- *Analytics*: In SAP FI, SAP now ships financial planning with *SAP Analytics Cloud (SAC)*. This helps finance professionals to analyze financial and non-financial information in a transparent way, based on the universal journal and the single source of truth.
- *Universal Allocation*: The new 'Universal Allocation' functionality, along with the universal journal, improves the operational setup and execution of allocations, as well as the transparency and traceability of costs across the organization.
- *Contract and Lease Management*: The new enhancements in the Contract and Lease Management will help users in simplifying lease processing and reporting with help of the integrated SAC.

We shall discuss more about these innovations is SAP S/4HANA Finance in Chapter 3. With this, let us have discuss the implementation options for SAP S/4HANA in the next Section.

2.5 Implementation

You can opt for a new installation of SAP S/4HANA or a system conversion (migration):

- Often referred to as the *'greenfield implementation'*, a new installation of SAP S/4HANA (on-premise or in-cloud) needs to run on the SAP HANA database. You can enhance this very simple landscape with the *SAP Cloud solutions* and *SAP Business Suite* products. to suit your specific business needs.
- You can also integrate SAP S/4HANA into an existing *SAP Business Suite* (ECC) landscape by replacing the SAP ERP with SAP S/4HANA. When performing this *conversion* in your system landscape, you need to do some adaptations; for example, you need to convert some of your existing business processes to the simplified SAP S/4HANA processes. You also need to be aware that some of the existing processes are no longer supported in SAP S/4HANA, some have changed, and there are new processes. Accordingly, you need to convert your existing processes to the SAP S/4HANA processes.

To move from SAP ECC to SAP S/4HANA, earlier, you had to follow an extended path to migrate. However, with system conversion option, now, it is possible to move directly from ECC 6.0 to SAP S/4HANA (say, 1909) on HANA 2 database, without going through the intermediary steps, irrespective of whether you plan to be in-cloud or on-premise (Figure 2.4)

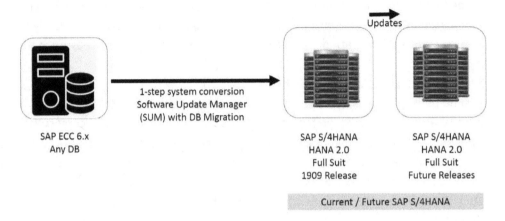

Figure 2.4: System Conversion to SAP S/4HANA

Let us discuss, next, the integration aspects of SAP S/4HANA with the other SAP solutions.

2.6 Integration with SAP Solutions

By integrating various SAP solutions with SAP S/4HANA, you can leverage those SAP solutions for making your business enterprise an efficient one. Let us see some of the solutions that you can integrate with SAP S/4HANA:

- SAP SuccessFactors Employee Central
  SAP S/4HANA will be the backend system on premise, when you use *SAP SuccessFactors Employee Central* as your system of records for HR master data. Here, SAP offers a 'full cloud' deployment and integration with predefined integration content. Supporting initial and delta data loads, the integration is web-service based and can be a scheduled middleware job.

- *SAP Fieldglass*
  SAP S/4HANA supports end-to-end business process integration for contingent labour and invoice-to-pay. This integration enables electronic transfer of master data (like, cost objects and organizational data) from SAP S/4HANA to *SAP Fieldglass* automatically.

- SAP Ariba Network
  You can leverage the purchase order and invoice automation scenario that offers business process integration between SAP S/4HANA (deployed on-premise), and the *SAP Ariba Network* cloud-based solution.

- SAP Hybris Cloud for Customer
  The integration of SAP Hybris Cloud with SAP S/4HANA enables you to transfer all master and transactional data, required for the opportunity-to-order processes. You can extract data like accounts, contacts, materials, prices etc. from SAP S/4HANA and transfer the same to SAP Hybris Cloud for Customer so that it is available for opportunity-to-order processes.

- SAP Financial Services Network
  You can connect your SAP S/4HANA system to *the SAP Financial Services Network* via *SAP HANA Cloud Integration* (HCI), enabling integrating A/P and A/R data for payment processes. The data such as payment collections is extracted from the SAP S/4HANA Financials system and transferred via the SAP Financials Service Network, which then connects you to your relationship banks so that the data is available for financial transaction interaction processes.

This completes our discussion on SAP S/4HANA.

2.7 Conclusion

You have, in this Chapter, learned that SAP S/4HANA is the digital core of the modern business enterprise, which consolidates internal and external elements into a single structure connecting all the processes, and providing you with live information and insights. You learned about the major benefits and its capabilities. You also learned about the deployment options (on-premise or in-cloud) of SAP S/4HANA with the associated advantages in each case, the release and maintenance strategy for SAP S/4HANA, the innovations that are brought into the release 1909, and the implementation considerations as to whether to go in for a greenfield project or system conversion. You also found out how you can integrate SAP S/4HANA with some of the key SAP solutions like SAP SuccessFactors Employee Central, SAP Ariba Network, SAP Hybris, SAP Fieldglass etc.

Let us now mow on to learn about SAP S/4HANA Finance, in the next Chapter.

3 SAP S/4HANA Finance

The finance & accounting processes and the erstwhile technical platforms, on which an ERP solution was running in the last couple of decades, were not agile enough and were simply not aimed at today's digital world. They were marked by disconnected silos of data processing and reporting that called for manual intervention at every step. The legacy technologies and the different ERP products limited the seamless integration across finance and other enterprise resource modules resulting in integration issues, outdated reports, data entry repetition, closing delays etc that prevented the businesses from taking timely actions.

SAP launched *SAP S/4HANA Finance* (formerly '*SAP Simple Finance*'), in 2015, to reimagine finance for the digital world. This ERP application is a simplified business suite, combining the functionalities of ERP, CRM, SRM and others into a single HANA system, replacing the earlier SAP system. Running on the in-memory platform of SAP HANA, this solution supports financial planning, general accounting, management accounting, accounts payable, accounts receivable, treasury & cash management, risk management, financial close and much more.

In this Chapter, you will learn about the overview, capabilities and benefits for SAP S/4HANA Finance. Let us start, first, with the overview of SAP S/4HANA Finance.

3.1 Overview

SAP S/4HANA Finance is a set of comprehensive financial solutions designed to help your business to meet the demands of today's digital economy. It is a part of the finance solution portfolio from SAP, that is built on a modern digital core of in-memory SAP HANA platform. It is the platform for the modern digital enterprise with advanced digital data architecture. This platform enables future innovations, a single source of the truth for both transactions and analytics, and a digital 'core' that integrates workforce, network, customer, and application extensions like as SAP Ariba, Concur, SAP SuccessFactors, and SAP Fieldglass solutions.

SAP S/4HANA Finance solution (a) covers all areas of finance enabling your finance professionals to transform the business / processes to compete in digital economy, (b) helps to remove bottlenecks in integration, and (c) enables an innovation-driven enterprise–wide simpler and more efficient IT operations. It delivers instant insights with real-time analysis across all dimensions of financial data, empowering you with contextual, live information for faster and better decision making.

SAP S/4HANA Finance comes equipped with a simple and intuitive user experience, offering one common, real-time view of financial and operational data for enterprise-wide consistency and reduces reconciliation time and errors. It also comes with the built-in ability to use prediction, simulation, and analysis to evaluate financial implications while optimizing business processes. It can deliver end-to-end business benefits across the five solution areas (=capabilities) within finance (see Section 3.2, for more details) besides improving the overall operations supporting business transformation.

SAP S/4HANA Finance is available for on-premise, in-cloud and hybrid deployments for both new implementation and existing business (conversion). With massive simplification and optimization within SAP S/4HANA, you can deploy SAP S/4HANA Finance with minimal business disruption and eliminate overly complex processes. You can achieve additional value by deploying solutions and templates within the *SAP Activate* methodology, standardizing master data using the *SAP Master Data Governance* application and focusing on the reduction or elimination of legacy custom code.

With this overview of SAP S/4HANA Finance, let us move on to understand its capabilities.

3.2   Capabilities

The primary capabilities of SAP S/4HANA Finance are depicted in Figure 3.1.

Figure 3.1: Primary Capabilities of SAP S/4HANA Finance

Let us understand them in detail:

3.2.1 Accounting and Financial Close

With the traditional ERP finance, you will encounter several pain points like (i) delayed closing activities that do not begin until period-end, (ii) several manual reconciliations / eliminations, required due to the prevalence of multiple ledgers / subledgers, preventing error-free depiction of intra-period business performance, (iii) delays in batch processing and post-closing activities leading delays in the completion of downstream dependent activities, (iv) separate closing and consolidation activities as the ERP and consolidation systems are often distributed, (v) inability to perform real-time inventory valuation as the valuation data resides in multiple aggregated tables, (vi) manual intervention during currency conversion due to limitation in number of local currencies and (vii) delayed reporting and lack of flexibility to respond to regulatory changes.

SAP S/4HANA Finance alleviates the above pain points as it (i) provides a foundation for soft-close with significant reduction in the need for period-end batch processing with the availability of single-source of data, extension ledger and the ability to derive profitability characteristics in real-time, (ii) comes with a single *universal journal* for data entry of G/L, controlling, asset accounting, material management etc, and revenue recognition process within the universal journal, enabling continuous and real-time reconciliation, (iii) enables more efficient consolidation process through the universal journal with its embedded real-time consolidation, (iv) removes redundancies and aggregates, with all inventory valuation data existing in material ledger, enabling faster actual costing (due to optimized code of SAP HANA), (v) provides for expanded currency support with real-time currency conversion, for all currency types, together with the freely definable currency functionality, (vi) enables live reporting with its predefined reports and configurable reporting tools leveraging G/L, subledgers etc, and (vii) streamlines reporting through a statutory reporting framework.

3.2.2 Finance Operations

Traditionally, the business processes (clearing, bad debt identification, credit risk management, invoice processing, vendor management etc) in various FI components like accounts receivable (A/R), accounts payable (A/P) etc, are often manual, disjointed across multiple solutions, reactive and consume significant time and effort. Also, there are difficulties in (i) setting up a single interconnected process to address some of these pain points, (ii) integrating 3rd party data for an end-to-end back-office processing in shared services, (iii) managing expense related processes that are often handled off-line across different systems making it nearly impossible to forecast, monitor or control expenses in real-time, and (v) managing the real-estate business processes that are disparate across multiple solutions, forcing the enterprises to spend unnecessary lease payments and the associated difficulties in adhering to IFRS 16 standards.

SAP S/4HANA Finance helps in addressing the bottlenecks in finance operations by (i) integrating with external data providers and other data sources to simplify and improve operations besides providing an intuitive user experience (UX) through *SAP Fiori*, (ii) streamlining payment processes through the *SAP Biller Direct*, (iii) integrating multiple A/P systems for a consolidated view of multiple invoices, suppliers, and vendors, (iv) a centralized liquidity planning leveraging SAP C*entral Finance* function, (v) integrating with *SAP Ariba* for invoice and discount management, integration of payment capability with supply chain finance for supporting end-to-end fulfilment, (vi) providing S*hared Services Framework* that improves operational excellence by standardizing best practices across various business departments, including procurement (*SAP Ariba* solutions), HR (*SAP SuccessFactors*), and travel expenses (*Concur*), (vii) bringing together expense information (from multiple systems) for making more informed and real-time decisions through *SAP Real Spend* solution, (Viii) increased compliance reporting for managing real estate with *SAP Real Estate Management*, and (ix) using *SAP Lease Administration* for simplified equipment lease accounting.

3.2.3 Planning and Predictive Analysis

Prior to SAP S/4HANA Finance, there have been (i) separate and disconnected tools and processes for planning, manual and static budget allocations, (ii) alternate hierarchies and planning master data maintained outside of ERP, (iii) difficulties to model / simulate business innovation, costs, and structural changes to assess financial impacts, and (iv) difficulties in drill-down of financial metrics as data were stored in multiple / disparate systems.

In SAP S/4HANA Finance, you will notice that (i) the planning processes and functions are integrated into transactional system, allowing for closed-loop planning and execution, (ii) there is a single consolidated view of all planning and forecasting information with simplified user experience through *SAP Business Objects Planning and Consolidation* application that enables planning at any level, (iii) the real-time 'what-if' analysis and simulations help to model & test the impact of changes to profitability before committing to plans, with managerial views derived from income statement, obviating manual reconciliation, (iv) the central finance deployment enables faster integration during restructuring, merger and acquisitions, and (v) the real-time access to financial data (with the ability to drill down to line-item levels), merger of FI and CO for a single source of truth (with *universal journal*).

3.2.4 Treasury and Financial Risk Management

The ERP on a traditional database is characterised by its (i) limited capabilities to integrate data from multiple treasury systems and external bank interfaces, (ii) manual and offline cash forecasting processes that often resulted in inaccurate and/or delayed planning and forecasting with limited or no analytical capability, (iii) difficulty to centrally manage exposure and mitigate risk with forecasting and controlling foreign exchange (FX), commodity price fluctuation, and contractual information requiring separate add-on solutions, and (iv) basic & manual bank account management capabilities.

SAP S/4HANA Finance comes with integrated liquidity management, including cash flow analysis and embedded liquidity planning. The *SAP Cash Management* enables complete lifecycle management of liquidity. It uses prediction, simulation, and analysis functionality to support an informed and automated forecasting process. Its 'one exposure' functionality enables central storage of all actual / forecast operational transactions. It also comes with additional enhancements in FX risk management and supports hedge accounting as per IFRS 9. It enables simplified yet automated bank reconciliations & workflows, and improved integration with *SAP Bank Communication Management* and *SAP In-House Cash* applications.

3.2.5   Financial Governance and Compliance

Traditionally, the data samples needed to be manually extracted, from multiple systems and analysed to detect a potential fraud. The fragmented compliance processes, across the organization, resulted in lack of transparency and accountability. There has been no link between 'governance, risk and compliance' (GRC) activities and business strategy. The basic audit management capabilities have been through separate offline solutions that are difficult to scale with business expansion. It has been difficult for managing compliance across international trades, as the basic functionalities are from separate offline solutions.

SAP S/4HANA Finance with its cloud / LoB extension enhancements like *SAP Fraud Management* analytic application enables full lifecycle of fraud management from detection, investigation, quantification, and remediation with the ability to monitor performance and optimize the investigation process. The streamlined automated controls, aligning risk to business value drivers, regulations, and policies through the use of the *SAP Process Control* and *SAP Risk Management* applications, in combination with the *SAP Audit Management*, helps in building an effective 3-tier defence framework.

Let us, next, look at the benefits that will accrue to businesses, from SAP S/4HANA Finance.

3.3   Benefits

The major benefits of SAP S/4HANA Finance include:

1. *Single Source of Truth*: with massive process and technology simplification, and with a system that removes data replications, reconciliations, and redundancies, you are always with a 'single source of truth' that enables faster and real-time financial decisions, to keep up with the competition and technology.
2. *Flexible Business Processes*: you can redesign and optimise processes to focus on exceptions and critical tasks, and easily change processes as your business evolves.

3. Best Practices: you can leverage and benefit from cross-company self-learning data, with various roles access to embedded statistics, reporting, and benchmarking.

In quantifying terms, SAP S/4HANA Finance may help in, among others, 5–10% reduction in bank fees, 5–10% reduction in business, operations analysis and reporting costs outside of finance, 5–10% reduction in days sales outstanding, 5–25% reduction in A/R write-offs, 10–40% improvement in invoice processing productivity, 15–20% reduction in single, high-value fraud categories (such as travel expense fraud), 20–40% reduction in audit cost, 20–40% reduction in G/L and financial closing costs, 20–40% reduction in treasury and cash management cost etc.

This completes our discussion on SAP S/4HANA Finance.

3.4 Conclusion

You understood SAP S/4HANA Finance in detail in this Chapter.

First, you learned about the overview of SAP S/4HANA Finance as to how it is different from the erstwhile and traditional ERP applications with its digital SAP HANA core, its new and improved set of comprehensive financial solutions designed to help business to meet the demands of today's digital economy, and its improved but intuitive user interface and experience.

Second, you learned about the major capabilities of SAP S/4HANA Finance in accounting and financial close, financial operations, planning and predictive analysis, treasury & risk management, and financial governance & compliance. You understood how this new solution helps to overcome the age-old pains like delayed period-ends and closing, inability to perform real-time inventory valuation, manual reconciliations, issues in integrating multiple A/P systems, difficulties to model and simulate business innovation, costs, and structural changes in the organization to assess the financial impacts etc.

Third, you learned about the major benefits that will accrue to businesses from SAP S/4HANA Finance solution, with its single source of truth, flexible business processes and a plethora of best practices that you can lean on to leverage. You further learned that you will be able save substantially as this solution will help in reducing the bank fees, A/R write-offs, audit cost, cash management cost, days required to close the books etc.

With this background of SAP HANA, SAP S/4HANA and SAP S/4HANA Finance, let us move on to our discussion on configuring SAP Financial Accounting (SAP FI), for a typical business.

Before discussing SAP Financial Accounting, in detail, let us look at the case study in the next Chapter, that will be the basis of discussion for the reminder of the book.

4 Case Study

You will come across two case studies in this book:

- Project Dolphin
- Project Oyster

The *Project Dolphin* is the main case study, that will cover most of the configuration in this book and will relate to BESTM Corporate. The *Project Oyster* is a mini case study, that has been used to discuss inflation accounting as a part of configuring SAP FI.

Let us discuss each of the projects, in the Sections below:

4.1 Project Dolphin

BEST Machinery, also known as BESTM group, is the corporate group having companies operating out of both United States of America (USA) and India, among other countries. The case study is, however, limited to the operations in USA and India. BESTM group has three companies namely, BESTM Agro, BESTM Construction and BESTM Drives. All the three companies are operating out of USA from the same address as that of the corporate group at Glen Ridge, New Jersey:

- ✓ BESTM Agro is the flagship company and is made up of four company codes – two in USA and two in India. This company, through its various legal entities, is in the business of manufacturing, supplying and servicing tractors for agricultural and other uses, agricultural implements, lawn & garden mowers, and equipments required by the forestry industry.
- ✓ BESTM Construction manufactures and services all kinds of trucks and heavy machinery used in the construction industry like dump trucks, track & crawler loaders, excavators, dozers etc. It has two company codes both of which are operating out of USA.
- ✓ BESTM Drives is in the business of making and servicing industrial diesel engines including diesel generators, and drivetrain related equipments like transmissions, axles, gear drives etc. This company is comprising of two USA-based company codes.

BESTM group had been using a variety of software applications, built and bought over a period of years, to meet all their business requirements. Because of a plethora of applications, which were often different between USA and India, the corporate was finding it difficult to integrate the information that hampered their decision making. Calling for a lot of manual interventions and time-consuming reconciliations, they were finding it hard to close their books in time. Also, there were lot of redundancies and duplicity as the applications were not fully integrated. Hence, the corporate group was thinking of to go in for an ERP that would overcome all these shortcomings, and they wanted to bring in the latest in ERP so that they would have an enterprise solution that would not only be state-of-the-art, but also insulate them from becoming obsolete in the near future. Accordingly, the management had taken decision to implement the SAP S/4HANA suite of applications, and it was decided to deploy the application on-premise.

BESTM decided to partner with a leading IT firm to manage the implementation and the transition to SAP S/4HANA. The implementation was code named as ‘*Project Dolphin*’. The project team had several discussions and workshops with the BESTM management at various levels, and what you see in the following pages is the outcome of those discussions / workshops.

The project team will define three *companies* in SAP, as shown in Table 4.1:

Company	Company ID	Country	Currency
BESTM Agro	B1000	USA	USD
BESTM Construction	B2000	USA	USD
BESTM Drives	B3000	USA	USD

Table 4:1 BESTM - Companies

BESTM Agro company has the following legal entities (company codes) operating out of USA:
1. BESTM Farm Machinery
2. BESTM Garden & Forestry Equipments

BESTM Agro also operates in India through the following company codes:
1. BESTM Farm Machinery
2. BESTM Garden & Forestry Equipments

BESTM Construction company is made up of the following legal units functioning out of USA:
1. BESTM Trucks
2. BESTM Other Construction Equipments

BESTM Drives manages the following legal units:
1. BESTM Drives
2. BESTM Engines

All the *company codes*, except the ones in India, will have USD as their company code currency; the ones in India will have INR as the company code currency. All the company codes will use English as the official language. Each of these company codes will have 4-digit numerical identifier as indicated in the Table 4.2.

Company Code	Company Code ID	Country	Currency
BESTM Farm Machinery	1110	USA	USD
BESTM Garden & Forestry Equipments	1120	USA	USD
BESTM Farm Machinery	1210	India	INR
BESTM Garden & Forestry Equipments	1220	India	INR
BESTM Trucks	2100	USA	USD
BESTM Other Construction Equipments	2200	USA	USD
BESTM Drives	3100	USA	USD
BESTM Engines	3200	USA	USD

Table 4:2 BESTM - Company Codes, Country and Currency

There will be a total of four *credit control areas*: one each for the companies B2000 (BESTM Construction) and B3000 (BESTM Drives), and two credit control areas for company B1000 (BESTM Agro). These credit control areas will be denoted by a 4-character numeric identifier. The details of credit control area, currency etc will be as shown in Table 4.3

Company	Company Code	Credit Control Area (CCA)	CCA Currency	Default Credit Limit
B1000	1110	1100	USD	10,000
	1120			
	1210	1200	INR	700,000
	1220			
B2000	2100	2000	USD	20,000
	2200			
B3000	3100	3000	USD	30,000
	3200			

Table 4:3 BESTM – Credit Control Areas

Since it has been decided to default some of the credit control data while creating the customer master records in each of the company codes, a default credit limit has been mentioned per credit control area as denoted in the table above. BESTM wants the users not to be allowed to change the default credit control area during document posting.

BESTM group requires several *business areas* cutting across company codes (Table 4.4) to report and monitor the operations of different operational areas like agri. tractor business, agri. equipments, after-sales services, garden equipments etc.

Business Area	Business Area Identifier
Agri Tractor Business	ATRA
Agri Equipments	AEQP
After-sales Service	ASER
Garden Equipments	GEQP
Forestry Equipments	FEQP
Construction Machinery	CONM
Drives & Engines	DREN
Military Sales	MILI

Table 4:4 BESTM – Business Areas

BESTM group plans to create their own *functional areas* with easy-to-remember IDs. The project team shall copy the SAP supplied functional areas into the new ones, like BM20 (Production), BM25 (Consulting/Services), BM30 (Sales & Distribution) and so on. BESTM wants the project team to configure the system to derive the functional areas automatically.

BESTM requires the following four FM (Financial Management) areas:
- BF11: FM area for USA-based company codes of BESTM Agro
- BF12: FM area for India-based company codes of BESTM Agro
- BF21: FM area for USA-based company codes of BESTM
- BF31: FM area for USA-based company codes of BESTM Drives

BESTM requires the following business segments to be defined for segment reporting. BESTM wants to have a 10-character alpha-numeric ID segments, with the first three indicating the company code (say, B11/B12/B13 for company B1000, B21/B22 for company 2000 and so on), and the last seven characters, a meaningful abbreviation of the segment description.

- B11FMTRACT   Farm Tractors
- B12HARCOMB   Harvester Combines
- B12FMIMPLE   Farm Implements
- B12FORESTY   Forestry Equipments
- B13LANTRAC   Lawn Tractors
- B13LANMOWR   Lawn Mowers
- B13GRDNUTL   Garden Utility Vehicles
- B13GOLFSPR   Golf and Sports Equipments
- B21LODRDOZ   Loaders and Dozers
- B22EXCAVAT   Excavators and other Construction Equipments
- B31DRVTRAN   Drivetrain Components
- B32GENERAT   Generators
- B33INDSENGN   Industrial Diesel Engines
- B33MARENGN   Marine Engines

BESTM group has decided to have three controlling areas, BESTM Agro (B1000), BESTM Construction (B2000) and BESTM Drives (B3000) with USD as CO area currency. They will need to be denoted as B100, B200 and B300 respectively.

BESTM group has indicated that they need profit centers, defined in such a way, to represent the actual internal management as in Table 4.5:

Controlling Area	Profit Center Group	Profit Center
B100	Tractors	Farm Tractors
		Lawn Tractors
		Speciality Tractors
	Farm Equipments	Cultivators & Planters
		Harvesters
		Seeding / Fertilizing Equipments
		Sprayers & Liquid Systems
	Garden Equipments	Lawn Movers
		Garden Utility Vehicles
	Others	Misc. Farm / Garden Equipments
		Forest Machinery
		Others (B100)
B200	Light Machinery	Compact Machines
		Building Equipments
	Heavy Machinery	Heavy Equipments
		Road Machinery
		Mining Equipments
	Others	Miscellaneous Construction Machinery
		Others (B200)
B300	Drives	Gear Drives
		Pump Drives
		Transmissions
	Engines	Industrial Engines
		Commercial Marine Engines
		Pleasure Marine Engines
	Generators	Stationary Generators
		Portable Generators
	Others	Military Solutions
		Others (B300)

Table 4:5 BESTM – Profit Centers / Profit Center Groups

Looking at the SAP-supplied transaction types in the system, the Dolphin Project team has decided not to add any new transaction type for consolidation for BESTM. They have also decided not to add any new coding fields in the system. This has been finalised after a thorough study of the SAP defined standard coding fields.

The project team has decided to use a single field status variant (FSV), B100, in all the company codes of BESTM. They have further recommended that (a) 'Business Area' and 'Functional Area' fields to be set as 'required' for data entry, and (b) 'Payment Reference' field as 'optional entry' field.

The team has recommended to use different ledgers to meet the different statutory requirements of the company codes: (1) BESTM group of companies will use the SAP supplied standard ledger 0L as their leading ledger and that will meet the International Accounting Standards (IAS), (2) US-based company codes will use a non-leading ledger (BU) to meet the local accounting requirements (US GAAP) and (3) India-based company codes will use another leading ledger (BI) to meet India's legal reporting (Ind-AS). BESTM management is of the opinion that the project team combines the leading ledger (0L) and the non-leading ledger (BU) into a ledger group called B1 as the accounting principles of IAS (0L) and US GAAP (BU) are the same as there will almost be identical postings to both of these accounting principles.

BESTM wants to leverage the 'extension edger' functionality of SAP S/4HANA. Accordingly, the project team has proposed to define four extension ledgers: one for general purpose, the other for simulation, the third for prediction & commitment and the fourth for valuation purposes accounting for valuation differences. In all the cases, BESTM wants manual postings.

BESTM does not want to create new fiscal year variants (FYVs), but shall use the SAP supplied ones. Accordingly, FYV 'K4' will be used for all the US-based company codes and V3 will be used by India-based company codes. To simplify opening and closing of posting periods in the system without much complications, it has been decided to define separate posting period variant (PPV) per company code.

There will be two new charts of accounts defined in the system, BEUS for US-based company codes and BEIN for India-based company codes. The respective Financial Statement Version will also be created in the same name as that of the chart of accounts. For all the US-based company codes, both the operative and country chart of accounts will be the same: BEUS. In the case of India-based company codes, the operative chart of accounts will be BEUS and the country chart of accounts will be BEIN. A suitable document entry screen variant that facilitates country-specific processing of withholding tax needs to be used in all the US-based company codes.

If there is a difference in currency translation due to exchange rate fluctuations during transaction posting, then, a maximum of 10% has to be allowed as the permitted deviation.

However, this will not be applicable to the tax postings as all the tax items have to be translated using the exchange rate from the document header. All the US-based company codes will use a single variant as the workflow variant. It has been decided to allow negative postings, thereby avoiding inflated trial balance.

BESTM wants to activate *Cost of Sales* (CoS) *accounting*, in all the company codes, to understand the outflow of economic resources engaged in making the company's revenue. It has also been decided that suitable configuration to be made to enable drawing up of financial statements per business area. Further, it has been requested that the system should clear the foreign currency open items into local currency using the prevailing exchange rate instead of using the original exchange rate; any gain/loss arising out of this, needs to be posted to the designated G/L accounts.

BESTM does not want the system to propose fiscal year during document change or document display functions, as it expects all the company codes to work with year-independent document numbers. However, the current date can be defaulted to as the 'value date' while entering the line items in a document.

Since USA makes use of the jurisdiction codes for tax calculation, BESTM wants the tax base to remain at the jurisdiction code level, for all the US-based company codes. For the company codes in India, the tax base has to be configured as the net of discount of the invoice amount.

BESTM does not want to define any new document type, and has decided to use the standard ones. It has also been decided to use the same document type for document reversals. To restrict the access to the closing operations, BESTM wants to make use of user authorization through document type CL. To make cross-verification easier, the project team has decided to make the 'Reference' field mandatory for data input for invoice postings and credit memos. There will be no change in the default document type / posting key for the common transactions. The posting date = system date, when posting a parked document.

BESTM does not want to define any new posting keys in the system. However, BESTM has requested to configure the posting keys in such a way that (a) 'Invoice Reference' to be made mandatory for all payment transactions, (b) 'Payment Reference' is optional for document reversals and (c) a valid reason to be mandatory for all payment difference postings.

BESTM wants numerical number ranges for all the document types, in all the company codes. The project team has decided to define a number range 91 (9100000000 to 9199999999) for document type CL in non-leading ledgers. All the number ranges are to have a validity of 9,999 years, so as to overcome any additional configurations every year.

BESTM management has indicated that it requires two additional tolerance groups, besides the null tolerance group, to be configured in the system: the tolerance group TGUS will be for all the US-based company codes, and TGIN for the India-based company codes. It is further stipulated that these special tolerance groups will have only a handful of employees assigned, in each company code, to handle special situations and high-value customers / vendors, as these additional groups will have liberal tolerances in comparison to the null group.

All the employees who are allocated to the tolerance group TGUS will be allowed to post accounting documents of maximum value USD 999,999,999 per document, with a limit of USD 99,999,999 per open item. However, they can process cash discounts at 5% per line item, with the system allowing a maximum payment difference of 3%, subject to an absolute maximum of USD 500. The cash discount adjustment amount will be USD 100.

As already indicated, the tolerance group TGIN will be for the two India-based company codes (1210 and 1220). The select employees who are part of this group will be allowed to post accounting documents of maximum value INR 999,999,999 per document with a limit of INR 99,999,999 per open item. However, they can process cash discounts at 5% per line item, with the system allowing a maximum payment difference of 3%, subject to an absolute maximum of INR 5,000. The cash discount adjustment amount will be INR 1,000.

The null tolerance group will be applicable for all the employees, and will be the default tolerance group for all the company codes of BESTM, both in USA and India:

- ✓ For all the US-based company codes, this null tolerance group will enable posting of accounting documents with values not exceeding USD 999,000 per document with a limit of USD 99,000 per open item. The maximum cash discount allowed is 2% per line item, and the maximum payment difference is 1%, with an amount cap of USD 50. The cash discount adjustment limit has to be set at USD 5.
- ✓ In the case of India-based company codes, the null group enables posting of accounting documents of value up to INR 1,500,000 per document with the line item limit of INR 1,000,000. The maximum cash discount allowed will be 2% per line item, with the maximum allowed payment difference of 1% with an amount cap of INR 1,000. The cash discount adjustment limit will be at INR 100.

BESTM wanted to know if they can go in for the summarization functionality of SAP. However, the project team, after careful consideration of the current and future data volume for each of the company codes, has advised the management that this functionality will be useful only in the case of exceptionally large volume of data, as in the case of – for example – companies operating in telecommunications, and not for BESTM entities.

BESTM wants to implement the following changes (Table 4.6) to the standard messages:

Message description	Changes to be made for	
	Online processing	Batch input processing
Amount is zero - line item will be ignored	Warning (W)	Switch off message (-)
Check whether document has already been entered under number & & &	Warning (W)	Error (E)
Vendor is subject to withholding tax	Note in window (I)	Switch off message (-)
Terms of payment changed; Check	Warning (W)	Warning (W)

Table 4:6 BESTM – Standard Messages and Changes Required for BESTM

BESTM has requested to explore the possibility of using validation rules for preventing posting of documents, based on certain pre-defined account assignment combinations. For example, they have indicated that for the cost center 11101101 and G/L account 11001099 combination, the validation rule set in the system should reject the posting. Similar combinations are to be built in for various cost center-G/L account combinations, as decided by the FI Manager of various company codes for BESTM. This is to prevent posting with incorrect account assignment combinations.

To enable auditing and other purposes, BESTM corporate has decided that the documents / accounts should not be archived until they cross a minimum life of 1000 days (about 3 years), as it was felt that SAP's default of 9,999 days may put pressure on system performance. However, it was clarified, that even after archiving, the documents / accounts need to be fetched faster from respective archives, at least, for another year (365 days).

The project management team has recommended to make use of standard correspondence types supplied by SAP. Accordingly, it has been decided not to create any new correspondence type except a few like SAP01, SAP06 and SAP08 which will be copied into new correspondence types namely YB01, YB06 and YB08 for use in cross-company code correspondence, for company codes 2100 and 2200. Also, the project team has recommended using standard print programs associated with the correspondence types, in all the company codes of BESTM but use different variants to meet individual company code's reporting requirements. To make use of 'cross-company code correspondence' functionality in respect of company codes 2100 and 2200, the company code 2100 needs to be designated as the 'correspondence company code' that will manage the correspondence for company code 2200 as well.

The BESTM management has recommended to make use of the standard settings in SAP for tax calculation and posting, for both India and USA. As regards USA, the team has planned to take care of the jurisdiction requirement of taxation, by interfacing with the external tax system, 'Vertex'. The project team will properly structure the tax jurisdiction code identification in the SAP system to make it fully compatible with Vertex. The project team, accordingly, indicated that the tax on sales and purchases, for all the US-based company codes, is to be calculated at the line item level. Any decision to tax a particular transaction has to come from Vertex. As the tax calculation is from this external tax application, no user is required to enter the tax amount in SAP system. If that is not the case, the system needs to issue a warning, if the tax amount entered by the user is different from the amount calculated automatically in Vertex. No new tax code will be defined by the project team. The posting date will be the baseline date, for tax calculation. The tax amounts should be translated using the exchange rate of the tax base amounts.

The BESTM management has requested the project team to complete the required configurations settings for *extended withholding tax* (EWT) in the system. They have requested the project team to make use of the standard (a) withholding tax keys, (b) reasons for exemptions and (c) recipient types in the system for EWT. The project team, per instructions from BESTM management, has decided to configure the message control to be valid for all users; no separate configuration will be done for individual users. For online transactions, the project team will configure message control in such a way to enable the system to issue warning messages, yet allowing users to correct errors, if any. For batch input processing, the project team will make use of standard message control settings of SAP, for all the message numbers relevant for withholding tax processing.

The Dolphin project team has decided to define the following withholding tax types to support invoice posting:

- 42: 1042 Compensation
- FW: 1099 Federal Withholding Tax
- IN: 1099 Independent Contractor Status
- SW: 1099 State Withholding Tax
- EW: Exempted from WT

BESTM has instructed the project team to make it possible to manually enter the withholding base amount / tax amount, to provide some flexibility in transaction posting. However, these fields should not be made as 'required' in the relevant field status settings, so as not to hold up a transaction. The management also indicated that the minimum / maximum amount settings to be done at the tax code level and not at the tax type level.

BESTM management has informed the project team to define the required withholding tax types for payment postings relating to government payments (1099-G). Accordingly, the project team has decided to define two withholding tax types for payment posting: GX - 1099G reporting excluding WT and GN - 1099G reporting including WT. Besides, BESTM made it clear to the project team that all the company codes will be using the exchange rate of payment, when translating the withholding tax from foreign currency to a local currency.

BESTM has indicated to the project team to make use of standard default withholding tax codes relating to 1099-MISC reporting. If any additional tax codes (to comply with 1099-G, 1099-INT etc) are required, BESTM suggested that the project team creates them in accordance with the reporting requirements in USA, to cover both the federal and state provisions.

The Dolphin project team has recommended to BESTM management to have separate G/L accounts (from 21613000 to 21614000), differentiated by withholding tax types. However, they also indicated that it may not be required to have these accounts separated according to the tax codes for all the third-party transactions. It has also been recommended to have a single account (21603000) for self-withholding tax. No explicit withholding tax certificate numbering is required for withholding tax reporting in USA as the requirement is fulfilled through TIN, EIN, and SSN numbers.

The project team has been instructed by the BESTM management to configure only one retained earnings account for each of the company codes. Accordingly, the G/L account 33000000 has been designated as the retained earnings account (in the chart of accounts area) of the operative chart of accounts BEUS.

The project team has suggested to the BESTM management to make use of sample accounts in creating some of the G/L account master records, to facilitate quicker and easier master data creation. Accordingly, it has been agreed to use sample accounts, in all the company codes, to create G/L account master records for bank accounts. The project team will create the required data transfer rules. Two sample rule types (or sample rule variants) will be created; one for the US-based company codes, and the other for Indian based company codes.

For the rule type for US-based company codes, following data transfer rules will be applicable:

- ✓ The FSG 'YB32' (bank accounts with obligatory value / due dates) set in the sample account, will be transferred to the newly created G/L account but the users will not be able to change the values in the newly created G/L accounts. So also, with the field 'Valuation Group'. However, the fields 'Exchange Rate Difference Key', 'Account Currency', 'Sort Key' and 'House Bank' will be configured in such a way that the non-blank value in the sample account will be transferred and can be overwritten, after transfer to the new G/L account master record that is being created.

For the rule type for all the Indian-based company codes, the above data transfer rules will also apply, except that the reconciliation account ('Recon. Account for Account Type') will be transferred from the sample account which can be changed, if required, after the transfer.

BESTM wants the project team to have thorough validation of all the G/L accounts of the chart of accounts BEUS, to ensure that (a) the accounts have been properly identified as B/S or P&L type, (b) the correct functional area has been assigned to them and (c) the account groups are correct for each of the accounts. Also, the short / long texts need to be properly modified; for example: instead of 'Bank1 Main Account', it should be changed to 'BoA Main Account'. Bank 2 should be renamed as 'Chase', Bank 3 as 'Citi', Bank 4 as 'PNC' and so on. BESTM requires a similar verification be done, in the company code area data as well, to ensure that the accounts have been correctly identified for open item management, line item display, balance in local currency etc.

BESTM wants to make use of document splitting functionality for all the company codes, both in US and India. Accordingly, the project team has suggested the following, which was later agreed upon with the BESTM management:

- ✓ The configuration will make use of SAP's default and standard document splitting method 0000000012; no new method will be defined. Also, no new item categories, document types, business transactions, and business transaction types will be defined as the project feels that the standard offerings from SAP will be enough to meet all the document splitting requirements of BESTM company codes. The 'Business Area', 'Profit Center' and the 'Segment' will be used as the document splitting characteristics, with a zero-balance setting. Additionally, the team will make appropriate settings for 'Segment', as BESTM requires a complete balance sheet, per segment, for which inaccuracies due to non-assigned postings cannot be tolerated. The characteristics 'Order', 'Cost Center' and 'WBS Element' need to be used as the document splitting characteristics for CO. The cash discount that is applied in the payment of an asset-relevant invoice should be capitalized to the asset.

The BESTM Corporate wants to take care of cross-company code transactions as the company code 1110 will be the central purchasing organization for all the company codes in US. Besides, the company code 1120 will make sales of their products through company code 1110 which will act as the merchandiser. A similar scenario was envisaged for India-based company codes, as well, with regard to the central purchasing by the company code 1210.

The Dolphin Project team has recommended, to the BESTM management, that there is no need to define any new clearing procedures. They also recommended not to change any of the default posting keys for these procedures, as tinkering with the standard posting keys may result in system-wide unforeseen discrepancies.

The project team suggested using a single set of accounts, to take care of automatic posting of the exchange rate differences realized in clearing open items: for loss it will be 72010000, and for the gains it will be 72510000. For valuation adjustments, the loss will be posted to 72040000 and the gains to 72540000; B/S adjustments will go to the G/L account 11001099.

The Dolphin Project team has recommended not to go for any additional clearing grouping criteria. The BESTM management, after some discussion with the project team, requested to configure four more user-criteria for grouping clearing items for automatic clearing, for more flexibility: 'Assignment Number', 'Business Area', 'Trading Partner' and 'Contract Number' for customer and vendor, and 'Segment' (in the place of 'Contract Number') for G/L accounts. The project team has suggested to configure two separate G/L accounts for posting of clearing differences: G/L account 52080000 will be configured for debits and 52580000 for credits.

The project team has been advised by the BESTM management to configure three G/L tolerance groups: a null tolerance group and two special tolerance groups:

a) The *null tolerance group* will be applicable for all employees, and will be the default tolerance group for all the company codes of BESTM, both in USA and India. This will have a tolerance of USD 1 (in absolute terms), with 0.5% as the limit for US-based company codes; the absolute limit will be INR 10 and the percentage limit will be the same at 0.5%, for Indian company codes.

Besides the null tolerance group, there will be two more special tolerance groups defined in the system: one for US-based company codes, and the other for India-based company codes:

b) BGLU: This will be for the selected employees of US-based company codes allowing a tolerance of USD 10, in absolute terms, both for debit and credit transactions; in percentage terms the limit will be 1%.

c) BGLI: This will be for the India-based company codes; the percentage will be the same at 1%, but the absolute amount in INR will be 100.

In all the three tolerance groups, lower of the absolute amount or percentage will apply.

BESTM has decided to use two different interest indicators, besides the standard. The new interest indicators will be used for calculating account balance interest on staff loan accounts; one indicator for US-based company codes and the other for India-based company codes.

BESTM management wants the two new interest indicators with the details as under:

✓ The interest calculation frequency is to be set at six months for the staff loans, for both India and USA. The Gregorian calendar needs to be used for interest calculations. The interest settlement should be configured to be on the last day of the month. The interest needs to be charged on a graduated scale for all the staff loan accounts, for US-based company codes, at 2% interest up to $10,000; 3% up to $25,000; and 4% in excess of $25,000; for India, the corresponding figures will be: 8% for loans up to INR 200,000, 9% up to INR 500,000 and 10.5% for above INR 500,000. The interest will have to be settled when the interest amount calculated is in excess of $10 and INR 100, respectively for US and India-based company codes. The interest needs to be paid within 10 days of interest posting to the respective accounts. The interest posting is to be made to the appropriate G/L accounts, one for interest paid (71100000) and another for interest received (70100000). The system should use the document type SA for interest posting.

In addition to allowing negative postings in all the company codes of BESTM, the project team has been asked to configure suitable 'document reversal reasons' in the system, to handle the reversal transactions. It has been clarified to the team that:

- If reversal is happening in the current period, then, the system should allow negative posting; but, should not allow to change posting date (of the document to be reversed).
- If reversal is to happen in a closed period, then, following conditions should be met:
  - Negative postings can be allowed, but without altering the posting date (of the document to be reversed).
  - Negative postings cannot be allowed, but the posting date (of the document to be reversed) can be altered.

BESTM Corporate wants to have single valuation method that will be used worldwide. However, there needs to be different valuation areas to take care of the different valuation needs and requirements of each of the accounting principles. Besides, the corporate also wants to make use of the 'delta logic' functionality in foreign currency valuation to ensure that the system does not execute any reversal postings, for the valuation postings in the subsequent period. Besides the default account assignment fields for foreign currency valuation, BESTM wants to include 'Functional Area' and 'Cost Center' as the additional account assignments to have more flexibility.

BESTM management has indicated to the project team that they want to set up appropriate adjustment accounts to post the results of P&L and B/S adjustments, so as to assign line items to specific account assignment objects like 'Business Area', 'Profit Center' etc. This is to avoid posting the adjustment line items to the original accounts.

In closing, for regrouping receivables and payables, BESM wants the configuration team to stick to the SAP's standard sort method. The team has been tasked to assign the suitable G/L accounts as adjustment accounts for this default sort method.

The BESTM management has indicated that they want additional account assignments during carryforward, in the case of B/S accounts, on 'Order Number' and 'Account Type', besides the standard account assignments in the system. In the case of P&L accounts, BESTM does not want to have any additional account assignments than that of the standard settings.

4.1. Project Oyster

NJ Corporate is involved in mining operations worldwide. Though headquartered in the USA, it operates in most of the countries including countries like Peru, Mexico and Venezuela. The company code (NJ10) in Venezuela has been operating out of Valencia, and is involved in mining of raw materials required for cement manufacturing. As it is in a high-inflation country, and as required by the local laws, *Inflation Accounting* has been activated for the company code.

The *Oyster* project team, after making a thorough study of the standard inflation indexes provided by SAP, has recommended to the management to make use of the general (GI00) and specific (SI00) inflation indexes without defining anything new. Accordingly, they have requested maintaining the index values, manually, as soon as the same has been published by the local government. No composite inflation index will be used for this company code.

It has also been recommended by the project team to make use of the standard 'time base and exposure to inflation variants' (TBE variants) that has been delivered with the standard SAP. And, it has been further decided to have the validity of this variant RE to last for ever, that will obviate the need to maintain the posting intervals every year. Additionally, the posting intervals are to coincide with the calendar months. The team has also recommended to post revaluation every month, on the last day of that calendar month.

When defining the inflation key, it has been decided to use the 'Balance Method', as the 'Adjustment Method' for calculation. By doing this, the adjustment is done at the account balance level and the system creates one inflation adjustment document for the G/L account.

As regards the 'Inflation Key' field in the G/L accounts, the project team has decided to make that field with the field status 'Optional Entry' for both create and change activities; however, the status will only be 'Display' for the document display activity. Additionally, it has instructed the configuration team to take utmost care while maintaining the field status of 'Inflation Key' per account group in a such a way that it does not conflict with the field status per activity.

The project team has requested the configurators that for every account they want to adjust for inflation, they need to make sure that they are entering the Inflation Key on the 'Control Data' tab of the G/L account master record, without fail.

While maintaining the inflation methods, it has been clarified by the management, that inflation revaluation needs to be posted to the leading ledger and not to any non-leading ledger. Also, it has been indicated that the system should not post all inflation adjustment amounts in their entirety to the general inflation gain / loss account; instead, the system needs to split the inflation adjustment amount between two separate accounts: one representing the general inflation rate, and other representing the price level change for that G/L account. The management also requested to define separate document types (one for local currency, and another for foreign currency) to take care of inflation adjustment documents. And, necessary settings be also made for FI-AA and MM components as well, besides FI.

Finally, the management has indicated that the accounting clerks should not be allowed to manually assign inflation indexes to specific G/L line items; instead, the index defined in the inflation key should always be used.

5 Enterprise Structure

The *'enterprise structure'* in SAP reflects the business organization, consisting of various structures in financial accounting (FI), controlling (CO), sales & distribution (SD), material management (MM), plant maintenance (PM), etc. The definition of an enterprise structure is the fundamental step, and is the starting point of system configuration. Being the crucial piece in the entire project implementation, this forms the foundation for all other configuration activities. Upon completion, this will bring out the enterprise structure (of your business) comprising of organizational units and their linkages enabling interaction between various components of the SAP application.

In this Chapter, we shall discuss the following:

- FI/CO Organizational Units
- Localization of Organizational Units
- Definition of FI/CO Organizational Units
- Assignment of FI/CO Organizational Units

Before discussing the localization of organizational units, let us understand the FI organizational structure and its units.

5.1 FI/CO Organizational Units

The *'FI organizational structure'* relates to the definition and assignment of various organizational units that you will require in FI (*Financial Accounting*) and CO (*Controlling*) for your day-to-day operations of recording the accounting data. These units also facilitate external and internal reporting besides enabling the control requirements of the business, for data integrity. Before you actually define the important FI/CO organizational units, you need to have a clear understanding of the current organizational structure of your business, the future requirements arising out of growth in the business etc. Unless you capture these details correctly, you may not have a very representative organizational structure which may come in the way of defining additional organizational units later in the system.

> **i** The definition of FI enterprise / organization structure is mandatory and is the backbone, without which you will neither be able implement FI component nor will be able to integrate other modules with FI.

Not all the organizational units provided by SAP are mandatory for definition. There are a few units, like company, functional area etc that are optional for definition. The Table 5.1 lists out the most important FI/CO organizational units that are mandatory.

Mandatory to define	Optional to define
Client	Company (FI)
Company Code (FI)	Business Area (FI)
Credit Control Area (FI)	Financial Management Area (FI)
	Functional Area (FI)
	Profit Center (FI)
	Segment (FI)
	Controlling Area (CO)
	Operating Concern (CO)

Table 5:1 FI Organizational Units – Mandatory and Optional

> **i** The best practice in defining organizational units is to define what is really required. And, use what has been provided by SAP as much as possible; of course, you may need to rename them to suit your business.

Similar to FI organizational units, you will also be defining the required organizational elements when you implement other modules in SAP like Sales & Distribution (SD), Material Management (MM), Plant Maintenance (PM) etc. Though we will not discuss these units in detail, in this book, look at Table 5.2 to have an idea.

Sales & Distribution	Material Management	Logistics	Human Resources Management
*Sales Organization *Distribution Channel *Sales Office *Sales Group	*Storage Location *Purchasing Organization	*Plant *Division *Warehouse Number *Shipping Point *Loading Point *Transportation Planning Point	*Personnel Areas *Personnel Sub-areas *Employee Groups

Table 5:2 Important Organizational Units in Modules other than FI/CO

Once you complete defining the required organizational units in the system, you also need to 'assign' them appropriately to bring out the relationship among these units and to make sure the data flows from one to the other, as planned. Refer Section 5.4 for details on assignment.

With this background of organizational units and enterprise structure, let us now do the first step of localizing the sample organizational units in configuring the system for further activities.

5.2 Localize Sample Organizational Units

SAP comes delivered with sample organizational units, which you can copy to create your own organizational units. All the sample organizational units are country-independent, and therefore, before you copy them to create your own, you first have to localize them to meet your country's statutory requirements by applying the appropriate *country template*. As the standard SAP system comes delivered with company code and other organizational units like sales organization, plant etc (all denoted by 0001) with customizing relevant for standard chart of accounts (YCOA), they do not contain any specific country-relevant settings. Unless you localize them to a specific country, you will not be able to use them in that particular country.

So, the first step you should do is to run the *'country installation program'* that will localize the sample organizational units by applying the appropriate country template (SAP has 40 such templates). When initiated, this country installation program makes changes in the chart of accounts, account determination, financial statement version, tax procedures, payment methods, cost elements, chart of depreciation etc, to the sample organizational units (0001) and creates country-specific sample organizational units for that particular country. Now, as these sample organizational units will meet the legal requirements of the country for which the country localization was done, you may use them to create your own organizational units to meet your specific business needs.

> **i** Execute this IMG activity only if you have not changed any settings in the standard SAP system. Do not execute this in your production client, as it will overwrite the settings for any organizational units named 0001. And, run it only once in your production preparation client.

If you need to localize organizational units for several countries, you just need to repeat the country localization activity for all the required countries, one-by-one; in this case, you do not need to reset the company code 0001, every time you run the program.

> **i** Before we actually discuss a Customizing (or configuration) activity in any Chapter of this book, we shall provide you with the case-study (Project Dolphin) details, relevant for that activity, to provide you with the appropriate business perspective for that system activity.

Project Dolphin

BEST Machinery, also known as BESTM group, is the corporate company group having companies operating out of both United States of America (USA) and India, among other countries. Since the case study is limited to the operations in USA and India, the standard system needs to be localized for these two countries to take care of the country-specific settings that would be required for the legal entities in these two countries.

Let us start with the IMG activity of localizing the sample organizational units for USA:

i. Follow the menu path: SAP Customizing Implementation Guide > Enterprise Structure > Localize Sample Organizational Units. You can also use Transaction O035.

ii. On the 'Country version – general' screen, click on 'Country version' button and you will be taken to 'Customizing: Country Version' screen.

iii. Now, select the country key (US) for USA from the drop-down list, for 'Country to install' field, select 'Test run' check-box (Figure 5.1), and 'Execute' (F8) the function.

Customizing: Country Version

Country to install   US

☑ Test run

Figure 5.1 Initial Customizing Screen for Country Localization

iv. When the execution is completed, you will see the results of the test run ('Results Log') as to what will all be localized as shown in the Figure 5.2.

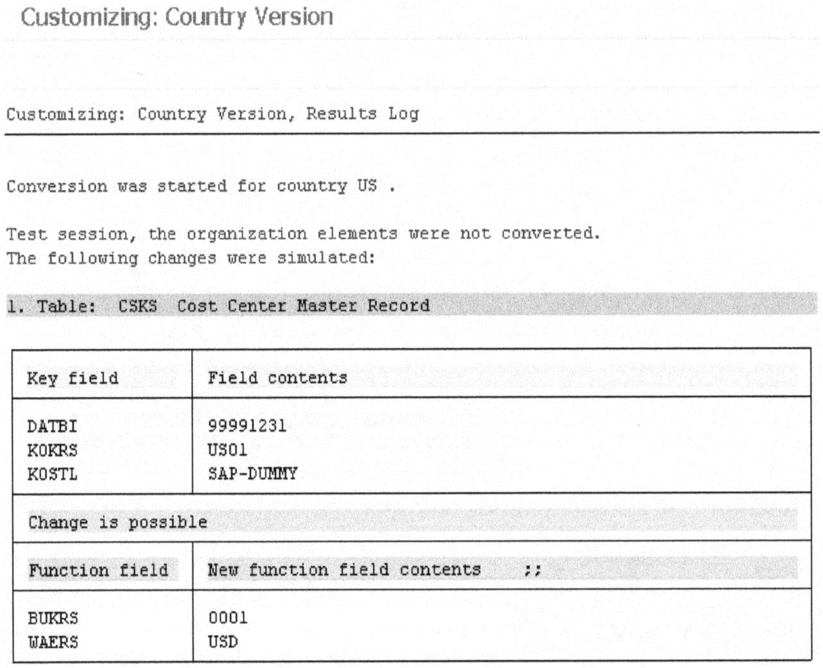

Customizing: Country Version

Customizing: Country Version, Results Log

Conversion was started for country US .

Test session, the organization elements were not converted.
The following changes were simulated:

1. Table: CSKS Cost Center Master Record

Key field	Field contents
DATBI	99991231
KOKRS	US01
KOSTL	SAP-DUMMY

Change is possible

Function field	New function field contents ;;
BUKRS	0001
WAERS	USD

Figure 5.2 Results of Country Localization Test Run

Note that there have not been any changes made to the system yet, as this was only a test run. If system shows any error, take the help of your SAP Basis System Administrator to restore the original settings of 0001, and run the program again.

v.   When satisfied and ready to proceed, go back to the previous screen, deselect the 'Test run' check-box and 'Execute' again. Now, the system will localize the sample organizational units for USA.

vi.   Repeat the steps for localizing the sample units for India.

With the localization of organizational units completed, let us move on to define the different FI/CO organizational units that will eventually form the FI/CO enterprise structure for BESTM corporate. Let us start with the definition of the company.

5.3   Definition of FI / CO Organizational Units

As discussed in Section 5.1, there are several organizational units, both in FI and CO, that needs to be defined to structure your business enterprise in the SAP system. Before we start defining the first organizational unit, let us first understand the concept of 'client' (in SAP), which sits at the top of any enterprise structure.

A *'client'*, in SAP, is a self-contained commercial, organizational, and technical unit within the system. Since you can have more than one client, SAP ensures that all business data within a client is protected from other clients. Each client has its own data, which can be considered as the exclusive property of that client. However, the SAP offers a system solution that is implemented for all clients in a central repository and cross-client tables (central data source).

The client concept allows you to split an SAP system into multiple logical sub-systems (= clients). You can isolate these sub-systems and operate them as separate business units. All the data in a system, with multiple clients, is located in a common database. The client is included in the data model as a mapping of your business entity, in addition to the business application solution. The client does not contribute to the modeling of the application solution, but it makes sure that all data created during business processes is assigned exclusively to the client.

The client-specific data includes all application tables as well as all the Customizing settings. The application tables hold business data such as master data or transaction data; this data can be created, changed, or deleted at any time by regular business processes. The Customizing tables are business-relevant which include the data representing organizational structures of the enterprise, and the parameters that control business processes. In addition to the client-specific customizing tables, there is also a range of cross-client customizing tables. Since, often there are strong mutual dependencies between Customizing tables, these tables are not maintained individually, but as Customizing objects.

A Customizing object can contain both client-specific tables and cross-client tables: a client-specific object is one wherein if all tables maintained through that object are client-specific; if at least one cross-client table maintained through that object can be changed, then that object is called cross-client.

> **i** The SAP System is delivered with the clients 000 and 001, containing default settings.

With the understanding of client concept in SAP, we are now ready to define the company.

5.3.1 Define Company

A '*company*', in SAP, is an independent organizational unit for which you will be able to draw independent financial statements according to the commercial law requirements of a particular country. Though optional, it is recommended that you define this organizational unit so that you will be able to draw consolidated balance sheet for the corporate group as whole when there are more than one company (as in the case of BESTM corporate).

> **i** Recommended that you keep the SAP delivered company 'G00000' if you require only one company, so as to reduce the number of tables that are required when you define more than one company.

When defined, a company can contain one or more company codes but they all need to work with the same operative chart of accounts and fiscal year variant (FYV) even though each one of them can have a different company code currency.

Project Dolphin

BESTM group has three companies namely, BESTM Agro, BESTM Construction and BESTM Drives. All the three companies are operating out of USA from the same address as that of the corporate group at Glen Ridge, New Jersey.

BESTM Agro is the flagship company and is made up of four company codes – two in USA and two in India. This company, through its various company codes, is in the business of manufacturing, supplying and servicing tractors for agricultural and other uses, agricultural implements, lawn & garden mowers, and equipments required by the forestry industry.

BESTM Construction manufactures and services all kinds of trucks and heavy machinery used in the construction industry like dump trucks, track & crawler loaders, excavators, dozers etc. It has two company codes, both of which are operating out of USA.

BESTM Drives is in the business of making and servicing industrial diesel engines including diesel generators, and drivetrain related equipments like transmissions, axles, gear drives etc.

This company has two USA-based company codes. The configuration details of these companies will be, as shown in Table 5.3.

Company	Company ID	Country	Currency
BESTM Agro	B1000	USA	USD
BESTM Construction	B2000	USA	USD
BESTM Drives	B3000	USA	USD

Table 5:3 Configuration Settings for Company

To create these companies in the system, follow the steps listed below:

i.   Follow the menu path: SAP Customizing Implementation Guide > Enterprise Structure > Definition > Financial Accounting > Define Company, or Transaction OX15.

ii.   On the resulting screen, click on 'New Entries'.

iii.   On the next screen (Figure 5.3), maintain the values for the various fields:

Figure 5.3 Creation of Company B1000

- Company: This is the company ID and you can have ID length of 6 and this can be numeric or alphanumeric. Enter B1000 to denote BESTM Agro.
- In the 'Company name' and 'Name of company 2' fields, enter the appropriate information.
- Provide the door number and street name in 'Street', and enter the postal code (zip code in USA) in 'Postal code' field.
- Input Glen Ridge in 'City' field and select the country key US for the 'Country' field which is the only required field on this screen.
- Select EN as 'Language Key' from the given list in the drop-down box.

> **i** The language key though represented as a 2-character identifier (for example EN), is internally stored as a single character (E) of data of type LANG.

- Now select USD as the 'Currency' from the drop-down list, and note that this is the local currency of this company.
- 'Save' entries.

iv.   The company B1000 is now created (Figure 5.3).

v.   Go back to the initial screen, and create the remaining two companies (B2000 and B3000), either by copying or creating afresh. Now, you have created all the three companies in the system for BESTM corporate (Figure 5.4).

Change View "Internal trading partners": Overview

New Entries

Company	Company name	Name of company 2
B1000	BESTM Agro	BESTM Agro Incorporated
B2000	BESTM Construction	BESTM Construction Incorporate
B3000	BESTM Drives	BESTM Drives Incorporated

Figure 5.4 Companies under BESTM Corporate

With the completion of defining of all the three companies under Project Dolphin, for BESTM, it is time to define the respective company codes.

5.3.2 Define Company Code

The *'company code'* is the smallest central organizational unit, in SAP, for which you can maintain a complete and self-contained set of accounts, besides drawing up the external financial statements (balance sheet and profit & loss account) to meet the legal and statutory requirements of the country in which the company code operates. It is possible that you can create a legally independent company, in SAP, with just one company code. In case you want to manage accounting for more than one company simultaneously, then, you need to have more than one company code in the system. Unlike company (which is optional to define), it is mandatory to have at least one company code in the system to take care of the financial accounting of your business. You can also create a legally independent company code abroad to represent the operations in that country. As already discussed in Section 5.3.1 of this Chapter, you will need to set up a company when you want to consolidate financial operations for more than one company code: in this case, these company codes are all attached to the company defined in the system.

In order to integrate with other modules in SAP, you need to make assignments between the company code(s) and the organizational units in FI and also in other application areas like material management, sales & distribution etc. Unless this is done, you will not be able to make the data flow from these components into FI. Besides this, when you are implementing Controlling (CO), you need to make necessary assignments between the company code(s) and the 'Controlling Area' which is the central organizational element in CO (more detail, in Section 5.4, of this Chapter).

> **i** You need to define at least one company code per client in the SAP system. You can set up more than one company code in the same client.

Project Dolphin

BESTM Agro company has the following entities (company codes) operating out of USA:
- BESTM Farm Machinery
- BESTM Garden & Forestry Equipments

BESTM Agro also operates in India through the following company codes:
- BESTM Farm Machinery
- BESTM Garden & Forestry Equipments

BESTM Construction company is made up of the following units functioning out of USA:
1. BESTM Trucks
2. BESTM Other Construction Equipments

BESTM Drives manages the following legal units:
- BESTM Drives
- BESTM Engines

All the company codes, except the ones in India, will have USD as their company code currency; the ones in India will have INR as the company code currency. All the company codes will use English as the official language. Each of these company codes will have 4-digit numerical identifier as indicated in the Table 5.4.

Company Code	Company Code ID	Country	Currency
BESTM Farm Machinery	1110	USA	USD
BESTM Garden & Forestry Equipments	1120	USA	USD
BESTM Farm Machinery	1210	India	INR
BESTM Garden & Forestry Equipments	1220	India	INR
BESTM Trucks	2100	USA	USD
BESTM Other Construction Equipments	2200	USA	USD
BESTM Drives	3100	USA	USD
BESTM Engines	3200	USA	USD

Table 5:4 Configuration Settings for Company Code

You can define (=create) company codes in two ways:

- Create a new company code by copying an existing company code
- Create a new company code afresh

We already have a USA-localized company code (0001) in the system. Let us start creating a company code 1110 by using the 'copy' option by copying from the sample company code.

5.3.2.1   Create Company Code by 'Copy'

To create a company code, by copying from an existing one in the system:

i.   Go to the menu path: SAP Customizing Implementation Guide > Enterprise Structure > Definition > Financial Accounting > Edit, Copy, Delete, Check company code. Or use Transaction EC01.

ii.   On the 'Select Activity' pop-up screen, double-click on 'Copy, delete, check company code'. On the 'Organizational object Company code' screen, click on 'Copy' button.

iii. You will see the 'Copy' pop-up screen; enter 0001 in 'From Company Code' field and enter 1110 in 'To Company Code'. Press 'Enter'.

iv.   On the 'G/L accounts in company code 1110' pop-up screen (Figure 5.5), press 'Yes' as you want the same G/L accounts (company code data) to be copied to the new company code from the sample one.

Figure 5.5 Pop-up Screen for Copying G/L Company Code Data, from 'Source' to 'Target'

v.   On the next pop-screen, you are asked whether you want to allocate a different company code currency than that of the source. Since USD is the source company code's currency and as you want the same currency for the target (1110) as well, you need to press 'No'.

vi.   On the next pop-up, you may notice an information that some data were not copied. Press 'Enter' to continue.

> **i** When you copy a company code, not all the settings are copied automatically from the source to the target: for example, the data that is unique for each company code, assignment between company code and controlling area etc, are not copied.

> After copying the company code data, you need to manually maintain appropriate data in these fields in the target company code. You can get this information by pressing the 'Question Mark' on the pop-up screen.

vii. On the 'Transport number ranges and addresses' pop-up screen, press 'Enter'. You can maintain the details manually later. On the 'Number range management messages' pop-up screen, press 'No'.

viii. The next pop-up screen will indicate that the copying action has been completed (with or without errors). Press 'Enter', and you will see the final confirmation screen as shown in Figure 5.6. On the 'Completed activities' tab, you will see the message that company code 0001 has been copied to the target company code 1110.

ix. At this point you may press F8 or 'Check.org object' button on the 'Organizational object Company code screen' to check for inconsistencies, if any. On the resulting pop-up screen enter the company code which need to be checked (say, 1110). On the next pop-up screen, you may display the log to understand the details.

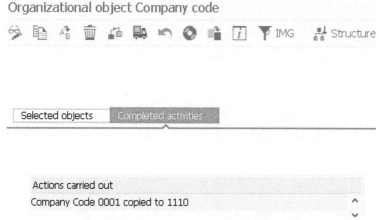

Figure 5.6 Confirmation of Company Code creation by 'Copy' function

x. To look at the new company code created, you need to go back to the initial 'Select Activity' pop-up screen and double click on the second row 'Edit Company Code Data'. And, you will see that the new company code (1110) has also been created with the same name as that of the source company code.

xi. Double-click on the specific row containing the company code 1110; on the resulting 'Change View: Company Code Details' screen, change the required information and 'Save'. You can also use Transaction OX02 to make these changes.

This completes the creation of the company code 1110 (BESTM Tractors) under the company B1000 (BESTM Agro). Now, let us see how to create another company code from the scratch, without using the 'copy' option.

5.3.2.2   Create Company Code afresh (not using the 'Copy' option)

You will, normally, resort to this option when you do not find any suitable sample company code to be copied. In our case, though we have the sample organizational units for both USA and India (refer Section 5.2 of this Chapter), we will use this option to create another new company code from scratch so as to familiarise yourself with this option as well:

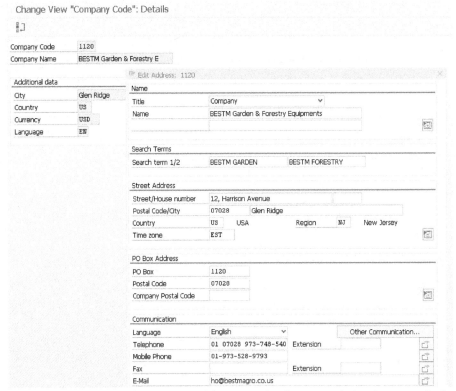

Figure 5.7 Company Code Creation, without Copying from an Existing Company Code

    i.   Go to the menu path: SAP Customizing Implementation Guide > Enterprise Structure > Definition > Financial Accounting > Edit, Copy, Delete, Check company code.

    ii.   On the 'Select Activity' pop-up screen, double-click on 'Edit Company Code Data'.

    iii.   You will be taken to 'Change View "Company Code": Overview' screen (you can also reach this screen directly through Transaction OX02). Click on 'New Entries' button.

    iv.   On the 'New Entries: Details of Added Entries' screen, maintain the details for the fields 'Company Code' (1120), 'Company Name' (BESTM Garden & Forestry Equipments) and other details including the 'Currency' (USD) which is the only mandatory field under 'Additional data' block.

    v.   Press 'Save'. The system will bring up a pop-up to fill up the address details.

    vi.   On the 'Edit Address: 1120' pop-up screen, fill up the fields with the required information (Figure 5.7). When completed press, 'Save'.

> **i** You will not be able to maintain values for both 'Postal Code' and 'Company Postal Code' fields; you can maintain either one of the fields.

We have now completed creation of two company codes (Figure 5.8), one (1110) through the 'copy' functionality and the other (1120) without using the 'copy' option. We will not be creating the remaining company codes now; instead, we will do so when we complete the configuration of company code global parameters, as outlined in Section 6.8 of Chapter 6. This way, it will be easy to create fully configured company codes by 'copy' option, as this will reduce the efforts significantly.

Figure 5.8 Creation of Company Codes 1110 and 1120

With this, let us move further on to create the rest of FI/CO organizational units. Let us define the credit control area, next.

5.3.3 Define Credit Control Area

The *'credit control area'* is an organizational unit (with 4-character alphanumeric identifier), in SAP, that represents an area responsible for granting and monitoring of credit. You can have one or more credit control areas defined in a client. Every company code needs to be attached to one (only one) credit control area. While it is possible that a single credit control area can cater to more than one company code, the converse is not true.

> **i** You cannot define credit limits in different currencies to the customers within a specific credit control area: all the limits have to be in the same currency. If a customer is created in different company codes, with those company codes assigned to different credit control areas, then the customer is provided with separate credit limits in each of these areas in different currencies.

Used in SAP FI-Accounts Receivable (A/R) and SAP SD, the credit control area monitors and manages the customer-wise credit information. However, it is interesting to know that there is no permanent linkage between a credit control area and company code(s): the credit control area in the company code table (through the 'company code-credit control area' assignment) acts to derive the default credit control from the assigned company code area when there is no other way of determining the same. There are multiple ways of entering the credit control area: you can enter the credit control area when you make a transaction posting or the same can be derived when you enter an order, from business area & sales area segment of a payer's master record or through user exits. As in all other sample organizational units, SAP comes delivered with a credit control area denoted as 0001.

Project Dolphin

There will be a total of four credit control areas: one each for the companies B2000 (BESTM Construction) and B3000 (BESTM Drives), and two credit control areas for company B1000 (BESTM Agro). These credit control areas will be denoted by a 4-character numeric identifier. The details of credit control area, currency etc., are as in Table 5.5. Since it has been decided to default some of the credit control data while creating the customer master records in each of the company codes, a default credit limit has been mentioned for each of these credit control areas as outlined in the table.

Company	Company Code	Credit Control Area (CCA)	CCA Currency	Default Credit Limit
B1000	1110	1100	USD	10,000
	1120			
	1210	1200	INR	700,000
	1220			
B2000	2100	2000	USD	20,000
	2200			
B3000	3100	3000	USD	30,000
	3200			

Table 5:5 Company Code – Credit Control Area Details

> **i** The system can automatically a create credit master record (for a customer) when at least any one of the fields, say 'Risk category', 'Rep. group' and 'Credit limit', is maintained in the respective credit control area.

Let us define the credit control areas for BESTM group:

i. Use the menu path: SAP Customizing Implementation Guide > Enterprise Structure > Definition > Financial Accounting > Maintain Credit Control Area, or Transaction OB45.

ii. On the 'Change View "Credit Control Areas": Overview' screen, press 'New Entries'.

iii. On the ensuing screen, fill-up the fields with the relevant information:

- In the 'Credit.Contr.Area', input the 4-digit identifier of the credit control area. In our case, you will be entering 1100 as this is the credit control area for all the USA-based company codes of BESTM Agro. Note that you will not yet be able to enter a name of the credit control area at this point as the field is greyed out; you can do that later.

- Enter USD in the 'Currency' field
- In the 'Update' field under the section 'Data for updating SD', select the suitable value from the drop-down list: which will decide at what point of time the system updates the values of open sales orders, deliveries and the billing documents. We will leave that as blank so as not to set any limitation.

The system determines the available credit limit based on the *'update group'* maintained in the 'Update' field of the credit control area. The limit is arrived at the system in the following manner: available credit limit = credit limit – (value of open orders + value of open deliveries + value of open billing documents not yet billed + A/R balance of the account). The least of the controls is exercised, when you do not specify an update group: here, the system ignores SD documents when determining the credit availability, and the available credit limit is equal to the A/R balance. The most stringent update group is 000012 (Table 5.6).

Update Group	Sales Order	Delivery	Billing Document	Financial Journal Entry
<blank>	No update	No update	No update	No update
000012	Increases open order value from delivery-relevant schedule lines	Reduces open order value from delivery-relevant schedule lines	Reduces open delivery value	Reduces open billing document value
		Increases open delivery value	Increases open delivery value	Increases open items
000015		Increases open delivery value	Reduces open delivery value	
			Increases open billing document value	
000018	Increases open delivery value		Reduces open delivery value	Reduces open billing document value
			Increases open billing document value	Increases open items

Table 5:6 Update Groups in Credit Control Area

> **i** Even when you specify an 'update group' for default processing of sales orders, the system does not always go by that group in actual processing; instead, it determines the next suitable update group option, when it is not possible to process further using the default one.

Consider, for example, that the default update group is 000012, but the system encounters a situation that one item in the order is not delivery-relevant. Though, by default, the system is supposed to increase open delivery value and reduce open order value from delivery relevant schedule lines of the order, the system skips using 000012 (since one of the items is not delivery-relevant) but uses update group 000018 which will increase the open delivery value of the order item by using the confirmed quantity of delivery-related schedule lines up to the order value.

- Do not enter a value in the 'FY Variant' field at this point of time; we shall do it later. The fiscal year variant (FYV) is used in determining the posting period from the posting date and fiscal year entered in an accounting document. The FYV is necessary when a credit control area covers multiple company codes whose fiscal years are different and the value of open orders is updated by posting period.
- In the field 'Risk category' under the 'Default data for automatically creating new customers' section, enter the appropriate category; in our case, let us leave that blank for the time being as we do not want this to be automatically copied to the credit master record.

> **i** The 'risk category' entered (while defining the credit control area) is carried on to the credit master automatically, when a new customer is created in the company code. As you already know (we discussed this earlier) that this is one of the three fields that is looked into by the system when automatically creating a credit master record; the other two fields being 'Credit limit' and 'Rep. group'.

- In the 'Credit limit' field enter 10,000 as that is the minimum credit envisaged for the credit control area 1100 by the Project Dolphin.
- Also known as the *credit management representative group*, the 'Rep. group' field is used to denote a group of employees of your company who are vested with the credit management operations for the credit control area. You may leave this blank.
- Next, under the 'Organizational data' section, you will see a check-box called 'All CoCodes'. By selecting this check-box, you tell the system that this credit

control area is permitted for postings in every company code that you have defined. This means, when making evaluations, if data (say, balances, open items, dunning data etc.) for a credit control area is to be displayed, then the system selects and displays the data relating to every company code that has been defined. Do not select this check-box for BESTM, as we have several other company codes that will not use this particular credit control area.

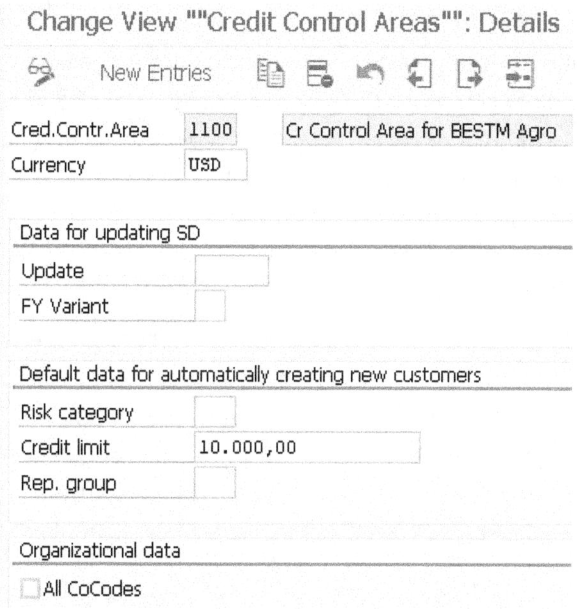

Figure 5.9 Creation for Credit Control Area 1100

iv.   Now, 'Save' the entries (Figure 5.9).

v.   Go back, to the initial screen, and enter the name (Cr Control Area for BESTM Agro - USA) under the field 'Description'.

vi.   You can copy credit control area 1100, to create rest of the credit control areas: for the USA-based credit control areas 2000 and 3000, you just need to change the default credit limit as 20,000 and 30,000 respectively. For the credit control area 1200, you need to change the currency to INR and the credit limit to 700,000 as this will be used by all the India-based company codes.

This completes our discussion of defining the credit control areas for BESTM. Let us now continue to define the other organizational units.

5.3.4   Define Business Area

A *'business area'* is a FI organizational unit representing an area of responsibility or operations of your business. Besides enabling creation of financial statements (balance sheet and profit & loss statement) below the level of a company code, the business areas help you with segment reporting as you can define them based on geographical areas, products, product lines etc. Denoted by using a 4-character alphanumeric identifier, you can use a business area across several company codes (in the same client), even if these company codes operate with different chart of accounts. In cases of cross-company code transactions, SAP creates only one document when you post to more than one business area spread across many company codes. The main purpose of business area, thus, is to report on similar activities or operations that span across multiple company codes.

 It is not mandatory to define a business area.

Business areas help in differentiating the transactions that originate from different points, product lines, or locations in the business. Though you will normally input (or assign) a business area only during transaction processing, you can assign balance sheet items (like fixed assets, receivables, payables, and stock), and profit & loss statement items directly to business areas. However, you can only indirectly assign banks, equity, and taxes to business areas manually.

Once you assign an asset to a business area in the asset master record (in FI-AA), you then need not make any further manual account assignment (for that business area) during any transaction like acquisition, depreciation, retirement etc., as the system automatically updates all the asset balance sheet accounts for that business area, besides passing down the details to all the connected line items of that asset. In case, you need to transfer an existing asset to a new business area, do that by creating a new asset master and maintain the required business area in that master.

Though it is not mandatory to link business area with FI organizational units, we recommend you link them in the system for obvious business benefits: for example, linking the business areas to sales areas ensures that revenue postings are made to correct business areas when your sales organizations sell a single grouping of products. Note that the financial statements for business areas are normally unbalanced as it may not be always possible match the debit and credit entries of a transaction to the same business area. These statements are, therefore, appropriate only for internal reporting.

> **i** Enable the 'Business Area Balance Sheet' indicator in the company code, to make business area as a required field for transactions in FI-AA (Asset Accounting).

Though you can achieve the business-area functionality by using SAP EC-PCA (Profit Center Accounting), beware of the implications: while profit centers are areas of internal responsibility for achieving profits, the main aim of business areas is internal reporting for a set of similar operations / activities. You normally use profit centers to delegate authority / responsibility for decentralized decision making and control. Though many a new implementation favour use of profit centers, it is up to you to decide what to use: business area or profitability center; but, that decision has to be made early in the design phase of project implementation to avoid complications at a later stage. Of course, the factors like (i) the need to report business lines across company codes, (ii) the need to have a full balance sheets at business line (or divisional) level, and (iii) the costs and benefits associated with the each of the alternatives, will help you in taking a correct decision that is just right for your business.

Project Dolphin

BESTM group requires the business areas, as in Table 5.7, cutting across company codes (Figure 5.10) to report and monitor the operations of different operational areas like agri. tractor business, agri. equipments, after-sales services, garden equipments etc. The business area identifier will be a 4-character ID which by itself will meaningfully convey the name of the business area, so that it will be easy to remember for data entry and report interpretation

Business Area	Business Area Identifier
Agri Tractor Business	ATRA
Agri Equipments	AEQP
After-sales Service	ASER
Garden Equipments	GEQP
Forestry Equipments	FEQP
Construction Machinery	CONM
Drives & Engines	DREN
Military Sales	MILI

Table 5:7 BESTM – Business Areas

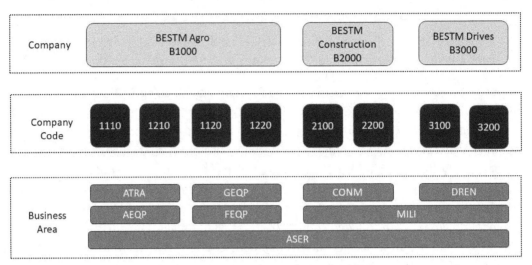

Figure 5.10 Company Code – Business Area Relationship, for BESTM Group

Let us configure the business areas, in the system.

i.   Use the menu path: SAP Customizing Implementation Guide > Enterprise Structure > Definition > Financial Accounting > Define Business Area, or Transaction OX03.

ii.   On the 'Change View "Business areas": Overview' screen:

- Input the business area identifier, say ATRA, in 'Business area' field.
- Enter a suitable name in the 'Description' field.

iii. Repeat step (ii) for the other business areas; when completed, 'Save' the entries; you have now created all the business areas for BESTM group (Figure 5.11).

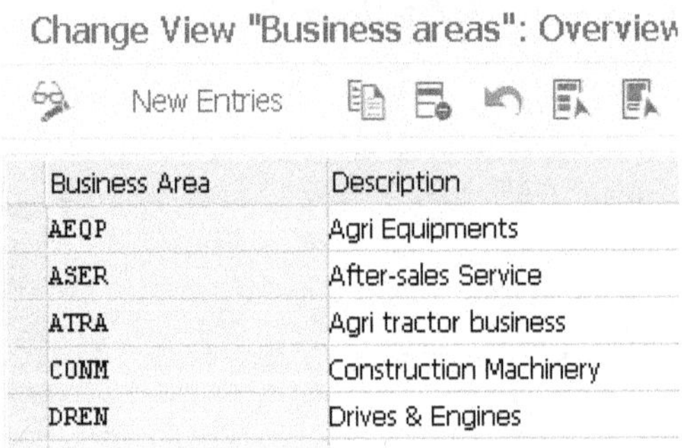

Change View "Business areas": Overview

   New Entries   🖺 🖺 ↶ 🖺 🖺

Business Area	Description
AEQP	Agri Equipments
ASER	After-sales Service
ATRA	Agri tractor business
CONM	Construction Machinery
DREN	Drives & Engines

Figure 5.11 Business Areas for BESTM Group

This completes our discussion on defining a business area. We can now move on to create the functional area, next.

5.3.5   Define Functional Area

Used in *cost-of-sales accounting* and SAP Funds Management, a *'functional area'* is a FI organizational element (unit) that classifies expenses of your business, based on the functions (like, administration, marketing, sales etc) performed by your employees. Though the typical functional areas supplied by SAP (all starting with 'Y') like administration (YB40), production (YB10), marketing (YB35), sales & distribution (YB30), research & development (YB50) etc., will serve most of the business' needs, you can define your own functional areas to meet your specific requirements, if any.

After creating the required functional areas, you also need to assign them to the cost center categories using the menu path: SAP Customizing Implementation Guide > Controlling > Cost Center Accounting > Master Data > Cost Centers > Define Cost Center Categories (or Transaction OKA2) to enable the system to derive the required functional area when an expense is posted.

> **i** It is recommended to derive functional areas automatically, instead of allowing the users to select an area during data entry so as to avoid manual mistakes in assignments.

Project Dolphin

BESTM group plans to create their own functional areas with easy-to-remember functional area IDs. Accordingly, the following functional areas need to be created in the system. The project team has decided to copy the SAP supplied functional areas (starting with 'Y') into the new ones and name them starting with 'BM' like BM20 (Production), BM25(Consulting/Services), BM30 (Sales & Distribution) and so on. The BESTM corporate also wants the project team to make necessary configuration settings in the system to derive the functional areas automatically, instead of manually entering the same, when an expense transaction is posted.

You will need to follow the steps mentioned below to create the functional areas:

i.   Use the menu path: SAP Customizing Implementation Guide > Enterprise Structure > Definition > Financial Accounting > Define Functional Area, or Transaction OKBD.

ii.   On the ensuing 'Change View "Functional areas": Overview' screen, press 'New Entries' and maintain (a) 'Functional Area' ID and (b) description in the 'Name' field.

iii. You may also copy the SAP supplied standard functional areas (starting with 'Y') and create the new ones (as we have done). In this case, on the 'Change View "Functional areas": Overview' screen, select the rows to be copied and press 'Copy As' and change the details, as required. When completed, 'Save' the details. You have now completed the creation of functional areas for BESTM group (Figure 5.12)

Change View "Functional areas": Overview

New Entries

Functional areas

Functional Area	Name
BM10	Sales Revenue
BM15	Sales discounts and allow
BM20	Production
BM25	Consulting/Services
BM30	Sales and Distribution
BM35	Marketing
BM40	Administration
BM50	Research & Development
BM70	Other gains
BM75	Other expenses
BM77	Gain from investments
BM79	Gain from shares & loans
BM81	Interest & similar gains
BM83	Amort.curr.Fin.Assets;Sec
BM85	Interest & similar costs
BM87	Extraordinary gain
BM89	Extraordinary expense
BM90	Taxes from income and rev
BM98	Other Taxes
BM99	Dummy functional area

Figure 5.12 Functional Areas for BESTM Group

This completes defining the functional areas, for BESTM. As regards the configuration settings to derive the functional areas automatically, we shall complete that later. With this, we are now ready define the next organizational unit namely financial management area (FM area).

5.3.6 Maintain Financial Management Area (FM Area)

You will use the *'financial management area'* (FM area) to structure the business organization from the perspective of SAP Cash Budget Management and SAP Funds Management. You need to define the characteristics of FM areas, separately for both SAP Cash Management and SAP Funds Management, and link these areas with other organizational units in the system. The system derives the FM area from the company code, when you assign a company code to an FM area; you can assign more than one company code to a single FM area (refer Section 5.4.3).

It is not necessary that the FM area currency should be the same as that of company code currency of the assigned company code. If you want to change FM area's currency, later, you will not be able to do that if you have already posted any actual data to that specific FM area.

Project Dolphin

BESTM requires four FM areas to cover their companies. Accordingly, the following FM areas need to be created in the system (Figure 5.13):

- BF11: FM area for USA-based company codes of BESTM Agro (covering company codes 1110 and 1120).
- BF12: FM area for India-based company codes of BESTM Agro (covering company codes 1210 and 1220).
- BF21: FM area for USA-based company codes of BESTM Construction (covering company codes 2100 and 2200).
- BF31: FM area for USA-based company codes of BESTM Drives (covering company codes 3100 and 3200).

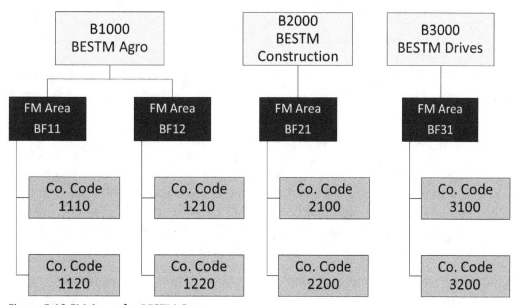

Figure 5.13 FM Areas for BESTM Group

Let us define the FM areas for BESTM:

i.   Use the menu path: SAP Customizing Implementation Guide > Enterprise Structure > Definition > Financial Accounting > Define FM Area.

ii.   On the 'Change View "Create FM areas": Overview' screen, press 'New Entries' and input the details: enter the area identifier (say, BF11) in 'FM Area' field, provide a name (say, FM Area BESTM Agro – USA) in 'Name of FM Area' field and select the appropriate currency (say, USD) for 'FM Area Currency' field. You have entered the details for creating the FM area BF11.

iii.   Repeat entering the details for creating the other FM areas for BESTM group, and 'Save' the entries.

You have, now, completed creating all the four FM areas for BESTM group (Figure 5.14)

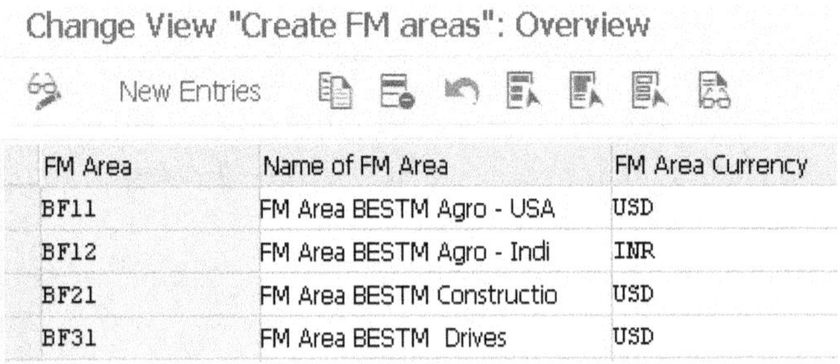

Change View "Create FM areas": Overview

New Entries

FM Area	Name of FM Area	FM Area Currency
BF11	FM Area BESTM Agro - USA	USD
BF12	FM Area BESTM Agro - Indi	INR
BF21	FM Area BESTM Constructio	USD
BF31	FM Area BESTM Drives	USD

Figure 5.14: Functional Areas for BESTM Group

> **i** If you assign an accounting document to an SAP Funds Management object such as a commitment item or funds center, the system has to determine an FM area so as to record the data in SAP Funds Management; for this, you must specify how the appropriate FM area is to be determined.

As we have completed the definition of FM are, let us now understand the usage of functional area Vs FM area.

5.3.6.1   Functional Area and FM Area

Unlike account assignment elements, funds center and commitment item, you can use the functional area in SAP FI-AA, SAP CO and in SAP HRMS as an independent account assignment object, as soon as you activate the functional area for SAP Public Sector Management under the menu path SAP Customizing and Implementation Guide > Public Sector Management > Global Settings > Activate Account Assignment Elements.

In FI-AA, activating the functional area enables you to handle the assets with the correct function (like, asset acquisition, depreciation posting, displaying asset history sheet etc.). With postings in FI-AA, the funds center and the commitment item can be entered either manually (using the coding block) or derived from other account assignments.

The functional area is always transferred automatically from the master asset When you activate the fund in CO, the system ensures that costs and revenues are assigned to the correct fund in Cost Center Accounting; now, functional area, along with controlling objects, becomes another account assignment object that you can specify as sender and receiver for all types of internal clearing. In SAP HRMS, when you activate the fund, it ensures that personnel expenses, time sheet and travel expenses are assigned to the correct fund in Cost Center Accounting. In SAP Funds Management, the functional area is passed on through the whole organizational and functional grouping structure.

You derive budget usage from postings made using the FM area account assignment containing the functional area. Note that funds reservations, earmarked funds and business transactions entered in the feeder components (such as SAP FI and SAP MM) also affect the budget. For posting data from the feeder systems to be updated in SAP Funds Management, you must always specify a complete funds management account assignment in the posting transaction. You can minimize manual entry expenditure by assigning the fund to other account assignment elements, for the system to automatically derive the functional area.

Let us, now, understand how to define a segment which is another FI organizational unit.

5.3.7 Define Segment

You use *'segments'*, in SAP, for segment reporting to meet the requirements of IAS (International Accounting Standards), IFRS (International Financial Reporting Standards) and US GAAP (Generally Accepted Accounting Principles) for a, say, geographical area or line of business. A *business segment*, as per IAS, is a component of a business entity providing a single product (and/or service) or a group of related products (and/or services) that is different from other business segments in terms of risks and returns. Based either on the location of the business entity's assets or customers, a *geographical segment* is a component that provides products (and/or services) within a particular economic environment and is subject to risks and returns that are different from the rest of the components operating in other economic environments.

You need to look into the organizational structure and internal reporting system to identify reportable segments because IAS-14, in particular, presumes that segmentation in internal financial reports (prepared for the board of directors and CFO / CEO) should normally determine the segments for external financial reporting. So, you will infer that your business' reportable segments are its business and geographical segments where a majority of revenue is earned from sales to external customers. You may combine related segments (that are too small for separate reporting) with each other. You can manually enter the segment information during transactions or derive the same automatically.

---

i Define the segments first, before defining profit centers so that you can enter segment in profit center master record, for automatic derivation of the associated segment.

After defining segments here in this section, you need to complete the remaining customizing steps (listed below), before you can make use of a segment in the system:

- *Derive the Segments*: There are three ways with which you can derive / update segment information during posting of financial transactions: (i) by manually updating the segment in transaction processing, (ii) by making use of the 'Segment' field in the profit center master data to automatically derive a segment, and (iii) by deriving a segment automatically through custom derivation rules using the BAdI 'FAL_DERIVE_SEGMENT', instead of updating the profit center master data.

  If you plan to take the BAdI route, note that (a) if no segment is entered during manual posting, the system determines the segment from this substitution, and (b) if the system cannot determine the segment from the substitution, the segment is derived from the profit center. Further, in the implementation of this BAdI, you can choose whether you want to implement a *user exit* or create a formula. To derive a segment through BAdI, use the menu path: SAP Customizing Implementation Guide > Financial Accounting > Financial Accounting Global Settings > Tools > Customer Enhancements > Business Add-Ins (BAdIs) > Segment Derivation > Derive Segment.

> **i** *Business Add-In*, also commonly as 'BAdI', consists of a BAdI interface (which replaced the erstwhile 'function exits' or 'function module exits'), a set of filters, and various settings. They are the basis for enhancements where BAdI methods in object plug-ins are called from ABAP programs; the caller decides which BAdI implementations are used by specifying the filter values. You can define BAdIs as screen or menu enhancements for Dynpros or GUI statuses. Located in the namespace of the global classes, you can edit BAdIs as enhancement spot element definitions in the *Enhancement Builder*. You can switch BAdI implementations 'on' and 'off' by using the *Switch Framework*. You can also edit the classic BAdIs directly in *BAdI Builder*.

- *Maintain the Field Status Group in the FI accounts*: You will find the 'Segment' field under the group 'Additional account assignments'; maintain the field status as 'required' against the 'Segment'. Use the menu path: SAP Customizing Implementation Guide > Financial Accounting > Financial Accounting Global Settings > Ledgers > Fields > Define Field Status Variants, or Transaction OBC4.

Project Dolphin

BESTM requires the business segments to be defined to ensure internal reporting for these segments. BESTM wants to have a 10-character alpha numeric ID for each of the segments, with the first three indicating the company code (say, B11 indicates company B1000 and the last seven characters a meaningful abbreviation of the segment description):

- B11FMTRACT   Farm Tractors (including speciality tractors)
- B12HARCOMB   Harvester Combines
- B12FMIMPLE   Farm Implements (ploughs, sub-soilers etc.)
- B12FORESTY   Forestry Equipments (bunchers, forwarders, skidders etc)
- B13LANTRAC   Lawn Tractors
- B13LANMOWR   Lawn Mowers
- B13GRDNUTL   Garden Utility Vehicles
- B13GOLFSPR   Golf and Sports Equipments
- B21LODRDOZ   Loaders and Dozers
- B22EXCAVAT   Excavators and other Construction Equipments
- B31DRVTRAN   Drivetrain Components
- B32GENERAT   Generators
- B33INDSENGN   Industrial Diesel Engines
- B33MARENGN   Marine Engines

Let us define the business segments required for BESTM:

i.   Use the menu path: SAP Customizing Implementation Guide > Enterprise Structure > Definition > Financial Accounting > Define Segment.

ii.   On the 'Change View "Segments for Segment Reporting": Overview' screen, create new entries using the 'New Entries' button: enter the segment identifier (up to 10-character alphanumeric) in the 'Segment' field (say, B11FMTRACT) and provide a 'Description' (say, Farm Tractors).

iii. Repeat the entries for creating the other segments, and 'Save' the entries. You have now created the required segments for BESTM group (Figure 5.15).

Change View "Segments for Segment Reporting": Overview

New Entries

Segments for Segment Reporting

Segment	Description
B11FMTRACT	Farm Tractors
B12FMIMPLE	Farm Implements
B12FORESTY	Farm Equipements
B12HARCOMB	Harvester combines
B13GOLFSPR	Golf and sports equipments
B13GRDNUTL	Garden utility vehicles
B13LANMOWR	Lawn mowers
B13LANTRAC	Lawn tractors
B21LODRDOZ	Loaders and dozers
B22EXCAVAT	Excavators & other construction equipments
B31DRVTRAN	Drivetrain components
B32GENERAT	Generators

Figure 5.15: Segments for BESTM Group

We are now left with the creation of last FI organizational unit namely, the profit center. However, you cannot create a profit center without having a controlling area in place in the system. Hence, let us complete the definition of controlling area next.

5.3.8 Maintain Controlling Area

You use *'controlling area'*, the central organizational structure in SAP Controlling (CO), to sub-divide your business organization from the cost-accounting perspective. Used in internal reporting, it is a self-contained cost accounting entity, like a company code in FI.

The controlling area ensures that the internal business transactions (such as, primary costs) are transferred from external accounting (FI) and classified according to internal managerial accounting (CO) perspectives. The *primary costs* (or direct costs) are assigned to cost objects like projects. The *secondary costs* (or overheads) are assigned to cost centers or overhead cost orders, which are then allocated using internal allocation techniques according to their source. Similarly, postings in FI-AA (like, depreciation) are also passed on to CO. All your revenue postings in FI would result in postings in Profitability Analysis (CO-PA) and also in Profit Center Accounting (EC-PCA).

You already know that SAP SD, SAP MM, and SAP PP modules have many integration points in CO, with a 'goods issue' (GI) to a controlling object or a 'goods receipt' (GR) from a production order. These modules are so tightly integrated that consumption activities, cost of goods issued, overhead charges, material costs etc., are passed on to the production objects like PP production order or SD sales order. The WIP (work-in-progress) together with the variances, if any, are settled to CO-PA, EC-PCA and also to FI at the period end. If a sales order is a cost object item, then, you post revenues directly when you generate billing documents in SAP SD.

> **i** You can have one or more controlling areas in a single client. You will assign one or more controlling areas to an *operating concern*. You can assign one or more company codes to a single controlling area.

You can embed the controlling area in the organizational structure either with the 1:1 or 1: n relationship with company code:

- *1: n Relationship*
  You assign a controlling area to more than one company code, and this arrangement is known as *cross-company code cost accounting*. In such an arrangement, all the data relevant to cost accounting appears in a common controlling area that is further available for allocations and evaluations. Here, you need to assign the group currency as *controlling area currency*. You also need to make sure that all the company codes use the same *operative chart of accounts*. You will go for this kind of relationship when a business corporate, for example, is made up of several independent subsidiaries and the corporate entity undertakes centralized cost accounting for all.

- *1:1 Relationship*
  You assign a controlling area to only one company code, with both the controlling area and the company code having the same identifier. In this arrangement, the controlling area defaults to the currency, the fiscal year variant and the chart of accounts of the assigned company code.

> **i** We recommend that you use the controlling area 0001, supplied by SAP, if you need just one controlling area, as all the preliminary settings such as the definition of number ranges are already maintained for this controlling area. Unlike company codes wherein you need to create your own company codes, by copying the country localized sample one, you can straight away use SAP supplied controlling area 0001; you may just need to rename that.
>
> You may also copy SAP supplied controlling area 0001, to your own controlling area(s) and then make the required adjustments to suit your exact needs.

Project Dolphin

BESTM group has decided to have three controlling areas, one each for the three companies BESTM Agro (B1000), BESTM Construction (B2000) and BESTM Drives (B3000). They will need to be denoted as B100, B200 and B300 respectively. All the three controlling areas will have USD as the controlling area currency.

Let us create the controlling areas required for BESTM group:

i.   Use the menu path: SAP Customizing Implementation Guide > Enterprise Structure > Definition > Controlling > Maintain Controlling Area.

ii.   On the 'Choose Activity' pop-up screen, double click on 'Maintain Controlling Area'. You can use Transaction OX06 as well.

iii. On the 'Change View "Basic Data": Overview' screen, press 'New Entries' and you will be taken to the 'New Entries: Details of Added Entries' screen (Figure 5.16):

- Enter a 4-character alphanumeric identifier in the 'Controlling Area' field. If you want to have a 1:1 relationship with controlling area and company code, you may accordingly select the company code ID by clicking on the magnifying glass adjacent to the field. Since we will not have 1:1 relationship, enter the ID (say, B100).

  When you opt for 1:1 relationship by clicking on 'COArea = CCode' adjacent to the magnifying glass, the system will bring a pop-up to select the company code, and will automatically set the 'Currency Type' to 10 (company code currency) besides filling up the company code currency of the selected company code in the 'Currency' field. Also, the check-box 'Diff. CCode Currency' will be deselected.

- Enter the name of the controlling area in the 'Name' field (CO area for Company B1000).

- Enter the name of the person who will manage this controlling area in 'Person Responsible' field.

- Under 'Assignment Control', you will see two options (namely, 'Controlling area same as the company code' and 'Cross-company-code cost accounting') for the field 'CoCd -> CO Area'; select the 2nd option 'Cross-company-code cost accounting' to meet BESTM requirements.

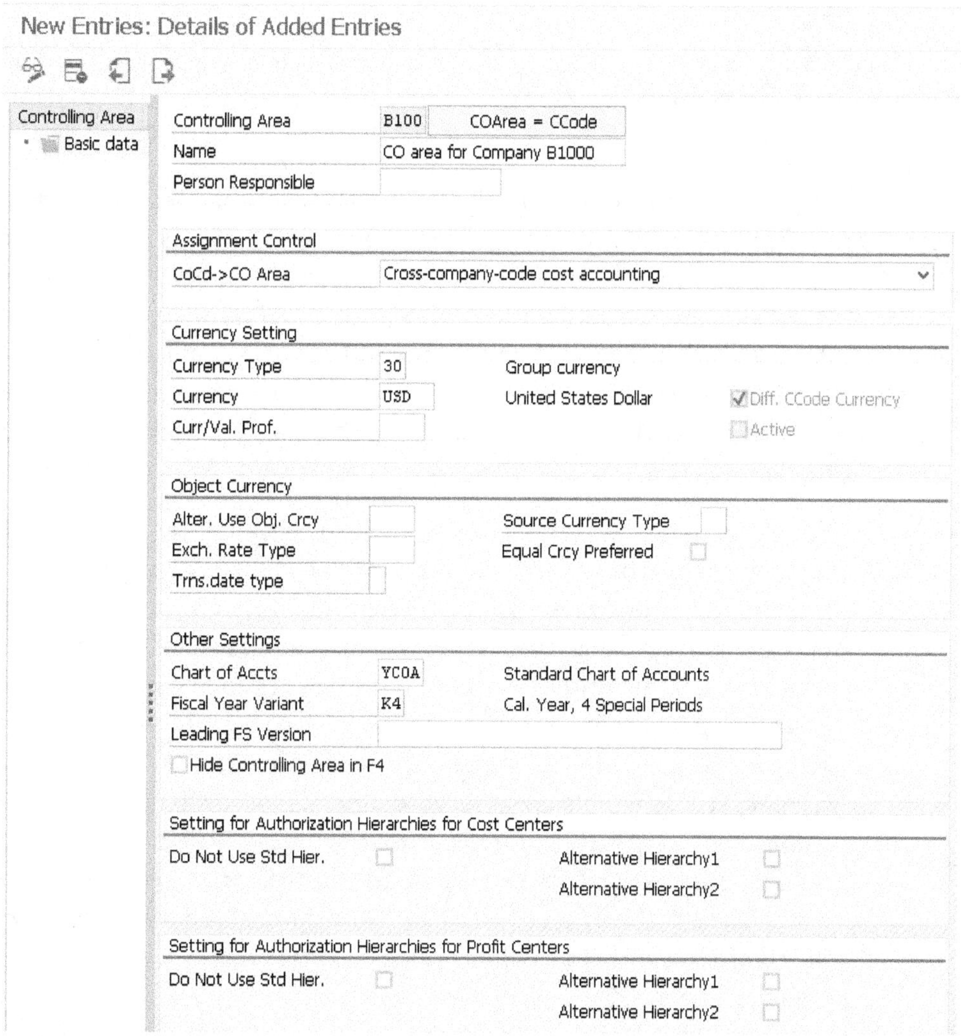

New Entries: Details of Added Entries

Controlling Area	Controlling Area	B100	COArea = CCode
Basic data	Name	CO area for Company B1000
	Person Responsible		

Assignment Control

| CoCd->CO Area | Cross-company-code cost accounting | ⌄ |

Currency Setting

Currency Type	30	Group currency	
Currency	USD	United States Dollar	☑ Diff. CCode Currency
Curr/Val. Prof.			☐ Active

Object Currency

Alter. Use Obj. Crcy		Source Currency Type	
Exch. Rate Type		Equal Crcy Preferred	☐
Trns.date type			

Other Settings

Chart of Accts	YCOA	Standard Chart of Accounts
Fiscal Year Variant	K4	Cal. Year, 4 Special Periods
Leading FS Version		
☐ Hide Controlling Area in F4		

Setting for Authorization Hierarchies for Cost Centers

| Do Not Use Std Hier. | ☐ | Alternative Hierarchy1 | ☐ |
| | | Alternative Hierarchy2 | ☐ |

Setting for Authorization Hierarchies for Profit Centers

| Do Not Use Std Hier. | ☐ | Alternative Hierarchy1 | ☐ |
| | | Alternative Hierarchy2 | ☐ |

Figure 5.16: CO Area B100

- Under 'Currency Setting' section, select 30 (group currency) from the drop-down list for the 'Currency Type' field. We have selected 30 as this controlling area B100 will be used by both US-based company codes with USD as the company code currency, and India-based company codes with INR as the company code currency; the other options for 'Currency Type' include: 10-company code currency, 20-controlling area currency, 40-hard currency, 50-index-based currency and 60-global company currency. For CO area B200 and B300, you need to select 10 (company code currency) as the controlling area currency and company code are the same (USD).

> **i** You will select 10-company code currency if you have selected 'Controlling area same as the company code' for 'CoCd -> CO Area' field under the 'Assignment Control' section.
>
> The *company code currency* (also known as *local currency* or *transaction currency*) is the currency of the country in which the company code is operating. You will select 40-*hard currency* (or the *country-specific second currency)* to valuate transactions in an inflationary economic situation; you will use this for your subsidiaries if they are operating in countries with high level of inflation. You may go in for currency type 50 (*index-based currency*), again, in the case of subsidiaries in countries with high inflation; you will use this for statutory reporting. You need to select 60 if you want to use the currency of the company or consolidated company.
>
> You use currency type 10 (company code currency) as the controlling area currency when all the company codes use the same local currency; even here, you can define a different controlling area currency – then, the system automatically selects the 'Diff. CCode Currency' check-box. When the company codes assigned to the controlling area use different local currencies (as in the case of company B1000 in which the USA-based company codes use USD as the company code currency, and all the India-based company codes use INR as the company code currency), you need to select 30 as the currency type to denote that the *group currency* will be the controlling area currency. Use currency type 20 (*controlling area currency*), if you want to record the CO transactions in a currency other than that of the company code's currency; To use either of the currency types 40 or 50, all or some of the company codes assigned to the controlling area should in the same country; or, if they are in different countries, then these countries should use the same hard currency or index-based currency. For selecting 60 as the currency type, you need to make sure that the company codes are belonging to the same company; or, the companies must use the same currency. If your company code-controlling area relationship is 1:1, you cannot define any other currency type than 10.

- Now, enter USD in the 'Currency' field as you have selected 30 for the 'Currency Type' field. In case you have entered 40 or 50 or 60 in 'Currency type', make sure to enter a value in this 'Currency' field before assigning any of the company codes to the controlling area; else, you will see the system automatically defaulting to the respective currencies (hard currency, index-based currency, or global company currency). As already discussed, if you have entered 10 in 'Currency Type' field, the company code currency will be defaulted to in the 'Currency' field.

- Use the 'Curr. /Val. Prof' field to assign the appropriate valuation profiles; but only when you plan to have multiple valuations stored in the system. Since we are not planning for multiple valuations, we have left this as blank.

- The system automatically selects the 'Diff. CCode Currency' check-box when 'Currency Type' entered is 30 (group currency). Remember we will be using this controlling area B100 for US-based company codes (currency=USD) and India-based company codes (currency=INR) of the company B1000.

- The check-box 'Active' indicates as to whether a controlling area allows transfer prices for company codes or profit centers.

- Under 'Other settings' section, enter the chart of accounts to be used by the controlling area in 'Chart of Accts' field. In the case of a 1:1 relationship between company code and controlling area, the system defaults to the company code's chart of accounts; you need to enter a value only when the relationship is 1:n, as in ours. As we have not yet created a separate chart of accounts for BESTM, select the standard chart of accounts YCOA for the time being as a place holder. When we adapt YCOA into a new chart of accounts suitable for BESTM US-based company codes, we shall revisit and change this value, after we maintain the company code global parameters in Section 6.8 of Chapter 6.

> **i** All company codes assigned to the same controlling area (in cross-company code cost accounting) should use the same *operative chart of accounts*; they can, of course, can have different *country chart of accounts* to meet that particular country's legal requirements. We will discuss more about chart of accounts in a later Chapter in which you understand the different charts of accounts.

- As we plan to use the SAP supplied 'Fiscal Year Variant' (FYV) K4 (calendar year with four special periods) as the FYV for the controlling area B100, enter K4. You can have a different number of special periods in the company codes than that of the controlling area, but you need to have the same number of posting periods with the same start/end limits for each of the posting periods. We will discuss more about FYV, in Section 6.4 of Chapter 6.

- Select 'Do Not Use Std. Hier.' check-box under 'Setting for Authorization Hierarchies for Cost Centers' when you do not want the system to check authorizations (for cost centers) with the current calendar year and the valid hierarchies, in the order in which they were entered (standard hierarchy is checked first, followed by the first alternative hierarchy and then the second one). When you select this check-box, you also need to indicate whether the system is to check 'Alternative Hierarchy1' and 'Alternative Hierarchy2' by selecting / de-selecting the relevant check-boxes. Since we will not be using the alternate hierarchies, we will not select this check-box for our case study. We shall also maintain some controlling area settings, when we define the standard hierarchy (refer Section 5.3.9.3).

---

i Since SAP has introduced the new authorization concept in SAP Overhead Cost Controlling, you can now inherit authorizations within a hierarchy. The authorization objects K_CCA, K_PCA, K_ABC and K_ORDER, enable you to enter standard hierarchy groups. If a user is authorized for one of these groups then he/she is also authorized for all objects in this group. All hierarchies that were entered with a date five years in the past and the future in the customizing for the controlling area can be used in the authorization maintenance.

This inheritance logic previously only applied to the standard hierarchy. You can now, however, use the settings in the controlling area to name up to two more alternative hierarchies (according to fiscal year) that are used in the authorization checks in the same way as the standard hierarchy (with the inheritance logic). You can also deactivate the standard hierarchy as the authorization hierarchy, and use only the alternative hierarchies. This logic has been implemented for cost centers (K_CCA and K_ORDER) and profit centers (K_PCA).

- Now, 'Save' the details; you have completed creation of the controlling area B100 (Figure 5.16).
- Create the remaining two controlling areas namely, B200 and B300, by repeating the steps above.

This completes our discussion on maintaining the controlling areas. We are now ready to define the last organizational element, namely profit center.

5.3.9 Define Profit Center

A *'profit center'* is, primarily, an area of responsibility within a company for revenues and expenses; sometimes, it is responsible for assets and liabilities as well. A *'standard hierarchy'* is used to depict all the profit centers coming under a particular controlling (CO) area.

The SAP Profit Center Accounting (EC-PCA) is made up of profit centers which takes transaction data from other SAP components and represents the same from a profit-center-oriented point of view. Since the profit center itself is not an account assignment object in CO, the postings in EC-PCA are all statistical postings: either as original postings or as additional postings. The integration of various SAP components enables automatic posting of profit-relevant data to EC-PCA as soon as a transaction is posted. Primarily used for performance reporting of responsibility areas (=profit centers), EC-PCA is aimed at preparation of P&L statements.

You can structure EC-PCA for your business on any of the following lines:

- Functional Divisions (production, marketing, R&D etc)
- Geographical Divisions (regions, locations etc)
- Product Divisions (product lines etc)
- Mixed Divisions (combinations of the above three divisions)

You can create profit centers in SAP either by copying the cost centers (and making the required changes, later) or creating them from scratch.

Project Dolphin

BESTM group has indicated that they need profit centers, defined in such a way, to represent the actual internal management. Accordingly, it has been decided to have profit centers (and profit center groups) under each of the controlling areas, as in Table 5.8.

Controlling Area	Profit Center Group	Profit Center
B100	Tractors	Farm Tractors
		Lawn Tractors
		Speciality Tractors
	Farm Equipments	Cultivators & Planters
		Harvesters
		Seeding / Fertilizing Equipments
		Sprayers & Liquid Systems
	Garden Equipments	Lawn Movers
		Garden Utility Vehicles
	Others	Misc. Farm / Garden Equipments
		Forest Machinery
		Others (B100)
B200	Light Machinery	Compact Machines
		Building Equipments
	Heavy Machinery	Heavy Equipments
		Road Machinery
		Mining Equipments
	Others	Miscellaneous Construction Machinery
		Others (B200)

B300	Drives	Gear Drives
		Pump Drives
		Transmissions
	Engines	Industrial Engines
		Commercial Marine Engines
		Pleasure Marine Engines
	Generators	Stationary Generators
		Portable Generators
	Others	Military Solutions
		Others (B300)

Table 5:8 Profit Centers / Profit Center Groups

Before creating the profit centers required for BESTM group, we need to complete the following customizing steps:

- Define Profit Center Standard Hierarchy
- Define Profit Center Groups
- Maintain Standard Hierarchy Details
- Define Profit Center

Let us first create the profit center standard hierarchy.

5.3.9.1   Define Profit Center Standard Hierarchy

The '*standard hierarchy*' is a tree structure for organizing all the profit centers belonging to a controlling area. In this step, we just define the profit center standard hierarchy. We shall discuss the actual tree structure (containing the profit center groups and profit centers), later, in 'Maintain Standard Hierarchy Details' step. Now, follow the steps listed below, to define the profit center standard hierarchy for the controlling area B100:

i.   Use the menu path: SAP Customizing Implementation Guide > Financial Accounting > General Ledger Accounting > Master Data > Profit Center > Define Profit Center Standard Hierarchy in Controlling Area.

ii.   On the 'Change View "Define Profit Center Standard Hierarchy in Controlling Area" Overview' screen, enter the hierarchy identifier (B1000) against the CO area B100 (Figure 5.17).

iii. Repeat step (ii) for the other hierarchies (B2000 and B3000), and 'Save'.

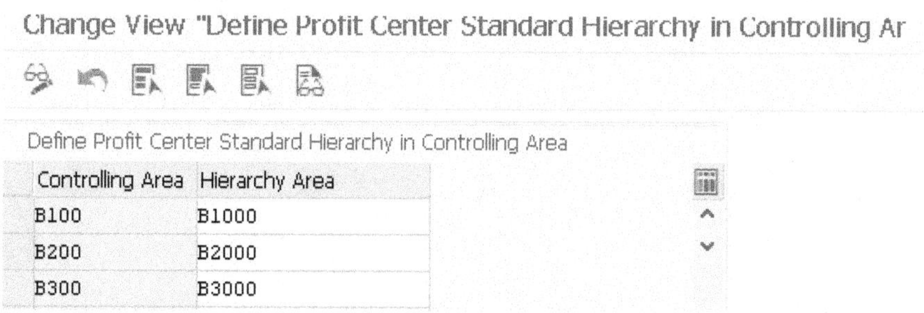

Change View "Define Profit Center Standard Hierarchy in Controlling Ar

Define Profit Center Standard Hierarchy in Controlling Area

Controlling Area	Hierarchy Area
B100	B1000
B200	B2000
B300	B3000

Figure 5.17: Standard Hierarchy in CO Area for BESTM

Let us now move on to define the profit center groups without which you will not be able to create the individual profit centers.

5.3.9.2   Define Profit Center Groups

A *'profit center group'* is used to group the various profit centers, with similar characteristics. Unlike the standard hierarchy, the profit center groups do not have to contain all the profit centers in the controlling area. You can have several profit center groups that helps in grouping all your profit centers in a meaningful way.

Use the following steps to create the profit center groups:

i.   Use the menu path: SAP Customizing Implementation Guide > Financial Accounting > General Ledger Accounting > Master Data > Profit Center > Define Profit Center Groups, or Transaction KCH1. You may also use the menu path: SAP Customizing Implementation Guide > Controlling > Profit Center Accounting > Master Data > Profit Center > Define Profit Center Groups.

> **i** When you enter the transaction, you may get a pop-up informing that you have not yet assigned any company code to the controlling area B100. Refer Section 5.4.4 and assign the company codes suitably, before proceeding further. Also, you may encounter a situation of not able to assign the company code to the controlling area as some of the important company code parameters have not yet been maintained; if that is the case, use Transaction OBY6 and maintain those essential details like chart of accounts, FSV etc. In our case, we have gone ahead and assigned YCOA as the chart of account, K4 as the FYV etc for the company code 1110. Refer Section 6.8.1 of Chapter 6, for more details on company code global parameters.

ii.   On the 'Create Profit Center Group: Initial Screen', enter the group identifier in 'Profit Center Group' (say, TRACTORS).

iii.   Click on 'Hierarchy' icon, enter a description for the group, and 'Save' (Figure 5.18).

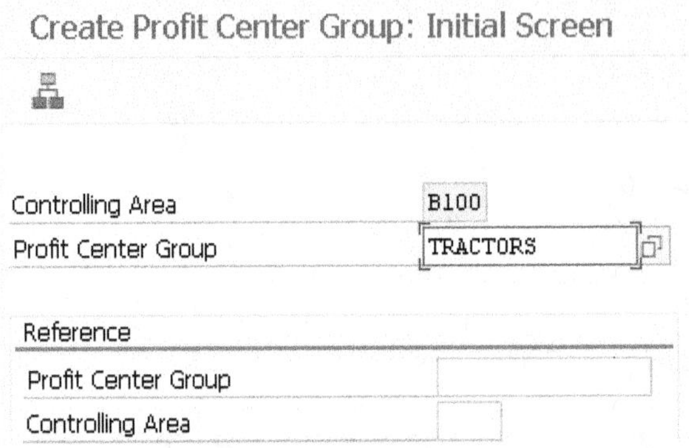

Create Profit Center Group: Initial Screen

Controlling Area	B100
Profit Center Group	TRACTORS

Reference

Profit Center Group	
Controlling Area	

Figure 5.18: Creation of Profit Center Group (TRACTORS)

iv.   Repeat creating other profit center groups

> **i** You need to define the profit center groups, before you actually create a profit center, as 'Profit Center Group' is a required field in creating the master data for a profit center.

The next logical step is assigning the profit center groups to the standard hierarchy.

5.3.9.3   Maintain Standard Hierarchy Details

As already mentioned, the standard hierarchy is a tree structure for organizing all the profit centers belonging to a controlling area. You can have two types of nodes as structure elements in the standard hierarchy: (a) *profit centers* that are directly assigned an end node, and (b) *summarization nodes* that do not themselves contain profit centers, but summarize other nodes (*end nodes*). The system divides the nodes into these two types, automatically. If you have already assigned profit centers to a node, you can no longer attach any sub-nodes to it; also, you cannot assign profit centers to a node that already contains sub-nodes. You can copy the standard hierarchy of SAP Cost Center Accounting and use that as a template in creating the standard hierarchy.

Let us now assign the profit center groups to the standard hierarchy that we have already defined in Section 5.3.9.1.

i.   Use the menu path: SAP Customizing Implementation Guide > Financial Accounting > General Ledger Accounting > Master Data > Profit Center > Define Standard Hierarchy.

ii.   On the 'Change Standard Hierarchy (Profit Center Group): Structure' screen you will see the standard hierarchy B1000. Enter the name for the standard hierarchy (Standard Hierarchy for CO Area B100).

iii.   Place the cursor on B1000, and click on 'Lower Level'. At that level, select the profit center group (say, GEQUIP). Now this profit center group is attached to the standard hierarchy. Continue and assign the other profit center groups as well (Figure 5.19).

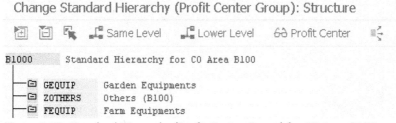

Figure 5.19: Standard Hierarchy (Profit Center Group) for CO Area B100

Now that we have completed assigning the profit center groups to the standard hierarchy, we can now proceed to define the profit centers for BESTM. However, we need to complete one more configuration activity: we need to maintain additional configuration settings for the controlling area B100, which enable tying up the controlling area a with a *dummy profit center* and standard hierarchy:

i.   Use the menu path: SAP Customizing Implementation Guide > Controlling > Profit Center Accounting > Basic Settings > Controlling Area Settings > Maintain Controlling Area Settings. Or, use Transaction OKE5.

ii.   On the 'Change View "EC-PCA: Controlling Area Settings": Overview' screen (Figure 5.20):

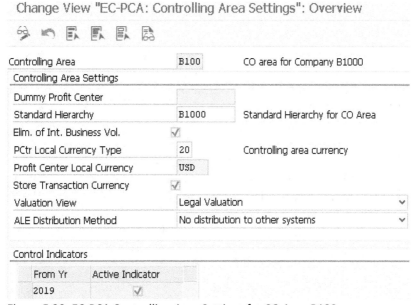

Figure 5.20: EC-PCA Controlling Area Settings for CO Area B100

- You will see a greyed-out 'Dummy Profit Center' field. The system uses this dummy profit center to post transactions when the original account assignment object (say, an object or an order) is not assigned to any profit center ensuring that the data in EC-PCA is complete. You can, later, transfer these data from the dummy profit center to the correct profit center, either through assessment or distribution.

> **i** You can create dummy profit centers using the menu path: SAP Customizing Implementation Guide > Controlling > Profit Center Accounting > Master Data > Profit Center > Create Dummy Profit Center, or Transaction KE59.

- Enter a name in "Standard Hierarchy' field (say, B1000).
- Select 'Elim. of Int. Business Vol' check-box, to eliminate internal business volume in your controlling area.
- Select the appropriate currency type from the drop-down list to fill the 'PCtr Local Currency Type' field. This sets the type of local currency you will be using for the profit center. You can select 30 (group currency), 20 (controlling area currency), or 90 (special profit center currency that you specify). When you select either 20 or 30, then, the system will automatically bring up the 'Profit Center Local Currency' field for input; if you select 90, then, you need to enter the currency here in this field. We will go with currency type 20, and the system will automatically fill USD in 'Profit Center Local Currency' field.
- Select 'Store Transaction Currency' check-box, so that the system updates the transaction data in EC-PCA in the transaction currency. However, this setting works only when you select 'legal valuation' option for the 'Valuation view' field. If you deselect 'Store Transaction Currency' check-box, though this will help in reducing the data volume, you will not be able to analyze the data in the transaction currency.

> **i** When you need a consolidated group viewpoint, you will use the 'group valuation' view in which the intercompany profits are eliminated between internal trading partners; the goods movements are posted at the group production cost price which is used for clearing within a group without transfer price surcharges.

Go for 'profit center valuation' view when you want to reproduce business transactions between profit centers for internal management purposes; goods movements are posted between profit centers at negotiated transfer prices which are used for internal profit determination and corporate management.

Select 'legal valuation' view to have the individual enterprise's view point wherein a business transaction between the internal trading partners is reproduced for external prices; the goods movements are posted between profit centers at the sales price which was agreed between the internal trading partners who produce a balance sheet / profit and loss statement independently.

iii.   'Save' the details (Figure 5.20). You may repeat the steps and configure the other two controlling areas (B200 and B300).

Now, we can define the profit centers.

5.3.9.4   Define Profit Center

Follow the steps listed below to create all the profit centers that are required:

i.   Use the menu path: SAP Customizing Implementation Guide > Controlling > Profit Center Accounting > Master Data > Profit Center > Define Profit Center.

ii.   On the 'Select Activity' pop-up screen, double-click on the first entry 'EC-PCA: Create profit center'. You may also use Transaction KE51. If you want to make change to an already created profit center, double-click on the second entry 'EC-PCA: Change profit center' on the 'Select Activity' pop-up screen or use Transaction KE52.

iii.   On the 'Create Profit Center' screen, enter the profit center identifier in the 'Profit Center' field (FARMTRACT).

iv.   Ensure that the system is showing the correct 'CO Area' (B100).

v.   Now, click on 'Master Data', and maintain the required details on the next screen, 'Create Profit Center' (Figure 5.21):

- Under the 'Basic Data' tab, under 'Descriptions' section, the system has proposed the 'Analysis Period'; if you are not fine with the date(s) proposed, you can change the same.

- Enter a meaningful name for the profit center, in 'Name' field; you may also enter a 'Long Text', if required.

- Under 'Basic Data' section, enter the person who will manage the profit center under 'Person Respons.' field, and select the appropriate profit center group in 'Profit Ctr Group' field. You may also enter the 'Segment'.

- You may maintain the details in other tabs.

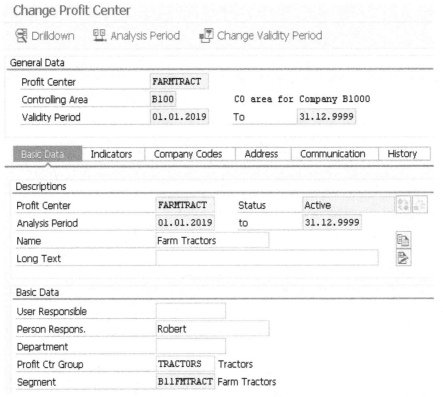

Figure 5.21: Creation of Profit Center (FARMTRACT)

- Now, 'Save' the entry and activate by pressing 'Activate' button. You have now created the profit center FARMTRACT under the profit center group TRACTORS (Figure 5.21).

iv.   Repeat the steps to create the remaining profit centers.

This completes creation of profit centers as required by BESTM management. Let us, now, look at the standard hierarchy, to see how it looks like with the assignment of profit centers to the profit center groups:

i.   Use the menu path SAP Customizing Implementation Guide > Controlling > Profit Center Accounting > Master Data > Profit Center > Define Standard Hierarchy, or Transaction KCH4. You may also use the other menu path: SAP Customizing Implementation Guide > Financial Accounting > General Ledger Accounting > Master Data > Profit Center > Define Standard Hierarchy.

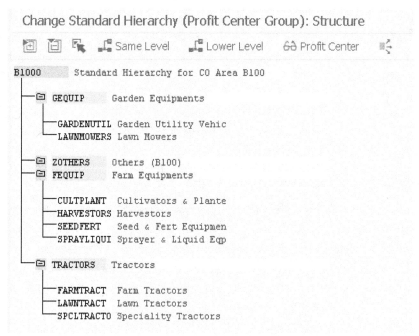

Figure 5.22: Tress Structure of the Standard Hierarchy B1000

ii. On the 'Change Standard Hierarchy (Profit Center Group): Structure' screen (Figure 5.22), you will see the standard hierarchy details that we have defined for controlling area B100, in a tree like structure with the top most node denoting the standard hierarchy (B1000), the profit center groups at the second level (sub-node) and the individual profit centers at the third level (node). You can display the corresponding profit center by positioning the cursor in the appropriate profit center identifier and clicking on 'Display Profit Center' button; you can also just double-click on the profit center identifier.

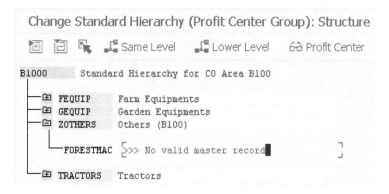

Figure 5.23: Profit Center with 'No Valid Master Record' Comment

> **i** Unless you activate a profit center when defining, you will see a comment that 'No valid master record' against that profit center identifier in the standard hierarchy (Figure 5.23).

This completes our discussion of creating the profit center, and also the definition of organizational elements that are required in FI/CO enterprise structure. We are now ready to connect these elements to establish the relationship for a meaningful data flow across them.

5.4   Assign FI / CO Organizational Units

You need to establish the relationship among the organizational units by making suitable assignments: for example, you need to assign the company codes to a company to enable group accounting, company codes to credit control area for effective credit management, company code to financial management area to derive FM area from the assigned company code, and so on. Let us start, first, with the assignment of company code to company.

5.4.1   Assign Company Code to Company

As already discussed in Section 5.3.1, we have three companies that have already been defined for Project Dolphin. And, we have also defined the required company codes in Section 5.3.2: four company codes (1110, 1120, 1210 & 1220) to be grouped under the company B1000, two company codes (2100 & 2200) to come under B2000, and two more company codes (3100 & 3200) to form the company B3000. The 'company-company code' relationship is depicted in Figure 5.24.

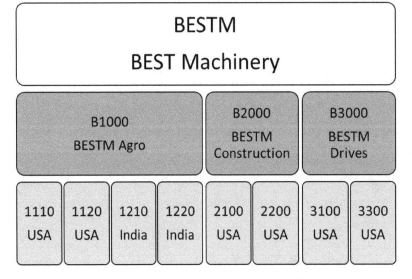

Figure 5.24: Company – Company Code Relationship for BESTM Group

Let us, now, complete the assignment:

i. Use the menu path: SAP Customizing Implementation Guide > Enterprise Structure > Assignment > Financial Accounting > Assign company code to company; or, you may use Transaction OX16.

ii. On the 'Change View "Assign Company Code -> Company": Overview' screen, select the appropriate company for the 'Company' field from the drop-down list against the respective company codes, and 'Save' (Figure 5.25).

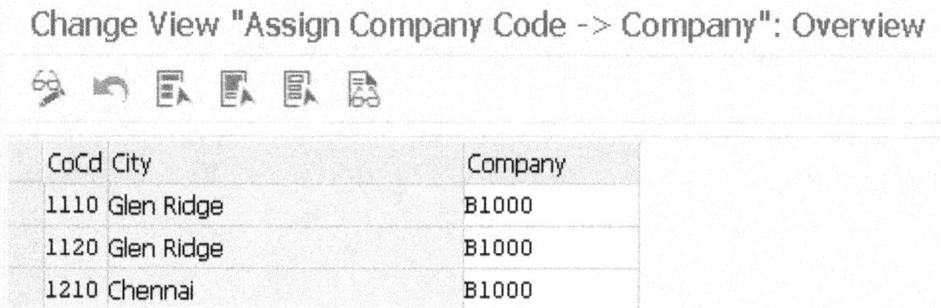

Change View "Assign Company Code -> Company": Overview

CoCd	City	Company
1110	Glen Ridge	B1000
1120	Glen Ridge	B1000
1210	Chennai	B1000

Figure 5.25: Company – Company Code Assignment

> **i** While doing the 'company code – company' assignments, when you try assigning a company code having a currency that is different than that of the company, you will then see a message to remind you that the currencies are different.

With the completion of 'company code–company' assignment, we are now ready move on to the next task of assigning company codes to credit control area.

5.4.2 Assign Company Code to Credit Control Area

We have already seen in Section 5.3.3, while defining the credit control area, that every company code needs to be attached to one (only one) credit control area, even though you can have a single credit control area catering to more than one company code.

When you assign only one company code to a credit control area, then the credit control area's currency is the same as that of the company code. But, if you assign several company codes to a single credit control area, then, the currency of the credit control area can be from any of the assigned company codes with also the possibility that the credit control area's currency is different from that of any the assigned company codes. In such a case, the receivables (FI-A/R) will all be converted to match the currency of the credit control area.

For the Project Dolphin, there are four credit control areas which we have already defined in Section 5.3.3: one each for the companies B2000 (BESTM Construction) and B3000 (BESTM Drives), and two credit control areas for B1000 (BESTM Agro). The 'company code-credit control area' relationship for BESTM group is shown in Figure 5.26.

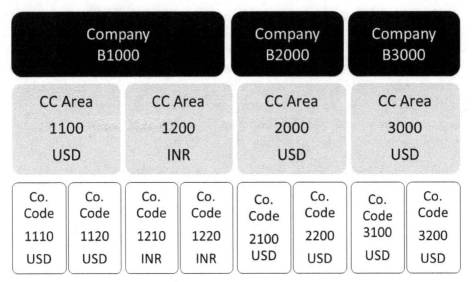

Figure 5.26: Company Code – Credit Control Area Assignment Overview for BESTM Group

Project Dolphin

BESTM wants the users not to be allowed to change the default credit control area during document posting.

Follow the steps listed below to assign a company code to a credit control area:

i.   Use the menu path: SAP Customizing Implementation Guide > Enterprise Structure > Assignment > Financial Accounting > Assign company code to credit control area or, Transaction OB38.

ii.   On the 'Change View "Assign company code -> credit control area": Overview' screen, select the appropriate credit control area for the 'CCAr' field, from the drop-down list against the respective company codes.

iii. Since BESTM does not want to change the default credit control area, you will not select the 'CCAR Can Be Overwritten' check-box; if you select this check-box, then, you can manually overwrite the credit control area defaulted (during document posting) from the company code's global data. 'Save' the entries now (Figure 5.27).

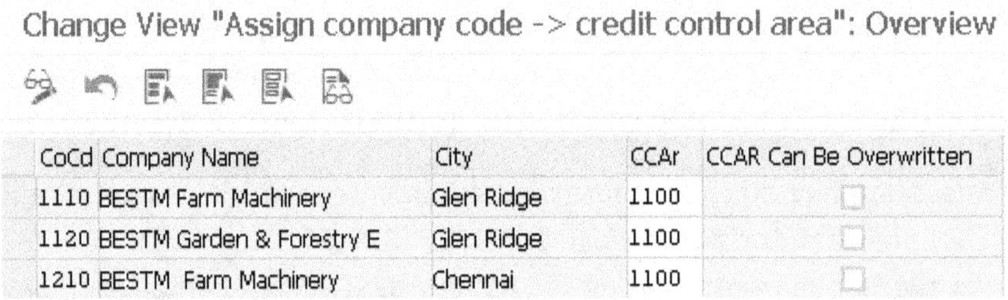

Change View "Assign company code -> credit control area": Overview

CoCd	Company Name	City	CCAr	CCAR Can Be Overwritten
1110	BESTM Farm Machinery	Glen Ridge	1100	☐
1120	BESTM Garden & Forestry E	Glen Ridge	1100	☐
1210	BESTM Farm Machinery	Chennai	1100	☐

Figure 5.27: Company Code – Credit Control Area Assignment

> **i** You can also assign credit control area to company code while maintain the global parameters for a company code (Transaction OBY6; menu path: SAP Customizing Implementation Guide > Financial Accounting > Financial Accounting Global Settings > Global Parameters for Company Code > Enter Global Parameters).

Let us move on, next, to complete assigning of FM area to company code.

5.4.3   Assign Company Code to FM Area

We need the 'company code–FM area assignment' completed to enable the system deriving the appropriate FM area from the company code to which it is assigned. It is possible that you can assign more than one company code to a single FM area. We have already defined the required FM areas in Section 5.3.6, and we can now assign them to the company codes:

> **i** You can have a FM area's currency that is different from that of the assigned company code; you cannot change the FM area's currency if you have already posted to that FM area.

i.   Use the menu path: SAP Customizing Implementation Guide > Enterprise Structure > Assignment > Financial Accounting > Assign company code to financial management area or, use Transaction OF18.

ii.   On the 'Change View "Assigning Company Codes to FM Areas": Overview' screen, select the appropriate FM area for the 'FM Area' field from the drop-down list against the respective company codes.

iii.   Even though you have already maintained the name for each of the FM area defined in Section 5.3.6, you may see that 'FMA text' is blank; enter the details and 'Save'. You have now completed the 'company code-FM area' assignment (Figure 5.28).

Change View "Assigning Company Codes to FM Areas": Overview

Assigning Company Codes to FM Areas

CoCode	Name	FM Area	FMA text
1110	BESTM Farm Machinery	BF11	FM Area BESTM Agro - USA
1120	BESTM Garden & Forestry E	BF11	FM Area BESTM Agro - USA
1210	BESTM Farm Machinery	BF12	FM Area BESTM Agro - Indi

Figure 5.28: Company Code – FM Area Assignment

With this, now, we can make the assignment between company code and controlling area.

5.4.4   Assign Company Code to Controlling Area

You have already learned in Section 5.3.8 that you can have either 1:1 or 1:n arrangement between controlling area and company code. We have adopted the 1:n arrangement for Project Dolphin, to display cross-company code CO postings like assessments, activity allocation etc. in the reconciliation ledger.

> **i** Use 1:n 'CO area-company code' assignment, for multilevel product cost management, cutting across multiple company codes, for processing cross-company code transactions in a single CO area, and to make use of EC-PCA (and transfer prices) besides group costing.

Follow the steps listed below to complete the assignment:

i.   Use the menu path: SAP Customizing Implementation Guide > Enterprise Structure > Assignment > Controlling > Assign company code to controlling area or Transaction OX19.

ii. On the 'Change View "Basic data": Overview' screen, select the appropriate controlling area (B100), and double-click on 'Assignment of company code(s)', on the left-hand 'Controlling Area' pane.

iii. On the 'Change View "Assignment of company code(s)": Overview' screen, click on 'New Entries'.

iv. On the 'New Entries: Overview of Added Entries' screen, enter the company codes (say, 1110, 1120 etc) in 'CoCd' field that need to be assigned to the controlling area (B100), selected in step (ii) above.

v.   When completed, 'Save' the details (Figure 5.29).

vi. Repeat the steps (ii) to (v) to assign the company codes to other controlling areas (say, B200 and B300).

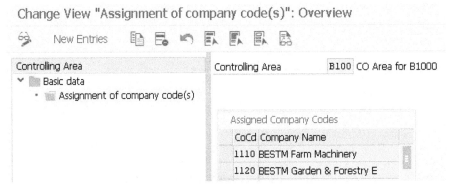

Figure 5.29: Company Code – CO Area Assignment

Now that we have completed assigning company codes to the required CO areas, let us move on to complete the final assignment between company code and profit center.

5.4.5   Assign Company Code to Profit Center

You have seen that we have already defined the required profit centers / profit center groups / standard hierarchy in Section 5.3.9. Let us now look at how to assign a company code to a profit center / profit center group or standard hierarchy.

i.   Use the menu path: SAP Customizing Implementation Guide > Enterprise Structure > Assignment > Financial Accounting > Assign profit center to company code or Transaction KE56.

ii.   On the ensuing pop-up screen, set the controlling area to B100.

iii.   On the 'Assignment of Profit Centers to Company Codes – Change' screen, you have the option of assigning the standard hierarchy or profit center groups to company code(s). Select the appropriate radio button ('Standard Hierarchy' or 'Profit center grp.') and select the company codes for 'CoCode' and 'To' fields.

iv.   When you select 'Profit center grp.' radio button, you will see the list of profit centers under the particular profit center group assigned to the company codes represented by the tick-mark in the check-boxes for the respective company codes.

v.   You can select / de-select the tick-mark appropriately before 'Saving' (Figure 5.30).

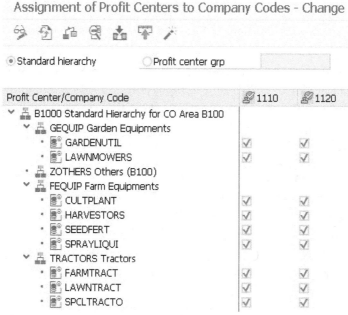

Figure 5.30: Company Code – Profit Center Assignment

With this we have completed the required assignments among the organizational units.

5.5   Conclusion

You started this Chapter with a discussion on the various organizational units (forming the enterprise structure) that you would need to create in the SAP system, to configure SAP FI and SAP CO; you understood what are all the organizational units that need to be mandatorily defined and what could be optional. You, then, went on to understand about country localization: why it is necessary, how to do that etc. You went through the steps to localize the SAP's sample organizational units to meet your specific requirements, for USA and India.

You, in the later Sections of the Chapter, learned about defining the important organizational units like, company, company code, credit control area, business area, FM (financial management) area, segment, controlling area and profit center. While defining each of these organizational units, you learned about the characteristics of that particular organizational unit, why it is important to have that defined, how to define etc. In the process, you understood that the 'client' sits at the top of the SAP system, with one or more companies below, and each company comprising of at least one company code.

You learned that a company code is the smallest mandatory central organizational unit, in SAP, for which you can maintain a complete and self-contained set of accounts, besides drawing up the external financial statements (balance sheet and profit & loss account) to meet the legal and statutory requirements of the country in which the company code operates. You learned that you can have one or more credit control areas defined to suit your credit management. Your, further, learned that a business area in FI represents an area of responsibility (or operations) of the business, and that it enables creation of financial statements below the level of a company code. You also learned that a functional area in FI classifies expenses of the business, based on the functions like, administration, marketing etc performed by employees of the organization.

While learning about FM areas that are used to structure the business organization from the perspective of SAP Cash Budget Management and SAP Funds Management, you understood the difference between a functional area and a FM area. You, then, went on to learn about the segments that are used in segment reporting to meet the statutory requirements IAS, IFRS and US GAAP; and, that these segments are based normally on the location of a business entity's assets or customers or a geographical segment.

You understood that the controlling area is a self-contained cost accounting entity (like a company code in FI) that is central to the organizational structure in SAP CO, and is used to subdivide your business from the cost-accounting viewpoint, for bringing out internal reporting. Finally, you learned about defining the profit centers that are areas of responsibility within a company for revenues and expenses; while on profit centers, you also learned about profit center groups and standard hierarchy.

In the last part of the Chapter, you learned about assigning the various organizational units among themselves, to bring out the functional relationship between two units that will enable process and data flow in SAP. You learned that you can assign one or more company codes to a company, one or more company codes to a credit control area, one or more FM areas to a company code and so on. In the case of assignment of company code to controlling area, you learned that the assignment can be 1:1 or 1:n between the controlling area and company code(s). Lastly, you saw the assignment of profit centers (profit center groups and standard hierarchy) to a company code.

This completes our discussion on enterprise structure. We can, now, move on to the next Chapter to discuss about FI global settings. In fact, we shall discuss FI global settings in the next three Chapters, starting with Chapter 6.

6   FI Global Settings – I

You need to configure *Financial Accounting (FI) global settings* to ensure that the SAP component of FI (Financial Accounting) is properly set up in the system, to meet your specific business requirements. By doing this configuration, you decide - for example - what ledgers you want to use to record the FI transactions, what fiscal year and posting period(s) are to be used by the company codes, how the screen fields should behave during transaction processing, what are the ground rules for changing / parking documents, what numbering should the system allot to the various types documents, how the system should calculate and post the taxes, how to handle the correspondence with the business partners etc.

As there are several global settings, we have divided the discussion of FI global settings into three Chapters:

- *Chapter 6* will be dealing with fields, ledgers, fiscal year, posting period, parallel accounting, integration of CO with FI and company code global parameters.
- *Chapter 7* will discuss mainly the documents (types, numbering, posting keys, variants for document entry, rules for changing documents, tolerance groups, texts for document entry, default values, recurring entries, document parking etc). It will also discuss inflation accounting, correspondence and integration of SAP S/4HANA with SAP Shared Services.
- *Chapter 8* will deal with the remaining FI global settings namely, tax on sales/purchases, withholding tax and SEPA (Single Euro Payment Area).

Let us start discussing the FI global settings that we will be dealing in this Chapter; let us begin with the fields.

6.1   Fields

SAP comes delivered with several fields, known as '*standard fields*' (or dimensions), such as business area, profit center, segment etc. Besides tailoring these fields to meet your specific reporting needs, you can make use of the SAP-provided extensive functions and integrations to process them in your transactions in FI. However, you may find that these standard fields may not be sufficient to meet your exact business needs; in such cases, you may consider using fields (not supplied by SAP) called '*customer fields*' that you define yourself to meet the requirements. So, a customer field is a database table field that is created and defined by you (the customer), the inclusion of which has effects across the whole system (and across all clients) because these customer fields entail repository changes. However, it is not mandatory that you need to use these customer fields in all the clients.

You can use customer fields as (a) product-related or activity-related characteristics such as product groups (say: new cars, pre-owned cars, leased cars etc), vehicle categories (say: medium, small, heavy etc), characteristics for maintenance works, characteristics for customer service etc, (b) organizational or managerial characteristics such as geographical regions (say: Asia, Middle East, Europe etc), characteristics for specific business areas that cannot be otherwise covered by either profit centers or cost centers, and (c) characteristics arising out of legal / statutory or industry requirements such as contract types or other contract characteristics in the area of insurance and financial services.

> **i** You cannot delete a customer field once it has been created, by using standard means.

You can use customer fields for analysing information at an aggregated level. You can also use customer fields to assign specific documents or line items to a customer-specific characteristic; in such cases, you may not need to assign the complete document volume, but just the selected posting data. In the most basic case, you will use a customer field for storing structured information that is not stored in the standard fields. SAP G/L Accounting enables you to combine customer fields with the available *standard fields* so that you can, for example, create P&L statements by profit center and special criteria within your company.

> **i** Do not use any of the SAP-supplied standard fields for alternative purposes (including deriving a customer field), just to store information in documents, as at a later date you may want to use some of these standard fields. It will really become a problem, at that point, if you had already used those fields for some other purposes.

You can include customer fields, in FI, in the *'coding block'* so as to broaden the scope of SAP G/L Accounting either by adding new customer fields or by combining such fields with the existing standard fields. This way, you can adapt the information in SAP G/L Accounting to the specific reporting requirements of your business. However, note to deliberate beforehand whether you really want to use customer fields; if so, how you want to define them. This is because of the significance that more the number of customer fields you create, more will be the fields in the system that you need to fill-in when you enter or transfer documents. Besides manual postings, this will also have an impact on automatic postings that are made through interfaces. The use of customer fields, therefore, is not to replace the standard scenarios; for example, if you want to perform segment reporting in accordance with IAS (International Accounting Standards) or IFRS (International Financial Reporting Standards) or US GAAP

(Generally Accepted Accounting Principles), you should use the standard 'Segment' field that is designed for that purpose.

> **i** It is possible to use G/L accounts instead of customer fields, to achieve the same result. However, this approach leads to redundant G/L accounts and consequently inflating the coding block. Also, such a solution is generally not acceptable, because it may cause problems if you use the account approach for parallel accounting as that may for making additional differentiation of accounts.

The inclusion of customer fields does not automatically affect or trigger subsequent process in the SAP standard system. From the perspective of FI, certain actions (such as the creation of correspondence or informing designated employees / departments within the company) are triggered by values that you enter in customer fields. You could implement such subsequent processes, separately (if necessary), in the relevant application, using enhancements or workflows. You can only assign customer fields, in the coding block, to G/L account items (accounts for financial statements). Hence, you cannot use the customer fields in FI for open item accounting (in FI-A/R, FI-AP), even though you can use enhancements to include customer fields in the master data.

With this understanding of standard and customer fields, let us proceed to configure the two important customizing tasks involving standard fields namely (a) maintaining transaction types for consolidation and (b) assign asset transaction types.

6.1.1   Maintain Transaction Types for Consolidation

You will use the *'consolidation transaction types'* to represent transaction types during consolidation. You will use them for showing the horizontal development of balance sheet items (like, changes in fixed assets from opening to closing balance, changes in appropriations etc).

In FI-AA, you use them to classify business transactions (such as, asset acquisition, asset retirement, and asset transfer), and to determine how to process them in the system. Forming the basis for the assignment of business transactions to a column in the asset history sheet, every transaction type belongs to a specific transaction type group.

The standard SAP system comes delivered with a range of transaction types for consolidation (Figure 6.1), and it is highly unlikely that you will need anything more.

Project Dolphin

Looking at the SAP-supplied transaction types in the system, the Dolphin Project team has decided not to add any new transaction type for consolidation, for BESTM.

Change View "Consolidation transaction types": Overview

New Entries

Transactn type	Description
900	Opening balance
901	Incoming units
902	Cons Mthd Chg(Old)
903	Cons Mthd Chg(New)
904	Equity Mthd Rate Chg
906	Dividends
909	Change in accounting
915	Net variation
920	Increase/ Purchase
925	Increase in deprecia

Figure 6.1 Standard Transaction Types

As the Project Dolphin does not require any new transaction types for consolidation, we will not define anything new. However, should you need a new transaction type, follow the steps listed below to define the new one:

i.   Use the menu path: SAP Customizing Implementation Guide > Financial Accounting > Financial Accounting Global Settings > Ledgers > Fields > Standard Fields > Maintain Transaction Types for Consolidation. You may also use Transaction OC08.

ii.   On the 'Change View "Consolidation transaction types": Overview' screen (Figure 6.2), press 'New Entries', and maintain the required details on the next screen:

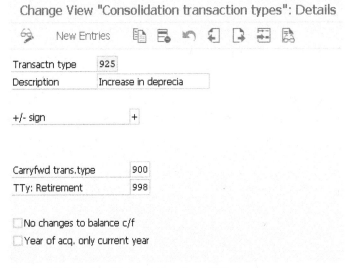

Change View "Consolidation transaction types": Details

New Entries

Transactn type   925
Description   Increase in deprecia

+/- sign   +

Carryfwd trans.type   900
TTy: Retirement   998

☐ No changes to balance c/f
☐ Year of acq. only current year

Figure 6.2 Details of Transaction Type 925

- For each new transaction type, you specify + or - in the '+/- sign' field, so that you can make data entry without a sign, but the system internally stores the data with that sign.
- Also, maintain the 'Carryfwd trans.type' field that defines the transaction type to which the system posts the balance forward in the new period.
- Select 'No changes to balance c/f' check-box if the transaction type should not be changed by entering data. This will come handy after the balance carried forward for the opening balances, to prevent these being changed manually.
- Select 'Year of acq. only current year' check-box, if a transaction type should only be entered for the current year, despite data entry by year of acquisition.
- 'Save' the details, you have now created a new transaction type. Note that we have not created any new transaction type, but have provided the screen-shot to provide a clarity on what needs to be filled to create new (Figure 6.2).

If you have created a new transaction type, then, you need to move on to the next step of assigning the new asset transaction types to consolidation transaction type.

6.1.2 Assign Asset Transaction Types

Use the menu path: SAP Customizing Implementation Guide > Financial Accounting > Financial Accounting Global Settings > Ledgers > Fields > Standard Fields > Assign Asset Transaction Types. On the 'Change View "Asset transaction types -> Consolidation": Overview' screen, enter the transaction type in the 'Cons TType' field for each of the new transaction types created. In the standard SAP system, the consolidation transaction types are already assigned to asset transaction types (Figure 6.3).

Change View "Asset transaction types -> Consolidation": Overview

Trans. Type	Transaction Type Name	Cons TType
000	Formal transctn type for migration (000,398,399)	
100	External asset acquisition	920
101	Acquisition for a negative asset	920
102	External asset acquisition – set changeover year	920
103	Incidental costs, non-deduct. input tax (fol.yrs)	920
105	Credit memo in invoice year	920
106	Credit memo in invoice year to affiliated company	920
107	Gross acquisition of prior year balances (merger)	920
108	Gross acquisition of curren year balances (merger)	920
110	In-house acquisition	920

Figure 6.3 Assigning Transaction Types to Consolidation Type

This completes our discussion on the customizing activities relating to the standard fields. Let us now move on to discuss what needs to be done to make customer fields ready or available for posting the transactions:

- Edit Coding Block
- Define Master Data Check
- Include Customer Fields in Enjoy Transactions

Let us start with editing the coding block.

6.1.3 Edit Coding Block

Create your own customer fields in the coding block of the system, and use these *'coding fields'* in G/L accounts in SAP FI, inventory management & purchasing in SAP MM, and for updating the line items created in SAP CO. The newly created customer fields are, then, updated by the system during automatic postings. To enable you to post these fields manually in SAP Enjoy Transactions, you must assign them to the entry variants, in the Enjoy posting transactions (we shall discuss this later when we configure the 3rd task namely 'Include Customer Fields in Enjoy Transactions'). You will need a test system, and the following authorizations (Table 6.1) to include the coding fields:

Task	Authorization Required
New field inclusion in coding block	X_COBLMOD
Maintenance of cross-client tables	S_TABU_CLI
Dictionary authorization	S_DEVELOP
Transport authorization	T S_TRANSPRT

Table 6:1 Authorizations Required for including the Coding Fields

> **i** We recommend that you start with a clear-cut concept or strategy for your own coding fields, before making the necessary changes to the coding block. Check whether a suitable standard SAP coding field already exists fulfilling your requirements: if yes, use that field; else, create a new coding field. But, define the final format (data type and length) for the new coding field, as soon as possible; you cannot make any changes to the field format or delete a coding field using standard methods, subsequently, once it has been included.

Once you complete editing the coding block for including the new customer fields, and as soon as you flag the client as 'productive' in the system, the *'Include fields'* function is locked for that system, and you can no longer make any subsequent changes. Now, the system adds the newly included coding fields to the ABAP Dictionary.

Project Dolphin

The Dolphin Project team has decided not to add any new coding fields in the system. This has been finalised, after a thorough study of the SAP defined standard coding fields that are already available in the coding block.

Though we will not create any new coding fields, as indicated by the implementation team of Project Dolphin, let us understand the how to do that in the system should you require one.

i.   Use the menu path: SAP Customizing Implementation Guide > Financial Accounting > Financial Accounting Global Settings > Ledgers > Fields > Customer Fields > Edit Coding Block. You may also use Transaction OXK3.

ii. You will see a pop-up screen warning you that the changes you are about to make involves extending central Dictionary tables, besides making entries in tables that affect all the clients in the system. It also warns to save your data before making an 'update run' for adding a field or making changes to the Dictionary. Press 'Continue'.

iii. On the 'Maintain User-Defined Coding Block Fields: List' screen, you will see a tree-structure with 'Coding Block' at the top, and two child entries namely 'SAP Standard Account Assignments' and 'Customer-Defined Account Assignments' below that.

iv. When you expand 'SAP Standard Account Assignments', you will see more than 70 standard coding fields like ANBWA (Transaction Type), ANLN1 (Asset), BUKRS (Company Code), FIKRS (FM Area) and so on, as shown in Figure 6.4.

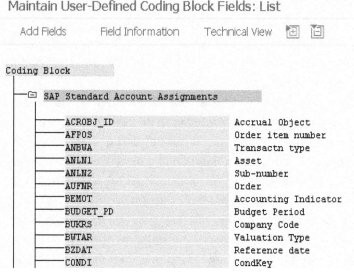

Figure 6.4 Coding Block: SAP Standard Account Assignments

v.   Expand 'Customer-Defined Account Assignments' and you will see 'Customer Include Structure' and 'Customer APPEND Structures' (Figure 6.5).

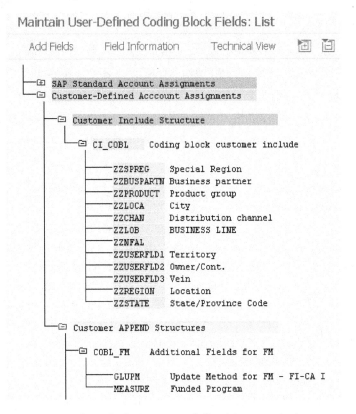

Figure 6.5 Coding Block: Customer-defined Account Assignments

vi.   Expand the 'Customer Include Structure', and you will reach CI_COBL which is the coding block for customer include. Expand CI_COBL, and you will see several new coding fields that have already been defined in the system (Figure 6.5). You can make use of these SAP supplied coding fields. Or, if you need a new one:

- Click on 'Add Fields'. For this specific customizing task, let us create a new field called 'YYMOREINFO' which can be used to add more information when posting a G/L line item. Note this is not part of the Project Dolphin.

- On the 'Maintain User-Defined Coding Block Fields: New Field' screen, select the 'Test Run' check-box. You will deselect this when the test-run is over, and when you are ready to do the production update.

- Now, enter the 'Development Class' that you have created for extending the coding block. Make sure that the development class is assigned to a transport layer that has the same target system as that of the SAP standard objects.

- Enter the field in 'Field Name' starting with the customer-allowed namespace of 'ZZ' or 'YY' (Figure 6.6).

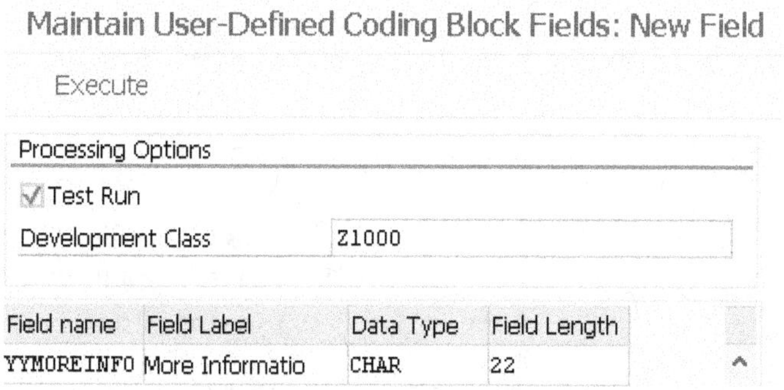

Maintain User-Defined Coding Block Fields: New Field

Execute

Processing Options

☑ Test Run

Development Class   Z1000

Field name	Field Label	Data Type	Field Length	
YYMOREINFO	More Informatio	CHAR	22	^

Figure 6.6 Adding a new Coding Field

- Enter the 'Field Label', 'Data Type' (CHAR or NUMC), and 'Field Length'. Ensure that you are not entering a field length of more than 22.
- Now, 'Execute'. The system creates a test-run and will throw errors, if any. If there are no errors, and if you are satisfied with the results of the test-run (=production simulation), deselect the 'Test Run', and 'Execute' again.
- Enter a correction number and a repair number for table BSEG. Note that it is important to have both the specifications in the same transport request to import the enhancement correctly into the *Electronic Data Interchange* (EDI) sub-system. The new field has now been included in the coding block, and the system creates a log of all the changes that has been done; this will help in analysing errors, if any, that have occurred in the dictionary functions while performing this transaction.

> **i** Run a data backup and proceed as per SAP guidelines, before you proceed to create a customer field in the system. Also, note that no postings should occur, while the field is being created and while transporting the same to the production system.

This completes our discussion on editing coding block. Let us, now, move on to the next configuration task of defining the master data check.

6.1.4 Define Master Data Check

You will use this configuration task to determine how the check is to be carried out for the *integrated master data* that you use for planning and allocation. This is necessary because this data is not always created in the SAP G/L, such as a G/L account, rather is created during SAP system integration, such as cost center. Consider that you are entering certain G/L account during planning, in one of your company codes; the system, then checks, to ascertain if the entered account is a valid one and if it is a valid 'company code-account' combination.

> **i** *Integrated master data* refers to all master data that is used as dimensions in SAP G/L Accounting.

The standard SAP system comes delivered with check routines for the most important fields; that is, for the fields that can be activated when setting up scenarios. These standard check routines will be more than sufficient to meet your business requirements. However, in case you need a new check routine to be defined, follow the steps listed below:

i. Use the menu path: SAP Customizing Implementation Guide > Financial Accounting > Financial Accounting Global Settings > Ledgers > Fields > Customer Fields > Define Master Data Check. You may also use Transaction GLGCS1.

ii. On the resulting 'Change View "Field for Master Data Check": Overview' screen, you will see the default check routines ('Check') defined by SAP (Figure 6.7).

Change View "Fields for Master Data Check": Overview

Table	Field Name	Check
ACDOCA	ACCASTY	=76
ACDOCA	AUFNR	=13
ACDOCA	AWTYP	
ACDOCA	BTTYPE	
ACDOCA	CATEGORY	
ACDOCA	KOKRS	=04
ACDOCA	LSTAR	=10
ACDOCA	OBJNR	=53

Figure 6.7 Standard Settings for Master Data Check

iii. Click on the 'New Entries' if you define a new check routine. On the next screen (Figure 6.8):

- Enter the appropriate totals table (ACDOCA) from the drop-down list in the 'Totals Table' field. We shall discuss ACDOCA, later, in detail in Section 6.3.3.
- Select the appropriate field for 'Field Name', for which you want the check to be created, from the drop-down list.
- Under the 'Master Data Validation Block', under 'Validation Using Exit or FI-SL Master Data Table' block, enter the appropriate 'Exit/Table' for all SAP fields where the validation is not done through value tables. For all SAP fields (and customer fields) where validation is done through a value table, enter the required details in the 'Validation Using Value Table' block (Figure 6.8).

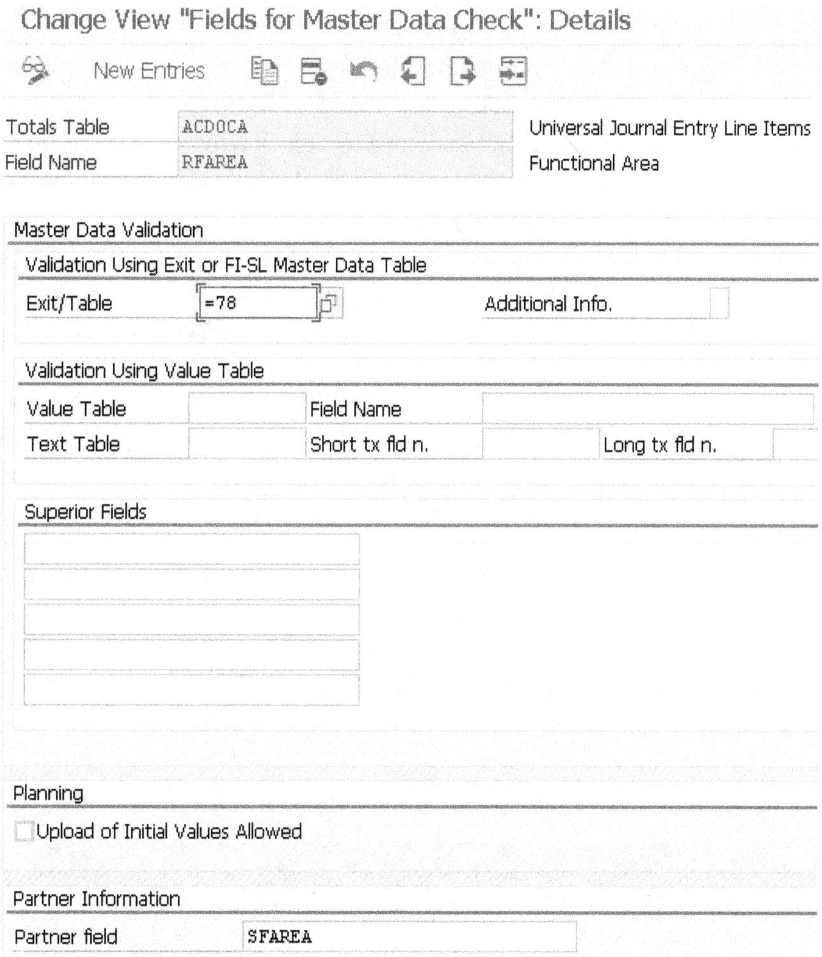

Change View "Fields for Master Data Check": Details

63.   New Entries   📑 🖪 ↩ ⬅ 📤 ➡️

| Totals Table | ACDOCA | Universal Journal Entry Line Items |
| Field Name | RFAREA | Functional Area |

Master Data Validation

Validation Using Exit or FI-SL Master Data Table

| Exit/Table | =78 | 📋 | Additional Info. | |

Validation Using Value Table

| Value Table | | Field Name | |
| Text Table | | Short tx fld n. | Long tx fld n. |

Superior Fields

| |
| |
| |
| |
| |

Planning

☐ Upload of Initial Values Allowed

Partner Information

| Partner field | SFAREA |

Figure 6.8 Defining new Master Data Check

> **ℹ** The exit will be in the form of '= NN', where N stands for a number, in the 'Exit/Table' field. For example, 04 represents KOKRS (CO area), 05 COST_ELEM (cost element), 06 RCNTR (cost center), and so on. The exit routine itself is stored in program SAPLGUMD. Unless you enter a 'Field Name', the system will not propose the possible entries for 'Exit/Table' field: for example, if you enter RBUKRS in 'Field Name' the system will show you the relevant exit (=03) for the drop-down list for the field 'Exit/Table'; if the 'Field Name' is RYEAR, then the exit will be =08, and so on.

- Now, select the appropriate value for 'Additional Info.' field. Maintain this field only for validations with an exit, as it controls whether the exit retrieves other values as well besides the validation: for example, when validating a cost center, you need to retrieve other values as well. You have three options here: 0-no exit for additional values, 1-exit for period-independent values and 2-exit for period-dependent values.

- If the field (say, G/L account) for which you are creating a check is dependent on another field (say, company code), then you need to enter that field name (that is, company code) under 'Superior Fields'. You must always enter the field name of the summary table field (such as RBUKRS) in the superior field.
- 'Save' the details, when completed, and you have now created a new master data check for the field that you have entered initially.

> **i** Note that what we have shown Figure 6.8 is only for providing information as to what needs to be entered and to give you a feel how the screen looks like. We have not created this check afresh.

Let us now look at the last task of including the customer fields in SAP Enjoy Transactions, under configuring the customer fields.

6.1.5 Include Customer Fields in Enjoy Transactions

Use this Customizing task to assign your customer fields to a screen variant for the G/L account items (screen 100 in program SAPLFSKB) of SAP Enjoy Transactions, to enable the use of these customer fields when making manual postings for account assignment (Table 6.2):

Enjoy Transaction	Transaction
G/L account posting and parking	FB50, FV50, FV50, FV50L
Invoice entry and parking	FB70 and FB60, or FV70 and FV60
Credit memo entry and parking	FB75 and FB65, or FV75 and FV65
Incoming invoice	MIRO, MIR7

Table 6:2 Enjoy Transactions in which you can use Customer Fields

You cannot directly select customer fields when creating a screen variant for the G/L account items. Because, in the element list on the screen, you only see generic fields like ACGL_ITEM_GEN-GEN_CHAR1, as placeholder in the screen variant in place of the customer field. However, during runtime, the generic fields are replaced in the screen by your customer fields; only fields with the type CHAR are considered, and other formats (such as DATS) are not supported. Hence, when editing the screen variant, specify the maximum number of visible customer fields (up to five) and their column position/sequence. Then, specify which fields are displayed in the screen variant in place of generic fields and in which sequence.

> **i** If you do not make an assignment for a screen variant, the customer fields are displayed, up to the maximum number specified in the variant and in the same sequence as they are defined in the coding block.

You can also include your customer fields in a screen as a modification (for example, if more than five customer fields need to be entered in one screen variant). In this way, you do not need to execute this configuration activity described in this Section, and you can hide the generic fields in screen 100 when editing the screen variant.

Let us now configure the activity:

i. Use the menu path: SAP Customizing Implementation Guide > Financial Accounting > Financial Accounting Global Settings > Ledgers > Fields > Customer Fields > Include Customer Fields in Enjoy Transactions.
ii. On the resulting 'Determine Work Area: Entry' pop-up screen, select the appropriate screen variant (say, STANDARD 1_0100).
iii. Press 'Enter'. On the 'Change View "Define Assignment of Customer Fields to Screen Variants": Overview' screen, click 'New Entries'.
iv. On the next screen (Figure 6.9):

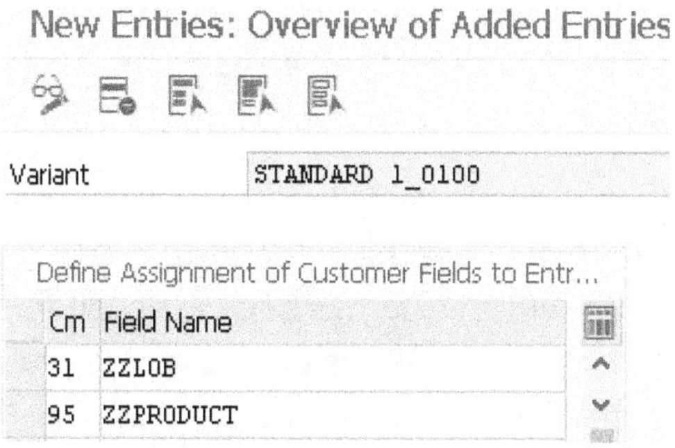

New Entries: Overview of Added Entries

Variant   STANDARD 1_0100

Define Assignment of Customer Fields to Entr...

Cm	Field Name
31	ZZLOB
95	ZZPRODUCT

Figure 6.9 Including Customer Fields in Screen Variant

- Enter starting position for the field in question, in 'Cm' field.
- Select the customer field from the drop-down list for 'Field Name'
- Repeat the above for all the customer fields, in the sequence you want, that need to be included in the screen variant, and 'Save' (Figure 6.9).

This completes our discussion on configuring the customer fields in the system. And, we are, now, ready to discuss the field status variants.

6.2   Field Status Variants

Before discussing *'field status variant'* (FSV), let us first understand what is a *'field status'*, and what is a *'field status group'* (FSG). As you might be aware of, every field has a 'status' which controls the behaviour of that field on a screen: whether it is displayed or hidden (suppressed), and whether that field is a required (mandatory) or optional for data entry. Hence, the 'field status' refers to the characteristic or behaviour of a field on a data entry screen as to its display and/or receiving a data entry input. Though all fields on a form will normally have a field status, there are some fields - for example, fields on a document header - for which you cannot attach a field status; however, you can define some fields from the document header also as 'required' or 'optional' fields in the document type.

> **i** Keep only the most important fields as 'required entry' or 'suppressed', with all others as 'optional entry' to prevent unnecessary issues while transaction entry.

A *'field status group'* (FSG) is a collection of field statuses, defined in the company code data of G/L account, and is used to determine which fields are ready for data entry input (required/mandatory or optional), and which needs to be hidden. By default, every field is displayed; only by applying one of the three statuses, you decide if that field needs to be required one, optional or suppressed (hidden). Additional account assignments (for example, cost centers or orders), if any, are only possible if the corresponding fields are ready for input. The FSG that you enter in the reconciliation accounts affects the corresponding customer / vendor accounts when posting.

In addition to the FSG, the other factors that influence the field status are the (a) posting key and (b) document type. The status 'optional entry' field has been assigned to the standard G/L account posting keys 40 and 50 in the standard SAP system. As regards document type, you can – for example - specify that a 'reference number' and a 'document header' must always be entered. There are several FSGs defined in the standard SAP system, all starting with 'Y': for example, YB01 (General with text & assignment), YB05 (Bank Accounts), YB29 (Revenue Accounts) and so on (Figure 6.10).

Each FSG is made up of sub-groups that include general data, additional account assignments, materials management, payment transactions, asset accounting, taxes, foreign payments, consolidation, real estate management and financial assets management that group the associated fields. You will see sub-groups in both blue and black letters: the fields in black groups will all have the 'suppressed' field status because they are not relevant to that particular FSG.

Field status group	Text
SEC0	All Fields optional
SECC	Secondary GL
YB01	General (with text & assignment)
YB03	Material consumption accounts
YB04	Cost accounts
YB05	Bank accounts (obligatory value date)
YB06	Material accounts
YB07	Asset accts (w/o accumulated depreciatn)
YB08	Assets area clearing accounts
YB09	Bank accounts (obligatory due date)
YB11	Clearing accounts (with settlement per.)
YB12	Receivables/payables clearing
YB13	General (obligatory text)
YB14	MM adjustment accounts
YB17	Freight/customs provisions/clearing (MM)
YB18	Scrapping (MM)
YB19	Other receivables/payables
YB23	Plant maintenance accounts

Figure 6.10 Standard Field Status Groups (FSG)

Make sure that you control the field status properly through posting keys and FSGs; conflicting field statuses between an FSG attached to an account and the FSG attached to the underlying posting keys may result in chaos. If not properly controlled, you will end up with a situation, for example, wherein you would have inadvertently assigned both 'suppressed' and 'required entry' statuses to the same field. SAP uses *'link rules'* to overcome this conflicting situation. The details of the link rules are outlined in Figure 6.11: when one field status is 'suppressed' and the other is 'optional entry', the resulting field status is always 'suppressed'. A combination of 'suppressed' and 'required entry' always result in an error due to conflict. Hence, the link rule determines what should be the final status of a field if there are two conflicting statuses for the same.

---

i You cannot directly enter an FSG in customer / vendor accounts; they are determined from their respective reconciliation accounts (via the G/L account number), in their respective master records.

You group several FSGs in one field status variant (FSV), and then assign that FSV to a company code. By this, you will be able to work with the same FSGs in multiple company codes. These FSVs use FSGs to specify which fields are ready for input, which fields must be filled, or which fields are suppressed (hidden) when entering postings.

Field Status in Posting Key and G/L Account		Field Status in Posting Key			Final Field Status as per Link Rules
		Suppressed	Required Entry	Optional Entry	
Field Status in G/L Account	Suppressed	○			Suppressed
			○		Error (Conflict)
				○	Error (Conflict)
	Required Entry	○			Error (Conflict)
			○		Required Entry
				○	Error (Conflict)
	Optional Entry	○			Suppressed
			○		Required Entry
				○	Optional Entry

Figure 6.11 SAP Link Rules to resolve conflicting Field Statuses

With this we are now ready to define the FSV.

6.2.1 Define Field Status Variant

As in other customizing objects, SAP comes delivered with a standard FSV (0010). Look at that and decide if you really need a new one. The easiest way to create a new one, is to copy a standard FSV, make the changes in the field statuses to suit your need.

Project Dolphin

The Dolphin Project implementation team has decided to use a single FSV across all the company codes of BESTM. They have further recommended that (a) 'Business Area' and 'Functional Area' fields to be set as 'required' for data entry, and (b) 'Payment Reference' field to be set as 'optional entry' field so as to enable the users to input payment reference, if any, while undertaking the payment transactions.

Let us now define the FSV for BESTM:

i.   Use the menu path: SAP Customizing Implementation Guide > Financial Accounting > Financial Accounting Global Settings > Ledgers > Fields > Define Field Status Variants. You may also use Transaction OBC4.

ii. On the 'Change View "Field status variants": Overview' screen, select the FSV row 0010, and click on 'Copy as' button.

iii. You will now be taken to 'Change View "Field status variants": Overview of Selected Set' screen. Rename the 'FStV' (say, B100) and 'Field Status Name' fields to suit your naming conventions.

iv. Press 'Enter' and go ahead with 'Copy All'; the system completes copying all the dependent entries; they are nothing but the FSGs associated with this FSV. 'Save' (Figure 6.12).

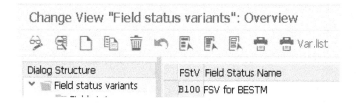

Figure 6.12 Defining FSV 'B100' for BESTM

v.   Now, select the row containing the FSV B100. You can double-click on 'Field status group' folder on the dialog-box on the left pane.

vi. You are now looking at the 'Change View "Field status groups": Overview' screen. You can see all the FSGs associated with the FSV B100, on the right-hand side of the dialog box (Figure 6.13).

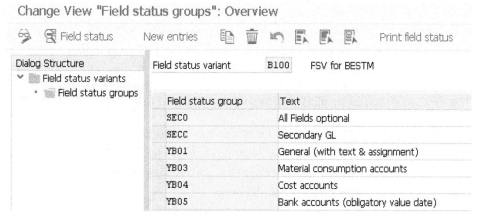

Figure 6.13 FSGs associated with FSV 'B100'

vii.   Double-click on the FSG 'YB01'. You will reach 'Maintain Field Status Group: Overview' screen; double-click on 'Additional account assignments' under 'Select Group' block.

viii. On the next screen 'Maintain Field Status Group: Additional account assignments', you will see that the fields 'Business Area' and 'Functional Area' have 'suppressed' field status at this point of time. Since, you need to make them 'required' for BESTM, select the 'Req. Entry' radio button against these fields.

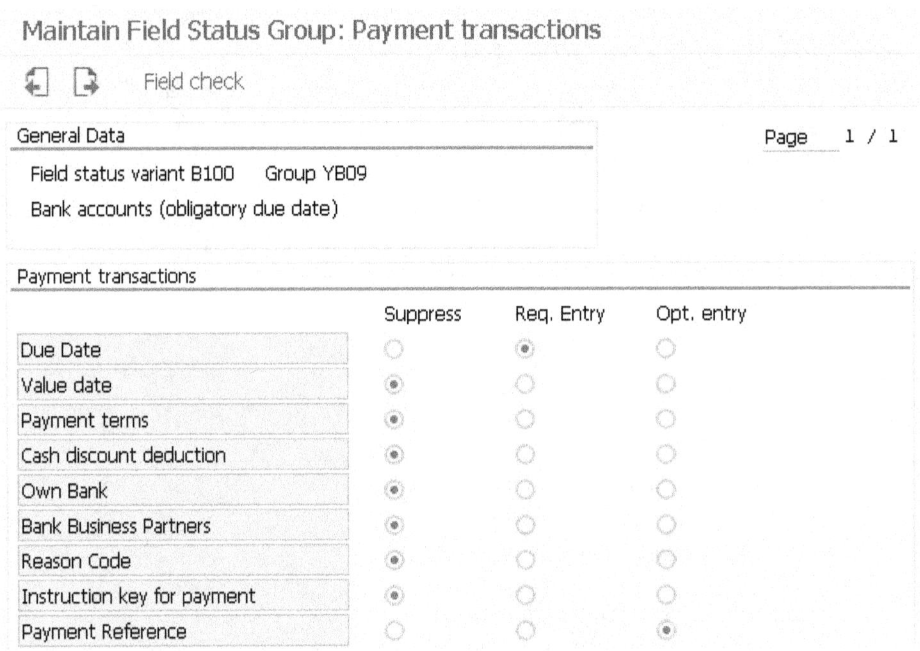

Maintain Field Status Group: Payment transactions

⬅ ➡   Field check

General Data			Page 1 / 1

Field status variant B100   Group YB09
Bank accounts (obligatory due date)

Payment transactions

	Suppress	Req. Entry	Opt. entry
Due Date	○	⦿	○
Value date	⦿	○	○
Payment terms	⦿	○	○
Cash discount deduction	⦿	○	○
Own Bank	⦿	○	○
Bank Business Partners	⦿	○	○
Reason Code	⦿	○	○
Instruction key for payment	⦿	○	○
Payment Reference	○	○	⦿

Figure 6.14 Field Status change for 'Payment Reference' field

ix.   'Save', and you are taken back to 'Change View "Field status groups": Overview' screen. Now, double-click on the FSG YB09 {Bank accounts (obligatory due date)}, on the next screen double-click 'Payment transactions' group, and change the 'suppressed' field status of 'Payment Reference' to 'optional entry' by selecting the 'Opt. entry' radio button against this field. And, 'Save' (Figure 6.14).

You have now defined the FSV 'B100' and made the required field status changes to some of the fields as required by BESTM. Now, we are ready to assign this FSV to the company codes.

6.2.2 Assign Company Code Field Status Variants

Now that we have defined the FSV in the previous Section 6.2.1, it is time we assign the company codes to this FSV, so that they can use the variant. As already indicated, you can use the same FSV across multiple company codes:

i.   Use the menu path: SAP Customizing Implementation Guide > Financial Accounting >
     Financial Accounting Global Settings > Ledgers > Fields > Assign Company Code to
     Field Status Variants. You may also use Transaction OBC5.

ii. On the 'Change View "Assign Company Code -> Field Status Variant": Overview'
     screen, select the FSV 'B100' under the column 'Fld stat. var.' against the appropriate
     company codes (1110, 1120 etc) and 'Save'. You have now assigned the company
     codes to the FSV (Figure 6.15).

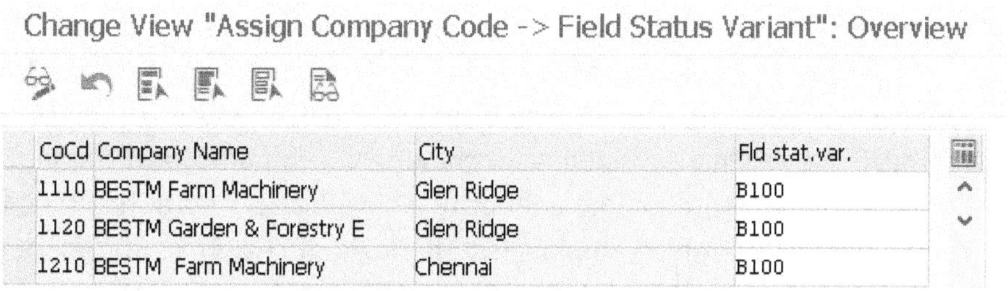

Change View "Assign Company Code -> Field Status Variant": Overview

CoCd	Company Name	City	Fld stat.var.	
1110	BESTM Farm Machinery	Glen Ridge	B100	
1120	BESTM Garden & Forestry E	Glen Ridge	B100	
1210	BESTM Farm Machinery	Chennai	B100	

Figure 6.15 FSV – Company Code Assignment

> **i** You can also assign the FSV to a company code while maintaining the company code global parameters (Transaction OBY6). Refer <u>Section 6.8.1</u> of this Chapter.

Let us now move on to complete the final configuration step for 'Fields': defining subscreens
for coding blocks.

6.2.3 Define Subscreens for Coding Blocks

The account assignment transactions, in SAP, use subscreens containing the various account
assignment fields. The system, when generating the data entry screens for these transactions,
searches for the most suitable subscreen (containing the most 'required' fields), and brings
up that for data entry. If there is no such subscreen that contains all the necessary fields, the
system will force you to enter the additional fields in a separate dialog box. By defining your
own subscreens, you can structure these subscreens to suit your own requirements, thereby
avoiding the need to enter the account assignment fields in an additional dialog box.

> **i** As this is a client-independent configuration activity, note that any changes you make here will apply in all clients and for all the transactions that use that particular coding block. You will need the authorization S_TABU_CLI to maintain the subscreens.

We will not be defining any new subscreen for BESTM; however, let us see the steps should you decide to create a new subscreen:

i. To define your own subscreens, use the menu path: SAP Customizing Implementation Guide > Financial Accounting > Financial Accounting Global Settings > Ledgers > Fields > Define Subscreens for Coding Blocks. You may also use Transaction OXK1.

ii. On the 'Maintain Coding Block Subscreens: Overview' screen, you will see all the standard SAP subscreens, listed in a table. On this screen, note that you can either create your own subscreens or change the one already defined in the system. However, you will be able to change only the 'Priority' and 'Active' flag on the SAP supplied subscreens, and nothing else. As already mentioned, the system searches through the existing subscreens for the one which fulfils most of the requirements, using the values entered in the 'Priority' field which serves to fine tune the search: 1 is the highest priority, 9 the lowest. The logic of search is: (a) first, it searches for subscreens containing all 'required' account assignment fields; if there is more than one, it selects the one with the highest priority, (b) if that is unsuccessful, the system then looks for subscreens containing all of the 'optional entry' fields, or as many of them as possible; the subscreen containing the most 'optional entry' fields is selected, and (c) if two subscreens contain the same number of 'optional entry' fields, then the one containing the most 'required' account assignment fields is selected; if there is still more than one, the selection is made according to the priority.

> **i** You can use a subscreen in the individual account assignment transactions only when the 'Active' flag is set. Since you cannot delete SAP supplied subscreens, you can deactivate them using this flag, enabling the system to use your own subscreens instead of the standard one.

iii. If you want to define new a subscreen, click on the 'Create' button on the initial 'Maintain Coding Block Subscreens: Overview' screen.

iv. On the 'Maintain Coding Block Subscreens: Details' screen, maintain the details:

  • Enter the number for the 'Subscreen', the number can be anything between 9000 and 9999; note that system proposes '9000' if you have not created a new subscreen earlier. And, enter the name for the subscreen in the adjoining text field.

> **i** When numbering the new subscreens, note to use the numbers between 9000 and 9999 for your own subscreens. SAP will not allow a numbering between 0001 and 8999 as this range is used for SAP delivered subscreens.

- Set the 'Priority', any value between 1 and 9; by default, system proposes 9.
- Select the 'Active' flag; unless you activate, you cannot use the newly defined subscreen.
- Enter the field's starting position in 'Position' against the fields listed on the left. Each subscreen can accommodate a maximum of 10 fields. The positions are numbered from 1 (1st line left) to 10 (5th line right). For certain fields, you can display master data texts for the field values; for this, select the 'With text' check-box. In such cases, note that, you will need an entire row for that field.
- 'Generate' and 'Save', when completed (Figure 6.16). The system, now, adds this new subscreen under 'Customer Subscreens' on the initial 'Maintain Coding Block Subscreens: Overview' screen.

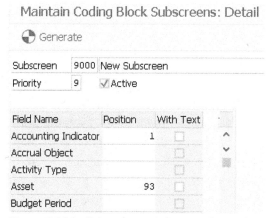

Figure 6.16 Defining a new Subscreen for Coding Block

This completes our discussion on defining new subscreen, and our discussion on configuring the fields. Let us now move on to discuss the ledgers in the next section.

6.3 Ledgers

A 'ledger' is used to record classified and summarized financial information from journals (also called as the 'books of first entry') as debits and credits in a structured way, and showing their current balances. It is also known as 'book of final entry'.

A 'general ledger' (G/L) provides you with a record of each financial transaction that takes place during the life of an operating company. It holds the account information that is needed to prepare the company's financial statements. The transaction data is segregated by various types like assets, liabilities, owners' equity, revenues, and expenses. It is the foundation of financial accounting, and these transactions are posted to individual G/L accounts which form a part of the company's chart of accounts. The transactions are then closed out or summarized to the G/L.

In SAP G/L Accounting, you can use several ledgers in parallel thereby producing, for example, financial statements according to different accounting principles. You, therefore, create a ledger for the each of the G/L you are using.

6.3.1 Ledger Types

There are two types of ledgers
- Standard Ledgers
- Extension Ledgers

A 'standard ledger' contains a full set of journal entries for all business transactions. It can be designated either as a 'leading ledger' or 'non-leading ledger'. You must designate one standard ledger as the 'leading ledger' (you cannot have more than one leading ledger). Along with the leading ledger, you can have any number of other ledgers known 'non-leading ledgers' and/or 'extension ledgers.'

In the standard SAP system, the 'leading ledger' is designated as 0L. This ledger is updated in all company codes, as it is assigned to all company codes, by default. The document numbers assigned in this ledger apply for all dependent ledgers. The leading ledger contains the complete set of document items in table ACDOCA (we shall discuss ACDOCA, later, in detail in Section 6.3.3). In each company code, the leading ledger receives exactly the same settings that apply to that company code: the currencies, the fiscal year variant, and the posting period variant. You can define a second and third parallel currency for your leading ledger, for each company code. The leading ledger is integrated with SAP CO and therefore also forms the basis for CO actual data. Hence, the CO actual version VERSN 0 is essentially the same as that of the leading ledger.

The 'non-leading ledgers' are 'parallel ledgers' to the leading ledger. They can be based on a local accounting principle, for example. You have to activate a non-leading ledger for the individual company codes. The non-leading ledgers also contain the complete set of document items in table ACDOCA. These ledgers can have different fiscal year variants and different posting period variants, in each company code than that of the leading ledger of that company code. You do not need to compulsorily have a second and third currency in non-leading ledgers; they are optional. However, if you plan to have the second and third currency for the non-leading ledger, then it must be a currency that is managed as second or third currency in the respective company code; any other currency is not allowed.

> **i** If you use the account approach for parallel accounting, you will need only one ledger; that is automatically the leading ledger.

An *'extension ledger'* is a non-leading ledger created based on an underlying standard ledger. The postings to the underlying ledger also apply for the extension ledger. However, the postings made explicitly to an extension ledger are visible only in that extension ledger but not in the underlying standard ledger. This is to avoid duplication of journal entries if many business transactions are valid for both ledgers and only a few adjustments are required in the extension ledger. When you run reports for an extension ledger, the data of the underlying ledger is also called; that is, it inherits all journal entries of the underlying standard ledger for reporting. Therefore, only the manual postings made directly in the extension ledger are stored physically on the database. Hence, you will use the extension ledgers for providing information from a management viewpoint, without the need for touching the data of the underlying ledger. You can create different extension ledgers that are based on the same underlying ledger. You can also define an extension ledger based on another extension ledger. While assigning company code to extension ledger, it is possible to assign a different posting period variant to the extension ledger than that of the underlying standard ledger. However, the currency settings and the fiscal year variant are not allowed to differ from that of the underlying ledger.

With this background on ledgers, let us, now, compare a standard ledger with an extension ledger.

6.3.2   Standard Ledger Vs Extension Ledger

The Table 6.3 brings out a comparison between a standard ledger and an extension ledger:

Standard Ledger	Extension Ledger
This is an independent ledger, and is the leading ledger	This is a non-leading ledger with an underlying standard ledger.
The postings made to a standard ledger will only be reflected in the standard ledger.	The postings made to standard ledger will form part of reports of extension ledgers linked to the standard ledger.
Total Balance = Balance in standard ledger	Total Balance = Balance in standard ledger + Balance in extension ledger
Postings can be specifically made in standard ledger.	Postings can be specifically made in extension ledger.

If you are on Classic G/L and migrating to SAP S/4HANA, you cannot activate standard ledgers on day1, even though subsequent activation is possible.	Extension ledgers can be activated in SAP S/4HANA on day1, even if you were on classic GL in SAP ECC.
You can define standard ledgers for reporting to meet different requirements, with one of the ledgers designated as the leading ledger and others as non-leading.	You can add more than one extension ledger on top of a single underlying standard ledger.

Prior to SAP S/4HANA, there were several separate configuration steps (to define ledgers for G/L accounting, to define currencies for leading ledger and to define & activate non-leading ledgers) for ledger configuration. However, all these tasks have now been bundled into a single Customizing task (Figure 6.17) namely 'Define Settings for Ledgers and Currency Types' (Transaction FINSC_LEDGER), in SAP S/4HANA.

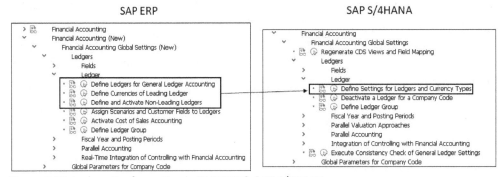

Figure 6.17 Ledger Configuration in SAP ERP & SAP S/4HANA

Besides, note that SAP has dropped the customizing node 'Assign Scenarios to Ledgers' in SAP S/4HANA as this is no more relevant: this was there, earlier, to reduce the data volume in FAGLEXA table as processing was time-consuming. As SAP S/4HANA can now process huge volumes of data, with minimal processing time, this customizing activity is no longer considered required and hence deleted from the IMG.

Before proceeding to understand how to define the required settings for ledgers and currency types, we need to take a look at a new concept in SAP S/4HANA: the universal journal.

6.3.3 Universal Journal

The 'Universal Journal' is actually an enhanced financial document in SAP S/4HANA, that is created whenever you post something to SAP FI from any of the SAP modules. ACDOCA is the name of the SAP FI's important new S/4HANA table (Figure 6.18), which is based on the

universal journal line items, containing all of the financial fields, as well as a lot of information
from other sub-modules of SAP FI namely FI-G/L, SAP CO, CO-PA, FI-AA etc.

Dictionary: Display Table

⬅ ➡ 🔍 🔧 📋 📎 🖊 🔻 🔲 🔳 📊 🗒 ⅰ ⅰ🔳 🔳 Technical Settings Append Structure...

Transparent Table   ACDOCA   Active
Short Description   Universal Journal Entry Line Items

| Attributes | Delivery and Maintenance | Fields | Input Help/Check | Currency/Quantity Fields | Indexes |

✂ 📋 🔲 🔲 🔲   ≫ 🔲 🔲 🔺   🔍 Search   Built-In Type   502

Field	Key	Ini...	Data element	Data Type	Length	Deci...	Short Description
HBKID	☐	☐	HBKID	CHAR	5	0	Short key for a house bank
HKTID	☐	☐	HKTID	CHAR	5	0	ID for account details
XOPVW	☐	☐	XOPVW	CHAR	1	0	Indicator: Open Item Management?
AUGDT	☐	☐	AUGDT	DATS	8	0	Clearing Date
AUGBL	☐	☐	AUGBL	CHAR	10	0	Document Number of the Clearing Document
AUGGJ	☐	☐	AUGGJ	NUMC	4	0	Fiscal Year of Clearing Document
.INCLUDE	☐	✓	ACDOC_SI_FAA	STRU	0	0	Universal Journal Entry: Fields for Asset Accounting
AFABE	☐	☐	AFABER	NUMC	2	0	Depreciation Area Real or Derived
ANLN1	☐	☐	ANLN1	CHAR	12	0	Main Asset Number
ANLN2	☐	☐	ANLN2	CHAR	4	0	Asset Subnumber
BZDAT	☐	☐	BZDAT	DATS	8	0	Asset Value Date
ANBWA	☐	☐	ANBWA	CHAR	3	0	Asset Transaction Type
MOVCAT	☐	☐	FAA_MOVCAT	CHAR	2	0	Transaction Type Category
DEPR_PERIOD	☐	☐	PERAF	NUMC	3	0	Posting Period of Depreciation
ANLGR	☐	☐	ANLGR	CHAR	12	0	Group Asset
ANLGR2	☐	☐	ANLGR2	CHAR	4	0	Subnumber of Group Asset
SETTLEMENT_RULE	☐	☐	BUREG	NUMC	3	0	Distribution Rule Group
ANLKL	☐	☐	ANLKL	CHAR	8	0	Asset Class
KTOGR	☐	☐	KTOGR	CHAR	8	0	Account determination
PANL1	☐	☐	PANL1	CHAR	12	0	Main number partner asset (intercompany transfer)
PANL2	☐	☐	PANL2	CHAR	4	0	Partner asset subnumber (intercompany transfer)
.INCLU-_PN	☐	☐	FAA_S_ACDOC_ITE..	STRU	0	0	Source Document Fields FIAA of Line Item Accounting Document
UBZDT_PN	☐	☐	UBZDT	DATS	8	0	Original Value Date of Transaction
XVABG_PN	☐	☐	XVABG	CHAR	1	0	Indicator: Post Complete Retirement
PROZS_PN	☐	☐	PROZS	DEC	5	2	Asset retirement: Percentage rate
XMANPROPVAL_PN	☐	☐	XMANPROPVAL	CHAR	1	0	Indicator Proportional Values Entered Manually

Figure 6.18 Universal Journal

The table ACDOCA brings in most of the sub-modules of FI together. This, coupled with the
data validation at the table level, obviates the need for reconciliation between FI and its other
sub-modules. With the SAP HANA database, this is easily taken care of in spite of processing
of large data volumes. ACDOCA also aims at removing duplication and redundancy arising out
of multiple totals / index tables. For example:

- Tables BSIS (index for G/L accounts) and BSAS (index for G/L cleared items) hold
  information that is already available in table BSEG. However, BSIS / BSAS holds the
  secondary index enabling quicker reporting and processing.
- Tables BSID (index for customers) and BSIL (index for vendors) holds information on
  customer / vendor open items, respectively, most of that (information) is already
  available in BSEG.

- Table GLT0 (G/L totals) holds redundant data from table BSEG. Though you can query directly from BSEG, SAP has been keeping GLT0 to avoid performance issues while totalling.
- Tables KNC1 (customer transaction figures) and LFC1 (vendor transaction figures) contain the totals of customer / vendor transactions, respectively, period/fiscal year wise. Though, you can – technically – get these details from BSEG table itself, the duplication was necessary to avoid issues in performance.

Accordingly, with the introduction of the table ACDOCA, the index tables such as BSIS, BSAS, BSID, BSAD, BSIK, BSAK, BSIM, FAGLBSIS and FAGLBSAS, as well as aggregate tables such as GLT0, GLT3, FAGLFLEXT, KNC1, LFC1, KNC3, LFC3, COSS, COSP are no longer required and have been removed. FAGLFLEXA and some other New GL tables are also now made obsolete.

The universal journal is the 'single source of truth' for SAP FI and CO, and includes all the cost objects traditionally found in SAP CO such as cost centers, internal orders and WBS elements as well as columns for the standard CO-PA characteristics, and up to 50 additional characteristics. The journal also enables faster reconciliation with FI-AA as important details like asset, subnumber, asset value date, depreciation area etc., are now available in table ACDOCA itself. Since this is a ledger-based table, it is multi-GAAP enabled.

You can display this journal as before, using the display document Transaction FB03. Many of the journal entry, invoice entry and other posting transactions are still available in the SAP GUI, so you can still, for example, use Transaction FB50 or FB50L (by ledger) to post a journal.

With the understanding of universal journal, we can now move on to learn how to configure the ledgers in SAP.

6.3.4 Define Settings for Ledgers and Currency Types

This is a composite customizing activity that takes care of configuring the ledgers and currency. We shall start with the ledgers first:

Project Dolphin

The Dolphin Project has decided to use different ledgers to meet the different statutory requirements of the company codes: (1) BESTM group of companies will use the SAP supplied standard ledger 0L as their leading ledger and that will meet the International Accounting Standards (IAS), (2) US-based company codes will use a non-leading ledger (BU) to meet the local accounting requirements (US GAAP) and (3) India-based company codes will use another leading ledger (BI) to meet India's legal reporting (Ind-AS).

BESTM wants to leverage the 'extension edger' functionality of SAP S/4HANA. Accordingly, the project team has proposed to define four extension ledgers: one for general purpose, another for simulation, the third for prediction / commitment and the fourth for valuation purposes accounting for the valuation differences. In all the four cases, BESTM wants manual postings.

6.3.4.1 Define Ledgers

As indicated by Project Dolphin's implementation team, we will not create a new leading ledger, but use the one supplied by SAP. Accordingly, 0L will be the leading ledger for all the company codes of BESTM group.

Now, follow the steps below, to create the non-leading ledgers required for BESTM, to meet the reporting requirements of company codes operating out of US and India:

i.   Use the menu path: SAP Customizing Implementation Guide > Financial Accounting > Financial Accounting Global Settings > Ledgers > Ledger > Define Settings for Ledgers and Currency Types. You may also use Transaction FINSC_LEDGER.

ii.   You will be taken to the 'Change View "Ledgers": Overview' screen; you will notice that the folder 'Ledger' has already been highlighted under the 'Dialog Structure' on the left pane.

iii.   Now, click on 'New Entries' and maintain the details, on the next screen:
   * Enter a ledger identifier in 'Ledger' field. Let that be BU. This will be the non-leading ledger to be used by all the US-based company codes for BESTM.
   * Enter a name under 'Ledger Name' field. Let this be 'Non-Leading (US)'.
   * Do not select the 'Leading' check-box as this will be a non-leading ledger.
   * For the 'Ledger Type' filed, select 'Standard Ledger' from the drop-down list.
   * You do not need to select a value for the field 'Extn. Ledger Type' as this is not relevant for a non-leading ledger. However, you will notice that this field has a default value as 'Standard journal entries'.

> **i** Between release SAP S/4HANA 1809 and 1909, you will see a difference in the naming of the classification of 'extension ledger type'. In release 1809 the types were named as (1) extension ledger, (2) simulation, (3) prediction and commitments and (4) valuation. However, in 1909 the types names have been changed to (1) standard journal entries, (2) line items with technical numbers / deletion possible, (3) line items with technical numbers / no deletion possible, and (4) journal entries for valuation differences.

   * Leave 'Underlying Ledger' field as well blank, as this is valid only for the extension ledger.
   * Do not select the 'Man.Pstgs. Not Allwd' check-box, as this is only a non-leading ledger.

- Leave the 'AcctgPrinc of Ledger' as blank; we shall maintain the same later.
- Repeat the entries for the other non-leading ledger (BI), and 'Save'. You have now created two non-leading ledgers (BU and BI) for BESTM (Figure 6.19).

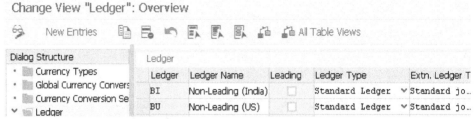

Figure 6.19 Defining Non-Leading Ledgers for BESTM

> **i** When you 'Save' the entries in defining the entries, the system creates a ledger group as well, with the same name of the non-leading ledger.

Now that we have defined the non-leading ledgers for BESTM, let us understand how to define an extension ledger.

i. Go back to the 'Change View "Ledgers": Overview' screen.
ii. Now, click on 'New Entries' and maintain the details, on the next screen:

    a. Enter a ledger identifier in 'Ledger' field. Let that be ER. The other three extension ledgers will be named as ES, EP and EV.

    b. Enter a name under 'Ledger Name' field. Let this be 'Extn Ledger for BESTM - General' for the ledger ER.

    c. Do not select the 'Leading' check-box as this will be an extension ledger.

    d. For the 'Ledger Type' filed, select 'Extension Ledger'.

    e. For the 'Extn. Ledger Type' field, select 'Standard journal entries' for the ledger ER from the drop-down list to indicate that this will be a regular all-purpose extension ledger that will allow standard journal entries.

    f. In the 'Underlying Ledger' field as enter '0L'.

    g. Do not select the 'Man.Pstgs. Not Allwd' check-box, to allow manual postings.

    h. Repeat the entries for the other three extension ledgers (ES, EP and EV): Note that you need to select 'Line items with technical numbers / deletion possible' for the extension ledger ES (simulation purposes), 'Line items with technical numbers / deletion not possible' for the extension ledger EP (prediction & commitment purposes), and 'Journal entries for valuation differences' for the extension ledger EV (valuation purposes), in 'Extn. Ledger Type' field. The two extension ledgers ES and EP can be used for simulation postings (without any actual postings), and predicting the financial results, respectively.

i.   'Save'. You have now created all the four extensions ledgers (ER, ES, EP and EV) for BESTM (Figure 6.20).

Figure 6.20 Defining Extension Ledgers for BESTM

> **i** When you 'Save' the entries in defining the extension ledgers, the system creates a ledger group with the same name of the ledger, as in the case of non-leading ledgers.

Now that we have defined the required ledgers for BESTM, both non-leading and extension, let us maintain the company code settings for these ledgers.

6.3.4.2   Company Code Settings for the Ledger

In this step, you will assign company code(s) to a ledger. You can also complete the other activities like maintaining fiscal year variant and posting period variant.

i.   On the 'Change View "Ledgers": Overview' screen, highlight the ledger for which you need to maintain the company code settings. Let that be BU.

ii. Double-click on 'Company Code Settings for the Ledger', on the left-hand side 'Dialog-Structure'.

iii. You will be taken to 'Change View "Company Code Settings for the Ledger": Overview' screen.

iv. Click on 'New Entries' and maintain the details, on the next 'New Entries: Details of Added Entries' screen:

- Enter the company code that needs to be attached to this ledger in 'Company Code' field. Say, 1110.
- You may maintain the fiscal year and posting period variants in the respective fields. This is only for the non-leading ledger; if it is an extension ledger, you will not be able to change the system-proposed fiscal year variant but, you can change the posting period variant.

> **i** In the case of non-leading ledgers, you can have a fiscal year variant and/or a posting period variant that are different than that of the attached company code.
>
> However, in the case of an extension ledger, note that the system picks up the fiscal year variant from the underlying standard ledger, when you assign the company code to that ledger; you will not be able to change it. Also, you will not be able to change the currency settings as they are also taken from the underlying standard ledger. Of course, you are free to assign a different posting period variant here.

- Do not select the 'Parallel Accounting Using G/L Accounts' check-box. You will select this only if you plan parallel accounting using G/L accounts (instead of using different ledgers). Also, you will select this, when you are most likely to assign more than one accounting principle to this combination of ledger and company code. By doing this, you make the system suppresses the corresponding message that 'you have assigned too many accounting principles to the same combination of ledger and company code'.
- Press 'Enter'; the system will fill up all the currency related information in the respective fields.
- You can click on 'Add Currency' at the bottom right-hand side of the screen and continue adding freely defined currencies.

> **i** You can add up to eight additional currencies in addition to the 1st FI currency (local currency) and 2nd FI currency (global currency).

- 'Save' the details (Figure 6.21).
- Click on 'Next Entry', and enter the next company code that needs to be assigned to this ledger; repeat this to complete the ledger assignment for all the remaining company codes.
- Once done, go back to the initial 'Change View "Ledgers": Overview' screen, and repeat the steps for the next ledger. Complete this for both non-leading and extension ledgers.

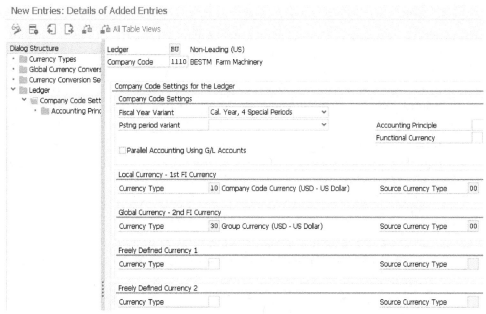

Figure 6.21 Maintaining Company Code Settings for the Ledger

Our next task is to assign the accounting principles for the 'ledger-company code' combination. However, to accomplish this we should have completed defining the accounting principles in the system. So, let us do that now.

6.3.4.3 Define Accounting Principles

The '*accounting principles*' are the rules and guidelines that companies must follow when reporting financial data. These principles govern accounting, according to general rules and concepts by forming the groundwork for the more complicated, detailed and legalistic rules of accounting. There are several accounting principles including the revenue-recognition principle, going-concern principle, accrual principle and matching principle.

---

i The accounting principles differ from country to country: for example, you have IAS (International Accounting Standards), IFRS (International Financial Reporting Standards), US GAAP (Generally Accepted Accounting Principles), Indian Accounting Standard (Ind-AS) etc.

The common set of U.S. accounting principles is the Generally Accepted Accounting Principles (US GAAP) that is based on three important sets of rules: the basic accounting principles & guidelines, the generally accepted industry practices, and the detailed rules & standards that have been issued by the Financial Accounting Standards Board (FASB) and the Accounting Principles Board (APB). All the US-based companies are required to follow US GAAP when releasing their financial statements to the public.

Ind-AS is the accounting standard adopted by companies in India that is issued under the supervision of Accounting Standards Board (ASB). The Ind-AS is named and numbered in the same way as that of the International Financial Reporting Standards (IFRS).

In SAP, you can combine several different accounting principles in one entry; for example, you can create one accounting principle for IAS/US GAAP. This can be useful when the postings derived from the data are identical for each of the accounting principles. With leading valuation stored in the leading ledger, the system uses additional non-leading ledgers (say, BU and BI as in our Project Dolphin) to store data for each of the additional (parallel) accounting principles

Let us configure this customizing activity:

i.   Use the menu path: SAP Customizing Implementation Guide > Financial Accounting > Financial Accounting Global Settings > Ledgers > Parallel Accounting > Define Accounting Principles.

ii.   On the 'Change View "Accounting Principles": Overview' screen, click on 'New Entries' and maintain the details on the next screen.

iii. 'Save' and you have now created the required accounting principles (Figure 6.22).

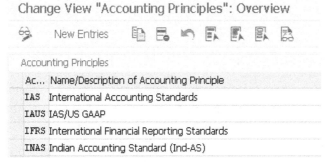

Figure 6.22 Accounting Principles

With the definition of accounting principles completed, we are now ready to assign the accounting principles for the ledgers (leading, non-leading and extension) and the company code combination.

6.3.4.4   Accounting Principles for Ledger and Company Code

Follow the steps listed below, to assign the accounting principles to the 'ledger-company code' combinations:

i.   Use the menu path: SAP Customizing Implementation Guide > Financial Accounting > Financial Accounting Global Settings > Ledgers > Ledger > Define Settings for Ledgers and Currency Types. You may also use Transaction FINSC_LEDGER.

ii. You will be taken to the 'Change View "Ledgers": Overview' screen; select the row containing the ledger for which you need to assign the accounting principles. Say, BI.

iii. Double-click on 'Accounting Principles for Ledger and Company Code' on the left-hand side 'Dialog Structure' pane.

iv. On the 'Determine Work Area: Entry' pop-up screen, input the 'Company Code'; enter or select 1210. Press 'Enter'.

v. On the 'Change View "Accounting Principles for Ledger and Company Code": Overview' screen, press 'New Entries'.

vi. On the next screen, enter the ID for the accounting principles (say, INAS) and 'Save' (Figure 6.23). You have now assigned the appropriate accounting principles for the particular ledger (BI) for the India-based company code (1210).

Figure 6.23 Accounting Principles for Ledger and Company Code

vii. Go back to the initial 'Change View "Ledgers": Overview' screen, repeat the above steps and complete assignment of company code 1220 to the non-leading ledger BI.

viii. Repeat the steps and assign all the US-based company codes (1110, 1120, 2100, 2200, 3100 and 3200) to the other non-leading ledger BU.

ix. Continue with the assignment and complete the exercise for the leading (0L) and extension ledgers (E1, E2 and E3). In the case of leading ledger (0L), you may assign IAS (or IAUS) as the accounting principles for all the US-based company codes, and assign INAS for India-based company codes. You will do similar assignments for the 'ledger-company code' combinations for all the extension ledger as well.

Remember, when we defined the ledgers (Section 6.3.4.1), we had left the 'AcctgPrinc of Ledger' field as blank. You can revisit the activity now and maintain the appropriate accounting principles against each of those ledgers. When you maintain an accounting principle for a ledger in this step, then this accounting principle will be valid for all the company codes that are assigned to that ledger.

This completes our discussion on assigning accounting principles to the 'ledger-company code' combinations. Let us, now, move on to define the ledger groups.

6.3.4.5   Define Ledger Groups

The 'ledger group', in SAP, is a combination of ledgers that helps in simplifying SAP G/L account processing, as you can apply certain functions to the ledger group as a whole instead applying them individually to each of the ledgers. We have already seen, when defining a ledger, that the system creates a ledger group automatically with the same name as that of the ledger. Of course, you can create your own ledger group(s) if you want a different grouping. Within a ledger group, you designate one ledger as the 'representative ledger' for that group, which will determine whether the posting period is open for posting. As long as the posting period of the representative ledger is open, then the system posts to all the ledgers (even if the period is not open in some of the non-leading ledgers of that ledger group). If the ledger group contains only one ledger, then that ledger will also be the representative ledger. The Figure 6.23 provides you with the details as to which will be the representative ledger in different situations (numbered 1 to 4):

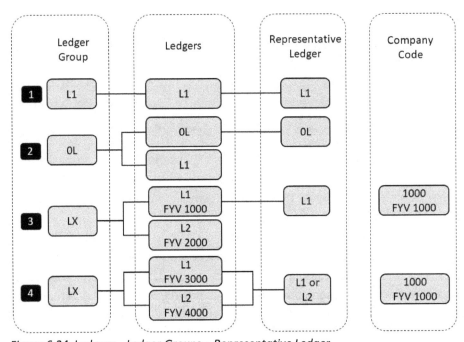

Figure 6.24 Ledgers – Ledger Groups – Representative Ledger

1. If the ledger group contains only one ledger (L1), then, it will be the representative ledger (L1).
2. If there are more than one ledger (OL and L1) in a ledger group (OL), with one of the ledgers being the leading edger (OL), then, the leading ledger will be the representative ledger (OL).

3. If there are more than one ledger (L1 and L2) in a ledger group (LX) and neither of the ledgers is a leading ledger, then, the ledger with the FYV same as that of the FYV of the attached company code will be the representative ledger (L1).
4. If there are more than one ledger (L1 and L2) in a ledger group (LX) with neither of the ledgers being a leading ledger, and each one having an FYV that is different than that of the FYV of the attached company code, then, either of the ledgers can be the representative ledger (L1 or L2).

Project Dolphin

BESTM management is of the opinion that the project team combine the leading ledger (OL) and the non-leading ledger (BU) into a ledger group called B1 as the accounting principles of IAS (OL) and US GAAP (BU) are the same as there will almost be identical postings to both of these accounting principles.

Let us look at how to configure the ledger groups:

i. Use the menu path: SAP Customizing Implementation Guide > Financial Accounting > Financial Accounting Global Settings > Ledgers > Ledger > Define Ledger Group.
ii. On the resulting 'Change View "Ledger Group": Overview' screen, you will notice that the system has already created the ledgers groups like OL, BI, BU, EP, ER etc. Since we want to combine the ledgers that will use IAS and GAAP into a ledger group, click on 'New Entries'.
iii. On the next screen, enter the ledger group identifier (say, G1) in the 'Ledger Grp' field, and enter a suitable 'Description'. Press, 'Enter'.
iv. Now, select this row containing G1, and double-click on 'Ledger Assignment' on the left-hand side 'Dialog Structure' pane.

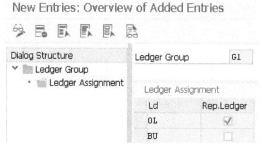

Figure 6.25 Defining a Ledger Group

v. On the 'Change View "Ledger Assignment": Overview' screen, click on 'New Entries', select the ledgers that need to be grouped in 'Ld' field, on the next screen.
vi. Select the 'Rep.Ledger' check-box against OL to make that as the representative ledger, and 'Save' the entries. You have now created a ledger group in the name G1 with the OL as the representative ledger of the group (Figure 6.25).

> **i** Instead of assigning accounting principles to individual ledgers, you can assign the same to a ledger group. For this you need to follow the menu path: SAP Customizing Implementation Guide > Financial Accounting > Financial Accounting Global Settings > Ledgers > Parallel Accounting > Assign Accounting Principle to Ledger Groups (refer Section 6.5.2).

With this, we are, now, ready to discuss configuring the currency types in the system.

6.3.5 Currency Types

Before discussing the '*currency type*' let us understand the usage of currency in SAP:

When you enter a monetary amount in your SAP system, you need to specify a currency (which is the legal means of payment in a country). You will enter currencies as per the ISO standards, like INR for Indian Rupees, USD for US dollar and so on. To enable the system to translate amounts into various currencies, you need to have *exchange rates* set up in the system; for each currency pair, you can define different exchange rates and then differentiate between them by using *exchange rate types*.

The '*exchange rate*', defined at the client level and valid for all company codes, denotes the relationship between two currencies and is used to translate an amount into another currency. You need to define exchange rates in the system for (a) posting and clearing (to translate amounts posted or cleared in foreign currency, or to check a manually entered exchange rate during posting or clearing), (b) taking care of exchange rate differences (to determine gain / loss from exchange rate differences) and (c) foreign currency valuation (to valuate foreign currency open items and foreign currency balance sheet accounts as part of the closing operations).

You define exchange rates in Customizing using the menu path: SAP Customizing Implementation Guide > SAP NetWeaver > General Settings > Currencies > Enter Exchange Rates. For each foreign currency, specify the exchange rate in the local currency in the system. Additionally, specify (a) an exchange rate type (say, M) and (b) time restrictions for the exchange rate to take care of exchange rate fluctuations. You need to use the validity date ('Valid From') to indicate the date from which the exchange rate should apply; the system, then, refers either to the posting date or the translation date and uses the current exchange rate from the system.

You can use either direct or indirect quotation to specify exchange rates. You also need to specify the relationship of the exchange rate, for example, USD/INR exchange rates are normally specified 1:1, SGD/TZS exchange rates in the relationship 1:1000. You do not have to enter all exchange rates; there are various tools that you can use to automatically determine other exchange rates from existing ones. Of course, you have to specify the tool (say, *'inversion'* where you calculate the opposite rate from a defined exchange rate) to be used for each exchange rate type.

---

i SAP recommends using the *reference currency* and *exchange rate spread* as tools.

The *'reference currency'* is the currency key used to carry out all foreign currency translations for a specific exchange rate type. You can assign a reference currency to an exchange rate type. For every other currency, you enter the exchange rate in the reference currency. All other translations are carried out using the reference currency. For example, you specify USD as the reference currency; to translate from GBP to INR, the system uses the GBP/USD and INR/USD exchange rate specifications. you can only use the reference currency for exchange rate type M (average rate), and not for bank buying or bank selling exchange rate types.

The *'exchange rate spread'* is the constant difference between the average rate and the buying rate (or between the average rate and the bank selling rate). Per exchange rate type, define the fixed exchange rate spreads between average rate and buying rate, as well as between average rate and bank selling rate. Then, you just need to enter exchange rates for the average rate: the system calculates the exchange rates for the buying rate and bank selling rate by adding / subtracting the exchange rate spread for the average rate.

SAP recommends defining a reference currency for the average rate and then entering exchange rate spreads for the buying and bank selling rates. This combination is most efficient and enables you to enter exchange rates (for the individual currencies) to the reference currency for the average rate (exchange rate type) as the system calculates all the other exchange rates.

The *'exchange rate type'* is the key used to define exchange rates in the system. Define different exchange rates for each currency pair and then differentiate between these exchange rates using the exchange rate type that you define in Customizing, using the menu path: SAP Customizing Implementation Guide > SAP NetWeaver > General Settings > Currencies > Check Exchange Rate Types. The standard SAP system comes delivered with several exchange rate types like average rate (M), bank buying rate, bank selling rate, key date exchange rate and historical exchange rate. For posting and clearing, the standard system uses the exchange rate type M (average rate).

With this understanding about the currency, let us now discuss the currency type.

A *'currency type'*, in SAP, refers to the currency usage in the system like the currency that is entered in the document header (known as the *document currency*), the currency that is associated with the company code (known as the *company code currency* or *local currency*), the currency that is used in a Controlling area (known as the *controlling area currency*) and so on. The standard SAP comes delivered with several currency types, as outlined in Table 6.3:

Currency Type	Description	Remarks, if any
00	Document Currency	
10	Company Code Currency	The currency of the country in which the company code is located. This is also known as 'local currency' or 'transaction currency'. You also have currency types 11 (Company Code Currency – Group Valuation) and 12 (Company Code Currency – Profit Center Valuation)
20	Controlling Area Currency	
30	Group Currency	You also have two more here for meeting different valuation requirements: 31 (Group Currency – Group Valuation) and 32 (Group Currency – Profit Center Valuation)
40	Hard Currency	The currency that is used in countries with high-inflation
50	Index-based Currency	The fictitious currency that is used in high-inflation countries
60	Global Company Currency	
70	CO Object Currency	This is the currency defined in the master record of a CO object; you can assign this only if your CO area currency type is 10. You also have 71 (Controlling Object Currency – Group Valuation) and 72 (Controlling Object Currency – Profit Center Valuation)
80	Ledger Currency	You also have two more currency types: 81 (Ledger Currency – Group Valuation) and 82 (Ledger Currency – Profit Center Valuation)
90	Profit Center Invoice Currency	There is one more currency type for profit center: 92 (Profit Center Accounting currency - Profit Center Valuation)

Table 6:3 Standard Currency Types

We have already discussed about the important currency types in Chapter 5, Section 5.3.8 while discussing the currency for the controlling area. In all probability, you will not need a new currency type, as the SAP supplied currency types will be more than sufficient to meet all your business requirements. However, if you really need to define a new currency type (say, to meet some reporting requirements), note that:

- The new currency types should begin with the letter Y or Z but can consist of letters or letters and digits like Y1, YA, Z2 etc.
- You need to decide, for each new currency type you define, whether you want the corresponding currency conversion settings to be valid globally (for all company codes) or only at the company code-level.

> **i** You cannot make any changes in the currency conversion settings to the standard currency types 00 and 10. However, for the other standard currency types, you can define whether the currency conversion settings are valid globally or on company code-level.

For defining a new currency type:

i. Use the menu path: SAP Customizing Implementation Guide > Financial Accounting > Financial Accounting Global Settings > Ledgers > Ledger > Define Settings for Ledgers and Currency Types. You may also use Transaction FINSC_LEDGER.

ii. You will be taken to the 'Change View "Ledgers": Overview' screen; double-click on 'Currency Types' under the 'Dialog Structure' on the left pane.

iii. You will now be on the 'Change View "Currency Types": Overview' screen. Click on 'New Entries' to define your own currency types.

iv. On the next screen, enter 2-character a 'Currency Type' identifier (starting with Y or Z), enter a 'Description', also a 'Short Description' and select either 'Global' or 'Company Code-Specific' for the field 'Settings Def. Level'. The selected value decides how you proceed with the definition of your currency conversion settings in the later steps of the configuration: if you select the 'Global' option, you will define the currency conversion settings once, for each of your own currency types; if it is the 'Company Code-Specific' option, you define the corresponding settings, for each combination of company code and your own currency types.

v. 'Save' the details (Figure 6.26). We have created two new currency types, for demonstration purpose: one for the currency conversion settings at global level and the other for the company code level.

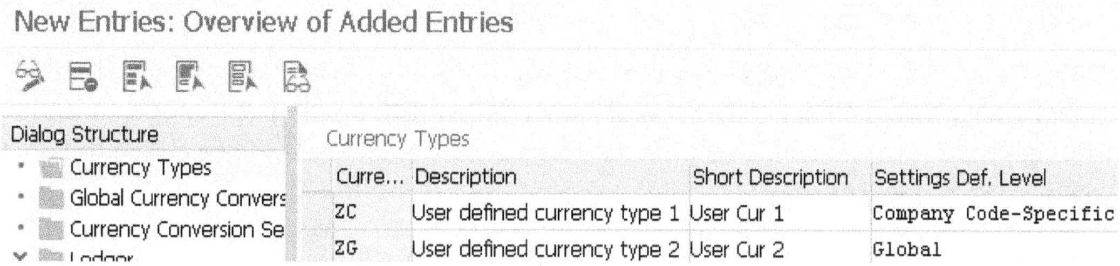

New Entries: Overview of Added Entries

Curre...	Description	Short Description	Settings Def. Level
ZC	User defined currency type 1	User Cur 1	Company Code-Specific
ZG	User defined currency type 2	User Cur 2	Global

Figure 6.26 Defining New Currency Types

vi.   Now, highlight the appropriate row, and double-click either on the 'Global Currency Conversion Settings' or 'Currency Conversion Settings for Company Codes' and maintain the appropriate details on the next screen and 'Save'.

In the case of settings for global conversion, enter the currency into which the conversion is to be made ('Currency' field), and the currency from which currency conversion is to be made ('Source Currency' field). In addition, enter the appropriate exchange rate type (in 'Exch. Rate Type' field) and the date on which the translation is to be carried out (document date, posting date, or translation date) in 'Trans.Date Type' field. You can also decide whether the currency conversion shall be done in real-time by selecting the 'Real-Time Conversion' check-box; if you do not select the 'Real-time Conversion' checkbox, you can do this at period-end closing using the foreign currency re-measurement run.

In the case currency conversion settings for company codes, you need to maintain the above settings for each of the company codes for which you will be using this new currency type.

---

i   If you need to add new currency types to a combination of 'company code and ledger' that are already productive, note that the system configuration will become inconsistent; use Transaction FINS_ADAPT_CTP (Adaption of transactional data for new currency types), to update the new currency key to existing transaction data. Better, avoid such a situation; and, add the required currency types before becoming productive!

However, to add a new currency for company codes and ledgers that are already in production, you may use the functionality 'Manage Currencies' which we have described in the next Section 6.3.6.

6.3.6 Manage Currencies

You can use 'Manage Currencies' functionality in SAP to introduce new currencies for company codes and ledgers that are already used in your production system. Once introduced, these new currencies are available in the Universal Journal (ACDOCA table) and you can use them in, both accounting-specific processes and reporting. When you introduce a new currency, both the new currency and its calculated value are added to all journal entries, which are available in the system. However, the system will not enrich the archived data with the new currency.

You can access the 'Manage Currencies' configuration step by using the menu path: SAP Customizing Implementation Guide > Financial Accounting > Financial Accounting Global Settings > Tools > Manage Currencies. This includes several activities, which provide you with the necessary configuration and conversion steps to introduce a new currency. You can find the configuration steps in the 'Preparatory Phase' and the conversion steps (including 'Cockpit: Manage Currencies') in the 'Execution Phase'. You must complete these steps to ensure that new currencies are consistently introduced. Using 'Manage Currencies', you can reconcile SAP G/L Accounting data as well as the journal entries that were posted in the current fiscal year; that is, the journal entries and entities that are used for reporting in external accounting, are completely reconciled and rounding differences are posted.

> **i** The 'Manage Currencies' functionality does not include reconciliation for entities in FI-AA, CO, and inventory accounting. Also, note that you cannot change an existing currency, which is already in use, using 'Manage Currencies' functionality.

This completes our discussion on ledgers. Let us move on to discuss the fiscal year, fiscal year variant, posting period, posting period variant etc., in the next Section.

6.4   Fiscal Year and Posting Periods

A *'fiscal year'* is an accounting period, normally made up of 12 months. Each month in a fiscal year is known as a *'period'*. Each period, within a fiscal year, is known as a *'posting period'*. In SAP, when you post a transaction, each transaction is assigned and added to a particular posting period, identified by the month and year of the fiscal year. Besides posting periods, SAP also uses a concept known called *'special period'*: you will use special periods to manage activities like period-end / year-end closings. Though a fiscal year usually runs for 12 months, there may be instances wherein you may need a fiscal year that is made up of lesser number of months; in such cases, the fiscal year is known as *'shortened fiscal year'*.

6.4.1   Types of Fiscal Years

SAP supports different types of fiscal years to meet varying business requirements. The following are the types of fiscal years that are supported in the system (Figure 6.27):

- *Calendar Fiscal Year*
  A *'calendar fiscal year'* is nothing but a calendar year, with 12 posting periods corresponding to the 12 calendar months. You do not need to define the individual posting periods, when the fiscal year is the calendar year. The first posting period will always be January and the last will be December. The start and end date of each of the posting periods, will be the same as that of the corresponding calendar month. Looking at the posting date, the system will assign the correct posting period to an underlying transaction.

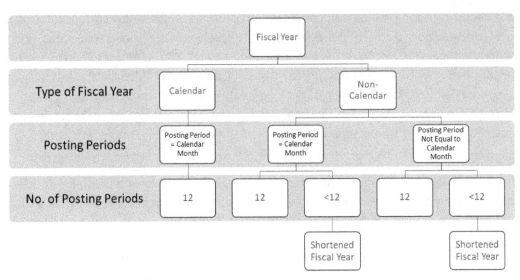

Figure 6.27 Types of Fiscal Year

- *Non-Calendar Fiscal Year*

  A fiscal year that does not correspond to a calendar year, is known as the *'non-calendar fiscal year'*. The posting periods may or may not correspond to the calendar months. A non-calendar fiscal year, for example, may start on 1st of April and end on 31st March of the following year; or it may start on 16th July and end on 15th July of the following year. There could be instances wherein the non-calendar fiscal year does not have 12 posting periods, but have lesser number of periods. In such cases, as already discussed, the fiscal year is called as *'shortened fiscal year'*. So, it is always required that you need to define the number of posting periods for a non-calendar fiscal year. Besides, you need to instruct the system as to how it needs to determine the posting period and the associated fiscal year, as there is a possibility that the posting period is either the same as that of a calendar month or the posting period does not correspond to a calendar month.

  <u>When the posting periods are the same as that of the calendar months</u>, specify the calendar month for the posting period and the day limit for each of the periods. Also, specify a *'year displacement factor'* or *'year shift'* (0 or -1, or +1) for each of the posting periods, to adjust the fiscal year as it is not equal to calendar year (Table 6.4).

Calendar Year	Calendar Month	Fiscal Year	Posting Period	Start Date	End Date	Year Shift
2019	7	2019	1	01-Jul	31-Jul	0
2019	8	2019	2	01-Aug	31-Aug	0
2019	9	2019	3	01-Sep	30-Sep	0
2019	10	2019	4	01-Oct	31-Oct	0
2019	11	2019	5	01-Nov	30-Nov	0
2019	12	2019	6	01-Dec	31-Dec	0
2020	1	2019	7	01-Jan	31-Jan	−1
2020	2	2019	8	01-Feb	29-Feb	−1
2020	3	2019	9	01-Mar	31-Mar	−1
2020	4	2019	10	01-Apr	30-Apr	−1
2020	5	2019	11	01-May	31-May	−1
2020	6	2019	12	01-Jun	30-Jun	−1

Table 6:4 Non-Calendar Fiscal Year with Posting Periods same as that of Calendar Months

Consider that you make a transaction on 15th March, 2020; when posting the transaction, the system reads the posting period as 9 (calendar month = 3), and uses of the year shift (-1) to correctly identify the fiscal year as 2019 (= 2020 – 1).

> **i** For the month of February, specify the end date of the posting period as 29th, so as to enable the system to post transactions correctly. Else, when you maintain the end date as 28th, then a transaction made on the 29th will be posted to the next posting period.

<u>When the posting period is not the same as that of the calendar month</u>, and when the start date and end date of posting periods does not match with the starting and ending of calendar months, you need to maintain the difference by specifying the date of the *period-end* (Table 6.5).

Consider that your non-calendar fiscal year starts on 16th July, 2019 and ends on 15th July 2020. As the start date and end date of the posting periods differ from the starting and ending of the calendar months, you need to maintain the period-end specifications for each of the periods as in Table 6.5. For the posting period 6, you will need two periods: one ending on 31st December, 2019 (for the 12th calendar month, December), and the other ending on 15th January, 2020 (for the 1st calendar month, January). Unless you specify the end dates, the system will have issues in identifying the correct posting period for the transactions falling between 1st January, 2020 and 15th January, 2020. Now, with these specifications, both a transaction dated on 26th

December, 2019 and another dated 10th January, 2020, will correctly be identified as transactions belonging to the posting period 6 of the fiscal year 2019 (= 2020 – 1).

Calendar Year	Calendar Month	Fiscal Year	Posting Period	Period-End	Year Shift
2019	8	2019	1	15-Aug	0
2019	9	2019	2	15-Sep	0
2019	10	2019	3	15-Oct	0
2019	11	2019	4	15-Nov	0
2019	12	2019	5	15-Dec	0
2019	12	2019	6	31-Dec	0
2020	1	2019	6	15-Jan	−1
2020	2	2019	7	15-Feb	−1
2020	4	2019	8	15-Mar	−1
2020	4	2019	9	15-Apr	−1
2020	5	2019	10	15-May	−1
2020	6	2019	11	15-Jun	−1
2020	7	2019	12	15-Jul	−1

Table 6:5 Non-Calendar Fiscal Year with Posting Periods not equal to Calendar Months

- *Shortened Fiscal Year*
  A fiscal year that is less than 12 posting periods in duration is called a *'shortened fiscal year'*. It is *year-dependent* and has always to be followed or preceded by a full fiscal year with 12 periods. You must always define an entire calendar year when defining a FYV: the year-related FYV therefore contains not only the periods from the shortened fiscal year, but also other periods from the previous or subsequent fiscal year. You may need such a shortened fiscal year during the initial periods of company formation, (a) when you want to switch from a calendar fiscal year to a non-calendar year or vice versa, (b) when you combine your company to be a part of a new enterprise and so on. In the standard SAP system, you will notice that there are two variants (R1 and AM) for shortened fiscal years: use R1 in SAP FI and AM in FI-AA.

> **i** Since you define your shortened fiscal year and the following normal fiscal years under the same FYV, ensure that it is possible to post to previous fiscal years.
>
> Also, you need to keep the year-dependent fiscal year variant for as long as you are posting in or prior to a shortened fiscal year, or if you are transferring old data from this period. Year-dependent definitions will be deleted as soon as you convert the fiscal year variants from year-dependent to year-independent.

You may define a shortened fiscal year, in two ways:

1. When you use SAP FI without FI-AA, you can begin a fiscal year with any period. For example, if your shortened fiscal year is from January to September, you can assign periods 004 to 012; you then assign the periods 001 to 003 of the new fiscal year to the months October to December. You need to specify the number of periods for the FYV (12 in this example). Keep in mind, that the last period of a fiscal year must correspond to the number of periods in that year: that is, if you want to define 12 periods, the last period in that year must be number 12.

2. If you also implement the FI-AA or another application component such as SAP-MM or SAP-CO, then, each fiscal year must begin with period number 001, to allow correct asset depreciation calculations in the system. For a FYV, you specify the periods and the number of periods the shortened fiscal year has. This way, each fiscal year of the variant can begin with period 001. For example, if you define a fiscal year with twelve periods, it can contain a shortened year with nine periods (from 001 to 009); the remaining calendar year will contain the first three periods (periods 001 to 003) of the new fiscal year.

> **i** The FYV is used in multiple application components in SAP like FI, FI-AA, CO, SD, MM, or HR. In some of these application components, the calendar-year-dependent definition of fiscal periods and years is necessary even if the shortened fiscal year is in the past. If such a shortened fiscal year exists in your system, it must always be indicated as year-specific. You should not change this setting under any circumstances, even if the shortened fiscal year is already in the past.

- *Special Period*
  A '*special period*' is a part of the last posting period, in a fiscal year, that you will use for carrying out period-end closing operations. You can divide the last posting period into several special periods to facilitate such tasks. Alternatively, when you do not need all the 12 posting periods in a fiscal year, you can designate the unused regular posting periods as special periods. But, the special periods created by subdividing the last posting period (into one or more) does not in any way create new posting periods (Figure 6.28). With these special periods in place, you will be able to create more than one supplementary financial statement, all within the same fiscal year.

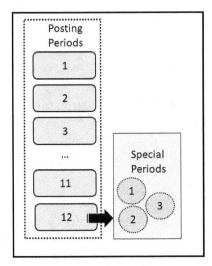

Figure 6.28 Special Periods

When entering a transaction, you need to input the special period in the document header in the 'Period' field as the system cannot automatically determine the special periods. Besides, ensure that the posting date of the transaction you are entering is within the last regular posting period.

> **i** In SAP G/L Accounting, you can have a maximum of 16 periods, including four special periods. However, in Special Purpose Ledgers (FI-SL), you can use a maximum of 366 posting periods.

Now that we have an understanding on fiscal years and posting periods, let us now move on to configure the FYV in the system.

6.4.2 Maintain Fiscal Year Variant

You will use a *'fiscal year variant'* (FYV), in SAP, to manage the fiscal year and the posting periods. It is made up of the number of posting periods in a fiscal year, and the number of special periods you may want. It enables the system to determine how the posting period should be ascertained during transaction postings.

The standard SAP system comes delivered with several FYVs to meet differing business needs: K0 to K4 representing the calendar year FYVs with 0 to 4 special periods, V3 (April to March with 4 special periods), V6 (July to June with 4 special periods), V9 (October to September with 4 special periods), WK (calendar weeks), R1 etc.

Project Dolphin

BESTM does not want to create new FYVs, but wants to use the SAP supplied ones. Accordingly, FYV 'K4' will be used for all the US-based company codes and 'V3' will be used by India-based company codes.

If you want to define a new FYV, you may follow the steps listed below:

i.   Use the menu path: SAP Customizing Implementation Guide > Financial Accounting > Financial Accounting Global Settings > Ledgers > Fiscal Year and Posting Periods > Maintain Fiscal Year Variant. You may also use Transaction OB29.

ii. You will be taken to the 'Change View "Fiscal year variants": Overview' screen; you will see all the standard FYVs defined in the system on the right-hand side, on the left you will see the 'Dialog Structure' to select the appropriate function.

iii. Click on 'New Entries', and maintain the details on the next screen:

- Enter the 2-character identifier in the 'FYV' field. Say, F4. Note that we are creating this new FYV for demonstrating how to create a new FYV; this is not required for the BESTM business case we are working with.
- Maintain the name in 'Description'.
- Select the 'Calendar Year' check-box, if this is a calendar year fiscal year. If it is not a calendar year fiscal year but year-dependent one, then select the other check-box namely 'Year-dependent'. Since we are creating a non-calendar year fiscal year (April-May), let us select this.
- Enter the 'Number of posting periods' (let that be 12 for our example), and 'No. of special periods' (4 in our case). You may leave all other fields as blank (Figure 6.29).

Figure 6.29 Defining a new FYV: F4

- Now, select this row containing the FYV 'F4', and double-click on 'Periods' on the left pane.
- On the ensuing 'Calendar yr' pop-up screen, you will see that the system has proposed the current calendar year (2019) for the 'Calendar yr' field. Change that, if required; else, press 'Enter' to proceed further.

- You will now be on the 'Change View "Periods": Overview' screen. Maintain the details as shown in Figure 6.30, after clicking on 'New Entries'.

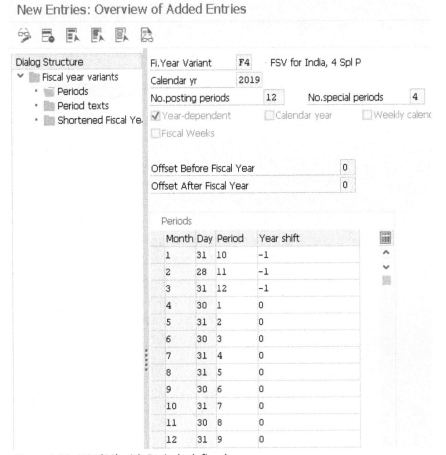

Figure 6.30 FYV 'F4' with Periods defined

- When completed, double-click on 'Period texts' on the left-hand side 'Dialog Structure' and maintain the details as indicated in Figure 6.31.
- If this is a shortened fiscal year, then you will define the required details by double-clicking on 'Shortened Fiscal Year' on the left pane.
- Now, 'Save' the entries; you have created a non-calendar FYV 'F4' in the system.

Figure 6.31 FYV F4 with Period texts defined

This completes our discussion on defining a new FYV. Let us, in the next task, see how to edit the fiscal year calendar for FYVs.

6.4.3   Edit Fiscal Year Calendar

You need to carry out this task, to maintain a fiscal calendar based on the FYV configuration. You need to execute this report only when setting up your system, or if you introduce a new FYV in between. In a running system, the fiscal calendar data are automatically determined by the *'balance carryforward'* functionality, and there is no need for this specific task. If you still execute this report, with the same or other selection data, the fiscal calendar data information, from the previous run are deleted and updated from the selection data of the current report run.

When run, the report determines - for a specific FYV - the fiscal calendar data, such as the fiscal year, period and quarters with start and end dates for a calendar date. These fiscal calendar data is used in analytical applications, such as the *Trial Balance* Fiori app, or in other Fiori apps that integrate the date picker component to let users choose the last fiscal year, period or quarter.

To edit fiscal year calendar:

i.   Use the menu path: SAP Customizing Implementation Guide > Financial Accounting > Financial Accounting Global Settings > Ledgers > Fiscal Year and Posting Periods > Edit Fiscal Year Calendar. You may also use Transaction OB_FCAL.

ii. On the 'Calculate attributes of fiscal periods', maintain the range of FYVs in 'Fiscal Year Variant' and 'to' fields; you may also maintain any single value selection (say, K4) by clicking on 'Multiple selection' arrow to the right of the 'to' field (Figure 6.32).

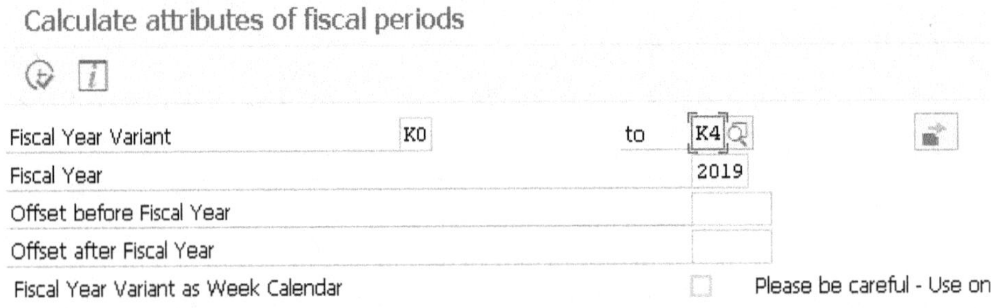

Calculate attributes of fiscal periods

	KO	to	K4	
Fiscal Year Variant	KO	to	K4	
Fiscal Year			2019	
Offset before Fiscal Year				
Offset after Fiscal Year				
Fiscal Year Variant as Week Calendar			☐	Please be careful - Use on

Figure 6.32 Edit Fiscal Year Calendar function

iii. Fill in the required 'Fiscal year' (the system defaults the current fiscal year), and 'Execute' (F8). The system now determines, for the given FYVs, the fiscal calendar data, such as the fiscal year and periods with start / end dates for the calendar year.

Let us, now, move further to assign the company codes to FYV in the next step.

6.4.4 Assign Company Code to a Fiscal Year Variant

Unless you assign a company code to a FYV, you will not be able post any transactions in the system. You can assign more than one company code to the same FYV, but the converse is not possible. We have already seen that for Project Dolphin, the FYV 'K4' needs to be assigned to all the US-based company codes, and 'V3' for the India-based ones.

To assign company code to a fiscal year variant:

i.   Use the menu path: SAP Customizing Implementation Guide > Financial Accounting > Financial Accounting Global Settings > Ledgers > Fiscal Year and Posting Periods > Assign Company Code to a Fiscal Year Variant. You may also use Transaction OB37.

ii. On the 'Change View "Assign Comp. Code -> Fiscal Year Variant": Overview' screen, enter the FYV against the respective company codes (Figure 6.33), and 'Save'. You have now assigned the FYV to the appropriate company codes.

Change View "Assign Comp.Code -> Fiscal Year Variant": Overview

CoCd	Company Name	Fiscal Year Variant	Description
1110	BESTM Farm Machinery	K4	Cal. Year, 4 Special Periods
1120	BESTM Garden & Forestry E	K4	Cal. Year, 4 Special Periods
1210	BESTM Farm Machinery	V3	Apr.- March, 4 special periods

Figure 6.33 Assigning Company Code to FYV

This completes our discussion on FYVs. Let us, now, discuss the posting period variants (PPV) in the next section.

6.4.5   Define Variants for Open Posting Periods

SAP manages opening and closing of posting periods in the system using the '*posting period variant*' (PPV). Using a PPV, you can control which period is to be opened and in which company code. In a standard system, SAP uses a separate variant for posting periods, for each of the company codes, with the name of the PPV same as that of the company code. So, every company code has its own PPV. This way, it is easier to manage the opening and closing of the posting periods for specific company codes. You, normally, will have the current posting period open and all other periods closed in the system, though you can have several posting periods open at any point of time.

> **i** Once the system becomes productive, you need to restrict access for opening and closing posting periods to avoid complications. You shall open the special periods only during closing operations.

Project Dolphin

The project team of Dolphin has been asked to simplify opening and closing of posting periods in the system without much complications. Accordingly, they have decided to define separate posting period variant for each of the company codes, in the same name as that of the company code, so that it becomes easier to manage the same in the individual company codes.

To define posting period variant:

i.   Use the menu path: SAP Customizing Implementation Guide > Financial Accounting > Financial Accounting Global Settings > Ledgers > Fiscal Year and Posting Periods > Posting Periods > Define Variants for Open Posting Periods. You may also use Transaction OBBO.

ii.   On the 'Change View "Posting Periods: Define Variants": Overview' screen, click on 'New Entries'.

iii.   On the next screen, enter the identifier for the PPV (same as that of the company code, in our case) in the 'Variant' field, and provide a description in 'Name' field. 'Save' the details. You have now created the PPVs in the same name as that of the company codes for BESTM group (Figure 6.34)

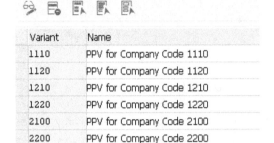

New Entries: Overview of Added Entries

Variant	Name
1110	PPV for Company Code 1110
1120	PPV for Company Code 1120
1210	PPV for Company Code 1210
1220	PPV for Company Code 1220
2100	PPV for Company Code 2100
2200	PPV for Company Code 2200

Figure 6.34 Defining Posting Period Variants for BESTM

With the definition of PPVs completed, we are ready to assign the company code to a PPV.

6.4.6 Assign Variants to Company Code

Let us assign the company codes to the respective PPV, using this customizing activity.

i.   Use the menu path: SAP Customizing Implementation Guide > Financial Accounting > Financial Accounting Global Settings > Ledgers > Fiscal Year and Posting Periods > Posting Periods > Assign Variants Company Code. Or Transaction OBBP.

ii.   On the 'Change View "Assign Comp. Code -> Posting Period Variants": Overview' screen, enter the appropriate PPV in the 'Variant' field, and 'Save' (Figure 6.35).

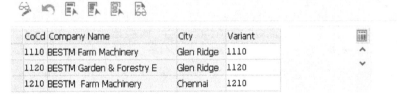

Change View "Assign Comp.Code -> Posting Period Variants": Overview

CoCd	Company Name	City	Variant
1110	BESTM Farm Machinery	Glen Ridge	1110
1120	BESTM Garden & Forestry E	Glen Ridge	1120
1210	BESTM Farm Machinery	Chennai	1210

Figure 6.35 Assigning Company Codes to Posting Period Variants

As already indicated, it is possible to assign a single PPV to multiple company codes; in that case, you will enter the same PPV in the 'Variant' field for several company codes. You will, of course, use this only when you plan simultaneous opening and closing of posting periods, across multiple company codes.

> **i** You cannot assign more than one PPV to a company code, but you can assign several company codes to a single PPV (normally, not recommended).

With the assignment of company to PPV completed, let us now understand how to control the opening and closing of posting periods.

6.4.7 Open and Close Posting Periods

Using this configuration step, you can specify - for each PPV - which posting periods are open for posting. For this to be done, you need choose between period intervals 1 to 3 on the configuration screen (Figure 6.36). Use period intervals 1 and 2 for all normal postings in regular and special periods. You will use period interval 3, for postings from SAP CO to FI. If you do not make an entry for period interval 3, the check on these postings is made from SAP CO against period intervals 1 and 2. If you make an entry for period interval 3, the check on these postings is only made against period interval 3. Specify a lower limit, an upper limit, and the fiscal year for each of these intervals. Maintain the SAP G/L account numbers ('From Account' and 'To Account') for the specifications. For the sub-ledger accounts, define the permitted posting periods using the relevant reconciliation accounts: specify the account type (D or K) and provide the 'From Account' and 'To Account' details.

You can open (a) selected accounts for posting in an already-closed posting period, and/or (b) posting periods to select users by making appropriate authorization settings. You will accomplish this in the authorization object F_BKPF_BUP; assign an authorization group (for those permitted posting periods) to a group of users, so that in month-end or year-end closing, you can open some of the posting periods only for select users. This is possible, of course, only in time period 1.

You can close a period by selecting the period specifications in such a way that the period you want to close does not fall within them.

> **i** Note that there must at least be a minimum of one entry for each PPV: this entry must have + in column A, and the columns 'From Account' and 'To Account' must not contain entries. In the columns for the posting periods, specify the periods you want to always be open for this PPV. With further entries, you define more specifically which periods are to be open for which accounts.

Let us understand how to configure this in the system:

i.   Use the menu path: SAP Customizing Implementation Guide > Financial Accounting > Financial Accounting Global Settings > Ledgers > Fiscal Year and Posting Periods > Posting Periods > Open and Close Posting Periods, or Transaction OB52.

ii.   On the 'Determine Work Area: Entry' pop-up screen, enter the PPV (1110), and press 'Continue'.

iii. On the 'Change View "Posting Periods: Specify Time Intervals": Overview' screen, press 'New Entries'.

iv.   On the next screen, note that column 'A' is used for account type or masking: a '+' on the first row in this column signifies the minimum required entry for opening the periods for all your accounts. You will use other rows for entering various account types: A (asset accounts), D (customers), K(vendors), M (material accounts), S (G/L accounts), and V (Contract accounts) as shown in Figure 6.36:

New Entries: Overview of Added Entries

Pstng period variant   1110

Posting Periods: Specify Time Intervals

A	From Acct	To Account	From Per.1	Year	To Per. 1	Year	AuGr	From Per.2	Year	To Per. 2	Year	From Per.3	Year	To Per. 3	Year
+			1	2019	12	2019		13	2019	16	2019				
A		ZZZZZZZZZZ	1	2019	12	2019		13	2019	16	2019				
D		ZZZZZZZZZZ	1	2019	12	2019		13	2019	16	2019				
K		ZZZZZZZZZZ	1	2019	12	2019		13	2019	16	2019				
M		ZZZZZZZZZZ	1	2019	12	2019		13	2019	16	2019				
S		ZZZZZZZZZZ	1	2019	12	2019		13	2019	16	2019				
V			1	2019	12	2019		13	2019	16	2019				

Figure 6.36 Open / Close Posting Period configuration for PPV 1110

- Enter + in column A. Leave 'From acct' and 'To Account' fields as blank for this row. The field 'From acct' is used to enter the lower limit of the accounts, and 'To Account' is for the upper limit of the accounts.

- Use 'From per. 1' to enter the number of the period that needs to be open. Enter '1' to open the first period i.e. January (in a calendar fiscal year). In the 'Year' column, enter the fiscal year of 'From per. 1' that you want to open (2019, in our case, for example). In conjunction with 'From per. 1', the entry in 'To period' helps to keep open one or more periods: enter '12' to keep open January to December, for PPV 1110. The 'Year' column represents the fiscal year corresponding to the entry in the column 'To period' (2019).

- Enter the authorization group, if required, in 'AuGr' to allow only select users the access for particular posting periods. Let us leave this as blank.

- Use the column 'From per. 2' to open the special periods. Enter the beginning of the special period (13). Maintain the fiscal year in 'Year' (2019), input the ending special period (16) in 'To period' and complete the settings of period 2 by entering the fiscal year corresponding to 'To period' in 'Year' column (2019).

- The columns relating to period 3 are meant for maintaining the posting period settings for enabling CO to FI postings. If you do not maintain any value in these columns, then, the period-check is made against intervals maintained for periods 1 and 2. However, if you maintain the intervals for period 3, the check on CO to FI postings is done against this interval only. Leave these columns as blank.

- Now we have completed the settings for the minimum required entry signified by the + in column A in the first row. Let us continue to configure the other rows as detailed below.
- In the second row, enter A (for Assets) under column A. Leave 'From acct' as blank. Enter ZZZZZZZZZZ in 'To Account' to include the maximum possible end number of a number range, both numeric and non-numeric. For rest of the columns, you may enter the values as that of the first row; you can, of course, maintain different periods as well. You have now completed the settings for opening/closing of posting periods for asset accounts (A).
- Configure the other rows (D, K, M, S and V) as explained in the previous step. However, for the row containing V (Contract accounts) leave the 'To Account' as blank.
- 'Save' when completed. You have, now, completed the settings for opening the periods 1 to 12 for regular postings for the fiscal year 2019, for the PPV 1110. You have also opened all the four special periods for that year in the system (Figure 6.36).

> **i** Enter 9999 in the 'Year' field to keep open the posting periods permanently. Even though the system permits this, this is not recommended.

v. Now, go back to the Transaction. On the initial 'Determine Work Area: Entry' pop-up screen, do not enter a PPV, but click on 'Maintain All'.

vi. On the resulting 'Change View "Posting Periods: Specify Time Intervals": Overview' screen, select all the seven rows of PPV 1110 and press 'Copy As'.

vii. On the next screen, change the PPV from 1110 to 1120 for all the seven rows. You can, of course, modify the 'From Per.1', 'To Per.1' etc to suit the requirements of this PPV for the company code 1120.

viii. 'Save' your entries. You have now created the required settings for PPV 1120 (Figure 6.37) for opening/closing of posting periods, by copying from the PPV 1110.

ix. Repeat the steps (v to vii) above to copy the settings to other posting period variants like, 1210, 1220, 2100, 2200 etc, and 'Save'. You have now made the required settings for opening / closing of posting periods for the different PPVs of BESTM.

New Entries: Overview of Added Entries

New Entries

Posting Periods: Specify Time Intervals

Var.	A	From Acco...	To Account	From Per.1	Year	To Per. 1	Year	AuGr	From Per.2	Year	To Per. 2	Year	From Per.3
1120	+			1	2019	12	2019	13		2019	16	2019	
1120	A		ZZZZZZZZZZ	1	2019	12	2019	13		2019	16	2019	
1120	D		ZZZZZZZZZZ	1	2019	12	2019	13		2019	16	2019	
1120	K		ZZZZZZZZZZ	1	2019	12	2019	13		2019	16	2019	
1120	M		ZZZZZZZZZZ	1	2019	12	2019	13		2019	16	2019	
1120	S		ZZZZZZZZZZ	1	2019	12	2019	13		2019	16	2019	
1120	V			1	2019	12	2019	13		2019	16	2019	

Figure 6.37 Open / Close Posting Period configuration for PPV 1120 (Copied from 1110)

This completes our discussion on opening / closing of posting periods using posting period variants. Let us, now, look at how to open a new fiscal year in the system.

6.4.8   Open a New Fiscal Year

You will open a new fiscal year, in your SAP system, with either (a) your first posting in that fiscal year or (b) a balance carryforward to that fiscal year. It is not required that you close the old fiscal year to be able to post in the new fiscal year. It is also not required open / close financial statements. However, to ensure that you can post in a new fiscal year, you need to have the following prerequisites in place:

- If you use year-specific FYVs, then you need have the appropriate FYV in place for this new fiscal year, and it must have been assigned to the company code (s).
- If you use year-dependent document numbering, you need to ensure that the document number ranges for the new year have been already created (refer Section 7.1.5 of Chapter 7, for more details).
- The posting periods are open for the new fiscal year.

This completes our discussion on fiscal year variants, posting period variants, opening/closing of posting period(s) and opening a new fiscal year. Let us, now, understand parallel accounting.

6.5   Parallel Accounting

The *'parallel accounting'*, in SAP, enables you to perform the valuations and closing operations for a company code according to the accounting principles of the group, as well as other accounting principles, such as local accounting principle. You can portray parallel accounting in the SAP system, using *parallel ledgers* ('ledger approach'). If your accounting principles do not differ much, then, you can also use *'additional accounts'* as an alternative approach ('account approach') to parallel accounting instead of parallel ledgers.

You can perform parallel accounting by running several parallel ledgers (G/L) for different accounting principles. During posting, you can post data to all ledgers, to a specified selection of ledgers, or to a single ledger. The data required according to the accounting principle for the consolidated financial statements is managed in the leading ledger (0L) of the G/L. As we have seen already, the leading ledger is integrated with Controlling (CO) and is updated in all company codes. For each additional (parallel) accounting principle, you will create an additional (non-leading) ledger in the relevant company codes. It is also possible to assign the same ledger to different accounting principles in several company codes. By doing this, for example, you can bundle all local accounting principles of the different countries in one ledger. However, you have to ensure that the same accounting principle is not assigned to different ledgers if they are used in several company codes.

> **i** It is recommended that you implement *parallel ledger* approach for parallel accounting if the number of G/L accounts would otherwise be unmanageable with the account approach. The advantages of using parallel ledgers include: (a) in each company code, you manage a separate ledger for each accounting principle, (b) you can use standard reporting for the leading ledger and all other parallel ledgers, (c) you can portray different FYVs and (d) the number of G/L accounts is manageable. Of course, you need to live with the fact that the use of parallel ledgers will increase the data volume in the system.

For parallel accounting through parallel ledgers, you need to make various settings (like, defining the accounting principles and assigning accounting principle to ledger groups) for automatic posting to the parallel ledgers. The first step is to define the accounting principles.

6.5.1 Define Accounting Principles

You will use an *'accounting principle'* to designate the legal regulations, of a country, and to draw the financial statements to meet those legal requirements. The *'accounting principle'*, thus, helps in simplifying the depiction of parallel accounting in the system as it is possible to post data for different accounting principles in separate ledgers. With leading valuation stored in the leading ledger (0L), you will see that the system uses additional non-leading ledgers (say: BI, BU) to store data, for each of the additional (parallel) accounting principles.

We have already completed this activity of defining the accounting principles in Section 6.3.4.3 (of this Chapter), when we configured the settings for ledgers. We have, also, completed assigning the accounting principles, so defined, for the required 'ledger-company code' combination as detailed out in Section 6.3.4.4 of this Chapter. And, we have defined the required ledger groups as well in Section 6.3.4.5. The next step will be to assign the accounting principle to ledger groups.

6.5.2 Assign Accounting Principle to Ledger Groups

We have already created the required ledger groups (G1) earlier in Section 6.3.4.5. Let us now assign the appropriate accounting principle to this ledger group:

i.   Use the menu path: SAP Customizing Implementation Guide > Financial Accounting > Financial Accounting Global Settings > Ledgers > Parallel Accounting > Assign Accounting Principle to Ledger Groups.

ii.   On the 'Change View "Assignment of Accounting Principle to Target Ledger Group": Overview, click on 'New Entries' and maintain the details on the next screen: Enter the 'Accounting Principle' (IAUS), select the 'Target Ledger Group' (G1).

iii. 'Save' and you have now created the required accounting principles (Figure 6.38).

Figure 6.38 Assigning Accounting Principle to Ledger Group

This completes our discussion on parallel accounting. With this, we are now ready to discuss CO integration with FI.

6.6   Integration of Controlling with FI

Historically, FI (*external accounting* or financial accounting) and CO (*internal accounting* or *management accounting*) were kept as independent areas in terms of content, with the posting of data into two different SAP components in different detail, in different structures etc., allowing and calling for local correction, reconciliation and manipulation of data. The result has been differing numbers in some of the reports, even after several rounds of reconciliation, although these two areas are supposed to provide the same financial information / result based on the underlying business processes.

With today's management demand for a holistic financial overview combining both financial accounting and management accounting, and with the new era of big data providing for larger and richer content, besides unmatched data processing capabilities, it is the by-word now to provide inputs for faster decision making, on the fly, without any tedious reconciliations.

Accordingly, SAP FI and CO are now merged, by getting rid of data redundancies and the need for reconciliations, and making visible – in real time - the internal CO actual postings in FI. Hence, the real-time FI-CO integration is now obsolete: the CO data is now stored in the new finance table ACDOCA along with the FI data. This has been achieved by several ways: for example, to have only one field available in the universal journal for both the G/L account and cost element numbers, the cost elements are now dovetailed inside the G/L account master records, by defining four types of G/L account (1-balance sheet account, 2-non-operating expense or income, 3-primary costs or revenue and 4-secondary costs) instead of the previous two (balance sheet and profit & loss). Also, the G/L account mapping of CO real-time integration with the new G/L is now rendered obsolete: the secondary cost elements are now created as G/L accounts and are part of the chart of accounts.

With the simplified settings for CO integration with FI, you just need to (a) define the document types that you want to use for posting in CO and (b) set the required indicator for G/L. You will, then, link these document types to the CO business transaction, via a document type mapping variant (Figure 6.39).

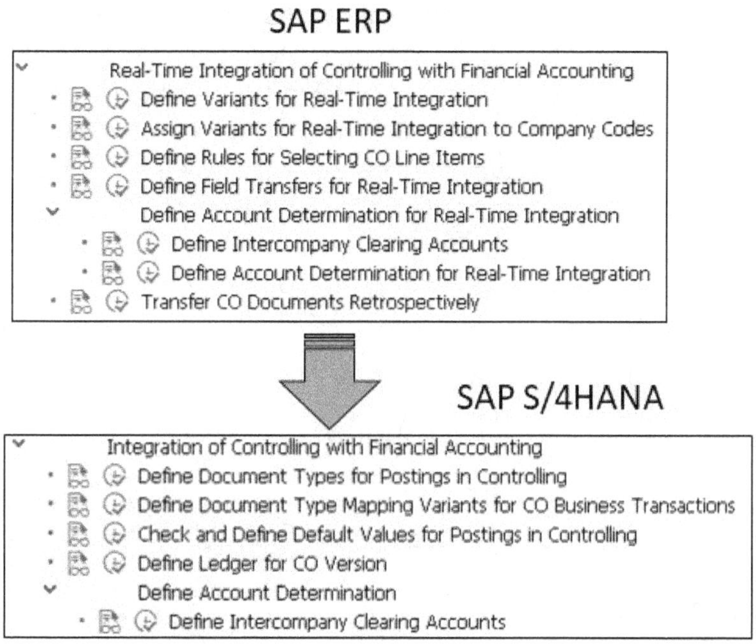

Figure 6.39 CO Integration Configuration between SAP ERP and SAP S/4HANA

Let us proceed to configure the settings required for integrating CO with FI.

6.6.1 Define Document Types for Postings in Controlling

You can create new document types for postings in CO. For example, you may want to create a document type that you can use for the manual reposting of primary costs. We shall use the SAP-defined standard document types (CC, CO etc).

Project Dolphin

Project Dolphin does not want to create any new document types for postings in CO. Instead, they have favoured using the SAP defined standard document type CO and CC.

However, if you need to define new document types for postings in CO, you may follow the steps listed below:

i.   Use the menu path: SAP Customizing Implementation Guide > Financial Accounting > Financial Accounting Global Settings > Ledgers > Integration of Controlling with Financial Accounting > Define Document Types for Postings in Controlling.

ii.   On the 'Change View "Document Types": Overview' screen (Figure 6.40), click on 'New Entries' to create the new document types. Enter the details and 'Save'.

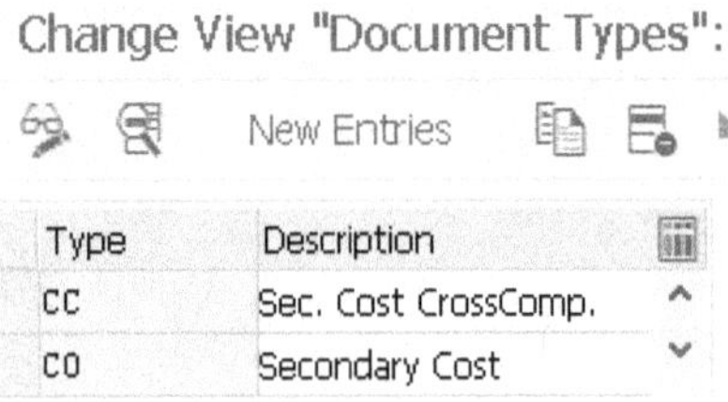

Figure 6.40 Document Type(s) for CO Integration with FI

iii. Now, double-click on the row containing the new document type, and maintain the required details (number range, reverse document type etc) on the next screen (Figure 6.41):

- 'Number range': Assign an appropriate number range; to see the number range information, for a company code, click on 'Number range information'.
- 'Reverse Document Type': The system uses the reverse document type, during document reversals. If you do not specify the reverse document type, the system assigns the reverse document the same document type of the original document. We shall discuss more about document types, in Section 7.1.2 of Chapter 7, when we discuss the documents.

iv.   Select the appropriate 'account type allowed' check-boxes. For example, for the document type CO, the check-boxes 'G/L Account' and 'Secondary Costs' need to be selected (Figure 6.41). You may also configure the required 'Control data' on this screen. And 'Save', when completed.

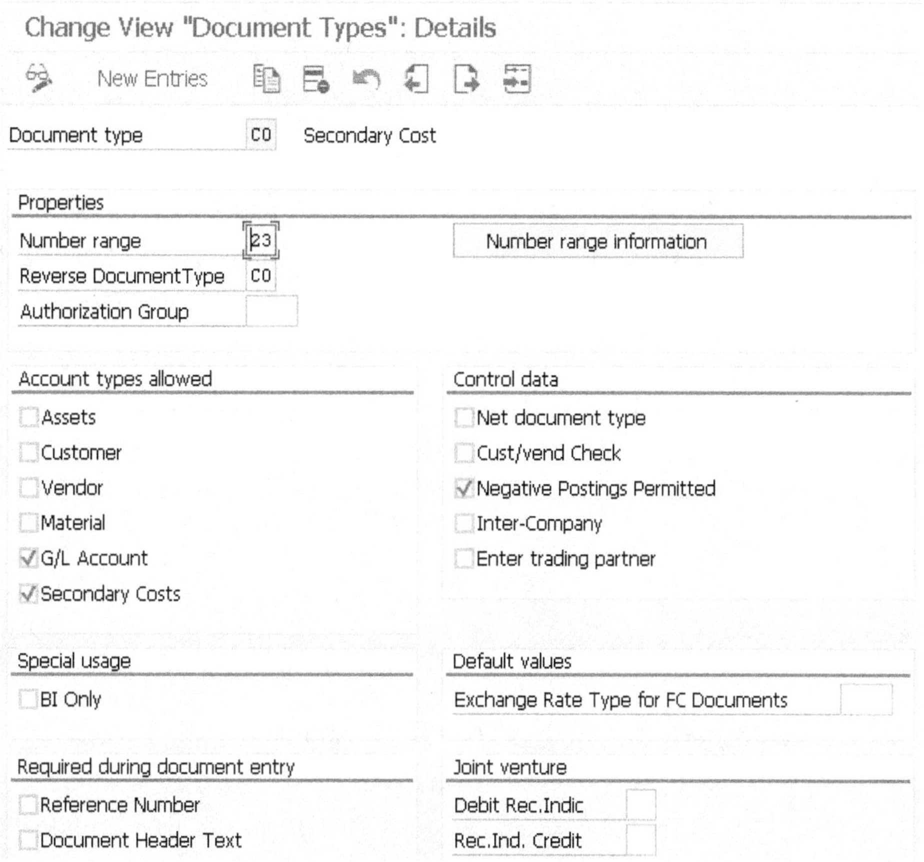

Change View "Document Types": Details

⚒   New Entries   📑 📇 ↩ ⏎ ➡ ⬈

Document type   CO   Secondary Cost

Properties

Number range	23	Number range information
Reverse DocumentType	CO	
Authorization Group		

Account types allowed

☐ Assets
☐ Customer
☐ Vendor
☐ Material
☑ G/L Account
☑ Secondary Costs

Control data

☐ Net document type
☐ Cust/vend Check
☑ Negative Postings Permitted
☐ Inter-Company
☐ Enter trading partner

Special usage

☐ BI Only

Default values

Exchange Rate Type for FC Documents

Required during document entry

☐ Reference Number
☐ Document Header Text

Joint venture

Debit Rec.Indic
Rec.Ind. Credit

Figure 6.41 Detailed Configuration for Document Type 'CO'

ℹ️ Set the indicator 'G/L Account', for all the documents types used in CO.

The next step is to map the document types with the variants for CO business transactions.

6.6.2 Define Document Type Mapping Variants for CO Business Transactions

You have to define a 'document mapping variant' that maps CO business transactions to document types, that you have defined the previous configuration step. You need to complete this mapping, for all CO business transactions that do actual postings. However, note that for actual settlement of internal orders with a settlement rule that specifies settlement to a G/L account, the mapping defined in this activity is overridden by the 'Document Type' setting under 'Other Parameters' in the configuration activity under the menu path: SAP Customizing Implementation Guide > Controlling > Internal Orders > Actual Postings > Settlement > Maintain Settlement Profiles.

> **ℹ** You can use the sample mapping variant 0000000001 without the need to create a new one. It maps all CO business transactions to the document type CO, and cross-company code document type CC.

Go through the steps listed below to complete the configuration of defining mapping variants:

i.   Use the menu path: SAP Customizing Implementation Guide > Financial Accounting > Financial Accounting Global Settings > Ledgers > Integration of Controlling with Financial Accounting > Define Document Type Mapping Variants for CO Business Transactions.

ii.   On the 'Change View "Variant for Mapping CO Transct. to Doc. Types": Overview' screen, you will see the sample mapping variant 0000000001. Make it as the 'Default Variant' by selecting that check-box' (Figure 6.42).

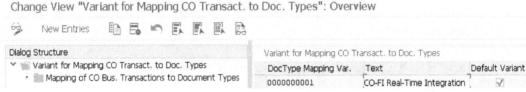

Figure 6.42 Mapping Variant for CO Business Transactions

iii. Now, select the row containing the sample mapping variant and double-click on 'Mapping of CO Bus. Transactions to Document Types' on the left-hand side 'Dialog Structure'.

iv.   Maintain the appropriate 'Document Type' (CO) and 'Cross-company Document Type' (CC), on the next screen against business transactions, and 'Save' (Figure 6.43).

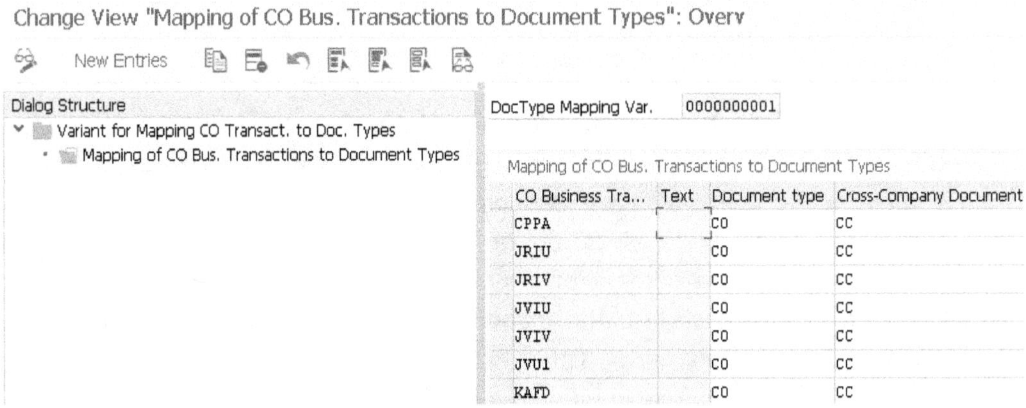

Change View "Mapping of CO Bus. Transactions to Document Types": Overv

🔧 New Entries 📄 📑 ⤺ 📊 📊 📊 📇

Dialog Structure
∨ ▦ Variant for Mapping CO Transact. to Doc. Types
  • ▦ Mapping of CO Bus. Transactions to Document Types

DocType Mapping Var.   0000000001

Mapping of CO Bus. Transactions to Document Types

CO Business Tra...	Text	Document type	Cross-Company Document
CPPA		CO	CC
JRIU		CO	CC
JRIV		CO	CC
JVIU		CO	CC
JVIV		CO	CC
JVU1		CO	CC
KAFD		CO	CC

Figure 6.43 Mapping CO Business Transactions to Document Types

It is important that you assign a mapping variant to each company code that contains CO documents; this means, that if no mapping variant exists yet, you need to manually create one and enter a document type for all CO business transactions.

The next task is to define the default values for postings in CO.

6.6.3   Check and Define Default Values for Postings in Controlling

In this configuration activity, you will map each of the company codes to a mapping variant and default ledger group besides maintaining the 'Valid From' date.

i.   Use the menu path: SAP Customizing Implementation Guide > Financial Accounting > Financial Accounting Global Settings > Ledgers > Integration of Controlling with Financial Accounting > Check and Define Default Values for Postings in Controlling.

ii.   On the 'Change View "Default Values for Postings in Controlling": Overview' screen, click on 'New Entries' and maintain 'Company Code', 'Valid From', 'Default Ledger Group' and the default 'DocType Mapping Var.' on the next screen, and 'Save' your details (Figure 6.44).

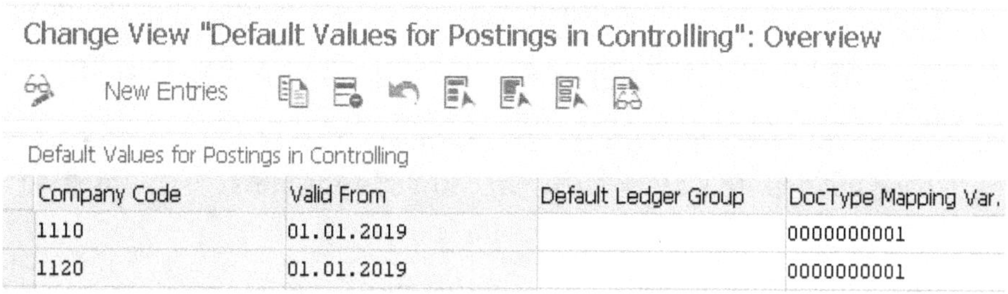

Change View "Default Values for Postings in Controlling": Overview

    New Entries

Default Values for Postings in Controlling

Company Code	Valid From	Default Ledger Group	DocType Mapping Var.
1110	01.01.2019		0000000001
1120	01.01.2019		0000000001

Figure 6.44 Default Values for Posting in CO

In cross company code postings, the system generates company code clearing items automatically. If you want to use customer accounts or supplier accounts for this item, you need to leave the 'Default Ledger Group' field as blank so that all CO postings are done to all the G/L ledgers. If you enter the leading ledger 0L in 'Default Ledger Group', the system will issue a warning while executing the consistency check of G/L settings which we discuss later in Section 6.7. We now need to assign G/L ledgers to CO versions.

6.6.4   Define Ledger for CO Version

Here, in this activity, you need assign G/L ledgers to CO versions, to enable CO to read the actual data (postings) from the G/L ledgers you specify here. It is important that all company codes must have the same fiscal year variant as that of the CO area. CO version 000 should be assigned to the leading ledger.

i.   Use the menu path: SAP Customizing Implementation Guide > Financial Accounting > Financial Accounting Global Settings > Ledgers > Integration of Controlling with Financial Accounting > Define Ledger for CO Version.

ii.   On the 'Change View "Ledger From Which CO Reads Actual Data": Overview' screen, click on 'New Entries'. On the next screen, enter 'CO Area' (B100), 'Version' (000) and 'Ledger (Compat.)' (0L); and 'Save'. You have now assigned the CO version 000 (displayed as 0) to the leading ledger 0L for the controlling area B100 (Figure 6.45).

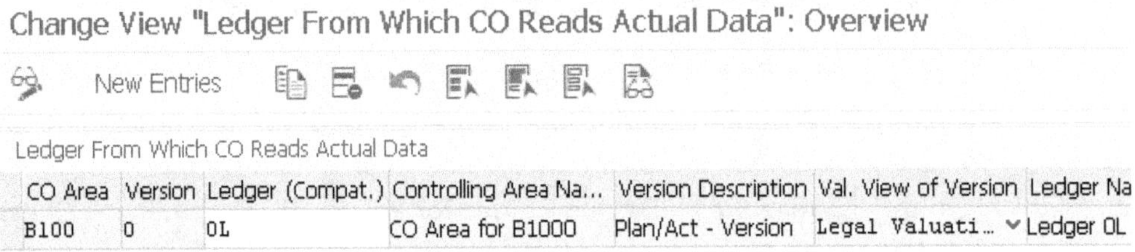

Change View "Ledger From Which CO Reads Actual Data": Overview

New Entries

Ledger From Which CO Reads Actual Data

CO Area	Version	Ledger (Compat.)	Controlling Area Na...	Version Description	Val. View of Version	Ledger Na
B100	0	0L	CO Area for B1000	Plan/Act - Version	Legal Valuati...	Ledger 0L

Figure 6.45 Defining Ledger for CO Version

This completes our discussion on configuring CO integration with FI. Let us discuss, next, about the consistency check of G/L settings, before discussing global parameters for company code.

6.7   Execute Consistency Check of General Ledger Settings

Using this activity, you will be checking the configuration settings for the ledgers that have already been defined. This check must run without error messages before you can continue further:

i.   Use the menu path: SAP Customizing Implementation Guide > Financial Accounting > Financial Accounting Global Settings > Ledgers > Execute Consistency Check of General Ledger Settings.

ii.   You will see inconsistencies, if any, on the next screen ('Messages') grouped under terminations, errors, warnings and information with differently shaped and coloured icons, for all the company codes.

As long as inconsistencies exists, the posting of journal entries will not be possible in the affected company codes and ledgers. If there are inconsistencies, correct your Customizing settings to solve the issues. Once the inconsistencies are resolved, you will be able to post the journal entries.

You can check the consistency of the Customizing settings using:

- Transaction FINS_CUST_CONS_CHK, for all company codes and ledgers
- Transaction FINS_CUST_CONS_CHK_P, for a single company code and ledger group.

> **i** Within Customizing activities, the system sends only warning message instead of error messages, for the detected inconsistencies to enable saving the Customizing settings despite those existing inconsistencies. But, if you try to post a journal entry, the system will regard the inconsistencies as errors, and will stop you from proceeding further.

We have executed Transaction FINS_CUST_CONS_CHK_P for company code 1110, and the results are as shown in Figure 6.46.

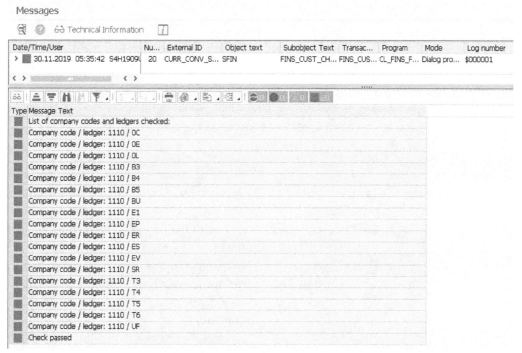

Figure 6.46 Consistency Check for G/L Ledger Settings

With the consistency check for G/L ledger group completed, we are ready to configure the global parameters for company codes.

6.8   Global Parameters for Company Code

You use the company code global parameters to control how a company code behaves, in your SAP system. You will be configuring about 35 global parameters, in all, grouped into two categories: accounting organization and processing parameters:

Accounting Organization: There are 11 parameters as listed below (Table 6.6):

Chart of accounts	External company code	Country chart of accounts	Global company code
Company	Is company code productive	FM area	VAT registration number
Credit control area	Hide company code in F4	Fiscal year variant	

Table 6:6 Accounting Organization: Global Parameters for Company Code

Processing Parameters: There are 24 global processing parameters (Table 6.7):

Document entry screen variant	Inflation method	Business area financial statements	Financial asset management active
Fields status variant	Tax currency translation	Propose fiscal year	Purchase account processing is active
Posting period variant	Co. Code -> CO Area	Define default value date	JV accounting active
Max. exchange rate deviation	Cost of sales accounting status	No exchange rate difference when clearing in local currency	Hedge request active
Sample account rules variant	Negative postings permitted	Tax base is net value	Enable amount split
Workflow variant	Manage posting period	Discount base is net value	Tax reporting date active

Table 6:7 Processing Parameters: Global Parameters for Company Code

Besides, there are 19 more parameters that you can be configure under 'Additional Data'. If you have not already maintained the 'Address' information while defining the company codes (Chapter 5, Section 5.3.2.2), then, you can maintain them now in this activity.

You will use all these parameters to characterize the particular company code and influence the way the system processes the business transactions for that company code.

Let us complete configuring these company code global parameters for the company codes of BESTM that we have already defined in Section 5.3.2, of Chapter 5.

6.8.1 Enter Global Parameters

Let us understand how to enter the global parameters for company codes.

Project Dolphin

BESTM wants the following to be configured properly for the appropriate company codes:

It has already been mentioned, while configuring the controlling area for BESTM, that the SAP supplied standard chart of accounts YCOA has to be copied and adapted into two new charts of accounts, BEUS for US-based company codes and BEIN for India-based company codes. Accordingly, these two charts need to be created for BESTM in the system. The respective Financial Statement Version will also be created in the same name as that of the chart of accounts.

For all the US-based company codes, both the operative and country chart of accounts will be the same: BEUS. In the case of India-based company codes, the operative chart of accounts will be BEUS and the country chart of accounts will be BEIN. All the US-based company codes will use K4 as their FYV, and the India-based ones will use V3. A suitable document entry screen variant that facilitates country-specific processing of withholding tax needs to be used in all the US-based company codes. A common field status variant (FSV), B100, will be used in all company codes. As regards the PPV is concerned, each company code will use the specific PPV that has already been created with the same identifier as that of these company codes.

If there is a difference in currency translation due to exchange rate fluctuations during transaction posting, then, a maximum of 10% has to be allowed as the permitted deviation. However, this will not be applicable to the tax postings as all the tax items have to be translated using the exchange rate from the document header. All the US-based company codes will use a single variant US01 (copied from SAP standard variant 0001 but configured for USD) as the workflow variant. It has been decided to allow negative postings, thereby avoiding inflated trial balance.

BESTM wants to activate Cost of Sales (CoS) accounting in all the company codes to understand the outflow of economic resources engaged in making the company's revenue. It has also been decided that suitable configuration to be made to enable drawing up financial statements per business area. Further, it has been requested that the system should clear the foreign currency open items into local currency using the prevailing exchange rate, instead of using the original exchange rate; any gain/loss arising out of this, needs to be posted to the designated G/L accounts.

BESTM does not want the system to propose fiscal year during document change or document display functions as it expects all the company codes to work with year-independent document numbers. However, the current date can be defaulted to as the value date for entering the line items in a document.

Since USA makes use of the jurisdiction codes for tax calculation, BESTM wants the tax base to remain at the jurisdiction code level, for all the US-based company codes. For all other company codes (that is, for the ones in India) the tax base has to be configured as the net of discount of the invoice amount.

Before we actually proceed to configure the company code global settings, let us create the chart of accounts for BESTM. As outlined in the case study, we will need two charts of accounts BEUS (for US-based company codes) and BEIN (for India-based company codes. It has been decided by the project management team, to copy the SAP supplied standard chart of accounts YCOA in creating these two charts of accounts for BESTM.

A *'Chart of Accounts'* is a list of G/L accounts that provides the framework for recording accounting transactions for a business entity in a formal and organised manner. Each G/L account, in the chart of accounts, is made up of an account number, account name, and some control parameters. The control parameters (like G/L account type, account group etc) decides how an account is created and posted to.

There are different types of charts of accounts:

Operating Chart of Accounts: You will use the 'operating chart of accounts' for recording the day-to-day transactions in a company code. Though you can use the same chart of accounts across several company codes, each company code must work with only one operating chart of accounts. This can be different from the 'country chart of accounts'. The operating chart of accounts goes by various names including *operative chart of accounts*, *standard chart of accounts* or just chart of accounts,

Country Chart of Accounts: You will use the 'country chart of accounts' to meet the statutory / legal requirements of the country in which your company code is operating. Though optional to assign to a company code, you will need such a chart when you work with a different operating chart of accounts (say, as in the case of the company codes in India for BESTM Corporate). When you use a country chart, you need to establish the link with the operating chart by entering the country chart's G/L account number in the 'Alternate Account Number' field of the G/L master record in the 'Co. Code' section of the operating chart of accounts. You have to enter the country chart of accounts, if different from the operating chart, while maintaining the company code global parameters (Transaction OBY6). You can also do the same when you assign the company code to chart of accounts, using Transaction OB62.

Group Chart of Accounts: You will use the 'group chart of accounts' for consolidating all company codes operating with different operating charts of accounts, but belonging to a same company. Also known as the *'corporate chart of accounts'*, you will establish the link with the operating chart of accounts by entering the ID of this chart of accounts in the 'Group Chart of Accounts' field under 'Consolidation' when creating the chart of accounts.

We will discuss the chart of accounts and G/L accounts in detail in Chapter 9. However, for the present, we shall restrict ourselves in creating the required charts of accounts for BESTM.

You can create a new chart of accounts by following two methods:

1) You can create a new chart of accounts through 'Edit Chart of Accounts List' configuration task. You need to use the menu path: SAP Customizing Implementation Guide > Financial Accounting > General Ledger Accounting > Master Data > G/L Accounts > Preparations > Edit Chart of Accounts List. Or, you may use Transaction OB13.

   In this method, you can (a) create a new chart of accounts afresh or (b) you can copy an existing one and create the new. In either case, you will maintain settings like the chart of accounts ID, chart of accounts description, maintenance language and the length of the G/L account number. You may also maintain the group chart of accounts. If you are not using the SAP supplied consolidation group chart of accounts, and want to create that as well new, it is better you create this group chart first before creating the rest of the charts of accounts as you need to select the group chart from the drop-down list when creating a new chart. Here, in this method you are just creating the new chart of accounts, but you are not creating / copying the chart of accounts data for the new chart. Though you can create the chart of accounts area data (G/L accounts, account determinations etc) later, it is easier and recommended to create a new chart of accounts along with the chart of accounts data by copying from a suitable standard chart. As you are aware that there is a standard chart of accounts (YCOA) supplied by SAP which can be copied into creating the new ones, together with the chart of accounts area data, we will not use this method (1) to create the new charts but the other method which is detailed below in (2).

2) In this method of creating a new chart of accounts, you can actually create the new chart of accounts together with the chart of accounts area data by copying from a source (or reference) chart of accounts. While doing this you actually copy and create all the G/L accounts in the chart of accounts area, from the *reference chart of accounts*, associated account determinations (for FI, AM, CO, MM, HR & SD) and the financial statement version. You can then adapt the new chart of accounts by making the required minor changes. You can also create the company code data later. In our

case, as already outlined, we will be creating the new charts together with the account determination and financial statement version, for BESTM by copying the standard chart of accounts YCOA supplied by SAP.

Let us understand how to create the new charts of accounts, together with the chart of accounts area data by copying from an existing chart of accounts:

i. You need use the menu path: SAP Customizing Implementation Guide > Financial Accounting > General Ledger Accounting > Master Data > G/L Accounts > G/L Account Creation and Processing > Alternative Methods > Copy G/L Accounts > Copy Chart of Accounts. Or, you may use Transaction OBY7.

ii. On the ensuing pop-up screen, select all that need to be copied. We have selected all including the financial statement version. Click 'Enter' to proceed.

iii. On the next screen (Figure 6.47):

Copy Chart of Accounts-Dependent Table Entries

🔒 Copying capability   ↩ New selection

Chart of accounts	BEUS
Chart of accounts name	BESTM - US Standard Chart of Accounts
FS Version	BEUS
Fin. stmt version name	BESTM-Financial Statement Version US

Reference

Chart of accounts	YCOA	Standard Chart of Accounts
FS Version	$US2	Financial Statement Version US

Figure 6.47 Copying Chart of Accounts using a Reference Chart of Accounts

- Enter the identifier for the new 'Chart of accounts'. Say, BEUS.
- Enter a name for the new chart.
- Enter the identifier for the new financial statement version in 'FS Version' field. Enter BEUS, as we want to have the same identifier as that of the new chart of accounts.
- Enter a name of the financial statement version.
- Under 'Reference', enter the 'Chart of accounts' (YCOA) and the 'FS Version' that we are copying from.

iv. Now, click on 'Copying capability'. The system takes you to the next screen, 'Copy Chart of Accounts: Proposal List', with the details of a proposal as to what will all be copied (Figure 6.48).

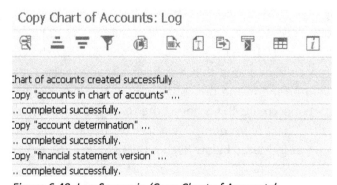

Figure 6.48 Proposal List in 'Copy Chart of Accounts' Activity

v.   The system copies all the data in the chart of accounts area including the G/L accounts, account determination etc., to the new chart of accounts BEUS along with the new financial statement version BEUS (Figure 6.49).

vi. You can create the other chart of accounts BEIN as well, by repeating the steps.

Figure 6.49 Log Screen in 'Copy Chart of Accounts'

We have now created all the required the new charts of accounts for BESTM group (Figure 6.50) that we can use in configuring company code global parameters, which we will discuss next.

Figure 6.50 List of Charts of Accounts for BESTM

To configure the company code global parameters for a company code, say 1110:

i.   Use the menu path: SAP Customizing Implementation Guide > Financial Accounting > Financial Accounting Global Settings > Global Parameters for Company Code > Enter Company Code Global Parameters. You may also use Transaction OBY6.

ii. On the 'Change View "Company Code Global Data": Overview' screen, double-click on the row containing the company code (1110) for which you are about to maintain the company code global parameters.

iii. On the 'Change View "Company Code Global Data": Details' screen, you will see that the system has already filled up the header data (Figure 6.51) including the 'Country Key', 'Currency' and 'Language Key'.

Figure 6.51 Header data in Company Code Global Parameters

iv. Under 'Accounting organisation', you will notice that the system has already pre-filled some of the fields like 'Chart of accounts' (YCOA), 'Company' (B1000), 'Credit control area' (1100), 'FM Area' (BF11) and 'Fiscal Year Variant' (K4) for the company code 1110, based on the configurations that we have already made (in the previous Sections of this Chapter and in the previous Chapter 5). Since we plan to use the BESTM-specific chart of accounts BEUS, for all the US-based company codes, change YCOA to BEUS in the 'Chart of accounts' field. Let us maintain the settings for the remaining fields now, as indicated below (Figure 6.53):

- 'External CoCode': You will select this checkbox only when defining the specified local company code as an external company code; this is necessary only if you are using the document entry function for external SAP systems (ICT).
- 'Company Code Is Productive': Select this check-box only when the company code is about to become 'productive' to prevent deletion programs from re-setting data in this company code by mistake. This you will do as the last step of configuration in any implementation, when every other configuration setting has been completed. Leave this as blank for now.
- If you select 'Hide Company Code in F4', the system will not display the company code when displaying the possible entries for F4. Do not select this check-box.
- 'Country Chart/Accts': You will enter the country chart of accounts in this field, if that is different from the operative chart. We will leave this field as blank for company code 1110, as both the operative and country charts are one and the same (BEUS); when you 'Save', the system will fill this field with BEUS. However, you will, for example, enter BEIN in this field, for India-based company codes like 1210 and 1220 as the operative and country charts is different for these entities.

---

i If you have earlier created a company code with a different chart of accounts and want to change the same now or later, then, you need to follow the below listed steps:

Step1: Use the menu path: SAP Customizing Implementation Guide > Financial Accounting > General Ledger Accounting > Preparation for Productive Start > New Installation > Delete Test Data > Delete Transaction Data > Delete Company Code Data or Transaction OBR1 to delete or to re-set company code data, if any. The pre-conditions include that the company code for which you are trying to delete the data should not have been flagged as 'productive'. You may delete the transaction data for individual company codes by using the deletion program SAPF020. For this, you need authorization F_002 for object S_PROGRAM.

Step2: Re-set company code-dependent SAP G/L account master data (without the general master data) by using menu path SAP Customizing Implementation Guide > Financial Accounting > General Ledger Accounting > Preparation for Productive Start > New Installation > Delete Test Data > Delete Master Data > Delete G/L Account or Transaction OBR2. When executing, ensure that there are no problems listed in the 'test-run' log. The program will not delete the chart of accounts section of an SAP G/L, if the account is also a primary cost element in CO; you need to, then, use the program RKSCUS03 to accomplish the task.

- 'Global CoCde': This works in conjunction with the field 'External CoCode'. The global company codes are involved in document entry for external SAP systems as the sender or receiver, and this kind of company code must have – for example - a cross-system company code ID (such as EUROPA) in addition to their local company code ID (such as 0001). You will set these company codes up for ALE distribution scenarios.

- 'VAT Registration No.': You will enter the information in this field only for company codes in Europe, as this number is used within the European Union for tax-exempt deliveries for the European Commission (EC) sales list. Leave this as blank for 1110.

v.   Let us now complete the settings, for the company code 1110, under 'Processing parameters':

- 'Document Entry Screen Variant': You need to select an appropriate screen variant for entering accounting documents. There are four standard variants available: <blank>, 1, 2 and 3. There are country-specific settings in some of the variants: 1 for Austria & Switzerland, 3 for countries with classic withholding tax, and 2 for France and other countries with (extended) withholding tax. Since, we are configuring this for a US company code, you need to select 2 here.

- The system has already pre-populated both the 'Field status variant' (B100) and 'Pstng period variant' (1100).

- In 'Max. exchange rate deviation', enter 10 as indicated in the case study. The system maintains the exchange rates in the exchange rate table for accurate currency translation. However, it also enables you to enter a foreign currency exchange while carrying out a transaction. Should there be a difference between these two rates, then, you need to instruct the system regarding the maximum exchange rate deviation that can be allowed to complete the transaction. Beyond that limit (10% in our case), the system will issue a warning, and you cannot proceed further with that transaction.

- 'Sample Acct. Rules Var.': You will use the variant entered in this field while creating SAP G/L accounts from sample accounts: the variant entered here will point to a template from which you can transfer, via *data transfer rules*, certain data to the newly created SAP G/L accounts. An entry in this field is necessary only if you want to work with sample accounts when creating G/L accounts. We shall discuss more about this when we cover sample accounts, Section 9.3.1.6 in Chapter 9. Leave this as blank for the time being.

- 'Workflow variant': A workflow variant (for the payment release) allows you to group and route the documents processing of several company codes for payment release. Though SAP comes delivered with a sample workflow (0001), you cannot straightaway use this unless the workflow variant's currency is the same as that of your company code's currency. In our case, we need the workflow currency in USD but the standard workflow is in EUR. Hence, we have defined the required workflow variants (US01 and IN01); enter the newly defined workflow variant US01 here in this field for the US company code 1110.

Let us just side-step a little to understand how to define a workflow variant (for the payment release) in the system, before we continue with the setting up of rest of the company code global parameters:

While defining the workflow for the release of payment, you can make specifications as to (a) if a release is required (the system triggers a workflow within the release for payment), and (b) the amount limit beyond which the release for payment is to take place. Once defined, you can attach the variant(s) to the appropriate company codes. SAP comes delivered with the standard workflow 0001 that can be copied and required changes made to suit your requirements.

a) You will define a workflow using the menu path: SAP Customizing Implementation Guide > Financial Accounting > Accounts Receivable and Accounts Payable > Business Transactions > Release for Payment > Create Workflow Variant for Release for Payment, or Transaction OBWA.

b) On the 'Change view "Preliminary Posting Workflow Link": Overview' screen, you can highlight the row containing the variant 0001 and press 'Copy As'. On the next screen, enter the details:
   • Provide the identifier for the workflow variant in "Workflow var." field (US01).
   • Change the 'Currency' to USD if the currency is other than USD.
   • Enter a 'Name'.

c) Under 'Preliminary posting release', select the 'Posting Release' check-box if you want to ensure that a release has to take place before a document can be posted Do not enter the subworkflow which we will do later when we discuss payment release in FI-A/R and A/P in Section 10.3.1.2 and 10.3.2 of Chapter 10 (Volume II of this book), wherein we shall control both the document release and payment release through release groups and approval paths for various payment levels (single level, two level and three level) of control.

d) Under 'Payment release', set the indicator 'Release Payts' to ensure that a payment release must take place before you can pay a document (if the indicator is not set, no payment release is necessary).

e) 'Save' the details, and you have now created the workflow variant US01 for the release of payment for BESTM (Figure 6.52). Repeat the steps and create another variant, by copying US01, in the name IN01 to be used by Indian company codes of BESTM.

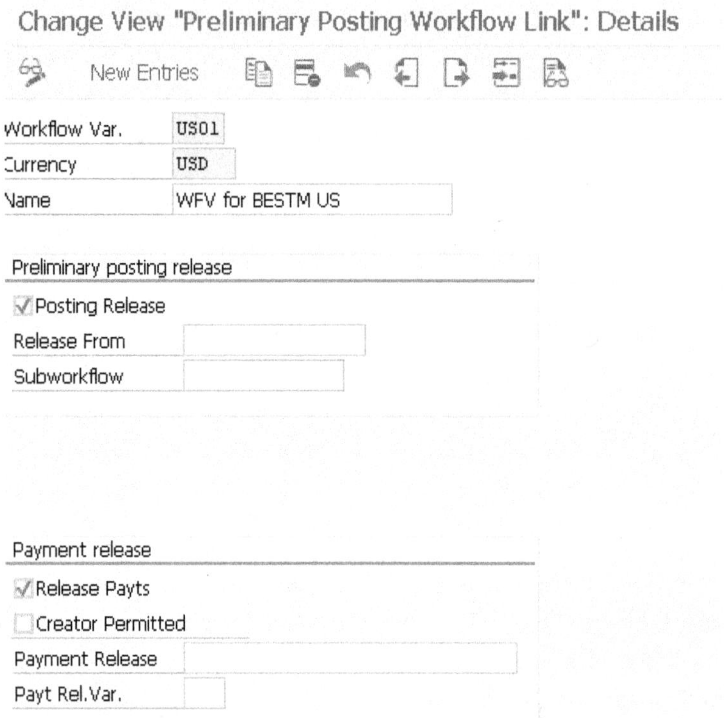

Figure 6.52 Defining Workflow Variant US01

This completes our discussion on creating a new workflow variant. Let us continue with the configuration of other company code global parameters (Figure 6.53):

- 'Inflation Method': You are required fill this field only when you use 'Inflation Accounting Solution' for this company code. That not being the case, leave this as blank.

- 'Tax Crcy Translation': The value entered here will influence how the system takes up foreign currency translation for tax Items. As you are aware, the tax amounts are normally translated using the exchange rate prescribed by the tax base amount. When you want to enter or have the system propose a different exchange rate for translation, you then need to select the appropriate settings, for this option from the drop-down values; there are five options available : <blank> is the default option wherein the exchange rate is picked up from the document header, 1 allows for manual entry of exchange rate, 2 is for picking up the exchange rate based on the posting date, 3 is to decide the exchange rate based on document date, 4 is similar to that of option 2 but with a provision to distribute the differences, if any, and 5 is for determining the exchange rate based on tax reporting date. The alternate exchange rate selected will result in a local currency balance in the document, and that balance is posted automatically to a separate account. You will leave this as blank as BESTM wants to have the foreign exchange rate picked up from the document header for translating the tax items.

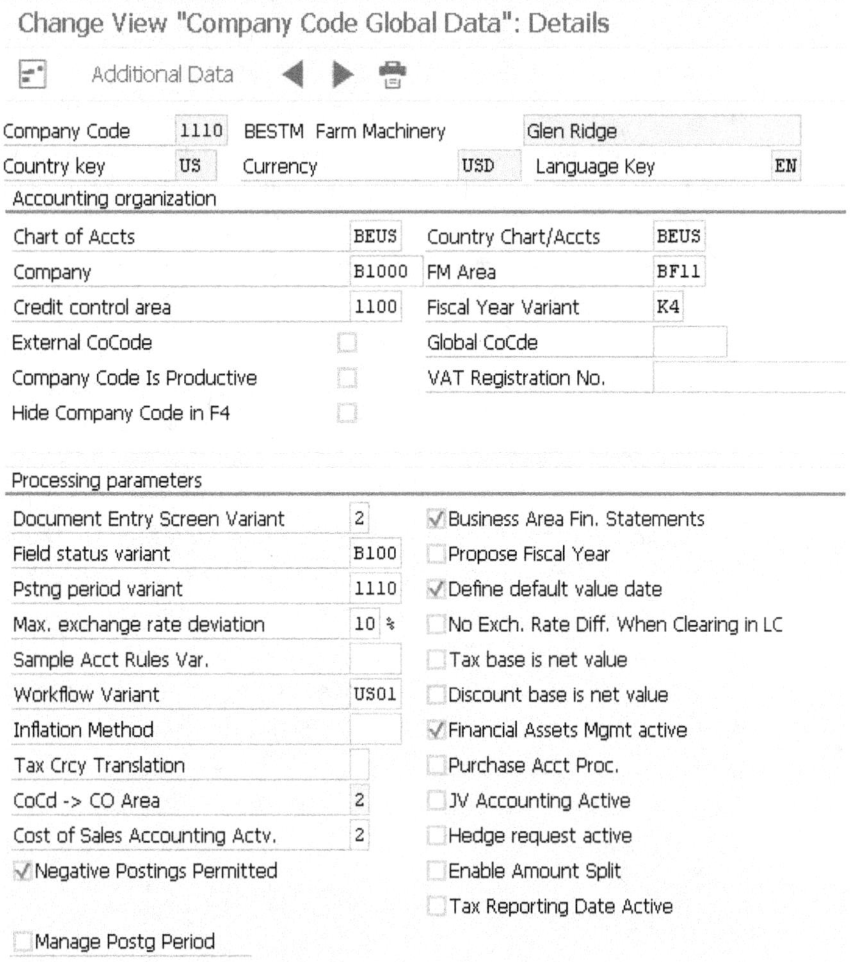

Figure 6.53 Company Code Global Parameters for 1110

- 'CoCd -> CO Area': The system has already populated this field with 2 indicating cross-company code cost accounting of assigning more than one company code to a single controlling area. Recall that we have discussed this in detail in Chapter 5 in Section 5.3.8 when defining the CO area, and in Section 5.4.4 of Chapter 5, when assigning company code to CO area. You would have noticed that the field has been greyed-out indicating that you will not be able to change the 'company code – controlling area' assignment here.

- 'Cost of Sales Accounting Actv.': *Cost of Sales accounting* (CoS) is a type of P & L statement that matches the sales revenues to the costs (or expenses) involved in making the cost of sales (=revenue). The costs are listed in the functional area like manufacturing, management, sales & distribution, R & D etc. Through CoS accounting, you can show how your business is incurring the expenses. Enter 2 in the field to activate CoS accounting for the company code 1110. When 'active' (for postings in this company code), the functional areas are derived and updated. The other two statuses are: <blank> inactive and 1 in-preparation. If the field is set to the value 1 (in-preparation), the field functional area is then ready for input in the master data of the G/L accounts, cost elements and certain CO account assignment objects; this means that you can enter the functional area in the master data.

- 'Negative Postings Permitted': When you select this check-box, it signals to the system that the transaction figures on the original side of the account are reset, rather than being increased on the other side of the account, when documents are reversed. In other words, the system makes an entry with an opposite sign for reversals instead of posting to the opposite side of the account. Because of this, the account balance of the account in question is represented as though the document had never been posted after the document is reversed. Otherwise, the transaction figures of the account would be increased by the same amount on the debit and on the credit side due to the reversal document. This is also called as '*true reversal*'. However, to enable negative postings, you need to have the appropriate document types defined in the system so as to allow the line items to be flagged individually as negative postings. Enabling negative postings is per company code, and you also need to define reversal reasons in the system using the menu path: SAP Customizing Implementation Guide > Financial Accounting > General Ledger Accounting > Business Transactions > Adjustment Posting/Reversal > Define Reasons for Reversal (we shall discuss this configuration step in detail, in a later Chapter, when we discuss about G/L accounting).

> **i** If the reversal is posted using a posting date other than the one for the document to be reversed, the settings you make here does not take effect.

- 'Manage Postg Period': This check-box field is used to decide if the posting period check is also to be undertaken for non-representative ledgers. You will use this indicator, if you want to define posting periods and fiscal year variants for non-representative ledgers that differ from the settings of the representative ledger. In this case, postings to a ledger group are made by the system, if the relevant posting period is open in all ledgers of the ledger group. The recommended setting is not to activate this flag; because, when set, there is an increase in system resource usage during the checking depending on the number of ledgers that you have defined.

- 'Business Are Fin. Statements': You need to select this check-box if you want to draw financial statements per business area. A tick-mark in this check-box makes the 'Business Area' field as mandatory for data entry during postings.

> **i** When you enable business area financial statements here, you are in effect overriding all other settings in posting keys or accounts made elsewhere for the business area.

- 'Propose Fiscal Year': Use this indicator to control whether the fiscal year is defaulted for document display and change transactions. You will select this check-box only for company codes that work mainly with year-dependent document numbers. By selecting this check-box, you enable the system to display (and default) not only the last document number processed but also the corresponding fiscal year. When you work company codes that use non-year-dependent document number assignment (like, 1110), you should leave the field blank; then, the system searches only for documents via the document number.
- 'Define default value date': Select this check-box to enable the system to indicate that the current date is used as the default value date when entering line items. You can, of course, change the date during document entry.
- 'No Exch. Rate Diff. When Clearing in LC': This check-box controls how foreign currency open items are cleared in local currency. When the check-box is selected, the system clears the foreign currency open items using the prevailing exchange rate when those open items were originally created. If you do not select this check-box (as in the case of the company code 1110), then, the system uses the foreign exchange rate as on the date of clearing (payment), by converting the original open items into the local currency value, and then clearing the same with the incoming payment in the local currency. The difference (gain or loss), if any, arising out of the exchange rate variation between these two dates, is automatically posted to appropriate G/L accounts that have been designated for the purpose.
- 'Tax base is net value': The tax base (on an expense or a revenue item) used in tax calculation, can include or exclude a cash discount. The tax base is known as 'gross' when you include the cash discount; otherwise, the base is known as 'net'. The whole invoice is taken as the base for tax calculation when it is 'gross'; you will not deduct the cash discount in arriving at the tax base. On the other hand, when it is 'net', you will deduct the discount from the value of the goods, and this reduced amount will be the tax base. For all the company codes in USA, the entry

made here does not influence the system as tax is calculated at the jurisdiction level. However, you will need select this check-box for company codes operating in countries like UK, India etc., where the tax base is calculated on the 'net'. Accordingly, leave this field as blank for all US-based company codes including 1110, and select the check-box for India-based company codes including 1210.

- 'Discount base is net value': The 'net' discount base system of discount calculation is followed in countries like France. When you select this check-box, you enable the system to ignore the tax amount – if any - in arriving at the discount base for calculating the discount. The discount, now, is on the invoice amount less the tax. If you do not select the check-box, the system includes the tax amount also in arriving at the discount base ('gross'). The setting here does not affect company codes where the discount calculation is configured at the jurisdiction code level, as in US-based company codes including 1110. Hence, leave this as blank; but select the same for India-based company codes.

> **i** When the cash discount base is 'net', note that SAP does not take into account the freight and setup charges also. On the other hand, these charges along with the input tax, are all considered while arriving at the discount base, when the cash discount base is 'gross'. If the tax base is 'net', the discount base also needs to be 'net'.

- 'Financial Assets Mgmt. Active': This is used to pass on payment information especially to the 'Loans' sub-component of SAP Treasury & Risk Management, when using bank account statement processing and the payment program. There, the field controls the reporting and processing of incoming payments and their clearing in the customer area. Select the check box for 1110.

- 'Purchase Acct Proc.': This check-box specifies if 'purchase account management' is active in the system. Note that a purchase account is required in some countries, to record the value at which externally obtained materials should be posted. When active, additional postings are carried out by the system during the posting of receipts of goods (GR) and invoices (IR): (a) the same amount is posted to the purchase account as to the balance sheet account; the offsetting entry is made to the purchasing offsetting account, and (b) a freight purchase account has been defined, similar to the purchase account; it documents the posted delivery costs of externally obtained materials. Not to be selected for BESTM company codes.

- 'JV Accounting Active': SAP JVA (*Joint Venture Accounting*) is a complete accounting system for joint ventures. In a joint venture (JV), companies typically form partnerships to minimize risks involved in capital intensive operations that demand a long payback period. A joint venture partnership consists of an 'operating partner' (operator) and one or more 'non-operating partners' who combine monetary or personnel resources to share a project's expenses and revenues. The operator manages the venture, arranges venture activities, and maintains accounting records, besides remitting venture expenses, collecting revenues, and distributing to the partners, according to their ownership shares. Do not select this checkbox, as BESTM company codes will not be into JVA.

- 'Hedge request active': SAP E-HA (SAP Hedge Accounting for Exposures) can manage hedging relationships with which you document how you use financial instruments to hedge your risk positions (exposures) against foreign exchange risks, interest rate risks, and commodity price risks. As BESTM will not be using hedge accounting, you do not need to select this check-box for the any of the company codes.

- 'Enable amount split': This check-box enables you to split the final amount of invoice or credit memo. Set the indicator if, for example, you want to split an amount according to different withholding tax information; then, the system brings up the screen (for entering invoices or credit memos) containing an additional tab for the amount split. You can also split the amount according to payment method or terms of payment. If you have entered a payment method, this entry has priority over the payment method in the terms of payment. As this functionality has not been required by BESTM, do not select this check-box.

> **i** This 'amount split' function is only possible in the invoice/credit memo entry single-screen transaction developed as an Enjoy Transaction.

- 'Tax Reporting Date Active': You do not need to select this check-box for any of the company codes of BESTM; leave this as blank.

vi. You can now 'Save' the data (Figure 6.53). When you are trying to save, the system throws a message that the chart of accounts in controlling area and the company code 1110 is different. This is because when we created the controlling area, we had the chart of accounts YCOA for the company code, which we have changed now to BEUS. Press 'Enter' and continue to save the details; we shall change the chart of accounts in controlling area B100, later, when we have maintained the global company code parameters for the other company code 1120.

vii. You have now configured all the important global parameters for the company code 1110. You may also click on 'Address' if you have not maintained that earlier.

> **i** Even though you see a button 'Additional Data' to maintain additional details, note that you will not be able to that from this Transaction. To maintain the additional details, use the menu path: SAP Customizing Implementation Guide > Financial Accounting > Financial Accounting Global Settings > Global Parameters for Company Code > Maintain Additional Parameters. You may also use Transaction OBY6. On the 'Display "View Company Code": Overview' screen, select the company code row and double-click on 'Additional Data' on the left-hand side dialog-box. Maintain the required details and 'Save'.

This completes configuring the company code global parameters for the company code 1110. Repeat the steps and maintain the details for company codes 1120 and 1210. Once done, you can use either 1110 or 1120 as the source to copy and create rest of the US-based company codes (2100, 2200, 3100 and 3200) by using the configuration step already discussed in Section 5.3.2.1 of Chapter 5. Similarly, you can use 1210 as the source to copy and create the other India-based company code (1220).

Before proceeding further, revisit the configuration activity that you have used to maintain the controlling area (Section 5.3.8 of Chapter 5), and change the chart of accounts of the controlling area B100 from YCOA to BEUS. Do change the chart of accounts in other controlling areas (B200 & B300) as well, if required.

This completes our discussion on the financial accounting global settings relating to fields, ledgers, FSV, PPV, parallel accounting, CO integration with FI and company code global parameters.

6.9   Conclusion

As the first part of configuring the FI global settings, here in this Chapter, we started with the configuration of fields: you understood the difference between standard and customer fields, learned how to define the customer fields and also learned about including the customer fields in the coding block to make them available in data-entry screens for transaction processing. You also learned about field status, field status group (FSG) and field status variant (FSV). You understood that an FSG is a collection of field statuses, defined in the company code data of G/L account, and is used to determine which fields are ready for data entry input (required or mandatory / optional), and which needs to be hidden. You also learned that SAP uses 'link rules' to overcome conflicting field status situations. You understood that you can group several FSGs in one field status variant (FSV), and then assign that FSV to a company code. By this, you learned that, you will be able to work with the same FSGs in multiple company codes.

You, then, moved on to understand the ledger concept in SAP. You learned that there are two different ledger types: standard and extension ledgers. You learned that a standard ledger is one that contains a full set of journal entries for all business transactions, and it can be designated either as a 'leading ledger' or 'non-leading ledger'. You understood that you must designate one (only one) standard ledger as the 'leading ledger'. Along with the leading ledger, you learned that, you can have other ledgers known 'non-leading ledger' and/or 'extension ledger'. You, also learned that the non-leading ledgers are parallel ledgers to the leading ledger, and they can be – for example - based on a local accounting principle. You learned that an extension ledger is a non-leading ledger, created based on an underlying standard ledger, and the postings to the underlying ledger also apply for the extension ledger, even though the postings made explicitly to an extension ledger are visible only in that extension ledger but not in the underlying standard ledger. You, then, learned about the 'universal journal' that is actually an enhanced financial document in S/4HANA created whenever you post to SAP FI from any of the SAP modules. You understood that ACDOCA is SAP FI's important new S/4HANA table that is based on the universal journal line items, containing all of the financial fields, as well as a lot of information from other sub-modules of SAP. You, then, proceeded to define and configure the ledgers in the system besides configuring the currency settings for the ledgers defined.

You, later, learned about the fiscal year, posting period and special periods. You learned about the different types of fiscal years (calendar, non-calendar and shortened fiscal years). You learned that a 'calendar fiscal year' is nothing but a calendar year with 12 posting periods corresponding to the 12 calendar months, and a fiscal year that does not correspond to a calendar year is known as the 'non-calendar fiscal year'. You understood that the posting periods may or may not correspond to the calendar months in a non-calendar fiscal year. You also understood that a fiscal year that is less than 12 posting periods in duration, is called a 'shortened fiscal year', and is year-dependent and has always to be followed or preceded by a full fiscal year with 12 periods. You, then, went on to learn and configure fiscal year variant (FYV), assigning company codes to FYV and finally learned about opening and closing of posting periods through posting period variant (PPV).

You moved on to learn about parallel accounting. You learned that unlike the erstwhile classic G/L, wherein parallel accounting has to be performed through the accounting approach, using several parallel G/L accounts and special-purpose ledgers, you can now use the alternative approach for parallel accounting in SAP G/L using the parallel ledger concept. You learned how to define the accounting principles, and assign them to ledger groups.

You, then, learned about the configuration settings that are required for the integration of CO with FI. In the process, you learned to define the document types for postings in CO, assigning document types to mapping variants and defining the default values for CO postings.

You, then, moved on to check the configuration settings for the ledgers that have already been defined. You learned that this check must run without errors before continuing, for example, with the migration of transaction data or any other activities. You understood that as long as inconsistencies exist, you will not be able to post journal entries in the affected company codes / ledgers.

You, finally, moved on to configure the global parameters for company codes. You learned that these company code global parameters control how a company code behaves in your SAP system, besides controlling the associated transaction processing. You understood that you are required to configure about 35 global parameters, grouped into two categories: accounting organization and processing parameters. You learned, in detail, about each of these parameters, and what value they need to be configured with and why. You also learned about creating a new chart of accounts while configuring the company code global parameters.

This completes our discussion of 1st part of the FI global settings. Let us move on to the next Chapter to discuss about the 2nd part of FI global settings, that relates mostly to documents.

7 FI Global Settings – II

In Chapter 6, we discussed the 1st set of FI global settings namely fields, ledgers, fiscal year, posting period, parallel accounting, integration of CO with FI and company code global parameters. Let us now, in this Chapter, discuss the 2nd set of FI global settings relating mainly to documents: types, numbering, posting keys, variants for document entry, rules for changing documents, tolerance groups, texts for document entry, default values, recurring entries, document parking, archiving etc. We shall also discuss inflation accounting, correspondence and integration of SAP S/4HANA with the shared services.

Let us start with documents.

7.1 Documents

The transaction processing, in SAP, is based on the '*document*' principle. A unique document is generated every time you make a posting in the system. The document becomes a record of a posting in FI. This is to maintain the integrity of the posted transaction; else, there will be chaos and confusion as to which transaction is correct. Once you post a transaction, and once a document is generated by the system (identified by a unique document number), you will not be able to change (or modify) that document, except for the descriptive text. However, should you need to modify the important information (say: account, amount, tax code etc) of an already posted document, you can do that by posting a new document and reversing the original one (*document reversal*). The accuracy of postings in the compact journal and the G/L can only be checked on the basis of documents. The documents are the link in FI, between the business transaction and the posting.

A business transaction, in general, is identified by two kinds of documents: (a) original documents (b) processing documents. The *original documents* signify the origin of the transaction and are, for example, receipts, invoices, bank statements, cheques etc. The *processing documents* are the end documents in a business transaction which are accounting documents, recurring entry documents, sample documents etc. The *accounting documents* represent the original documents in the system. The *recurring entry documents* and *sample documents* are also known as '*special documents*' in SAP. These special documents simplify the document entry during a transaction.

> **i** The '*data aging function*' available for accounting documents enables you to move large amounts of data within a database so as to gain more working memory. The data is moved into a 'historical area'. The data aging enables you to perform queries on large numbers of data in a much shorter time. In FI, you can use data aging to move data relating to journal entry (aging object = FI_DOCUMENT). When executing aging for journal entries, the corresponding database tables are moved into the historical part of the database. A number of conditions (say: document type retention time exceeded; document has been in the system for the minimum number of days; sample, recurring and some parked documents not included etc) must be met to ensure that only the 'aged' documents, that are no longer needed for operational purposes, are moved.

SAP comes delivered with several standard document types. Each document in the system is uniquely numbered from a predefined number range. The number range can be internal (system-generated) or external (user-supplied).

A document in SAP is made up of a document header and line items (at least two). While the document header identifies a document, the line items represent the transactions.

Let us understand more on the document structure, now.

7.1.1 Document Structure

As already mentioned, a document is made up of two components: the header and the line items. There should be a minimum of two line items in a document: a debit entry and a corresponding credit entry, making the document total to zero. Unless this condition of zero total is ensured, you will not be able to post the document; of course, you can 'park' the same.

> **i** You can post only a complete document in the system: a document is said to be 'complete' when its debit total = credit total (with the balance as zero). You must enter the minimum account assignments (for example: document date, posting date, document type, posting key, account number, and amount) in the document as designated by the system. You can, of course, also enter other fields that have been defined as 'required' fields for that transaction screen while maintaining the configuration settings.

Document Header

The '*document header*' is valid for the entire document. It helps in the identification of a document. It has two tabs: basic data and details. The 'Basic Data' tab normally consists of the following elements / fields (Figure 7.1):

- 'Document date': The document date represents the date of the business transaction. That is, for example, when the invoicing happened or when the payment was done and so on. A mandatory field for data entry, this signifies the date of the original document, and is usually on or prior to the posting date.

- 'Posting date': This denotes the date on which the transaction is accounted for in the system. Another mandatory field for data entry, this date is normally after the document date; it can also be on the same date.

> **i** If you have selected the 'Propose Value Date' check-box while configuring the company code global parameters (Section 6.8.1 in Chapter 6), the system proposes the current system date as the posting date which is also known as the 'value date'; you can, of course, change the system proposed date.

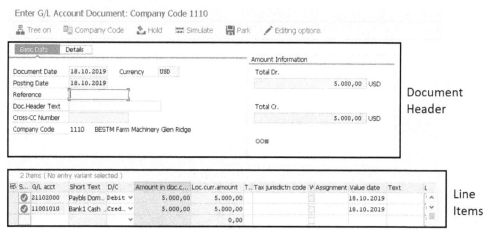

Figure 7.1: Document: Header (Basic Data) and Line Items

- 'Reference': You will normally use the reference (document) number as a 'search criterion' when displaying or changing documents. It can contain the document number of the customer or vendor, for example. It may, also, contain a different value like invoice number, payment reference etc. In correspondence, the reference document number is sometimes printed in the place of the document number.
- 'Doc. Header Text': You can enter explanations or notes that apply to the entire document and not only for certain line items (also see Section 7.1.11, 'Texts and Text Identifiers for Documents').
- 'Cross-CC Number': In cross-company code document entry, as you are aware, several documents will be created in different company codes. This field represents a common transaction number indicating that the documents belong together logically. This number can be assigned by the system or manually. If automatic, the system creates the Cross-CC document number as 000000471110032019 (00000047-1110-03-2019), for example, denoting the document number 00000047, company code 1110, posting period 03 and fiscal year 2019.

- 'Company code': This is defaulted to the entry you made on the pop-up screen when you initiated the transaction. You can switch to another company code by clicking on 'Switch Company Code'.
- 'Currency': This is defaulted from the company code settings. You will not be able to change.

Under the 'Details' tab, you will see some more fields (Figure 7.2):

Figure 7.2: Document: Header (Details)

- 'Exchange rate': This field is used for the translation between foreign currency and local currency. You will specify the exchange rate only when you want a different rate to the table rate.
- 'Translation date': The translation date is used for determining the exchange rate that is to be applied for the translation. You do not need to enter a date, unless the date in question is not the same as the document entry date.
- 'Trading part. BA': You will use this field to enter the business area of the trading partner. Together with the business area to which the posting is made, there is a sender/receiver relationship in each line item. This relationship enables the elimination of inter-company (IC) sales at business area level, within business area consolidation.
- 'Tax Reporting Date': This represents the date on which the tax on sales and purchases is due, or the date on which that tax must be reported to the tax authority. This date can be equal to the posting date / the document date. You also can define your own rules to determine the date.
- 'Calculate Tax': If you select this check-box, the system calculates the taxes automatically, during simulation or posting.

Under the 'Amount Information' block on the right-hand side of the document, you will see the 'Total Dr.' and 'Total Cr.' details, both of which should be equal making the document balance as zero; else, the document is considered as 'incomplete' and you need to correct the line items, as the system will not allow you to post a document where the document balance is not zero. When the document balance is zero you will see the green icon glowing.

You can 'hold' a document (*hold document*) at any point of time, if you are not ready to post the document for different reasons like, you want to add more line items or when the document balance is not zero etc. You can come back later and post the document. When you hold an incomplete document, the system will store that document with the temporary document number. You can also 'park' the document (*park document*): the system generates a document number which you can use later to retrieve the same. You may retrieve the parked document at any time, and mark that as 'complete' by clicking on 'Save as Complete' after making the required changes, if any. You may also press 'Simulate' to see, how the document will look like including automatically posted line items, if any, like tax etc. You will not be allowed to simulate an incomplete document.

Below the document header, you will see the line items (Figure 7.1).

Line Items

A *'line item'* is defined as that part of a document that contains information about an item. This includes an amount, an account number, the credit or debit assignment (via posting keys), and additional details specific to the transaction [say: tax code, assignment number, value date, text (both short and long), trading partner, business area, negative posting indicator, cost center, profit center, fund, grant, cost object etc] that is being posted. As already mentioned, there should at least be two line items in a document: one debit and one credit. You may have up to 999 line items in a single document. All the line items in a document should total out to zero satisfying debits = credits.

You can make the system to automatically create some of the line items, such as tax on sales or purchases (while entering customer/vendor invoice), payables and receivables between company codes when posting cross-company code transactions, gain or loss arising out of exchange rate differences between invoice and payment for customer/vendor, cash discount paid or received (during payment postings), residual items or bank charges (while posting a customer or vendor payment and clearing open items) , tax adjustment postings (for a down payment) and so on. You can add text to a tax item (on sales or purchases) in addition to making additional account assignments to the automatically generated line items.

With this background on document structure, let us move on to discuss the various types of documents.

7.1.2 Document Types

The *'document type'*, in SAP, is used to classify accounting documents and distinguish between business transactions to be posted. Entered in the document header, it applies to the whole document. You define your document types at the client level. You will specify a number range key for each document type. You create the desired number range intervals, for each number range key based on the company code.

A document type helps to:

- Differentiate between business transactions: you can always tell what type of business transaction is involved, as the document type is shown for every line item. You can also use the document type for evaluation purposes.
- Control the posting to the appropriate account types: the document type controls as to what type of account namely vendor, customer, or G/L, you can post to.
- Assign document numbers: you will assign a number range to every document type. The document numbers are chosen from this number range. You can use the same number range for several document types.
- Apply the vendor net procedure: the applicable discount and the net amount are calculated (and posted) when the vendor invoice is posted.

> **i** You can establish the link between the original document and the processing document, by storing them correctly. If you want to store original documents (paper documents) along with their corresponding processing documents (EDP documents) generated in the system, then, store all them together with the same document type. If you want to store several document types together, assign a separate number range to each document type. For example, suppose you want to store the original invoice (say, CD-2019-44444) along with the processing document (8888899999) posted in SAP for invoice posting. You just need to enter CD-2019-44444 in the 'Reference' field of the document 8888899999. In doing so, you can always cross-reference these two documents, besides using the 'Reference' field in the search criteria.
>
> Store your original documents (paper documents) under the EDP number of the SAP System. You should write the EDP document number (say, 8888899999) on the original document (say, CD-2019-44444). In this way, the original document for a business transaction can be found at any time.

As in other cases, SAP comes delivered with several (40+, actually) standard document types (Table 7.1), that you can use as such or change to create new. The standard document types cover business transactions relating to G/L accounting, A/R, A/P, AA and consolidation in SAP

FI. In SAP MM & SD, there are standard documents to meet business transactions involving GR/IR, invoicing (incoming and outgoing), stock taking (inventory) etc.

Type	Description	Type	Description
AA	Asset Posting	KR	Vendor Invoice
AB	Journal Entry	KZ	Vendor payment
AD	Accruals/Deferrals	ML	ML Settlement
AF	Depreciation Pstngs	PR	Price Change
AN	Net Asset Posting	RA	Sub.Cred.Memo Stlmt
AP	Periodic asset post	RE	Invoice - Gross
CC	Sec. Cost CrossComp.	RK	Invoice Reduction
CL	CL/OP FY Postings	RN	Invoice - Net
CO	Secondary Cost	RV	Billing doc.transfer
DA	Customer document	SA	G/L Account Document
DG	Customer credit memo	SB	G/L Account Posting
DR	Customer invoice	SC	Transfer P&L to B/S
DV	Customer interests	SE	Inventory Postings
DZ	Customer Payment	SK	Cash Document
ER	Manual Expense Travel	SU	Intercomp./Clearing
EU	Euro Rounding Diff.	UE	Data Transfer
EX	External Number	WA	Goods Issue
KA	Vendor Document	WE	Goods Receipt
KG	Vendor Credit Memo	WI	Inventory Document
KN	Net vendors	WL	Goods Issue/Delivery
KP	Account maintenance	WN	Net Goods Receipt

Table 7:1 Default Document Types

> **i** If you want to delete any of the already available document types in system, check if it is currently being used. If already in use, you will not be able to delete those document types.

Project Dolphin

BESTM does not want to define any new document type, and has decided to use the standard ones available in the system. It has also been decided to use the same document type for document reversals. To restrict the access to the closing operations, BESTM wants to make use of user authorization through document type CL. To make cross-verification easier, the project team has recommended to the BESTM management to make the 'Reference' field mandatory for data input for invoice postings (customer and vendor) and credit memos.

Let us configure the settings relating to document types.

7.1.3   Define Document Types

Since BESTM does not want to have any new document types, we do not need to configure this activity for Project Dolphin. However, we have given the details below to make you understand how to create a new one:

i.   Use the menu path: SAP Customizing Implementation Guide > Financial Accounting > Financial Accounting Global Settings > Document > Document Types > Define Document Types. Or, you may use Transaction OBA7.

ii.   On the 'Change View "Document Types": Overview' screen, select the appropriate row containing the standard document type (say, ER).

iii. Click on 'Copy As'. You will be taken to the 'Change View "Document Types": Details of Selected Set' screen:

- Change the 'Document Type' from ER to a new identifier; say, YR.
- You can now keep the 'Number range' proposed by the system; or, change it to a new one by maintaining the required number range for the company code by clicking on 'Number range information'.
- Enter the 'Reverse Document Type': if you want the same document type for the reversal documents also, you can just leave that as blank. You may also a enter a different document type.
- Leave the 'Authorization Group' as blank, or enter the group identifier should you wish to control the document entry for select group of users.
- Select the appropriate check-boxes (say: vendor, G/L account etc) under 'Account types allowed' and 'Control data' blocks.
- You may also maintain other details like 'Reference Number' and 'Document Header Text': if you select these check-boxes, then the system will expect an input for these fields while posting this document.

iv.   'Save' when completed. You have now created the new document type YR. You need to go back to the initial screen to change the 'Description'. 'Save' again (Figure 7.3).

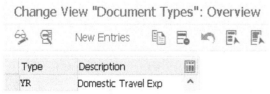

Figure 7.3: New Document Type (YR)

Now that you have understood how to create a new document type, let us move on to configure the specific requirements of BESTM for the various document types:

i.   Use the menu path: SAP Customizing Implementation Guide > Financial Accounting > Financial Accounting Global Settings > Document > Document Types > Define Document Types. Or, you may use Transaction OBA7.

ii.   On the 'Change View "Document Types": Overview' screen, select the appropriate row containing the standard document type (say, CL).

iii.   Click on 'Details'. On the next screen, enter the desired 'Authorization Group' under the 'Properties' block. The authorization group allows extended authorization protection for particular objects. The authorization groups are freely definable. The authorization groups usually occur in authorization objects together with an activity. Enter B100. (You have to create this authorization group in the specific authorization object, and attach the required users to this authorization group to make this effective). 'Save'.

iv.   Now, go back to the initial 'Change View "Document Types": Overview' screen, double-click on the row DR. On the next screen, select the 'Reference Number' check-box under 'Required during document entry' block, and 'Save' (Figure 7.4).

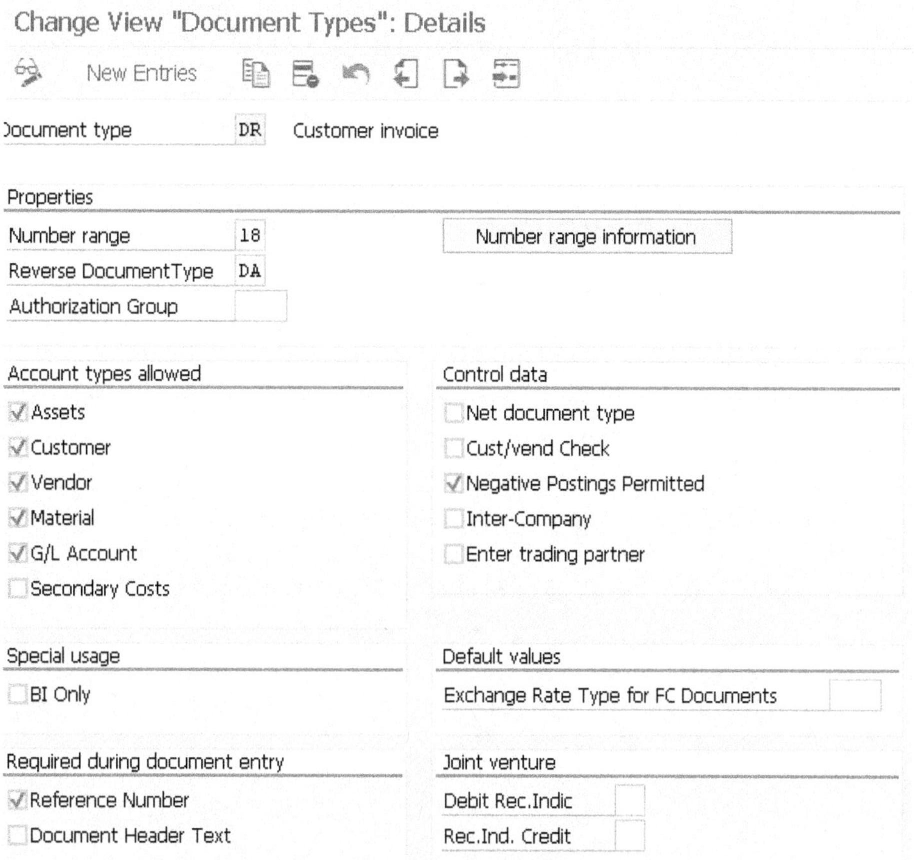

Change View "Document Types": Details

New Entries

Document type   DR   Customer invoice

Properties
Number range   18   Number range information
Reverse DocumentType   DA
Authorization Group

Account types allowed   Control data
✓ Assets   Net document type
✓ Customer   Cust/vend Check
✓ Vendor   ✓ Negative Postings Permitted
✓ Material   Inter-Company
✓ G/L Account   Enter trading partner
Secondary Costs

Special usage   Default values
BI Only   Exchange Rate Type for FC Documents

Required during document entry   Joint venture
✓ Reference Number   Debit Rec.Indic
Document Header Text   Rec.Ind. Credit

Figure 7.4: Making 'Reference Number' as Required Entry for Document Type DR

v.   Repeat the steps and select the 'Reference Number' check-box for the remaining document types (KR, DG and KG).

You have now made the 'Reference Number' (displayed as 'Reference' in the document header) as a mandatory field for data entry for document types DR, KR, DG and KG as required by BESTM management.

Let us move on to define the document types in a ledger, for posting to non-leading ledgers

7.1.4 Define Document Types in a Ledger

You specify the document type for postings to non-leading ledgers, here in this task. You need to set up a separate document type for these postings, and assign a unique number range to this document type, for each non-leading ledger (say: BU and BI). By encapsulating the ledger-related postings for the non-leading ledgers in a separate number range, you are ensuring contiguous assignment of document numbers, at the ledger level for each number range.

> **i** Since the representative ledger determines the document types and number ranges applied within a ledger group, you cannot perform this configuration activity for a ledger group. If you use a ledger group to make account assignments for postings, it is only possible to verify that document numbers are assigned contiguously at the ledger level for the representative ledger.

To define document types for postings to non-leading ledgers:

i.   Use the menu path: SAP Customizing Implementation Guide > Financial Accounting > Financial Accounting Global Settings > Document > Document Types > Define Document Types in a Ledger.

ii.   On the 'Determine Work Area: Entry' pop-up screen, select the appropriate non-leading ledger (say, BI), and press 'Continue'.

iii. On the 'Change View "Document Types for Entry View in a Ledger": Overview' screen, click on 'New Entries', and on the next screen (Figure 7.5):

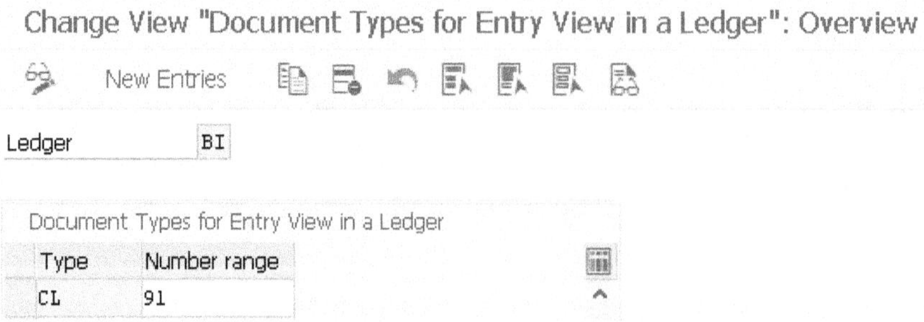

Change View "Document Types for Entry View in a Ledger": Overview

New Entries

Ledger   BI

Document Types for Entry View in a Ledger

Type	Number range
CL	91

Figure 7.5: Document Type Specification for Non-Leading Ledger (BI)

- Select document type for the 'Type' field from the drop-down list (say, CL).
- Enter the 'Number Range'
- Repeat for any other document type, and 'Save' (Figure 7.5).

iv.   Repeat the steps (ii) and (iii) for all the non-leading ledgers, and 'Save' your settings.

You have now specified the document types for entry view for all non-leading ledgers. We can now discuss the document number ranges.

7.1.5 Document Number Ranges

A 'document number', in SAP, helps in identifying a particular document relating to a company code and fiscal year. You will define a *document number range* (for each of the document types), from which the system assigns a unique number, to each of the documents (of a particular document type) that are posted during a transaction. The number ranges are defined per company code; you need to transport the defined company codes to the target systems. The document number range can be either *numeric* or *alphanumeric* but the length is uniformly kept at 10 digits (Figure 7.6). If you define a document number that is less than 10 digits in length, then the system prefixes the shortage with leading zeros, for all the numeric number ranges, and suffixes with zeros for alphanumeric number ranges.

> **i** You can specify the same number ranges for both master records and other documents; or, you can define different number ranges. Since the document number ranges are defined per company code, you can use the same number range for the same document type across company codes.

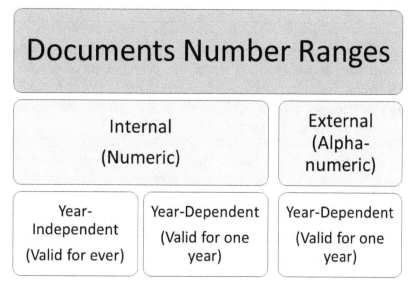

Figure 7.6: Document Number Range

You should define separate number intervals for special documents like sample documents and recurring entry documents. SAP recommends using the number range identifier X1 for recurring entry documents and X2 for sample documents. Do not use these identifiers for any other document number ranges.

7.1.5.1 Number Range Assignment

SAP allows two types of number range assignments (Figure 7.6) in the system:

- Internal numbering
- External numbering

In *internal numbering* or number assignment, you make the system to automatically assign a document number sequentially from a pre-defined number range for that document type. If you resort to internal number range assignment, then, you need to define only a numeric number range. This way, it is easier for the system to bring up the next number, sequentially, for the new document. The last number assigned to a document (of a particular document type) is stored in 'Current Number' field.

In the case of *external numbering*, you will be required to supply a new and unique number every time you create a new document. The system does not bring up the next number automatically, as it does not store the last number (in 'Current Number' field). However, it is possible that you can configure the system to input the numbers, automatically, from a pre-invoicing system. The external number intervals can only contain either letters or numbers, as sorting can differ between platforms. You can have, for example, 000001 to 999999 or AAAAAA to ZZZZZZ. But you cannot have a combination like AAAAAA to 999999.

> **i** You may find it useful to resort to alphanumeric document number ranges when you plan for external number range assignment. This type of numbering would be suitable when you transfer documents from a feeder system. These numbers must be unique. As the number range is not displayed for external number assignment, ensure that you do not skip any numbers, in between, when assigning document numbers manually.

As in the case of new documents, you may specify separate number ranges all the *reversal documents*. By default, the system makes use of the same number range (as that of the main document) for reversal document as well unless you specify that a separate internal number range needs to be used for reversal documents. Even in the case of documents with external numbering, as far as reversal is concerned you need to maintain an internal number range for these reversal documents; else, the system will throw errors.

7.1.5.2   Number Range Validity

Each number range has a pre-defined validity in the system. You can define the number ranges either as year dependent or year independent (Figure 7.6):

- You will define the *'year-independent number ranges'* only once in the system, and they will be valid for ever (9,999 years, to be specific). When defining this kind of validity, you need to make sure that you define a fairly large interval for each of the document types, so that you do not exhaust the numbers in the near future. Normally, you will define year-independent number ranges together with internal numbering (with numeric number range), enabling the system to assign the next number from the already defined number range, without any break, in all the fiscal years.
- The *'year-dependent number ranges'* are relevant only for a specific fiscal year. You need to define them every year, at the start of the new fiscal year. You will normally define the external number ranges as year dependent; but you can define internal number ranges also as year-dependent. Since, the number ranges are valid only for a year, it is sufficient to have a small range. You can repeat the same number range every year, as the system identifies the document using the document number and fiscal year.

7.1.5.3   Number Range Change

You may come across a situation that you may need to change the number interval or validity period or both, of an already defined number range. It is possible that you can change the lower and upper limits. You can change the lower limit in a number range (with internal number assignment) only when the number has not yet been assigned. Before changing the upper limit of a number range, you need to ensure that the new number is not less than the current number. When you change the intervals, the system will, of course, ensure that the intervals will not overlap after the change.

7.1.5.4   Number Range Deletion

You should normally avoid deleting a number range after the same has been defined, even though it is possible to delete a number range. The system will allow you to delete an already defined range as long as that has not been used. In the case of internal number assignment, you will not be able to delete a range once a number has been assigned already, from that range. However, you can delete an external number range at any point of time; if the range is already in use, the system issues a warning, but you can still go ahead and delete.

With this understanding on document number ranges, let us move on to configure the same in the system for Project Dolphin. The sequence of configuring involves (a) defining document number ranges, (b) determining which intervals of the defined document number ranges are to be copied from one company code into another and (c) determining which intervals of document number ranges are to be copied from one fiscal year into another. Let us start with the definition of number ranges.

7.1.5.5   Define Document Number Ranges

Using this configuration step, you create number ranges (stored in Table NRIV) for the journal entries. For each number range, you specify a number interval from which the document numbers are to be chosen and the type of number assignment (internal or external). You will then assign one or more document types to each number range. The number range becomes effective, via the document type when you are entering or posting a document. As already discussed, you can use one number range for several document types.

Project Dolphin

BESTM wants numerical number ranges for all the document types in all the company codes. The project team has decided to define a number range 91 (9100000000 to 9199999999) to take care of document type CL in non-leading ledgers. It has also been decided that all the number ranges are to have a validity of 9,999 years so as to overcome any additional configurations every year.

Recall that we have copied the number ranges also while we were creating the company code 1110 by copying from 0001. However, since we created the company code 1120 anew without copying from an existing company code, we are yet to define the number ranges for 1120. Let us do that now:

i.   Use the menu path: SAP Customizing Implementation Guide > Financial Accounting > Financial Accounting Global Settings > Document > Document Number Ranges > Define Document Number Ranges. Or, you may use Transaction FBN1.

ii.   On the 'Edit Intervals: Accounting Document, Object RF_BELEG' screen, click on 'Copy Subobject' button.

iii.   On the ensuing pop-up screen, enter the 'From' (1110) and 'To' (1120) fields; press 'Copy' to continue.

iv.   Click 'Continue' on the 'Number Range Interval Transport' pop-up screen.

v.   You will see a message that 'CoCode 1110 copied to 1120'.

vi.   Now enter 1120 in the 'Company Code' field, and click on 'Display Intervals' to display the number range information.

vii.   You can also click on 'Change intervals' to edit. You will be taken to 'Edit Intervals: Accounting Document, Object RF_BELEG, Subobject 1120' screen; here you can add or delete a number range, for example.

viii.   While defining the document type for non-leading ledgers (Section 7.1.4), recall we have configured the system to have number range 91 for the document type CL. As there is no number range with number range key 91 already defined in the system for company code 1120, let us insert this number range now:

- Click on 'Insert line' or press F6. The system inserts a blank row at the top of the table, above the row 00.
- Enter 91 as number range identifier in 'No' field.
- Enter 9999 in 'Year' field. This represents the 'to year' till the number range is valid.
- Enter the starting number of the number range in 'From No' (9100000000). Enter the ending number of the number range in 'To Number' field (9199999999). When you press 'Enter' the system may prompt with a message that the number ranges are overlapping, if there is an overlapping. If you closely look at, the new number range (91) we have entered is overlapping with the default number range of X1 (9100000000 to 9199999999). Let us now edit the number ranges of X1 and X2 suitably, as shown below, to avoid the overlapping:

Document Type	Original Number Range		Revised Number Range	
	From	To	From	To
X1	9100000000	9199999999	9200000000	9299999999
X2	9299999999	9399999999	9300000000	9399999999

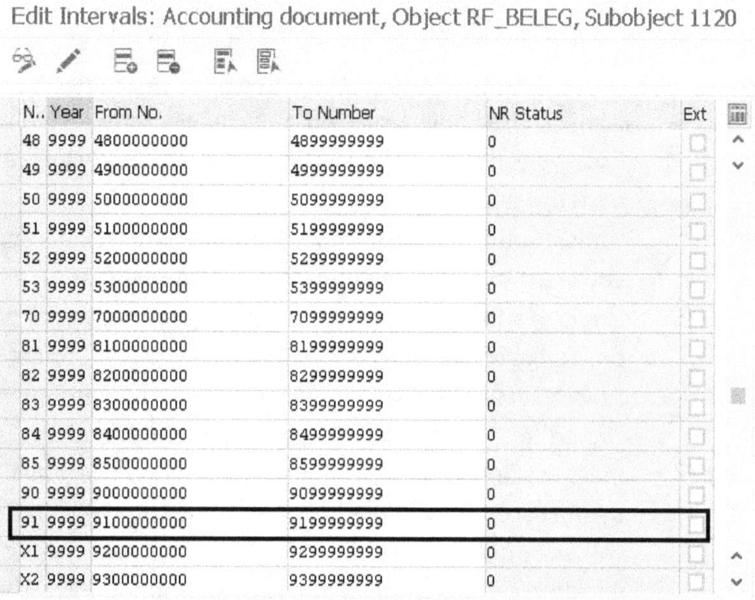

Edit Intervals: Accounting document, Object RF_BELEG, Subobject 1120

N..	Year	From No.	To Number	NR Status	Ext
48	9999	4800000000	4899999999	0	
49	9999	4900000000	4999999999	0	
50	9999	5000000000	5099999999	0	
51	9999	5100000000	5199999999	0	
52	9999	5200000000	5299999999	0	
53	9999	5300000000	5399999999	0	
70	9999	7000000000	7099999999	0	
81	9999	8100000000	8199999999	0	
82	9999	8200000000	8299999999	0	
83	9999	8300000000	8399999999	0	
84	9999	8400000000	8499999999	0	
85	9999	8500000000	8599999999	0	
90	9999	9000000000	9099999999	0	
91	9999	9100000000	9199999999	0	
X1	9999	9200000000	9299999999	0	
X2	9999	9300000000	9399999999	0	

Figure 7.7: Document Number Ranges for Company Code 1120

- You will see a 0 in the 'NR Status' denoting that no number from this number range is used yet. You can modify the NR Status for any of the number ranges by clicking on 'Change interval limits' button.
- Do not select the 'Ext' check-box as this not an external number range.

ix.   'Save' the details. You have now added the number range interval 91 for the company code 1120 with a validity of 9,999 years (Figure 7.7).

x.   You can maintain number ranges for any other company code by going back to the initial screen and repeating the steps listed above.

Using the next step, you can copy one or more or all the number ranges in a company code to another company code.

7.1.5.6   Copy to Company Code

If you have already copied a company code from a source company code along with all the number ranges, this step is not required. However, if you define a new number range in any of your company codes, and want that range to be copied to all other company codes, you may use this configuration activity to accomplish that in one step.

i.   Use the menu path: SAP Customizing Implementation Guide > Financial Accounting > Financial Accounting Global Settings > Document > Document Number Ranges > Copy to Company Code. Or, you may use Transaction OBH1.

ii.   Click 'Continue' on the pop-up screen, and enter the required details on the 'Document Number Ranges: Copying to Company Code' screen:

- Under 'General selections', enter the specific number range numbers if you want to copy only select number ranges; else, leave that as blank. Enter the fiscal year details, if you want to restrict copying of ranges only for specified period; else, leave that as well as blank.
- Under 'Source company code details', enter the 'Company code' from which you want to copy the number range intervals.
- Under 'Target company code details', you may enter a single company code or a range of company codes to which you want to copy the desired intervals.
- Now 'Execute'. You can see the details of number ranges that have been copied to the target company code(s) on the resulting screen: you will see a message 'Interval added' under 'Status text' against all intervals that have been successfully copied to the target company code from the source. You will see 'Interval cannot be added' message under 'Status text' with an explanation like 'Interval already exists' under 'Message text' in cases where you are trying to copy an interval range that is already existing in the target company code(s).

For all the company codes in BESTM wherein we have used the 'copy' function to copy from one company code (say, 1110 or 1120 or 1210) to others (say, 2100, 2200, 3100, 3200 and 1220), we have copied all the configuration settings including the number ranges. Hence, we are not making use of this configuration functionality for BESTM. However, if any number range is defined new, at a later date, in any of these company codes and that needs to be copied to other company codes, you may use this activity.

Let us move on to understand how to copy number ranges to one or more fiscal years.

7.1.5.7 Copy to Fiscal Year

When the number ranges are valid for ever (= 9,999 years) it is not normally required to carry out this activity. However, if you have defined a new number range with the new validity which is not 9,999 years, but restricted to a specific fiscal year, you may use this configuration step to copy the same to one or more fiscal years in future.

i. Use the menu path: SAP Customizing Implementation Guide > Financial Accounting > Financial Accounting Global Settings > Document > Document Number Ranges > Copy to Fiscal Year. Or, you may use Transaction OBH2.

ii. Click 'Continue' on the 'Transport Number Range Intervals' pop-up screen, and enter the required details on the 'Document Number Ranges: Copying to Fiscal Year' screen:
   - Under 'General selections', enter a single company code or range of company codes and enter specific number range numbers, if you want to copy only some specified number ranges; else, leave that as blank.
   - Under 'Source fiscal year details', enter the source fiscal year to be copied.
   - Under 'Target fiscal year details', you may enter the target fiscal year.
   - Now 'Execute'. You can see the details of number ranges that have been added / not added to the target fiscal year, on the next screen. As in the case of 'Copy to Company Code' function, in Section 7.1.5.6, that we have seen earlier, you will see appropriate messages under 'Result' and 'Explanation' columns. The number ranges are only copied into a target company code, if no such number ranges exist there within the selected 'To fiscal year' interval.

This completes our discussion on document number ranges. We shall now proceed to discuss the posting keys.

7.1.6 Define Posting Keys

The *'posting key'* controls how a line item is entered and processed in a document. You will specify a posting key, for each of the line items in a document. For each posting key, you will define (a) which side of an account it can post to, (b) which type of account it can post to and (c) which fields the system should display on the entry screen and whether an entry must be made (field status). SAP comes delivered with several standard posting keys (Table 7.2).

Posting Key	Name	Cr/Dr Indicator	A/c Type	Reversal Key
01	Invoice	Debit	Customer (D)	12
02	Reverse Credit Memo	Debit	Customer (D)	11
03	Bank Charges	Debit	Customer (D)	13
04	Other receivables	Debit	Customer (D)	14
05	Outgoing payment	Debit	Customer (D)	15
06	Payment difference	Debit	Customer (D)	16
07	Other clearing	Debit	Customer (D)	17
08	Payment clearing	Debit	Customer (D)	18
09	Special G/L debit	Debit	Customer (D)	19
0A	Bill.doc. Deb	Debit	Customer (D)	1A
0B	CH Cancel.Cred.memoD	Debit	Customer (D)	1B
0C	CH Clearing Deb	Debit	Customer (D)	1C
0X	CH Clearing Cred	Debit	Customer (D)	1X
0Y	CH Credit memo Cred	Debit	Customer (D)	1Y
0Z	CH Cancel.BillDocDeb	Debit	Customer (D)	1Z
11	Credit memo	Credit	Customer (D)	02
12	Reverse invoice	Credit	Customer (D)	01
13	Reverse charges	Credit	Customer (D)	03
14	Other payables	Credit	Customer (D)	04
15	Incoming payment	Credit	Customer (D)	05
16	Payment difference	Credit	Customer (D)	06
17	Other clearing	Credit	Customer (D)	07
18	Payment clearing	Credit	Customer (D)	08
19	Special G/L credit	Credit	Customer (D)	09
1A	C CH Cancel.Bill.docDe	Credit	Customer (D)	0A
1B	CH Credit memo Deb	Credit	Customer (D)	0B
1C	CH Credit memo Deb	Credit	Customer (D)	0C
1X	CH Clearing Cred	Credit	Customer (D)	0X
1Y	CH Cancel.Cr.memo C	Credit	Customer (D)	0Y
1Z	CH Bill.doc. Cred	Credit	Customer (D)	0Z

21	Credit Memo	Debit	Vendor (K)	32
22	Reverse invoice	Debit	Vendor (K)	31
24	Other receivables	Debit	Vendor (K)	34
25	Outgoing payment	Debit	Vendor (K)	35
26	Payment difference	Debit	Vendor (K)	36
27	Clearing	Debit	Vendor (K)	37
28	Payment clearing	Debit	Vendor (K)	38
29	Special G/L debit	Debit	Vendor (K)	39
31	Invoice	Credit	Vendor (K)	22
32	Reverse credit memo	Credit	Vendor (K)	21
34	Other payables	Credit	Vendor (K)	24
35	Incoming payment	Credit	Vendor (K)	25
36	Payment difference	Credit	Vendor (K)	26
37	Other clearing	Credit	Vendor (K)	27
38	Payment clearing	Credit	Vendor (K)	28
39	Special G/L credit	Credit	Vendor (K)	29
40	Debit entry	Debit	G/L (S)	50
50	Credit entry	Credit	G/L (S)	40
70	Debit asset	Debit	Assets (A)	75
75	Credit asset	Credit	Assets (A)	70
80	Inventory taking	Debit	G/L (S)	90
81	Costs	Debit	G/L (S)	91
82	Inventory difference	Debit	G/L (S)	92
83	Price difference	Debit	G/L (S)	93
84	Consumption	Debit	G/L (S)	94
85	Change in stock	Debit	G/L (S)	95
86	GR/IR debit	Debit	G/L (S)	96
89	Stock inward movement	Debit	Material(M)	99
90	Inventory taking	Credit	G/L (S)	80
91	Costs	Credit	G/L (S)	81
92	Inventory difference	Credit	G/L (S)	82
93	Price difference	Credit	G/L (S)	83
94	Consumption	Credit	G/L (S)	84
95	Change in stock	Credit	G/L (S)	85
96	GR/IR credit	Credit	G/L (S)	86
99	Stock outward movement	Credit	Material (M)	89

Table 7:2 Default Posting Keys
(The standard SAP posting key for account assignment model is 00)

> **i** It is strongly recommended to use the SAP supplied standard posting keys, without resorting to creating new ones.

Project Dolphin

BESTM does not want to define any new posting keys in the system, as the project team has explained to the management that the standard keys supplied by SAP will be good enough to meet the business processing requirements of the company. However, BESTM has requested to configure the posting keys in such a way that (a) 'Invoice Reference' to be made mandatory for all payment transactions, (b) 'Payment Reference' is optional for document reversals and (c) a valid reason to be mandatory for all payment difference postings.

You may not need to define a new posting key in the system. However, should you want to create a new posting key:

i.   Use the menu path: SAP Customizing Implementation Guide > Financial Accounting > Financial Accounting Global Settings > Document > Define Posting Keys. Or, you may use Transaction OB41.

ii.   On the 'Maintain Accounting Configuration: Posting Keys – List' screen, you will see the list of SAP supplied standard posting keys that are already available in the system (Figure 7.8), arranged according to the account type.

Maintain Accounting Configuration : Posting Keys - List

Posting K...	Name	Debit/Credit	Account Type
15	Incoming payment	Credit	Customer
16	Payment difference	Credit	Customer
17	Other clearing	Credit	Customer
18	Payment clearing	Credit	Customer
19	Special G/L credit	Credit	Customer
1A	CH Cancel.Bill.docDe	Credit	Customer
1B	CH Credit memo Deb	Credit	Customer
1C	CH Credit memo Deb	Credit	Customer
1X	CH Clearing Cred	Credit	Customer
1Y	CH Cancel.Cr.memo C	Credit	Customer
1Z	CH Bill.doc. Cred	Credit	Customer
21	Credit memo	Debit	Vendor
22	Reverse invoice	Debit	Vendor

Figure 7.8: Standard Posting Keys

iii.   Double-click on any of the rows, to see the details of the configuration settings for that posting key (Figure 7.9) on the 'Maintain Accounting Configuration: Posting Keys – Details Screen':

Maintain Accounting Configuration : Posting Keys - Detail Screen

Maintain Field Status   ⊞

Posting Key   15   Incoming payment

Debit/credit indicator
○ Debit
◉ Credit

Account type
◉ Customer
○ Vendor
○ G/L account
○ Assets
○ Material

Other attributes
☐ Sales-Related
☐ Special G/L
Reversal Posting Key   05
☑ Payment Transaction

Figure 7.9: Settings for a Posting Key

- You will see the 'Debit/credit Indicator' indicating to which side of the account the posting key posts to.
- You will also see the 'Account type' indicating to which account, the key posts to. Each posting key can be used for a specific account type. In setting the account type indicator, you specify whether the document type is valid for asset accounts (A), material accounts (M), customer accounts (D), vendor accounts (K), or G/L accounts (S).
- You will see other details including the 'Reversal Posting Key' and whether this relates to 'Payment Transaction'.

iv.   Click on 'Create' on the initial 'Maintain Accounting Configuration: Posting Keys – List' screen, to define a new posting key.

v.   On the ensuing 'Create posting key' pop-up screen, enter an identifier for the new posting key in 'Posting Key' field, and input an explanation in 'Posting Key Name'.

vi.   Click 'Enter'.

vii.   On the next 'Maintain Accounting Configuration: Posting Keys – Details Screen', maintain the settings as already discussed in step (iii).

viii.   Now, click on 'Maintain Field Status' and make the required settings for the new posting key, for each category under the 'Select Group' block (refer Section 6.2 of Chapter 6, for more details).

ix.   'Save' the entry; you have now created a new posting key along with the appropriate field status setting for that key.

Let us look at configuring the specific requirements for BESTM for some of the posting keys: since(a) 'Invoice Reference' is to be made mandatory for all payment transactions, (b) 'Payment Reference' is to be made optional for reversals and (c) a valid reason is to be mandatory for all payment difference postings, we need to make the changes in field status as described in Table 7.3:

Transaction	Posting Key	Field Name	Default Field Status	Field Status required for BESTM
Outgoing payment (Customer)	05	**Invoice Reference**	Optional entry	Required entry
Incoming payment (Customer)	15	**Invoice Reference**	Optional entry	Required entry
Outgoing payment (Vendor)	25	**Invoice Reference**	Optional entry	Required entry
Incoming payment (Vendor)	35	**Invoice Reference**	Optional entry	Required entry
Reverse credit memo (Customer)	02	Payment Reference	Suppressed	Optional Entry
Reverse invoice (Customer)	12	Payment Reference	Suppressed	Optional Entry
Reverse invoice (Vendor)	22	Payment Reference	Suppressed	Optional Entry
Reverse credit memo (Vendor)	32	Payment Reference	Suppressed	Optional Entry
Payment difference (Customer)	06	**Reason Code**	Optional entry	Required entry
Payment difference (Vendor)	26	**Reason Code**	Optional entry	Required entry

Table 7:3 Field Status Configuration for Posting Keys for BESTM

To make the required changes for BESTM:

i.   Use the menu path: SAP Customizing Implementation Guide > Financial Accounting > Financial Accounting Global Settings > Document > Define Posting Keys. Or, you may use Transaction OB41.

i.   On the 'Maintain Accounting Configuration: Posting Keys – List' screen, double-click on the row containing the posting key 05.

ii.   On the next 'Maintain Accounting Configuration: Posting Keys – Details Screen', click on 'Maintain Field Status'.

iii. On the 'Field Status Group: Overview' screen, double-click on 'General data' FSG under the 'Select group' block.

iv.   On the 'Field Status Group: General Data' screen, change the 'Invoice Reference' radio button from 'Opt. entry' to 'Req. Entry' and 'Save' (Figure 7.10)

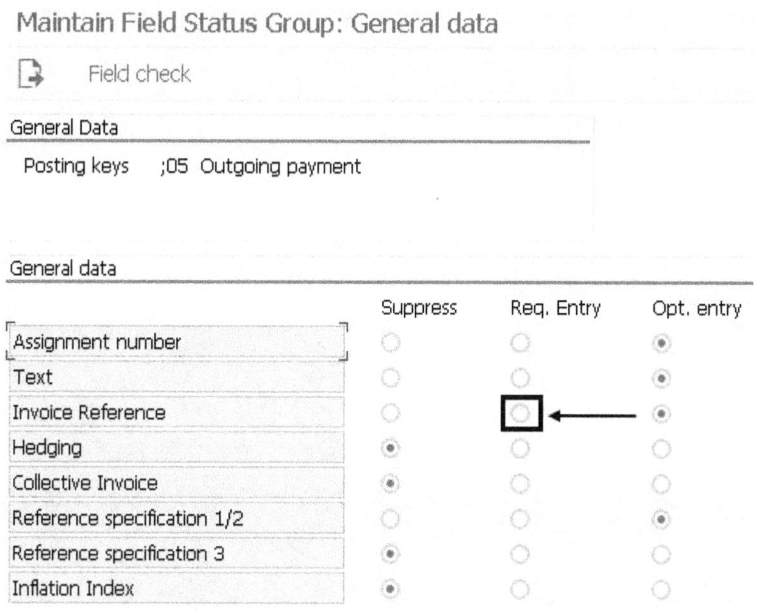

Maintain Field Status Group: General data

Field check

General Data

Posting keys   ;05 Outgoing payment

General data

	Suppress	Req. Entry	Opt. entry
Assignment number	○	○	◉
Text	○	○	◉
Invoice Reference	○	[○] ←	◉
Hedging	◉	○	○
Collective Invoice	◉	○	○
Reference specification 1/2	○	○	◉
Reference specification 3	◉	○	○
Inflation Index	◉	○	○

Figure 7.10: Settings for Posting Key 05

v.   Repeat the steps for making the required changes for posting keys 15, 25 and 35. Now, you have made 'Invoice Reference' as a mandatory field for all the payment transaction postings.

vi.   You need to repeat the steps above for configuring the other posting keys:
   • For posting key 02, 12, 22 and 32 you will see that the 'Payment Reference' field is available under the FSG 'Payment transaction' under the 'Select group' block, on the 'Field Status Group: General Data' screen. You will see that the field 'Payment Reference' is having a default field status as 'Suppress'; you need to change that to 'Opt. entry' (Figure 7.11)

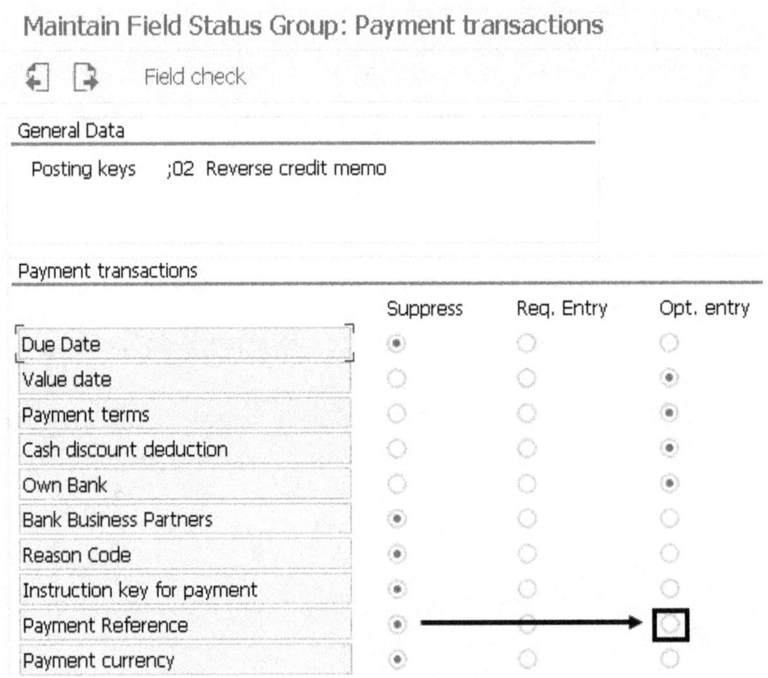

Maintain Field Status Group: Payment transactions

Field check

General Data

Posting keys   ;02 Reverse credit memo

Payment transactions

	Suppress	Req. Entry	Opt. entry
Due Date	●	○	○
Value date	○	○	●
Payment terms	○	○	●
Cash discount deduction	○	○	●
Own Bank	○	○	●
Bank Business Partners	●	○	○
Reason Code	●	○	○
Instruction key for payment	●	○	○
Payment Reference	●	○	○
Payment currency	●	○	○

Figure 7.11: Settings for Posting Key 02

- For posting keys 06 and 26, we need to make the field 'Reason Code' as a mandatory for input.

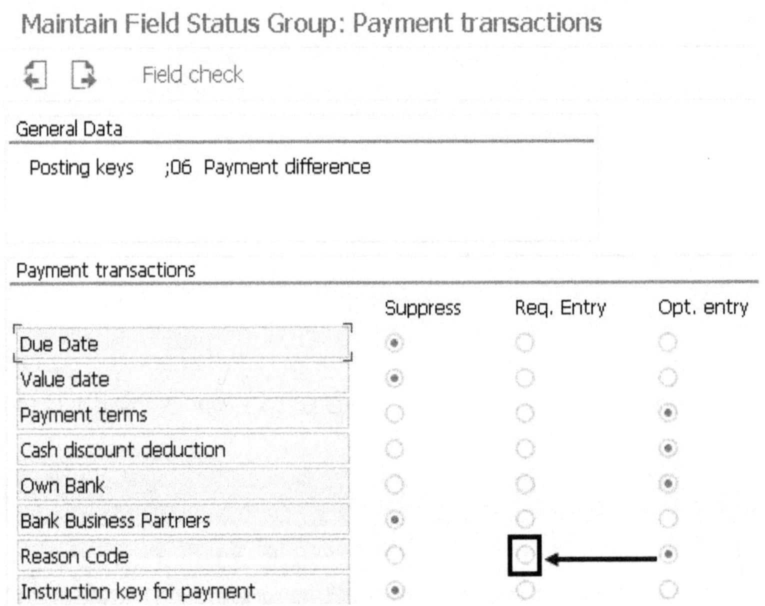

Maintain Field Status Group: Payment transactions

Field check

General Data

Posting keys   ;06 Payment difference

Payment transactions

	Suppress	Req. Entry	Opt. entry
Due Date	●	○	○
Value date	●	○	○
Payment terms	○	○	●
Cash discount deduction	○	○	●
Own Bank	○	○	●
Bank Business Partners	●	○	○
Reason Code	○	○	●
Instruction key for payment	●	○	○

Figure 7.12: Field Status Settings for Posting Key 06

You will see that this field is available under the FSG 'Payment transaction' under the 'Select group' block, on the 'Field Status Group: General Data' screen. You will see that the field is having a default field status as 'Opt. entry'; you need to change that to 'Req. Entry' (Figure 7.12).

We have, thus, configured posting keys as required by BESTM. This completes our discussion on posting keys. Let us now understand configuring the screen variants for document entry.

7.1.7 Screen Variants for Document Entry

The *'screen variant'*, specified per company code, controls the special screens (if any) for documents, for several specific functions. We have already seen (in Section 6.8 of Chapter 6) while configuring the company code global parameters that SAP comes delivered with four standard variants for document entry (Table 7.4):

Variant	Description
	Standard version
1	For Austria and Switzerland
2	For France and countries with withholding tax
3	Countries with classic withholding tax

Table 7:4 Standard Screen Variants for Document Entry

We have already configured this for company code 1110 with screen variant 2, as this variant will be the most suitable one for all the US-based company codes. Since we used this company code to copy to other US-based company codes like 1120, 2100 etc, this configuration has already been completed. For company codes in India, the standard version is the right one.

However, to assign/change the screen variant for document entry, then:

i.   Use the menu path: SAP Customizing Implementation Guide > Financial Accounting > Financial Accounting Global Settings > Document > Screen Variants for Document Entry.

ii.   On the 'Change View "Document Entry Screen Variant": Overview' screen, select the appropriate screen variant for the company codes, and 'Save' (Figure 7.13).

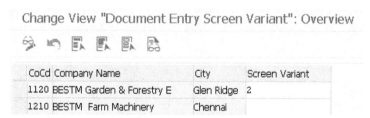

Figure 7.13: Screen Variant for Document Entry

Let us move on to discuss the rules for changing documents, next.

7.1.8 Rules for Changing Documents

In general, it is not recommended to try changing an already posted document, as that goes against the document principle of maintaining and preserving the integrity of documents. The system itself determines, for a number of fields, that you can no longer change them after posting. This includes all the fields - like, the amount posted and the account - which are central to the principles of orderly accounting. However, there could be instances when you may want to change the contents of some of the fields, of an already posted document, without undermining the document principle. SAP's *document change rules* will help you in those circumstances. Even with these rules, the system will prevent you from changing the update objects like cost center, profit center, business area etc., in an already posted document.

> **i** The *update objects* are elements in the system, for which transaction figures or line items are updated. You shall enter them, as additional account assignments during posting.

There are two rules for changing documents: (a) rules for changing the header and (b) rules for changing the line items.

Let us start with the rules for changing the header.

7.1.8.1 Document Change Rules, Document Header

The document change rules have special provisions only for transaction types A (down payments) and W (bills of exchange). For all other transaction types, you will use the <blank> rule for transaction type. If you make entries for document change rules with transaction types other than <blank>, A or W, then the system will ignore that.

It is recommended that you do not change the default document change rules (for document header) which you can display using the menu path: SAP Customizing Implementation Guide > Financial Accounting > Financial Accounting Global Settings > Document > Rules for Changing Documents > Document Change Rules, Document Header. Or Transaction OB32. From the 'Change View "Rules for Changing Documents": Overview', you will see that you can change the contents of the fields 'Text' (document header text) and 'Reference' in a document header, even after posting (Figure 7.14)

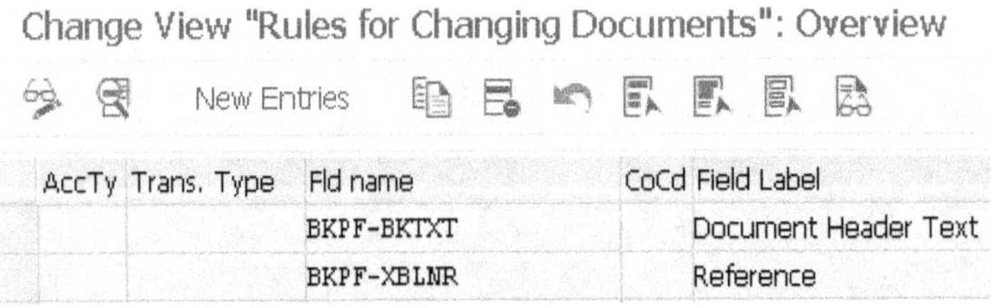

Change View "Rules for Changing Documents": Overview

New Entries

AccTy	Trans. Type	Fld name	CoCd	Field Label
		BKPF-BKTXT		Document Header Text
		BKPF-XBLNR		Reference

Figure 7.14: Document Change Rules for Document Header

You may use an appropriate Transaction, for example, for changing a document, like FB02. When you call up a document, using this Transaction, the system brings up the last document that you have posted in the system. You may press F5 to bring up the document header. On the 'Document Header: 1110 Company Code' pop-up screen, you can see that the fields 'Doc. Header Text' and 'Reference' as editable (Figure 7.15) in line with the document change rules (for document header), that we have discussed earlier in this Section.

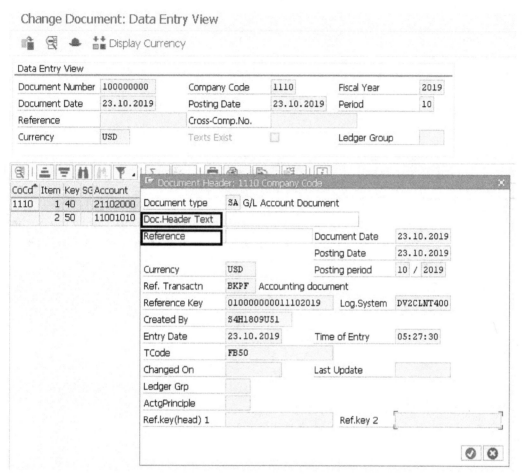

Figure 7.15: Document Change: Editable Fields in Document Header

Let us now understand the document changes rules, for line items in a document.

7.1.8.2   Document Change Rules, Line Item

Unlike document header, the default document change rules for line item allow you to change the contents of a number of fields (185 to be exact), for various account types / transaction types, except the ones that are central to the document principle (like, account, amount, posting key etc). The entire list of fields which you can modify can be seen when you execute the configuration activity using the menu path: SAP Customizing Implementation Guide > Financial Accounting > Financial Accounting Global Settings > Document > Rules for Changing Documents > Document Change Rules, Line Item. On the 'Change View "Rules for Changing Documents": Overview', you will see the list of fields which you can modify, even after you have posted a document (Figure 7.16).

Change View "Rules for Changing Documents": Overview

New Entries

AccTy	Trans. Type	Fld name	CoCd	Field Label
A		BSEG-SGTXT		Text
A		BSEG-ZUONR		Assignment
D		BSEC-BANKL		Bank Key
D		BSEC-BANKN		Bank Account
D		BSEC-BANKS		Bank Country
D		BSEC-BKONT		Bank control key
D		BSEC-DTAMS		DME indicator

Figure 7.16: Document Change Rules for Line Item (Sample List)

As in the case of document header, when you use Transaction FB02 to change the document, press F2 to get into the line items. And, you will see that you can change fields like 'Text' (BSEG-SGTXT), 'Assignment' (BSEG-ZUNOR) etc., for the line items (Figure 7.17).

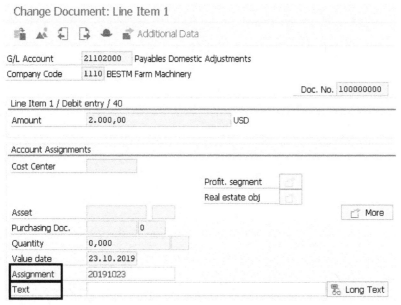

Figure 7.17: Document Change: Editable Fields in a Line Item

This completes our discussion on rules for changing documents. Let us, now, see the settings required for bar code entry, next.

7.1.9   Bar Code Entry

Here, you will make the necessary settings to archive the documents using bar codes. The system supports five types of bar codes (like, EAN 8, EAN13, UPC A etc). You need to complete two activities: (a) specifying the control parameters for bar code entry and (b) maintaining the document types for bar code entry.

Let us understand the first activity of specifying the control parameters.

7.1.9.1   Specify Control Parameters for Bar Code Entry

Here, you specify the settings to archive documents using bar codes. You need to enter the bar code details for object type BKPF and your document type. You can enter them for all users or individual users. You must select the 'Bar code active' option so that the additional pop-up screen for entering the bar code is displayed, when a document is posted:

i. Use the menu path: SAP Customizing Implementation Guide > Financial Accounting > Financial Accounting Global Settings > Document > Bar Code Entry > Specify Control Parameters for Bar Code Entry.

ii. On the 'Change View "Settings for Bar Code Entry": Overview' screen, click on 'New Entries'.

iii. On the next screen:

- Select the 'Object type' from the drop-down list, say, incoming invoice. You will use this field to specify what document types can be archived using bar codes. The object type in the non-coded information documents has been defined for each document type. Only those document types which are assigned to the object type can be archived using bar code.

- Select the appropriate 'Document type'; the standard document type FIINVOICE is used for all document types for which you do not make any specifications. If you want to use bar code entry for document type XY only, for example, you would have to create a new document type and select 'Bar code active' option for it. If you, however, want to use bar code entry for all document types apart from document XY, you would have to create a new document type, select the 'Bar code active' option for it, and select the 'Bar code active' option for the standard document type FIINVOICE. This means that you can make settings so that only the exceptions to your normal situation are made in the customizing table.

- By specifying the 'User' you can limit the users whose original documents can be archived using bar codes with a specific document type.

- Under the 'Settings for Bar Code Entry':
    - Select the 'BCode Type': SAP provides you with five bar code types (2/5 Interleaved, EAN 13, EAN 8, UPC A und UPC E) to select from. Select the appropriate one.

> **i**
>
> *Interleaved 2 of 5 (ITF)* is a continuous two-width bar code symbology encoding digits. It is a numeric only barcode used to encode pairs of numbers into a self-checking, high-density barcode format. In this symbology, every two digits are interleaved with each other, to create a single symbol. It is used commercially on 135 film, for ITF-14 bar codes, and on cartons of some products, while the products inside are labelled with UPC (Universal Product Code, technically known as UPC-A) or EAN (European Article Number).
>
> *EAN-8* is an EAN/UPC symbology bar code and is derived from the longer International Article Number code. It was introduced for use on small packages where an EAN-13 barcode would be too large; for example, on cigarettes, pencils, and chewing gum packets.
>
> *EAN-13* is a numeric, continuous and fixed-length bar code. The EAN-13 symbol contains the same number of digits as UPC-A. It also includes a thirteenth digit as a check character, calculated using the Modulo 10 algorithm.
>
> The *UPC-A bar code* is a 12-digit, numeric symbology used in retail applications and is by far the most common and well-known barcode symbology in the United States. It is designed to uniquely identify a product and its manufacturer. You will find UPC-A barcode on virtually every consumer good at your local supermarket, as well as on books, magazines, and newspapers.
>
> *UPC-E bar code* (also known as the 'zero suppression version'), is a variation of UPC-A that allows manufactures to encode a limited number of unique 12-digit product codes in six digits allowing for a more compact barcode. The six digits are enclosed between two left-hand guard bars and three right-hand guard bars. Since the resulting UPC-E barcode is about half the size as an UPC-A barcode, it is widely used on products with very small packaging where a full UPC-A barcode may not fit.

o The 'Bar code active' check-box is used to flag whether or not the bar code entry function is active, for the maintained combination of object type/ document type/user name.

o Select the 'Check is active' check-box to specify that bar code verification is active. When selected, in bar code verification, the maintained check function module corresponding to the bar code type is called up.

o You can use 'No cancel' flag to specify whether the bar code entered by the user can be cancelled or not.

o You will use the 'Multiple entry' flag to specify whether or not the bar code entered by the user can be used more than once.

o 'Popup in workflow': when selected, this activates the bar code entry dialog box for the specified document type, although an entry scenario using SAP Business Workflow is active. Normally no bar code is used when entering documents using workflow, because linking the application document and the document is carried out by an automatic assignment.

o The 'Doc. Type Not Modifiable' check-box determines whether a document type can be modified in the bar code entry popup.

- 'Save' when completed (Figure 7.18).

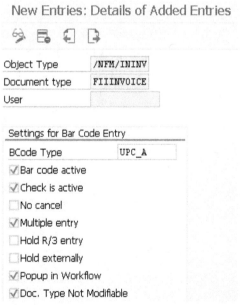

Figure 7.18: Control Parameters for Bar Code Entry

iv.   Repeat the same, if required, for various 'object type-document type-user' combinations (Figure 7.19).

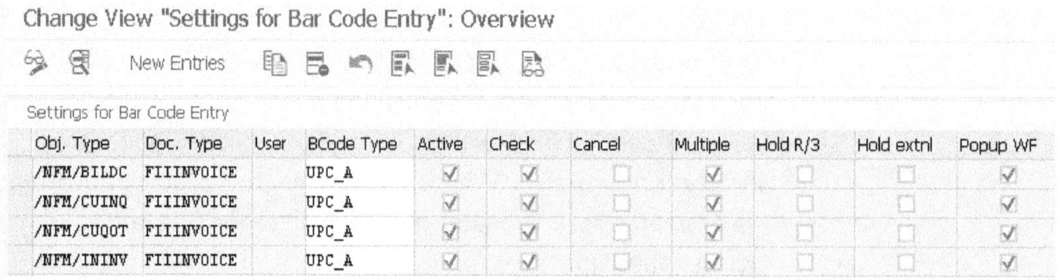

Change View "Settings for Bar Code Entry": Overview

New Entries

Settings for Bar Code Entry

Obj. Type	Doc. Type	User	BCode Type	Active	Check	Cancel	Multiple	Hold R/3	Hold extnl	Popup WF
/NFM/BILDC	FIIINVOICE		UPC_A	✓	✓	☐	✓	☐	☐	✓
/NFM/CUINQ	FIIINVOICE		UPC_A	✓	✓	☐	✓	☐	☐	✓
/NFM/CUQOT	FIIINVOICE		UPC_A	✓	✓	☐	✓	☐	☐	✓
/NFM/ININV	FIIINVOICE		UPC_A	✓	✓	☐	✓	☐	☐	✓

Figure 7.19: Control Parameters for Bar Code Entry: Overview Screen

In the next activity, you will determine the document type, for bar code entry using the 'company code and document type' combinations. Depending on the combination, you can thus control whether the pop-up window for inputting the bar code is displayed or not, when entering a document.

7.1.9.2   Maintain Document Types for Bar Code Entry

In this configuration step, you can maintain the settings at various levels:

- Completely specifying the company code and document type
- Specifying the company code without a document type
- Specifying the document type but no company code
- Specifying neither the company code nor document type

You may configure using the menu path: SAP Customizing Implementation Guide > Financial Accounting > Financial Accounting Global Settings > Document > Bar Code Entry > Maintain Document Types for Bar Code Entry. On the 'Change View "Object Types for Early Entry in Financial Acctng": Overview' screen, click on 'New Entries' and just specify the company codes under 'CoCd' and 'Save' (Figure 7.20).

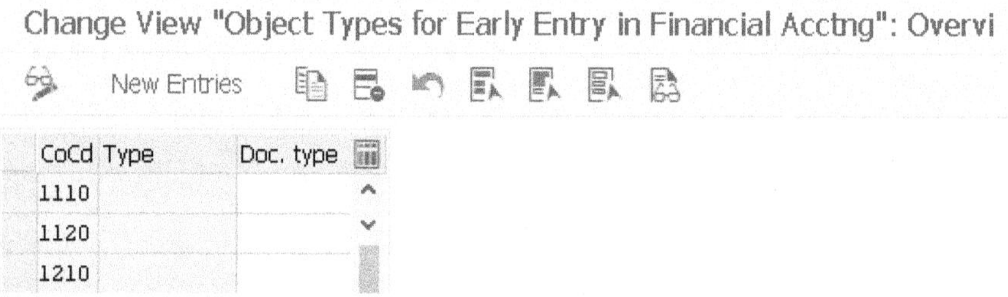

Change View "Object Types for Early Entry in Financial Acctng": Overvi

New Entries

CoCd	Type	Doc. type
1110		
1120		
1210		

Figure 7.20: Maintaining Document Types for Bar Code Entry

This completes our discussion on bar code entry. We are now ready to discuss tolerance groups.

7.1.10 Tolerance Groups

You need to define a *'tolerance'* in the system for dealing with the payment differences arising out of transaction posting in FI. By defining a tolerance, you are instructing the system as to how to proceed further: (a) what are the amounts or percentage rates up to which the system is to automatically post to a separate expense or revenue account, if it is not possible to correct the cash discount or (b) up to what difference amounts the system is to correct the cash discount; the cash discount is automatically increased or decreased by the amount in difference using 'tolerance groups'.

You will come across three types of tolerances:

- Employee tolerance
- Customer / vendor tolerance
- G/L account clearing tolerance

In SAP, you manage the tolerances through *tolerance group*. Since the same rules usually apply to a group of employees, you can maintain the values per employee group. This way you can then enter amount limits and tolerances, per employee group and company code. You can also define tolerances without specifying a tolerance group: the stored tolerances are then valid for all employees who are not allocated to a group. As it is possible to specify tolerances for clearing procedures for your customers / vendors, the system takes into account the lower limits from the customer/vendor specifications and employee group during clearing transactions.

SAP comes delivered with sample tolerances which you can copy and tailor to your own requirements. You can also additionally differentiate these settings by company code: there should at least be one entry per company code (usually a blank in the tolerance group field, called the *'null tolerance group'*) to enable transaction posting without any glitch.

Let us now understand how to define the tolerance groups for employees.

7.1.10.1 Define Tolerance Groups for Employees

For every company code, you need to find out which tolerances are to be determined and whether a differentiation according to employee group is necessary. If you want to define different tolerances for your employees, specify the amount limits for each of the groups. If the tolerance limits are to apply to all employees, leave the 'Group' field empty. Define the tolerances correspondingly. You pre-define various amount limits for your employees with which you determine:

- The maximum document amount the employee is authorized to post.
- The maximum amount the employee can enter as a line item in a customer or vendor account.

- The maximum cash discount percentage the employee can grant in a line item.
- The maximum acceptable tolerance for payment differences for the employee.

If you have defined different tolerance groups, you then have to assign your employees to a certain tolerance group. To do this, select the activity 'Assign users to tolerance groups' and enter your employees under the relevant groups. You should also define separate tolerances for employees and business partners. When clearing the open items, the system checks both the tolerances and clears the transaction with the lowest tolerance.

> **i** It is possible that you can manage payment difference transactions with just one tolerance group (also known as 'null tolerance group') per company code, that is applicable to all the employees. However, we recommend that you to have at least one more tolerance group, attached to a select group of employees, with relatively larger tolerances to handle special situations or your most valued customers / vendors. Your null tolerance group, of course, will be the most restrictive one and will apply to most of the employees.

Project Dolphin

BESTM management has indicated that it requires two additional tolerance groups, besides the null tolerance group, to be configured in the system: one will be for taking care of all the US-based company codes, and the other for the India-based company codes. It is further stipulated that these special tolerance groups will have only a handful of employees assigned, in each company code, to handle special situations and high-value customers / vendors as these groups will have liberal tolerances in comparison to the null group.

Accordingly, the project has decided to have the following tolerance groups: TGUS and TGIN.

The tolerance group TGUS will be for all the US-based company codes. All the employees who are allocated to this group will be allowed to post accounting documents of maximum value USD 999,999,999 per document, with a limit of USD 99,999,999 per open item. However, they can process cash discounts at 5% per line item, with the system allowing a maximum payment difference of 3%, subject to an absolute maximum of USD 500. The cash discount adjustment amount will be USD 100.

The tolerance group TGIN will be for the two India-based company codes (1210 and 1220). The select employees who are part of this group will be allowed to post accounting documents of maximum value INR 999,999,999, per document with a limit of INR 99,999,999 per open item. However, they can process cash discounts at 5% per line item, with the system allowing a maximum payment difference of 3%, subject to an absolute maximum of INR 5,000. The cash discount adjustment amount will be INR 1,000.

The null tolerance group will be applicable for all the employee, and will be the default tolerance group for all the company codes of BESTM, both in USA and India:

(a) For all the US-based company codes, this null group will enable posting of accounting documents with values not exceeding USD 999,000, per document with a limit of USD 99,000 per open item. The maximum cash discount allowed is 2% per line item, and the maximum payment difference is 1%, with an amount cap of USD 50. The cash discount adjustment limit has to be set at USD 5.

(b) In the case of India-based company codes, the null group enables posting of accounting documents of value up to INR 1,500,000, per document with the line item limit of INR 1,000,000. The maximum cash discount allowed will be 2% per line item, with the maximum allowed payment difference of 1% with an amount cap of INR 1,000. The cash discount adjustment limit will be at INR 100.

Let us define the tolerance groups, for BESTM, as detailed out below:

i.   Use the menu path: SAP Customizing Implementation Guide > Financial Accounting > Financial Accounting Global Settings > Document > Tolerance Groups > Define Tolerance Groups for Employees. You may also use Transaction OBA4.

ii. On the 'Change View "FI Tolerance Group for Users": Overview' screen, click on 'New Entries'. On the next screen (Figure 7.21):

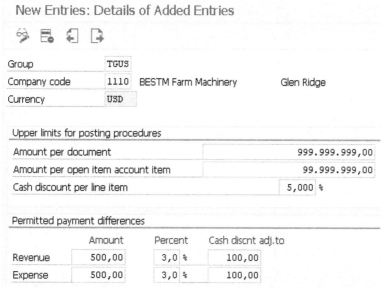

Figure 7.21: Tolerance Group TGUS for Company Code 1110

• Enter the identifier for the tolerance group in 'Group', say, TGUS.
• Enter the 'Company code'. Let that be 1110.

- Enter the 'Amount per document' as 999,999,999 under 'Upper limits for posting procedures' block; enter the 'Amount per open item account item' as 99,999,999; the 'Cash discount per line item' will be 5%. Note that the maximum permitted amount entered in the 'Amount per open item account item' field will not apply to the automatically created line items, as in the case of line items created by automatic payment program.
- Maintain the 'Permitted Payment Differences' as set out in Figure 7.21:
  - The 'Revenue' row describes the settings controlling overpayments from customers. A payment difference handled in this row, is to the advantage of the specific company code as it increases the revenue, and is posted automatically to a revenue account. For BESTM, enter 500 in the 'Amount' field and enter 3 in 'Percent' field. Specify the 'Cash discnt.adj.to' (100 in our case) which is normally set to be lower than the 'Amount' field: the system uses this field to adjust the payment difference up to this amount, which is then posted using a cash discount adjustment.
  - Similar to the 'Revenue', the 'Expense' row denotes customer underpayment that lowers your revenue, and is handled and posted automatically to an expense account. You may maintain the same amount or percentage limit as that of the revenue row or you can define different amount / percentage. The 'Cash discnt.adj.to' field in 'Expense' row is, again, similar to that of the 'Cash discnt.adj.to' field in the 'Revenue' row.
- Once completed, 'Save' your entries.

iii. You have defined the tolerance group TGUS.

iv. Go back to the initial 'Change View "FI Tolerance Group for Users": Overview' screen, and you will see that the tolerance group TGUS attached to the company code 1110.

v. Select the row containing TGUS /1110, and click on 'Copy As'. On the next screen, change the company code to 1120, and 'Save'. You have now copied the tolerance group TGUS to the company code 1120. Repeat this step to copy TGUS to all the US-based company codes.

vi. Now, configure the null tolerance group, as required by BESTM, for company code 1110 by following the steps explained above and then copy this null/1110 to other US-based company codes (Figure 7.22).

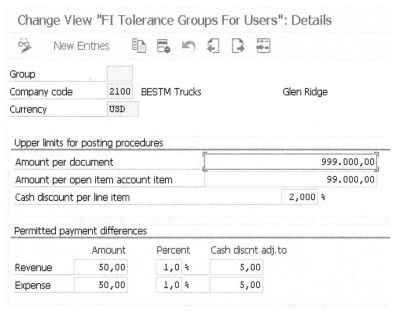

Figure 7.22: Null Tolerance Group for Company Code 2100

vii.   Repeat the steps above to define the tolerance group TGIN for the company code 1210 with the specifications as stipulated by BESTM, and then copy this to the other India-based company code 1220.

viii.   Maintain the details for the null tolerance group as well for the company code 1210; once configured, use this to copy to the other India-based company code 1220.

ix.   'Save' when completed. You have now completed all the configuration settings for the required tolerance groups for BESTM.

---

i So, how the tolerance settings work in a real-life situation?

Take the case of null tolerance group for the company code 1110. Consider that you have an invoice is for USD 10,000; You now know that 'Cash discnt.adj.to' is USD 5 for both revenue and expense items. You also know that the maximum permitted payment difference ('Amount') is USD 50 and the allowed percentage ('Percent') is 1 for this tolerance group.

Now, consider the <u>scenario 1</u> in which you have received an incoming payment of USD 9,980. Because this an underpayment, the system will make checks based on the 'Expense' row settings. First, it checks whether cash discount can be adjusted to accommodate the payment difference: because the difference (USD 20) exceeds the cash discount adjustment limit ('Cash discnt.adj.to' field) of USD 5, the discount is not adjusted. Next, the system looks up the 'Amount' and 'Percent' field values: 1% of USD 10,000 = USD 100, and the maximum allowed difference amount is USD 50. Since the actual payment difference is only USD 20 (= 10,000 – 9,980), which is well within the upper limit of USD 50 specified in the 'Amount' field, the system proceeds to book the loss of USD 20 to an expense account, and the transaction is posted through.

Consider the scenario 2 in which the incoming payment is USD 9,890. Because this also an underpayment, as in the case of scenario 1, the system will make checks based on the 'Expense' row settings. First, the system checks whether the cash discount can be adjusted to accommodate the payment difference: as the difference (USD 110) exceeds the maximum permitted cash discount adjustment limit ('Cash discnt.adj.to' field) of USD 5, the system does not adjust the discount. Now, the system looks up the 'Amount' and 'Percent' field values: 1% of 10,000 = 100, and the maximum allowed difference in amount is USD 50; but the actual payment difference is USD 110 (= 10,000 – 9,890). As the system can tolerate only to a maximum of USD 50, the system does not allow posting the transaction.

Let us consider another situation (scenario 3), wherein the incoming payment is USD 9,998. Because this also an underpayment, as in the case of scenarios 1 & 2, the system will make checks based on the 'Expense' row settings. First, the system checks whether the cash discount can be adjusted to accommodate the payment difference: as the payment difference is only USD 2 which is well within the maximum permitted ('Cash discnt.adj.to') amount of USD 5, the cash discount amount is adjusted to USD 2, and the transaction is posted to.

Now, consider the scenario 4 in which the incoming payment is USD 10,040. Being an overpayment, the system will take into account the settings specified in 'Revenue' row. The system, first, checks whether the cash discount can be adjusted to accommodate the payment difference: since the difference (USD 40) exceeds the maximum permitted cash discount adjustment limit of USD 5 ('Cash discnt.adj.to' field), the system does not adjust the cash discount. Instead, the system now looks up the 'Amount' and 'Percent' field values: 1% of 10,000 = 100, and the maximum allowed payment difference in amount is USD 50; but the actual payment difference is an overpayment of USD 40 (= 10,040 - 10,000). As the system can allow overpayments up to a maximum of USD 50, the system books the profit by posting USD 40 to a revenue account and clears the payment transaction.

Now, consider yet another situation (scenario 5) in which the incoming payment is USD 10,070. Being an overpayment as in scenario 4, the system will take into account the settings specified in 'Revenue' row. The system, first, checks whether the cash discount can be adjusted to accommodate the payment difference: since the difference (USD 70) exceeds the maximum permitted cash discount adjustment limit of USD 5 ('Cash discnt.adj.to' field), the system does not adjust the cash discount. Instead, the system now looks up the 'Amount' and 'Percent' field values: 1% of 10,000 = 100, and the maximum allowed payment difference in amount is USD 50; but the actual payment difference is an overpayment of USD 70 (= 10,070 - 10,000). As the system can tolerate overpayments only up to a maximum of USD 50, the system does not allow you to proceed further with the transaction.

Let us consider the final scenario (scenario 6), wherein the incoming payment is USD 10,003. Because this an overpayment, as in the case of scenarios 4 & 5, the system will make checks based on the 'Revenue' row settings. First, the system checks whether the cash discount can be adjusted to accommodate the payment difference: as the payment difference is only USD 3 which is well within the maximum permitted ('Cash discnt.adj.to') amount of USD 5, the cash discount amount is adjusted to USD 3, and the transaction is posted to.

In short, the system tolerates an underpayment or overpayment to a maximum of USD 50, which can be represented as 9,950 < 10,000 > 10,050; the invoice amount being USD 10,000. Anything below USD 9,950 or above USD 10,050 is not tolerated in the system and those transactions will be blocked from posting.

You can treat the payment differences, exceeding the tolerance limits set for automatic clearing, either as *partial payments* or *residual items*:

- In the case of *'partial payments'*, the system will not clear the original receivable, but will post the payment with an invoice reference, by entering the invoice number in the 'Invoice Reference' field in the payment items. The system determines the due date of the payment, by calculating the net due date for the invoice, and this due date is then entered in the 'Baseline Date' field of the payment. The dunning program, then, includes this payment on the dunning run on this date.
- However, in the case of *'residual items'*, you can use the payment to clear the original receivable and post the remaining amount (payment difference) to the customer account as a residual item. The system enters this payment amount in the line item, for the original receivable. You may also clear such original receivable and post the (payment) difference to an expense account, in case of underpayment.

Now that we have defined the tolerance groups, and understood how it actually works in transaction processing, let us proceed with the next task of assigning users to the tolerance groups.

7.1.10.2 Assign User/Tolerance Groups

Once you have defined the tolerance groups, you then need to assign FI users, to whom you wish to give special tolerances to the special tolerance group (in our case, TGUS or TGIN). Since the null tolerance group will be the default tolerance group in a company code, and applicable for all the employees / users, you do not need to explicitly assign the users to that.

i.   Use the menu path: SAP Customizing Implementation Guide > Financial Accounting > Financial Accounting Global Settings > Document > Tolerance Groups > Assign User/Tolerance Groups. You may also use Transaction OB57.

ii.   On the 'Change View "Assign Users → Tolerance Groups": Overview' screen, you will notice that there is an entry with a * in 'User name' field against a blank 'Tolerance Group', indicating that all the users are a part of this null tolerance group, by default.

iii.   To assign select users to a tolerance group, other than the null tolerance group, click on 'New Entries'.

iv.   On the ensuing screen, enter the 'User name' for the specific tolerance group (say, TGUS). You will not see a drop-down list to select the users, but just a field to input the names.

v.   'Save' when completed (Figure 7.23). The system attaches these users to this specific tolerance group. While saving, the system will not check whether the entered user is already defined or active in the system. However, it validates if the entered tolerance group is already defined; if not, it throws a warning message but still allows to save and proceed.

vi.   Repeat this for the other tolerance groups, as well (say, TGIN).

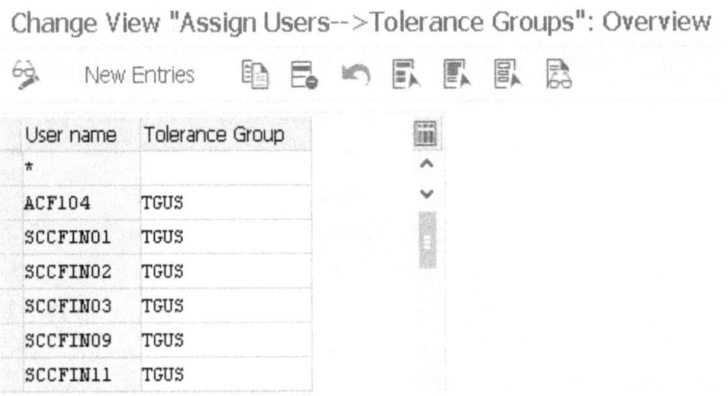

Change View "Assign Users-->Tolerance Groups": Overview

New Entries

User name	Tolerance Group
*	
ACF104	TGUS
SCCFIN01	TGUS
SCCFIN02	TGUS
SCCFIN03	TGUS
SCCFIN09	TGUS
SCCFIN11	TGUS

Figure 7.23: Assigning Users to a Tolerance Group

This completes our discussion on tolerance and tolerance groups. Let us, now, discuss the texts and text identifiers for documents in the next section.

7.1.11 Texts and Text Identifiers for Documents

It is possible that you can define text IDs for both document header and line items, to store additional or detailed information for a document header or for the line items during document entry, as you cannot have all the information stored in the long text field.

- In the case of 'text IDs for a document', you define the text IDs for the long texts. During document entry, you can enter detailed texts for a text ID by calling the 'Texts in Accounting Document' pop-up screen (Extras > Document texts) and proceeding further (Figure 7.24) to store additional information relating to the document by clicking on 'Detailed text' on the pop-screen: a text editor opens up and you can enter the details therein for a later reference. When you maintain additional information, you will see that the check-box 'M' selected on the pop-up screen indicating that there are more texts available.

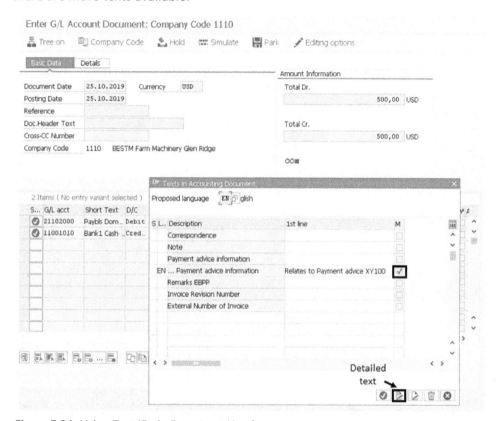

Figure 7.24: Using Text IDs in Document Header

- Similar to the text IDs for the document, you can also create the 'text IDs for the line items' to note down additional information for that particular line item. This is over and above the line item text that you will enter during a line item entry. During document entry, when you are entering the line items, you can click on the 'Long Text' icon for a line item, and you will see a pop-up screen displaying the text IDs. You may click on 'Editor' to input additional details. When done, you will see that the check-box 'T' selected, on the pop-up, indicating that there are more texts for this line item (Figure 7.25).

You can also define text identifiers (also known as 'keys') for line items, which you can enter in the line item text field, instead of inputting the details to save time. The actual texts associated with the text key will transferred, later, to the line item.

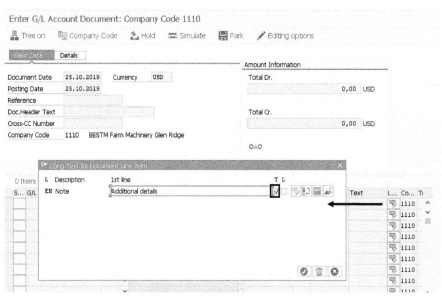

Figure 7.25: Using Text IDs in a Line Item

Let us first see how to define the text IDs for documents

7.1.11.1 Define Text IDs for Documents

The text IDs defined for documents are valid across the system, and SAP comes delivered with a number of text IDs which you can make use of. If you want to define new text IDs:

i.   Use the menu path SAP Customizing Implementation Guide > Financial Accounting > Financial Accounting Global Settings > Document > Texts and Text Identifiers for Documents > Define Text IDs for Documents, or Transaction OBT8.

ii.   On the 'Maintain Text Determination Configuration: List' screen, click on 'Create'.

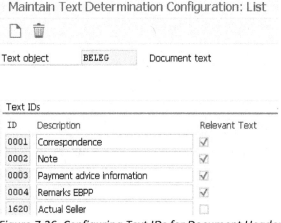

Figure 7.26: Configuring Text IDs for Document Header

iii.   On the ensuing pop-up screen, enter a text ID (4 character) and provide 'Description'. Press 'Enter' to continue and the new text ID will now be added to the already available standard text IDs provided by SAP.

iv.   Unless you select the 'Relevant Text' check-box for a specific text ID on the initial screen, you will not see this screen on the document entry screen when you reach the list the text IDs through 'Extras > Document texts' as already shown in Figure 7.24.

v.   When completed, 'Save' your entries; you have now created new text IDs that you can use to enter additional information for the document header while entering a document (Figure 7.26).

Let us now understand how to create a new text ID, for line items in a document.

7.1.11.2 Define Text Identifications for Line Items

Using this configuration activity, you can define the text identifications (text IDs) for long texts at line item level. When you, then, enter a document, you can enter additional text or information for each of the text ID, thereby providing more information that concerns the line items in that particular document. As in the case of text IDs for document, these are also valid across clients. SAP delivers one text ID as a default setting.

To define a new one:

i.   Use the menu path SAP Customizing Implementation Guide > Financial Accounting > Financial Accounting Global Settings > Document > Texts and Text Identifiers for Documents > Define Text Identifications for Line Items, or Transaction OBT10.

ii.   On the 'Maintain Text Determination Configuration: List' screen (Figure 7.27), click on 'Create'.

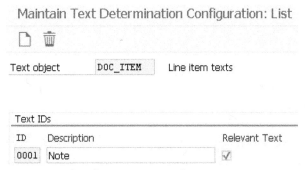

Figure 7.27: Configuring Text IDs for Line Items

iii.   On the ensuing pop-up screen, enter a text ID (4 character) and provide 'Description'. Press 'Enter' to continue and the new text ID will now be added to the already available standard text IDs provided by SAP.

iv.   Unless you select the 'Relevant Text' check-box for a specific text ID on the initial screen, you will not see the list the text IDs when you click on the 'Long Text' icon against a line item as already described in Figure 7.25.

v.   When completed, 'Save' your entries; you have now created new text IDs that you can use to enter additional information for the line items while entering them in a document (Figure 7.27).

With this, we are now ready to see how to configure the texts for line items that can be stored under text keys or identifiers.

7.1.11.3 Define Texts for Line Items

Using this activity, you can store texts under 'keys' which can then be transferred to the line item. When entering a document, you just need to enter the key instead of the whole text. You can also configure this in such a way that these texts care transferred to the customers in payment notices.

For configuring this:

i.   Use the menu path SAP Customizing Implementation Guide > Financial Accounting > Financial Accounting Global Settings > Document > Texts and Text Identifiers for Documents > Define Texts for Line Items. You may also use Transaction OB56.

ii.   On the 'Change View "Line Item Text Templates": Overview' screen, click on 'New Entries'.

iii.   On the next screen:

- Enter a 4-character 'ID'.
- In the 'Text Edit Format' field enter the long text (not exceeding 50 characters) that will be input when the user enters the ID. The text may contain the following variables which are replaced in each case by the current value:
  - $BLD Document date
  - $BUD Posting date
  - $ZFB Baseline date for payment
  - $BUP Posting period
  - $XBL Reference document number

> **i** During document entry, you need enter the text variable (identifier or ID) in the line item text with a prefixed equals sign (for example, =B100). The system then copies the associated text, automatically to the text field.

- Use the 'Control Display' check-box to indicate that the text transferred during document entry is to be displayed for control purposes. This means that when the flag is set, you can check and to adapt the text as required.

iv. 'Save' when completed. You have now created text keys that you can use while entering line items in a document to quicken document entry (Figure 7.28).

Change View "Line Item Text Templates": Overview

New Entries

ID	Text Edit Format	Control Display
ONLP	On-line publicity expenses including Facebook etc	✓
SADV	Salary in Advance for Supervisiors	✓
WADV	Wage in Advance for Workmen	✓

Figure 7.28: Texts for Line Items

This completes our discussion on configuring texts and text IDs for quicker document entry, besides maintaining additional information for a document header and for line items. Let us move on to discuss summarization.

7.1.12 Summarization

Summarization is essentially the summarization of journal entries and profitability segments. This functionality is intended only when you anticipate exceptionally large data volumes that may cause critical performance and data storage issues. This is a purely technical function which is intended, to allow customers with very large data volumes to optimize their system performance, by reducing the number of G/L line items in table ACDOCA and the number of profitability segments in table CE4XXXX (where XXXX denotes the operating concern). You should use this only when absolutely necessary, as it restricts the flexibility of reporting.

> **i** Once you decide to use this function, you will not be able to reverse its effect on the system. You will also see undesirable effects, if you do not use this function correctly.

Project Dolphin

BESTM wanted to know if they can go in for the summarization functionality of SAP in Project Dolphin. However, the project team, after careful consideration of the current and future data volume for each of the company codes, has advised the management that this functionality will be useful only in the case of exceptionally large volume of data and not for BESTM entities.

The summarization is the same regardless of whether you are using account-based or costing-based profitability analysis: since the level of summarization in table ACDOCA should be the same as that of the profitability segments, the summarization settings are used for account-based profitability segment determination; in costing-based profitability analysis, the corresponding profitability segment determination utilizes these settings as well. Even if you define a summarization of fields for table ACDOCA, costing-based line items continue to be posted to table CE1XXXX. The settings defined here also apply to distributed CO-PA: the same level of summarization is used with regard to profitability segments in distributed scenario.

If only costing-based profitability analysis (CO-PA) is activated in an operating concern, the system then posts line items in table ACDOCA to aggregated objects, called 'reconciliation objects' (ACDOCA-OBJNR 'AO….'). The system does not generate any characteristic to table ACDOCA for this operating concern. However, if there is another operating concern existing with which account-based CO-PA activated, then, the system can generate characteristics (that are also contained in the costing-based operating concern) into table ACDOCA. The system does not fill characteristics, for the G/L line items in the costing-based operating concern, in table ACDOCA and hence no summarization is needed. An exception to this is certain fixed characteristics that are already predefined in table ACDOCA (which are filled by a sending application, even if only costing-based CO-PA is active), for example, the fields Sales Organization (VKORG) or Distribution Channel (VTWEG) of an SD billing document. In order to summarize such fields, use 'Dependent Summarization of General Ledger View activity'.

The summarization of G/L line item table ACDOCA and profitability segments can be of two types:

- Dependent Summarization
- Independent Summarization

In *'dependent summarisation'*, you can summarize a field based on a combination of the fields: 'Reference Transaction' (AWTYP), 'Document Type' (BLART), 'Company Code' (BUKRS) and 'Ledger' (RLDNR). This allows, for example, to summarize a field only in a particular document type and ledger. You will find this configuration under the menu path SAP Customizing Implementation Guide > Financial Accounting > Financial Accounting Global Settings > Document > Summarization > Dependent Summarization of General Ledger View. However, this feature is not available for all fields: you can only summarize CO-PA fields in table ACDOCA, based on the 'Reference Transaction', 'Document Type', 'Company Code', and 'Ledger', if account-based CO-PA is not active in the company code in which you want to summarize the field. If account-based CO-PA is active in the company code (in which you want to summarize the field), the field cannot be summarized based on the 'Reference Transaction', 'Document Type', or 'Ledger', but only based on the 'Operating Concern' (ERKRS) and 'Company Code', as described below under independent summarization.

The *'independent summarization'* depends on the operating concern. Here, you can use a field for summarization based only on the 'Operating Concern' (ERKRS) and the 'Company Code' (BUKRS). You need to use this option for all the fields which are part of an operating concern, since profitability analysis does not recognize most of above-mentioned dimensions at the time of determining the profitability segment. The fields offered for independent summarization include customer-defined CO-PA characteristics and some fixed characteristics, such as, 'Sales Organization' (VKORG), 'Distribution Channel' (VTWEG), and 'Division' (SPART), which are contained in every operating concern. If a field is defined here, it is summarized in distributed CO-PA regardless of whether summarization is restricted to certain company codes or not. You will find this configuration step under the menu path SAP Customizing Implementation Guide > Financial Accounting > Financial Accounting Global Settings > Document > Summarization > Independent Summarization of General Ledger View and Profitability Segments. If profitability analysis is not active at all in a company code, these settings under the above menu path are not used.

> **i** To avoid performance problems, it is recommended to exclude the frequently occurring fields that have a different value with each posting (like, the 'Sales Order Number' for a repetitive manufacturer, or the 'Customer' and 'Material' for a retailer) and which are therefore not relevant for analysis. This can improve performance considerably. It is further recommended that you use document summarization of table BSEG, and reduce the number of G/L line items in table ACDOCA as much as possible.

The fields you define for the summarization of G/L line item table ACDOCA and profitability segments are not summarized in the following cases:

- Line items relevant to the Material Ledger when Material Ledger is active.
- Line items relevant to fixed assets.
- The Customer Number (KUNNR) on debtor line items or if the customer is an affiliated party.
- True and statistical account assignments are never summarized in table ACDOCA. For example, if you choose to summarize the 'Cost Center' (RCNTR) field, this would not be initialized in G/L line items with true or statistical account assignment to cost center. For profitability segments containing the cost center characteristic, the summarization takes place for both the G/L line item and the profitability segment, if the cost center is not a statistical account assignment, since the profitability segment is always a true account assignment.
- 'Sales Order' (KDAUF) and 'Sales Order Item' (KDPOS) are never summarized on line items relevant to event-based revenue recognition.

This completes our discussion on summarization. Let us proceed to discuss default values.

7.1.13 Default Values

Instead of inputting certain data like fiscal year, document type, posting date, posting key etc., every time you create a document, you can setup the system to propose these inputs. Using the different configuration steps, you can make the system to propose (a) default document type and posting key during a transaction, (b) default fiscal year, (c) default value date and (d) a message control.

Let us start with the configuration of default values.

7.1.13.1 Define Default Values

You may define the default document type and posting key for a Transaction (like, F-02, F-05, F-31, F-47 etc), so that you do not need to enter them during document entry. For example, when posting customer invoices (Transaction F-22), you need to use the document type DR and posting key 01. You can store this information using this configuration step, so as to make the system to propose them, when you call up the relevant Transaction. This is a cross-client customizing step and is valid across the clients.

You can use SAP's default settings (Figure 7.29) as such that cover most of the Transactions.

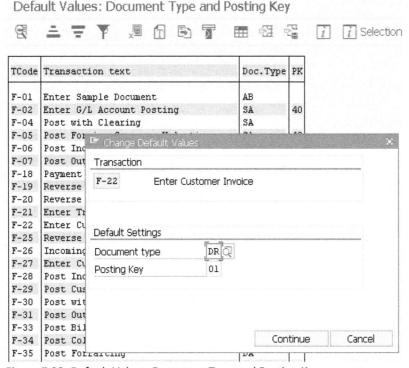

Figure 7.29: Default Values: Document Type and Posting Key

Project Dolphin

The project team, as suggested by BESTM, will not make any change to the SAP standard defaults relating the document type and posting key for the common transactions.

However, if you want to change the defaults, use the menu path SAP Customizing Implementation Guide > Financial Accounting > Financial Accounting Global Settings > Document > Default Values > Define Default Values. Or use Transaction OBU1. To change the defaults, double-click on a row and make changes on 'Change Default Values' pop-up screen.

> **i** Do not to change the default values provided by SAP for any of the Transactions.

Let us proceed to make the settings for enabling fiscal year default.

7.1.13.2 Enable Fiscal Year Default

You can make the system to propose the fiscal year during document display / change. The system will bring up the last fiscal year that was used by a user in his work session.

> **i** You will use this only when you work with company codes using year-dependent document number ranges.

Use the menu path SAP Customizing Implementation Guide > Financial Accounting > Financial Accounting Global Settings > Document > Default Values > Enable Fiscal Year Default. Or use Transaction OB63. On the 'Change View "Default Fiscal Year": Overview' screen, select the 'Propose Fiscal Year' check-box, for the company codes for which you want the system to propose the fiscal year during document entry or change functions, and 'Save' your entries. Since, BESTM will not use year-dependent document number ranges, we will not be selecting the 'Propose Fiscal Year' check-box for any of the company codes (Figure 7.30).

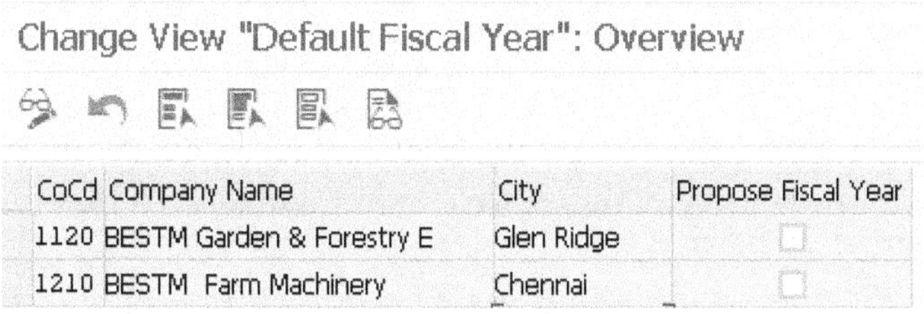

Change View "Default Fiscal Year": Overview

CoCd	Company Name	City	Propose Fiscal Year
1120	BESTM Garden & Forestry E	Glen Ridge	☐
1210	BESTM Farm Machinery	Chennai	☐

Figure 7.30: Enable Fiscal Year Default

Recall that we have already made this configuration while maintaining the global parameters for company codes (Transaction OBY6) for BESTM in Chapter 6 (Section 6.8.1).

We can now proceed to discuss how to make the settings to propose a default value date.

7.1.13.3 Default Value Date

You may need to enter a value date when you enter line items in a document. By making suitable settings, you make the system to determine, per company code, whether the CPU date is defaulted as the value date.

Use the menu path SAP Customizing Implementation Guide > Financial Accounting > Financial Accounting Global Settings > Document > Default Values > Default Value Date. Or use Transaction OB68. On the 'Change View "Default Fiscal Year": Overview' screen, select 'Propose Value Date' check-box, for the company codes for which you want the system to propose the CPU date as the default value during document entry, and 'Save' your entries (Figure 7.31). We have already made this configuration while maintaining the global parameters for company codes (Transaction OBY6) for BESTM in Chapter 6 (Section 6.8.1).

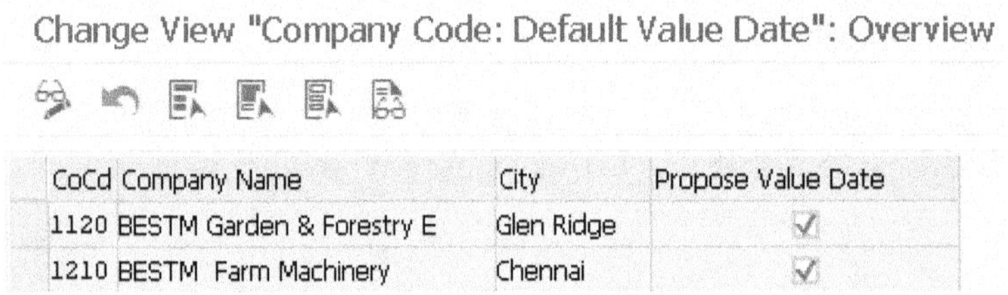

Change View "Company Code: Default Value Date": Overview

CoCd	Company Name	City	Propose Value Date
1120	BESTM Garden & Forestry E	Glen Ridge	✓
1210	BESTM Farm Machinery	Chennai	✓

Figure 7.31: Default Value Date

The last configuration step in defining the default values is setting up the message control for document processing. Let us discuss that now.

7.1.13.4 Change Message Control for Document Processing

You can configure the appearance of system messages, according to your requirements, using this configuration activity. You can (a) determine whether a message is output as a note in a dialog box or in the footer, (b) change warnings to error messages and (c) deactivate warnings and error messages. The system uses message classes F5 and F5A for document processing in SAP FI.

> **i** You can make different specifications for dialog processing and batch input processing (in the background). You can make the specifications for a client or for individual users.

Project Dolphin

BESTM wants the project team to make the following changes (as in Table 7.5) to some of the standard messages.

Message description	Changes to be made for	
	Online processing	Batch input processing
Amount is zero - line item will be ignored	Warning (W)	Switch off message (-)
Check whether document has already been entered under number & & &	Warning (W)	Error (E)
Vendor is subject to withholding tax	Note in window (I)	Switch off message (-)
Terms of payment changed; Check	Warning (W)	Warning (W)

Table 7:5 BESTM – Standard Messages and Changes Required for BESTM

To configure the system messages to suit BESTM's requirements:

i.   Use the menu path SAP Customizing Implementation Guide > Financial Accounting > Financial Accounting Global Settings > Document > Default Values > Change Message Control for Document Processing. Or use Transaction OBA5.

ii.   On the 'Determine Work Area: Entry' pop-up screen, select the appropriate 'Application Area' from the drop-down list (say, F5). Click 'Continue'.

iii. On 'Change View "Message Control by User": Overview' screen, click on 'New Entries'.

iv.   On the next screen, maintain a new message or change the message type for online or batch input processing. You may also restrict this for a given user by entering the user id in 'User Name'; if you leave this field as blank, then the settings are valid for all the users.

v.   We have re-configured the message type for online and batch input for some of the message numbers (like, 097, 117, 122, 231 etc) as depicted in Figure 7.32 as required by BESTM management. 'Save' when completed.

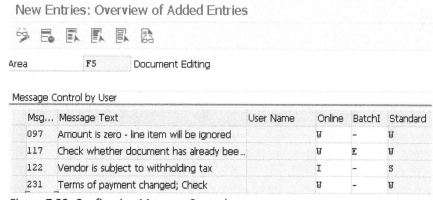

Figure 7.32: Configuring Message Control

This completes our discussion on configuring the default values. Let us discuss the transaction types, next.

7.1.14 Edit Business Transaction Types

The *business transaction type* is an important classification of journal entry items. SAP comes delivered with several (about 100) standard business transaction types. The system derives one business transaction type for each journal entry, at the header level. You can create your own business transaction types in the customer namespace Y*, if the SAP supplied standard ones do not serve your purpose.

    i.   Use the menu path SAP Customizing Implementation Guide > Financial Accounting > Financial Accounting Global Settings > Document > Edit Business Transaction Types. Or use Transaction FINSC_BTTYPE.

    ii.   On the 'Change View "Business Transaction Type": Overview' screen, you will see all the standard business transaction types supplied by SAP (Figure 7.33).

    iii.   If you need a new business transaction type, click on 'New Entries' and proceed.

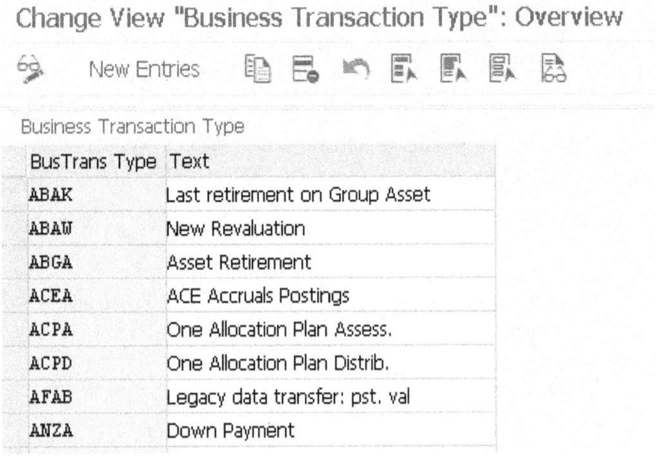

Change View "Business Transaction Type": Overview

    New Entries

Business Transaction Type

BusTrans Type	Text
ABAK	Last retirement on Group Asset
ABAW	New Revaluation
ABGA	Asset Retirement
ACEA	ACE Accruals Postings
ACPA	One Allocation Plan Assess.
ACPD	One Allocation Plan Distrib.
AFAB	Legacy data transfer: pst. val
ANZA	Down Payment

Figure 7.33: Standard Business Transaction Types

> **i** Instead of creating a new one, you can overwrite the default logic of a particular business transaction type to suit your own requirement by implementing BAdI BADI_FINS_ACDOC_POSTING_EVENTS to fill ET_ACDOC_SUBST-BTTYPE in method SUBST_ACDOCA_EXTENSION_FIELDS. You can do this for all business transactions triggering journal entry postings. Besides, you can specify your own business transaction type in the external interface BAPI AcctngDocument.POST (BAPI_ACC_DOCUMENT_POST). There is no dedicated field available in this BAPI, but you can map any extension field of parameter EXTENSION2 to the business transaction type, by implementing BAdI BADI_ACC_DOCUMENT to fill C_ACCIT-BTTYPE in method CHANGE.

Let us proceed to discuss recurring entries, in the next section.

7.1.15 Recurring Entries

You will come across that there are several business transactions like rental payment, utility payment etc that occur periodically in any business. You will be repeating some of the details, every time when you process these *recurring entries*. SAP helps in automating these efforts, instead of manually entering them in every period, through *reference documents* which include '*account assignment model*' and '*recurring document*'.

The '*account assignment model*', in SAP, is a 'reference method' used in document entry, when you want to repeat distributing the same amounts to several company codes, cost centers, G/L accounts etc. Instead of manually distributing the amount among accounts or company codes, you may use *equivalence numbers* for distributing the amount. You can use this model to distribute both the credit and debit amounts. You can also create a cross-company code account assignment model. The model can be used across several company codes, and can even include company codes from non-SAP systems. The account assignment model may contain any number of G/L accounts. Unlike a 'sample document' (which is a template used to copy into new documents and posted in the system) an account assignment model may be incomplete, and can be completed during document entry by adding or deleting or changing the data that have already been saved in the model.

 Use Transaction FKMT to create a new account assignment model.

Let us now understand the configuration of document entry screen variants for account assignment models.

7.1.15.1 Account Assignment Models: Define Entry Screen Templates

Using this activity, you can define your own screen templates for line-by-line document entry, via an account assignment model that is similar to the *fast entry* of G/L account items. SAP comes delivered with standard screen variants like SAP01, SAP02 etc. You may look at these and decide if you can use them as such; or, you can customize them to meet your own requirements. To do this, select the fields that you require for your screen template, by double-clicking on them from a list of available fields:

i.   Use the menu path SAP Customizing Implementation Guide > Financial Accounting > Financial Accounting Global Settings > Document > Recurring Entries > Account Assignment Models: Define Entry Screen Templates. Or use Transaction O7E3.

ii. On the 'Maintain Screen Variant: List' screen, you will see all the screen variants for account assignment models (Figure 7.34).

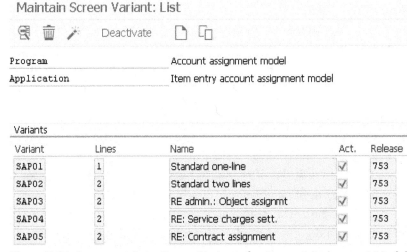

Figure 7.34: Document Entry Screen Variants for Account Assignment Model

iii.   You can copy and create a new one, or you can create a new one from the scratch; you can select the fields you require for your screen template, by double-clicking on them from a list of available fields.

> **i** You will not be able to make any modification to the SAP supplied standard screen variants.

iv.   You can 'Activate' / 'Deactivate' these standard ones.
v.   If you want to assign a screen template to a user, enter the value as a parameter in their user master record.

With this, let us understand the recurring documents.

The *'recurring documents'* automate the periodic payments with a fixed run schedule. This is similar to the standing order you will give to your bank to deduct your rental, premium payments, or loan repayments. The recurring entry original document contains all repetitive data necessary for posting the periodic (monthly, quarterly etc) accounting documents. You will ensure that the recurring entry program is started regularly based on the periodicity. The system creates a run schedule, and a batch input file containing all recurring documents to be generated. When you run the batch input session, the system posts the documents, there by updating the expenses and open items.

> **i** Use Transaction FBD1 to create a recurring entry document.

Let us see how to define the run schedules for recurring entry program am in the system.

7.1.15.2 Define Run Schedules

We have already seen that the postings which recur periodically can be made using the recurring entry program. To accomplish this, you need to enter a recurring entry document and then execute the recurring entry program at desired intervals or you can schedule it for automatic execution. You can specify when an accounting document is to be created, from a recurring entry document (Figure 7.35):

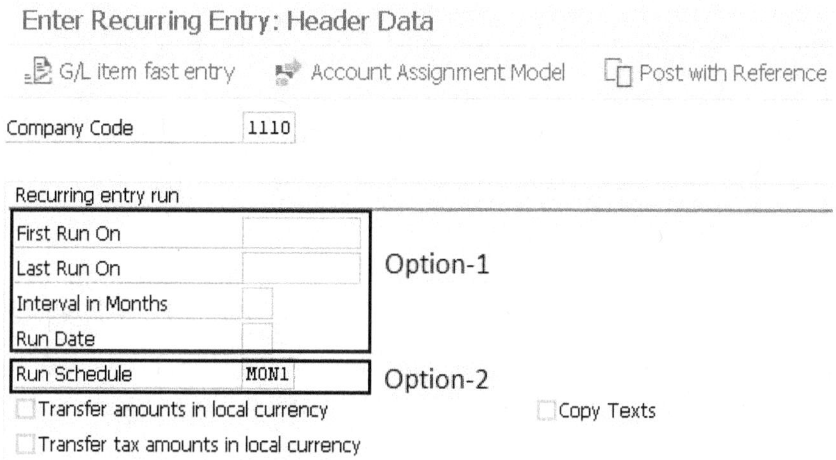

Figure 7.35: Options for Recurring Entry

- *Option-1*: you can enter the interval in the recurring entry document, by specifying a date for the first run and a date for the last run. You also enter the run intervals in months. By specifying a calendar day, you can determine the day on which the program is to be executed. This is useful if the postings are to be made at monthly intervals (calendar months).
- *Option-2*: you can define a run schedule in the system, and specify in the recurring entry document which schedule the system uses for the document. This procedure is useful if the postings cannot be made at monthly intervals: the postings that are to be carried out in 13 periods or every other week, for example, can only be made by scheduling the run.

Use this configuration activity to define the run schedules by specifying a key and a description. In the next activity, you will enter the required dates for each schedule.

i. Use the menu path SAP Customizing Implementation Guide > Financial Accounting > Financial Accounting Global Settings > Document > Recurring Entries > Define Run Schedules.

ii. On the 'Change View "Recurring Entries: Run Schedules": Overview' screen, click on 'New Entries'.

iii.   Enter the identifier for the run schedule in 'Run Sched.', and enter a 'Description'. 'Save' when completed. You have now created a run schedule (Figure 7.36) which you will use in the next step to configure the dates.

Figure 7.36: Defining Run Schedule

iv.   You can specify this run schedule in the recurring entry document (refer Figure 7.35).

With this, let us understand how to configure the run dates for this schedule.

7.1.15.3 Enter Run Dates

Let us follow the steps listed below to configure the run dates for a given run schedule.

i.   Use the menu path SAP Customizing Implementation Guide > Financial Accounting > Financial Accounting Global Settings > Document > Recurring Entries > Enter Run Dates.
ii.   On the 'Determine Work Area: Entry' pop-up screen, select the 'Run Schedule' and press 'Continue'.
iii.   On the 'Change View "Recurring Entries: Run Dates": Overview' screen, click on 'New Entries'.
iv.   Enter the 'Run Date' in the correct date format and 'Save'. You have now created the run dates for the run schedule MON1 (Figure 7.37).

Figure 7.37: Defining Run Dates

This completes our discussion on recurring entries. Let us now move on to discuss document parking.

7.1.16 Document Parking

The *'document parking'* functionality in SAP enables you to enter and 'park' (store) incomplete documents in the system without extensive entry checks. You can, later on, recall the parked document and add to, check, and post the same. You can also enable another user to do this. The settings you make in this step, relate mainly to releasing the parked documents. You can define whether the parked document must be released and who should release it. The document release uses the SAP Business Workflow component.

Let us start with the first activity of making the settings for changing the posting date of a parked document.

7.1.16.1 Change Posting Date for Parking Documents

Through this step, you define how the posting date is to be set for posting parked documents. For each company code, you can specify whether the posting date is to remain unchanged or to be overwritten with the system date. You can choose from several procedures (<blank>, 1 and 2). You can only use this function for the classic FI parking transactions, as this function is not active in the new 'FI Enjoy single screen transactions' since the user can change the posting date at any time.

Project Dolphin

BESTM has requested the project team to configure the system in such way that the posting date should be the system date, in cases of posting a parked document.

To configure the posting date for parking documents:

i. Use the menu path SAP Customizing Implementation Guide > Financial Accounting > Financial Accounting Global Settings > Document > Document Parking > Change Posting Date for Parking Documents. You may also use Transaction OBD1.

ii. On the 'Change View "Posting Date for Document Parking": Overview' screen, select the appropriate option for 'Prk Pst Dt' field. The options are:
  - <blank> Posting date is not changed during posting
  - 1 Posting date is changed to system date
  - 2 Same as 1 only if the posting period is closed

As required by BESTM, enter 1 in the field to enable changing the posting date to the system date when posted.

> **i** If changing of the posting date results in a new fiscal year, the system keeps the posting date as it is without changing to the system date (options 1 & 2).

iii.   'Save' your entries. (Figure 7.38).

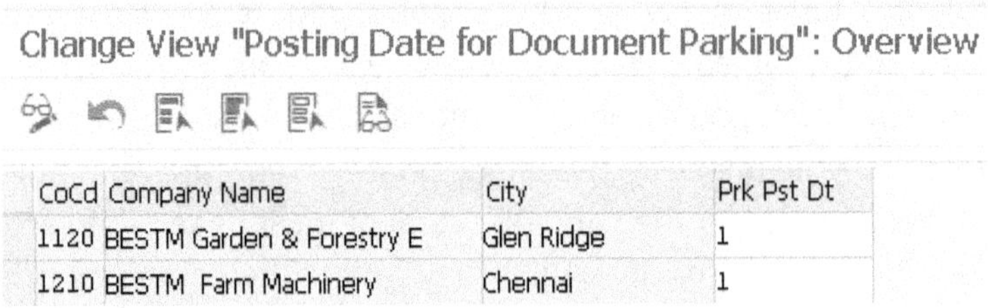

Change View "Posting Date for Document Parking": Overview

CoCd	Company Name	City	Prk Pst Dt
1120	BESTM Garden & Forestry E	Glen Ridge	1
1210	BESTM Farm Machinery	Chennai	1

Figure 7.38: Change Posting Date for Parked Documents

Let us see the other configuration activity for document parking.

7.1.16.2 Develop Enhancements for Parking Documents

You may use the SAP enhancements that are available for the 'Document Release Workflow' (SAPLF040) for the release of parked documents. You can use the menu path: SAP Customizing Implementation Guide > Financial Accounting > Financial Accounting Global Settings > Document > Document Parking > Develop Enhancements for Parking Documents, or Transaction CMOD, to create your enhancement. You can either create a new project or use an existing one. You can, then, modify the source code for a transaction delivered by SAP, by adding the elements you need. SAP provides you with the necessary function modules with short text, interface, and documentation to be able to do this. A sample source code created by SAP may exist for user exits which can be copied (and changed), if required. When completed, 'activate' the project: this allows the ABAP source code to run.

This completes our discussion on the settings that are required to configure the release of parked documents. Let us now understand the validation of account assignment combinations.

7.1.17 Validation of Account Assignment Combinations

When a document needs to be posted, the system applies the *validation rules* you defined together with the account assignments specified in the document, classifies the document as invalid if applicable, and rejects the posting. These additional checks you define for accounting documents helps in minimizing data entry errors.

Let us discuss how to define the validation rule for account assignment combination.

7.1.17.1 Define Validation Rule for Account Assignment Combinations

Here, you can define rules for classifying account assignment combinations as valid or invalid. After defining validation rules as part of a validation strategy, you can assign them to a company code as a default validation strategy or assign them directly to a specific ledger group. SAP uses the authorization object, F_FAGL_DRU, for validating account assignment combinations. To update the groups used in the validation rules (such as, cost center groups), you need to schedule the program 'Adjustment of Derivation Rules After Changes to Groups' (FAGL_VAL_DERIVATION_TOOL) periodically.

> **i** For example, in your company, you decide that postings should not be made to the account assignment combination 'Cost Center 11100 and G/L Account 44500000'. For this, you define a validation strategy with the validation type 'Invalid Account Assignment Combination', and create a derivation step with the source fields 'Cost Center' and 'G/L Account'. As rule entries, you specify 'Cost Center' = 11100 and 'G/L Account' = 44500000. If you now assign this validation strategy to a company code as a default validation strategy, documents with this account assignment combination are rejected. The validation type, thus specifies how the system subsequently needs to interpret the rule, when posting the document.

In this configuration activity, you (a) create a *validation strategy*, and define *derivation rules* with the desired account assignment combinations. When creating the validation strategy, you have to select the desired *validation type* (invalid or valid account assignment combinations). The validation type specifies whether the validity of the defined rules or account assignment entries need to be checked (see the example above). If validation rules have already been created for a validation strategy, the validation type can no longer be changed. Now, (b) in combination with the definition of the derivation rule, specify the objects to be checked, such as cost center 11100, G/L account etc., (rule entries). Later, (c) assign the validation strategy to a company code (or to a ledger group). Note that the validation strategies can be assigned to multiple company codes or ledger groups. Finally (d) 'activate' the validation strategy for the company code and save your entries.

Project Dolphin

BESTM has requested Project Dolphin to explore the possibility of using validation rules for preventing posting of documents based on certain pre-defined account assignment combinations. For example, they have indicated that for a cost center (11101101 and G/L account (11001099) combination like, the validation rule set in the system should reject a posting. Similar combinations are to be built in for various cost center-G/L account combinations as decided by the FI Manager of various company codes for BESTM. This is to prevent posting with incorrect account assignment combinations.

Let us see how to do this in the system for Project Dolphin:

i.   Use the menu path SAP Customizing Implementation Guide > Financial Accounting > Financial Accounting Global Settings > Document > Document Parking > Define Validation Rule for Account Assignment Combinations.

ii.   On the 'Display IMG' screen, ensure that the 'Validation Strategy' is highlighted on the left pane under the 'Dialog Structure'. Click on 'New Entries'. On the next screen:

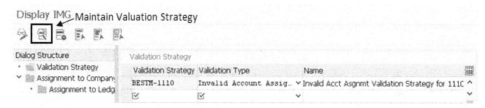

Figure 7.39: Define Validation Strategy (Initial Screen)

- Enter a 'Validation Strategy' identifier (BESTM-1110).
- Select the 'Validation Type'; Let this be 'Invalid Account Assignment Combination'. The other option is 'Valid Account Assignment Combination.
- Provide a description in the 'Name' field (Figure 7.39)

iii.   'Save' the details. Select the row, and click on 'Maintain Validation Strategy'.

iv.   On the 'BESTM-1110 - Invalid Acct Asgmnt Validation Strategy for 1110: Display' screen, click on 'Change' and then press 'Create'. Then, select the 'Derivation Rule' radio button on the 'Create Step' pop-up screen.

v.   On the next screen (Figure 7.40), enter the 'Step Description' and enter the 'Name' (KOSTL) under 'Source Fields' in the 'Definition' tab.

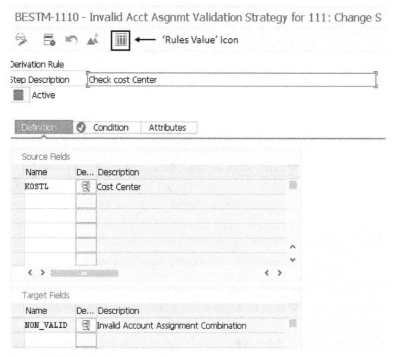

Figure 7.40: Define Derivation Rule

vi. Go to the 'Condition' tab, select the 'Link' rule (AND), enter the 'Name' (HKONT) for G/L account and select the operator '=' under 'Op' and enter the G/L account in 'Value' (11001099) field.

vii. Click on 'Rule Values' icon, and select the appropriate cost center (11101101).

viii. 'Save' the details; you have now created the derivation rule and defined the required rule values (Figure 7.41).

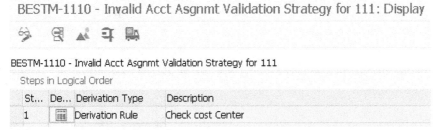

BESTM-1110 - Invalid Acct Asgnmt Validation Strategy for 111: Display

BESTM-1110 - Invalid Acct Asgnmt Validation Strategy for 111

Steps in Logical Order

St...	De...	Derivation Type	Description
1		Derivation Rule	Check cost Center

Figure 7.41: Steps in Rule Entries

ix. The next step is to assign the validation strategy to the company code. On the initial 'Display IMG' screen, select the row containing the required validation strategy, double-click on 'Assignment to Company Code' on left-hand side 'Dialog Structure'.

x. On the 'Change View "Assignment to Company Code": Overview' screen, click on 'New Entries'.

xi. Enter the company code (1110) in 'CoCd' field, select the 'Active' check-box and select BESTM-1110 as the 'Default Validation Strategy'. Then, 'Save' (Figure 7.42). You may also assign this validation strategy to a ledger group by clicking on 'Assignment to Ledger Group' on the left pane.

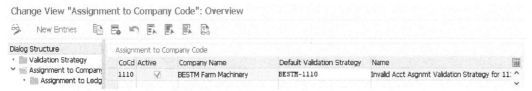

Change View "Assignment to Company Code": Overview

New Entries

Dialog Structure	Assignment to Company Code				
• Validation Strategy	CoCd	Active	Company Name	Default Validation Strategy	Name
˅ Assignment to Company	1110	✓	BESTM Farm Machinery	BESTM-1110	Invalid Acct Asgnmt Validation Strategy for 11:
• Assignment to Ledg					

Figure 7.42: Assignment of Validation Strategy to a Company Code

We have now created a validation strategy for company code 1110 with the validation rule that documents with account assignment combination of 'Cost Center 11101101 and G/L Account 11001099' will be rejected as invalid for posting into the system.

This completes our discussion on defining validation rule for account assignment combinations. Let us now move to discuss account document archiving.

7.1.18 Account Document Archiving

Using *'archiving'*, you can delete and archive documents that are no longer required on line. You can specify the minimum number of days that an accounting document, and the respective secondary indexes must be in the system, before you can archive them. You will make these settings, per document type / account type.

To delete (and archive) the account master data from the system, you must set the 'Mark for Deletion' flag in the respective master records (Figure 7.43): the deletion must be carried out using the program for archiving G/L account master data. This program archives the master records that have been marked for deletion, provided there is no dependent data remaining in the system. However, you should only use this program to delete test data before you 'go live' with the system.

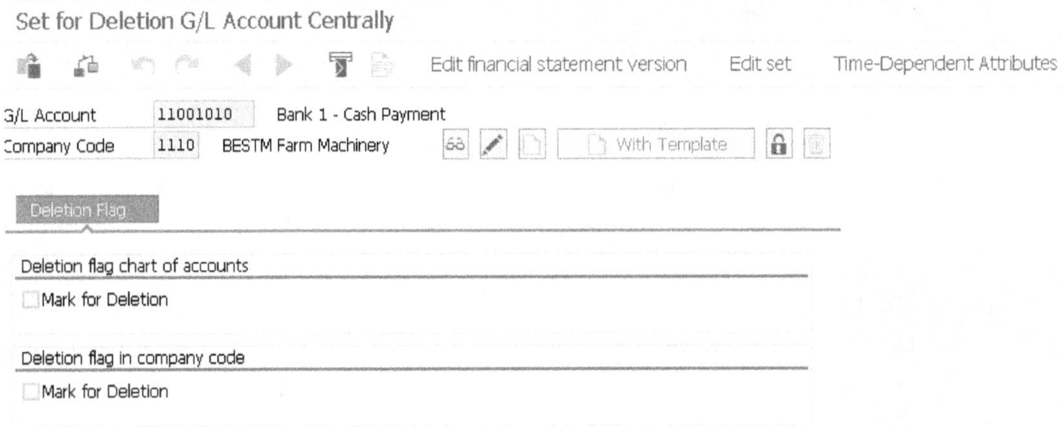

Set for Deletion G/L Account Centrally

G/L Account   11001010   Bank 1 - Cash Payment
Company Code   1110   BESTM Farm Machinery   With Template

Deletion Flag

Deletion flag chart of accounts
Mark for Deletion

Deletion flag in company code
Mark for Deletion

Figure 7.43: Deletion Flag in G/L Master Record

Let us understand archiving, in detail.

7.1.18.1 Archiving, Account Type Life

Here, you specify a *minimum life* for accounts in days, so that during archiving of documents, the system checks whether this minimum life is reached or not. To define the *account life*, you specify account number intervals: for the account types D (customer) and K (vendor), enter the number of the reconciliation accounts. The system always uses the most exact entry for an account: this means that entries with an * are not exact and specialization decreases with the length of the respective G/L account interval. A special role comes into force in a situation where, for one account, an entry exists with company code * and a particular account type (say, D) as well as an entry with account type * and a particular company code (say, 1110). Since it is not possible to say which of the two options is more exact in this situation, the system takes the entry with the maximum number of days. Before this, the system searches for the shortest relevant G/L account interval, in both company code/account type combinations.

You may also define '*index lives*': these index lives must always be after or the same as the account type life. The system contains the following indexes for FI: (a) *secondary indexes* and (b) *archiving indexes*. The information on the document is held in parallel to the actual document data, in the secondary indexes of G/L accounts, customer accounts, and vendor accounts. By means of the secondary index life, you can now determine how many days (related to the clearing date and archiving key date) a secondary index for a document is to remain in the system. When the index life is longer than the account type (document type) life, you can archive and delete the document from the database, but the secondary index information remains in the system, until they are deleted by the post-processing program in accordance with the secondary index life.

Project Dolphin

To enable auditing and other purposes, BESTM corporate has decided that the documents / accounts should not be archived until they cross a minimum life of 1000 days (about 3 years), since it was felt that SAP's default of 9,999 days may put pressure on the system performance and hence the recommendation. However, it was clarified, that even after archiving the documents / accounts need to be fetched faster from the respective archives, at least, for another year (365 days).

Let us configure the details in the system:

i.   Use the menu path SAP Customizing Implementation Guide > Financial Accounting > Financial Accounting Global Settings > Tools > Archiving > Accounting Document Archiving > Archiving, Account Type Life. Or, you may use Transaction OBR7.

ii.   On the 'Change View "Document Archiving, Account Life": Overview' screen, click on 'New Entries'.

iii. On the next screen:
- Enter * in the 'Comp' (company code) field if the settings are to be valid for all the company codes. Since, BESTM wants the same settings for all the company codes, we will not create separate rows for different company codes.
- This field 'Accou' is used to denote the affected account types for the archiving settings: if you enter *, then it takes care of all the account types. Else, you need to specify the settings for each of the account types (S, A, D, K and M) in separate rows. As we have decided that the settings will be valid for all the account types, you just stop with * entry.

- Enter the starting account number in the 'From Acct' field. Enter the reconciliation account number in case of sub-ledgers like K, D etc. Enter 0.
- In the 'To Account' field, enter the upper limit of the account number. Say, 9999999999.
- Now, specify the days after which the FI documents need to be archived in the 'Life' field; enter 1,000 for BESTM company codes.
- The 'SecondaryIdxRunTime' field denotes the life of the secondary index. Set this to 1,365 days (=1000+365). This means, even after archiving of documents / accounts from the database, the information stored in the secondary index is available in the system for another 365 days
- 'Save' the entries. You have created the account type life for all the company codes, all the document types with the numeric number range of 0 to 99999999999.
- Copy this entry and create another row to cover the non-numeric number ranges: Enter the starting account number in the 'From Acct' field. Enter A.
- In the 'To Account' field, enter the upper limit of the account number. Say, ZZZZZZZZZZ.

iv.   You have now configured the archiving settings using account life for all the company codes of BESTM (Figure 7.44)

Comp	Accou	From Acct	To Account	Life	SecondaryIdxRunTme
*	*	0	9999999999	1000	1365
*	*	A	ZZZZZZZZZZ	1000	1365

Figure 7.44: Archiving Settings using Account Type Life

> **i** You may click on 'Archive test' button on the 'Change View "Document Archiving, Account Life": Overview' screen (or Transaction FB99), to see / check whether documents can be archived for a given company code.

Let us proceed to discuss the settings for archiving using document type life.

7.1.18.2 Archiving, Document Type Life

For archiving accounting documents based on *document type life*, specify a minimum document life in days depending on the document type. When archiving documents, the system checks whether this minimum life is adhered to and decides what to be archived and what not. Besides the document type life, you can also determine the *archiving index life* for document types. The archiving indexes represent the link between the FI data and the archives. As long as the system knows these document-oriented archiving indexes, it is possible to display documents from the archive. This function also applies to displaying line items from the document archive. Here also, the system always uses the most exact entry for a document type. The system sees entries with an * as not being exact or specific. As stated earlier while discussing archiving based on account type life, here also a special role comes into force in situations where, for one document type, an entry exists with company code * and a particular document type (say, KG) as well as an entry with document type * and a particular company code (say,1110): in this case, the system takes the entry with the maximum number of days.

To make the archiving settings for document type life:

i. Use the menu path SAP Customizing Implementation Guide > Financial Accounting > Financial Accounting Global Settings > Tools > Archiving > Accounting Document Archiving > Archiving, Document Type Life. Or, you may use Transaction OBR8.

ii. On the 'Change View "Document Archiving: Document Life": Overview' screen, click on 'New Entries'.

iii. On the next screen:
- Enter * in the 'Company Code' field if the settings are to be valid for all the company codes. Since, BESTM wants the same settings for all the company codes, we will not create separate rows for different company codes.
- This field 'Doc. Type' is used to denote the affected document types for the archiving settings: if you enter *, then it takes care of all the document types. Else, you need to specify settings for each of the account types (AA, AB, AD, AF, DA, DG, DR, DZ, KA, KG, KR, KZ, RE, RK, RN, SA, SB and so on) in separate rows. As we have decided that the settings will be valid for all the document types, you just stop with * entry.
- In 'Document Life' field, specify days after which the FI documents of a particular document type can be archived by the system. You can set the 'life' individually for different document types or set the same 'life' for all the document types. As required in Project Dolphin, enter 1,000 as the document life for all the document types.
- 'FBRA Check': select the check-box, if you want to execute Transactions FBRA (reset cleared items) and FCH8 (cancel check payment), for a document in which the document archiving life (1,000 days in our case) has been reached. When selected, the system examines in detail whether the document is contained in a current archiving run: if this is not the case, the re-setting of cleared items is allowed. If the check-box is not selected and the document

archiving life has been reached, the re-setting of cleared items is always rejected. Select this check-box for BESTM.

iv.   We have now configured archiving settings based on document type life for BESTM (Figure 7.45)

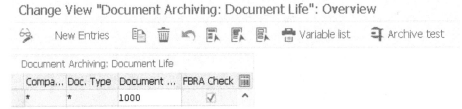

Figure 7.45: Archiving Settings using Document Type Life

Now, let us understand how to develop enhancements for archiving.

7.1.18.3 Develop Enhancements for Archiving

SAP provides you with FARC0001 as the enhancement for FI archiving programs. However, you can create your own enhancement / modify an existing one using the menu path: SAP Customizing Implementation Guide > Financial Accounting > Financial Accounting Global Settings > Tools > Archiving > Accounting Document Archiving > Develop Enhancements for Archiving, or Transaction CMOD. In the first step, create your enhancement: either create a new project or use an existing one. Modify the source code for a transaction delivered by SAP by adding the elements you need. SAP provides you with the necessary function modules with short text, interface, and documentation to be able to do this. A sample source code created by SAP may exist for user exits which can be copied (and changed) if required. When you complete defining the project, activate the same so as to allow the ABAP source code to run.

This completes our discussion on archiving of accounting documents. We can now move on to understand inflation accounting, in the next Section.

7.2   Inflation Accounting

Inflation, as defined in economics, is a sustained increase in the general price level of goods and services, in an economy over a period of time. With the inflation, the general price level rises, and each unit of your currency buys fewer goods and services. As a result, inflation leads to a reduction in the purchasing power, per unit of money. With the inflation the real value of money goes down and the actual income (say, USD 10,000 per annum) is not the same as that of the real income (say, USD 9,000) after adjusting for the inflation (of, say, 10%). If the inflation is very high, then it is called *hyper-inflation*.

'Inflation Accounting' is the process of adjusting the financial statements of a company to show the real financial position during periods of high inflation. It requires adjustment of financial statements according to the current price index of the country. This form of

accounting takes care of the problems of historical cost accounting, in times of high inflation. This involves recording the business transactions at the current value, to analyse the impact of changes in price on costs / revenues and assets / liabilities of a company.

You will resort to inflation accounting, if you are operating in countries that are with high inflation (or hyper-inflation). You will use this in countries like, Columbia, Chile, Turkey, Peru etc., where the country's local law requires use of inflation accounting for financial and asset accounting, to adjust the value of fixed assets for inflation, on a regular basis. This is achieved by adjusting the historical cost of the fixed assets and depreciation using an *inflation index*, as a part of normal closing activities of the business. In essence, you will be adjusting your SAP G/L accounts for inflation, adjusting the open receivables/payables, and preparing inflation-adjusted financial statements, to project the right financial health of the company.

To complete inflation accounting in the system, you have to (a) maintain or define inflation indexes, time bases, inflation keys, inflation methods etc., (b) assign the inflation keys to respective SAP G/L accounts for inflation adjustment, (c) adjust specific line items that require inflation adjustment when they are posted to the system using a specific inflation index besides running the specific programs to revaluate the SAP G/L accounts and open items (both in local and foreign currency) and (d) customize your SAP system to bring out two sets of financial statements: adjusted (for inflation) and unadjusted.

Project Oyster

NJ Corporate is involved in mining operations worldwide. Though headquartered in the USA, it operates in most of the countries including countries like Peru, Mexico and Venezuela. The company code (NJ10) in Venezuela has been operating out of Valencia, and is involved in mining of raw materials required for cement manufacturing. As it is in a high-inflation country, and as required by the local laws, Inflation Accounting has been activated for the company.

The project team, after making a thorough study of the standard inflation indexes provided by SAP, has recommended to the management to make use of the general (GI00) and specific (SI00) inflation indexes without defining anything new. Accordingly, they have requested maintaining the index values, manually, as soon as the same has been published by the local government. No composite inflation index will be used for this company code.

It has also been recommended by the project team to make use of the standard 'time base and exposure to inflation variants' (also known as TBE variants) that has been delivered with the standard SAP. And, it has been further decided to have the validity of this variant RE to last for ever, that will obviate the need to maintain the posting intervals every year. Additionally, the posting intervals are to coincide with the calendar months. The team has also recommended to post revaluation every month, on the last day of that calendar month.

When defining the 'Inflation Key', it has been decided to use the 'balance method', as the 'adjustment method' for calculation. By doing this, the adjustment is done at the account balance level and the system creates one inflation adjustment document for the G/L account.

As regards the 'Inflation Key' field in the G/L accounts, the project team has decided to make that field with the field status 'Optional Entry' for both create and change activities; however, the status will only be 'Display' for the document display activity. Additionally, it has instructed the configuration team to take utmost care while maintaining the field status of 'Inflation Key', per account group in a such a way that it does not conflict with the field status, per activity.

The project team has requested the configurators that for every account hey want to adjust for inflation, they need to make sure that they are entering the inflation key on the 'Control Data' tab of the G/L account master record, without fail.

While maintaining the inflation methods, it has been clarified by the management, that inflation revaluation needs to be posted to the leading ledger and not to any non-leading ledger. Also, it has been indicated that the system should not post all inflation adjustment amounts in their entirety to the general inflation gain / loss account; instead, it needs to split the inflation adjustment amount between two separate accounts: one representing the general inflation rate, and other representing the price level change for that G/L account. The management also requested to define separate document types (one for local currency, and another for foreign currency) to take care of inflation adjustment documents. And, necessary settings be also made for FI-AA and MM components as well, besides FI.

Finally, the management has indicated that the accounting clerks should not be allowed to manually assign inflation indexes to specific G/L line items; instead, the index defined in the inflation key should always be used.

Let us now understand the configuration settings that you will require, to set up inflation accounting for NJ Corporate in the system. The first step is to maintain the inflation indexes.

7.2.1 Maintain Inflation Indexes

The *'inflation index'* is the statistics that show, how much the prices of goods and services have increased over a specific period of time. It is compiled by recording the price increases on a specific selection (or basket) of goods. In countries with high inflation, you are allowed to adjust some G/L accounts when preparing financial statements to allow for the rate of inflation shown by the inflation index.

In this configuration step, you will maintain the inflation indexes that you will use to adjust your accounts for inflation. You must define (a) one index to represent the *'general inflation index'* and (b) another index for each *'specific inflation index'* that you will use. You will use the general inflation index to adjust most of your SAP G/L accounts and a specific inflation index, to adjust specific accounts based on the local government regulations. Maintain these values (mostly on a monthly basis) as they are published in the country of your operation.

SAP comes delivered with sample inflation indexes for a number of country versions. You can use these indexes as such after changing the inflation index values as provided by the local government, or you can use them as the basis for creating new inflation indexes.

i. Use the menu path SAP Customizing Implementation Guide > Financial Accounting > Financial Accounting Global Settings > Inflation Accounting > Maintain Inflation Indexes.

ii. On the 'Change View "Header: Overview' screen, you will see the standard indexes defined by SAP (Figure 7.46). GI00 and SI00 denote the general and specific inflation indexes, respectively.

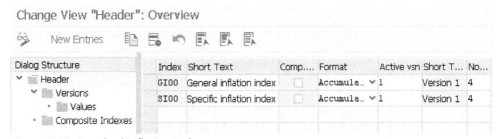

Figure 7.46: Standard Inflation Indexes

iii. When you decide to use the standard ones supplied by SAP, you may enter them manually by using the 'Values' option on the left-hand side pane, after maintaining the appropriate 'Versions' (Figure 7.47).

> **ℹ** When you first create an index, enter the index value from the first date that you want to adjust your accounts for, and the value before that. The system needs this information in order to be able to calculate the net inflation rate. For example, if you create a new monthly index at the beginning of 2019, enter the values for 31 January 2019 and for 31 December 2018.

iv. If you want to create your own indexes, the easiest way is to copy an existing entry on the 'Change View "Header: Overview' screen and then creating your own:
- Provide a 4-character identifier in 'Index', and enter a 'Short Text'.
- Select the 'Comp. Ind.' Check-box, if you want to define a composite index, and then specify which indexes it is composed of under 'Composite Indexes' on the left-hand side dialog box.

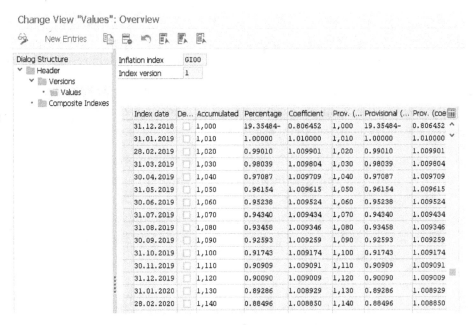

Figure 7.47: Values for Standard Inflation Index GI00

> **i** A '*composite index*' is an inflation index that is composed of two or more other inflation indexes. It enables you to adjust G/L accounts and line items for inflation, if you need to adjust them using more than one inflation index. For example, if your company is required by law to adjust you real estate accounts using an inflation index that combines the (a) specific inflation index for real estate and (b) general inflation index. In this case, you will use a composite inflation index.

- Select the appropriate 'Format' (normally, 'Accumulated') that determines the format for maintaining the inflation values.
- Enter the appropriate version in the 'Active vsn' field and maintain required number of decimal points in the last column (No. dec).

v.   'Save' your settings. You have now created a new inflation index. Repeat the step (iii) and complete the set up.

The next step is to maintain the time base and the associated settings.

7.2.2 Maintain Time Base and Exposure to Inflation Variants

The '*Time Base and Exposure to Inflation Variant*' (TBE variant) is a system object, in inflation accounting, that instructs the system how often to adjust any given item for inflation, and how to adjust items posted partway through a given interval. The default interval for inflation adjustment is at a periodicity such as one day, one month, six months, and one year.

> **ℹ** Consider that you are required to adjust your assets for inflation every half-year, and to treat new assets, as if you posted them on the last day of the half year. You define a TBE variant to this effect. Suppose that you acquire a new asset on 16 May. When you adjust your accounts for inflation on 30 June, the TBE variant instructs the system to treat the asset as if you posted it on 30 June. However, the asset is subject to a full six months' inflation on 31 December.

As with most of the settings, SAP comes delivered with standard TBE variants which you can use as such. However, if you want to create your own variants, you may do so:

i.   Use the menu path SAP Customizing Implementation Guide > Financial Accounting > Financial Accounting Global Settings > Inflation Accounting > Maintain Time Base and Exposure to Inflation Variants.

ii. On the 'Change View "Time Base and Exposure to Inflation Variant: Overview' screen, you will see the standard TBE variants defined by SAP (Figure 7.48). RE represents the regular variant and TR, a special variant. You can create your own variants by selecting an existing variant and clicking on 'Copy As'; in that case, enter an identifier for the new 'Variant', provide a 'Text', maintain a posting variant (Pstg var.). 'Save' the details.

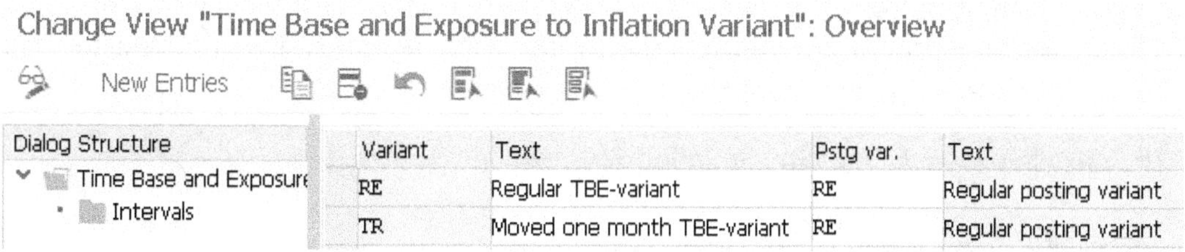

Change View "Time Base and Exposure to Inflation Variant": Overview

🔍   New Entries   📄 📑 ↩ 📝 📝 📝

Dialog Structure	Variant	Text	Pstg var.	Text
⌄ 🗃 Time Base and Exposure	RE	Regular TBE-variant	RE	Regular posting variant
• 📁 Intervals	TR	Moved one month TBE-variant	RE	Regular posting variant

Figure 7.48: Standard TBE Variants

iii. Now, select a row (say, RE) and click on 'Intervals' on the left-hand side dialog structure, to see the intervals (Figure 7.49). If you want to maintain different intervals, then, click on 'New Entries'.

iv. The intervals table provide you with the 'Year' up to which the variant is valid, and you can maintain the 'Month', 'Day' details here. When you enter 9,999 in 'Year' field, you denote that the settings are valid for ever, and there is no need to maintain them every year.

v.   Select the 'Post' check-box if you have to revaluate your assets on this date. When selected, this flag instructs the Asset Revaluation (Inflation) program to create inflation adjustment documents when you run it for this date. Otherwise, it only calculates the revaluation amounts but does not post them.

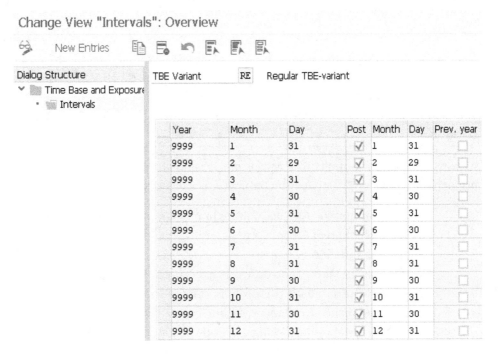

Figure 7.49: Intervals for TBE Variant 'RE'

vi.   You will use the 'Prev. year' check-box to denote if system needs to use the index from the previous year for the same month and day interval. Do not select this flag as the entries are configured to valid forever ('Year' = 9,999).

The next step is to maintain the inflation keys.

7.2.3 Inflation Key

'Inflation key' is a system object that instructs the system on how to adjust a G/L account for inflation, including what inflation index is to be applied, whether the balance only is to be adjusted, or whether all the line items in the account are to be adjusted separately. You need to define inflation keys while configuring the system, and then assign them to different G/L accounts. Once you define the keys, you need to make sure that the 'Inflation Key' field is displayed in the respective accounts for entering the inflation key at a later step.

Let us see the various configuration steps:

7.2.3.1 Maintain Inflation Key

Using this configuration step, you will maintain the inflation keys that you need and assign them to each account that you want to adjust for inflation. These accounts include (a) every G/L account that you want to adjust using the Inflation Adjustment of G/L Accounts program:

here, the program only adjusts G/L accounts that you have assigned an inflation key to, and (b) every customer / vendor reconciliation account that you want to adjust using the following programs:

- Inflation Adjustment of Open Receivables in Local Currency
- Inflation Adjustment of Open Payables in Local Currency
- Inflation Adjustment of Open Items in Foreign Currency

Create one inflation key for each group of G/L accounts that has to be adjusted in the same way. For example, if some G/L accounts need to be adjusted using the general index (say, GI00), and others using a specific index (say, SI00), you would have to create two inflation keys. If you want to adjust open items for inflation, define yet another inflation key in which the 'adjustment method' is set to reconciliation account:

i.   Use the menu path SAP Customizing Implementation Guide > Financial Accounting > Financial Accounting Global Settings > Inflation Accounting > Inflation Key > Maintain Inflation Key.

ii. On the 'Determine Work Area: Entry' pop-up screen, select the country ID for which you want to define the inflation keys. Let this be VE (Venezuela). Press 'Continue'.

iii. On the Change View "Inflation Keys": Overview' screen, click on 'New Entries'. On the next screen (Figure 7.50):

Figure 7.50: Configuring Inflation Key

- Enter an identifier in the 'Inflation Key' field and maintain a short description.
- Do not select the 'Monetary Items' check-box: if selected, this denotes that this account contains monetary items.

> **i** The Inflation Adjustment of G/L Accounts program, by default, adjusts accounts only with non-monetary items; that is, those with an inflation key where this indicator is not selected. However, if you need, you can also run the report for monetary items instead. In that case, the report only adjusts the G/L accounts, with an inflation key where you have selected this indicator.

- Under 'Calculation' select the appropriate adjustment method for the field 'Adj. Method'): select the balance method.

> **i** If you want the adjustment to happen at the line item level, but you need a document for each of the adjusted line items, select the 'Line Item Method (One Document Per Line Item)' from the drop-down values. If you need only one document for all the line items, then select the 'Other Line Item Method (One Document Per Account'). When you select the 'Balance Method', note that the adjustment is done at the account balance level and the system creates one inflation adjustment document for the G/L account.
>
> Note that you can only use the line item method for G/L accounts that meet both the criteria that (a) they are managed on an open item basis and (b) they allow line item display

- Enter the appropriate inflation index in 'Inflation In' field and select the appropriate 'TBE Variant'.
- Under the 'Posting' block, select the 'Post adjustmnts' check-box if you want to create inflation adjustment documents for the SAP G/L accounts (to enable the Inflation Adjustment of SAP G/L Accounts program). Even if you do not select this check-box, the program still calculates the inflation adjustment amounts, and displays them in the output list, but will not create any inflation adjustment documents.

iv.   'Save' the entries; you have now created a new inflation key (VE01).

v.   Repeat the steps if you want to create another inflation key, for example, based on another inflation index like SI00.

Now that we have defined the required inflation keys, the next step is to make sure that the inflation key is displayed in G/L the accounts.

7.2.3.2   Display Inflation Key Field in G/L Account (Per Activity)

Before we can assign inflation keys to G/L accounts, it is important to make sure that the 'Inflation Key' field is displayed in those accounts when you create / change a G/L account master record. The settings you make here apply to all G/L account master records. You will, in the next activity, also specify a field status for each account group and thereby control the 'Inflation Key' field at account group level. When you maintain a G/L account master record, the system will check the settings, per activity, against those per account group. If the settings are different, it takes whichever of the following settings comes first:

- Suppress
- Display
- Required entry
- Optional entry

ℹ️ Assume that you have set the 'Inflation Key' field as an optional entry when creating G/L account master records in general, but suppress the field for a given account group. When you, then, create a G/L master record in that account group, the system will suppress the field completely.

Let us configure the required settings in the system:

i.   Use the menu path SAP Customizing Implementation Guide > Financial Accounting > Financial Accounting Global Settings > Inflation Accounting > Inflation Key > Display Inflation Key Field in G/L Account (Per Activity).

ii.   On the 'Change View "Field Selection by Activity (G/L Accts)": Overview' screen, double-click on 'Display' under 'Activity category'.

iii.   On the 'Maintain Field Status Group: Overview' screen, double-click on 'Account control' under 'Select Group'.

iv.   On the next screen, make sure that the field status of 'Inflation Key' field is set to 'Display' radio button.

v.   'Save'. Go back to the initial screen, repeat the steps (ii) to (v) for the other two activity categories namely 'Change' and 'Create', but change the field status to optional entry (Opt. entry') for these two activity categories (Figure 7.51)

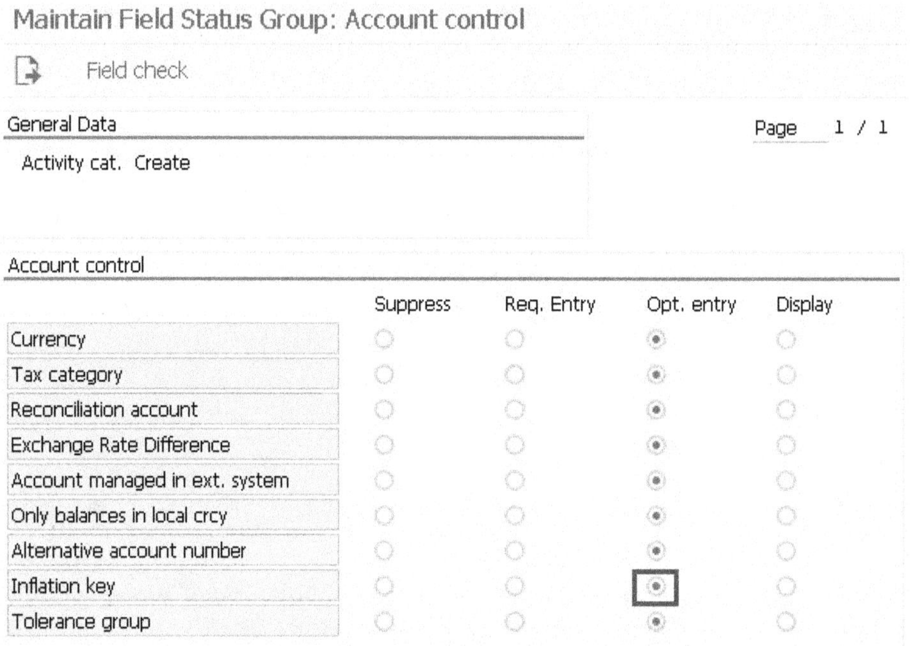

Maintain Field Status Group: Account control

⮞ Field check

General Data		Page 1 / 1
Activity cat. Create		

Account control

	Suppress	Req. Entry	Opt. entry	Display
Currency	○	○	◉	○
Tax category	○	○	◉	○
Reconciliation account	○	○	◉	○
Exchange Rate Difference	○	○	◉	○
Account managed in ext. system	○	○	◉	○
Only balances in local crcy	○	○	◉	○
Alternative account number	○	○	◉	○
Inflation key	○	○	◉	○
Tolerance group	○	○	◉	○

Figure 7.51: Settings to Display Inflation Key in G/L Accounts per Activity

We have, now, maintained the required field settings to the G/L accounts ensuring the display of the 'Inflation Key' field and has set the same to 'optional entry' field status for change / create activity. The next step is to control the field status at the account group level.

7.2.3.3   Display Inflation Key Field in G/L Account (Per Acct Group)

Let us, now, configure the G/L account groups so that the system displays the 'Inflation Key' field in the G/L accounts that need to be adjusted, so that you will be able to assign an inflation key to the G/L accounts as required (in the next step):

i.   Use the menu path SAP Customizing Implementation Guide > Financial Accounting > Financial Accounting Global Settings > Inflation Accounting > Inflation Key > Display Inflation Key Field in G/L Account (Per Acct Group).

ii.   On the 'Change View "G/L Account Groups": Overview' screen, double-click on 'Acct. Group' for a given chart of accounts.

iii.   On the 'Maintain Field Status Group: Overview' screen, double-click on 'Account control' under 'Select Group'.

iv.   On the next screen, make sure that the field status of 'Inflation Key' field is set to optional entry ('Opt. entry') radio button.

v.   'Save'. Go back to the initial screen, repeat the steps (ii) to (v) for any other account group for which you maintain this field status (Figure 7.52).

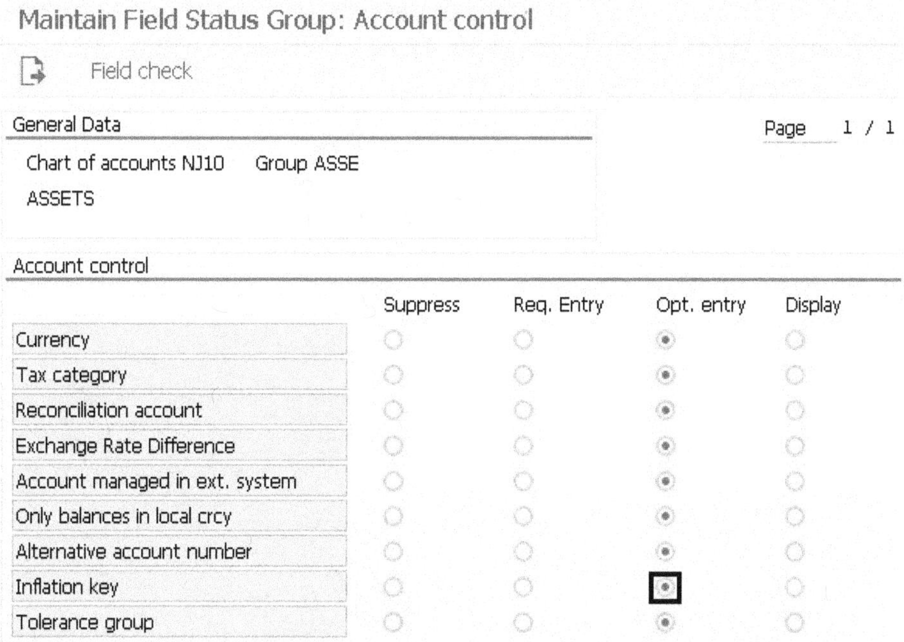

Maintain Field Status Group: Account control

🡢   Field check

General Data   Page   1 / 1

Chart of accounts NJ10   Group ASSE
ASSETS

Account control

	Suppress	Req. Entry	Opt. entry	Display
Currency	○	○	◉	○
Tax category	○	○	◉	○
Reconciliation account	○	○	◉	○
Exchange Rate Difference	○	○	◉	○
Account managed in ext. system	○	○	◉	○
Only balances in local crcy	○	○	◉	○
Alternative account number	○	○	◉	○
Inflation key	○	○	◉	○
Tolerance group	○	○	◉	○

Figure 7.52: Settings to Display Inflation Key in G/L Accounts per Account Group

So, the final field status of the 'Inflation Key' field for G/L accounts will be as in Table 7.6:

G/L activity	Field status per activity	Field status per account group	Final field status in G/L account
Display	Display	Optional entry	Display
Create	Optional entry	Optional entry	Optional entry
Change	Optional entry	Optional entry	Optional entry

Table 7:6 Standard Screen Variants for Document Entry

We are now ready to assign the inflation keys to the respective accounts: you may assign one key at the company code level to every SAP G/L account that needs to be adjusted. However, to adjust FI-A/R and FI-A/P, the inflation key is to be entered into the appropriate reconciliation account(s).

7.2.3.4 Assign Inflation Keys to G/L Accounts

Using this activity, you can assign the inflation keys that you have defined in the previous activity (Section 7.2.3.1) to the appropriate G/L accounts. For every account that you want to adjust, you have to enter the inflation key on the 'Control Data' tab of G/L account master.

Use the menu path SAP Customizing Implementation Guide > Financial Accounting > Financial Accounting Global Settings > Inflation Accounting > Inflation Key > Assign Inflation Keys to G/L Accounts. You may also use Transaction FSS0. On the 'Edit G/L Account Company Code Data' screen, select the 'G/L Account' and 'Company Code', and click on 'Create'. Enter the 'Inflation Key' (say, VE01) under 'Control Data' tab (Figure 7.53). Repeat entering the key for all the required G/L accounts and 'Save'.

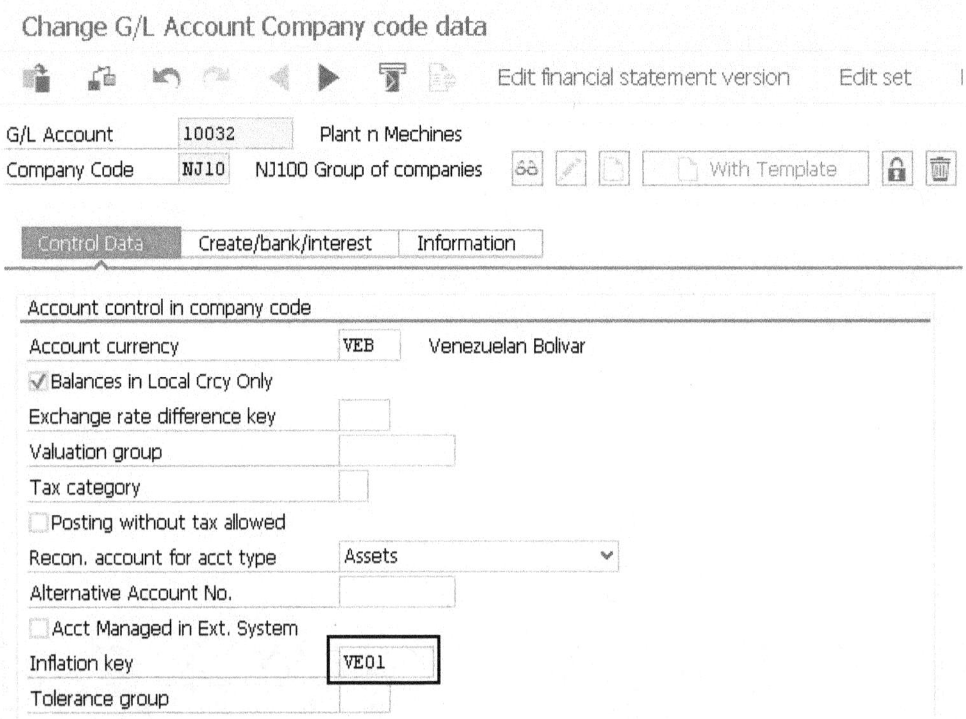

Figure 7.53: Assign Inflation Key to G/L Account

This completes the discussion on inflation keys. Let us move on to understand the inflation methods

7.2.4 Inflation Methods

The 'inflation method', in SAP, controls the inflation accounting settings, relating to a given company code like the accounts that are to be adjusted for inflation (in FI, FI-AA and MM), what general inflation index to use, what TBE variant to use, what document type is to use to post inflation adjustment documents and so on. You need to (a) maintain inflation methods and (b) assign an inflation method to a company code.

Let us start with the maintenance of inflation methods.

7.2.4.1 Maintain Inflation Methods

Using this configuration step, you can define the required inflation methods. The standard SAP system comes delivered with sample inflation methods for each country version, which you can use as the basis for your own inflation methods. The inflation method consists of three parts, one each for the different components (FI, FI-AA and MM) affected by inflation.

Let us look at the settings that required for maintaining the inflation methods:

i. Use the menu path SAP Customizing Implementation Guide > Financial Accounting > Financial Accounting Global Settings > Inflation Accounting > Inflation Methods > Maintain Inflation Methods.

ii. On the 'Determine Work Area: Entry' pop-up screen, enter the country ID. Click 'Continue'.

iii. On the 'Change View "Inflation Methods": Overview' screen, click on 'New Entries'. On the next screen (Figure 7.54):

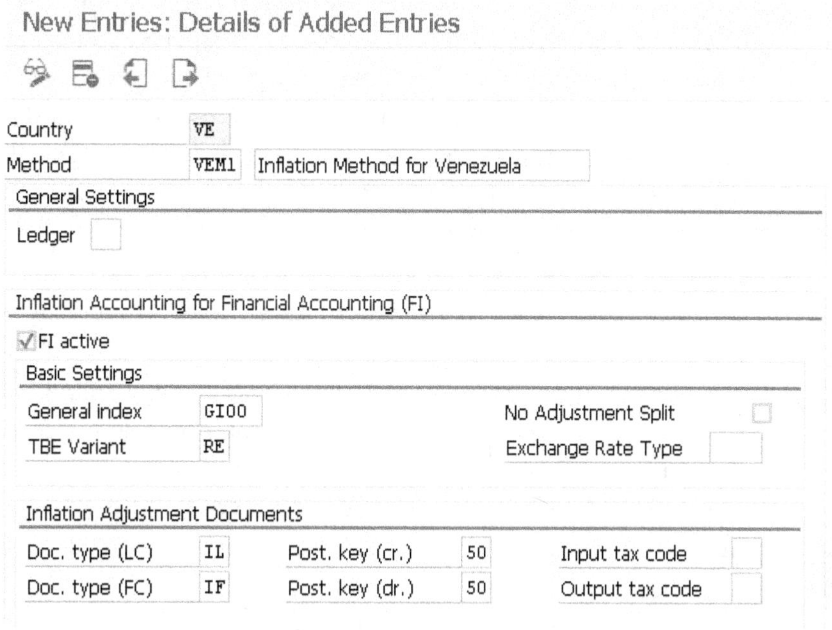

New Entries: Details of Added Entries

Country	VE
Method	VEM1 Inflation Method for Venezuela

General Settings

Ledger [ ]

Inflation Accounting for Financial Accounting (FI)

✓ FI active

Basic Settings

General index	GI00		No Adjustment Split	[ ]
TBE Variant	RE		Exchange Rate Type	[ ]

Inflation Adjustment Documents

Doc. type (LC)	IL	Post. key (cr.)	50	Input tax code	[ ]
Doc. type (FC)	IF	Post. key (dr.)	50	Output tax code	[ ]

Figure 7.54: Maintaining Inflation Method

- Enter an identifier for inflation method in 'Method' field; say, VEM1; enter a short description.
- In the 'Ledger' field, specify the ledger that you want the Inflation Management reports use to adjust G/L account balances and material stocks for inflation. By default, the system uses the leading ledger for the revaluation, and you do not need to make an entry here if you go with that. However, if you want the system to post the inflation adjustments to a non-leading ledger, then specify it in this field.

iv.   To make the settings for inflation accounting for FI:
- Select the 'FI active' check-box. Now you will see that all the fields under this block are ready for input. Before the flag was set, all these fields were not ready for data input.
- Under 'Basic Settings', select the 'General index' (GI00), and enter the 'TBE Variant' (RE).
- When you select 'No Adjustment Split' check-box, the system posts all inflation adjustment amounts, in their entirety, to the general inflation gain or loss account. When not selected, the system splits the inflation adjustment amount between two separate accounts: one representing the general inflation rate, and other representing the price level change for that G/L account. Do not select this, as we want the adjustment to be split.
- 'Exchange Rate Type': This is used to specify which exchange rate type the Inflation Adjustment of G/L Accounts program should use, to convert amounts in foreign currencies. If you want to use M (standard translation at average rate), leave this field as blank. Only enter a rate type, if you need to use an exchange rate type other than M.

v.   For Inflation Adjustment Documents:
- Enter the document type for local currency {'Doc. Type (LC)} as well as foreign currency {'Doc. Type (FC)}. It helps to have two different document types for this purpose.
- Specify which credit / debit posting key (for postings to G/L accounts only) the inflation accounting programs use for credit line items in inflation adjustment documents.
- Maintain the input / output tax code, if required.

vi.   Do similar or the required settings for FI-AA and MM data blocks. And, 'Save' the details.

You have now created the inflation method, which you can use, in the next step, to assign to the appropriate company codes.

7.2.4.2   Assign Inflation Methods to Company Codes

Using this configuration activity, you will assign an inflation method to each company code, that works with the inflation accounting solution. By doing so, you specify the default settings for the inflation accounting programs for these company codes.

Use the menu path SAP Customizing Implementation Guide > Financial Accounting > Financial Accounting Global Settings > Inflation Accounting > Inflation Methods > Assign Inflation Methods to Company Codes. You may also use Transaction OBY6.

Under the 'Processing Parameters', enter the inflation method (say, VEM1) in the 'Inflation Method' field for the selected 'Company Code' (say, NJ10). Continue to assign the 'Inflation Method' if there are more than one company code that uses inflation accounting solution.

Let us now understand the assignment of inflation indexes to line items.

7.2.5 Assignment of Inflation Indexes to Line Items

Here, you will make the settings that will allow inflation indexes to be assigned to individual line items, in a given accounting document. For these purposes, you have to open the 'Inflation Index' field, for each permutation of (a) G/L account that such line items are to be posted to and (b) Posting key that is to be used to create such line items.

You need to use this function, only if you want (a) your accounting clerks to manually assign inflation indexes to specific G/L line items, and (b) to adjust open receivables and payables that are denominated in your local currency. Since, we will not be using both the above options, we can skip the configuration steps (i) Maintain Posting Keys, and (ii) Maintain Field Status Variants under this step.

With this we are now ready to look at the last bucket of configuration for inflation accounting.

7.2.6 Account Determination

Here, you make the settings to ensure that when the system adjusts a G/L account for inflation, it posts the inflation adjustment amounts to the correct G/L accounts. This involves (a) creating the inflation adjustment accounts and (b) specifying, for each G/L account to be adjusted, which inflation adjustment accounts are to be used. When you set up inflation adjustment accounts, for A/R and A/P in local currency, you must ensure that they allow postings with tax codes. Also, when setting up the accounts for A/R and A/P items in foreign currency, ensure that they allow postings without tax codes, since taxes are not supported by the Inflation Adjustment of Open Items in Foreign Currency program.

---

i   To assign inflation adjustment amounts to cost centers, you must assign the inflation adjustment accounts a field status that allows cost centers.

Let us look at defining the inflation adjustment accounts now:

7.2.6.1 Maintain Inflation Adjustment Accounts

Use the menu path SAP Customizing Implementation Guide > Financial Accounting > Financial Accounting Global Settings > Inflation Accounting > Account Determination > Maintain Inflation Adjustment Accounts, or use Transaction FS00 and define the required inflation adjustment accounts. The next step is to maintain the G/L accounts for inflation postings.

7.2.6.2 Maintain G/L Accounts for Inflation Postings

Once you have defined the inflation adjustment accounts, you then specify, for each G/L account that you want to adjust, which inflation adjustment accounts you want to use by following the menu path SAP Customizing Implementation Guide > Financial Accounting > Financial Accounting Global Settings > Inflation Accounting > Account Determination > Maintain G/L Accounts for Inflation Postings.

This completes our discussion on configuring the system for inflation accounting. Let us, now, understand how the system calculates the inflation using the inflation accounting program.

7.2.7 Inflation Calculation

In inflation accounting, the system calculation the inflation using the inflation accounting program as detailed below:

To start with, the system selects the appropriate inflation index to be used: the program validates this at the line item level. If you have maintained the inflation index at the line item level, then the system adjusts the line items with that index. Else, it uses the index that you have defined in the inflation key. If the system does not come across any inflation index in the inflation key, then the program goes further to use the one that you have maintained in the inflation method.

Then, the system calculates the net inflation rate: it takes into account the inflation index value per last adjustment date and from the date that you have entered on the program selection screen. If there is no inflation index value for a particular date, the system, then, determines the same for that date automatically, by assuming that inflation progresses at a constant linear rate between any two inflation values. For example, if the inflation index value for January 31 was 1,000, and the index for March 31 was 1,100, but you want to determine inflation for February 15, the system then calculates that to be 1,050 on that date.

This completes our discussion of inflation accounting. Let us move on to discuss correspondence in SAP in the next section.

7.3 Correspondence

The 'correspondence' function, in SAP, is to set up the system for corresponding with your business partners and for internal purposes. The correspondence includes:

- Account statements
- Balance confirmations
- Bill of exchange charges statements
- Document extracts
- Individual letters

- Internal documents
- Payment notifications

First, you make the fundamental specifications for the above correspondence types. Then, you make the specific definitions for each correspondence type at other points in the IMG.

> **i** To make settings for fax or e-mail correspondence, you need to configure the activity 'Develop enhancements for correspondence' using the menu path: SAP Customizing Implementation Guide > Financial Accounting > Financial Accounting Global Settings > Correspondence > Develop Enhancements for Correspondence, or Transaction CMOD.

Let us start with the definition of correspondence types.

7.3.1 Define Correspondence Types

A 'correspondence type' is type of letter in the system, which determines what data is required for creating a letter and how that data is entered into. The correspondence types are offered to the user, by the system for selection, when processing business transactions (more details in Section 7.3.6) or created automatically according to rules defined by the user or always created automatically by the system. For example, you can select the correspondence type 'payment notice' when entering incoming payments; a bill of exchange charges statement is created automatically for your customers' payments per bill of exchange, if charges to be passed on were posted. You will determine which data is necessary for creating the letters for the correspondence types. The following data is required (either entered manually by the user or is determined automatically by the system after you have selected the relevant correspondence type) for the correspondences (Table 7.8). For example, if you select the correspondence type 'payment notice without line items' in the account display, then, you must specify a document number, since the correspondence type requires this. If you have specified, in the customer master record, that the payment notices are to be created automatically, then the system determines the necessary data when posting an incoming payment.

Correspondence Type	Required Data
Account statements	Account number and date specifications
Bill of exchange charges statements	Document number
Document extracts	Document number
Internal documents	Document number
Individual letters	Account number
Payment notices	Document number

Table 7:7 Correspondence Types and the Required Data

As with other configuration settings, SAP comes delivered with several standard correspondence types (like, payment notice with line items, payment notice without line items, document extract, account statement etc), all starting with 'SAP' (Figure 7.55) which you can use as such; however, if you need to create your own type, it is recommended to copy and make changes to those standard correspondence types supplied by SAP.

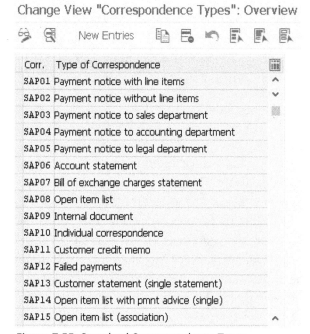

Figure 7.55: Standard Correspondence Types

Project Dolphin

The project management team has recommended to the BESTM management to make use of the standard correspondence types supplied by SAP. Accordingly, it has been decided not to create any new correspondence type except a few like SAP01, SAP06 and SAP08 which will be copied into new correspondence types namely YB01, YB06 and YB08 so as to use them in cross-company code correspondence for company codes 2100 and 2200. Also, the project team has recommended to use the same standard print programs associated with the correspondence types for automatic correspondence in all the company codes of BESTM but use different variants to meet individual company code's varying reporting requirements.

Follow the steps listed below to create a new correspondence types as required by BESTM:

i.   Use the menu path: SAP Customizing Implementation Guide > Financial Accounting > Financial Accounting Global Settings > Correspondence > Define Correspondence Types, or use Transaction OB77.

ii.   On the 'Change View "Correspondence Types": Overview' screen, select the appropriate row (say, SAP01) and click 'Copy As'.

iii.   On the next screen, provide a new identifier for the 'Correspondence' type, and enter a description in 'Correspond. Type' field.

iv.   Under 'General data', select the appropriate check-boxes to stipulate the required or necessary data for this new correspondence. You need to select 'Cross-Comp.Code' check-box if you want to include this correspondence type in a cross-company code correspondence (discussed later in Section 7.3.4).

v.   Under 'Date details', enter the number of date fields required for the new correspondence type as a parameter (for example, key date for the account statement) in 'No.Date.Specif' field and provide the name for 'Date 1 Name' and/or 'Date 2 Name' (Figure 7.56).

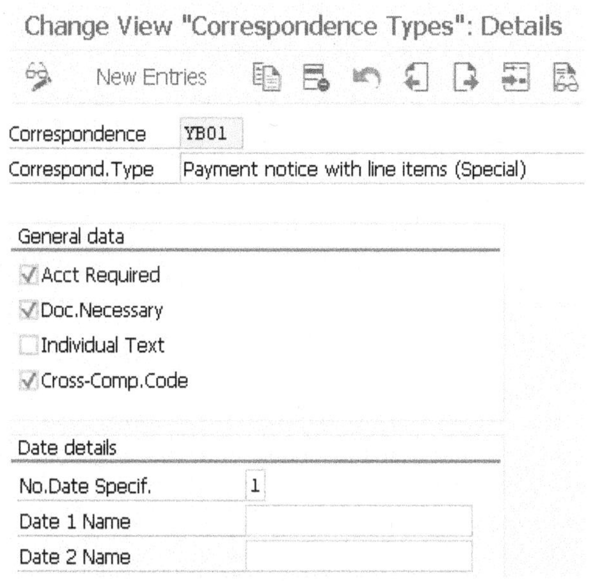

Figure 7.56: New Correspondence Type YB01

vi.   'Save' when completed. And, continue creating the other new correspondence types, YB06 and YB08, by repeating the steps above.

After you create your own correspondence types, you need assign them to the respective print programs besides creating the required report variants for executing the correspondence reports.

Let us look at creating report variants, first.

7.3.2 Create Report Variants for Correspondence

Use the menu path: SAP Customizing Implementation Guide > Financial Accounting > Financial Accounting Global Settings > Correspondence > Create Report Variants for Correspondence, or use Transaction SA38, to define the selection variants for the correspondence that you require. You will define the selection variants, independently of the company code and the type of correspondence. Usually only the fields in the 'Output control' and 'Print control' areas, as well as the field 'Correspondence' in the 'Test run' area, are of interest for a selection variant. The system makes use of the remaining fields in the 'Test run', only if the documents are to be output directly with the print program.

Find out the name of the appropriate print program: to search for standard programs, enter RFKORD*, or to search for customer-defined programs ZFKORD*, for example, on the 'ABAP: Program Execution' screen, upon entering the configuration activity. You will get an up-to-date list of programs displayed by the system. Now, select the required program (say, RFKORD00_PDF) from the list and run it. The system takes you to the 'Print Program: Payment Notice' selection screen in which you can either change an existing variant or create a new one. To change a standard variant, you can display the variant using the function 'Get Variant'. You can, then, change these variants and save them under your own name (customer name range). To create your own variant, enter the selection criteria directly and then save this variant under your own name (say, YB01 for new correspondence type YB01). Finally, in Customizing, specify report name / variant for report assignment for the correspondence type (next configuration activity 'Assign Programs for Correspondence Types').

7.3.3 Assign Programs for Correspondence Types

In this activity, you define the print program and the selection variant, corresponding to each correspondence type. You may use the selection when printing the requested correspondence. You can also distinguish your specifications by company code: this is usually necessary for companies with several company codes (as in BESTM), since you also enter the printer on which you want your correspondence to be issued in the selection variant. SAP comes delivered with the standard print programs, as listed in Table 7.9:

Correspondence	Print program
Account statements	RFKORD10
Bill of exchange charges statements	RFKORD20
Customer statement	RFKORD11
Document extracts	RFKORD50
Individual letters	RFKORD40
Internal documents	RFKORD30
Payment notices	RFKORD00

Table 7:8 Correspondence and the Print Programs

i.   Use the menu path: SAP Customizing Implementation Guide > Financial Accounting > Financial Accounting Global Settings > Correspondence > Assign Programs for Correspondence Types, or use Transaction OB78.

ii. On the ensuing 'Change View "Allocate Program for Automatic Correspondence": Overview' screen, select 'New Entries'.

iii. On the 'Change View "Allocate Program for Automatic Correspondence": Details' screen (Figure 7.57), enter 'Company Code' (1110) and 'Correspondence' type (SAP01).

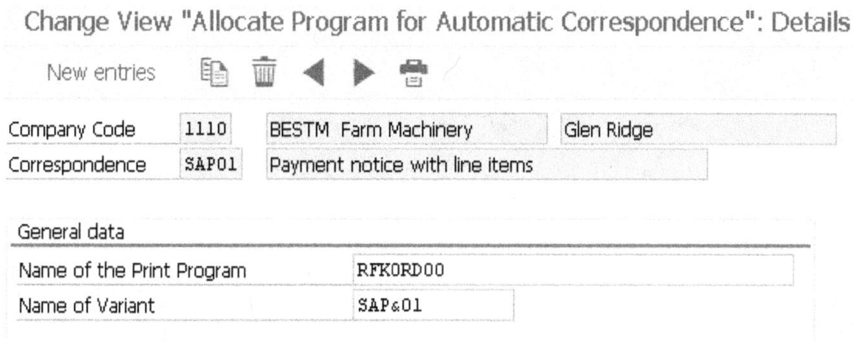

Change View "Allocate Program for Automatic Correspondence": Details

New entries

| Company Code | 1110 | BESTM Farm Machinery | Glen Ridge |
| Correspondence | SAP01 | Payment notice with line items | |

General data

| Name of the Print Program | RFKORD00 |
| Name of Variant | SAP&01 |

Figure 7.57: Program for Automatic Correspondence

iv. In 'General data', enter the 'Name of the Print Program' (RFKORD00) and enter the 'Name of the Variant' (SAP&01).

v.   'Save' the details; you have now allocated the print program RFKOD00 for automatic correspondence in company code 1110 with the standard variant SAP&01.

vi. Repeat the steps for other print programs and company codes.

Let us now look at designating a company, to handle correspondence on behalf of other company codes as well.

7.3.4 Assign Company Codes to Correspondence Company Codes

It is possible that you designate a particular company code as the 'correspondence company code' that, on behalf of all the participating company codes, will manage the correspondence in the system. Called as 'cross-company code correspondence', it will then be possible to send a customer, for example, data from different company codes together in one communication.

Project Dolphin

BESTM wants to make use of 'cross-company code correspondence' functionality in respect of company codes 2100 and 2200. Accordingly, the company code 2100 needs to be designated as the 'correspondence company code' that will manage the correspondence for company code 2200 as well.

To configure the correspondence company code:

i.   Use the menu path: SAP Customizing Implementation Guide > Financial Accounting > Financial Accounting Global Settings > Correspondence > Assign Company Codes for Correspondence Company Codes.

ii.   On the 'Change View "Company Code Details": Overview' screen, click on 'New Entries'.

iii.   On the next screen, enter the company code that will participate in cross-company code correspondence in 'CoCd' (2200) and enter 2100 as the correspondence company code in 'CCoCde' field.

iv.   'Save' the details (Figure 7.58).

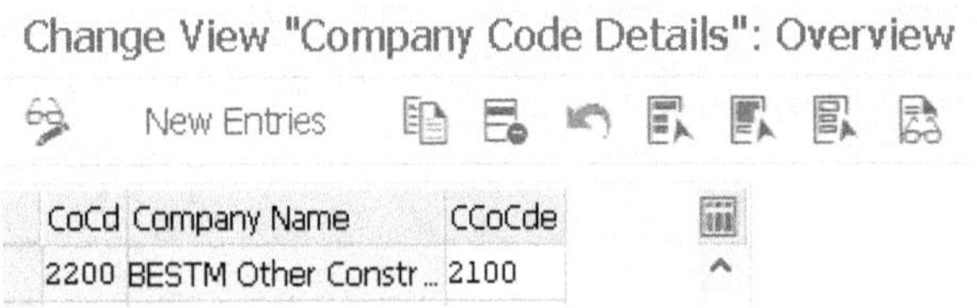

Figure 7.58: Configuring Correspondence Company Code

> **ℹ** You must define the correspondence types suitable for cross-company code use in order to use this function (refer Section 7.3.1).

The next step is to define the sender details for correspondence.

7.3.5 *Define Sender Details for Correspondence Form*

Using this activity, you will define which texts are to be used in the letter window and the signature line, for each of the company codes. This applies to the letter header, letter footer and sender address. This configuration is useful, when you do not define these details in the form (or use a pre-printed writing paper), and use the same form across several company codes. You will, of course, maintain the company code-specific texts separately using standard texts (text ID = ADRS).

To configure the required settings:

i.   Use the menu path: SAP Customizing Implementation Guide > Financial Accounting > Financial Accounting Global Settings > Correspondence > Define Sender Details for Correspondence Form. You may also use Transaction OBB1.

ii.   On the 'Change View "Sender Details for Correspondence": Overview' screen, click on 'New Entries'.

iii.   On the next screen, maintain the required details:
- If you want to use this across company codes, then leave the 'Company Code' as blank.
- Enter the print program in 'Program Name'.
- You may also leave the 'Sender Variant' as blank.
- Enter the 'Text ID' (ADRS), and maintain the standard texts as shown in Figure 7.59.
- You may also maintain the URL for 'Logo' / 'Graphics' under 'URL for PDF Graphics'.
- 'Save' when completed, and repeat the steps for other print programs.

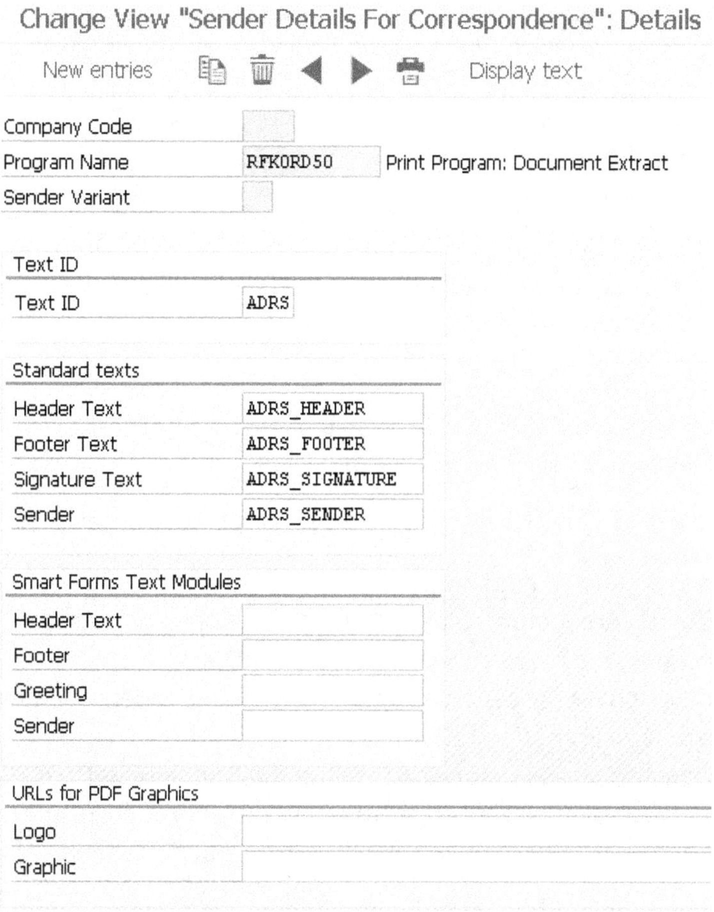

Change View "Sender Details For Correspondence": Details

New entries   Display text

Company Code	
Program Name	RFKORD50 Print Program: Document Extract
Sender Variant	

Text ID

Text ID	ADRS

Standard texts

Header Text	ADRS_HEADER
Footer Text	ADRS_FOOTER
Signature Text	ADRS_SIGNATURE
Sender	ADRS_SENDER

Smart Forms Text Modules

Header Text	
Footer	
Greeting	
Sender	

URLs for PDF Graphics

Logo	
Graphic	

Figure 7.59: Configuring Sender Details

The next step is to configure the system, for calling-up correspondence types online, while you are executing functions like document entry, payment settlement etc.

7.3.6 Determine Call-Up Functions

Using this activity, you may specify which correspondence types can be selected, online, while executing functions like document entry, payment settlement, document display / change, and account editing (balance display and line item processing). The specifications you make here, are dependent on company code; however, if no entry exists for a company code, the system offers the correspondence types specified without company code. As in other cases, SAP comes delivered with the standard settings which you can use as such (Figure 7.60). However, you can change them if required. But, ensure to include any new correspondence type that you would have already created (as in Section 7.3.1), and maintain the specifications for those types as well.

Change View "Call Options of Correspondence Types": Overview

New Entries

CoCd	Corr.	Correspondence Type	DocEnt	Payt	DocDsp	AccDsp
	SAP01	Payment notice with line items	☐	✓	☐	☐
	SAP02	Payment notice without line items	☐	✓	☐	☐
	SAP03	Payment notice to sales department	☐	✓	☐	☐
	SAP04	Payment notice to accounting depart...	☐	✓	☐	☐
	SAP05	Payment notice to legal department	☐	✓	☐	☐
	SAP06	Account statement	✓	✓	✓	✓
	SAP08	Open item list	✓	✓	✓	✓
	SAP09	Internal document	✓	☐	✓	✓
	SAP10	Individual correspondence	✓	✓	✓	✓

Figure 7.60: Standard Call-Up Function Settings

In case of including a new correspondence type in call-up function:

i.   Use the menu path: SAP Customizing Implementation Guide > Financial Accounting > Financial Accounting Global Settings > Correspondence > Determine Call-Up Functions. You may also use Transaction OB79.

ii. On the 'Change View "Call Options of Correspondence Types": Overview screen, select 'New Entries'.

iii. On the next screen (Figure 7.61), select the company code (2100) in 'CoCd', enter the new correspondence type you have created in 'Corr.' field, and select the appropriate check boxes ('DocEnt'-document entry, 'Payt'-payment transactions, 'DocDsp'-document display and 'AccDsp'-account display).

iv. 'Save' your entries. Repeat the steps for all the newly created correspondence types.

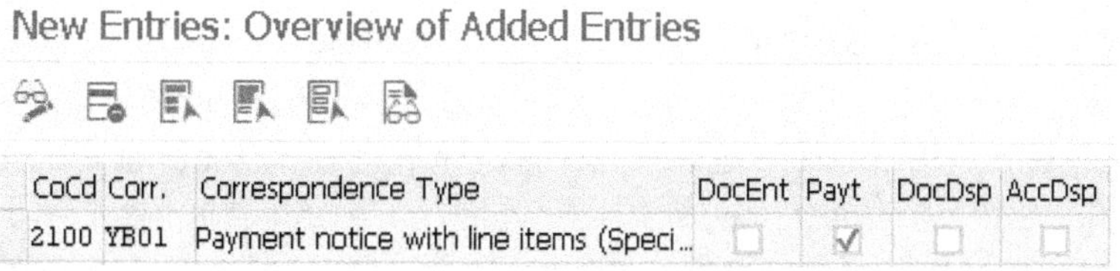

New Entries: Overview of Added Entries

CoCd	Corr.	Correspondence Type	DocEnt	Payt	DocDsp	AccDsp
2100	YB01	Payment notice with line items (Speci...	☐	☑	☐	☐

Figure 7.61: Configuring Call-Up Functions for New Correspondence Types

> **i** You can select only 'payment notices' for payment transactions; but, you can select account statements in all other functions. Also, you do not make a specification for the bill of exchange charges statement, as you cannot select the statement of bill of exchange charges: it is created automatically, for your customers, if bill of exchange charges were posted.

The last of piece of configuration is to create the forms for correspondence: the forms can be SAPscript-based or PDF-based.

7.3.7 Forms for Correspondence

As regards the forms for correspondence, you can maintain the settings using the following menu path. In both the cases, you need to complete two activities: 1. Define Forms for Correspondence and 2. Define Form Names for Correspondence Print.

- *SAPscript-based forms*: SAP Customizing Implementation Guide > Financial Accounting > Financial Accounting Global Settings > Correspondence > SAPscript-Based Forms.
- *PDF-based forms*: SAP Customizing Implementation Guide > Financial Accounting > Financial Accounting Global Settings > Correspondence > PDF-Based Forms.

> **i** You can also attach payment media (say, bank transfers that you send to your business partner together with their account statement or dunning notice) by making appropriate settings using the menu path: SAP Customizing Implementation Guide > Financial Accounting > Financial Accounting Global Settings > Correspondence > Attached Payment Media. The pre-requisite is that you have configured the payment methods and house bank determination, in the system.

This completes our discussion on correspondence. Let us now understand how to integrate SAP S/4HANA with SAP Shared Service Center.

7.4   Integration of SAP S/4HANA with SAP Shared Service Center

SAP's *Shared Service Framework* (SSF) serves as the software infrastructure underlying shared services developments, which are available across a range of functional areas, in one or a number of installed SAP systems. For companies which have offices located across numerous geographical locations, the implementation of a *Shared Services Center* (SSC) offers the possibility of integrating and unifying standard business procedures, which are common throughout the larger organization. This business benefits include reduced processing costs and improved efficiency & transparency. It also helps in quick and easy implementation of updates and best practices, across the organization at the same time.

The front end of an SSC may not always be in the same system. For example, there may be users whose own underlying business process (such as FI posting) are requested and processed by an SSC on a central system (that is, the system where the *CRM Interaction Center* or other applicable front end application is installed), but executed in a different, connected application system (such as SAP ERP). The SSF facilitates such interconnection, and cooperation across systems.

Project Dolphin

BESTM does not want to make use of SAP's shared service framework as the company's branches are all situated in USA except the two entities in India.

You can find the configuration relating to the foundation activities of SSF in the menu path: SAP Customizing Implementation Guide > Processes and Tools for Enterprise Applications > Shared Services Framework. You will then use SAP Customizing Implementation Guide > Financial Accounting > Financial Accounting Global Settings > Integration of SAP S/4HANA with SAP Shared Service Center > Activate Shared Services Center, to specify whether you want to integrate SAP S/4HANA with the on-premise release or the cloud release of SAP SSC.

We will not be configuring SAP's SSF for BESTM.

This completes our discussion on SAP shared services and the 2nd set of FI global settings.

7.5   Conclusion

We started this Chapter, with the discussion on documents in SAP. You learned that the transaction, in SAP, is based on the document principle and a unique document is generated every time you make a posting in the system. You understood the document structure: the document header and line items. You also understood that you can post a document only when it is 'complete' with the debit=credit. Then, you learned about the various document types, how they are used to differentiate business transactions, and how they control the posting to the appropriate account types (namely, vendor, customer, or G/L). You, then, went on to learn document number ranges: its assignment (internal and external), validity, change and deletion. You also learned about copying one or more number range to company code(s) and to fiscal year(s). Then, you learned about posting keys and how a posting key controls the entering / processing of a line item in a document. You, also, learned about the (a) screen variants that are required for document entry, (b) rules for changing a document and (c) bar code entry. You, then, moved on to understand tolerance and tolerance groups, how to define a tolerance group, how to use tolerance group in document processing and how to assign users to a tolerance group. You learned about defining texts / text identifiers for documents and their usage, in document processing. You learned how to make the required settings to make the system propose default values like default document type / posting key (for a transaction), value date and fiscal year. You went, further, on to understand the details of recurring entries, account assignment models and defining the run schedules. You also learned about document parking and how to change the posting date of a parked document. You, finally, learned about account document archiving: using the account type life and document type life.

You learned about inflation accounting: what is inflation, and when to use inflation accounting. You learned that the inflation accounting is the process of adjusting the financial statements of a company to show the real financial position, during periods of high inflation. During the discussion, you learned about defining and configuring the settings for inflation index, TBE variant, inflation key, inflation methods and inflation calculation.

You, then, moved on to discuss the correspondence in SAP. You learned that the correspondence function is to set the system up for mailing letters, for corresponding with your business partners and for internal purposes. You learned that the standard correspondence, in SAP, included account statements, balance confirmations, document extracts, payment notifications and so on. You went on to learn what is a correspondence type, how to define a new correspondence type, assigning print programs to correspondence types, how to denominate a particular company code as 'correspondence company code' and setting up of call-up functions to specify which correspondence types can be selected online, while executing certain business functions (like document entry, payment settlement etc).

You, at the end of the Chapter, learned about the SAP Shared Services Framework and how to integrate SAP S/4HANA with SAP Shared Service Center.

This completes our discussion on the 2nd set of the FI global settings that included documents, inflation accounting, correspondence and integration with SAP Shared Service Center. We are, now, ready move on to the next Chapter, to discuss the 3rd set of FI global settings, namely taxes.

8 FI Global Settings - III

Previously, in <u>Chapter 6</u>, we discussed the 1st set of FI global settings namely fields, ledgers, fiscal year, posting period, parallel accounting, integration of CO with FI, and company code global parameters. Later, in <u>Chapter 7</u>, we discussed the 2nd set of settings relating to documents (types, numbering, posting keys, variants for document entry, rules for changing documents, tolerance groups, texts for document entry, default values, recurring entries, document parking, archiving etc), inflation accounting, correspondence and integration of SAP S/4HANA with SAP Shared Services Center. Now, in this Chapter, we shall discuss the 3rd and final set of FI global settings consisting of tax on sales and purchases, and withholding tax.

You can use SAP FI (FI-G/L, FI-A/P and FI-A/R) for tax management involving calculation, posting, adjustment, and reporting of taxes. Using SAP, you can manage taxes at the (a) national level, as in countries like Europe or South Africa, or (b) regional and jurisdictional level as in USA, or (c) combined national and regional levels, as in Canada and India.

You will make the tax configuration, in the system, at the country level, as all legal entities in the same country need to follow the same taxation policies and GAAP, while preparing their financial statements. This ensures that any new company code that is created in that country can, then, automatically use the tax configuration of that country. The system allows you to either define the tax rates internally within SAP or fetch them from an external taxation system (like, Vertex), that is interfaced to your SAP system. You will store the tax configurations, in SAP, in the form of tax calculation procedures and tax codes, assign these procedures to different countries, and the company codes - in a particular country - can use the procedure that is relevant for that country in tax processing. You will maintain the tax rates in the tax codes for the various tax types, and define the tax calculation method in the tax calculation procedure.

SAP supports multiple taxation types: sales tax, tax on sales and purchases, and withholding tax (including extended withholding tax):

- The *'tax on sales and purchases'* (also known as *'sales and use tax'*) are levied on invoiced goods and services payable, in accordance with the principles of VAT (*value-added tax*). The *'sales tax'* is imposed on sales of goods, with the customer (buyer) bearing the tax while the vendor (seller) acts only as the collection agent for the area (jurisdiction in USA). While the sales tax is levied on the sale of taxable goods on the transactions occurring within a state, the *'use tax'*, on the other, is imposed on the purchaser; the seller is not liable for this tax. The purchaser pays the use tax on all the goods and services he uses, and the tax is remitted to the local tax authority where the goods or services have been consumed. The transaction is generally subject to either sales or use tax, but seldom both. The taxes on sales and purchases apply to input tax, output tax, additional tax, and acquisition tax:
  - While the *'input tax'* is calculated using the net invoice amount and charged by the vendor, the *'output tax'* is calculated using the net price of products and charged to the customer. It is possible to offset input tax against output tax and pay only the balance.
  - The *'additional tax'* is levied in addition to the taxes on sales and purchases, and is normally country specific (say, investment tax in Norway or sales equalization tax in Belgium).
  - The *'acquisition tax'* is applied by the receiving party at the local rate and is due on the cross-border movement of goods and services within the EU (European Union). You can also post this input tax.

> **i** In Italy, companies are required to register all their customer and vendor invoices about their sales and purchases, and to create tax reports according to VAT types. In the Philippines, the main tax on sales and purchases is VAT. In China, the taxes on sales and purchases include VAT, luxury tax, service tax and flat-rate tax. In Egypt, tax authorities impose tax on transactions pertaining to the sale and purchase of tangible property; as a general rule, the buyer pays the tax and the supplier collects the tax on behalf of the tax authorities; the transactions are generally subject to sales or purchases tax, but not both. In the Czech Republic, VAT is levied on most sales and purchases of goods and services; vendors are required to print VAT documents about down payments they receive from the customers. In Venezuela, the VAT is known as impuesto al valor agregado (IVA).

- In *'withholding tax'*, you withhold a portion of the invoice amount as tax from the vendor and report/pay the tax so withheld, directly to the taxation authorities. SAP supports two options in withholding tax: *classic withholding tax* and *extended withholding tax* (EWT). SAP recommends to go ahead with EWT if you are new to withholding tax. Alternatively, if you are already on classic withholding tax, you can changeover and migrate to EWT (refer Section 8.2.8, for more details on changeover).

Here, in this Chapter, we shall discuss the configuration settings, tax calculation procedure, posting, and reporting relating to two types of taxes namely, the tax on sales and purchases, and withholding tax. We shall also discuss the withholding tax changeover, from classic withholding tax to EWT.

Let us start with the tax on sales and purchases.

8.1   Tax on Sales and Purchases

As already outlined, SAP's FI-G/L, FI-A/P and FI-A/R application components support the calculation and posting of *tax on sales and purchases*. The 'tax on sales and purchases' is calculated through condition methods using a *tax calculation procedure* (also called as *tax procedure or calculation procedure*), tax codes, and jurisdiction codes, if any, and the system posts the tax so calculated during document processing:

- You define the tax rates for each of the tax codes, and associate them with the tax types in a tax procedure.
- The system makes use of the country-specific tax (calculation) procedures, and calculates the quantity of tax using tax codes that contain the tax rates. You will normally use the tax procedure, as a template to define the tax codes. The tax (calculation) procedure contains the necessary access sequence of the condition records (from the condition tables) for actual calculation of the tax.
- As the tax procedure is tagged to a G/L account master record, a particular tax procedure is accessed whenever that G/L account is used in document processing.
- The system posts the tax amount, thus calculated to the same side of the G/L containing the tax code. However, when there is an exchange rate difference due to tax adjustments in a foreign currency, the difference is normally posted to the specific accounts for exchange rate differences.

> **i** You can, of course, specify (for each company code) that the exchange rates for tax items can also be entered manually or determined by the posting / document date, and the resulting differences posted to a special account.

Technically, there are three ways by which you can calculate the tax on sales and purchases in SAP, and they are:

1) <u>Non-jurisdiction method</u>: this method is seldom used; here, you allocate percentage rates to tax codes.

2) <u>Jurisdiction method</u>: here, you manually define the jurisdiction for every region in which you do business. You will, then, use the standard tax calculation procedure (TAXUSJ for USA, for example) for calculating the tax.

3) <u>Jurisdiction method with external tax calculation system</u>: in this method, you automate tax compliance activities by using an interface to an external tax calculation system (like, Vertex). We will be discussing in detail about this method in the following Sections, as this is the method the BESTM corporate group (Project Dolphin) wants to follow for calculation of tax on sales and purchases in USA.

You can group all the configuration settings that are required for setting up of tax on sales and purchases into three broad areas:

- Basic settings
- Calculation
- Posting

Let us start with the basic settings for external calculation of taxes on sales and purchases.

8.1.1 Basic Settings

The important basic setting includes the following configuration activities:

- Check Calculation Procedure
- Assign Country to Calculation Procedure
- Check and Change Settings for Tax Processing
- Specify Structure for Tax Jurisdiction Code
- External Tax Calculation

The settings under 'External Tax Calculation' include several other steps like:

- Define Number Ranges for External Tax Returns
- Define Physical Destination
- Define Logical Destination
- Testing the Tax Data Retrieval in the External Tax System
- Activate External Tax Calculation
- Activate External Updating
- Define Connection with External Tax System

Let us start with the first configuration activity namely 'Check Calculation Procedure'.

8.1.1.1   Check Calculation Procedure

The *tax calculation procedure* contains the necessary specifications for the calculation and posting of taxes on sales and purchases, for various countries. Every calculation procedure groups several *tax types* together into a condition type (for example, output tax or input tax), and determines the calculation rules for it. The system brings up the condition types when you define a *tax code*. The *condition type,* within the calculation procedure, determines for which amount the individual condition types are to be calculated: this can be the base amount (total of the expense items and the revenue items) or a sub-total. The specifications necessary for calculating and posting the tax are defined in the condition type and *account key*.

> **i** It is recommended that you do not make changes to the default condition types and calculation procedures, provided in the standard SAP system. Check the standard condition types and calculation procedures, to see if you can use them without changing for your requirements; change only if you cannot make use of the standard settings as such.

Project Dolphin

The BESTM management has recommended to the project team to make use of the standard settings in, SAP, for tax calculation and posting for both India and USA. Accordingly, the project team has decided to use the standard tax calculation procedure TAXIN for India. As regards USA, the team has planned to use the procedure 0TXUSX, to take care of the jurisdiction requirement of taxation and also interfacing with the external tax system, Vertex.

Using this activity, you can check and, if necessary, change existing procedures for tax calculation to meet your own needs:

i.   Use the menu path: SAP Customizing Implementation Guide > Financial Accounting > Financial Accounting Global Settings > Tax on Sales/Purchases > Basic Settings > Check Calculation Procedure, and you will be taken to 'Select Activity' pop-up screen (You can also use Transaction OBYZ: this will take you directly to the 'Condition Element' pop-up screen, instead of the 'Select Activity' pop-up that you will reach using the menu path; the difference being the description and order of the activities).

ii.   Double-click on 'Define Procedures' on the 'Select Activity' pop-up screen.

iii. You will land on the 'Change View "Procedures": Overview' screen (you may also use Transaction OBQ3 to reach this screen directly). You will see several standard procedures listed under 'Procedures', with two listings for USA (0TXUSX and TAXUSJ) and one for India (TAXIN). The USA-specific procedure 0TXUSX provides for a standard tax interface system, that can pass all necessary data on to an external tax system. Use the other procedure TAXUSJ, when no external tax system is to be interfaced.

> **i** The external tax system (Vertex, Taxware etc) determines tax jurisdictions, calculates taxes, and returns the calculated results to SAP. This data transfer occurs during master data address maintenance to retrieve the appropriate tax jurisdiction codes; it also, occurs during order and invoice processing out of FI, MM, and SD, when tax rates and tax amounts are retrieved. The tax interface system also updates third party tax files with the appropriate tax information for legal reporting purposes.

iv. Now, select the row containing 0TXUSX and double-click on 'Control Data' on the left-hand side 'Dialog Structure'. You will, on the next screen, see the 'Reference Step Overview' under 'Control Data' (Figure 8.1):

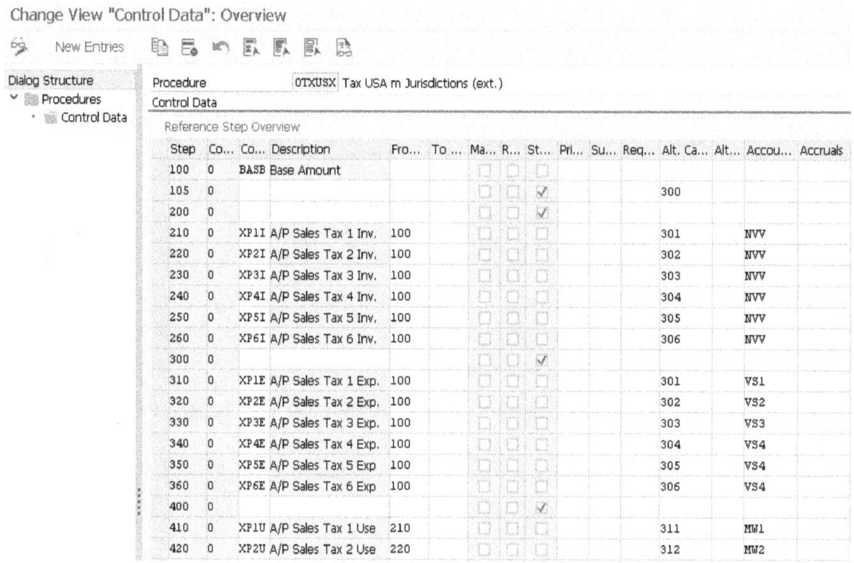

Step	Co...	Co...	Description	Fro...	To ...	Ma...	R...	St...	Pri...	Su...	Req...	Alt. Ca...	Alt...	Accou...	Accruals
100	0	BASB	Base Amount												
105	0							✓				300			
200	0							✓							
210	0	XP1I	A/P Sales Tax 1 Inv.	100								301		NVV	
220	0	XP2I	A/P Sales Tax 2 Inv.	100								302		NVV	
230	0	XP3I	A/P Sales Tax 3 Inv.	100								303		NVV	
240	0	XP4I	A/P Sales Tax 4 Inv.	100								304		NVV	
250	0	XP5I	A/P Sales Tax 5 Inv.	100								305		NVV	
260	0	XP6I	A/P Sales Tax 6 Inv.	100								306		NVV	
300	0							✓							
310	0	XP1E	A/P Sales Tax 1 Exp.	100								301		VS1	
320	0	XP2E	A/P Sales Tax 2 Exp.	100								302		VS2	
330	0	XP3E	A/P Sales Tax 3 Exp.	100								303		VS3	
340	0	XP4E	A/P Sales Tax 4 Exp.	100								304		VS4	
350	0	XP5E	A/P Sales Tax 5 Exp	100								305		VS4	
360	0	XP6E	A/P Sales Tax 6 Exp	100								306		VS4	
400	0							✓							
410	0	XP1U	A/P Sales Tax 1 Use	210								311		MW1	
420	0	XP2U	A/P Sales Tax 2 Use	220								312		MW2	

Figure 8.1: Tax Procedure 0TXUSX with the Control Data

- While the 'Step' denotes the sequence of conditions within a procedure, the 'Counter' denotes the *access sequence* within a condition.
- The 'Condition type' is used for different functions: in pricing, for example, the *condition type* lets you differentiate between different kinds of discount; in output determination, between different output types such as order confirmation or delivery note; in batch determination, between different strategy types. The condition type BASB represents the tax base, XP** the A/P sales tax, XR* the A/R sales tax, MWAS the output tax, MWS1 the sub-total and so on.
- The fields 'From Step' and 'To Step' represent the reference steps, from where the system obtains the value (like, the base amount) for calculation.

- The 'Manual only', 'Required', and 'Statistical' check-boxes can be used to indicate whether a condition is to be included for calculation when it is entered manually, whether the condition is required (or mandatory) when the system carries out pricing, or whether the calculated discount / surcharge is only for statistical purposes and not to be included in the pricing.

- The column 'Print Type' denotes the print ID for the condition lines. Enter 'a' to print condition lines at the item level (general), and 'A' to print them at the totals (general) level. You may leave this as blank, if you do not want to print them. You also have other options like 'B', 'C' & 'D' for printing the totals with specific instructions. Similarly, you get other options 'b', 'c' and 'd' for printing at the line item level.

- The 'Subtotal' column controls whether and in which fields the condition amounts or sub-totals (for example, a customer discount or the cost of a material) are stored. If the same fields are used to store different condition amounts, the system totals the individual amounts. These condition amounts or sub-totals are used as a starting point for further calculations. You may, for example, want a sub-total of all the discounts included in the pricing of a sales order. A blank here denotes that there will be no separate sub-totals.

- If the 'Requirement' is fulfilled (SY-SUBRC = 0), the relevant step is executed, which can be a step in the case of a pricing procedure or an access in the case of access sequence. A possible requirement would be, for example, that a difference should be made between document currency and local currency.

- The 'Alt. Calc.Cndn Amnt' (Alternative Calculation of Condition Amount) represents the alternative routine, to the routine in the standard system that determines a condition: 281 denotes excise tax, 300 represents the tax from the external system, 301 to 316 taxes and so on.

- The 'Alt. Cndn Base Value' represents the routine for determining the condition basis as an alternative to the standard one.

- The 'Account Key' identifies the type of G/L account. It enables the system to post amounts to certain types of revenue account. For example, the system can post freight charges (generated by the freight pricing condition) to the relevant freight revenue account. MW1 to MW4 denotes sales tax, MW5 is output tax GST, MWS the output tax, J1F the VAT, NAV the non-deductible input tax and so on.

- The 'Accruals' column denotes the account key that is used to identify various types of G/L accounts for accrual or provisioning. Using this account key, the system can post amounts to certain types of accruals accounts; for example, rebate accruals which are calculated from pricing conditions, can be posted to the corresponding account for rebate accruals.

Now that you have understood control data details of the calculation procedure 0TXUSX, let us move on to understand the condition types.

v. Go back the (ii) step; double-click on 'Define Condition Types' on the 'Select Activity' pop-up screen. You may also use Transaction OBQ1.

vi. On the 'Change View "Conditions: Condition Types" Overview screen (Figure 8.2), select a row (say, AR4) and double-click on the same.

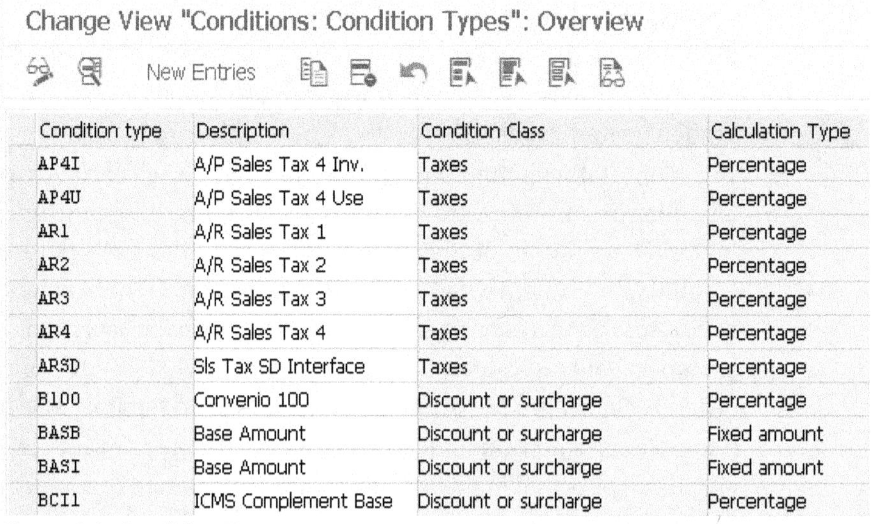

Change View "Conditions: Condition Types": Overview

Condition type	Description	Condition Class	Calculation Type
AP4I	A/P Sales Tax 4 Inv.	Taxes	Percentage
AP4U	A/P Sales Tax 4 Use	Taxes	Percentage
AR1	A/R Sales Tax 1	Taxes	Percentage
AR2	A/R Sales Tax 2	Taxes	Percentage
AR3	A/R Sales Tax 3	Taxes	Percentage
AR4	A/R Sales Tax 4	Taxes	Percentage
ARSD	Sls Tax SD Interface	Taxes	Percentage
B100	Convenio 100	Discount or surcharge	Percentage
BASB	Base Amount	Discount or surcharge	Fixed amount
BASI	Base Amount	Discount or surcharge	Fixed amount
BCI1	ICMS Complement Base	Discount or surcharge	Percentage

Figure 8.2: Condition Types

vii. You will reach the 'Change View "Conditions: Condition Types" Details' screen (Figure 8.3). You can notice that the 'Condition Type' AR4 is referring to the 'Access Sequence' MWST.

viii. Under 'Control Data1':
- You will see D (Taxes) has been selected as the 'Condition Class'. An 'A' here will denote discount or surcharge, B the price, C the expense reimbursement and so on.
- In 'Calculation Type', the 'Percentage' (A) has been selected. This can be fixed amount (B), quantity (C), gross weight (D) and so on.
- The 'Condition Category' has been selected as 'Tax' (D); the possible entries include cash discount (E), insurance (C), freight (F) and so on.
- The 'Rounding Rule' has been set to 'Commercial'.

ix. You will also see other data blocks namely, 'Group condition', 'Changes which can be made', 'Master Data'. 'Scales', 'Control Data 2' and 'Text Determination'.

Change View "Conditions: Condition Types": Details

New Entries

Condition Type	AR4	A/R Sales Tax 4		Access Sequence	MWST	Tax Classification
						Records for Access

Control Data 1

Condition Class	D	Taxes	Plus/Minus		positive and negative
Calculation Type	A	Percentage			
Condition Category	D	Tax			
Rounding Rule		Commercial			
Structure Condition		None			

Group Condition

Group Condition	☐	Group Cond. Routine	
RoundDiffComp	☐		

Changes which can be made

Manual Entries		No limitations	Amount/Percent	✓
Header Condition	☐		Quantity Relation	☐
Item Condition	✓		Value	✓
Delete	☐			

Master Data

Proposed Valid-From		Today's date	Pricing Procedure	
Proposed Valid-To		31.12.9999	Delete from DB	Do not delete (set the deletion
Ref. Condition Type			Condition Index	☐
Ref. Application				

Figure 8.3: Details of Condition Type AR4

x. Now, go back to step (ii) and double-click on 'Access Sequences' on the 'Select Activity' pop-up screen, to understand the configuration settings relating to access sequences.

xi. You will be taken to 'Change View "Access Sequences": Overview' screen (Figure 8.4). You can also use Transaction OBQ2 to reach this screen directly.

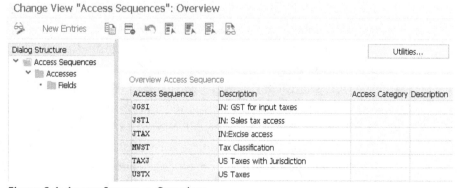

Change View "Access Sequences": Overview

New Entries

Dialog Structure
- ✓ Access Sequences
  - ✓ Accesses
    - • Fields

Utilities...

Overview Access Sequence

Access Sequence	Description	Access Category	Description
JGSI	IN: GST for input taxes		
JST1	IN: Sales tax access		
JTAX	IN:Excise access		
MWST	Tax Classification		
TAXJ	US Taxes with Jurisdiction		
USTX	US Taxes		

Figure 8.4: Access Sequence Overview

xii.   Select a row (say, USTX) and double-click on 'Accesses' on the left-hand side dialog-box.

xiii.   You will now be taken to the 'Change View "Accesses": Overview screen. Select a row and double-click on 'Fields' on the left-hand side.

xiv.   On the ensuing 'Change View "Fields": Overview' screen, you will see the 'Field Overview' table (Figure 8.5):

Figure 8.5: Fields Overview for Access USTX

- The name of the condition record is shown in the 'Condition' column.
- The 'I/O' column shows the symbol that indicates how the document data is used for the condition access, and how the data that is determined when the access is transferred back to the document. The 'arrows' indicate the direction of the data transfer. The 'equal' sign (=) stands for an access with a direct value or an initial value. The 'tools' symbol indicate that, when setting up pricing, the data transfer must be ensured by adapting the system using formulas and requirements. A green LED indicates automatic processing. A red LED signifies that data needed for correct processing is missing, for that particular line.
- The 'Document Structure' column specifies an internal table in which condition information about documents is stored.
- The 'Document Field' column determines the data dictionary characteristics for new fields in data dictionary structures. The reference fields are necessary for the generation of data dictionary structures for conditions and information structures. A reference structure and a reference field must always be entered.
- The 'Const. Value Source' field shows the value which the system automatically assigns to a field when it accesses the condition record.
- The 'Init' (Initial value allowed) check-box has two functions when you customize access sequences: first, it restricts the system from accessing the condition if the field in the document header/item is blank or 0; second, it

allows an initial value to be returned during automatic return transfer of data that was determined by the access.

- The 'Access Type' represents the processing type in access. The processing type determines how the corresponding field is used for the condition access. You can mark a field as belonging to the fixed (blank) or free key part (A) or as not relevant for the access (B) or as the data field is from condition table (C). All the fields defined, as data fields, for the definition of condition tables are automatically marked with an access type.
- The 'Priority' column represents the characteristics which can be used as fields, when you create condition tables or document fields for pricing. You can enter values from 01 (very high) to 99 (very low). The valuation controls how the system selects from the condition records determined from an access with a free key part. The more fields that are filled with a high priority in the key of a condition record, the more likely it is to be used for the document. If no two fields have the same value, then the access is guaranteed to determine exactly one condition record.

This completes our discussion on calculation procedure. The next task is to assign a country to the calculation procedure.

8.1.1.2   Assign Country to Calculation Procedure

Using this activity, you enter the key for the calculation procedure, per country, that determines the conditions that are allowed per document and that defines the sequence of the conditions in the document. We have already ensured, in the previous Section 8.1.1.1, that the calculation procedure we enter here contains the necessary specifications for calculating and posting the taxes on sales and purchases.

The steps to assign a country to a tax calculation procedure include:

i.   Use the menu path: SAP Customizing Implementation Guide > Financial Accounting > Financial Accounting Global Settings > Tax on Sales/Purchases > Basic Settings > Assign Country to Calculation Procedure. You may also use Transaction OBBG.

ii.   On the 'Change View "Assign Country -> Calculation Procedure": Overview' screen, enter TAXIN in the 'Proc.' column for India and 'OTXUSX' for USA (Figure 8.6).

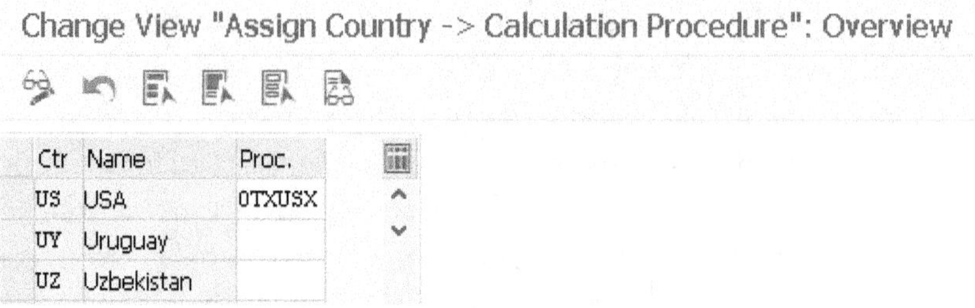

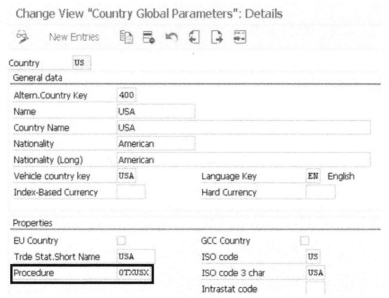

Figure 8.6: Assigning Country to Tax Calculation Procedure

> **i** You can also assign a tax calculation procedure to a country, while configuring the global parameters for that country. To do this, use Transaction OY01, and on the resulting 'Change View "Country Global Parameters": Details' screen, enter the tax procedure (Figure 8.7).

Figure 8.7: Tax Calculation Procedure in Country Global Parameters

Now that we have assigned India and US to the respective tax calculation procedures, let us move on to check (and change, if required) the settings for tax processing.

8.1.1.3   Check and Change Settings for Tax Processing

In this activity, you make the necessary specifications for posting taxes, by specifying tax type, whether not deductible, posting indicator etc., under a 'process key'.

> The *process keys*, with the most important characteristics for tax amounts, have already been set in the standard system. Do not change the standard settings. Check whether you can use these process keys for your company, without making a change. If you cannot use the standard settings, use new process keys and enter them in your calculation procedure.

Project Dolphin

The project management team has recommended using the standard process keys for tax processing. Accordingly, no new process key will be created for BESTM.

The following are the steps to check and change settings for tax processing:

i. Use the menu path: SAP Customizing Implementation Guide > Financial Accounting > Financial Accounting Global Settings > Tax on Sales/Purchases > Basic Settings > Check and Change Settings for Tax Processing. You may also use Transaction OBCN.

ii. On the 'Change View "Tax Processing in Accounting" Overview' screen, select a row (say, MW1) containing the process key ('Proc') and double-click to see the settings:

iii. On the 'Change View "Tax Processing in Accounting" Details' screen (Figure 8.8):

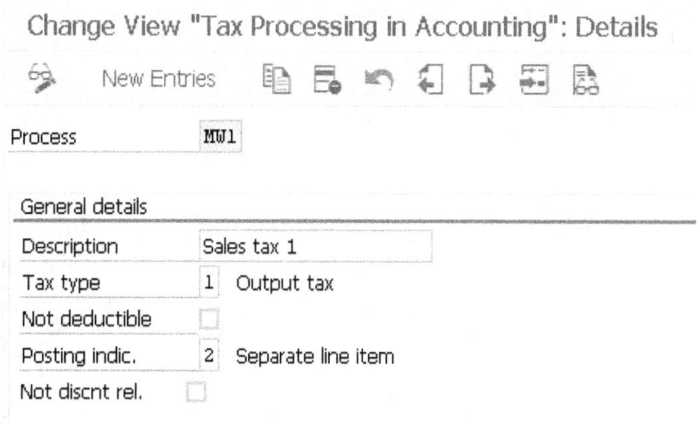

Change View "Tax Processing in Accounting": Details

New Entries

Process   MW1

General details

Description   Sales tax 1
Tax type   1   Output tax
Not deductible ☐
Posting indic. 2   Separate line item
Not discnt rel. ☐

Figure 8.8: Settings for Tax Processing

- You will see the 'Tax Type'. For the process key MW1 (Sales Tax 1), output tax (option1) has already been selected. The other options are: input tax (2), additional tax (3), and not relevant to tax (4).
- If you select the 'Not deductible' check-box, then tax amounts are marked as not deductible.
- The *posting indicator* ('Posting indic.') enables you to specify whether the tax amount is posted separately or distributed to expense / revenue items. You need to select option 1 when no posting is required, 2 to post separate line items and 3 to distribute to relevant revenue/expense items. Refer to Table

8.1, for the details as to for which process keys you should select 2 or 3 as the posting indicator.

Condition Type	Process Key	Posting indicator	Condition Type	Process Key	Posting Indicator
XP1I	NVV	3	XP1E	VS1	2
XP2I	NVV	3	XP2E	VS2	2
XP3I	NVV	3	XP3E	VS3	2
XP4I	NVV	3	XP4E	VS4	2
XP5I	NVV	3	XP5E	VS4	2
XP6I	NVV	3	XP6E	VS4	2
XP1U	MW1	2	XR1	MW1	2
XP2U	MW2	2	XR2	MW2	2
XP3U	MW3	2	XR3	MW3	2
XP4U	MW4	2	XR4	MW4	2
XP5U	MW4	2	XR5	MW4	2
XP6U	MW4	2	XR6	MW4	2

Table 8:1 Posting Indicator for Process Keys

- The 'Not discnt rel.' (not discount relevant) indicator is set only for Canada. When selected, the system does not take into account the corresponding tax amount during tax base determination.

Since we are not creating any new process key, we just saw the details of the settings in the above steps. In case, you want to create your own process key, select the appropriate row containing a standard process key in step (ii), click on 'Copy As' and change the settings as required by following the details in step (iii) above.

The next configuration step, under basic settings, is to specify structure for jurisdiction code.

8.1.1.4 Specify Structure for Tax Jurisdiction Code

Using this configuration step, you will determine the structure of the *tax jurisdiction code*, which is used for calculating taxes that are defined below the Federal level as in USA, Canada etc. You can divide the tax jurisdiction code into a maximum of four levels (for example, state/county/city/district), so that you can define the tax rate and also calculate the tax value per level. If a jurisdiction entry exists for a calculation procedure, then the system switches automatically to the tax jurisdiction code method of processing the tax using that calculation procedure. Here, you can also specify whether taxes are to be calculated at line item level or cumulated at 'tax code/tax jurisdiction code' level.

i You can make changes to your tax jurisdiction code structures in the quality system (Q system) and transport the same to the productive system (P system). Whenever you make changes to your jurisdiction code structures in the Q system, you need to create a transport request to the P system. Before this transport proceeds from the Q system to the P system, the system performs a *veto check* to ensure that the transport can proceed; else, it is blocked.

The veto check first looks to see whether there are any US tax postings in the table BSET. If yes, the transport will be blocked; else, the system permits the changes to be made in the Q system and communicates to the P system, that the changes can be made there, the transport proceeds and the changes are made in the P system.

If you are using the US external tax solution, and your tax jurisdiction code structure is not 2/3/4/1, you need to change the configuration of your tax jurisdiction code structure using the 'Specify Structure for Tax Jurisdiction Code' (Transaction OBCO) configuration step. Before you do so, verify your tax jurisdiction code structure with your external tax application provider. You cannot change the configuration of your tax jurisdiction code structure, if you are using the US internal tax calculation solution. Also, you cannot change the configuration of your tax jurisdiction code structure, if you have any US tax postings in your P system. If you have any US tax postings in your P system, any changes you make to your tax jurisdiction code structure in your Q system are not transported to your P system. The system will trigger the veto block, if you attempt to do such a transport.

Project Dolphin

BESTM management has requested the project team to properly structure the tax jurisdiction code identification in the SAP system to make it fully compatible with the external tax solution Vertex. The project team, accordingly, indicated that the tax on sales and purchases for all the US-based company codes is to be calculated at the line item level.

To configure structuring of tax jurisdiction code (USA), you need to follow steps listed below:

i.   Use the menu path: SAP Customizing Implementation Guide > Financial Accounting > Financial Accounting Global Settings > Tax on Sales/Purchases > Basic Settings > Specify Structure for Tax Jurisdiction Code. You may also use Transaction OBCO.

ii. On the 'Change View "Jurisdiction Code Structure": Overview screen (Figure 8.9), make the required settings for the 'Schema' 0TXUSX. The schema (also known as *costing sheet*), in Figure 8.9, is nothing but the tax calculation procedure:

   • The tax jurisdiction code is automatically divided into four parts with whose help the tax percentage is determined per tax authority. The field 'Lg' denotes the length of each part. Since BESTM wants to use Vertex, you need the structure as 2/3/4/1 that corresponds to the state code, county code, city code and local code.

> **i** If you use Taxware as your external tax solution for USA, then you need to have the jurisdiction structure set as 2/5/2/0. And, it will be 2/2/5/5 for ONESOURCE (Sabarix).

Change View "Jurisdiction Code Structure": Overview

New Entries

Schema	Name	Lg	Lg	Lg	Lg	Tx In
OTXUSX	External US Tax Jurisdiction Code	2	3	4	1	✓

Figure 8.9: Specifications for Tax Jurisdiction Structure

- Select 'Tx In' check-box to indicate that the tax needs to be determined by line item. When this indicator is selected, taxes are calculated on a line-by-line basis within MM and FI applications. This is necessary in order to pass on material specific data, such as material number and quantity, as well as to make sure that the taxes can be reported on a line item basis. A cumulative tax amount, based on the combination of tax code and jurisdiction does not apply here.

> **i** If the taxes are entered manually in the transaction, then 'calculate tax' function is deactivated and the check is performed on a cumulative basis, regardless of the fact that you have configured to determine taxes by line item, by selecting the 'Tx In' check-box.

iii.   'Save' the details when completed.

> **i** Though there are a couple of third-party or external tax application solutions for USA, the most important ones are Vertex, Taxware and ONESOURCE (known earlier as Sabrix) that you can interface with your SAP system, for tax calculation and reporting. Of all the three, Vertex is, by far, the most widely used one followed by Taxware and ONESOURCE in that order.

Vertex is the leading third-party tax application solution that is widely used to interface with SAP systems in USA. The solution simplifies tax management, streamlines taxation activities and automates tax calculations. It makes sales and use tax a seamless part of every transaction, connecting with your SAP systems. It manages tax in 11,000+ U.S. tax jurisdictions. With Vertex for SAP, the tax is calculated during the invoice or checkout process, based on the latest product taxability rules, ensuring that every transaction has the proper tax jurisdiction assignment to trigger the accurate tax calculation rules. Each new address entered is automatically cleansed for errors and the full 9-digit zip code and Tax Area ID is assigned. Vertex's integration benefits include: reliable tax rules and rates, calculation and compliance, exemption management, reporting, seamless integrations to SAP systems, flexible deployment options (on-demand, cloud, or on-premise).

Taxware provides global transaction-based tax calculation and compliance system, helping companies to correctly calculate and remit sales and use taxes in the United States, General Sales Tax (GST) and provincial taxes in Canada, and value-added taxes (VAT) in Europe, Asia, and South America. It integrates enterprise resource planning (ERP) solutions, point of sale systems, custom-billing applications, or web stores. It tracks and analyses tax law changes in approximately 13,000 state and local jurisdictions in the United States, and in nearly 200 other countries around the globe. It provides an end-to-end solution, offering clients the products and services they need to determine the correct rate for sales, use, and value-added tax compliance.

Thomson Reuters ONESOURCE Indirect Compliance tax solution (also known as Sabrix, earlier) streamlines the tax compliance process with real-time rates and rules, customizable tools, and support for e-filing plus powerful data reconciliation, adjustment, and reporting capabilities. You can choose federal, state, county, city, or district as necessary to meet the unique needs of your US business. For organizations operating globally, ONESOURCE Indirect Compliance automates the way you manage value-added tax (VAT), goods and services tax (GST), and other international tax returns and statutory filings.

With the specifications of the tax jurisdiction structure for the tax calculation procedure 0TXUSX, we have completed the important generic configurations under basic settings. From the next step onwards, let us configure the settings for interfacing the external tax application with your SAP system. But before doing that, let us understand how the tax is calculated when you connect your SAP system, with an external tax application solution.

8.1.1.5 External Tax Calculation Process - Overview

You can configure the SAP system to manage the tax sales and purchase (sales and use tax) in USA, either through manual calculation or automatically using an external tax application solution such as Vertex, Taxware etc.

In the automatic tax calculation environment, the external software - through built-in tax interfaces - determines tax jurisdictions, calculates taxes, and returns this information to the SAP system for updating in FI. Here, the interface determines the appropriate jurisdiction codes from the master data in SAP. Then, during order and invoice processing in FI, MM, and

SD application components, the system applies the appropriate tax rates and processes the tax values. The interface, then, updates the third-party tax software with the tax information for legal reporting. There must be an established connection between the SAP system and the external tax application using SAP's RFC *(Remote Function Call)* and tRFC *(Transaction RFC)*. SAP uses the standard tax calculation procedure 0TXUSX and the standard SD pricing procedure RVAXUS in external tax calculation.

In the tax calculation process in SAP MM and SAP FI, the sales or use tax can be computed by the system for each line item of the purchase order or invoice. Therefore, you need to maintain a ship-to tax jurisdiction code, as the system requires information as to where taxes are being charged. The tax calculation process includes the following steps:

1) The system looks for the ship-to tax jurisdiction code that resides on the plant, cost center, asset master, internal order, or project (WBS). If no jurisdiction code is maintained (on the asset, order, or project), then, the jurisdiction code of the responsible cost center maintained on the asset, order, or project defaults into the purchase order or invoice verification document at the time of document creation. This jurisdiction code is used as the ship-to destination.

> **i** In addition to the ship-to destination, taxability is also influenced by the ship-from destination. A jurisdiction code can be maintained in the vendor master record. This jurisdiction code is used as the ship-from tax destination.

2) The jurisdiction codes are automatically retrieved from the external tax package (say, Vertex) during creation or change of a plant, cost center, or vendor master record. This occurs after the address information has been entered on the master data. For an asset, internal order, and project, you can select F4 on the jurisdiction code field, to return a list of valid jurisdictions from the external tax system.

3) MM and FI use country and tax code to read the tax condition records. The tax calculation procedure 0TXUSX contains condition formulas (300 - 306, 311-316) which invoke the tax interface system.

4) Once the tax interface system is invoked, a communication structure is populated with the necessary data needed by your partner tax packages to calculate taxes.

5) This communication structure is passed to your tax partner's (say, Vertex) API through the RFC. The tax partner's API passes this data to its tax calculation package, which in return passes the tax data back to its API.

6) The tax partner's (say, Vertex) API, then, passes this information back to tax interface system onward to MM and FI.

> **i** The tax amounts and statistical rates apply to each of up to six levels of jurisdiction, denoted by condition types: XP1E - XP6E, XP1I - XP6I, and XP1U - XP6U.

In SAP SD, the sales orders and invoices reflect the tax applicability of each item and the total tax due on each line item is computed within the sales document. The appropriate tax amounts and tax rates are determined for both orders and invoices. There are several parameters that influence the tax amounts and tax rates determination, including delivering country (origin), tax class of the ship-to partner, tax class of the material being shipped, tax calculation date, jurisdiction code from ship-to-party (customer), jurisdiction code from ship-from address (plant), point-of-order acceptance and point-of-order origin. During the tax calculation:

1. The Jurisdiction codes are automatically retrieved from the external tax package during creation or change of a customer master record or a plant. This occurs after the address information has been entered on the master data.

> **i** SAP defaults the ship-from jurisdiction maintained on the plant as the point-of-order acceptance, and defaults the ship-to jurisdiction maintained on the customer as the point-of-order origin.

2. The system uses the country, customer tax indicator, and material tax indicator to read the tax condition records. During pricing execution in sales order processing, the system exits the normal pricing upon recognizing a condition type 1 (UTXJ). The tax condition records are then read using the country and tax code maintained in the pricing condition record.

3. The tax procedure 0TXUSX and the SD pricing procedure RVAXUS contain condition formulas (300 - 306 or 500, 510, 301 - 306 for document Max Tax calculation) which invoke the tax interface system.

4. Once the tax interface system is invoked, a communication structure with header and item data is filled with the necessary information needed by the partner's (say, Vertex) tax package to calculate taxes. This communication structure is then passed to your partner's (say, Vertex) API via an RFC.

5. The partner's (say, Vertex) API passes this data to its tax calculation package. The appropriate tax is calculated and returned back to the partner's (say, Vertex) API and then to the tax interface system.

6. These tax amounts and rates are applied to the SD document item's pricing at each of up to six levels of jurisdiction denoted by the condition types (XR1 - XR6).

Now that we have understood the process of external tax calculation in SAP, let us move on to configure the rest of the basic settings, relating to external tax calculation. Let us start with the first activity of defining the number ranges for external tax returns.

8.1.1.6   Define Number Ranges for External Tax Returns

An *external tax document* is created when an SD, MM or FI document is successfully posted to FI. This external tax document is the entity name for tax relevant information for one particular document. This information is to be updated into the external audit register file for legal reporting purposes.

There are two configuration steps relating to external tax document: (1) defining the number ranges for external tax returns or documents (which we will see now in this Section) and (2) activating external updating (nothing but activating the external tax document) which we shall see in Section 8.1.1.11).

In this activity, define the required number ranges for external tax documents: you should define the number range interval 01 that will be used for numbering the external tax returns.

> **i** It is recommended to take a wide range for the number range interval 01, for example, an interval between 000000000001 and 999999999999.

To define the number ranges:

i.   Use the menu path: SAP Customizing Implementation Guide > Financial Accounting > Financial Accounting Global Settings > Tax on Sales/Purchases > Basic Settings > External Tax Calculation > Define Number Ranges for External Tax Calculation. You may also use Transaction OBETX.

ii.   On the ensuing screen, click on 'Change intervals' and maintain the details on the next screen.

iii.   You will notice that the current number (NR Status) is set to 0 by default. You need to initialize this to 1 by clicking on 'Change interval limit' button.

iv.   'Save' the details (Figure 8.10).

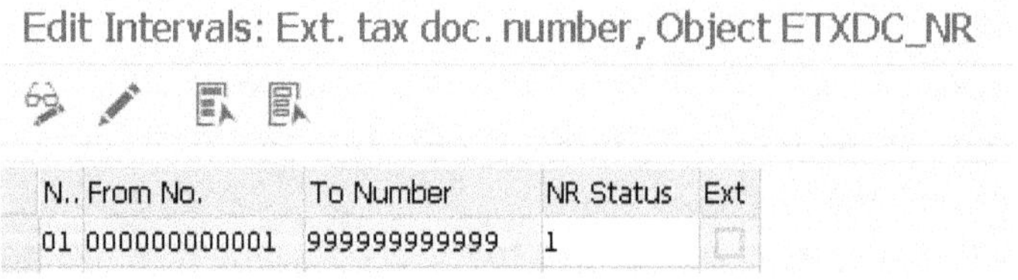

Edit Intervals: Ext. tax doc. number, Object ETXDC_NR

N..	From No.	To Number	NR Status	Ext
01	000000000001	999999999999	1	☐

Figure 8.10: Number Ranges for External Tax Returns

The next step is to define the physical destination for external tax calculation.

8.1.1.7 Define Physical Destination

The communication between the SAP system and an external tax application solution is established using RFC. Hence, you need to create an RFC destination, that specifies the type of communication and the directory path in which the tax package executable or shell scripts program is installed. You must set up the RFC destination as a TCP/IP communication protocol. The destination is user-defined. You need to be careful in making these settings as, many a time, this directory path setup is incorrectly configured and is a major area of concern.

> **i** The pre-requisite before carrying out this configuration activity is to ensure that the external tax system is already installed, configured and ready. You must also know the server path (provided by the supplier of the external system) on the target computer. As a user of SAP work process, you will require 'write' authorization for the external tax system's files.

Let us configure the physical destination as under:

i. Use the menu path: SAP Customizing Implementation Guide > Financial Accounting > Financial Accounting Global Settings > Tax on Sales/Purchases > Basic Settings > External Tax Calculation > Define Physical Destination, or Transaction SM59.

ii. On the 'Configuration of RFC Connections' screen, click on 'Create'.

iii. On the ensuing 'Create Destination' pop-up screen, enter a logical name for the RFC destination in the 'Destination' field (VERTEX or TAXWARE, for example), and select T (RFC connection to external program using TCP/IP), from the drop-down list for the field 'Connection type'. Press 'Continue'.

> **i** Enter the 'Destination' in upper-case letter (say, VERTEX).

iv. On the 'RFC Destination Vertex' screen, enter a short description in 'Description 1' under the 'Description' block.

v. Under 'Technical Settings' tab, you need to make the settings, for defining the directory path. There are two recommended methods (Figure 8.11) to define the directory path:

(1) <u>SAP and Tax Software Package reside on the same server</u>: If the SAP system and the external tax package were to reside on the same server, select 'Start on Application Server' radio-button (under 'Activation Type' data block), as the program location. In the field 'Program', under 'Start on Application Server' data block, specify the external tax package's executable or shell script program, along with the directory path in which it was installed.

(2) <u>SAP and Tax Software Package reside on different servers</u>: If the SAP system and the external tax package were to reside on different servers, then this is an explicit communication setup. Here, you need to select 'Start on Explicit Host' radio-button, under the 'Activation Type' data block. In the field 'Program', under 'Start on Explicit Host' data block, you now need to specify the external tax package's executable or shell script program along with the directory path in which it was installed. In the field 'Target Host', enter the host name of the server where the external tax package resides.

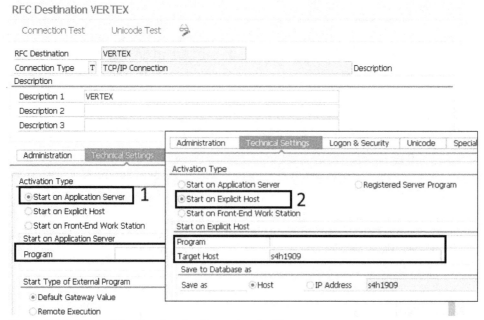

Figure 8.11: Physical Destination Configuration for Vertex

vi.   If necessary, set up the correct 'Gateway Host' and 'Gateway Service' under 'Gateway Options' block, and 'Save' the details.

vii.   You can test the connection by clicking on 'Connection Test'. If you encounter any errors, verify that the following conditions are true:

- The connection type is TCP/IP.
- Program location and host name are correctly specified.
- The directory path and the name of the executable program are correct.
- The Gateway host and service name is correctly specified.
- The external tax package has been installed correctly and is of the correct version.
- The external tax package's API for the SAP system tax interface is installed correctly and is of the correct version.
- The SAP system RFC libraries are of the correct version.

- The correct permissions are set for the user account.
- The user has read/write authority.

> **i** If this test fails, stop the installation and correct the errors before proceeding further. This test must be successful in order for the SAP system to communicate with the external tax package.

Now that we have defined the physical destination required for the correct functioning of the external tax application solution, it is time that we define the logical destination.

8.1.1.8   Define Logical Destination

To define the logical destination, use the menu path: SAP Customizing Implementation Guide > Financial Accounting > Financial Accounting Global Settings > Tax on Sales/Purchases > Basic Settings > External Tax Calculation > Define Logical Destination. SAP comes delivered with standard logical definitions which you can use as such (Figure 8.12).

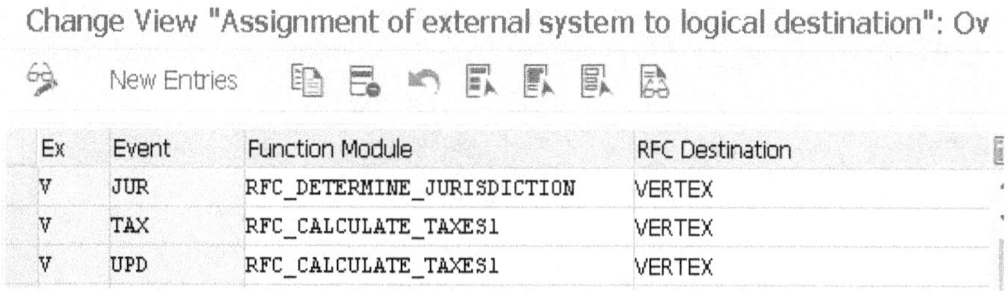

Change View "Assignment of external system to logical destination": Ov

New Entries

Ex	Event	Function Module	RFC Destination
V	JUR	RFC_DETERMINE_JURISDICTION	VERTEX
V	TAX	RFC_CALCULATE_TAXES1	VERTEX
V	UPD	RFC_CALCULATE_TAXES1	VERTEX

Figure 8.12: Logical Destination Configuration

Here, the column 'Ex' represents the external tax system identifier; V is used for Vertex. Under the column 'Event', you will see three business events namely JUR for determining jurisdiction, TAX for calculating taxes, and UPD for transmitting to the external system for updating. You need to enter the physical destination that you have defined in the previous configuration step (Section 8.1.1.7), in 'RFC Destination' field. 'Save' the details, when completed.

Now that we have defined both the physical and logical destinations, we need to test the tax data retrieval in the external system.

8.1.1.9   Testing the Tax Data Retrieval in the External Tax System

You must test the tax data retrieval in the external tax system, to ensure that the communication have been properly configured. In order to test the external tax system, dummy RFC-enabled function modules are available in the standard SAP system to simulate the external tax RFC functions. You can use the SAP Function Builder Test Utility (Transaction SE37), to test the RFC-enabled function modules (as listed out in Table 8.2):

Test Area	RFC-enabled Function Module
Jurisdiction code determination	RFC_DETERMINE_JURISDICTION
Tax calculation	RFC_CALCULATE_TAXES_DOC
Tax update	RFC_UPDATE_TAXES_DOC
Tax forced update	RFC_FORCE_TAXES_DOC

Table 8:2 RFC-enabled Function Modules to Test Tax Data Retrieval in External System

It is imperative to perform these tests and check the results, before continuing with the further configuration steps. With this, we are now ready to activate external tax calculation.

8.1.1.10 Activate External Tax Calculation

You will use this configuration step to define how the tax calculation procedure 0TXUSX accesses the external tax system, the external system ID, the RFC destination and the tax interface version so as to activate external tax calculation.

Let us define the settings in the system:

i.   Use the menu path: SAP Customizing Implementation Guide > Financial Accounting > Financial Accounting Global Settings > Tax on Sales/Purchases > Basic Settings > External Tax Calculation > Activate External Tax Calculation.

ii.   On the 'Change View "TTXD: View of External Systems": Overview' screen (Figure 8.13), enter the required details for the 'Schema' 0TXUSX:

Change View "TTXD: View of External System": Overview

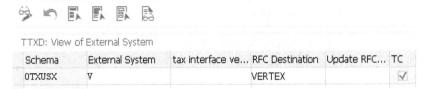

TTXD: View of External System

Schema	External System	tax interface ve...	RFC Destination	Update RFC...	TC
0TXUSX	V		VERTEX		☑

Figure 8.13: Settings for Activating External Tax Calculation

- Enter an identifier for the external tax system in 'External System' field: enter V for Vertex (and T for Taxware).
- Select the appropriate tax interface version in 'tax interface vers.' field. The tax interface version is the specific SAP API version, used by the external tax system for communicating with the SAP system. Each new SAP API version comes with new functions and usually corresponds to an SAP release. It is advisable that the external tax system supports the latest version. After you have installed the latest version of the external tax system API, you must set this field accordingly.

Leave this field as blank if the tax processing is to happen at the line item level as in our case for Project Dolphin; select TAXDOC00 if the tax calculation has to happen at the document level.

- Enter the 'RFC Destination' (VERTEX) which you have already configured in Section 8.1.1.7.
- Select the 'TC' check-box.

  If this customizing flag is NOT set: (a) If the tax jurisdiction code field is empty, the SAP System will attempt to determine a tax jurisdiction code, (b) If the tax jurisdiction code field contains a value, the SAP System checks this tax jurisdiction code against the respective address and (c) If this tax jurisdiction code is invalid, an error message is output.

  If this customizing flag is set: (a) If the tax jurisdiction code field is empty, the SAP System will attempt to determine a tax jurisdiction code, (b) If the tax jurisdiction code field contains a value, the SAP System checks this tax jurisdiction code against the respective address, and (c) If this check fails, the tax jurisdiction code for the respective address will be determined.

iii.   'Save' the details when completed.

You have now activated the external tax calculation in the system. However, a mere activation of external tax calculation is not sufficient; you also need to activate external updating for the tax data to be sent from FI to the tax interface. Let us complete that activity now.

8.1.1.11 Activate External Updating

Using this activity, you activate the updating facility for the external tax system. Once updated, the data is sent to the external system when the relevant items are posted to FI. Use the program RFYTXDISPLAY to display the current data.

To activate external updating:

i.   Use the menu path: SAP Customizing Implementation Guide > Financial Accounting > Financial Accounting Global Settings > Tax on Sales/Purchases > Basic Settings > External Tax Calculation > Activate External Updating.

ii.   On the 'Change View "View for Component EXTX": Overview' screen, select the 'Activ' check-box to activate external updating. This flag determines if an external tax document can be updated, into the external tax audit file for legal reporting purposes. The system reads this flag during the SD, MM and/or FI document posting process. If this flag is NOT set, the tax information is lost and there is no external tax document updated to the external audit file.

iii.   'Save' the settings (Figure 8.14).

Change View "View for Component EXTX": Overview

Component	To Year	Activ	
EXTX	2999	☑	^

Figure 8.14: Settings for Activating External Updating

The last activity, in basic settings, is to define the connection settings with the external tax application.

8.1.1.12 Define Connection with External Tax System

You can establish the connection to the external tax system (say, Vertex) using the settings defined in this step. As soon as you enter the missing logon data and 'Save' your entries, the system checks the connection to the external tax system. The result of the check is indicated in the 'Status' field and under 'Description'. Ensure that you have obtained the required logon data from the provider of the external tax system. The standard SAP system comes with an entry, in which an external tax system ID is filled and you are required to complete the remaining required fields.

To make the settings to define the connection with the external tax application system:

i.   Use the menu path: SAP Customizing Implementation Guide > Financial Accounting > Financial Accounting Global Settings > Tax on Sales/Purchases > Basic Settings > External Tax Calculation > Define Connection with External Tax System.

ii. On the 'Change View "Define Connection with the External Tax System": Overview' screen, you will see a row prefilled with the 'External Tax System ID' (Vertex). You now need to complete the entry in the other two fields: 'External Tax URL' and 'Trusted ID of Ext. System'; you have to obtain the details for both these fields from your external tax application partner, (Vertex, in this case).

iii. As soon as you enter the details and 'Save', the system will bring up the latest 'Status' along with the 'Description' for that status: when no connection is made the status will be 01 – Inactive; the other statuses include 02 – 'Activated, connection working', and 03 – 'Activated, connection not working' (Figure 8.15).

Change View "Define Connection with External Tax System": Overview

New Entries

Define Connection with External Tax System

External Tax System ID	External Tax URL	Trusted ID of Ext. System	Status	Description
Vertex ⌄			01	Inactive

Figure 8.15: Settings for Connection with External Tax System

This completes our discussion on the basic settings in configuring the tax on sales and purchases. Let us now move to on discuss the settings for tax calculation, in the next Section.

8.1.2   Calculation

You need to complete the following configuration settings in the system for calculation of tax on sales and purchases:

- Define Tax Codes for Sales and Purchases
- Assign Company Code to Document Date for Tax Determination
- Specify Base Amount
- Change Foreign Currency Translation

Let us start with the first activity of defining the required tax codes for sales and purchases:

8.1.2.1   Define Tax Codes for Sales and Purchases

For each country in which you operate, you need to define separate *tax codes* for sales/purchases. Each tax code contains one or more *tax rates* for the different *tax types*. If you have to report tax-exempt or non-taxable sales to the tax authorities, you need to define a tax rate with the value 0.

For each country, SAP delivers a calculation procedure (refer Section 8.1.1.1, for more details) for the tax calculation. The procedure comprises a list of all common tax types with rules for tax calculation. Check the standard tax codes shipped for your country and use them as such. You can add more tax codes, if necessary, and the recommended way will be to copy an existing one to create the new. Also, ensure that the tax accounts are defined for the automatic posting of taxes.

---

i   Do not delete or change any of the tax codes for sales/purchases tax and their definitions, as long as items with these tax codes already exist in the system. Otherwise, the system displays the tax amounts with incorrect tax rates, in the corresponding reports and determines incorrect amounts during a tax adjustment for payment transactions. If at all you want to change a tax code, do not use Transaction SM31 because the links to other tables are not maintained this way. Follow the menu path or use Transaction FTXP. Use transaction SM31 only for display purposes.

Project Dolphin

BESTM has indicated to the Dolphin project team that any decision to tax a particular transaction has to come from Vertex. As the tax calculation is from this external tax application, no user is required to enter the tax amount in SAP system. If that is not the case, BESTM wants to configure the system to issue a warning, if the tax amount entered by the user is different from the amount calculated automatically in Vertex. Also, no new tax code will be defined by the project team.

To maintain the tax codes:

i.   Use the menu path: SAP Customizing Implementation Guide > Financial Accounting > Financial Accounting Global Settings > Tax on Sales/Purchases > Calculation > Define Tax Codes for Sales and Purchases. Or, you may also use Transaction FTXP.

ii. On the 'Country' pop-up screen, enter the 'Country' (US), and press 'Continue'.

iii. On the next 'Maintain Tax Code: Initial Screen', enter the 'Tax Code' (say, I1) selected from the drop-down values. Press 'Enter'. If you want to create a new tax code by copying this, click on 'Copy'.

iv. On the 'Maintain Tax Code: Tax Rates' screen (Figure 8.16), you can see the details of the condition records, under 'Percentage rate' table, for the tax code I1. The plant's country (SD) or the company code's country (MM) along with the tax code, which was automatically determined from the SD/MM condition records, are used to read the tax condition records stored in table A003. The tax code can also be entered / changed, manually in both MM and FI.

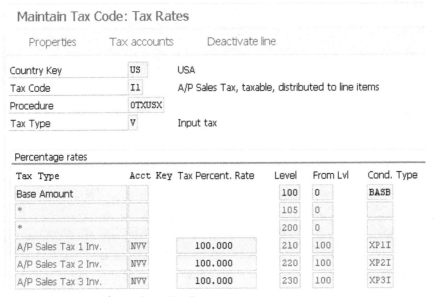

Figure 8.16: Tax Code Settings: Tax Rates

v.   Under 'Tax Percent. Rate' column, enter the tax percent rate as indicated in Table 8.3. For tax codes, which indicate use tax or self-assessment tax such as U1, the condition types XP1U - XP6U (marked with 100-) creates the credit entry to tax liability accounts and the condition types XP1I - XP6I (marked with 100) records the offset entry for the tax to the expense/inventory accounts.

Tax Code	Condition Type	Tax Percent. Rate	Tax Code	Condition Type	Tax Percent. Rate
I1 and I0	XP1I	100	U1	XP1I	100
I1 and I0	XP2I	100	U1	XP2I	100
I1 and I0	XP3I	100	U1	XP3I	100
I1 and I0	XP4I	100	U1	XP4I	100
I1 and I0	XP5I	100	U1	XP5I	100
I1 and I0	XP6I	100	U1	XP6I	100
O1 and O0	XR1	100	U1	XP1U	-100
O1 and O0	XR2	100	U1	XP2U	-100
O1 and O0	XR3	100	U1	XP3U	-100
O1 and O0	XR4	100	U1	XP4U	-100
O1 and O0	XR5	100	U1	XP5U	-100
O1 and O0	XR6	100	U1	XP6U	-100

Table 8:3 Properties for Tax Codes I0, I1, O0, O1 & U1

vi. You may click on 'Properties' (Figure 8.16) and understand the details (Figure 8.17):

- You will notice the 'Tax Type', for 'Tax Code' I1, has already been identified as V (input tax or A/P purchase tax). The other option is A, that is associated output tax or A/R sales tax.
- Leave the 'CheckID' check-box as blank indicating that the system will issue a warning (instead of an error message), when externally calculated and manually entered tax amounts differ with each other.

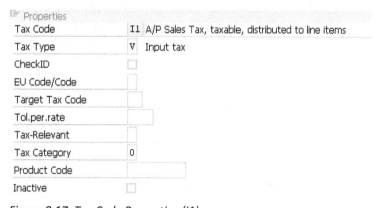

Figure 8.17: Tax Code Properties (I1)

- The field 'EU Code/Code' is not US-relevant; it classifies the output tax codes, that are to be taken into consideration in the *EU Sales List* (ESL). For taxation in Europe, set a proper value for in this code: if you do not set this as 1, then, none of the transactions with this code is picked up in the ESL, for that specific country. The value 1 denotes delivery of goods within the EU.

> **i** ESL listing (filed every month / quarter) provides you with the details of sales or transfers of goods and services to other VAT (value-added tax) registered companies within the EU. The tax offices in the EU use ESL, to confirm that VAT is being properly and fully declared by all parties in cross-border transactions.

- The 'Target Tax Code' is for deferred tax codes and is relevant in countries like France and Italy.
- The tolerance percentage rate ('Tol.per.rate') defines the rate that is accepted as tolerance, between automatically calculated value and a value that you have manually entered. The tolerance amount arises from the application of percentage rates to the amount determined by the system. If the difference between the tax value entered and the value calculated by the system is lower than the tolerance amount, the document is posted by the system and no warning or error message is issued.
- Leave 'Tax-Relevant' field as blank or select 0 to use the external system's decision engine, to decide whether a transaction is taxable or not. The other options include 1 and 2. When you select 1, the external tax application assumes that all the transactions are taxable; by doing so, you are ignoring the external system's tax decision engine, and the tax rates are, then, based solely on jurisdiction codes. When you select 2, the tax codes I0 and O0 force your SAP system, to impose a zero-tax bypassing the external tax system.
- Leave the 'Tax Category' field as zero or blank to indicate that this is a normal sales tax. The other options are consumer use tax (1), service tax (2), lease tax (3), and self-assessment use tax (4).
- You can use the field 'Product Code' to map the external tax system's product code in conjunction with SAP internal product code in table TTXP.
- When you select the 'Inactive' flag, you are effectively deactivating the tax code and that will be no longer displayed in the input help for making postings. However, you can still select this tax code from the input help for reporting (FI report RFUMSV00/RFUMSV10) purposes.

> **i** Although a deactivated tax code is not offered in the input help, you can still use that for posting, clearing, and making payments. The system does not check whether the tax code used is deactivated or otherwise.

vii.   You may use the Table 8.4 as a guideline to configure the properties of tax codes.

Tax Code	Tax Type	Details	Use	Condition Type	Tax-Relevant	Tax Category
O0	A (output tax)	A/P sales tax, exempt	Used mainly during sales orders, billings and A/R for (customer and/or material) exempt transactions	XR1 to XR6	2	0
I0	V (input tax)	A/P sales tax, exempt	Used mainly during purchase orders, invoice verifications and A/P for (ship-to location and/or material) exempt transactions	XP1I to XP6I	2	0
I1	V (input tax)	A/P sales tax, taxable, distributed to line items	Used mainly during purchase orders, invoice verification and A/P	XP1I to XP6I	0 or blank	0
O1	A (output tax)	A/R sales tax, taxable	Used mainly during sales orders, billings and A/R	XR1 to XR6	0 or blank	0
U1	V (input tax)	A/P use tax, self-assessed	Used mainly during purchase orders, invoice verifications and A/P	XP1I to XP6I / XP1U to XP6U	0 / 0	1 / 1

Table 8:4 Tax Code – Condition Type and other Properties

Tax codes I0 and O0 have the same settings as that of tax codes I1 and O1. The only difference is the 'Tax-Relevant' indicator set up that is part of the tax code properties. The 'Tax-Relevant' indicator must be set to 2 ('it is not relevant to tax; external system is not called') so that the tax rates and tax amounts are forced to zero for I0 and O0.

viii.   You can select a condition line (or row) and click on 'Deactivate line' to delete that.
ix.   'Save' the details, when completed.

With this understanding of the tax code settings, let us move on to assign the company codes to document date for tax determination.

8.1.2.2   Assign Company Code to Document Date for Tax Determination

You need to specify, per company code, whether the baseline date for determining the tax percentages should be the posting date (default date) or the document date, for processing taxes with jurisdiction codes. The system usually takes the posting date for this purpose. However, if you want the system to determine tax percentages on the basis of the document date, you must configure the system accordingly at this point.

Project Dolphin

BESTM management has instructed the project team to configure the system in such a way that the posting date will be the baseline date for tax calculation; it was also mentioned that the tax amounts should be translated using the exchange rate of the tax base amounts.

To assign a company code to document date for tax determination, use the menu path: SAP Customizing Implementation Guide > Financial Accounting > Financial Accounting Global Settings > Tax on Sales/Purchases > Calculation > Assign Company Code to Document Date for Tax Determination. Or, you may also use Transaction OBCK. Select the 'Tax Determ.with Doc.Date' check box, if you want the document date as the base date for processing taxes, against the appropriate company codes. Here for our case for BESTM, you will leave that as blank as we want the standard setting of posting date to be the base date and not the document date (Figure 8.18).

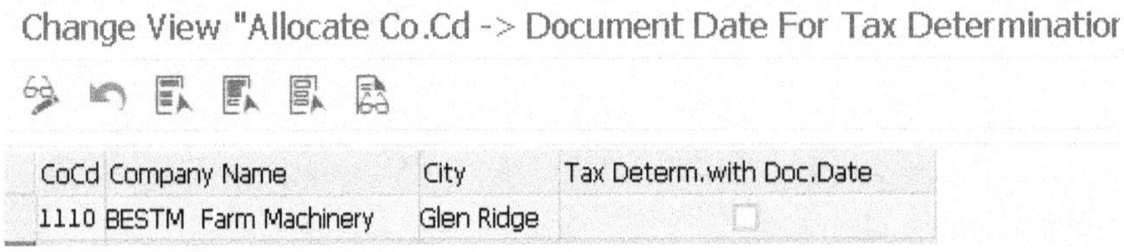

Change View "Allocate Co.Cd -> Document Date For Tax Determinatior

CoCd	Company Name	City	Tax Determ.with Doc.Date
1110	BESTM Farm Machinery	Glen Ridge	☐

Figure 8.18: Assigning Company Code to Document Date for Tax Determination

Let us now move on to specify the settings for base amount for tax determination.

8.1.2.3   Specify Base Amount

Using this activity, you will determine whether you want the cash discounts to be deducted from the *base amount,* used for calculating tax on sales/purchases for each company code. The rules for determining the base amount to calculate taxes on sales/purchases depend on the respective national laws. The base amount determination is controlled by using either the company code table or the jurisdiction code table.

We have already made the relevant settings for this specification when configuring the company code global parameters (Transaction OBY6) in <u>Section 6.8.1 of the Chapter 6</u>. In case you have not made the settings there, you can now do that by using the menu path: SAP Customizing Implementation Guide > Financial Accounting > Financial Accounting Global Settings > Tax on Sales/Purchases > Calculation > Specify Base Amount, or, Transaction OB69. If the cash discount amount should not be included in the base amount for tax calculation, select the 'TaxBaseNet' indicator (Figure 8.19). Since this is not the case for BESTM as the determination is controlled by the jurisdiction table, we have left the check-box as blank.

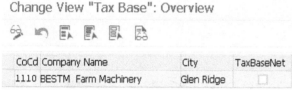

Change View "Tax Base": Overview

CoCd	Company Name	City	TaxBaseNet
1110	BESTM Farm Machinery	Glen Ridge	☐

Figure 8.19: Specification for Tax Base

With the base amount specification for tax calculation completed, we can now move on to define the final step in 'calculation' namely, the settings for translating the foreign currency.

8.1.2.4   Change Foreign Currency Translation

In general, the tax amounts are converted using the exchange rate that is specified by the tax base amounts. However, if you want to enter a different exchange rate when entering documents or you want to have the system propose one when you enter documents, then you need to make settings, here, in this activity. Here, you can specify, per company code, whether it is possible to enter a separate exchange rate for the currency conversion of the tax amounts, in the case of foreign currency postings. You can make settings that allows you to (a) enter tax exchange rate manually, or (b) determine exchange rate based on posting date, or (c) determine exchange rate based on document date or (d) determine exchange rate based on tax reporting date. If you do not make any settings here, then the currency is converted using the standard procedure with the exchange rate that is derived from base amounts in document (document header currency) and local currency, of the tax code.

To make the required settings, use the menu path: SAP Customizing Implementation Guide > Financial Accounting > Financial Accounting Global Settings > Tax on Sales/Purchases > Calculation > Change Foreign Currency Translation, or Transaction OBC8. On the next screen ('Change View "Foreign Currency Translation for Tax Items": Overview'), per company code, maintain the required values in the field 'Tx Crcy Tr' field. The options include leaving that as blank [exchange rate according to the document header (default)], or entering 1 (manual exchange rate entry possible), or 2 (exchange rate determined using posting date), or 3 (exchange rate determined using document date), or 4 (exchange rate determined using posting date with distribution of differences), or 5 (exchange rate determination according to tax reporting date). Since, BESTM wants to go ahead with the standard option of using the document header currency, you need to leave that field as blank (Figure 8.20).

Change View "Foreign Currency Translation for Tax Items": Overview

CoCd	Company Name	Tx Crcy Tr	Name
2100	BESTM Trucks		
2200	BESTM Other Construction		

Figure 8.20: Configuring Foreign Currency Translation of Tax

> **i** When using a different exchange rate other than the default (document header exchange rate), you need to define necessary account(s) for the purpose of handling exchange rate differences that may arise during transactions (refer Section 8.1.3.2).

With this, we have completed the required configuration settings for tax calculation. Let us, now, move on to discuss the settings that will be required to post the calculated tax.

8.1.3 Posting

You need to complete the following configuration activities to ensure that the tax amounts calculated are posted to the correct G/L accounts:

- Define Tax Accounts
- Define Account for Exchange Rate Difference Posting
- Assign Tax Codes for Non-Taxable Transactions
- Transfer Tax for Cross-Company Code Transactions

Let us start with the first activity of defining the required tax accounts in the system:

8.1.3.1 Define Tax Accounts

Using this activity, you need to specify the G/L accounts to which the different tax types are to be posted. The system determines these accounts for automatic postings.

The tax calculation procedure determines the G/L (tax liability) accounts to which the tax amounts are to be posted to accounting. The system uses three interconnected concepts (accounting key, process key and transaction key) in the tax calculation procedure to determine the desired G/L accounts per tax code:

- Each *'condition type'* amount, that is calculated during the tax procedure execution, is posted to the specified G/L account through the *accounting key* which is assigned for each relevant condition type in the tax procedure 0TXUSX.
- The *'process key'* defines, through the *posting indicator* (refer Section 8.1.1.3, for more details), if a tax liability account can be assigned for a tax code or if tax amounts are to be distributed to the expense items. You set the posting indicator to 2 (separate line item) for process keys for condition types XP1E - XP6E, XP1U - XP6U and XR1 - XR6. You set the posting indicator to 3 (distribute to relevant expense/revenue items) for process keys for condition types XP1I - XP6I.
- The *'transaction key'* defines the tax liability account (G/L account) and posting keys for line items that are created automatically during posting to FI. Only the process keys, which have the posting indicator not equal to 3, are also transaction keys. The transaction keys (or *account keys*) are defined per chart of accounts.

Here in this activity, you will verify that the transaction keys used, for example, VS1 - VS4 and MW1 - MW4 are already defined in the system. You can also confirm that transaction, such as NVV, with a posting indicator of 3 does not exist; this allows the system to book tax expense to the same account as the tax base. You need to configure (a) rules (tax liability account is the same for all tax codes or it differs per tax code), (b) G/L or cost element account assignment (liability or expense) and (c) posting keys (such as 40 or 50).

ℹ️ When you transport tax codes between different systems / clients, no tax accounts are transported. You need to manually adjust tax accounts in source and target system / client.

To define the tax G/L accounts:

i.   Use the menu path: SAP Customizing Implementation Guide > Financial Accounting > Financial Accounting Global Settings > Tax on Sales/Purchases > Posting > Define Tax Accounts. You may also use Transaction OB40.

ii.   On the 'Change View "Posting Key": Overview screen, you will see the posting key details (Debit / Credit) for each of the transaction keys ('Trs') in the 'Posting Key' table (Figure 8.21).

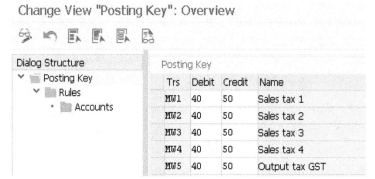

Figure 8.21: Details of Posting Keys for Transaction Keys

iii.   Select a transaction key row (say, MW1) and double-click on 'Rules' on the left-hand side 'Dialog Structure'.

iv.   You will see the 'Rules' table for the transaction MW1. You will see that the 'Tax Code' and 'Country' check-boxes have already been selected for the chart of accounts BEUS (Figure 8.22):

- The 'Country' flag, when selected indicates that the account determination for this transaction also depends on the country of the company code.
- The 'Tax Code' check-box, when selected, indicates that the account determination depends on a modification key for this procedure. For example, for posting the taxes on sales/purchases, you can determine an individual account per tax code; in this case, the tax code is used as the modification key for the account determination.

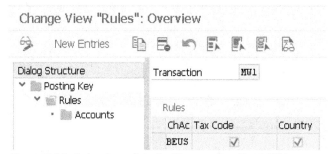

Figure 8.22: Rules Overview for Transaction Key MW1

v.   Now, select the chart of accounts BEUS row, and double-click on 'Accounts' on the left-hand side dialog structure.

vi.   You will be taken to the 'Change View "Accounts": Overview screen (Figure 8.23) on which you will see the G/L accounts that have been defined for the various tax codes ('Tx'), for the country US ('Ctr'), for the chart of accounts BEUS, for the 'Process key' (with the same name as that of the transaction key) MW1. Ensure that you have the G/L accounts defined, for each of the tax codes, for all the required process keys, for the selected chart of accounts (BEUS).

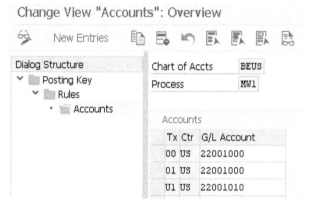

Figure 8.23: G/L Accounts for Tax Codes for a given Process Key

This completes our discussion on defining the G/L accounts for posting the tax. Let us move on to the next step, in which you will be defining the G/L accounts that are required to post the exchange rate differences.

8.1.3.2   Define Account for Exchange Rate Difference Posting

Remember, in Section 8.1.2.4, we have already configured the system in such a way to use the document header currency as the foreign currency for translation. While discussing that configuration step, we have also remarked that if you plan to use a different exchange rate other than the default settings (document header exchange rate), then, you need to define necessary account(s) for the purpose of handling exchange rate differences that may arise during transactions. We will not be requiring this step for BESTM, as it has been decided to use the default document header currency for forex translation.

With this, we can now move on to assign tax codes for non-taxable transactions.

8.1.3.3   Assign Tax Codes for Non-Taxable Transactions

Using this activity, you will define an input tax code and an output tax code per company code, to be used for posting non-taxable transactions (like, goods issue for delivery, goods movement, goods receipt for purchase order, goods receipt for production order, and order settlement) to tax-relevant accounts. You will also define a dummy tax jurisdiction code with the length, as defined earlier in Section 8.1.1.4. The veto check for this configuration step works the same way as it does for the 'Specify Structure for Tax Jurisdiction Code' configuration step.

To make the configuration settings:

i.   Use the menu path: SAP Customizing Implementation Guide > Financial Accounting > Financial Accounting Global Settings > Tax on Sales/Purchases > Posting > Assign Tax Codes for Non-Taxable Transactions. You may also use Transaction OBCL.

ii.   On the 'Change View "Allocate Co. Cd. -> Non-Taxable Transactions": Overview' screen (Figure 8.24), maintain the 'Input Tax Code (I0), 'Output Tax Code' (O0) and a default (dummy) 'Jurisdict. Code' (7700000000) for each of the US-based company codes, for taking care of non-taxable transactions.

iii.   'Save' the settings. You have now assigned, per company code, tax codes for non-taxable transactions.

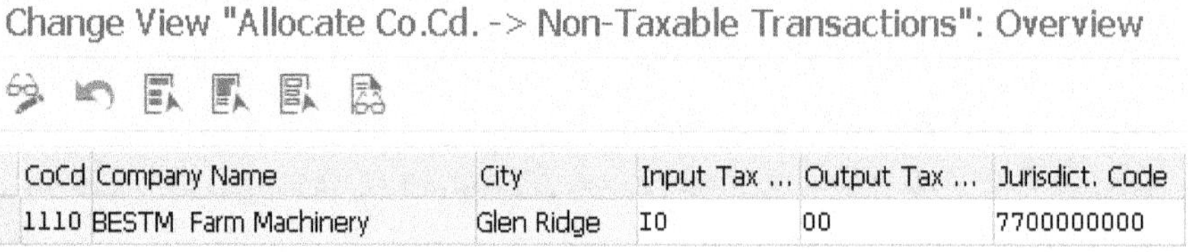

Change View "Allocate Co.Cd. -> Non-Taxable Transactions": Overview

CoCd	Company Name	City	Input Tax ...	Output Tax ...	Jurisdict. Code
1110	BESTM Farm Machinery	Glen Ridge	I0	O0	7700000000

Figure 8.24: Tax Codes for Non-Taxable Transactions

With this, we have just one more configuration step to be taken care of, to complete the settings for posting taxes on sales and purchases. Let us discuss that last step, now.

8.1.3.4 Transfer Tax for Cross-Company Code Transactions

Generally, in case of cross-company code transactions, the whole tax amount is posted to and displayed in the first company code only; the tax arising in other company codes is ignored. However, in certain countries such as Japan and Denmark, the tax amounts have to be displayed separately in each company code. In such cases, you will use this activity (menu path: SAP Customizing Implementation Guide > Financial Accounting > Financial Accounting Global Settings > Tax on Sales/Purchases > Posting > Transfer Tax for Cross-Company Code Transactions) to configure the settings so that the program (RFBUST10) creates a list of the respective tax amounts for which automatic transfer postings must later be made.

You will not carry out this activity as this is not required for BESTM.

This completes our discussion on posting of taxes, and that completes our discussion on tax on sales and purchases. We shall now move on to discuss the other important topic, the withholding tax.

8.2 Withholding Tax

By definition, '*withholding tax*' is the tax that is charged at the beginning of the payment flow in some countries (like the UK, USA, India, Argentina, Brazil etc). The party (vendor) that is subject to tax does not pay the withholding tax over to the tax authorities by himself, but a customer (that is authorized to deduct withholding tax, from invoices payable to the vendor) reduces the payment amount, by the withholding tax proportion, and pays the tax so withheld directly to the appropriate tax authorities (Figure 8.25). The withholding tax in India is known as the income tax in which the employer (customer) deducts the income tax at source (called as, TDS – Tax Deducted at Source) from the employee (vendor) and pays the same to the tax authorities. An exception to this rule is *self-withholding tax*: here, the vendor who is subject to tax, also has the right to pay the tax to the authorities by himself.

SAP provides two functions namely (a) *classic withholding tax* (all Releases of SAP) and (b) *extended withholding tax* (from SAP Release 4.0):

The '*classic withholding tax*' (or simply, the withholding tax) functionality has been in use before Release 4.0 of SAP R/3, supporting A/P. It allows withholding tax per vendor line item and supports the tax calculation during payment.

The '*extended withholding tax*' (EWT) supports assignment of more than one withholding tax type to a business partner and allows tax calculation for partial payments as well. In EWT, you can process withholding tax from both the vendor and customer view:

- In vendor (A/P) view, the vendor is subject to withholding tax, and your company code (as the customer) is liable to deduct and pay the withholding tax (as in Figure 8.25).
- On the other hand, in customer (A/R) view, your company code - as a vendor - is subject to withholding tax, and your customers deduct the withholding tax, from your invoice, for all the transactions you do with them, and then they pay the withholding tax to the tax authorities.

  In both cases, the business partner (of the person/entity subject to tax) deducts the tax and pays it over to the tax authorities. Due to legal requirements, the countries like USA, Argentina, Brazil, Chile, Columbia, Mexico, Peru, Venezuela, UK, Slovakia, Turkey, India, Philippines, South Korea and Thailand use EWT.

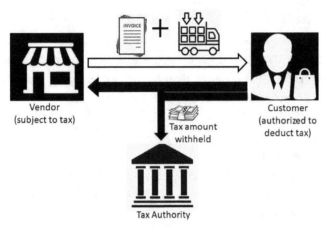

Figure 8.25: Overview of Withholding Tax

The Table 8.5 summarises the differences between the classic withholding tax and the EWT:

Functions		Classic Withholding Tax	EWT
Withholding tax on outgoing payment		X	X
Withholding tax on incoming payment			X
Withholding tax posting at time of payment		X	X
Withholding tax posting at time of invoice			X
Withholding tax posting on partial payment			X
Number of withholding taxes for each document item		Max. 1	Several
Withholding tax base	Net amount	X	X
	Modified net amount		X
	Gross amount	X	X
	Tax amount		X
	Modified tax amount		X
Rounding rule			X
Cash discount considered			X
Accumulation			X
Minimum/maximum amounts and exemption limits			X
Number assignment on document posting (certificate numbering)			X
Calculation formulas		X	X

Table 8:5 Tax Code Properties

> **i** For each company code, you can decide whether you want to use classic withholding tax or EWT. Since the EWT option includes all the functions of classic withholding tax, and as you can process withholding tax, from both vendor and customer views, SAP recommends EWT.
>
> If you have previously used classic withholding tax, and now wish to changeover to EWT, you must, first, convert the withholding tax data in all the affected company codes; do not activate EWT before you have converted the data. You may make use of the special tools from SAP, to complete the change-over from classic to EWT (refer Section 8.2.8, for more details).

The withholding tax is calculated and posted to the appropriate (withholding) tax accounts at different stages, depending on the legal requirements in each country. As a rule, withholding tax is posted at the same time that the payment is posted; in other words, the outgoing payment (A/P) or incoming payment (A/R) is reduced by the withholding tax amount. However, in countries such as Brazil, the Philippines, and Spain, the withholding tax can or must be posted, when the invoice is posted. This means that the amount of A/R or A/P is reduced by the withholding tax amount. The EWT, of course, supports both the above concepts.

The main concept in EWT is the distinction between *withholding tax type* and *withholding tax code*. While withholding tax types represent basic calculation rules, the specific features of these rules - in particular, the percentage rate - are represented by the withholding tax code. You can define any number of withholding tax codes for a given withholding tax type. If a particular transaction requires more than one kind of withholding tax, you can cover that in the system, by defining more than one withholding tax type. When entering a line item, you can enter the withholding tax data for each of these withholding tax types.

The EWT also supports special situations like:

- In some countries (such as Argentina and Italy), instead of the payment amount being reduced by the withholding tax amount, the withholding tax is posted as an offsetting entry to an expense account. You can make the relevant settings in the withholding tax code.
- Where cleared items are reset, the clearing document is automatically reversed, if it contains withholding tax data. For withholding tax types with accumulation, the accumulation base amount is adjusted, if the payment document is reversed.

Here, in this book, we will only be discussing the EWT, that too from A/P point of view relating to USA. Before we jump to the discussion relating to the configuration settings for EWT, let us first understand the process flow of withholding tax in A/P view.

8.2.1　Withholding Tax (A/P View) Process Flow

The withholding tax (A/P view) process flow is summarised as under:

A. During invoice entry:

- You can enter withholding tax data, for each vendor line item, during document entry. The withholding tax is calculated, and where necessary, posted, for each withholding tax type for which a withholding tax code is defined in the withholding tax dialog-box. If no withholding tax code exists for a withholding tax type, then, the system does not calculate withholding tax.

- You can also enter the withholding tax base and withholding tax amount manually (depending on the settings that you have made for the withholding tax type). If you do not enter any amount, the system calculates that automatically.

- Where withholding tax is to be calculated at the time of payment, only the base amount is calculated when the invoice is posted. Where withholding tax is to be calculated at the time of invoice posting, the system calculates both the base amount and the withholding tax amount when the invoice is posted.

B. During payment:

- For the withholding tax type 'posting at time of payment', the withholding tax is calculated using the data (withholding tax types, codes, and base amounts) in the open items. The payment amounts are reduced by the withholding tax amounts. This is irrespective of the fact, whether payment is made manually or automatically.

- Where outgoing payments are made manually or payment proposals created by the payment program are processed, the withholding tax amounts calculated can be displayed in detail, per open item. If you change your open item selection or edit the payment proposal, the withholding tax is recalculated automatically, if necessary.

C. The result is:

- When the payments are posted, the withholding tax data can be displayed in detail in the clearing line items in the payment document.

- The withholding tax types with posting on invoice entry are not taken into account for payments. This means that, there is no withholding tax data for these types in the payment document.

D. The prerequisite:

- For all the above to happen the pre-requisites include (a) activating EWT in your company code(s), (b) definition of withholding tax types and codes per country, (c) maintaining withholding tax type(s) in vendor master, (d) that the company code is authorized to deduct withholding tax for its vendors for these withholding tax types and (e) definition of withholding tax accounts for account determination.

Now, let us look at the various configuration steps that are required to set up the EWT in the system. These steps are grouped into:

- Basic Settings
- Calculation
- Company Code Settings
- Posting
- Advanced Compliance Reporting
- Withholding Tax Changeover

Project Dolphin

The BESTM management has requested the project team to complete the required configurations settings for EWT in the system.

Let us, first, discuss the various basic settings for configuring EWT in the system.

8.2.2   Basic Settings

Under the basic settings, you need to complete the following important configuration activities:

- Check Withholding Tax Countries
- Define Withholding Tax Keys
- Define Reasons for Exemption
- Check Recipient Types
- Change Message Control for Withholding Tax

Let us start with the first step of checking the withholding tax countries.

8.2.2.1   Check Withholding Tax Countries

You need a '*withholding tax country*' ID for printing the withholding tax form. The 'withholding tax country' is different from the country ID list, in the standard system, and follows the country requirements as per the withholding tax authorities. Since the list of country IDs prescribed by law may be different from the list in the system, you have to define the withholding tax countries again. Check the withholding country list delivered with the standard SAP system, and compare it with the official list from the tax authorities and make corrections, if necessary.

Use the menu path: SAP Customizing Implementation Guide > Financial Accounting > Financial Accounting Global Settings > Withholding Tax > Extended Withholding Tax > Basic Settings > Check Withholding Tax Countries. You may also use Transaction S_ALR_87003283.

On the 'Change View "Country Keys for Withholding Tax": Overview' screen (Figure 8.26), you will see the 'withholding tax country' ID or key in the field 'WCty' and the name of the country in the 'Description'. Compare this with the official list from the tax authorities and make corrections, if required.

Change View "Country Keys For Withholding Tax": Overview

New Entries

Ctr	WCty	Description
US	AA	Aruba
US	AC	Antigua&Barbuda
US	AE	Utd.Arab Emir.
US	AF	Afghanistan
US	AG	Algeria
US	AJ	Azerbaijan
US	AL	Albania

Figure 8.26: Country Keys for Withholding Tax

The second configuration activity is to define the withholding tax keys.

8.2.2.2   Define Withholding Tax Keys

The 'withholding tax keys' are the official descriptions of withholding tax codes, as defined by the particular country's national tax authorities. In a later step, you will assign these keys to each of the withholding tax codes. The withholding tax keys help you prepare the withholding tax returns.

SAP comes delivered with the standard settings for official withholding tax keys for (a) Argentina (here, the withholding tax keys delivered correspond to the keys used by the AFIP (state department for public revenues); in the DME files with the tax return to the AFIP created by the system, each record contains the relevant withholding tax key and that enables the AFIP to assign the withholding tax items), (b) India (the withholding tax keys correspond to the sections of the Income Tax Act according to which tax is withheld), (c) Italy (when you create a withholding tax return, the system displays the individual withholding tax items with the corresponding official withholding tax keys), (d) Colombia [the withholding tax keys delivered are used by the DIAN (state office for taxes and customs) in the withholding tax certificates; using this key, the system assigns the withholding tax items to the correct fields in the certificates], (e) Philippines [the withholding tax keys correspond to the ATC codes used by the BIR (office for internal revenues) in the withholding tax return], and (f) South Korea (the withholding tax keys are not used in any report delivered, but are used only for internal purposes).

Project Dolphin

The BESTM management has requested the project team to make use of the standard (a) withholding tax keys, (b) reasons for exemptions and (c) recipient types in the system for EWT.

To define the withholding tax keys:

i.   Use the menu path: SAP Customizing Implementation Guide > Financial Accounting > Financial Accounting Global Settings > Withholding Tax > Extended Withholding Tax > Basic Settings > Define Withholding Tax Keys. You may also use Transaction S_ALR_87003284.

ii. On the 'Determine Work Area: Entry' pop-up screen, enter the 'Country Key' (US) and 'Continue'.

iii. On the 'Change View "Official withholding tax key – Descriptions": Overview' screen (Figure 8.27), you will see the standard settings with the list of withholding tax keys ('Off. Key') along with the description ('Name'). The 'NatTaxCode' represents the official National Tax Code that belongs to each tax regulated by the federal tax office (AFIP in Argentina, for example). Using these values, you can classify every official tax key; this information is required on certain legal reports.

iv. You can use the standard settings as such, or use the 'Copy As' button to copy an existing entry and to create a new one. You can, of course, define a new key altogether. You will not be creating a new one as BESTM wants to go ahead with the standard settings.

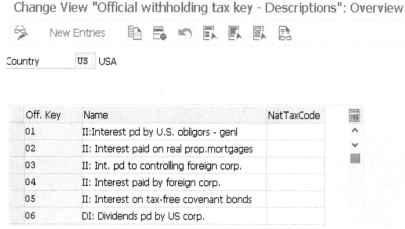

Change View "Official withholding tax key - Descriptions": Overview

New Entries

Country   US   USA

Off. Key	Name	NatTaxCode	
01	II:Interest pd by U.S. obligors - genl		
02	II: Interest paid on real prop.mortgages		
03	II: Int. pd to controlling foreign corp.		
04	II: Interest paid by foreign corp.		
05	II: Interest on tax-free covenant bonds		
06	DI: Dividends pd by US corp.		

Figure 8.27: Withholding Tax Keys

With the understanding of withholding tax keys, let us move on to discuss the reasons for exemptions.

8.2.2.3   Define Reasons for Exemption

Here, you can define 'reasons for exemption' from withholding tax. Once defined, you can enter this indicator, in the vendor master record or in the company code withholding tax master record information.

To define the reasons for exemptions:

i.   Use the menu path: SAP Customizing Implementation Guide > Financial Accounting > Financial Accounting Global Settings > Withholding Tax > Extended Withholding Tax > Basic Settings > Define Reasons for Exemptions. You may also use Transaction S_ALR_87003287.

ii.   On the 'Determine Work Area: Entry' pop-up screen, enter the 'Country Key' (US) and 'Continue'.

iii. On the 'Change View "Withholding tax type: Reasons for exemptions": Overview' screen (Figure 8.28), you will see a list of standard exemptions already available in the system. You may create your own exemption rows, if the standard settings are not sufficient.

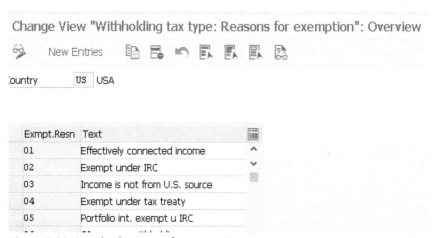

Figure 8.28: Standard Reasons for Exemptions

As already indicated, you can enter the exemption reason ID in the vendor master (Figure 8.29) in 'Exmpt. Resn' field, under 'Vendor: Withholding Tax' tab, for exempting a withholding tax type for a vendor.

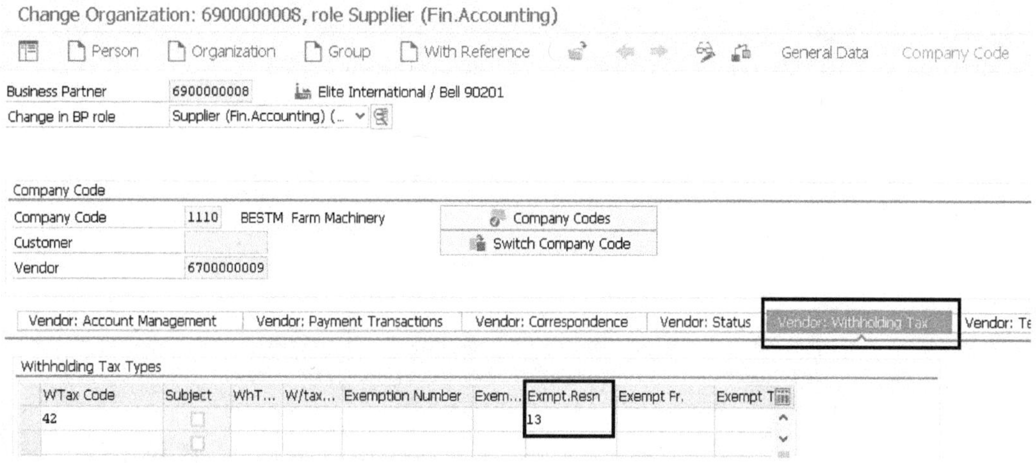

Figure 8.29: Entering Withholding Tax Exemption Reason Code in Vendor Master

Let us continue to configure the next activity under basic settings, checking of recipient types.

8.2.2.4   Check Recipient Types

You can use the withholding tax *recipient type* (for 1042 reporting in USA), to group vendors together according to particular characteristics such as occupations that may be subject to the same withholding tax type, but which are required to pay different percentage rates (as defined by the withholding tax code). You can use this activity to check the standard recipient types in the system, and create new if required.

Use the menu path: SAP Customizing Implementation Guide > Financial Accounting > Financial Accounting Global Settings > Withholding Tax > Extended Withholding Tax > Basic Settings > Check Recipient Types. Enter the 'Country Key' (US) on the ensuing pop-up screen and proceed to check the standard recipient types on 'Change View "Vendor types of recipient for withholding tax type": Overview' screen (Figure 8.30). We will not be creating any new recipient type ('Rec. Ty') for BESTM as the standard definitions can take care of the business needs of BESTM.

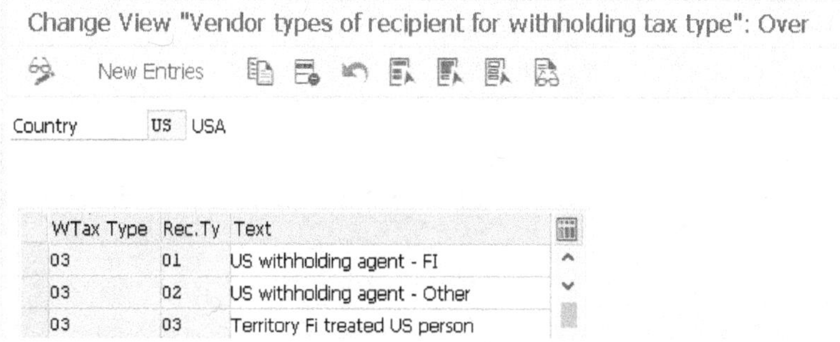

Figure 8.30: Standard Recipient Types

You can select the appropriate recipient type, while creating your vendor master. You will enter the recipient type in 'WhTaxC' field in the 'Withholding Tax Types' table in the 'Vendor: Withholding Tax' tab, under the 'Company Code' data (Figure 8.31).

Figure 8.31: Recipient Type in Vendor Master

The last configuration activity under basic settings is configuring the settings for message control for withholding tax.

8.2.2.5   Change Message Control for Withholding Tax

Using this activity, you can set system messages according to your specific requirements: You can, for example, determine if a message is issued as a note in the dialog-box or in the footer. You can also change or modify the settings to (a) change warnings into error messages or (b) switch off warnings and error messages. You will require different specifications for the online mode and for the batch input sessions processed in the background. It is also possible that you make the specifications for a client or, for individual users.

Project Dolphin

The project team, per instructions from BESTM management, has decided to configure the message control to be valid for all users. No separate configuration will be done for individual users. As far as the online transactions, the project team will configure message control in such a way, enabling the system to issue warning messages, but allowing users to correct errors, if any. In the case of batch input processing, the project team will make use of standard message control settings of SAP, for all the message numbers relevant for withholding tax processing.

You can configure the settings by:

i.   Using the menu path: SAP Customizing Implementation Guide > Financial Accounting > Financial Accounting Global Settings > Withholding Tax > Extended Withholding Tax > Basic Settings > Change Message Control for Withholding Tax.

ii.   On the 'Change View "Customizable Messages for Withholding Tax": Overview' screen, change the standard settings, say, from S (Note in the footer, standard) to W (Warning) for 'Online', for all the message numbers ('MsgNo'), and 'Save' the details (Figure 8.32).

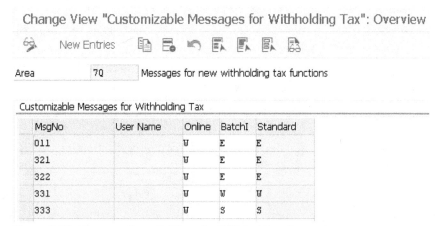

Figure 8.32: Message Type Settings for Withholding Tax

This completes our discussion on the basic settings. Let us move on to discuss the settings relating to calculation of withholding tax.

8.2.3 Calculation

Here, you will make the configuration settings relating to:

- Withholding Tax Type
- Withholding Tax Code
- Withholding Tax Base Amount
- Minimum and Maximum Amounts

Let us start with the first activity of maintaining the withholding tax types:

8.2.3.1 Withholding Tax Type

The 'withholding tax type' represents the various withholding taxes in a country. While it controls the essential calculation options for EWT, the withholding tax code only controls the percentage rate of the withholding tax. You will be required enter the withholding tax type in the customer/vendor withholding tax master data, and in the company code master data.

There are two categories of withholding tax type depending on when the withholding tax amounts are posted:

- Posting with Invoice
- Posting with Payment

Let us look at the settings that are required for both these categories; first, let us define the withholding tax types for invoice posting.

8.2.3.1.1   Define Withholding Tax Type for Invoice Posting

Here, you will define the withholding tax type for the posting at the time of entering an invoice. This withholding tax type does not have any effect on the payment. Since all the calculations for EWT are made in the first local currency of the respective company code, you have to maintain amounts in the company code country currency.

Project Dolphin

The Dolphin project team has decided to define the following withholding tax types to support invoice posting:

42: 1042 Compensation
FW: 1099 Federal Withholding Tax
IN: 1099 Independent Contractor Status
SW: 1099 State Withholding Tax
EW: Exempted from WT

BESTM has instructed the project team to make it possible to manually enter the withholding base amount / tax amount to provide some flexibility in transaction posting. However, these fields should not be made as 'required' in the relevant field status settings so as not to hold up a transaction. The management also indicated that the minimum / maximum amount settings to be done at the tax code level and not at the tax type level.

Follow the steps listed below to configure the withholding types for invoice posting:

i.   Use the menu path: SAP Customizing Implementation Guide > Financial Accounting > Financial Accounting Global Settings > Withholding Tax > Extended Withholding Tax > Calculation > Define Withholding Tax for Invoice Posting or Transaction S_ALR_87003264.

ii.   On the ensuing pop-up screen, enter the 'Country Key' (US) and proceed.

iii.   On the 'Change View "Define withholding tax: Posting at time of invoice": Overview' screen, click on 'New Entries' and maintain the details on the next screen (Figure 8.33).

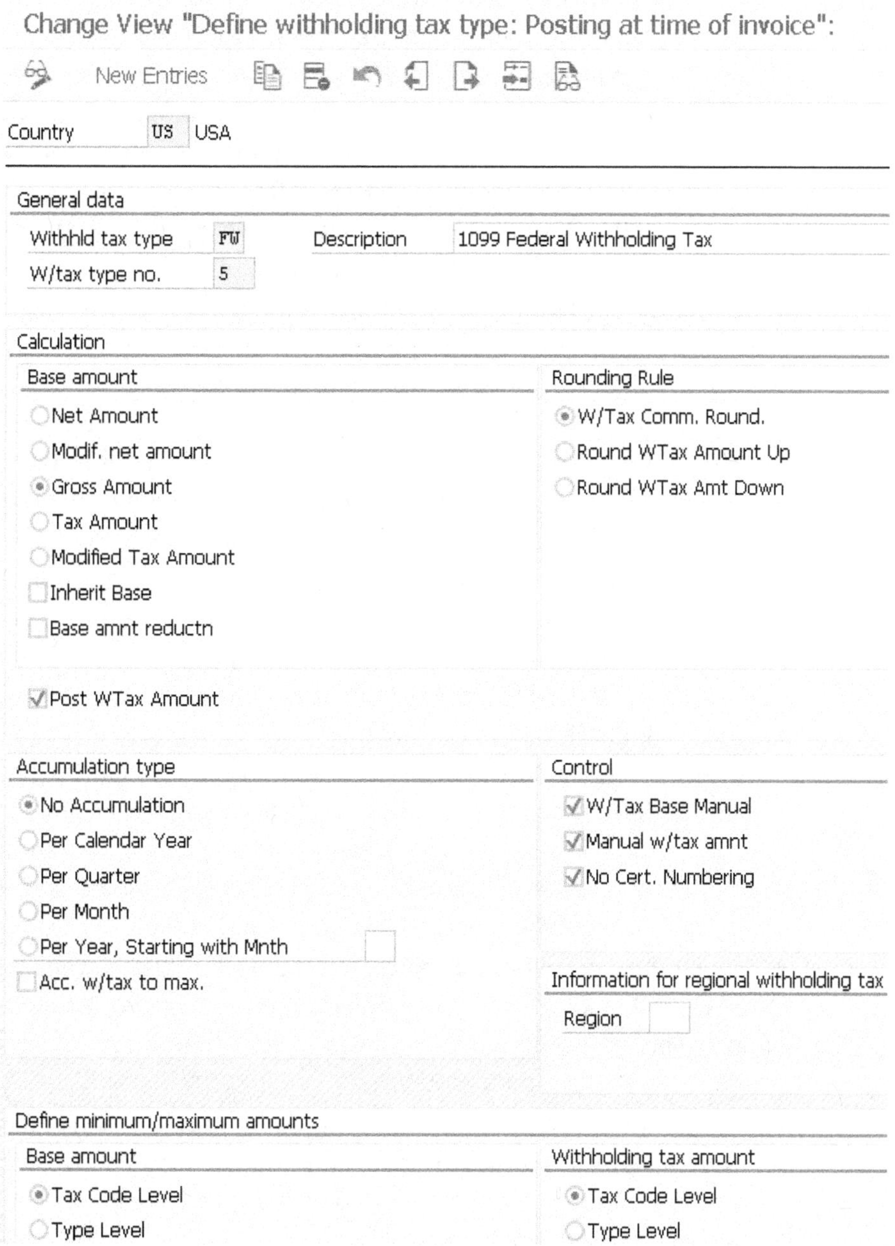

Change View "Define withholding tax type: Posting at time of invoice":

   New Entries

Country   US   USA

General data

Withhld tax type	FW	Description	1099 Federal Withholding Tax
W/tax type no.	5		

Calculation

Base amount	Rounding Rule
○ Net Amount	⦿ W/Tax Comm. Round.
○ Modif. net amount	○ Round WTax Amount Up
⦿ Gross Amount	○ Round WTax Amt Down
○ Tax Amount	
○ Modified Tax Amount	
☐ Inherit Base	
☐ Base amnt reductn	

☑ Post WTax Amount

Accumulation type	Control
⦿ No Accumulation	☑ W/Tax Base Manual
○ Per Calendar Year	☑ Manual w/tax amnt
○ Per Quarter	☑ No Cert. Numbering
○ Per Month	
○ Per Year, Starting with Mnth	
☐ Acc. w/tax to max.	**Information for regional withholding tax**
	Region

Define minimum/maximum amounts

Base amount	Withholding tax amount
⦿ Tax Code Level	⦿ Tax Code Level
○ Type Level	○ Type Level

Figure 8.33: Configuring Withholding Tax Type FW for Posting at the time of Invoice

- Under the 'General data' block:
  - Enter the 2-character identifier for the new withholding tax type in 'Wthhld tax type' field (say, FW); enter a suitable 'Description'.
  - The system generates a sequential number in the 'W/tax type no.' field. This number ensures to have the withholding tax calculated in a particular sequence when certain dependencies exist between different withholding tax types. The situation may arise in some countries (like Korea, Colombia etc) where the withholding tax base amount of one type is derived from the withholding tax amount of another type (see more, later when we discuss the indicators like 'Inherit base' and 'Base amnt reductn').
- Under the 'Calculation' block, under 'Base amount':
  - Select the appropriate radio-button. You have the options like net amount, modified net amount, gross amount, tax amount and modified tax amount. The 'modified net amount' means that an additional amount (consisting of the tax amount that is determined by one or more transaction keys that you define for the withholding tax base amount) is added to the net amount.
  - If you select 'Inherit base' check-box, then, the withholding tax base amount is set to be the same as the withholding tax amount of another type. Used in Korea, you need to maintain the sequence number of the type whose withholding tax amount is to be inherited and set as the base amount.
  - If you set the 'Base amnt reductn' indicator, then, the withholding tax base amount is reduced by the withholding tax amount of another withholding tax type, and you need to define the sequence number of the type whose withholding tax amount is to be used to reduce the output base amount. This is used in Colombia.
- Under the 'Rounding Rule' block, select the appropriate rounding rule for this new withholding tax type: select 'W/Tax Comm. Round' to activate commercial rounding. You may also select either 'Round WTax Amount Up' or 'Round WTax Amount Down'.
- Select 'Post WTax Amount' check-box, for both calculation and posting of the withholding tax. You will not select this for countries like Belgium and France, where there is no requirement to post the withholding tax that is calculated.
- Under 'Accumulation type' block:
  - Select the option as to whether withholding tax calculated is to be accumulated or not ('No Accumulation'). When accumulated, the accumulated withholding tax in the current period is added to the

withholding tax base amount of the line item, for which the withholding tax amount is to be calculated. If to be accumulated, you need to select at what interval this needs to be done (per quarter, per month, per calendar year etc).

- If you select 'Acc. w/tax to max.' check-box, then, withholding tax is not withheld once the accumulated withholding tax amount exceeds the maximum amount.

- Under 'Control' block, select the appropriate flags. You can make a manual entry of base amount when select the 'W/Tax Base Manual' check-box. You can also make the system to allow you to manually enter (during, document entry), a value in the field 'Withholding Tax Amount' for this withholding tax type, if you select 'Manual w/tax amnt' check-box. Both the fields 'Withholding Tax Base Amount' and 'Withholding Tax Amount' are not normally entered manually; however, by making the settings, here, you can allow manual entry in these field but you need to make sure that you have not made these fields as 'required' in the field status settings. If you select 'No Cert. Numbering' you make the system not to issue a number for the system generated tax certificate.

- The field 'Region' is used (in countries like USA, Canada, Italy, Brazil, Australia, and UK) to print the relevant state, region, and county, as a part of the address using the automatic address formatting function.

- Under 'Define minimum/maximum amounts' block, select the appropriate radio-button for base amount and withholding tax amount to define the minimum/maximum amounts either at the tax code level or at the tax type level.

iv.   'Save' the settings and create all other tax types (Figure 8. 34) as well.

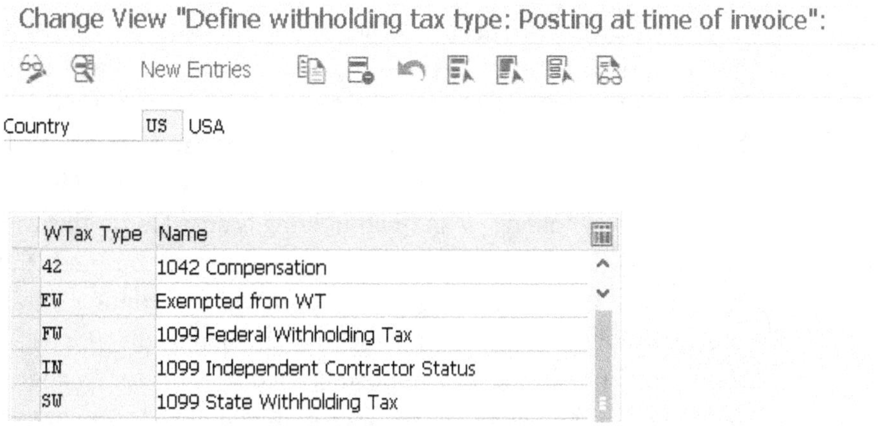

Change View "Define withholding tax type: Posting at time of invoice":

    New Entries

Country   US   USA

WTax Type	Name	
42	1042 Compensation	
EW	Exempted from WT	
FW	1099 Federal Withholding Tax	
IN	1099 Independent Contractor Status	
SW	1099 State Withholding Tax	

Figure 8.34: Withholding Tax Types (Invoice Posting)

Now, let us see define the withholding tax types for payment posting.

8.2.3.1.2   Define Withholding Tax Type for Payment Posting

Here, you define the withholding tax type, for posting at the time payment. You also have to enter withholding tax information, when entering the document for this withholding tax type.

Project Dolphin

BESTM management has informed the project team to define the required withholding tax types, for payment posting relating to government payments (1099-G). Accordingly, the project team has decided to define two withholding tax types for payment posting: GX - 1099G reporting excluding WT and GN - 1099G reporting including WT. Besides, BESTM made it clear to the project team that all the company codes will be using the exchange rate of payment, when translating the withholding tax from foreign currency to a local currency.

For making the required settings:

i.   Use the menu path: SAP Customizing Implementation Guide > Financial Accounting > Financial Accounting Global Settings > Withholding Tax > Extended Withholding Tax > Calculation > Define Withholding Tax for Payment Posting or Transaction S_ALR_87003266.

ii.   On the ensuing pop-up screen, enter the 'Country Key' (US) and proceed.

iii. On the 'Change View "Define withholding tax: Posting at time of payment": Overview' screen, click on 'New Entries' and maintain the details on the next screen (Figure 8.35). Most of the entries are similar to the one that we have already discussed in the previous Section 8.2.3.1.1, when we discussed the settings for defining the withholding tax type for invoice posting. We will discuss only fields that were not part of the screen, as in Figure 8.33:

- Under 'Calculation' block, you need to select the required option for 'Cash discount': select 'W/tax pre c/dis' option, if withholding tax is calculated before cash discount is calculated and deducted, or select 'C/dis pre w/tax', if cash discount is calculated and deducted (from the withholding tax base amount) before the calculation of withholding tax amount.

- Under the 'Control' block, you will see some more additional control flags: select 'Self-W/holding', if self-withholding is possible for this withholding tax type (self-withholding tax functions only apply to business transactions in A/R); select 'W/Tax Alrdy W/hd' for country like Argentina, wherein a part of the withholding tax has already been withheld by sub-suppliers and you can enter the same during invoice posting; select 'WTax for Payments', to enable entering withholding tax amount manually for incoming and outgoing payments.

Change View "Withholding tax type definition - posting at time of paym

🔧   New Entries   📄 📑 ↰ ⬅ ➡ 🔁 📇

Country   US   USA

General data

Withhld tax type	GN	Description	1099G reporting including WT
WTax Type No.	10		

Calculation

Base amount	Rounding Rule	Cash discount
⦿ Net Amount	⦿ W/Tax Comm. Round.	◯ W/tax pre c/dis
◯ Modif. net amount	◯ Round WTax Amount Up	⦿ C/disc pre W/tx
◯ Gross Amount	◯ Round WTax Amt Down	
◯ Tax Amount		
◯ Modified Tax Amount		
☐ Inherit Base		

☑ Post WTax Amount

Accumulation type	Control	
⦿ No Accumulation	☑ W/Tax Base Manual	☐ WTax Alrdy W/hd
◯ Per Calendar Year	☑ Manual w/tax amnt	☐ WTax for Payments
◯ Per Quarter	☐ Self-W/holding	☑ No Cert. Numbering
◯ Per Month		
◯ Per Year, Starting with Mnth		
☐ Combined accum.	**Information for regional withholding tax**	
☐ Acc. w/tax to max.	Region	

Define minimum/maximum amounts

Base amount	Withholding tax amount
⦿ Tax Code Level	⦿ Tax Code Level
◯ Type Level	◯ Type Level

Central invoice	Minimum Check
⦿ No Centr. Invoice	⦿ Minimum Check at Item Level
◯ Cent.inv.& 1st p.pmt	◯ Min. Base Amt Check at Payt Doc. Level
◯ Central Inv. Prop.	◯ Min.base amnt check at doc.invoice level

Figure 8.35: Configuring Withholding Tax Type GN for Posting at Payment

- Under 'Central invoice' block, you have options like 'no central invoice', 'central invoice and 1st partial payment' (along with the central invoice, the full withholding tax amount is deducted from the first partial payment in case of partial payment), and 'central invoice with proportionate distribution of withholding tax' (along with central invoicing, the withholding tax amount is divided and allocated to each partial payment pro rata in case of partial payments).

---

i The 'central invoicing' is a special method for dealing with line items that are linked to other dependent documents, like customer or vendor memos (credit memos, debit memos, down payment clearings or partial payments). This link is established when the dependent documents are posted by entering the invoice reference fields like document number, fiscal year, together with the line item (to which the reference is made).

Let us understand the options with some examples:

(1) *Withholding Tax with the 1st partial payment:*
Used for the VAT withholding tax in Argentina, here, the full withholding tax is posted in the first partial payment on the open item for this withholding type.

Consider an open item (invoice) together with some other open items (credit memos, debit memos, down payment clearing lines) related to it, via the invoice reference field. If this open item is paid together (with a subset of) the related items (some of the related items may not be selected due to special select options entered by the user), the systems uses the sum of the withholding tax base amounts of all these selected items for the calculation of the total withholding tax amount. For a withholding type with 'WT 1st part. payment', the total withholding tax amount is posted with the first partial payment. Also, for the withholding tax base minimum check, the system uses the total sum of the withholding tax base amounts of the open item together with all related items, selected or not.

(2) *Withholding Tax proportional distribution:*
Here, the withholding tax posted in a partial payment of an open item, is distributed proportionally to the payment amount on this open item for this withholding type. This is used for the 'Earning Tax' in Argentina.

Consider, again, the case of an open item (invoice) together with some other open items (credit memos, debit memos, down payment clearing lines) related to it, via the invoice reference field. If this open item is paid together (with a subset of) the related items (some of the related items may not be selected), the systems uses the sum of the withholding tax base amounts of all these selected items for the calculation of the total withholding tax amount. In a partial payment on the invoice, the related items are deactivated, and the total withholding tax base amount is weighted with the quotient of the partial payment amount and the total line item amount of the invoice and the selected related items. In contrast to the previous case 'Withholding Tax with the 1st partial payment', this withholding tax base amount is also used for the base amount minimum check.

- Under 'Minimum Check', you need to select the appropriate option like minimum check at the item level (if this option is selected, the withholding tax is calculated and posted only when the withholding tax base amount exceeds the minimum defined base amount, and the withholding tax amount exceeds the minimum withholding tax amount set in Customizing for each of the line items), minimum base amount check at the payment document level (when selected, the withholding tax amount is calculated and posted only if the withholding tax base amount exceeds the minimum base amount defined in Customizing), minimum base amount check at the payment invoice document level (when selected, the withholding tax amount is calculated and posted only if the withholding tax base amount exceeds the minimum base amount to be entered in the Customizing) etc.

iv.   'Save' when completed, and create the other withholding tax type GX also for payment posting (Figure 8.36).

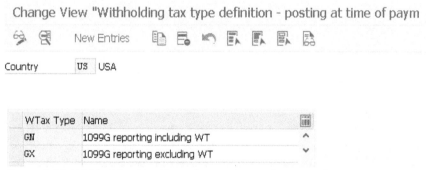

Figure 8.36: Withholding Tax Types for Posting at the time of Payment

Let us continue to discuss, and cover configuring exchange rate types for withholding types.

8.2.3.1.3   Define Exchange Rate Type for Withholding Tax Type

When calculating withholding tax for payments, you normally use the exchange rate of the payment, for translating the withholding tax amount from a foreign currency into the local currency. Some countries have legal requirements that specify which exchange rate is to be used: in Japan, for example, the bank selling rate (and not the average rate) must be used for translating the withholding tax. You, therefore, need to check whether there are any legal requirements, in your country, that require you to use an alternative exchange rate type to calculate withholding tax. If yes, you will define the exchange rate type for individual withholding tax types using menu path: SAP Customizing Implementation Guide > Financial Accounting > Financial Accounting Global Settings > Withholding Tax > Extended Withholding Tax > Calculation > Define Exchange Rate for Withholding Tax Type.

Since we will be using the exchange rate of payment, for BESTM, when translating the withholding tax from foreign currency to a local currency, you will not make any settings in this activity.

Let us now move on to discuss defining the rounding off rules for withholding types.

8.2.3.1.4   Define Rounding Rule for Withholding Tax Type
You need to define the *rounding rules,* for individual withholding tax types. The defined rounding rules only apply to the posting of withholding tax amounts in the appropriate company code; they do not apply to other amounts posted in that company code.

Use the menu path: SAP Customizing Implementation Guide > Financial Accounting > Financial Accounting Global Settings > Withholding Tax > Extended Withholding Tax > Calculation > Define Rounding Rule for Withholding Tax Type. On the next screen, click on 'New Entries' and maintain the rounding off details for each combination of 'company code – withholding tax type – currency'; for USA, enter 1 in the 'Unit' field (Figure 8.37), to round off the withholding tax to the whole dollar (enter 100 for India).

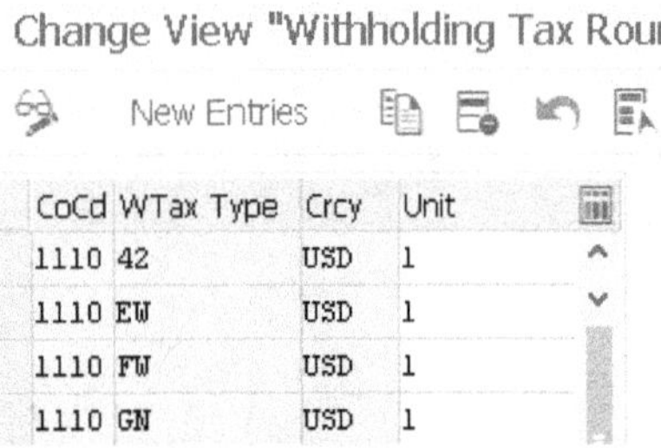

Change View "Withholding Tax Rounding Rules": Overview

CoCd	WTax Type	Crcy	Unit
1110	42	USD	1
1110	EW	USD	1
1110	FW	USD	1
1110	GN	USD	1

Figure 8.37: Rounding Rule for Withholding Tax Type

Let us now move on to the last configuration activity under withholding tax type.

8.2.3.1.5   Assign Condition Type to Withholding Tax Type
You will carry out this activity, if you are implementing FI together with SD. As you are aware, the withholding tax in FI is determined from the combination of withholding tax type and withholding tax code per customer/vendor. In contrast, the withholding tax in SD is determined from the combination of 'withholding tax condition type and withholding tax code' per material. It is therefore necessary to assign the withholding tax types from FI to the withholding tax condition types from SD. You can use the condition types in SD, to represent the withholding tax per customer and per material item. When posting from SD to FI, the system then converts (a) the withholding tax condition type into the withholding tax type and

(b) material items with different combinations of withholding tax condition type and withholding tax code into different customer items.

Let us move on to discuss the withholding tox code, next.

8.2.3.2   Withholding Tax Code

You use *'withholding tax code'* to determine the withholding tax percentage. In a withholding tax code, you will specify (a) the calculation of base amount for tax calculation, (b) the portion (or percentage) of the base that will be subject to tax, (c) the tax rate or reduced tax rate and (d) the posting of withholding tax. While specifying the calculation base, you will indicate if the invoice amount, including tax on sales/purchases, is to be used as the basis for the tax.

> **i** As in tax codes relating to tax on sales and purchases, you are not allowed to change or delete the definitions for withholding tax codes as long as open items exist in the system for those codes; else, you will encounter errors occur, during the payment transactions.

8.2.3.2.1   Define Withholding Tax Codes
Project Dolphin

BESTM has indicated to the project team to make use of standard default withholding tax codes relating to 1099-MISC reporting as in Figure 8.38. If any additional tax codes (to comply with 1099-G, 1099-INT etc) are required, BESTM suggested that the project team creates them, in accordance with the reporting requirements in US.

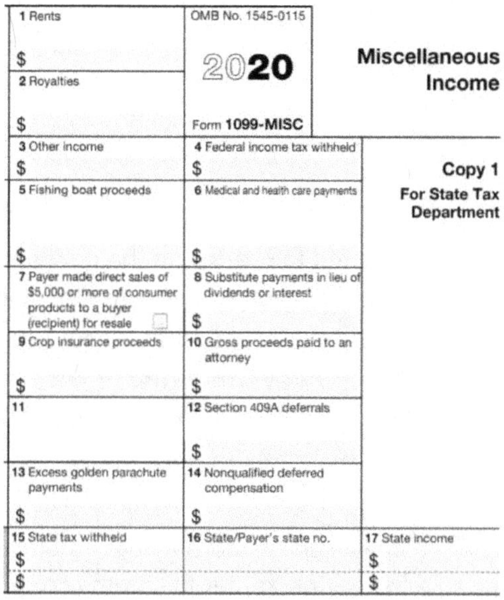

1 Rents $	OMB No. 1545-0115	
2 Royalties $	20**20** Form **1099-MISC**	**Miscellaneous Income**
3 Other income $	4 Federal income tax withheld $	**Copy 1**
5 Fishing boat proceeds $	6 Medical and health care payments $	**For State Tax Department**
7 Payer made direct sales of $5,000 or more of consumer products to a buyer (recipient) for resale ☐	8 Substitute payments in lieu of dividends or interest $	
9 Crop insurance proceeds $	10 Gross proceeds paid to an attorney $	
11	12 Section 409A deferrals $	
13 Excess golden parachute payments $	14 Nonqualified deferred compensation $	
15 State tax withheld $ $	16 State/Payer's state no.	17 State income $ $

Figure 8.38: Withholding Tax Codes for 1099-MISC reporting

To configure the new / view the standard withholding tax codes:

i.   Use the menu path: SAP Customizing Implementation Guide > Financial Accounting > Financial Accounting Global Settings > Withholding Tax > Extended Withholding Tax > Calculation > Define Withholding Tax Codes or Transaction S_ALR_87003617.

ii.   On the ensuing pop-up screen, enter the 'Country Key' (US) and proceed.

iii.   On the 'Change View "Withholding tax code": Overview' screen, you will see the default tax codes defined in the standard system. You need to copy them to the withholding tax types that we have created earlier in Section 8.2.3.1.1 and 8.2.3.1.2.

iv.   Select the rows and click on 'Copy As', and maintain the details on the next screen (Figure 8.39):

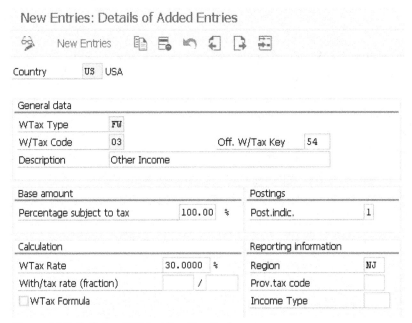

Figure 8.39: Defining Withholding Tax Code

- Change the 'WTax type' to FW for the selected tax codes on the next screen. You need to do that one by one. The system brings up the default 'Description', for each of the tax codes which you can change if required.
- Select the appropriate official withholding tax key, from the drop-down list for the field 'Off. W/Tax Key'; the key 54 represents 'OI: Other Income'.
- Under the 'Base amount' block, enter the 'Percentage subject to tax' (normally, 100).
- Under 'Postings', enter the posting indicator in 'Post.indic.' field: 1 for standard posting in which the bank / vendor / customer line item is reduced,

2 for offsetting entry to G/L account (grossing up) and 3 for offsetting entry to G/L account.

- Maintain the 'WTax Rate' under 'Calculation' block.
- You need to select 'WTax Formula' check-box, only when the withholding tax is not calculated using a constant rate, but by a special procedure. If this flag is set, the specifications necessary for the calculation are to be defined separately using the menu path: SAP Customizing Implementation Guide > Financial Accounting > Financial Accounting Global Settings > Withholding Tax > Extended Withholding Tax > Calculation > Define Formulas for Calculating Withholding Tax (refer the next <u>Section 8.2.3.2.2</u>). However, note that the special calculation cannot be used together with the 'grossing up' functionality as denoted by the posting indicator 2. We will, later, create a withholding tax code 42 (foreign vendor subject to withholding tax) to cover withholding tax type 42, wherein we will select this 'WTax Formula' check-box, to indicate that the withholding tax needs to be calculated using a special procedure.
- Maintain the details for 'Reporting information' block.
- 'Save' when completed, and continue maintaining the details for all other tax codes that are being created by copying, for the withholding type FW to cover 1099-MISC reporting.

v. You have now created all the required withholding tax codes for 1099-MISC reporting for withholding type FW for USA (Figure 8.40).

New Entries: Overview of Added Entries

New Entries

Country   US   USA

WTax Type	WTax Code	Name
FW	01	Rents
FW	02	Royalties
FW	03	Other Income
FW	05	Fishing Boat Proceeds
FW	06	Medical and Healthcare Payments
FW	07	Non-employee Compensation
FW	08	Substitute Paymn in Lieu of Dividends
FW	09	Direct Sales
FW	10	Crop Insurance Proceeds
FW	13	Excess Golden Parachute Payments
FW	14	Gross Proceeds Paid to an Attorney
FW	15	Section 409A deferrals
FW	16	State Tax Withheld

Figure 8.40: Withholding Tax Codes for 1099-MISC

vi. Define other withholding tax codes, if required, to cover 1099-G reporting (Table 8.6).

Withholding Tax Type for Payment Posting	Withholding Tax Code	Description
G1 1099-G reporting excluding WT	1G	Unemployment compensation of $10 or more
	2G	State or local income tax refunds, credits, or offsets of $10 or more
	5G	Other taxable grants of $600 and more
	6G	Taxable grants administered by a federal, state, or local program to provide subsidized energy financing
	7G	Agriculture subsidy payments
	8G	State or local income tax refunds, credits, or offsets on unincorporated businesses
GT 1099-G reporting including WT	1G	Unemployment compensation of $10 or more, if withholding tax is withheld
	2G	State or local income tax refunds, credits, or offsets of $10 or more, if withholding tax is withheld
	5G	Other taxable grants of $600 and more, if withholding tax is withheld
	6G	Taxable grants administered by a federal, state, or local program to provide subsidized energy financing, if withholding tax is withheld
	7G	Agriculture subsidy payments, if withholding tax is withheld
	8G	State or local income tax refunds, credits, or offsets on unincorporated businesses, if withholding tax is withheld

Table 8:6 Tax Codes – 1099-G Reporting

vii. Also, define withholding tax codes, if any, to cover 1099-INT reporting (Table 8.7).

Withholding Tax Type for Payment Posting	Withholding Tax Code	Description
II 1099-INT reporting excluding	1I	Interest amount to be reported in box 1 with a minimum amount of $600
	1J	Interest amount to be reported in box 1 with a minimum amount of $10

withholding tax	2I	Interest on early withdrawal penalty to be reported in box 2
	3I	Interest on U.S. Savings Bonds and Treasury Obligations to be reported in box 3
IT 1099-INT reporting including withholding tax	1I	Interest amount to be reported in box 1 with a minimum amount of $600, if withholding tax must be withheld
	1J	Interest amount to be reported in box 1 with a minimum amount of $10, if withholding tax must be withheld
	2I	Interest on early withdrawal penalty to be reported in box 2, if withholding tax must be withheld

Table 8:7 Tax Codes – 1099-INT Reporting

When we discussed the attributes of withholding tax codes, we saw that there could be situations, wherein you will use a special formula to calculate the tax (as in the case of withholding tax code 42), instead of using the single rate defined in the tax code. In the next Section, we will discuss how to create the formula to calculate the tax.

8.2.3.2.2   Define Formulas for Calculating Withholding Tax

Using this configuration activity, you will define the formulas (scales), for calculating withholding tax. These formulas consist of the currency key, withholding tax type, withholding tax code, withholding tax country key and validity date. In order to use a formula for calculating withholding tax, you should have entered the national currency in the 'Currency' key field, of the relevant company code. To use the formula for calculating withholding tax, you should have selected the 'WTax Formula' check-box, while defining the withholding tax code (refer the previous Section 8.2.3.2.1).

i.   Use the menu path: SAP Customizing Implementation Guide > Financial Accounting > Financial Accounting Global Settings > Withholding Tax > Extended Withholding Tax > Calculation > Define Formulas for Calculating Withholding Tax. You can also use Transaction S_ALR_87003618.

ii.   On the ensuing pop-up screen, enter the 'Country Key' (US) and proceed.

iii. On the 'Change View "Header data for formula maintenance": Overview' screen, click on 'New Entries' and maintain the header data for formula maintenance (Figure 8.41), and then define the formula itself. Note that the withholding tax country may differ from the vendor master record; we have entered AS (Australia). 'Save' the header data.

Figure 8.41: Header Data for Withholding Tax Formula

iv.   Now, select this row and double-click on 'Formulas for calculation' on the left hand-side dialog-box; click on 'New Entries' and maintain the settings as detailed in Figure 8.42. The decreased reduction of base amount ('Dec.Red.Base Amt') is nothing but the amount by which base amount is reduced, if exemption authorization exists on vendor master record

Figure 8.42: Withholding Tax Formula for Calculation

This completes our discussion on defining the withholding tax codes. Let us move on to discuss the minimum / maximum amounts

8.2.3.3   Minimum and Maximum Amounts

There are two configuration steps here: one for defining the minimum / maximum amounts for withholding types, and the other for defining the same for withholding tax codes. In both the cases, you can also maintain the minimum tax base amount: if the base amount calculated, when the invoice is posted is lower than this minimum, the system does not calculate any withholding tax, and no withholding tax is posted.

Let us now look at defining the minimum/maximum amounts for withholding tax types.

8.2.3.3.1   Define Min/Max Amounts for Withholding Tax Types

Here, you will define the minimum and maximum withholding tax amounts, per withholding tax type. This configuration step simplifies your withholding tax calculation, by enabling you to define minimum / maximum withholding tax amount for each tax type. You can also define a minimum tax base amount, below which no withholding tax will be calculated. If a journal entry with this tax type is posted, the system calculates the withholding tax amount based on the minimum and maximum settings you have defined, the tax base amount, and the tax rate.

Use the menu path: SAP Customizing Implementation Guide > Financial Accounting > Financial Accounting Global Settings > Withholding Tax > Extended Withholding Tax > Calculation > Define Min/Max Amounts for Withholding Tax Types.

When you have defined the minimum / maximum amounts for withholding tax types, you will encounter four scenarios during withholding tax calculation by the system:

1) If the calculated tax amount is less than the minimum amount defined, the withholding tax amount is zero.
2) If the expected tax amount lies between the minimum and maximum amounts you have defined, the calculated tax amount is the expected tax amount.
3) If the expected tax amount exceeds the maximum amount defined, the maximum tax amount is used as the withholding tax amount.
4) If the tax base amount in the document is less than the defined minimum tax base amount, no tax is deducted and the withholding tax amount is set to zero.

Having completed the definition of minimum/maximum amounts for withholding tax types, let us now look at defining the minimum/maximum amounts for withholding tax codes.

8.2.3.3.2   Define Min/Max Amounts for Withholding Tax Codes

This is similar to the previous activity, but the difference is that you define the minimum/maximum amounts, per withholding tax code. Besides maintaining the minimum base amount for calculation of withholding tax, you can also enter the withholding tax base exemption amount ('WTax Base Exem. Amt'), which is deducted while arriving at the withholding tax base. The amount of the tax exemption does not have any effect when matching the withholding tax base with the minimum, because the base amount and the minimum amount are matched before the tax-exempt amount is deducted.

Use the menu path: SAP Customizing Implementation Guide > Financial Accounting > Financial Accounting Global Settings > Withholding Tax > Extended Withholding Tax > Calculation > Define Min/Max Amounts for Withholding Tax Codes, to configure the required settings.

With this, we are, now, ready to look at the company code settings for withholding tax.

8.2.4 Company Code Settings

The company code settings for withholding tax include (a) assigning withholding tax types to company codes and (b) activating EWT.

Let us, first, look at the settings for assigning withholding tax types to company codes.

8.2.4.1 Assign Withholding Tax Types to Company Codes

Here in this activity, you assign withholding tax categories to company codes:

i. Use the menu path: SAP Customizing Implementation Guide > Financial Accounting > Financial Accounting Global Settings > Withholding Tax > Extended Withholding Tax > Company Code > Assign Withholding Tax Types to Company Codes. Or, you may use Transaction S_ALR_87003423.

ii. On the 'Change View "Withholding tax information for company code per w/type": Overview' screen, click on 'New Entries', and enter the details, on the next screen (Figure 8.43):

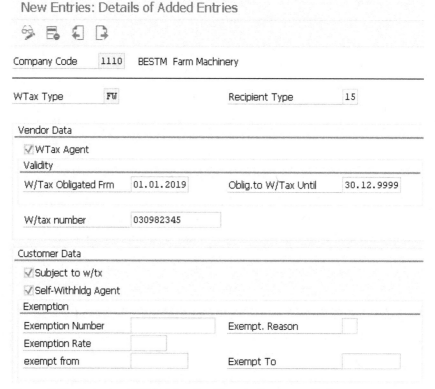

Figure 8.43: Assigning Withholding Tax Type to Company Code

- Enter the 'Company Code'.
- Enter the withholding tax type ('WTax Type').

- Select the 'Recipient Type' for the possible entries; 15 denotes that the recipient is a corporate.
- Under 'Vendor Data' block, select the 'WTax Agent' check-box, to indicate that for this withholding tax type, the company code is entitled to withhold tax, on behalf of a vendor. Under 'Validity', enter the from date ('W/Tax Obigated Frm'), to date ('Oblig.to W/Tax Until') and also the withholding tax number ('W/tax number'), if any. The withholding tax number ('W/tax number') is a number - the Tax Identification Number (TIN), Social Security Number (SSN), or Employer Identification Number (EIN)—issued by the tax authorities, per withholding tax type. You maintain this either as a part of withholding tax information of the company code or as a part of the withholding tax information of the customer or vendor master.
- Under 'Customer Data' block, select the 'Subject to w/tx' check-box, indicating that this company code is subject to withholding tax for this withholding tax type. The 'Self-withhldg Agent' check-box, when selected, indicates that this company code can withhold tax on its own behalf, for this withholding tax type. You can also make this setting in Customizing under the withholding tax information for the company code.
- Maintain the exemption related details under 'Exemption' data block.

iii. 'Save' the details, and click on 'Next Entry' to maintain the details for other withholding tax types, for the same company code. Repeat the steps and assign the withholding types to all the company codes.

The next activity under company code is to activate EWT.

8.2.4.2 Activate Extended Withholding Tax

You need to activate EWT, to use the functionality in the system. Use the menu path: SAP Customizing Implementation Guide > Financial Accounting > Financial Accounting Global Settings > Withholding Tax > Extended Withholding Tax > Company Code > Activate Extended Withholding Tax. On the 'Change View "Enhanced withholding tax functions active": Overview' screen, select the 'Ext.WTax' check-box against all the company codes wherein you want to use EWT. 'Save' the details (Figure 8.44).

---

i Once you decide to use EWT and activate the same, you have to migrate your master data and transaction data. It is, then, impossible to revert back to classical withholding tax.

Change View "Enhanced withholding tax functions active": Overview

CoCd	Company Name	Ext.WTax	
1110	BESTM Farm Machinery	✓	
1120	BESTM Garden & Forestry E	✓	
2100	BESTM Trucks	✓	
2200	BESTM Other Construction	✓	

Figure 8.44: Activating Extended Withholding Tax for Company Codes

This completes our discussion on the company code settings for EWT. Let us, now, move on to discuss the next set of configuration settings grouped under 'posting'.

8.2.5 Posting

Under posting, you will be configuring the settings relating to:

- Accounts for Withholding Tax
- Certificate Numbering for Withholding Tax

Let us start with the first activity of defining the G/L accounts for posting withholding tax:

8.2.5.1 Accounts for Withholding Tax

Here, you define the required G/L accounts for the account determination for posting withholding tax. Depending on whether you have set the posting indicator in the withholding tax code or if you use self-withholding, you need to define accounts for the following transactions:

a) Define Accounts for Withholding Tax to be Paid Over.
b) Define Accounts for Withholding Tax for "Gross. Up" Offsetting Entry.
c) Define Accounts for Self-Withholding tax.
d) Define Accounts for Withholding tax Offsetting Entry.

Let us understand and define the settings required for each of these four situations, in the following pages.

 Maintain the G/L accounts for posting the EWT on an open item basis, to enable clearing.

Project Dolphin

The Dolphin project team has recommended to BESTM management to have separate G/L accounts (from 21613000 to 21614000), differentiated by withholding tax types. However, they also indicated that it may not be required to have these accounts separated according to the tax codes for all the third-party transactions. It has also been recommended to have a single account (21603000) for self-withholding tax.

8.2.5.1.1 Define Accounts for Withholding Tax to be Paid Over

Here, you define accounts for the normal withholding tax transaction (WIT). This transaction is required for every withholding tax posting.

To define and configure the accounts for withholding tax to be paid over:

i. Use the menu path: SAP Customizing Implementation Guide > Financial Accounting > Financial Accounting Global Settings > Withholding Tax > Extended Withholding Tax > Posting > Accounts for Withholding Tax > Define Accounts for Withholding Tax to be Paid Over. Or, you may use Transaction OBWW.

ii. Enter the 'Chart of Accounts' on the ensuing pop-up screen, and 'Continue'.

iii. On the 'Configuration Accounting Maintain: Automatic Posts – Accounts' screen, click on 'Create' and enter the details on the next screen (Figure 8.45):

Figure 8.45: G/L Accounts for Witholding Tax to be Paid Over

- Enter the 'Withholding tax type' (say, FW), and enter the appropriate 'Withholding tax code' (say, 01) maintain the G/L account for 'Debit' (say, 21613000) and 'Credit' (say, 21613000). 'Save' the details. You have now defined the G/L account for posting withholding type FW for the withholding tax code 01.

- You may copy the above entry and maintain the details for all the withholding tax codes associated with the withholding tax type FW.
- Repeat the steps to create additional entries for all other withholding tax types like GN, GX etc. As required in Project Dolphin, you need to define separate G/L accounts for each of the withholding tax types.
- 'Save' the details when completed (Figure 8.45).

iv.   Now, click on 'Posting Key'. You will be taken to 'Configuration Accounting Maintain: Automatic Posts – Posting Keys' screen (Figure 8.46), wherein you will see the posting key details as to the 'Debit' / 'Credit' posting keys for the 'Transaction' WIT (Extended Withholding Tax).

Configuration Accounting Maintain : Automatic Posts - Posting Keys

Accounts	Rules

Transaction	WIT	Extended withholding tax

Posting Key	
Debit	40
Credit	50

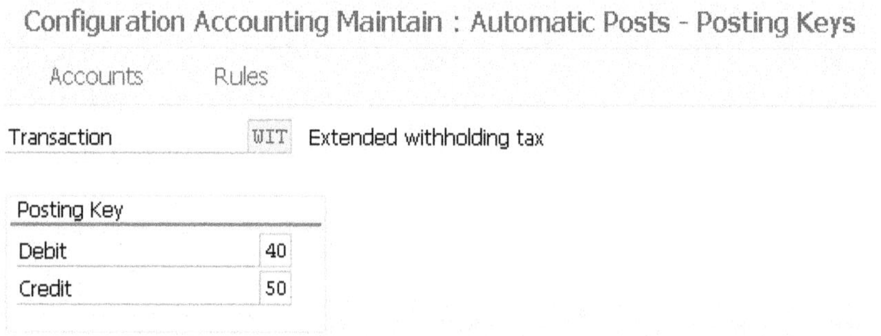

Figure 8.46: Posting Keys associated with Transaction WIT

v.   You may click on 'Rules'. On the 'Configuration Accounting Maintain: Automatic Posts – Rules' screen (Figure 8.47); you will see rules based on which the accounts are determined for posting the withholding tax.

Configuration Accounting Maintain : Automatic Posts - Rules

Accounts	Posting Key

Chart of Accounts	BEUS	BESTM - US Standard Chart of Accounts
Transaction	WIT	Extended withholding tax

Accounts are determined based on	
Debit/Credit	✓
Withholding tax code	✓
Withholding tax type	✓

Figure 8.47: Rules for Automatic Posting of Withholding Tax

Similar to the definition above, you can use the activities below to define the G/L account(s), for posting withholding tax under various situations:

8.2.5.1.2   Define Accts for W/hold.Tax for "Gross.Up" Offsetting Entry

Here, you will define accounts, if you have selected value 2 for the posting indicator in the withholding tax code (refer Section 8.2.3.2.1). An offsetting posting with the opposite +/- sign is, then, carried out for the withholding tax item (transaction GRU). The withholding tax amount is increased by a factor of $1/(1-p)$.

Use the menu path: SAP Customizing Implementation Guide > Financial Accounting > Financial Accounting Global Settings > Withholding Tax > Extended Withholding Tax > Posting > Accounts for Withholding Tax > Define Accts for W/hold.Tax for "Gross.Up" Offsetting Entry. Or, you may use Transaction OBWU.

8.2.5.1.3   Define Accounts for Self-Withholding Tax

For this, you will define accounts if you want to post self-withholding tax. An offsetting posting with the opposite +/- sign is then carried out for the withholding tax item (transaction OPO).

Use the menu path: SAP Customizing Implementation Guide > Financial Accounting > Financial Accounting Global Settings > Withholding Tax > Extended Withholding Tax > Posting > Accounts for Withholding Tax > Define Accounts for Self-Withholding Tax. Or, you may use Transaction OBWS.

8.2.5.1.4   Define Accounts for Withholding Tax Offsetting Entry

You need to define accounts, here, if you have selected value 3 for the posting indicator in the withholding tax code (refer Section 8.2.3.2.1). An offsetting posting with the opposite +/- sign is, then, carried out for the withholding tax item (transaction OFF).

Use the menu path: SAP Customizing Implementation Guide > Financial Accounting > Financial Accounting Global Settings > Withholding Tax > Extended Withholding Tax > Posting > Accounts for Withholding Tax > Define Accounts for Offsetting Entry. Or, you may use Transaction OBWO.

With the G/L account definition for posting of withholding tax completed, it is time to move on to discuss certificate numbering in the system for withholding tax.

8.2.5.2   Certificate Numbering for Withholding Tax

Using the following activities, you make the settings in the system for numbering the certificates for withholding tax:

- Define Numbering Classes
- Assign Numbering Group to Numbering Class
- Assign Numbering Concept to Company Code Country
- Numbering Concept Option 2: Assign Numbering Class

The numbering of the certificates is based on *numbering groups* and *numbering classes,* which can be assigned to organizational units and to withholding tax categories. The *numbering groups* are lots of numbers from one or more number ranges. The numbering groups are grouped into *numbering classes*. A number is determined, sequentially, from the corresponding numbering group, for each certification.

To exercise as much control as possible over the way withholding tax certificates are numbered, SAP provides a four-step concept for numbering the withholding tax certificates as exactly as possible:

1) *Concept 1* (K001): Assigning numbering class to company code(s).

Company Code	Numbering Class
9000	AA
9100	AA
9200	AA

2) *Concept 2* (K002): Assigning numbering class to combinations of withholding tax type/ company code.

Company Code	Withholding Tax Type	Numbering Class
9000	AA	AA
9100	AB	AB
9200	AA	AA

3) *Concept 3* (K003): Assigning numbering class to combinations of withholding tax type/branch/company code.

Company Code	Withholding Tax Type	Branch	Numbering Class
9000	AA	XXXX	AA
9100	AB	YYYY	AB
9200	AA	YYYY	AA

4) *Concept 4* (K004): Assigning numbering class to a combination of company code/branch/ recipient type/month.

You have to assign one of these four concepts to each company code country.

Project Dolphin

No explicit withholding tax certificate numbering is required for withholding tax reporting in USA, as the requirement is fulfilled through TIN, EIN, and SSN numbers.

> **i** We will be discussing the certificate numbering to make you understand how to configure the same, should you need that configuration, for other countries. Let us configure the numbering for the combination of 'withholding tax type and company code' (Concept 2, also known as K002), for easy monitoring and control.

Let us start with the first activity of defining the numbering classes.

8.2.5.2.1 Define Numbering Classes

While defining the numbering classes, it is helpful if you define numbering class with the same name (or identifier) as that of the withholding tax type when you use concept 2 (K002), so that just by looking at the numbering class, you know which withholding tax type the certificate relates to.

Use the menu path: SAP Customizing Implementation Guide > Financial Accounting > Financial Accounting Global Settings > Withholding Tax > Extended Withholding Tax > Posting > Certificate Numbering for Withholding Tax > Define Numbering Classes.

With the numbering classes defined, you can move on to assign the numbering groups to numbering class.

8.2.5.2.2 Assign Numbering Groups to Numbering Class

Once you have defined the numbering classes, you can assign numbering groups to numbering classes. You do not need to define the numbering groups or number ranges, prior to this step, as the system automatically creates the numbering group (for each combination of company code and numbering class) and the required number ranges during assignment.

You can configure this activity by following the steps listed below:

i.   Use the menu path: SAP Customizing Implementation Guide > Financial Accounting > Financial Accounting Global Settings > Withholding Tax > Extended Withholding Tax > Posting > Certificate Numbering for Withholding Tax > Assign Numbering Group to Numbering Class.

ii. On the resulting 'Change View "Allocation of numbering group to numbering class": Overview' screen, click on 'New Entries' and make the settings as under:
- Enter the 'Company Code' (say, 1210). And, enter the 'Numbering Class' that you have created in the previous step (say, SA).
- When you 'Save', the system automatically creates a 'Numbering Group' (000001), for the combination of company code and numbering class. The system also, automatically, populates the 'From number' and 'To number' denoting the number range interval from which the withholding certificates

will be numbered sequentially (Figure 8.48). You may click on 'Maintain no. range' if you need to modify the automatically created number range.

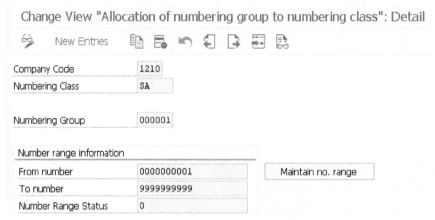

Figure 8.48: Assigning Numbering Group to Numbering Class

iii.   You can make similar assignments to all other company codes, wherein you want the system to issue serially numbered withholding tax certificates. You may use the 'Define Numbering Groups' or 'Define Number Ranges' configuration steps to make subsequent modifications, after the initial assignment of the numbering groups to numbering classes.

With this, we are now ready to assign the appropriate numbering concept (concept 2, in our case) to the company code country in the next step.

8.2.5.2.3   Assign Numbering Concept to Company Code Country

Use the menu path: SAP Customizing Implementation Guide > Financial Accounting > Financial Accounting Global Settings > Withholding Tax > Extended Withholding Tax > Posting > Certificate Numbering for Withholding Tax > Assign Numbering Concept to Company Code Country. On the next screen, enter the concept selected [say, Concept 2 (K002) – Company code/Withholding tax type] against the country row, and 'Save' the settings (Figure 8.49). You have now assigned the required numbering concept to the required company code country.

Change View "With/tax certificate numbering: Assign concept to country

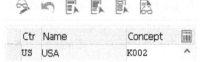

Figure 8.49: Assigning Numbering Concept to Company Code Country

The next step is to assign the numbering class to the numbering concept option.

8.2.5.2.4   Numbering Concept Option 2: Assign Numbering Class

Use the menu path: SAP Customizing Implementation Guide > Financial Accounting > Financial Accounting Global Settings > Withholding Tax > Extended Withholding Tax > Posting > Certificate Numbering for Withholding Tax > Numbering Concept Option 2: Assign Numbering Class. On the next screen, click on 'New Entries' and maintain the assignment settings for the 'company code – withholding tax type – numbering class' combination (Figure 8.50). Repeat the assignment for the other withholding tax types / numbering classes as well, for the same company code. And, repeat the steps for all other company codes, wherein you will be using the Concept 2.

Figure 8.50: Assigning Numbering Concept 2 to Numbering Class/Company Code Combination

This completes our discussion on withholding tax posting. The last configuration step, is to set up the system for advanced compliance reporting (to report withholding tax to tax authorities). Before discussing that, let us understand how do you undertake document entry / change / display involving EWT transactions.

8.2.6   Document Entry / Change / Display

The prerequisites for entering / changing / displaying withholding tax, in a transaction, include that (a) you have set up the field status for document entry in such a way that allows for withholding tax data to be entered, in at least one withholding tax fields, and (b) you select at least one withholding tax type.

8.2.6.1   Document Entry

When entering documents, you can enter withholding tax data for every customer/vendor line item. Once you have confirmed entry of the line item (on the customer or vendor screen), the system displays the dialog box, 'Enter Withholding Tax Information', which contains one line per withholding tax type. During document entry, this withholding tax dialog box appears each time you create a new customer or vendor line item. If you edit one of these customer or vendor line items again during document entry, you will need to access the withholding tax dialog box by choosing 'Extras > Withholding tax data'.

a) *Document Simulation and Posting*

The processing of withholding tax involves two separate activities, namely:

- *Calculation of the withholding tax base*: The system determines the withholding tax base amount (according to the Customizing settings) for the combination of withholding tax type and withholding tax code. There is, therefore, only an entry for withholding tax, once you simulate the document. The base amount can also be entered manually by the user (if the relevant Customizing settings have been made), and a manual entry overrides the amount calculated by the system. Where payments are made by instalments, the withholding tax base is apportioned across the new customer/vendor line items.

- *Calculation of the withholding tax amount*: The way in which withholding tax is calculated depends on the withholding tax type, and it controls when the withholding tax is calculated and posted, either when the invoice is entered or when payment is made. The withholding tax is, generally, calculated by the system. However, if you have made the appropriate settings in Customizing, you can also enter it manually; such a manual entry overrides the amount calculated by the system.

b) *Special Transactions*

The processing of special transactions takes place as indicated as under:

- *Down payment requests and payment requests*: When you post down payment requests and payment requests, the system only calculates the withholding tax base amounts.

- *Document parking*: The system does not calculate any withholding tax base amounts when you save or change parked documents; the calculation happens only when they are posted.

- *Document holding*: When documents are 'held', the system does not calculate any withholding tax amounts/base amounts.

- *Posting with reference*: When you post documents using a reference, the system defaults withholding tax base amounts, but not any existing withholding tax amounts. The system does not calculate any withholding tax base amounts/tax amounts, when you enter a reference document.

- *Recurring entry documents*: The system does not calculate any withholding tax base amounts/tax amounts, when you enter a recurring entry document.

8.2.6.2   Dcoument Change

You can change the withholding tax information in a document, if you have not already posted the withholding tax. This is only the case for withholding tax of the type 'posting at time of payment', and you can only make changes in transactions that are not relevant for payments. When you change the document, the system enables you to change the selection date in the withholding tax dialog box. If you have made changes in the relevant withholding tax types, the withholding tax fields for this type are ready for input. If you enter a new withholding tax code and do not enter the withholding tax base amount manually, then, the system recalculates the withholding tax base amount automatically. If you delete the withholding tax code, the system resets all withholding tax information for this withholding tax type. Whenever you change withholding tax information, the system creates change documents.

> **i** The settings you made in Customizing for the withholding tax type in question, determine whether the amount fields such as 'Withholding tax base', 'Withholding tax amount', and 'Withholding tax amount already withheld' can be changed or not.

8.2.6.3   Document Display

The same rules apply for displaying documents as for changing them, with the exception that you cannot enter any data in the fields. If, for example, when displaying the document, the list of relevant withholding tax types differs from the withholding tax types already defined in the withholding tax information for a line item, the same rules apply as for changing documents. When displaying documents, you can display the withholding tax base amount and withholding tax amount, in all the currencies maintained for that company code. You can call up the various currencies, in the withholding tax dialog box, by choosing the appropriate push-button.

With the understanding of the mechanics of document entry / change / display involving withholding tax in a transaction, we are now ready to discuss the advanced compliance reporting for EWT which will be the last and final step in setting up the system properly configured for EWT.

8.2.7   *Advanced Compliance Reporting*

Before proceeding to look at the specific withholding tax reports, for USA, you need to familiarise yourself with the three important concepts (in SAP S/4HANA) in advanced compliance reporting:

1) Report Category
2) Report Definition
3) Report Entity

Report Category

A '*report category*' groups versions of a report that are technically specified with the help of report definitions. The system uses the report category (for example, VAT Returns for UK, EC Sales List for the UK, USA Withholding Tax etc) to help you to create concrete reports for a specific period and specific company codes. For each of these report categories, the government may issue new versions, over time, to take care of the changes in the country's legislation. You can create independent report categories using the 'Define Advanced Compliance Reports' app (Figure 8.51), and assign country, phases, and organizational unit to a report category. You also assign activities to the report category. A report definition is then assigned to the reporting activity.

Figure 8.51: Define Advanced Compliance Reports App

Report Definition

A '*report definition*' describes the exact format in which the report is to be created (say, which tax balances are to be reported under which element names in an XML structure). The report definitions are identified by a report ID or report category ID (like, US_WHT_1042S). These definitions are repository content provided by SAP; of course, you can create your own (report) definitions, using the 'Define Advanced Compliance Reports' App (Figure 8.51), and assign them to report activities (discussed later in this Section).

Reporting Entity

A '*reporting entity*' is the legal entity within your organization that is obliged to submit certain compliance reports. It (say, US_RPG_ENT) can comprise of one or more organizational units (like business place, company code, section code, and tax jurisdiction). You will designate one of the organizational units, in the reporting entity, as the leading organizational unit. The assignment of the organizational unit to the reporting entity is time-dependent: if there is an organizational change that must only be considered as of a certain point in time, a new set of organizational codes must be assigned with the respective valid-from date. SAP provides you with the sample content for reporting entities; you can adapt this content to suit your own specific needs in Customizing or create new content altogether.

Besides the above three concepts, you should also understand the following in the context of advanced compliance reporting:

- *Reporting Activity*: These are steps that you need to perform to complete end-to-end compliance reporting process. They denote certain mandatory transactions to be performed by the system, before submitting your tax reports to the government. In the 'Define Advanced Compliance Reports' app (Figure 8.51), you can create new reporting activities and assign them to your report category (based on legal reporting requirements). You assign a report definition to the reporting activity.
- *Phases*: A phase is used to identify the 'type of report run' (declaration, correction, or additional correction) that is generated. When you generate a report run, by default, the report run type is 'declaration'. Based on the country-specific requirements, you can generate a 'correction' report, or 'additional correction' report for the documents from the previous submissions or for the documents that may have been omitted from the previous submissions or runs. When you generate a correction report, the report run type is set as 'correction'. You can display the documents omitted from the previous submissions using the 'Analyze Data' feature.

With this background on advanced compliance reporting, let us set up the compliance reporting, for USA, for withholding tax reporting for our case study (BESTM).

8.2.7.1 Setting Up Your Compliance Reporting

You need to set up the compliance reports to fulfil your country/region-specific compliance reporting requirements, and SAP provides the required report categories and report definitions for the same. In this configuration step, you make the connection between the reporting entities for which you should submit compliance reports. You need to complete the following activities, in the sequence, to set up the compliance reporting:

1) **Define Compliance Reporting Entities**: Enter a code and name for all the reporting entities that you need to fulfil the compliance requirements for your organization. To make things easier for your business users, enter a name (say, US_RPG_ENT). This text will be displayed on the user interface for the users running the reports.
   a. Assign Report Categories to a Reporting Entity: Select the report categories (say, US_WHT_1042S, US_WHT_1099INT etc) that you need for this reporting

entity. The report categories assigned to a reporting entity should have the same organizational units (say, company code) assigned. You create report categories in the 'Define Advanced Compliance Reports' app (Figure 8.51).

    i. *Set Periodicity of Report Category*: For each report category, you can define periodicity as per the government regulations. You need to define the 'Offset' (the number of days, after the period end, that the system uses to calculate the due date for submitting the report to the government) and 'Notify' (the number days, before the report due date, when the notification period for business users begins).

    ii. *Set Properties of Reporting Activity*: You can set the properties of the reporting activities assigned to the report category. You can set the valid from ('Valid From') and to ('Valid Until') dates for the report activity. You can set the activity due date using the 'Offset' field. The system calculates the activity due date by adding the report category due date and the specified offset value. You can also deactivate an activity. A deactivated activity does not appear in the 'Run Advanced Compliance Reports' app (Figure 8.60).

    iii. *Enter Parameters Specific to the Report Category*: Sometimes the system cannot find the data needed for the output of a specific report in your SAP system. Here, you enter the values for those parameters, to enable the system to create a complete and correct output document. In the search help for 'Parameter Name', you can only see the list of parameters that belong to the report category. In the 'Define Advanced Compliance Reports' app (Figure 8.51), you add parameters to a report definition. The report definition is then assigned to a reporting activity, and the reporting activity is assigned to the report category.

b. <u>Set Validity of Organizational Unit</u>: For each reporting entity, you should assign the organizational units that make up the legal entity required to submit the report, that is, whose data should be reported together to the government. This assignment is time-dependent. Enter a date from which the system should recognize the validity of these assignments. The system uses this date for certain consistency checks.

    i. *Assign Organizational Unit to a Reporting Entity*: Assign the organizational units (business place, business area, company code, section code, and tax jurisdiction) that make up this reporting entity. You can enter one or more organizational units, but must mark one of them as the *leading organizational unit*. The system takes data from the leading organizational unit master, to fill some of the fields in the report documents created for the government.

> **i** You can assign multiple organizational units to a reporting entity, but assign multiple values only to an organizational unit of a single type: for example, if you assign company code and tax jurisdiction to your reporting entity, you can enter multiple values for either the company code or tax jurisdiction, but not for both.

c. <u>Enter Parameters Specific to Reporting Entities:</u> If there is specific data related to a reporting entity that is valid for the output of several report categories but cannot be found in your SAP system, you need enter those missing values here.

With this, we are now ready to set up the compliance reporting for USA, for BESTM, for reporting withholding tax. You need to follow the steps listed below, in that order, to complete the configuration:

i. Use the menu path: SAP Customizing Implementation Guide > Financial Accounting > Advanced Compliance Reporting > Setting Up Your Compliance Reporting.

ii. On the 'Change View "Compliance Reporting Entities": Overview' screen, click on 'New Entries' to define a new compliance reporting entity for USA.

iii. On the next screen, enter an identifier for 'Rep Entity' (US_RPG_ENT) and enter a description in 'Reporting Entity Name'; 'Save' the details (Figure 8.52).

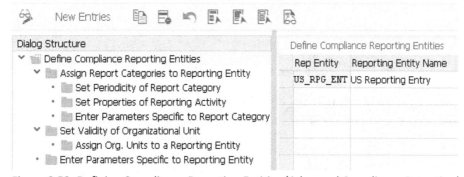

Figure 8.52: Defining Compliance Reporting Entities (Advanced Compliance Reporting)

iv. Now, select the row containing the entry US_RPG_ENT, and double-click on 'Assign Report Categories to Reporting Entity' on the left-hand side dialog-box.

v.   On the 'Change View "Assign Report Categories to Reporting Entity": Overview' screen, click on 'New Entries', enter all the reports, under 'Report Category ID', that you want to assign to the reporting entity US_RPG_ENT and 'Save' (Figure 8.53).

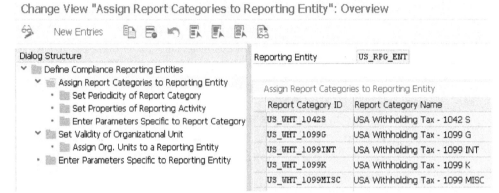

Figure 8.53: Assigning Report Categories to Reporting Entity (Advanced Compliance Reporting)

vi.   Now, select a report category row (say, US_WHT_1099MISC) and double-click on 'Set Periodicity of Report Category' on the left-hand side dialog-box.

vii.   On the 'Change View "Set Periodicity of Report Category": Overview' screen (Figure 8.54):

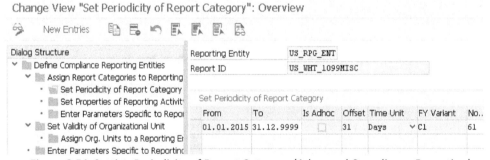

Figure 8.54: Setting Periodicity of Report Category (Advanced Compliance Reporting)

- Enter the 'From' and 'To' date of report validity.
- Select 'Is Adhoc' flag, to denote if the report as an adhoc one.

> **i** Adhoc reports will not have periodicity assigned to them. They may be requested by the government authorities on a non-regular basis. The reporting tasks are not generated automatically for adhoc reports in the 'Run Advanced Compliance Reports' app, but you can create your own reporting tasks in the app.

- Enter the 'Offset' limit in number of days: this is the number of days, after the period end, that the system uses to calculate the due date for submitting the report to the government.

> **i** Example: you submit a monthly report and the period ends on the last day of the calendar month. You decide that the due date for submitting the report should be 10 days after the period ends. You enter 10 as the value for 'Offset'. This means (for the first period of the year) that (a) the period ends on January 31, (b) the due date is displayed as February 10 and (c) the due date status changes to 'Overdue 1 Day' on February 11.

- You can set the 'Time Unit' for 'Offset' as days, weeks, months and years.
- In 'FY Variant' field, enter the appropriate FYV that the system should use, to determine how often (periodicity) the report should be submitted in a fiscal year. C1 denotes that the submission will be in the 1st period of the calendar year.
- In the 'Notify' period, enter the number days (before the report due date) when the notification period for business user should begin. The system calculates the due date using the value that you entered in the 'Offset' field. Then, the system subtracts the value that you enter, here, (in 'Notify') from the due date. The resulting date is when the system should first notify business users that the submission date is approaching. When the notification period begins, the due date status on the UI changes to 'Due Within 'n' Days'.

> **i** For example, you submit a monthly report and the period ends on the last day of the calendar month. You decide that the due date for submitting the report is 10 days after the period ends. You enter 10 as the value for 'Offset'. In the 'Notify' field, you enter 5, indicating that you want the business users to be notified 5 days before the due date. This means, for the first period of the calendar year, that (a) the first period of the year ends on January 31, (b) the due date is displayed on the UI as February 10, (c) before February 5, the due date status is 'Due Later' and (d) on February 5, the due date status is displayed as 'Due Within 5 Days'.

- Enter the 'Factory Calendar' ID of your company, if you have entered an exception rule for non-working days.

- Enter how the system should handle 'Due Date Adjustment' (like, previous working day, next working day etc) if the calculated due date falls on a non-working day.

viii. 'Save' the details.

ix. Double-click on 'Set Properties for Reporting Activity'. Click on 'New Entries' and enter the required details on the next screen (Figure 8.55):

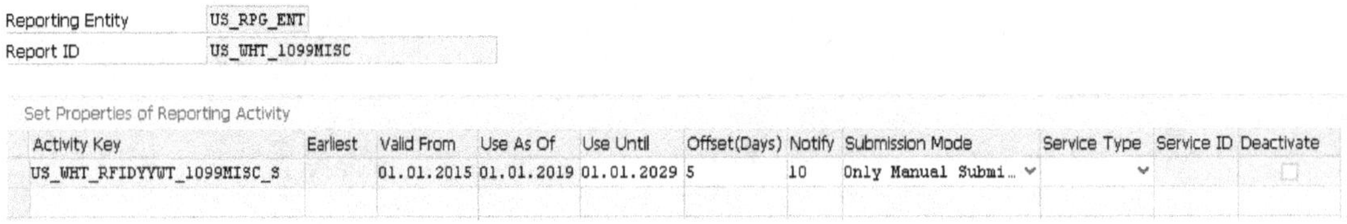

Reporting Entity   US_RPG_ENT
Report ID   US_WHT_1099MISC

Set Properties of Reporting Activity

Activity Key	Earliest	Valid From	Use As Of	Use Until	Offset(Days)	Notify	Submission Mode	Service Type	Service ID	Deactivate
US_WHT_RFIDYYWT_1099MISC_S		01.01.2015	01.01.2019	01.01.2029	5	10	Only Manual Submi... ⌄	⌄		☐

Figure 8.55: Setting Properties for Reporting Activity (Advanced Compliance Reporting)

- Select the required 'Activity Key'. Select US_WHT_RFIDYYWT_1099MISC_S, for normal 1099-MISC reporting or US_WHT_1099_MISC_V0_S, for enhanced 1099-MISC reporting.
- Enter the appropriate date for 'Use As Of' and 'Use Until' fields. Enter the required days for 'Offset (Days)' and 'Notify' fields.
- Select the 'Submission Mode'. If you want automatic submission, then, you need to maintain the appropriate details in 'Service Type' as RFC or SOAP.
- Provide the 'Service ID': ADS (Adobe Document Services) or FDT_XS_COMPILER, if you have selected automatic submission, in the previous step. Leave this as blank, if the submission is manual.
- Select 'Deactivate' if you want to deactivate an existing report activity and define a new one. The deactivated report activity will not appear in the corresponding tasks in the 'Run Advanced Compliance Reports' app (Figure 8.60).

x. Now, double-click on 'Enter Parameters Specific to Report Category' on the left-hand-side 'Dialog Structure', click on 'New Entries' and maintain the parameters as shown in Table 8.8 for the report 1099-MISC (Figure 8.56).

Parameter Name	Description	Sample Value
US_MIN_AMT_CHECK_01	Minimum invoice amount check, on royalty amount	600
US_MIN_AMT_CHECK_02	Minimum invoice amount check, on dividend amount	10
US_MIN_AMT_CHECK_03	Minimum invoice amount check, on the base amount of direct sales	5000

Table 8:8 Parameters specific to Report Category (US_WHT_1099MISC)

Change View "Enter Parameters Specific to Report Category": Overview o

New Entries

Dialog Structure			

Reporting Entity   US_RPG_ENT
Report ID   US_WHT_1099MISC

Dialog Structure
∨ Define Compliance Reporting Entities
  ∨ Assign Report Categories to Reporting Entity
    • Set Periodicity of Report Category
    • Set Properties of Reporting Activity
    • Enter Parameters Specific to Report Category
  ∨ Set Validity of Organizational Unit
    • Assign Org. Units to a Reporting Entity
  • Enter Parameters Specific to Reporting Entity

Enter Parameters Specific to Report Category

Parameter Name	Valid From	Parameter Value	
US_MIN_AMT_CHECK_01	01.01.2019	600	🔓
US_MIN_AMT_CHECK_02	01.01.2019	10	🔓
US_MIN_AMT_CHECK_03	01.01.2019	5000	🔓

Figure 8.56: Entering Parameters Specific to Report Category (Advanced Compliance Reporting)

You have, so far, completed defining the compliance reporting entity, assigned report categories to the reporting entity and maintained the (a) periodicity for the report category, (b) properties for the reporting activity and (c) parameters that are specific to a report category.

It is time, now, to set the validity of organizational units that are relevant for the reporting. Let us continue to make the settings as described below:

i.   Double-click on 'Set Validity of Organizational Unit' on the left-hand side 'Dialog Structure', click on 'New Entries' on the next screen, and maintain the 'Valid From' date and a 'Comment'. Now 'Save' (Figure 8.57).

New Entries: Overview of Added Entries

Dialog Structure
∨ Define Compliance Reporting Entities
  ∨ Assign Report Categories to Reporting Entity
    • Set Periodicity of Report Category
    • Set Properties of Reporting Activity
    • Enter Parameters Specific to Report Category
  ∨ Set Validity of Organizational Unit
    • Assign Org. Units to a Reporting Entity

Reporting Entity   US_RPG_ENT

Set Validity of Organizational Unit

Valid From	Comment
01.01.2019	Validity of oraganizational units

Figure 8.57: Setting Validity of Organizational Unit (Advanced Compliance Reporting)

With the validity set, you may now assign the organizational units (business place, business area, company code, section code, and tax jurisdiction) to the reporting entity.

ii.   Select a 'Valid From' row (Figure 8.57) from the previous activity, and double-click on 'Assign Org. Units to a Reporting Entity' on the left-hand side 'Dialog Structure'.

iii.   On the 'Change View "Assign Org. Units to a Reporting Entity": Overview' screen, click on 'New Entries' and enter the details on the next screen (Figure 8.58):

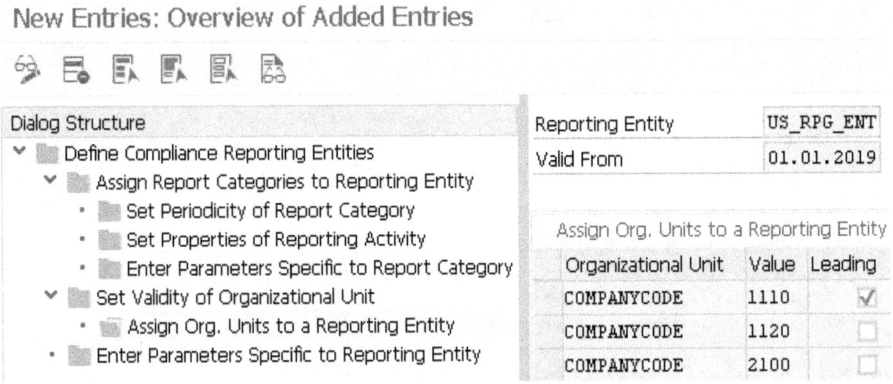

New Entries: Overview of Added Entries

Figure 8.58: Assign Organizational Units to Reporting Entity (Advanced Compliance Reporting)

- Select the type of 'Organizational Unit' from the drop-down values, and maintain the appropriate 'Value' (say, Company Code). Repeat to add more values of the same organizational unit type.
- Select 'Leading' check-box to denote that this company code will be the leading company code in this reporting entity.

> **i** You must mark one of the company codes (organizational unit) as the leading company code, even if there is only one company code in the reporting entity. The system uses the selected company code's data for the leading company code to fill some of the values in the report output.

iv. 'Save' the settings.

With this, we have reached the final step in configuring the settings for advanced compliance reporting, for USA, for reporting withholding tax for BESTM. Let us, now, complete setting up of the parameters specific to the reporting entity US_RPG_ENT.

v. Double-click on 'Enter Parameters Specific to Reporting Entity' on the left-hand side 'Dialog Structure' and click on 'New Entries'.

vi. Maintain the parameters relating the reporting entity (Figure 8.59) and 'Save' the settings. It may not be required to fill in values for all the parameters, but provide as much as details possible.

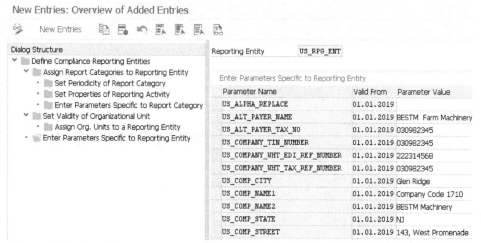

Figure 8.59: Entering Parameters specific to Reporting Entity (Advanced Compliance Reporting)

This completes our discussion on configuring advanced compliance reporting, for USA, for withholding tax reporting for BESTM (Project Dolphin). Let us move on to discuss the various withholding tax reports for compliance, now:

8.2.7.2   Withholding Tax Reports for USA

Let us discuss the following withholding tax compliance reports, in detail:

- Withholding Tax (1099-MISC) Report
- Withholding Tax (1099-G) Report
- Withholding Tax (1099-INT) Report
- Withholding Tax (1099-K) Report
- Withholding Tax (1042-S) Report

8.2.7.2.1   Withholding Tax (1099-MISC) Report

The Withholding Tax (1099-MISC) Report is generated based on the information collected from supplier documents, for example, supplier cleared invoices, supplier credit memos, open down payments, and so on. The system generates a TEXT file that you can submit to the government authorities. A PDF file for 1099-MISC Copy B is generated that you can send to the vendors. Also, a PDF pre-printed form, with the financial transaction data, is generated. You can print this data on a pre-printed Copy A form, and submit to the tax authorities. You can use the 'Run Advanced Compliance Reports' app (Figure 8.60) to generate the report.

As we already made the configuration and also maintained the relevant parameters for this specific report (Section 8.2.7.1), you may now follow the steps listed below, to generate the report:

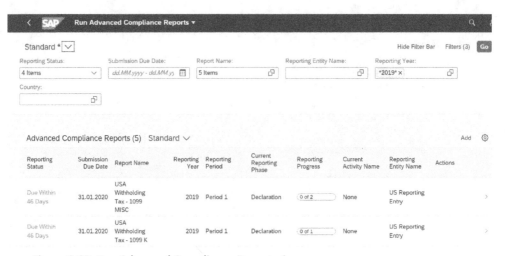

Figure 8.60: Run Advanced Compliance Reports App

1) To get a list of the reports that require actions, enter the selection parameters that define the reporting period and choose the US_WHT_1099MISC (USA Withholding Tax – 1099-MISC) report, in the search help of the 'Report Name' field [reporting entity: US_RPG_ENT (US Reporting Entity)].

2) Choose one or more 'Reporting Status' depending on how close the deadline of the report is to the actual calendar day. You can also enter additional filtering options, such as the "Submission Due Date", the 'Reporting Year', or the 'Country'.

3) Select the row for which you want to create the 1099-MISC legal documents.

4) Select 'Go'. The app displays a list of the reports for each reporting period that you can further process.

5) Click the row of the report you want to process and choose 'New Run'.

6) The app, now, opens the 'Generic Withholding Tax Reporting' program (RFIDYYT). Choose a 'Run Option': you can choose to generate the report run immediately or schedule the run for a later point in time. For report runs, that may take a long time to process, you can choose to run the reports in the background.

7) To run the report in 'Compatibility Mode', on the selection screen, choose the 'Process Type' as US_1099MISC, 'Output Group' as US1, and 'Country Key' as US. Enter a date in the 'Reporting Period' field.

8) Choose 'Run'. The app generates the run and displays it in the section 'Generated' on the screen. You can display the generated data by clicking the row of the generated run. If the run was successful, you can review the data in the TEXT file on the 'Legal Reporting' tab, by clicking the link in the 'Document Name' column. You can also download the generated document to your local computer, and submit it to the tax authorities as required (You can also configure the system to generate and send the report, automatically, to the tax authorities by maintaining the required settings in

'Submission Mode' in 'Set Parameters of Reporting Activity' under the configuration activity 'Setting Up your Compliance Reporting' discussed earlier in Section 8.2.7.1).

9) After the file has been generated, submit it to the tax authorities; when the authorities approved it, change the status of the 'Reporting Run' by choosing the row of the run and then click the 'Update Submission Status' button. Change the status manually to 'Accepted by Government'.

8.2.7.2.2   Withholding Tax (1099-G) Report

As in the case of withholding tax 1099-MISC report, for withholding tax (1099-G) report also, the system generates a TEXT file that you can submit to the government authorities. A PDF file for 1099-G Copy B is generated that you can send to the vendors. Also, a PDF pre-printed form, with the financial transaction data, is generated. You can print this data on a pre-printed Copy A form, and submit to the tax authorities. You can use the 'Run Advanced Compliance Reports' app (Figure 8.60) to generate the withholding tax report.

The steps to generate this report are similar to that of the 1099-MISC report, except that to get a list of the reports that require actions, you have to choose US_WHT_1099G (USA Withholding Tax – 1099 G) report in the search help of the 'Report Name' field, for the reporting entity US_RPG_ENT in the search help. And, when running the report in Compatibility Mode, on the selection screen, you will select the 'Process Type' as US_1099G; the other entries are similar to that 1099-MISC reporting.

8.2.7.2.3   Withholding Tax (1099-INT) Report

As in the case of withholding tax 1099-MISC report, for withholding tax (1099-INT) report also, the system generates a TEXT file that you can submit to the government authorities. A PDF file for 1099-INT Copy B is generated that you can send to the vendors. Also, a PDF pre-printed form, with the financial transaction data, is generated. You can print this data on a pre-printed Copy A form, and submit to the tax authorities. You can use the 'Run Advanced Compliance Reports' app (Figure 8.60) to generate the withholding tax report.

The steps to generate this report are similar to that of the 1099-MISC report, except that to get a list of the reports that require actions, you have to choose US_WHT_1099INT (USA Withholding Tax – 1099 INT) report in the search help of the 'Report Name' field for the reporting entity US_RPG_ENT in the search help. And, when running the report in Compatibility Mode, on the selection screen, you will select the 'Process Type' as US_1099INT; the other entries are similar to that 1099-MISC reporting.

8.2.7.2.4   Withholding Tax (1099-K) Report

As in the case of withholding tax 1099-MISC report, for withholding tax (1099-K) report also, the system generates a TEXT file that you can submit to the government authorities. A PDF file for 1099-K Copy B is generated that you can send to the vendors. Also, a PDF pre-printed form, with the financial transaction data, is generated. You can print this data on a pre-printed

Copy A form, and submit to the tax authorities. You can use the 'Run Advanced Compliance Reports' app (Figure 8.60) to generate the Withholding Tax report.

The steps to generate this report are similar to that of the 1099-MISC report, except that to get a list of the reports that require actions, you have to choose US_WHT_1099K (USA Withholding Tax – 1099 K) report in the search help of the 'Report Name' field for the reporting entity US_RPG_ENT in the search help. And, when running the report in Compatibility Mode, on the selection screen, you will select the 'Process Type' as US_1099K; the other entries are similar to that 1099-MISC reporting.

8.2.7.2.5   Withholding Tax (1042-S) Report

As in the case of withholding tax 1099-MISC report, for withholding tax (1042-S) report also, the system generates a TEXT file that you can submit to the government authorities. A PDF file for 1042-S Copy B is generated that you can send to the vendors. Also, a PDF pre-printed form, with the financial transaction data, is generated. You can print this data on a pre-printed Copy A form, and submit to the tax authorities. You can use the 'Run Advanced Compliance Reports' app (Figure 8.60) to generate the Withholding Tax report.

The steps to generate this report are similar to that of the 1099-MISC report except, that to get a list of the reports that require actions, you have to choose US_WHT_1042S (USA Withholding Tax – 1042S) report in the search help of the 'Report Name' field for the reporting entity US_RPG_ENT in the search help. And, when running the report in Compatibility Mode, on the selection screen, you will select the 'Process Type' as US_1042S; the other entries are similar to that 1099-MISC reporting.

However, you need to ensure that you have maintained the following parameters (Table 8.9), while defining the settings for advanced compliance reporting discussed already in Section 8.2.7.1, for 1042-S report:

Parameter Name	Description	Sample Value
US_1042_INT_CH3	Intermediary or FTE Chapter - 3 status code	X
US_1042_INT_TAXID	Intermediary or FTE Foreign Tax ID Number	666666666
US_CHP3	US Chapter - 3 reporting is available	X
US_FTIN	Foreign Tax Identification Number	1287111111111110
US_GIIN	Global Intermediary Identification Number	US1234567111111
US_STCD	Chapter 3 or Chapter 4 reporting status code	4

Table 8:9 Parameters specific to Report Category (US_WHT_1042S)

This completes our discussion on withholding tax reporting. Let us move on to discuss withholding tax change over.

8.2.8   Withholding Tax Changeover

To change over from classic withholding tax to EWT, it is not sufficient that you just activate EWT in the system, as you would not be able to carry out further processing to items that have previously been posted in the system. You need to convert all the relevant Customizing, master data, and transaction data so that it all can then be used in EWT. SAP provides you the necessary tool supporting the *withholding tax changeover,* by automatically converting all the existing and relevant withholding tax data in your current system.

You need to ensure that the prerequisites for the changeover has been carried out in full, before moving to the various process steps to make the actual changeover. Let us look at the prerequisites, first.

8.2.8.1   Prerequisites

The following are the prerequisites that you need to complete before actually starting the changeover:

i.   *Upgrade to Release 4.0 and Above*: It is essential that you complete all tasks relating to the Release upgrade, before starting the withholding tax changeover. Once you have converted the withholding tax data and activated the EWT functionality, the data conversion cannot be reversed. Hence, it is recommended that you first carry out the withholding tax data conversion in a test system. You need to activate EWT functionality, for the company codes for the changeover, only when you are explicitly directed to do so

ii.   *System Block*: You must ensure that no documents are posted in the company codes concerned, during the withholding tax changeover. It is recommended that you block your system for all the end users and carry out the conversion runs, preferably, on a weekend.

iii.   *Logistics Invoice Verification (LIV):* The EWT functionality is only supported by LIV; it is not supported by the conventional invoice verification. You can therefore no longer use the conventional invoice verification, once you have carried out the withholding tax changeover. Hence, you need to change over to LIV before converting the withholding tax data and changing over to EWT. If you do not use invoice verification in your organization, you do not need to take any action at this stage.

With the understanding of prerequisites for withholding tax changeover, we are now ready to discuss the various steps in the changeover process:

8.2.8.2   Changeover Process

The actual changeover process to EWT can be summarised as under:

i.   **Preparations:** The preparations include:
   a.   Carrying-out the FI Comparative Analysis
   b.   Archiving Cleared Items
   c.   Checking the System Settings for EWT: For the purposes of the changeover, the system settings for EWT should correspond to the settings for classic withholding tax. You need to define the official withholding tax keys, withholding tax types, withholding tax codes, withholding tax formulas and withholding tax minimum / maximum amounts. You do not need to make any settings for type of recipient for vendors, account determination and assignment of withholding tax types to company codes, as these system settings are automatically converted during 'Convert Customizing' activity (marked by A in Figure 8.62).
   d.   Setting Up Authorizations for the Withholding Tax Changeover: Here, you need to create authorization profiles for the people, who are involved in the withholding tax changeover. To create these profiles, use the authorization object 'Financial Accounting: Withholding Tax Changeover' (F_WTMG) provided by SAP. Once the withholding tax changeover is completed, take the precaution of withdrawing this change authorization for all these users, to prevent conversion being started while the system is being used for normal day-to-day activities.
   e.   Blocking Users: You must block the system for normal activities, while the conversion is being prepared and carried out. You should not post / process documents, and change master data; otherwise your accounting documents and system settings may result in serious discrepancies. Ensure that all users involved in the withholding tax changeover have the appropriate access authorizations, and block your SAP System for all other users.

> **i** If it is not possible to take measures to ensure that there are no users working in the system, you should block ALL the users and the WHOLE system throughout the organization: restart the system so that all users are logged off.

ii.   **Converting the Withholding Tax Data and Activating EWT**: To start the conversion of withholding tax data, you need to follow the menu path: SAP Customizing Implementation Guide > Financial Accounting > Financial Accounting Global Settings > Withholding Tax > Withholding Tax Changeover > Withholding Tax Changeover, or

Transaction WTM. You will be taken to the 'Withholding Tax Data Conversion: Initial Screen' (Figure 8.61).

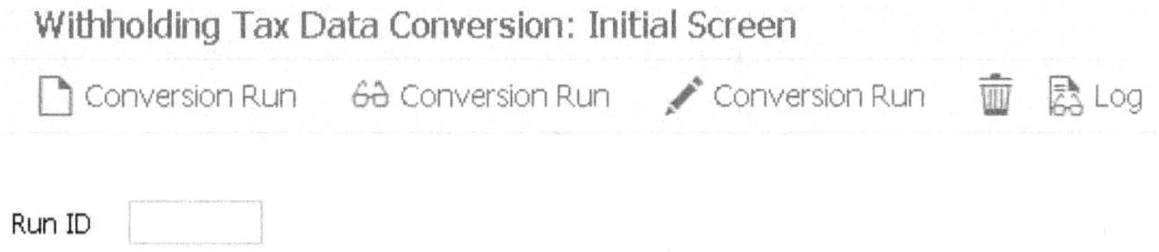

Withholding Tax Data Conversion: Initial Screen

📄 Conversion Run　　6ə Conversion Run　　✏ Conversion Run　　🗑　📇 Log

Run ID [　　　　]

Figure 8.61: Withholding Tax Changeover – Initial Screen

Then proceed as under:

a. <u>Creating and Editing a Conversion Run</u>: The withholding tax data can be converted in several conversion runs (Figure 8.62). In each *conversion run*, you can select one or more company codes for which you want to convert the withholding tax data. The system automatically adds company codes that are in the same country, and in which cross-company code clearing is possible. You cannot carry out any new conversion steps if conversion steps that have been started in other conversion runs have not yet been completed. The conversion of a previous run is considered complete when the 'Conversion Steps' namely Convert Customizing (A), Master Data Conversion (B), and Document Conversion (C) have been carried out without any errors, and EWT has been activated for the relevant company codes. In any one conversion run, data can only be converted from company codes that are all in the same country. It is not possible to convert company codes from different countries in the same conversion run.

b. <u>Preparation:</u> The preparations for data conversion include, in that order, (i) choosing the company code (s), (ii) assigning withholding tax types and withholding tax codes, (iii) analysing datasets and finally (iv) making the appropriate settings in vendor master records (as marked in Figure 8.62).

c. <u>Conversion</u>: The withholding tax data conversion is made up of three separate steps as shown in Figure 8.62: (A) Convert Customizing, (B) Master data conversion and (C) Document conversion. First carry out the individual conversion steps, as a test. A test checks the settings and picks up any errors that may exist. It is quicker to perform a test; if any errors are found, you can rectify them and then start the actual conversion step. To actually carry out the individual steps as a test, select the 'Test run' field and choose 'Execute'. If you discover any erroneous data, when you actually carry out a conversion step, you can 'reset' the conversion step and then correct the error.

> **i** You can only carry out the next conversion step when the preceding step has been successfully completed (with a green or yellow traffic light). Once you have activated EWT for the relevant company codes, it is no longer possible to reset any of the conversion steps that have actually been carried out.

d. Activating EWT: We have already discussed this, in Section 8.2.4.2.

Figure 8.62: Withholding Tax Changeover – Conversion Run Control Screen

iii. **Postprocessing:** The postprocessing activities include:
   a. Checking out and ensuring that you have completed all the system settings for EWT in the IMG.
   b. Manually postprocessing the exemption in the master data because, the information about withholding tax exemption in the master data for classic withholding tax is not automatically copied into the master data for EWT during the conversion. Hence, you have to define the information manually for each withholding tax type. Also, the 'Reduced rate' is defined at withholding tax code level for exemption in classic withholding tax; however, you need to maintain all information about exemption in the vendor master record (including the exemption percentage rate) for EWT, and do that for all the vendors concerned.
   c. Manual postprocessing of documents with reunification tax: in case you are changing over from a system with SAP Release lower than 4.6C, then, you have to define a separate withholding tax type for reunification tax and adjust the portion of the base amount or the withholding tax percentage rate subject to tax accordingly; in case of your system is with Release 4.6C or higher, then, you can define dependent withholding tax types when you post the payment; the 'Inherit base function' for the withholding tax base amount provides the withholding tax amount from another withholding tax type.
   d. Manually postprocess the documents and items (as in the case of recurring entry documents, sample documents and noted items) that were not automatically converted. After you have carried out the conversion run and the withholding tax changeover, you have to post these items again.
   e. Releasing the system: when you have successfully completed all the planned conversion runs and the necessary postprocessing, you have to release the system for the users so as to post documents again, and to carry out all other regular activities in the system.

This completes our discussion on withholding tax changeover, and also the discussion on withholding tax.

8.3   Conclusion

As the final set of FI global settings, we discussed the configuration relating to tax on sales and purchases, and withholding tax, in this Chapter.

You learned that you can use SAP FI (FI-G/L, FI-A/P and FI-A/R) for tax management involving calculation, posting, adjustment, and reporting of taxes. You also learned that, you can manage tax at the national level or at the regional / jurisdictional level or at the combined national and regional levels. You learned that you have to make the tax configuration at the country level as all legal entities in the same country need to follow the same taxation policies while preparing their financial statements. You understood that you can either define the tax rates internally within your SAP system or fetch them from an external taxation system (like, Vertex), via interfacing. You learned that SAP supports multiple taxation types like sales tax, tax on sales and purchases, and withholding tax (including extended withholding tax).

You understood that the 'tax on sales and purchases' (also known as 'sales and use tax') are levied on invoiced goods and services payable in accordance with the principles of VAT (value-added tax). You also understood that while the 'sales tax' is levied on the sale of taxable goods on the transactions occurring within a state, the 'use tax', on the other hand, is imposed on the purchaser; the seller is not liable for this tax. You further understood that the taxes on sales and purchases apply to 'input tax', 'output tax', 'additional tax', and 'acquisition tax'. You also understood that you can calculate the taxes on sales and purchases through three different ways: non-jurisdiction method, jurisdiction method and jurisdiction method with external tax calculation. You learned that the tax on sales and purchases is calculated through condition methods, in SAP, using a tax calculation procedure, tax codes, and jurisdiction codes, if any, and that the system posts the tax during document processing. You were then taken through the various configuration settings – grouped into basic settings, calculation and posting – that you need to make, in the system, for tax on sales and purchases. You understood that you can configure the SAP system to manage the tax sales and purchase for USA, either through manual calculation or automatically using an external tax application solution. You learned how to configure the settings for external tax calculation using Vertex.

Moving on to withholding tax, you learned that withholding tax is the tax that is charged at the beginning of the payment flow in some countries, and the party (vendor) that is subject to tax does not pay the withholding tax (to the tax authorities by himself), but a customer that is authorized to deduct reduces the payment amount by the withholding tax proportion and pays the tax, so withheld, directly to the appropriate tax authorities. You learned that SAP supports both classic withholding tax and extended withholding tax (EWT). You learned that EWT supports assignment of more than one withholding tax type to a business partner and allows tax calculation for partial payments as well, besides enabling processing the tax from both the vendor and customer views. You learned the various configuration settings (grouped under basic settings, calculation, posting and advanced compliance reporting) that enable you set up the EWT functionality in SAP to meet your business requirements including compliance reporting to the tax authorities. At the end, you understood how to make a changeover from classic withholding to EWT.

This completes our discussion on taxes on sales and services, and withholding tax. This also completes our discussion on FI global settings. We are all set, now, to discuss the G/L in the next Chapter.

9 General Ledger Accounting

The '*General Ledger*' (G/L) is the backbone of any accounting system which holds the financial data of an organization. It is, simply, a bookkeeping ledger serving as the central repository for accounting data transferred from all subledgers like accounts payable, accounts receivable, cash management, fixed assets, purchasing etc. Each account maintained by an organization is known as a ledger account, and the collection of all these accounts is known as the G/L.

The main purpose of *SAP G/L Accounting* is to represent external accounting in the statement of financial position (*balance sheet*) and the statement of income and expenditure (*profit and loss statement*). The SAP G/L Accounting records all business transactions, primary postings and settlements from internal accounting, in a software system that is fully integrated with all the other operational areas of a company. It ensures that the accounting data is always complete and accurate. Besides meeting the statutory / legal requirements of the country wherein your company operates, the SAP G/L Accounting also meets the modern day's accounting requirements like (a) parallel accounting (by running several parallel G/Ls for different accounting principles), (b) segment reporting (as required by the accounting principles of IFRS and US GAAP that are made possible by the 'Segment' dimension in the SAP G/L), (c) cost of sales accounting (through 'Functional Area' dimension in the SAP G/L) and (d) the integration of legal & management reporting (through the integration of SAP Profit Center Accounting with SAP G/L Accounting enabling financial statements for any dimension like profit center).

The SAP G/L Accounting comprises of several functions for entering and evaluating posting data, like (a) free choice of level like either the corporate group or the company, (b) automatic and simultaneous posting of all subledger items in G/L accounting (reconciliation accounts), (c) simultaneous updating of the parallel G/Ls and of the cost accounting areas, and (d) the real-time evaluation of and reporting on current posting data, in the form of account displays, financial statements with different balance sheet versions, and additional analyses.

The SAP G/L Accounting, hence, automatically serves as a complete record of all business transactions, with its centralized and up-to-date reference of the accounts. You can check the individual transactions at any time, in real-time, by displaying the original documents, line items, and monthly debits and credits at various levels like accounts, journals, total/transaction figures, and balance sheet / profit and loss evaluations.

The SAP G/L Accounting is integrated with all the following application components of the SAP system, generating posting data of relevance to G/L accounting:

- Asset Accounting (FI-AA)
- Accounts Receivable and Accounts Payable (FI-AP/AR)
- Controlling (CO)
- Materials Management (MM)
- Human Capital Management (HCM)
- Treasury and Risk Management (TRM)
- Travel Management (FI-TV)
- Public Sector Management - Funds Management Government (PSM-FM)

---

i The traditional G/L (or *classic G/L*) of SAP R/3 required reconciliation of multiple ledgers and/or several applications to meet modern day's accounting challenges as there was no unified functionality which can take care of, for example, parallel reporting, segment reporting etc. As a result, you had to interface several application components to meet the specific and varying requirements of a company or industry or accounting or legal framework. Also, there was no automatic reconciliation among these applications and the G/L accounting, necessitating manual interventions which resulted in delays in closing activities, finalisation of accounts and release of financial statements. The tools available for planning and forecasting were also limited, with no or minimal analytical support.

To overcome these obstacles, SAP introduced the New G/L as a part of SAP ERP offering, and tried providing the required flexibility in accounting and reporting, by addressing to overcome the shortcomings of the traditional G/L accounting of SAP. Since then, the New G/L functionalities in SAP-FI have been improved, with every major release of the application, and is now simply called as the SAP G/L Accounting, that takes care of most of the modern day's accounting / financial / legal reporting needs including document splitting, segment reporting, cost of sales accounting, parallel accounting etc., besides providing a tight integration between internal and external reporting. It also provides the business with a plethora of analytical tools and apps to plan, simulate and forecast, besides enabling quicker and timely decision making.

In this chapter, we will discuss the following:

- Features and Functionalities in SAP G/L Accounting
- Pre-requisites for Configuring SAP G/L Accounting
- Master Data
- Business Transactions
- Periodic Processing
- Preparation for Productive Start
- Information System

Let us start our discussion to understand the major features and functionalities of SAP G/L Accounting.

9.1   Features and Functionalities in SAP G/L accounting

The *SAP G/L Accounting*, now with its new structure (integrating several individual ledgers like cost of sales accounting ledger, profit center accounting ledger etc.), addresses the various new legal and reporting requirements for international and local accounting principles of almost all the countries in the world. With its unified user interface, for entering both FI and CO information in a single transaction, it obviates the duplicity of efforts and leads to increased efficiency in data entry, transaction posting, reconciliation and consolidation. With the improved functionality, it provides for on-the-fly document splitting, and automatic segment / functional area derivation, besides enabling financial statements for any dimension.   It provides you with the flexibility of going in either for the ledger-oriented parallel accounting through 'parallel ledgers' or the account-oriented parallel accounting through 'parallel accounts'. The new totals table (FAGLFLEXT) supports addition of your own fields (customer fields), besides a number of standard fields to provide the flexibility of bringing in additional information without any coding effort (we have already discussed this, in Chapter 6 in Sections 6.1.3, 6.1.4 and 6.1.5); this extensibility also brings in the required flexibility to add industry-specific fields as well. The Figure 9.1 shows the enhanced features and functionalities of SAP G/L in its current form.

Let us look at some of the enhanced features / functionalities of SAP G/L Accounting, in brief:

9.1.1   Extensibility

With SAP supplied *'standard fields'* (or *dimensions*), such as business area, profit center, segment etc, you can tailor them to meet your specific reporting needs, besides making use of them in your transactions in SAP G/L Accounting. If you find that these standard fields are not be sufficient to meet your needs, you may consider using your own fields (not supplied by SAP) called *'customer fields'* to meet those requirements. You can use customer fields as (a) product-related or activity-related characteristics such as product groups, (b) organizational or managerial characteristics such as geographical regions, and (c) characteristics arising out of legal / statutory or industry requirements such as contract. You can include customer fields, in FI, in the *'coding block'* and broaden the scope of SAP G/L Accounting, either by adding new customer fields or by combining such fields with the existing standard fields. This way, you can adapt the information in SAP G/L Accounting to the specific reporting requirements of your business.

Refer Sections 6.1.3 and 6.1.4, of Chapter 6, for more details on extensibility.

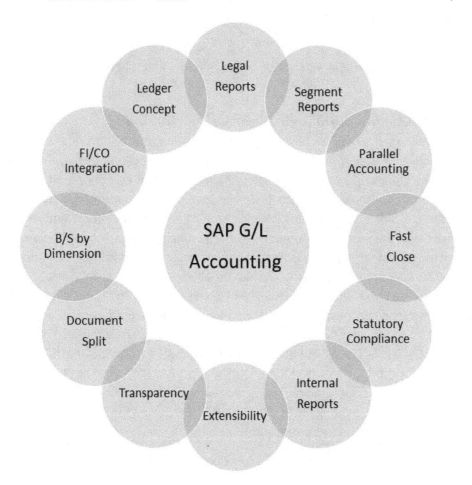

Figure 9.1 SAP G/L – Enhanced Features and Functionalities

9.1.2   Ledger Concept

Leveraging the SAP's Special Ledger (FI-SL) functionality to save the totals, the SAP G/L Accounting uses the ledger and ledger group concepts to model more than one valuation views.

There are two types of ledgers: *standard ledgers* and *extension ledgers*. The standard ledger contains a full set of journal entries for all business transactions, and can be designated either as the 'leading ledger' or 'non-leading ledger'. You will designate one standard ledger as the 'leading ledger'. You can have any number of other ledgers known 'non-leading ledgers' and/or 'extension ledgers' but you cannot have more than one leading ledger. You will designate the leading ledger as 0L, which is updated in all company codes, as it is assigned to all company codes, by default. The document numbers assigned in this ledger apply for all dependent ledgers. You will never be able to deactivate the leading ledger in the system. The non-leading ledgers are 'parallel ledgers' to the leading ledger, and can be based on a local accounting principle, for example. You have to activate a non-leading ledger for the individual company codes. An 'extension ledger' is a non-leading ledger created based on an underlying standard ledger. The postings to the underlying ledger also apply for the extension ledger; however, the postings made explicitly to an extension ledger are visible only in that extension ledger but not in the underlying standard ledger.

Refer Section 6.3, of Chapter 6, for more details.

When grouping the ledgers, if a ledger group contains the leading ledger, then you designate that leading ledger as the 'representative ledger' for that ledger group. However, if there is no leading ledger in a ledger group, you can designate one of the non-leading ledgers as the representative ledger. If the ledger group contains only one ledger, then, that ledger will also be the representative ledger.

Refer Section 6.3.4.5 of Chapter 6 for more details.

9.1.3 Document Splitting

The 'document splitting' functionality, in SAP G/L Accounting, helps you to automatically split line items for selected dimensions or to enable a zero-balance setting in the document for selected dimensions. As a result, it enables you to draw up complete financial statements, at any time, for various dimensions (including customer defined ones) like segments, profit centers, business areas, funds, receivables etc. When a document is split, the system creates additional clearing lines automatically. The illustration in Figure 9.2 shows how a document is split and additional lines items are generated by the system during document split.

> **i** Comparable with the document splitting for special purpose ledgers (FI-SL), this functionality has been available since the introduction of New G/L Accounting (as of SAP S/4HANA 5.0). It uses 'document splitting characteristics' (such as segment or profit center), as account assignment objects to portray the dimensions.

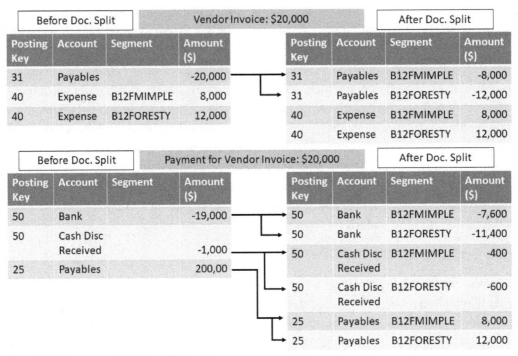

Figure 9.2 Document Splitting - Illustration

The document splitting (Figure 9.3) is based on the unique assignment of document types to predefined, non-modifiable 'business transactions' (or their attributes in a business transaction variant) as well as on the assignment of accounts to predefined, non-modifiable 'item categories'. The item categories are used to define 'document splitting rules', which, depending on the business transaction, determine which items of a document the system splits and how. A document splitting rule is assigned to a 'document splitting method'. To activate document splitting, assign a document splitting method that contains the document splitting rules.

The document splitting process is described below:

1) When you make a posting, the system determines (from the document type) the underlying business transaction, assigns the item category to the individual items within the document, and checks whether the item categories are permitted for that business transaction.

2) The system creates a reference to the preceding documents (such as, clearing and invoice reference). The system applies the account assignments that you have defined as document splitting characteristics for SAP G/L Accounting. This is called as *'passive document splitting'*.

3) Depending on the classification of the document, the system applies the related document splitting rule for the document, in which it is specified how the document is split and for which line items. This is known as *'active document splitting'*.

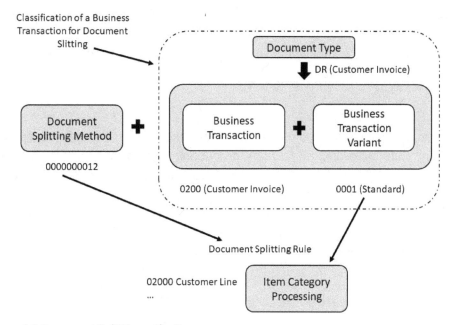

Figure 9.3 Document Splitting – the Process

4) If the system cannot determine the account assignments of the document splitting characteristics for individual line items, it can determine the account assignments either by inheritance or by using a standard account assignment. This may be necessary if the required information is not yet available when the posting occurs.

5) For individual document splitting characteristics for SAP G/L Accounting, you can define that the line items for these document splitting characteristics must be assigned to an account ('required entry' field). The system, then, checks whether the line items for these document splitting characteristics have an account assignment; if not, the system rejects the posting and issues an error message.

6) If the document does not produce zero-balance for the balancing dimensions, the system creates additional clearing items to ensure that the balancing dimensions in the document results in zero.

> **i** You can use document splitting only for documents that you can uniquely assign to a business process.

You can simulate the resulting postings, during document entry. From the simulation in the G/L view, you can call the 'expert mode' to obtain detailed information about the split document and the document splitting rules applied.

SAP comes delivered with a standard document splitting method that you can use, unchanged. However, you can also define your own document splitting rules and methods so as to adapt the standard document splitting method to meet your own specific requirements.

Refer to Section 9.4.1, for more details.

9.1.4 Parallel Accounting

The *'parallel accounting'* enables you to perform the valuations and closing operations, for a company code according to various accounting principles to meet varying reporting requirements like group reporting (or international reporting) and local reporting (in the country of operation). The SAP G/L Accounting supports two methods of parallel accounting: one using the concept of parallel ledgers (*ledger approach*) and the other using additional G/L accounts (*account approach*). The parallel accounting is supported in several of the SAP application components including FI, FI-AA, TRM (Treasury and Risk Management), CO and MM.

We have already discussed parallel accounting, in detail, in Section 6.5 of Chapter 6.

> **i** Consider, for example BESTM, the case of an Indian subsidiary of an American group company. The Indian subsidiary has to create financial statements according to the accounting principles of the group (US GAAP) as well as according to local accounting principles of India (IN-AS).

9.1.5 Segment Reporting

Required by some accounting principles (such as US GAAP and IFRS), you can use the *'segment reporting'*, in SAP G/L Accounting, by portraying the items in the financial statements by segment; the detailed results are then made available by segment, providing deeper insights into the financial health of a company. On the basis of the documents in SAP G/L Accounting, the system determines the segments that are relevant for the individual balance sheet items. The segment information is available in a document, only when document splitting is activated with the 'Segment' as the characteristic. In the case of documents that have been transferred from FI-CA (Contract Accounts Receivable and Payable), you will not be able to perform document splitting, subsequently, in SAP G/L Accounting. Hence, you need to ensure that those documents already contain the segment information before the transfer.

For more details on segment definition, derivation etc, refer to Section 5.3.7 of Chapter 5.

9.1.6 Integration of FI with Conrolling (CO)

With SAP S/4HANA Finance, 'Controlling' (CO) has now been tightly integrated with FI, by getting rid of data redundancies and the need for manual reconciliations, and making visible the internal CO actual postings in FI as well. Hence, the real-time FI-CO integration is now obsolete: the CO data is now stored in the new finance table ACDOCA along with the FI data.

The erstwhile totals tables are no longer required, because data can be aggregated from the line item table, which is also used for reporting. The actual data of COEP (WRTTP = '04') is now stored in ACDOCA. The actual statistical data of COEP (WRTTP = '11') is also stored in ACDOCA, using additional columns for the statistical account assignments and in COEP for compatibility access. The actual data needed for long-term orders/projects from COSP_BAK, COSS_BAK is now stored in table ACDOCA; this ensures (for primary postings) that there is a single source of truth, such that all G/L items with an assignment to cost centers, orders, WBS elements, business processes, or CO-PA characteristics are treated as one data record, enriched with the relevant profit center, functional area, segment, and so on. For secondary postings, this ensures that all sender-receiver relationships that are triggered by allocations, settlement etc., are now captured in the *Universal Journal* (refer Section 6.3.3 of Chapter 6, for more details), along with the partner profit centers, functional areas etc., that are affected by the allocation.

The cost elements are no longer required, separately, in SAP S/4HANA Finance, because they are now created as G/L accounts and are part of the chart of accounts. A new field for the 'cost element category' has been introduced in the G/L master record. You cannot, of course, maintain the cost elements in a time-dependent manner. The default account assignment is maintained using Transaction OKB9 (and not in the traditional cost element master data). The reports such as the trial balance, now, will display all postings (both primary and secondary) by account.

Also, refer to Section 6.6 of Chapter 6, to read more in detail about FI integration with CO, including the configuration that is required for setting that up.

9.1.7 Fast Close

The SAP G/L Accounting enables *'fast close'* for completing period-end closings much easier and quicker than ever before. Leveraging the SAP S/4HANA Financial Closing Cockpit, the fast close helps in (a) standardizing the closing cycle into a series of repeatable process steps and (b) managing those steps in accordance with best practices. It helps you in creation of non-consolidated balance sheet, at any time, at the characteristic's level, obviating the need to run additional programs to split the characteristics.

The SAP S/4HANA Financial Closing Cockpit helps you with the planning, execution, and analysis of closing operations, for the organizational units of your corporate group. The solution provides a structured user interface for recurring periodical tasks in the closing process in which several people may be involved. It supports various closing steps including Transactions, direct execution of programs, execution of programs in batch processing, workflows and manual steps. To optimize the closing process, the solution provides functions like (a) event-controlled organization of closing activities, (b) process overview and monitoring options and (c) analysis tools.

This completes our discussion on the main features / functionalities of SAP G/L Accounting. Let us move on to discuss the various pre-requisites for configuring SAP G/L Accounting, next.

9.2   Pre-requisites for Configuring SAP G/L Accounting

You need to complete some of the general settings for FI, before you can start working with the functions of SAP G/L Accounting: (a) you need to have the company codes and the Controlling area defined in the system, (b) you have to configure the ledgers that you will use in SAP G/L Accounting, (c) you will define the settings for fiscal year, posting period and currencies, (d) you set up the system for parallel accounting if required and (e) you make the necessary settings for integrating SAP FI with CO.

Let us look at, in detail, configuring those general settings for FI for making use of SAP G/L Accounting.

9.2.1   Definition of Company Code(s) and Controlling Area

As you are aware, we have already completed this configuration activity in Chapter 5 (Section 5.3.2 and Section 5.3.8) and defined the required company codes and controlling areas, while discussing the FI organization structure.

9.2.2   General settings for Fiscal Year, Posting Periods, and Currencies

We have already discussed and configured the required settings relating to fiscal year and posting periods in Chapter 6 (Section 6.4). We have defined the required fiscal year variants (FYV) and the posting period variants (PPV) and also discussed how to open / close posting periods. We have also discussed opening a new fiscal year in Section 6.4.8 of Chapter 6.

In SAP-FI, for each 'ledger-company code' combination, you have to specify the currencies in which your ledgers are to be managed (we have already made the required settings in Section 6.3.4 and 6.3.5 of Chapter 6). Recall that, in addition to managing ledgers in the company code currency (also, the national currency of the company code), you can manage ledgers in other currencies, such as the group currency or a hard currency.

9.2.3   Configuring Ledgers

To work with the functions of SAP G/L Accounting, you have to configure your ledgers. We have already configured the ledgers (leading, non-leading and extension ledgers), ledger groups and the associated settings (company code settings for ledgers, defining accounting principles etc) in Section 6.3 of Chapter 6. Once you have configured your ledgers for SAP G/L Accounting, you can then create your master data (chart of accounts, G/L accounts, segment, profit centers).

9.2.4 Settings for Parallel Accounting

We have already set up the parallel accounting for BESTM Corporate (Project Dolphin) using parallel ledgers as discussed in Section 6.5 of Chapter 6.

9.2.5 Integration of SAP FI with Controlling

We have made the required configuration settings for integrating FI with Controlling in Chapter 6 (Section 6.6).

This completes our discussion of the pre-requisites for configuring SAP G/L Accounting. Let us now move on to discuss the master data in SAP G/L Accounting.

9.3 Master Data

The G/L account master data defines how business transactions are posted on G/L accounts and how the posting data is processed. You need to have the master data for a G/L account, defined and available in the system, before you can make any posting to that account.

You can classify the G/L accounts into various types:

- *Balance Sheet Account*: This is an account to which you make postings from business transactions. The balance of a balance sheet account is carried forward at fiscal year-end.
- *Non-operating Expense and Income*: This is an income statement account that records expenses or gains from activities, that are not part of the main purpose of the company, such as gains realized from financial investments by a manufacturing company.
- *Primary Costs or Revenue*: This is an income statement account that functions as a cost element for primary costs or revenue. The primary costs reflect operating expenses such as payroll, selling expenses, or administration costs.
- *Secondary Costs*: This is an income statement account that functions as a cost element for secondary costs. The secondary costs result from value flows within the organization, such as internal activity cost allocations, overhead allocations, and settlement transactions.

The G/L account master record is divided into three areas (Figure 9.4):

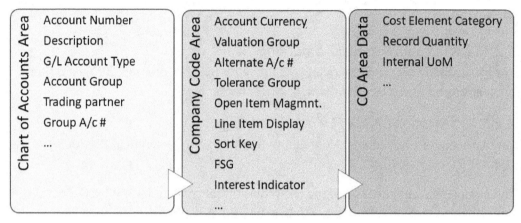

Figure 9.4 Structure of G/L Account Master Record

1) *Chart of Accounts Area*: This area contains the data that is valid across all the company codes that use a particular of chart of accounts. As a result, all that company codes with the same chart of accounts can use the same G/L accounts. The chart of accounts area also contains data that controls how a G/L account is created in the company code-specific area. This data includes, for example, the account number, description (short and long text), G/L account type, account group, functional area, trading partner number, group account number etc (Figure 9.5).

2) *Company Code Area*: This contains the data that is relevant only for the specific company code like account currency, tax category, balance in local currency only indicator, posting without tax allowed indicator, alternative account number, sort key and so on. It also contains information about created by, created on, group chart of accounts, country key, FM area, controlling area etc (Figure 9.5).

3) *Controlling Area Data*: The data in CO area that may vary from one controlling area to another. This portion of the data, used in cost accounting, is relevant only for accounts of the type Primary Costs or Revenue and Secondary Costs. The data may include cost element category, record quantity indicator, internal UoM etc (Figure 9.5).

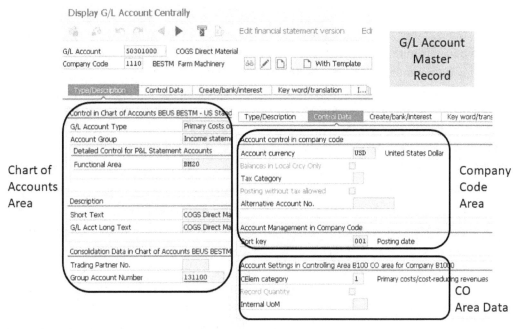

Figure 9.5 G/L Account Master Record – Example

Before we actually get into the details of how to create G/L account master data, we need to look at the preparations that will enable us in creating the master data later.

9.3.1   Preparations

You need to complete a couple of activities, as preparations, before actually creating the G/L account master records. These steps will help to rationalise and enable you to efficiently create only the required accounts that will meet your business needs. The activities include:

- Revise Chart of Accounts
- Edit Chart of Accounts List
- Assign Company Code to Chart of Accounts
- Define Account Group
- Define Retained Earnings Account
- Create Sample Accounts

Let us start with the first activity of revising the chart of accounts.

9.3.1.1   Revise Chart of Accounts

Recall that we have already discussed what a chart of account is and the types of charts of accounts in Chapter 6 (Section 6.8.1), while discussing the company code global parameters.

Now, start with the revision of your existing G/L accounts. Because, (a) you may want to reduce the number of G/L accounts that you are currently using, (b) you are thinking of moving away from the current way of numbering the G/L accounts into a more easier way of, say, using only numeric account identifiers or you just want to extend the length of numeric account numbers from, say, the current length of six digits to eight or more, (c) you want to have all your (legally independent) companies use a single chart of accounts instead of the current practice of using several different charts, and so on.

Hence, use this preparatory step to:

1) Decide on the type of account classification that you want to use for structuring your chart of accounts.
2) Discuss and find out, from your employees, which G/L accounts (a) are needed for which business transactions and which accounts they currently post to, and (b) are no longer required.
3) Determine which particular accounts are to be used for automatic postings in the SAP system, and finalise – by analysing the charts of accounts delivered with the standard SAP system - which of these you want to include in your revised chart of accounts.

Once you are through this important step, you can continue with the other preparatory activities. Let us now look at editing the chart of accounts list.

9.3.1.2   Edit Chart of Accounts List

Using this activity, check if you can use one of the charts of accounts supplied with the standard SAP system. In case you decide to have your own charts of accounts, you can maintain the necessary attributes for the charts of accounts, here, in this activity:

i.   Use the menu path: SAP Customizing Implementation Guide > Financial Accounting > General Ledger Accounting > Master Data > G/L Accounts > Preparations > Edit Chart of Accounts List, or Transaction OB13. You will see the sample chart of accounts (say, YCOA) in the standard system on the 'Change View "List of All Charts of Accounts": Overview' screen.
ii.   Double-click on a row, to see the details of the selected chart of accounts (say, BEUS).
iii. If you want to create your own, click on 'New Entries' or you can select the row containing the standard chart and click on 'Copy As' on the 'Change View "List of All Charts of Accounts": Overview' screen, and proceed to enter the details as shown in Figure 9.6.
iv.   Ensure that you have entered the 'Group Chart of Acct' (BEGR) for the two operative charts of accounts (BEUS and BEIN) to enable FI consolidation, for BESTM Corporate.

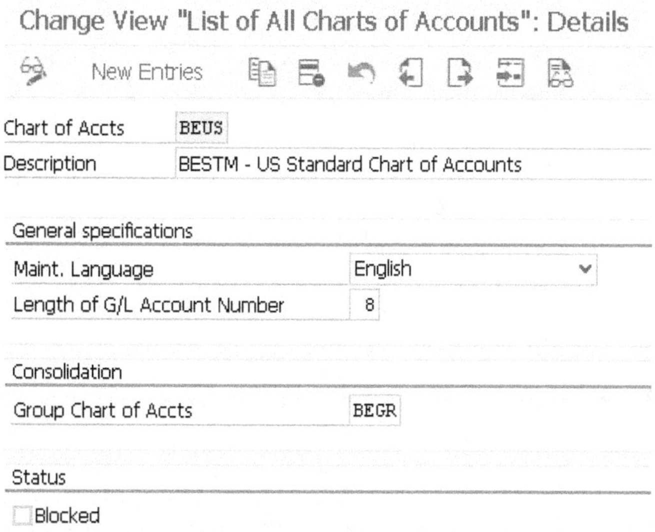

Change View "List of All Charts of Accounts": Details

   New Entries

| Chart of Accts | BEUS |
| Description | BESTM - US Standard Chart of Accounts |

General specifications

| Maint. Language | English |
| Length of G/L Account Number | 8 |

Consolidation

| Group Chart of Accts | BEGR |

Status

☐ Blocked

Figure 9.6 Chart of Accounts Details

Recall that we have already discussed and created three new charts of accounts (BEUS, BEIN and BEGR), to meet the exact requirements of BESTM Corporate, in Section 6.8.1 of Chapter 6, when we were configuring the company code global parameters for BESTM's company codes. Also recall, while doing so, that we have used the other activity 'Copy Chart of Accounts' (Transaction OBY7), to not only copy the standard chart of accounts but also to create all the G/L accounts in the chart of accounts area from the reference (standard) chart of accounts (YCOA), associated account determinations (for FI, AM, CO, MM, HR & SD) and the financial statement version. We, then, adapted the new charts of accounts, to meet the requirements of BESTM, by making the required (minor) changes.

Hence, let us proceed with the other activities of preparations.

9.3.1.3   Assign Company Code to Chart of Accounts

For each company code, you need to specify which chart of accounts is to be used. You already know that you can use the same chart of accounts for multiple company codes, if their requirements are the same.

To assign a company code to chart of accounts:

i.   Use the menu path: SAP Customizing Implementation Guide > Financial Accounting > General Ledger Accounting > Master Data > G/L Accounts > Preparations > Assign Company Code to Chart of Accounts, or Transaction OB62.

ii.   On the 'Change View "Assign Company Codes -> Chart of Accounts"; Overview' screen, enter the chart of accounts in 'Chrt/Accts' column against the appropriate company code. If the company code needs to use a separate country chart of accounts, then enter the same in the 'Cty ch/act' field (Figure 9.7). You may recall our discussion of different types of charts of accounts in Chapter 6 (Section 6.8.1).

iii.   Repeat this for all the company codes and 'Save'.

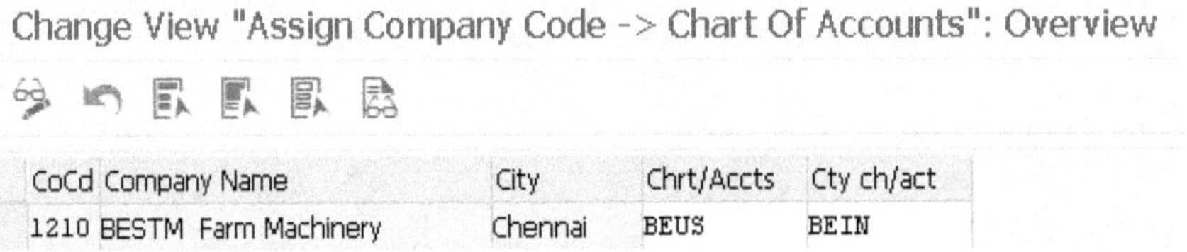

Change View "Assign Company Code -> Chart Of Accounts": Overview

CoCd	Company Name	City	Chrt/Accts	Cty ch/act
1210	BESTM Farm Machinery	Chennai	BEUS	BEIN

Figure 9.7 Assigning Company Code to Chart of Accounts

With this, let us now understand about the account groups.

9.3.1.4 Account Groups

An '*account group*' defines the criteria that affect how the G/L accounts in that group are created. The account groups allow you to group similar G/L accounts: for example, you can have bank accounts, petty cash accounts etc., in an account group called 'Liquid Assets'. The account group, also, defines the setup when creating a G/L account, in the company code and chart of accounts areas. The account group (with the definition of the allowed number range and field status) facilitates - besides simplifying - the process of creating G/L accounts, by reducing the number of entry fields. You need to specify an account group when creating a G/L account in the chart of accounts area.

> **i** When you define an *account group*, you also need to specify the number range that is allowed for the G/L accounts of that group. When creating a G/L account, of a particular account group, you cannot select an account number that falls outside the range defined for that group. For example, consider that you want the account numbers of bank accounts and petty cash accounts to begin with '1'. Accordingly, you have a defined an account group called 'Liquid Assets' for these accounts, and allowed a number range of 100000 to 129999 for the group. That being the case, if you now create a G/L account, with this account group, and specify the account number as 131000, the system will not allow it, since it is outside the allowed number range of this account group. However, the allowed number ranges for account groups can overlap; so, for G/L accounts that you do not want to assign to any special area, you can create a separate account group with a number range that has already been assigned to a different account group.

In the chart of accounts list, you have already defined the length of the account numbers ('Length of G/L Account Number' field) for the entire chart of accounts (Section 9.3.1.2). You can have the maximum length of account numbers as 10 characters. You can have the account numbers either in numeric or alphanumeric format. The numeric account numbers are automatically filled out with zeroes from the left, and alphanumeric account numbers are filled with spaces from the right. To achieve a logical system of account numbers, use account numbers of the same length and use either alphanumeric or numeric account numbers, but not both.

The required account groups have already been created (Figure 9.8), when we created the new charts of accounts, by copying the standard chart of accounts YCOA.

Change View "G/L Account Groups": Overview

🔍   🖳 Field status   New entries   📄 🗑 ↜ 📑 📑 📑   Print field status

Chrt/Accts	Acct Group	Name	From Acct	To Account
BEUS	ABST	Recon.account AP/AR		ZZZZZZZZZZ
BEUS	ANL.	Fixed assets accounts		ZZZZZZZZZZ
BEUS	ERG.	Income statement accounts		ZZZZZZZZZZ
BEUS	FIN.	Liquid funds accounts		ZZZZZZZZZZ
BEUS	MAT.	Materials management accounts		ZZZZZZZZZZ
BEUS	RECN	ReconAcct ARAP Ready for Input		ZZZZZZZZZZ
BEUS	SAKO	G/L accounts (general)		ZZZZZZZZZZ
BEUS	SASL	G/L accounts (ledger-spec. OI)		ZZZZZZZZZZ
BEUS	SECC	Secondary costs / revenues		ZZZZZZZZZZ

Figure 9.8 Account Groups in Chart of Accounts BEUS

If you want to create a new account group:

i.   Use the menu path: SAP Customizing Implementation Guide > Financial Accounting > General Ledger Accounting > Master Data > G/L Accounts > Preparations > Define Account Group, or Transaction OBD4.

ii.   On the 'Change View "G/L Account Groups": Overview' screen, click on 'New Entries' and enter the details on the next screen. You may also create by copying an existing account group by clicking on 'Copy As'.

iii. Select the row containing the account group and click on 'Field Status' to maintain the field status settings for the various fields.

iv.   'Save' the details. Repeat and create all the necessary account groups.

Once you have defined the required account groups, and at a later point of time you find out that the fields do not have the necessary field status for creating G/L accounts, you may need to change an existing account group. This is may be required, for example, if you want to implement a new application component that requires fields which originally were 'suppressed' but now needs to be defined as 'required entry' fields. You can achieve this by several means: (a) you may enter the account group of an existing G/L account: this changes the field status and the number range interval, (b) you just change the field status definition of the account group: the change affects the display and change mode for G/L account master records that were created with this account group; even though the current field status definition always applies, the field contents that were entered before the change remain in effect, even if the field in question is now 'hidden', and (c) you can change the number interval of an account group: for example, if the number interval is too small, you can increase it.

---

i Recommended to delete an account group, only if no G/L account master records exist for that account group; else, you would not be able to display or change these G/L accounts.

Let us continue with the next step in the preparations, namely, defining the retained earnings account.

9.3.1.5 Define Retained Earnings Account

You have to assign a *'retained earnings account'* to each of the P&L accounts by specifying a 'P&L statement account type', in the chart of accounts area of each P&L account. You can define more than one retained earnings account; in that case, select the retained earnings account for each of the P&L statement accounts, when you create the SAP G/L account master record. At the end of a fiscal year, the system carries forward the balance of the P&L account to the retained earnings account(s).

Project Dolphin

The project team has been instructed by the BESTM management to configure only one retained earnings account for each of the company codes. Accordingly, the G/L account 33000000 has been designated as the retained earnings account of the operative chart of accounts BEUS.

To define the retained earnings account:

i.   Use the menu path: SAP Customizing Implementation Guide > Financial Accounting > General Ledger Accounting > Master Data > G/L Accounts > Preparations > Define Retained Earnings Account, or Transaction OB53.

ii.   On the 'Enter Chart of Accounts' pop-up screen, enter the chart of accounts BEUS and press 'Continue'.

iii. On the 'Configuration Accounting Maintain: Automatic Posts – Accounts' screen, press 'New Entries'.

iv.   On the next screen, enter 33000000 under 'Account' and press 'Enter'; the system marks this account number as 'P&L statement account type' in the first column ('P&L statmt acct type').

v.   'Save' the details (Figure 9.9).

vi.   Repeat the steps for other charts of accounts as well.

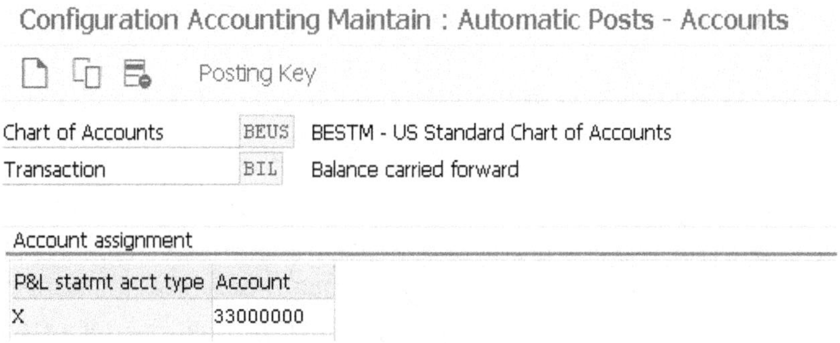

Configuration Accounting Maintain : Automatic Posts - Accounts

☐ ☐ ☐   Posting Key

| Chart of Accounts | BEUS | BESTM - US Standard Chart of Accounts |
| Transaction | BIL | Balance carried forward |

Account assignment

P&L statmt acct type	Account
X	33000000

Figure 9.9 Defining Retained Earnings Account

Let us, now, move on to discuss the sample accounts, as a part of preparations, which you can use later to create the G/L account master records.

9.3.1.6   Create Sample Accounts

Before you create a '*sample account*' in the system, you need to understand as to what is a sample account, how to create the same, and how to use sample accounts in the creation of G/L account master records.

A '*sample account*' is a master record, with some data, that can be used to create G/L account master records, in the company code area. Use of a sample account can save considerable time in the creation of G/L account master record. You can use a sample account only in the chart of accounts in which it is created. When you create a G/L account master record in the company code, using a sample account, the system transfers the data from the sample account to the newly created G/L account, using 'data transfer rules'.

> **i** You must not use sample accounts as regular G/L account master records. You can create as many sample accounts as you want. You cannot post to sample accounts. Use of sample accounts is optional.

To configure sample accounts, you need to complete the following IMG activities:

- Maintain List of Rule Types
- Define Data Transfer Rules
- Assign Company Code to Rule Type
- Create Sample Accounts

The '*data transfer rules*' determine which values are transferred from the sample account and how. You use the rules to specify, per company code, (a) the fields that are included in the sample account, (b) whether transferred field data (default value) can be overwritten and (c) whether transferred field data is mandatory (required value). You can transfer data in one company code as 'required values', and in another as 'default values'. If you do not want to apply the sample account (specified in the chart of accounts) to a particular company code, you simply do not enter a rule type for that company code.

You specify a rule for each field that is to be transferred, and the rules are grouped into *'rule types'*. You define a rule type (independent of the sample account) and, then, assign it to a company code. The rule types are company code-specific, and you can define as many rule types as you require. It is possible that more than one company code uses the same rule type. The rules come into effect when you create/change a G/L account master record in the corresponding company code.

Project Dolphin

The project team has suggested to the BESTM management to make use of sample accounts in creating some of the G/L account master records so as to facilitate quicker and easier master data creation. Accordingly, it has been agreed to use sample accounts, in all the company codes, to create G/L account master records for bank accounts. The project team will create the required data transfer rules. Two sample rule types (or sample rule variants) will be created; one for the US-based company codes, and the other for Indian based company codes.

For the rule type for the US-based company codes, the following data transfer rules will be applicable:

The FSG 'YB32' (bank accounts with obligatory value / due dates) set in the sample account, will be transferred to the newly created G/L account but the users will not be able to change the values in the newly created G/L accounts. So also, with the field 'Valuation Group'. However, the fields 'Exchange Rate Difference Key', 'Account Currency', 'Sort Key' and 'House Bank' will be configured in such a way that the non-blank value in the sample account will be transferred and can be overwritten. after transfer to the new G/L account master record that is being created.

For the rule type for all the Indian-based company codes, the above data transfer rules will also apply except that the reconciliation account ('Recon. Account for Account Type') will also be transferred from the sample account which can be changed, if required, after the transfer.

Let us start with the definition of list of rule types.

9.3.1.6.1   Maintain List of Rule Types

To maintain the list of rule types:

i. Use the menu path: SAP Customizing Implementation Guide > Financial Accounting > General Ledger Accounting > Master Data > G/L Accounts > Preparations > Additional Activities > Sample Accounts > Maintain List of Rule Types or Transaction OB15.

ii. On the 'Change View "Sample Accounts Rules Variants": Overview' screen, click on 'New Entries' and define the required details (Figure 9.10), and 'Save'. You will create two variants, one for US and another for India, to be used by the respective company codes of BESTM. You will, then, be using the variants defined here in the subsequent activities.

Figure 9.10 Defining Sample Account Rules Variant

Let us continue and define the data transfer rules.

9.3.1.6.2   Define Data Transfer Rules

The *'data transfer rules'* determine whether the values from the sample account can be changed in the newly created G/L account or not. If a rule is not specified for a field, the contents are not transferred. After you define the data transfer rules, you will assign the company codes (to which the rules apply). to a rule type in the next step. This way, the rules apply to a company code; if you do not assign the rules to a company code, the rules will not apply.

i. Use the menu path: SAP Customizing Implementation Guide > Financial Accounting > General Ledger Accounting > Master Data > G/L Accounts > Preparations > Additional Activities > Sample Accounts > Define Data Transfer Rules or Transaction FSK2.

ii. On the ensuing pop-up screen, enter or select the sample account rules variant that you have created in the previous step (say, SA1), and 'Continue'.

iii. On the 'Change View "Rules for sample accounts": Overview' screen, select the check-box against the appropriate fields:

- The 'Transfer Value' check-box determines if the value for the selected field should be transferred from the sample account for the creation of a new G/L account in the company code. If you do not select the check-box, then, the value of this field is not transferred from the sample account to the new G/L account that is being created. You need to select this check-box for all the six fields namely 'Field Status Group', 'Valuation group', 'House Bank', 'Account Currency', 'Sort Key' and 'Exchange Rate Difference Key' as we want to transfer the values of these fields from the sample account.

Change View "Rules for sample accounts": Overview

Sample Acct Rules   SA1   Sample Account Rules Variant1 (BESTM US)

Field	Transfer value	Cannot be changed if set	Cannot be changed if initial
Alternative Account No.	☐	☐	☐
Authorization Group	☐	☐	☐
Valuation Group	☑	☑	☐
Clerk Abbreviation	☐	☐	☐
Planning Level	☐	☐	☐
Commitment item	☐	☐	☐
Field status group	☑	☑	☐
House bank	☑	☐	☐
Account ID	☐	☐	☐
Inflation key	☐	☐	☐
Exchange Rate Difference Key	☑	☐	☑
Recon. Account for Acct Type	☐	☐	☐

Figure 9.11 Data Transfer Rules for Rules Variant SA1

- The 'Cannot be changed if set' check-box, when selected, determines that a field value from a sample account is transferred exactly as it is, if it is not left blank. That is, all non-blank field values are transferred to the newly created G/L account master exactly as in the sample account, and you cannot modify / change the values later. However, if you leave this field as blank in the sample account, then, you can enter a value in the newly created G/L account master record. Select this check-box for 'Account Currency', 'Field Status Group' and 'Valuation Group' fields, as we want to transfer the exact values from these fields in the sample account but do not want anyone to change the transferred values of in the newly created G/L account master records.

- When you select the 'Cannot be changed if initial' check-box, you can change the value in the new G/L account only if the field content is not blank in the sample account; if the field is blank (=initial) in the sample account, then you will not be able to enter anything in that field in the new G/L account master after the transfer. Select this check-box for 'Exchange Rate Difference Key', and 'Sort Key' fields.

iv.   'Save' the details (Figure 9.11).

v.   Repeat the steps for the other rule variant, SA2, as set out in the case study of 'Project Dolphin'.

To summarise the data transfer rules, refer to the explanation in Table 9.1.

Field Name of the Rule	Rule Details	How the Rule Works?
Transfer value	Value is transferred from sample account.	The value from the sample account is transferred into the new G/L account master record and can be overwritten.
Cannot be changed, if set	Field cannot be changed, if set.	If a value is contained in the field of the sample account, it can no longer be overwritten in the new G/L account master record.
Cannot be changed, if initial.	Field cannot be changed, if it contains an initial value.	If field is blank (=initial) in the sample account, nothing can be entered in the master record of the new G/L account. However, if the field content is non-blank, then, that value can be changed in the new G/L account master record after transfer.

Table 9:1 Data Transfer Rules Summary

With the data transfer rules defined and in place, we are now ready to assign the company codes to the rule types (or rule variants) defined earlier, in <u>Section 9.3.1.6.1</u>.

9.3.1.6.3 Assign Company Code to Rule Type

Use the following step to assign a company codes to a rule type. You can assign more than one company code to the same rule type, because the data transfer rule is always per company code.

i. Use the menu path: SAP Customizing Implementation Guide > Financial Accounting > General Ledger Accounting > Master Data > G/L Accounts > Preparations > Additional Activities > Sample Accounts > Assign Company Code to Rule Type or Transaction OB67.

ii. On the 'Change View "Assign Com. Code -> Sample Acct Rule Variants": Overview' screen (Figure 9.12), enter the appropriate rules variant ('Rules Var.') for each of the company codes, and 'Save' the details.

Figure 9.12 Assigning Company Code to Rule Type

With this, we are now ready to create the sample accounts.

9.3.1.6.4   Create Sample Accounts

To create a sample account:

i.   Use the menu path: SAP Customizing Implementation Guide > Financial Accounting > General Ledger Accounting > Master Data > G/L Accounts > Preparations > Additional Activities > Sample Accounts > Create Sample Accounts or Transaction FSM1.

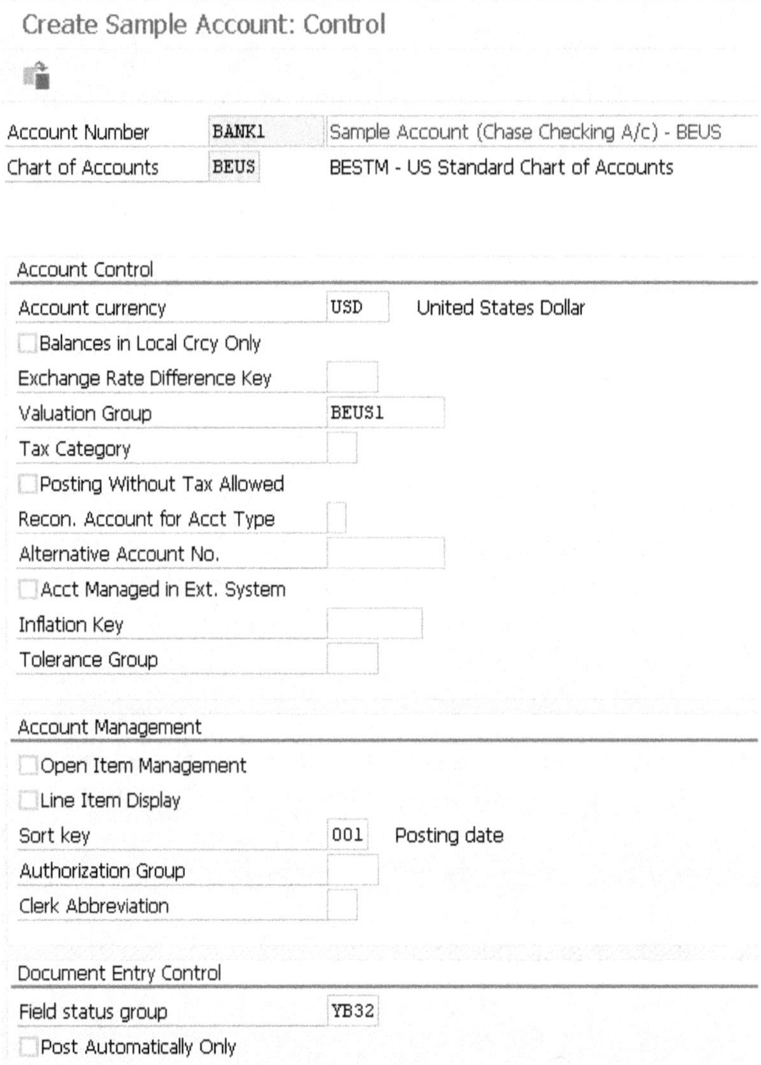

Figure 9.13 Creating a Sample Account

ii.   On the 'Create Sample Account: Initial Screen', enter an appropriate identifier for the sample account in the 'Sample Account' field (say, BANK1), enter the 'Chart of Accounts' and press 'Enter'.

iii.   On the 'Create Sample Account: Control' screen (Figure 9.13), maintain the required details:

- Enter USD as the 'Account Currency'.
- Enter the appropriate 'Exchange Rate Difference Key'; it is a blank for BEUS.
- Enter the 'Valuation Group'.
- Enter 001 as the 'Sort key'.
- Enter YB32 as the 'Field status group'.
- Enter the appropriate 'House Bank'.

iv.   When completed 'Save' the details.

v.   Repeat the steps to create the rest of the sample accounts, if any.

> **i**   When creating a sample account, it is recommended to use an easily recognizable mnemonic key, for example, BANK1. Do not use numeric values. This way, you can easily differentiate between an actual and a sample G/L account.

You can, now, use the sample accounts created in this Section, to define the new G/L account master records. With this, we are now ready to create the G/L accounts required for the BESTM company codes.

9.3.2 G/L Account Creation and Processing

SAP offers a couple of methods for creating G/L accounts, to meet the requirements of an enterprise. Based on your exact needs, you can select the appropriate method. The following are the different methods available in SAP to create and process G/L accounts:

1) Creating G/L Accounts with Reference

This method is useful when your chart of accounts is only slightly different from SAP's standard chart of accounts. You can resort to this reference method to copy G/L accounts, from a source company code into the new (target) company code, and then edit the accounts (by changing the account numbers and names). Before creating the G/L accounts, you can change the account numbers and names.

You have two options to edit and change the newly created G/L accounts:

- To change the master record for multiple G/L accounts, use the activity 'Collective Processing of G/L Accounts', and
- Use the option 'Change G/L Accounts Individually' if you want to make changes to a single master record, one-by-one.

2) Transferring G/L Accounts from an External System

If you are switching over to SAP, and already have the G/L accounts in a non-SAP system, you can transfer them to your SAP system. Use 'batch input method' when the number of G/L accounts is relatively high. As in the previous case, you can process newly created G/L accounts, either by collective processing or individual processing.

3) Copying G/L accounts (Alternative Method)

Use this alternative method if a chart of accounts in your system meets your needs exactly. Under this method you can copy the chart of accounts area data and company code area data separately.

Remember, we created the G/L accounts data in the chart of accounts area using the method (3) in Section 6.8.1 of Chapter 6, and later created the required master records in the company code area as well. Now that we have a chart of accounts (BEUS) and a company code with appropriate G/L master records, we can use the method (3) to create the G/L accounts in other company codes namely 1120, 2100 etc.

Project Dolphin

BESTM wants the project team to have thorough validation for all the G/L accounts of the chart of accounts BEUS, to ensure that (a) the accounts have been properly identified as B/S or P&L type, (b) the correct functional area has been assigned to them and (c) the account groups are correct for each of the accounts. Also, the short / long texts need to be properly modified; for example: instead of 'Bank1 Main Account', it should be changed to 'BoA Main Account'. Bank 2 should be renamed as 'Chase', Bank 3 as 'Citi', Bank 4 as 'PNC' and so on.

BESTM requires a similar verification be done, in the company code area data as well, to ensure that the accounts have been correctly identified for open item management, line item display, balance in local currency etc.

Let us use the collective maintenance option to edit the G/L accounts.

9.3.2.1 Change G/L Accounts Collectively

We can collectively edit / change the G/L accounts' data in four steps:

1) Change Chart of Accounts Data
2) Change Company Code Data
3) Change Account Name
4) Change or Create Controlling Area Data

Let us start with the first step of editing or changing the G/L accounts master records in the chart of accounts area.

9.3.2.1.1 Change Chart of Accounts Data

i. Use the menu path: SAP Customizing Implementation Guide > Financial Accounting > General Ledger Accounting > Master Data > G/L Accounts > G/L Account Creation and Processing > Change G/L Accounts Collectively > Change Chart of Accounts Data or Transaction OB_GLACC11.

ii. Read the 'Warning' message on the pop-up screen, press 'Enter' to continue.

iii. On the 'Mass Maintenance: G/L Account' screen, enter the chart of accounts, and maintain the range of G/L accounts if required. Press 'Execute'. The system brings up a pop-up indicating the number of records, and gives you the option of displaying all the records or change them in the background.

iv. Press 'Display All Records'.

v. The system brings up the next screen with all the G/L accounts already 'selected', by highlighting the rows. You will see two sections: the top header with two rows that is used to apply the same change to several accounts at one go, and the bottom section showing all G/L accounts selected by default (Figure 9.14).

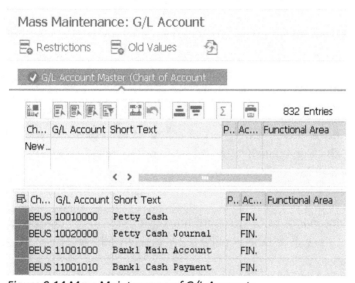

Figure 9.14 Mass Maintenance of G/L Accounts

vi. De-select all the accounts. Supposing that you want to change the functional area BM10 (Sales Revenue) for several accounts from 41000000 to 41001500, from the default functional area YB10, enter BM10 in 'Functional Area' in the 'New Values' row in the header (note to keep the correct values for the other two fields as well in the header), and click the 'Carry Out Mass Change' button or go to Edit > Apply Changes. The system replaces the functional area with the new value for all the selected records at one go.

vii.   Now, click on 'Display Old Values' button at the top of the screen, to display both the new and old values for each of the accounts which you will be changing. You can also click on 'Select Fields' to toggle the list of fields to change during this exercise; the default is three fields as displayed in the Figure 9.15.

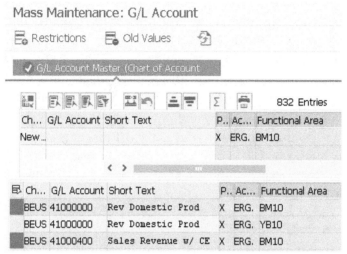

Figure 9.15 G/L Account Mass Maintenance: Displaying 'Old' and 'New' Values

viii.   Continue to make the required changes for the rest of the G/L accounts and 'Save' the details when completed.

With the changes you have made in the chart of accounts area of BEUS, you can now make the required changes, through collective (or mass) maintenance, in the G/L accounts in the company code area as well for company code 1110.

9.3.2.1.2   Change Company Code Data

Similar to the mass maintenance of G/L account master records in the chart of accounts area in the previous section, you will use this activity to collectively edit several of the G/L accounts in the company code area:

i.   Use the menu path: SAP Customizing Implementation Guide > Financial Accounting > General Ledger Accounting > Master Data > G/L Accounts > G/L Account Creation and Processing > Change G/L Accounts Collectively > Change Company Code Data or Transaction OB_GLACC12.

ii.   Maintain the required details like the company code, and range of G/L accounts on the initial 'Mass Maintenance: G/L Accounts' screen.

iii.   Upon 'Execution', you will be taken to the next screen (Figure 9.16) and you can select a block of accounts to carry out the required mass maintenance for the fields shown on the screen or you can add additional fields (maximum of 18) by clicking on 'Select field' button and edit the accounts collectively for all the desired fields:

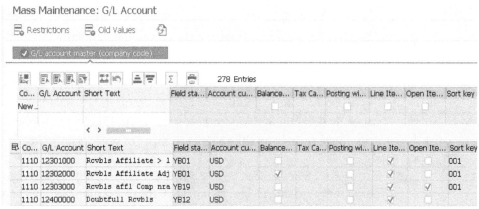

Figure 9.16 Mass Maintenance of G/L Accounts in Company Code Area

- You will use check-box 'Balances in Local Crcy Only' to indicate that balances are updated only in local currency when users post items to an account. You need to set this indicator in cash discount clearing accounts and in GR/IR clearing accounts. You usually set this for specific balance sheet accounts that (a) are not managed on an open item basis and not kept in foreign currencies and (b) are managed on an open item basis and have the same types of items posted in different currencies, but always allow clearing to be made if the local currency amounts correspond. Do not set this for reconciliation accounts for customers or vendors and setting it in all other cases is optional.

- The 'Tax Category' check-box in the G/L account master record is used to determine (a) if the account is tax-relevant, (b) is it a tax account and (c) is it a tax-relevant G/L account. If it is not tax-relevant, leave the field blank. If you decide that you will use this as tax account for posting taxes, then define it accordingly: enter < for input tax account, or > for output tax accounts. In case of tax-relevant G/L account, decide whether you want to use the account as a G/L account to which you make tax-relevant postings; specify the tax codes that can be used to post to the account; when posting to this account, the system checks whether the tax code in the line item is permitted for this account; if you only want to carry out a flat-rate check for the tax category, enter + (only output tax permitted), or – (only input tax permitted), or * (all tax types permitted).

- The 'Posting without tax allowed' flag indicates, when selected, that the account can still be posted to, even if a tax code has not been entered. If you do enter a tax code when posting to this account, the system checks the entry against the tax category.

- Use the 'Line Item Display' check-box to enable line item display for the account. When selected, an entry is saved in an index table for each line item;

the entry contains the connection between the line item and the account. You have to set this indicator if you want open item management; else, leave this as blank.

> **i** Do not set the indicator for tax accounts, receivables & payables and specific revenue & expense accounts, where line item display in dialog may not make sense due to the large number of postings.

- The items posted to accounts, managed on an open item basis, are marked as open or cleared. The balance of these accounts is always equal to the balance of the open items. The 'Open Item Management' check-box determines whether open items are managed for this account. There are two ways to set up these accounts: (a) setting up accounts with open item management if offsetting entries are to be assigned to the postings made to these accounts. The postings to these accounts represent incomplete transactions. For example, a goods receipt/invoice receipt (GR/IR) clearing account should be managed on an open item basis so that you can check at any time whether invoices have been received for the goods received for an order, and (b) setting up accounts without open item management, if no offsetting entry is to be made against a posting to this account.

> **i** The accounts that are normally managed on an open item basis include the clearing accounts (bank clearing account, payroll clearing account, cash discount clearing account and GR/IR clearing account). The accounts that are not managed on an open item basis include bank accounts, tax accounts, raw material accounts, reconciliation accounts (these are managed implicitly using the subledger open item function), P&L accounts and materials management (MM) accounts posted with a posting key that has account type as 'M'.

- The 'Sort Key' indicates the layout rule for the 'Allocation' field in the document line item. The system uses a standard sort sequence for displaying line items. It sorts, among other things, the items according to the content of the 'Allocation' field that is filled, either manually or automatically (by the system) when a document line item is entered. Hence, the system requires rules that determine which information is to be taken from the document header or from the document line item and placed in the field. The rules can be stored in the master record of an account, which enables you to determine the standard sort sequence on an account-specific basis.

iv.   Once you have completed editing the G/L accounts, 'Save' the details.

With the completion of mass or collective maintenance of G/L account master records both in the chart of accounts area and company code area, we can now move on to changing the G/L account name through collective maintenance.

9.3.2.1.3   Change Account Name

Here, using this activity, you can change the name of several G/L accounts in one step; the G/L accounts can be from different charts of accounts. You can restrict the data by (i) limiting the number of G/L accounts for which you want to change the names, (ii) entering the languages for which you want to change the account names, (iii) entering a chart of accounts or company code interval, and (iv) including additional selection fields. You can make changes to the displayed G/L accounts. After the change is made, you can display the old values along with the new values, for each the G/L accounts. Before saving, you can reverse your changes by choosing 'Reverse changes'; once saved, you cannot use 'Reverse changes' function again.

To work on editing / changing the name for multiple G/L accounts:

i.   Use the menu path: SAP Customizing Implementation Guide > Financial Accounting > General Ledger Accounting > Master Data > G/L Accounts > G/L Account Creation and Processing > Change G/L Accounts Collectively > Change Account Name or Transaction OB_GLACC13.

ii.   On the initial screen, enter the 'Language Key' and 'Chart of Accounts'; enter a range of 'G/L Accounts' if you want to restrict the number of accounts (Figure 9.17). Press 'Execute'.

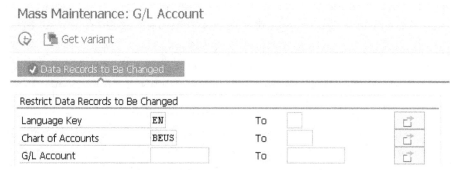

Figure 9.17 Change Name of multiple G/L Accounts – Initial Screen

iii.   On the next screen, carry out the required changes; for example, we have changed the name (both short and long texts) of the bank accounts as required by BESTM (Bank 1 to BoA, Bank 2 to Chase etc). 'Save' when completed (Figure 9.18).

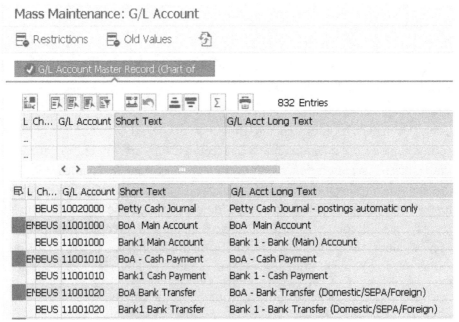

Figure 9.18 Changing the Name for multiple G/L Accounts

With this, we are, now, ready to change the data in the Controlling area for several G/L accounts using the collective maintenance. You may also create the required data, if that has not been done earlier.

9.3.2.1.4   Change or Create Controlling Area Data

Here, you can create / change the master data for multiple G/L accounts in the 'CO area data' at one go. Besides limiting the data selection (as in other cases of collective maintenance), you may also specify a G/L account that needs to be used as reference. All G/L accounts for the G/L account types 'Primary Costs' or 'Revenue or Secondary Costs' are selected within the specified intervals for which 'CO area-specific' data does not exist. When changing the 'CO-specific' data, select the 'Do Not Change Existing Data' check-box, if you do not have to change existing data:

i.   Use the menu path: SAP Customizing Implementation Guide > Financial Accounting > General Ledger Accounting > Master Data > G/L Accounts > G/L Account Creation and Processing > Change G/L Accounts Collectively > Change or Create Controlling Area Data or Transaction OB_GLACC14.

ii.   When you enter the Transaction, you are taken to the initial screen 'Mass Maintenance: G/L Account'. You have two options: one to change, and the other to create new data records.

- When you are in the 'change' mode ('Data Records to Be Changed'), you see that the 'Do Not Change Existing Data' check-box is unselected, and you will also see the data selection fields for restricting the data to be changed.
- When you are in the 'create' mode ('Data Records to Be Created'), besides the data selection fields and 'Do Not Create New Data' check-box, you will also see the reference fields ('Specify Values for the Reference') for input on the screen (Figure 9.19).

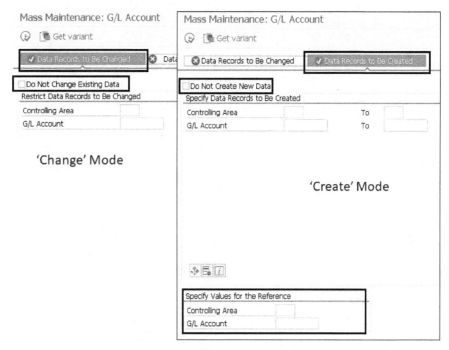

Figure 9.19 Changing CO Area-Specific Data – Initial Screen

iii. Maintain the required parameters for changing the data. Press 'Execute'.

iv. You will see the relevant data on the next screen. Make the required changes, with respect to the 'Cost Element Category', 'Record Quantity' and 'Internal UoM', for a block of G/L accounts, and apply the mass changes (Figure 9.20), then 'Save' the details.

v. Continue making changes for all the required G/L records. Once mass change is completed 'Save' and exit.

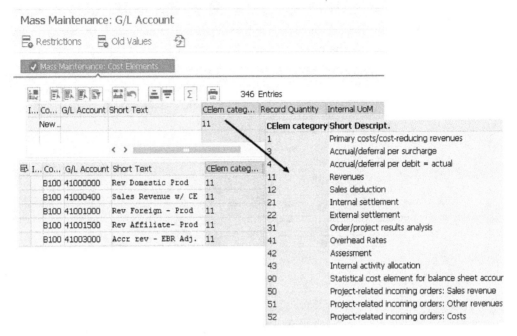

Figure 9.20 Changing CO Area-Specific Data – Mass Change Screen

---

The *'Cost Element Category'* determines which cost elements can be used for which business transactions. SAP has defined, in the standard system, various categories for primary and secondary cost elements.

The **Primary Cost Elements** include:

01: Primary costs/cost-reducing revenues
The cost elements of this category can be debited for all primary postings, for example, in FI and MM. The cost-reducing revenues are revenues that are handled in CO similar to that of overhead costs, and they reduce the prices of an activity type or the costs to be assessed; for example, rent revenues, which reduce the room costs to be assessed. The cash discount amounts and exchange rate amounts are also some of the cost-reducing revenues.

03: Accrual/deferral per surcharge
You can only use this cost element category for accrual calculation in Cost Center Accounting (CO-OM-CCA), when you are using the percentage method. You can post directly from FI to account the actual costs incurred. The system also uses cost elements of this category to post the accrual amounts within Cost Center Accounting.

04: Accrual/deferral per debit=actual

The cost elements of this category can only be used with the target=actual method of accrual calculation in Cost Center Accounting. You can post costs directly from FI to record actual costs. At the same time, cost elements of this category are used to post accrued costs within Cost Center Accounting.

11: Revenues

These are used to post revenues. These revenues are generally posted during make-to-stock-production, directly into the operating profit, or with make-to-order-production to the sales order. In CO, the revenues are displayed with negative sign; an exception is the costing-based Profitability Analysis (CO-PA), in which all values, including revenues, are displayed with a positive sign. The revenues posted to cost centers are only statistical; that is, they are shown only as information.

12: Sales deductions

These are revenue adjustments (or deduction postings), such as discounts and rebates. However, certain deductible items (such as freight charged separately, or surcharges for small quantities or special orders) are not classified as sales deductions but as revenue elements. You can use this category in the same manner as revenue elements (category 11). The, sales deductions posted to cost centers are also statistical, as that of the revenues posted to cost centers.

22: External settlement

The cost elements of this category are used to settle order costs, project costs, or cost object costs to objects outside of CO. These objects could be assets (FI-AA), materials (MM), or G/L accounts (FI). When you settle these objects, a journal entry is created automatically. You cannot use cost elements of this category for settlement to objects within CO, such as cost centers, orders, or projects; you need to use secondary cost element category 21 for this purpose. No journal entries are generated for settlement to objects within CO.

90: Statistical cost element for balance sheet account

When you create a G/L account, the cost elements of this category are created automatically if all conditions that (a) the account has the G/L account type B/S account, (b) the account is a reconciliation account for assets or materials, and (c) you selected the 'Apply Acct Assignments Statistically' in FI-AA / MM option, are met. The cost elements of category 90 allow you to track the costs of an order or project budget when acquiring fixed assets that can be directly capitalized: to achieve this, you need to enter the capital investment order or WBS element in the relevant field in the asset master.

The **Secondary Cost Elements** include:

21: Internal settlement
These are used for settling order and project costs objects within CO, such as orders, profitability segments, cost centers, and projects. The cost elements of this category cannot be used for settlement to objects outside of CO, such as assets or materials; you have to use primary cost element category 22 for this purpose.

31: Order/project results analysis
These cost elements enable order or project results analysis data to be saved to the relevant order or project.

41: Overhead rates
These are used for allocating overhead from cost centers to orders based on overhead rates.

42: Assessment
These are used for allocating costs using the assessment method.

43: Internal activity allocation
These cost elements are used for allocating costs during internal activity allocation and to allocate process costs.

50: Project-related incoming orders (Sales revenue)
These are used for sales revenues from sales orders with incoming orders in the current period of the project-related incoming orders.

51: Project-related incoming orders (Other revenues)
These are used for other revenues, such as imputed interest from sales orders with incoming orders in the current period of the project-related incoming orders.

52: Project-related incoming orders (Costs)
You will use this for the costs arising from sales orders with incoming orders in the current period of the project-related incoming orders.

61: Earned value
This is used for earned value analysis in the project system.

66: Reporting Cost Elements CO-PA
The cost elements of this category are only used for reports in combined Profitability Analysis (PA). They can be used in cost element hierarchies, but cannot be posted to.

This completes our discussion on changing/editing multiple G/L accounts using collective maintenance. We, now, have G/L accounts both in the chart of accounts area and company code area (of company code 1110), duly revised and edited, suitable for copying into other US-based company codes of BESTM. We shall use the alternative methods to accomplish this.

9.3.2.2 Alternative Methods

Using this method, you can copy an existing chart of accounts and, then, the company code specific area of an existing company code. As already outlined, you should only use this alternative method if a chart of accounts in your system meets your needs exactly. If, however, you need to make changes to an existing chart of accounts, you should use the copy with reference (method 1 outlined in Section 9.3.2) technique to create G/L accounts.

9.3.2.2.1 Copy Chart of Accounts

We have already discussed this when we created the chart of accounts data by copying the standard chart of accounts (refer Section 6.8.1 of Chapter 6). While doing so, we have created the required charts of accounts as well as the accounts, by copying an existing chart. We have copied the accounts from the reference chart of accounts along with the FI account determination and financial statement version.

Since we have a suitable chart of accounts (BEUS), fully configured and ready in the system, we can now proceed to copy the company code data from company code 1110 to the rest.

9.3.2.2.2 Copy Company Code

Here, using this activity you can copy G/L accounts from one company code to another, with the requirement being that there is no G/L account existing in the target company code, and the chart of accounts for the target company should be the same as that of the source company code. If no master data exists for G/L accounts in the chart of accounts area in the target company code, the system also copies the master data from the source company code's chart of accounts.

To copy the G/L accounts from the source to target:

i. Use the menu path: SAP Customizing Implementation Guide > Financial Accounting > General Ledger Accounting > Master Data > G/L Accounts > G/L Account Creation and Processing > Alternative Methods > Copy G/L Accounts > Copy Company Code or Transaction OBY2.

ii. On the 'Copy Company Code: G/L Accounts' screen, enter the target company code in 'Company code' field and maintain the source 'Company code' in the 'Copy from' data block.

iii. Select 'Test run' check-box (Figure 9.21), and press 'Execute'.

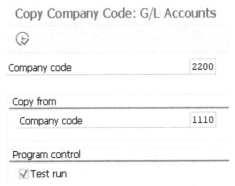

Figure 9.21 Copy Company Code: G/L Accounts – Initial Screen

iv.   The system brings up the next screen listing the G/L accounts that will be copied to the target company code. Please note that this is only a 'test run' and no accounts have been created in the target yet (Figure 9.22).

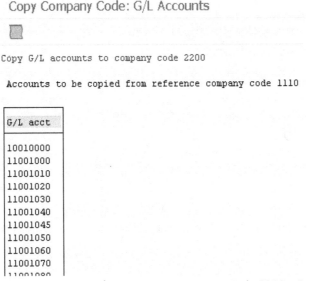

Figure 9.22 Copy G/L Accounts to Company Code 2200 – Proposal List

v.   Press 'Display Log' to view the log details, if any.

vi.   When you are satisfied with the proposal showing the G/L accounts that will be copied to the target company code, go back to the initial screen, deselect the 'Test run' check-box and 'Execute' again. The system will warn that you are making a production run.

vii.   Press 'Enter' and the system copies all the G/L accounts, as in the proposal, to the target company code (2200) from the source (1110).

This way, you can create the G/L account master data for rest of the company codes of BESTM wherever they use the chart of accounts BEUS. We have completed this for all the US-based company codes. We shall now use the method 1 of creating G/L accounts with reference, to create the G/L accounts for India-based company code 1210

9.3.2.3   Create G/L Accounts with Reference

Let us use this method to create the G/L accounts for the India-based company code 1210 to demonstrate how to use this reference method. Follow the steps listed below:

i. Use the menu path: SAP Customizing Implementation Guide > Financial Accounting > General Ledger Accounting > Master Data > G/L Accounts > G/L Account Creation and Processing > Create G/L Accounts with Reference or Transaction OB_GLACC01.

ii. On the 'Create G/L accounts with Reference – Overview' screen, under 'Table of the target company code', enter the target company code to which you want to copy the G/L accounts in 'Company Code' column, and enter the reference company code (source) from which you want to copy in 'Reference company code' column. 'Save', and, select this row.

iii. Now, click on 'Choose <detail>'.

iv. On the ensuing 'Create G/L accounts with Reference – Accounts' screen, click on 'Accounts from reference' button to transfer the required accounts that are to be copied.

v. You will notice that the system populates the 'Table of the G/L accounts in the company code' with all the selected G/L accounts. You can notice that the 'Account already created' check-box is un-checked for all the accounts at this point of time indicating that the G/L accounts have not yet been copied and created in the target company code. You will also see that the 'Account in acct determination' check-box is already checked for some of the accounts, showing that the automatic account determination assignments for those accounts. Select row(s) and use 'Delete Row' button, if you want to delete any of the proposed G/L accounts. Similarly, you can select row(s) and use 'Copy' and 'Paste' buttons to copy and add more G/L accounts (Figure 9.23).

vi. Make necessary changes in the G/L account number, short text, long text etc. Note that we have made the required changes with respect to the account name (both short and long text); for example, where ever the bank name is mentioned as BoA, we have changed that to SBI to suit Indian operations.

vii. Now, select all or a block of G/L accounts using the appropriate buttons. In our case, we have selected all the rows using the button 'Select All'.

Create G/L accounts with Reference - Accounts

Accounts from reference   G/L accounts   Account determination

Company Code   1210   BESTM Farm Machinery
Reference company code 1110   BESTM Farm Machinery

Table of the G/L accounts in the company code

G/L Account	Account al...	Account in acct ...	Short Text	G/L Acct Long Text	Reference G/L a...	Ref.acct in acct
10010000	☐	☑	Petty Cash	Petty Cash	10010000	☑
11001000	☐	☐	SBI Main Account	SBI Main Account	11001000	☐
11001010	☐	☐	SBI Cash Payment	SBI Cash Payment	11001010	☐
11001020	☐	☐	SBI Bank Transfer	SBI - Bank Transfer (Domestic/SEPA/Foreign)	11001020	☐
11001030	☐	☑	SBI Other Transfer	SBI - Other Interim Transfers	11001030	☑
11001040	☐	☐	SBI Direct Debit	SBI Direct Debit	11001040	☐
11001045	☐	☐	SBI Returns	SBI Returns	11001045	☐
11001050	☐	☐	SBI Checks Out	SBI Checks Out	11001050	☐
11001060	☐	☐	SBI Checks IN	SBI Checks IN	11001060	☐
11001070	☐	☐	SBI Check Clearing	SBI Checks Clearing	11001070	☐
11001080	☐	☑	SBI Cash Receipt	SBI Cash Receipt	11001080	☑
11001090	☐	☐	SBI Techn Account	SBI - Technical Account for Bank Statement	11001090	☐
11001099	☐	☑	SBI Forex Adjst Acco	SBI - Foreign Currency Adjustment	11001099	☑

Figure 9.23 Creating G/L Accounts with Reference: Accounts from Reference showing the Changes

viii.   Click on 'Create G/L accounts' button and the system displays a message that the G/L accounts have now been created in the new company code 1210. When you close the message pop-up screen, you will notice that the 'Account already created' check-box is now selected (Figure 9.24) for all the accounts displayed on the 'Create G/L accounts with Reference – Accounts' screen confirming G/L account creation.

Create G/L accounts with Reference - Accounts

Accounts from reference   G/L accounts   Account determination

Company Code   1210   BESTM Farm Machinery
Reference company code 1110   BESTM Farm Machinery

Table of the G/L accounts in the company code

G/L Account	Account al...	Account in acct ...	Short Text	G/L Acct Long Text	Reference G/L a...	Ref.acct in acc
10010000	☑	☑	Petty Cash	Petty Cash	10010000	☑
11001000	☑	☐	SBI Main Account	SBI Main Account	11001000	☐
11001010	☑	☐	SBI Cash Payment	SBI Cash Payment	11001010	☐
11001020	☑	☐	SBI Bank Transfer	SBI - Bank Transfer (Domestic/SEPA/Foreign)	11001020	☐
11001030	☑	☑	SBI Other Transfer	SBI - Other Interim Transfers	11001030	☑
11001040	☑	☐	SBI Direct Debit	SBI Direct Debit	11001040	☐

Figure 9.24 G/L Accounts Created in Company Code 1210 using Reference Method

ix.   Click on 'Check entries for consistency' button and ensure that there have not been any inconsistencies while creating the G/L accounts.

Now that we have created the G/L accounts in the company code area for the company code 1120, you can use collective maintenance as described in Section 9.3.2.1, to edit/change the

G/L accounts to suit India reporting and operations. Once done, you can use 'Copy Company Code' option as outlined in Section 9.3.2.2.2, to copy from 1210 to 1220.

In case, you want to edit a particular G/L account, at any point of time, you can do that by choosing the individual processing activity.

9.3.2.4   Edit G/L Account (Individual Processing)

Using this individual processing option, you can edit / change a G/L account master record (a) in the chart of accounts area or (b) in the company code area or (c) both in the chart of accounts area as well as the company code area, in one step.

- Use the menu path: SAP Customizing Implementation Guide > Financial Accounting > General Ledger Accounting > Master Data > G/L Accounts > G/L Account Creation and Processing > Edit G/L Account (Individual Processing) > Edit G/L Account Centrally or Transaction FS00, to change/edit a single G/L master record centrally, both in the chart of accounts area and company code area (Figure 9.25).

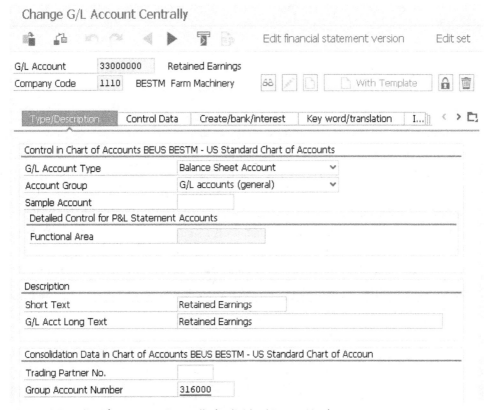

Figure 9.25 Edit G/L Account Centrally (Individual Processing)

- Use the menu path: SAP Customizing Implementation Guide > Financial Accounting > General Ledger Accounting > Master Data > G/L Accounts > G/L Account Creation and Processing > Edit G/L Account (Individual Processing) > Edit Chart of Accounts Data or Transaction FSP0, to change/edit a single G/L master record in the chart of accounts area.
- Use the menu path: SAP Customizing Implementation Guide > Financial Accounting > General Ledger Accounting > Master Data > G/L Accounts > G/L Account Creation and Processing > Edit G/L Account (Individual Processing) > Edit Company Code Data or Transaction FSS0, to change/edit a single G/L master record in the company code area.

This completes our discussion on creation and processing of G/L account master data. Let us, now, discuss the configuration settings relating to Financial Statement Structures.

9.3.3 *Financial Statement Structures*

The configuration settings under 'Financial Statement Structures' include (a) defining financial statement versions and (b) assigning accounting principles to the financial statement versions so defined.

Let us start with the definition of financial statement versions.

9.3.3.1 Define Financial Statement Versions

You need to define the *financial statement versions* for the balance sheet, and profit & loss statement. You can define versions for a specific chart of accounts, for a group chart of accounts, or without any specific assignment. You then determine the financial statement items for your version: you assign groups of accounts to the items at the lowest levels of the version. You can also use conditions to control in which item accounts are displayed: this enables you to assign accounts or a group of accounts to a specific item, depending on the respective balance. Alternatively, you can also assign functional area intervals at the lowest level of the version, instead of account intervals. Either account intervals or functional area intervals can be assigned to a balance sheet item. This financial statement version can, then, also be used by the notes to financial statement in the G/L account information system.

To define a financial statement version,

i.   Use the menu path: SAP Customizing Implementation Guide > Financial Accounting > General Ledger Accounting > Master Data > G/L Accounts > Financial Statement Structures > Define Financial Statement Versions or Transaction OB58 (or OB58_SM30).

ii.   On the 'Change View "Financial Statement Versions": Overview' screen, click on 'New Entries' and create the required versions. We have already created the required financial statement versions for BESTM as displayed in Figure 9.26 when creating the chart of accounts (Section 6.8.1 of Chapter 6).

Figure 9.26 Financial Statement Versions for BESTM

iii.   To look at the details of a financial statement version, double-click on the appropriate row and you can see the details for the version (Figure 9.27). By selecting the 'Fun.area perm' check-box, we have ensured that we can assign accounts or functional areas to the individual nodes of this financial statement version.

Change View "Financial Statement Versions": Details

Financial Statement Items	New Entries

FS Version	BEUS
Name	BESTM-Financial Statement Version US

General specifications

Maint. language	EN
Auto. Item Keys	☑
Chart of Accounts	BEUS
Group Account Number	☐
Fun.area perm.	☑

Figure 9.27 Financial Statement Version BEUS - Details

> **i** If you set the 'Fun.area perm.' indicator and reset it later, the system deletes the assigned functional areas from the financial statement version. Do not use a financial statement version to which functional areas are assigned, as the basis for planning in SAP G/L Accounting.

iv.   To look at the financial statement items, click on 'Financial Statement Items' and you will see the details of accounts / functional area assigned at the lower nodes of the tree structure (Figure 9.28).

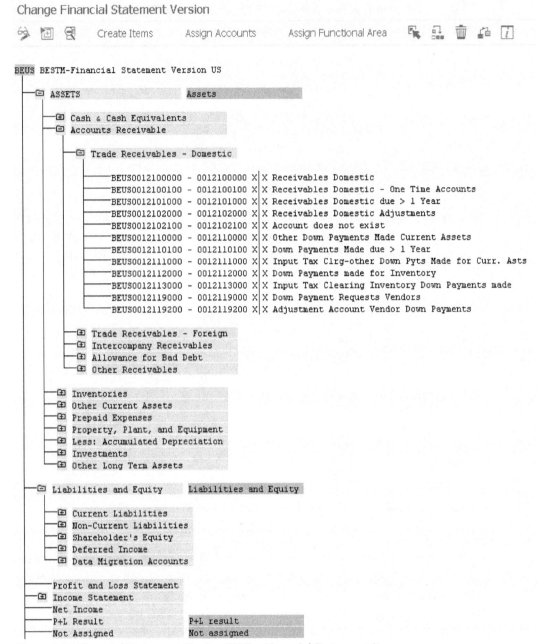

Figure 9.28 Financial Statement Version BEUS – Financial Statement Items

With this, we are now ready assign the financial statement versions to accounting principles that we have defined earlier, in Section 6.3.4.3 of Chapter 6.

9.3.3.2 Assign Financial Statement Versions to Accounting Principles

Use this assignment to determine the accounts to which the gains and losses of the foreign currency valuation are posted.

To assign a financial statement version to an accounting principle, use the menu path: SAP Customizing Implementation Guide > Financial Accounting > General Ledger Accounting > Master Data > G/L Accounts > Financial Statement Structures > Assign Financial Statement Versions to Accounting Principles.

This completes our discussion on G/L account master data. We shall now move on to discuss the settings relating to configuring the business transactions in SAP G/L Accounting.

9.4 Business Transactions

There are several business transactions that need correct configuration in the system to function properly. However, we will not be discussing all such transactions but restrict ourselves to the most important ones as listed below:

- Document Splitting
- Cross-Company Code Transactions
- Open Item Clearing
- Bank Account Interest Calculation
- Adjustment Posting / Reversals

Let us start with the document splitting

9.4.1 Document Splitting

We have already discussed the document splitting functionality in Section 9.1.3 of this Chapter. As you can recall, you can use the document splitting procedure to split up line items for selected dimensions (say, receivable lines by profit center) or to make a zero-balance setting in the document for selected dimensions (say, segment). This generates additional clearing lines in the document.

You can display the document with the generated clearing lines either in its original form in the entry view or from the perspective of a ledger in the G/L view. For document splitting to be possible, the individual document items and the documents must be classified, with each classification corresponding to a rule in which it is specified how document splitting is to occur and for which line items.

Project Dolphin

BESTM wants to make use of document splitting functionality for all the company codes, both in US and India. Accordingly, the project team has suggested the following which was later agreed upon with the BESTM management:

The configuration will make use of SAP's default and standard document splitting method 0000000012; no new method will be defined. Also, no new item categories, document types, business transactions, and business transaction types will be defined as the project feels that the standard offerings from SAP will be enough to meet all the document splitting requirements of BESTM company codes. The 'Business Area', 'Profit Center' and the 'Segment' will be used as the document splitting characteristics with a zero-balance setting. Additionally, the team will make appropriate settings for 'Segment', as BESTM indicated that it requires a complete balance sheet, per segment, for which inaccuracies due to non-assigned postings cannot be tolerated. The characteristics 'Order', 'Cost Center' and 'WBS Element' need to be used as the document splitting characteristics for CO. The cash discount that is applied in the payment of an asset-relevant invoice should be capitalized to the asset.

Let us use the *Document Splitting Wizards* to configure the required settings for US-based company codes of BESTM. There are two wizards:

- Wizard: Configure Document Splitting
- Wizard: Create Document Splitting Rule

The first one is for configuring the regular document splitting, and the other is for configuring *'Extended Document Splitting'*. Let us start with the first one to configure the normal document splitting functionality.

9.4.1.1   Wizard: Configure Document Splitting

You can make the required configuration settings for document splitting using this wizard from SAP. To facilitate and simplify the activity, this wizard combines all the necessary IMG activities in one interface. You can, also, use it to check the configuration settings.

> ℹ️ When you are using the wizard to set up document splitting configuration, you do not need to perform the individual IMG activities separately. All the relevant maintenance dialogs for configuration are linked to the wizard, and the data that you change in these maintenance dialogs are saved immediately. Hence, it is not possible to restore the initial status of the configuration settings; you can, of course, interrupt the wizard at any time, retaining the data that has been saved so far. If you have used the wizard, then, you should not make any configuration changes by navigating to an individual IMG activity (from a link in the system documentation) as it may result in configuration inconsistencies.

Let us use the wizard to configure document splitting functionality, as detailed below:

i.   Use the menu path: SAP Customizing Implementation Guide > Financial Accounting > General Ledger Accounting > Master Data > G/L Accounts > Business Transactions > Document Splitting > Wizards for Document Splitting > Wizard: Configure Document Splitting.

ii.   The system brings up the interface of the wizard: on the left pane you will see the tasks in the order in which they need to be performed, beginning with 'Start', and on the right-hand side pane, you will see the details / description of that step / task. When you enter the wizard, you will notice that all the tasks have a Red LED indicating that they are yet to be completed, and the 'Start' task will have Yellow LED indicating that it is in progress (Figure 9.29).

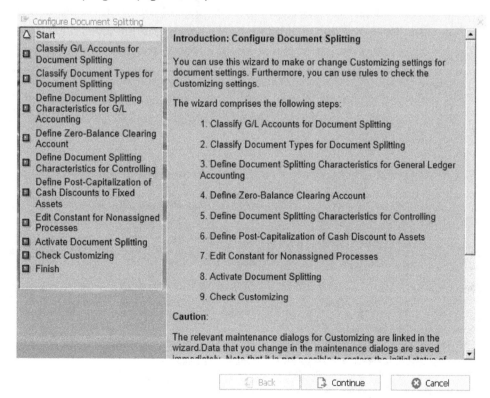

Figure 9.29 Doc. Splitting Wizard – Initial Screen

iii.   Press 'Continue'.

iv.   You will reach the first step: ***Classify G/L Accounts for Document Splitting***. Each business transaction that is entered is analysed (during the document splitting procedures) to determine - for each line item - whether it is an item that remains unchanged or an item that should be split. For this to happen, you need to classify the G/L accounts by assigning them to an '*item category*' (the standard item categories being customer, vendor, cash discount offsetting, material asset, expense and revenue). Using this step, you will assign the revenue / expense / bank or cash / balance sheet G/L accounts of a chart of accounts to the appropriate item category.

> **i** The classification of all other accounts is known to the system, so you do not have to enter them here. You can enter an account interval since the system recognizes SAP-specific classifications and does not allow SAP settings to be overwritten by your own settings.

Enter the chart of accounts by clicking on 'Switch ChtAccts' button. The system populates the G/L accounts. Click on 'Change Data' and enter the appropriate item category ('Cat') for a G/L account or a range of G/L accounts (Figure 9.30). You may also display the documentation in a separate window by clicking on the hyperlink 'Display Documentation in a Separate Window' at the top of the screen.

> **i** You cannot define any additional item categories, on you own. If the standard item categories included in the system are not meeting your requirements, get in touch with SAP.

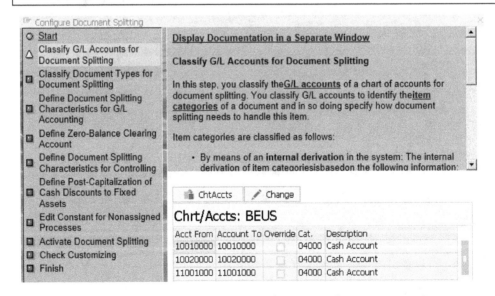

Figure 9.30 Doc. Splitting Wizard – Classifying G/L Accounts for Document Splitting

v. Press 'Continue'.

vi. The wizard moves to the 2nd step (*Classify Document Types for Document Splitting*) and displays the standard document types that are already in the system (Figure 9.31), together with the default business transaction and business transaction variant for each of the document types.

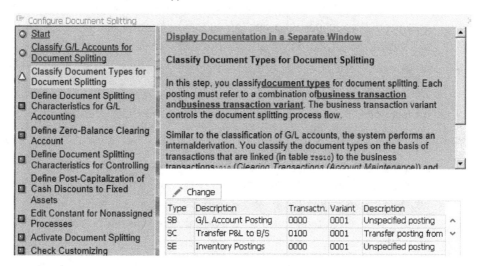

Figure 9.31 Doc. Splitting Wizard – Document Types

The document splitting is essentially controlled by the 'document type'. For the system to determine the splitting rule, you must assign a 'business transaction variant' to each document type. To ensure that a splitting rule is used appropriately, the relevant documents must meet certain requirements; these requirements relate in particular to certain item categories that either must or must not be available. This information is specified, per business transaction variant, and is checked against the current document during posting. If the document is not meeting these requirements, the system rejects the posting.

SAP includes the standard business transactions and business transaction variants in the system. The item categories that are allowed for each business (or accounting) transaction are also defined. The system uses the business transaction variants as additional limiting condition for an accounting transaction. The business transaction variant controls the document splitting process flow. Similar to the classification of G/L accounts, the system performs an internal derivation.

> **i** For the business transaction 0200 (customer invoice), for example, the business transaction variant 0001 is delivered as standard. In this business transaction, the

item categories namely customer, value added tax, withholding tax, expense, revenue, exchange rate differences, and company code clearing are allowed.

With the standard document types in the system, SAP delivers a classification for document splitting by proposing a 'document type-business transaction-business transaction variant' combination. Check, first, how your document types are organized. Also, check whether the classification or assignment of a document type to a business transaction variant will produce the desired result in document splitting.

> **i** As in the case of item categories, you cannot define additional business transactions. But, you can define your own business transaction variants to the standard business transactions.

At times, you may need to include more document types in the system to achieve your specific requirements. Consider that the document type SA is assigned to business transaction 0000 and business transaction variant 0001 ('Unspecified Posting'). By default, no splitting rules are defined for this business transaction variant (with the exception of company code clearing). Now, if you expect an account assignment on these documents, then, the assignment has to be specified for all line items because the system does not project any account assignments to non-assigned lines, due to the absence of a splitting rule. However, since the document type SA is generally used for a large variety of business transactions that would also have to be treated differently in document splitting, it is necessary that you define additional document types and to assign them to the specific fiscal year variants.

Now, assign the document types to an accounting transaction and a business transaction variant in this step: use 'Change Data' button to make the required changes.

vii.   Press 'Continue'.

viii.   On the next step (***Define Document Splitting Characteristics for Document Splitting***), you can maintain the document splitting characteristics for SAP G/L Accounting (Figure 9.32). You may add more fields if required by clicking on 'Change':

- Select the 'Zero Bal.' check-box, to enable the system to check whether the balance is zero for the selected characteristic when performing the posting. If the balance is not zero, the system creates additional clearing lines on clearing accounts that produce a zero-balance per specified characteristic(s). Select this indicator for all the three fields ('Business Area', 'Profit Center' and 'Segment') that are shown on the screen for BESTM.

- Select the 'Mandatory Field' check-box, to indicate that the field must contain a value after document splitting. You should set this indicator for fields for which you require a complete balance sheet and for which inaccuracies due to non-assigned postings cannot be allowed. When this indicator is set, any postings that, after document splitting, lack a value for the specified field are rejected and an error message is issued. Select this for 'Segment' for BESTM.

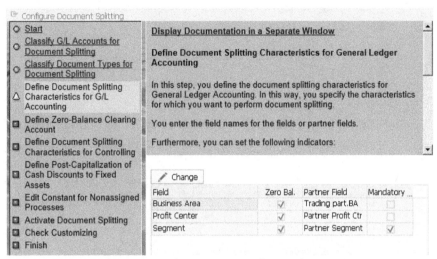

Figure 9.32 Doc. Splitting Wizard – Document Splitting Characteristics

ix.   Press 'Continue'.

x.   The wizard takes you to the next step (***Define Zero-Balance Clearing Account***) in which you will define the required G/L accounts for the zero-balance clearing account.

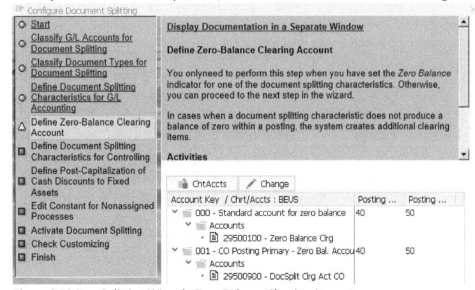

Figure 9.33 Doc. Splitting Wizard - Zero-Balance Clearing Account

For account assignment objects for which you want to have a zero-balance setting, the system checks whether the balance of account assignment object is zero after document splitting. If this is not the case, then, the system generates additional clearing items. Click on 'Change Data' and maintain the appropriate G/L account for each of the account keys (Figure 9.33) as we have set the 'Zero Bal.' indicator for three document splitting characteristics in the previous step.

> **i** You need to perform this step only when you have set the 'Zero Bal.' indicator for at least one of the 'document splitting characteristics' in the previous step; else, you can proceed to the next step.

xi. Press 'Continue'.

xii. On the next step (***Define Document Splitting Characteristics for Controlling***), you may specify the additional characteristics that you want to include in document splitting (Figure 9.34). These additional characteristics are not relevant for SAP G/L Accounting, but are relevant for other application components that transfer documents from SAP G/L Accounting (such as subcomponents from CO).

> **i** The selected characteristics are only transferred to the specified line items, when the account to which the postings are to be made can also take the characteristics. That is, these CO account assignments are only transferred when the account has also been set up as a cost element. As the field status definition of the account is explicitly excluded from this check, these characteristics are transferred (in manual entry) even when they are hidden by field status definition of the G/L account.

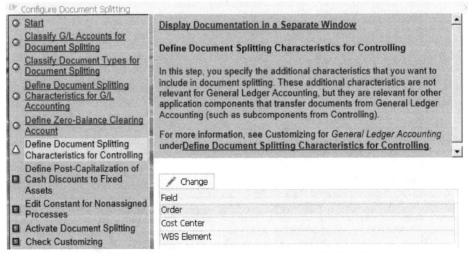

Figure 9.34 Doc. Splitting Wizard - Doc. Splitting Characteristics for CO

xiii.   Press 'Continue'.

xiv.   You will, now, move on to the next step (**Define Post-Capitalization of Cash Discounts to Fixed Assets**), to define the required post-capitalization discount settings for the fixed assets. Here, you define whether the cash discount that is applied in the payment of an asset-relevant invoice should be capitalized to the asset. When you select this setting, the cash discount amount is not posted to the cash discount account in the payment document, instead posted directly to the asset. Already, the field 'Asset' (AMNL1) has been defined as the standard settings (Figure 9.35).

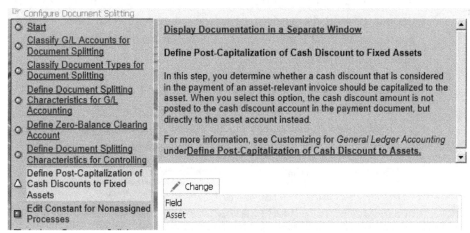

Figure 9.35 Doc. Splitting Wizard – Post-Capitalization of Cash Discounts to Fixed Assets

xv.   Press 'Continue'.

xvi.   The wizard takes you to the next step: **Edit Constant for Non-assigned Processes**, as shown in Figure 9.36.

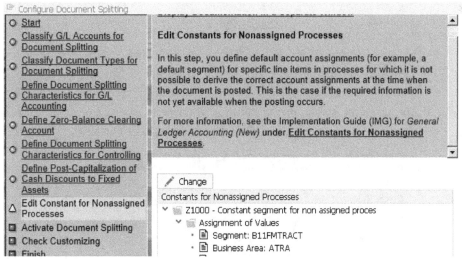

Figure 9.36 Doc. Splitting Wizard – Constants for Non-assigned Processes

Here, you define default account assignments (for example, a default segment) for specific line items in processes for which it is not possible to derive the correct account assignments at the time of document posting. This kind of assignment is useful when the required information is not yet available when the posting occurs. Use the 'Change Date' button to assign the required defaults for the document splitting characteristics under the constant Z1000 (Figure 9.36).

---

i Consider, for example, you have made the segment B13LANTRAC as the default account assignment object. For a cash receipt, from a customer, that is posted to a house bank account, it is not immediately known which invoices are to be paid by this cash receipt.

In step-1, to make the information concerning available financial means to the system within the shortest possible delay, a posting from checking account against cash receipt is made. Since no additional information is available for this, the account assignment is made to a default segment.

Account	Segment	Amount (USD)
Checking Account	B13LANTRAC	2,000
Cash Receipt	B13LANTRAC	-2,000

In step-2, the cash receipt account is then posted against the customer (with clearing of the customer). In this way, the correct segment is determined from the cleared invoice.

Account	Segment	Amount (USD)
Cash Receipt	B13GOLFSPR	2,000
Customer	B13GOLFSPR	2,000

In step-3, both items on the cash receipt account are cleared against each other. Since both positions are assigned to different segments, corresponding clearing items must be generated on the cash receipt account. In case zero-balance is required for a segment, additional line items making the document balance, per segment, to zero are generated on a clearing account already defined.

Account	Segment	Amount (USD)
Cash Receipt	B13LANTRAC	2,000
Cash Receipt	B13GOLFSPR	2,000
Clearing Account	B13GOLFSPR	2000
Clearing Account	B13LANTRAC	-2000

xvii.   Press 'Continue'.

xviii.   You will move to the next step '***Activate Document Splitting***' (Figure 9.37). Here, you activate document splitting with the standard splitting method (0000000012) containing the splitting rules for the different business transactions. If this splitting method does not meet your requirements, you can first define a new method and then activate the same. Using the 'Change Data' button, you can change the document splitting method and/or deactivate document splitting for specific company codes.

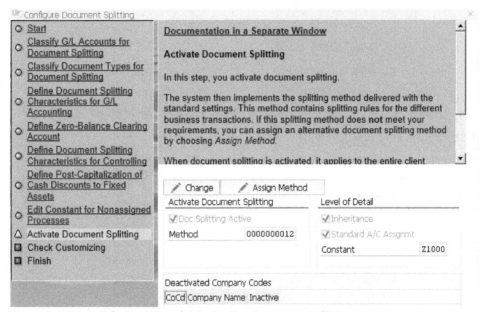

Figure 9.37 Doc. Splitting Wizard – Activating Document Splitting

> **i** The document splitting activation applies for the entire client; however, you can explicitly exclude individual company codes from document splitting by deselecting the 'Inactive' checkbox in Customizing.

xix.   Press 'Continue'.

xx.   The wizard takes you to the penultimate step (***Check Customizing***) in configuring the settings for document splitting (Figure 9.38). Press 'Check'; On the basis of the settings that you have made in the previous steps, the system checks the charts of accounts that you have used when you processed the steps in the wizard. If there are any errors or discrepancies, those are displayed on a pop-up log screen with the details.

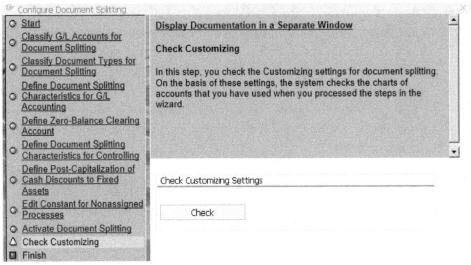

Figure 9.38 Doc. Splitting Wizard – Checking Customizing Settings

xxi.   Press 'Continue'.

xxii.   The wizard takes you to the final screen (Figure 9.39); press 'Complete'. At this stage you can notice that LED for all the previous steps is in Green indicating that you have successfully completed all the steps. When you press 'Complete', the wizard closes the interface and takes you back to the Customizing screen.

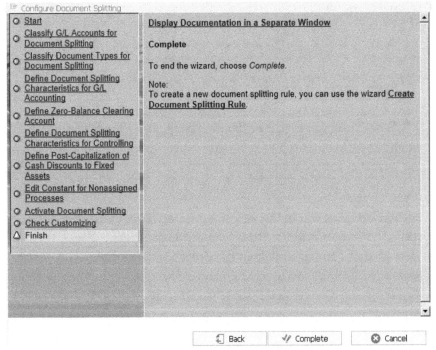

Figure 9.39 Doc. Splitting Wizard – Final Step in Configuring Document Splitting

With this, we are ready look at the second wizard, in document splitting, that you will use in case of extended document splitting functionality is required for your company codes.

9.4.1.2 Wizard: Create Document Splitting Rule

This wizard is a part of the functionality known as *'Extended Document Splitting'*. You will use this when the SAP-delivered general functions are not sufficient for your document splitting needs and you want to make changes or enhancements. For this, you will create your own set of rules appropriate to your needs and make the necessary settings so that the system applies the rules you defined and not the SAP standard rules. To make configuration simple, use this wizard and complete the steps listed (Figure 9.40), one-by-one, as we have done in the previous section.

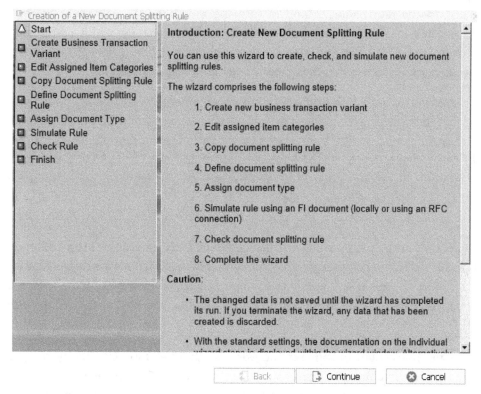

Figure 9.40 Doc. Splitting Wizard for Configuring Extended Document Splitting

Essentially, you will be creating a new rule for document splitting using this wizard. In the process, you will be creating a new business transaction variant, editing the assigned item categories, copying / defining the document splitting rule, assigning the document type, simulating the rule (using an FI document) and checking the newly defined document splitting rule for completeness and inconsistencies, before exiting the wizard. Since we will use only the SAP standard document splitting processing rules for BESTM, we will not be going through this wizard.

This completes our discussion on configuring document splitting functionality for BESTM. Let us, next, move on to discuss the settings required for cross-company code transactions.

9.4.2   Cross-Company Code Transactions

The cross-company code postings happen (a) when purchasing or payment is made centrally by a company code (say, 1110) on behalf of several company codes (say, 1120, 2100, 2200 etc) in a corporate group, and/or (b) if one of the company codes (say, company code 1120), of the corporate group, is a manufacturer and another (say, company code 1110) is a merchandiser (seller). In the manufacturer-merchandiser scenario, the manufacturer sells its products first to the merchandiser, and in turn the merchandiser sells them to the end customers. In this case, the system posts the transactions between the merchandising company code (say, 1110) and the manufacturing company code (say, 1210): the system creates two documents, one for each company code for every transaction.

You may also come across a situation where in the customers (of, say, company code 1120) make payment to the wrong company code (say, 1110) in the corporate group. In such cases, you can use cross-company code transactions to minimize the number of entries for posting this incorrect payment: you debit the bank account of company code 1110 and credit the customer account of company code 1120, and the system automatically generates clearing entries between these two company codes.

> **i** The company codes participating in cross-company code transactions should be part of the single legal entity. You can set up cross-company code transactions for clearing customer / vendor accounts as well as G/L accounts. If one of the participating company codes is an external one, you can only do this for G/L accounts clearing, and not for customer / vendor accounts.

Use this configuration activity to define the accounts for the clearing entries the system makes when posting cross-company code transactions. You will do the settings for a pair of company codes; if there are more than two company codes, then you need to define more than one pairing among themselves.

Project Dolphin

The BESTM Corporate has indicated to the project team that they need to take care of cross-company code transactions as the company code 1110 will be the central purchasing organization for rest of the company codes in US. Besides, it was further stated that the company code 1120 will make sales of their products through company code 1110 which will act as the merchandiser. A similar scenario was envisaged for India-based company codes, as well, with regard to the central purchasing by the company code 1210 for themselves and on behalf of the other company code 1220.

To configure cross-company code transactions:

i. Use the menu path: SAP Customizing Implementation Guide > Financial Accounting > General Ledger Accounting > Master Data > G/L Accounts > Business Transactions > Prepare Cross-Company Code Transactions.

ii. On the ensuing 'Company Code Clearing' pop-up screen, enter 1110 as 'Company code 1' and 1120 as 'Company code 2'. And, press 'Continue'.

iii. On the 'Configuration Accounting Maintain: Automatic Posts – Clearing Accounts' screen, maintain the required details as indicated below (Figure 9.41):

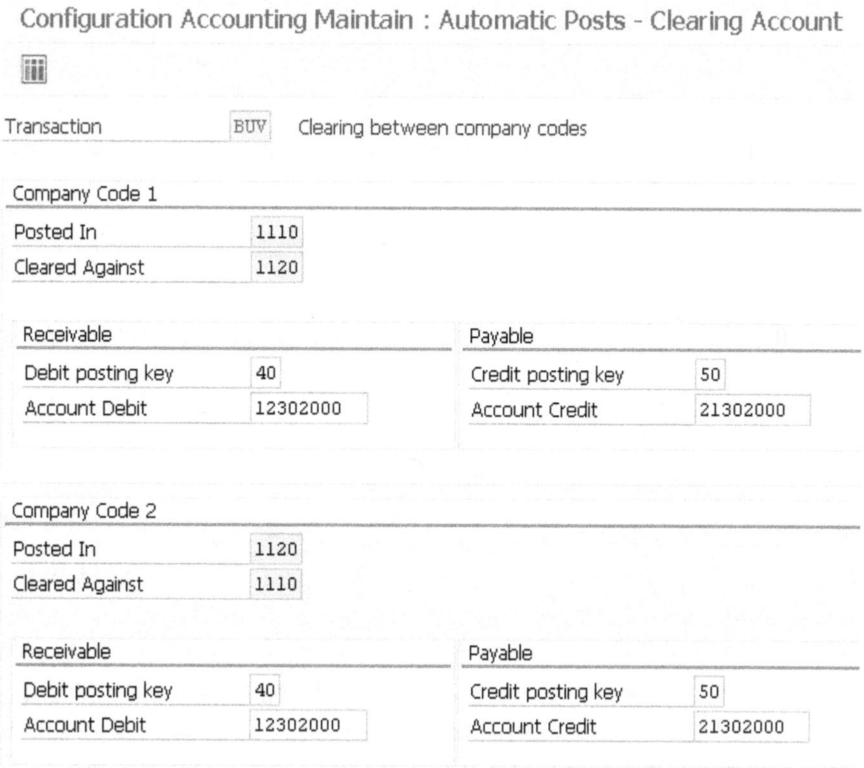

Configuration Accounting Maintain : Automatic Posts - Clearing Account

Transaction   BUV   Clearing between company codes

Company Code 1

Posted In	1110
Cleared Against	1120

Receivable		Payable	
Debit posting key	40	Credit posting key	50
Account Debit	12302000	Account Credit	21302000

Company Code 2

Posted In	1120
Cleared Against	1110

Receivable		Payable	
Debit posting key	40	Credit posting key	50
Account Debit	12302000	Account Credit	21302000

Figure 9.41 Cross-Company Code Transactions – Settings for Clearing between 110 and 1120

- Under 'Company code 1' block, for 'Posted In' the company code 1110 and 'Clearing Against' the 1120, enter the Debit and Credit posting keys (40 and 50 respectively). Also, enter the appropriate G/L account for receivable ('Receivables affiliated companies adjustments' - 12302000) and payable

('Payables affiliated companies adjustments' - 21302000) in the respective fields as shown in Figure 9.41.

- Repeat the entries for 'Company code 2' block for 'Posted In' the company code 1120 and 'Clearing Against' the company code 1110, and 'Save'.

iv.   Maintain similar configuration for other pairs of company codes as well. When completed, click on 'List' on the 'Configuration Accounting Maintain: Automatic Posts – Clearing Accounts' screen, to see the pairing of company codes for cross-company code transactions for BESTM (Figure 9.42). You may also use the 'Create' button on this screen to make settings between a pair of company codes.

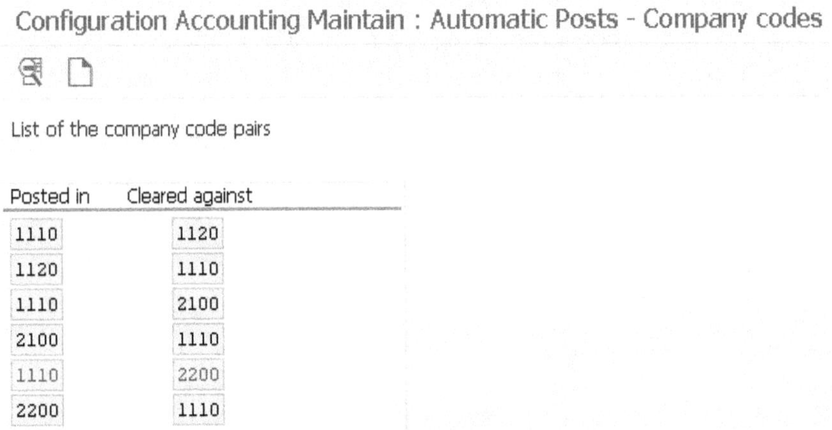

Configuration Accounting Maintain : Automatic Posts - Company codes

List of the company code pairs

Posted in	Cleared against
1110	1120
1120	1110
1110	2100
2100	1110
1110	2200
2200	1110

Figure 9.42 List of Company Codes paired for Cross-Company Code Transactions

This completes our discussion on preparing the company codes for cross-company code transactions. We can now move on to the next configuration activity under business transactions namely, open item clearing.

9.4.3   Open Item Clearing

An '*open item*' is an uncleared transaction (say, an unpaid invoice from a vendor) that can be cleared and closed, only when you post (say, a payment towards settling the vendor invoice) an offsetting amount to that account: when the offsetting amount is equal to the open item, then it is cleared in full; else, it is cleared partially as there is still a residual amount that is 'open'. In cases of partial clearing, the system stores the open residual amount for the item and the cleared amount. For the open item, you can enter a due date for net payment, due date for cash discount, or deferral date; when you enter a deferral date, the system does not process (by dunning or payment program) that open item until that date is passed. When clearing, the system enters a clearing document number and the clearing date in the open items.

You can process several accounts of different account types (G/L, vendor, and customer), including accounts from different company codes in a single clearing. The account balance is always the total of the open items, as the sum of the items involved in any clearing transaction is zero. The customer / vendor accounts are always managed on open item basis, allowing you to monitor the outstanding A/R and A/P, respectively, at any point of time. However, you need to define *open item management* for G/L accounts in their respective master records, and you will normally set this option, for example, for bank sub-accounts and clearing accounts so as to track whether the business transactions posted to these accounts are closed yet or not.

> **i** You will be able to move a document to the 'cold area' of the database only if all the open items have been cleared. This ensures that all the (open) items that are yet to be cleared are always available in the system.

You can clear the open items either in the local currency (of the open item) or using a foreign currency. When cleared in a foreign currency, the system translates the transaction using the average rate between the two currencies: first translates the document currency into the local currency, and then translates the local currency using the clearing currency. During such a translation, if the system encounters any difference (loss or gain) due to currency conversion, then, the system posts those differences (beyond the tolerance limits, as defined in configuration settings in Section 9.4.3.6) to the pre-defined G/L accounts.

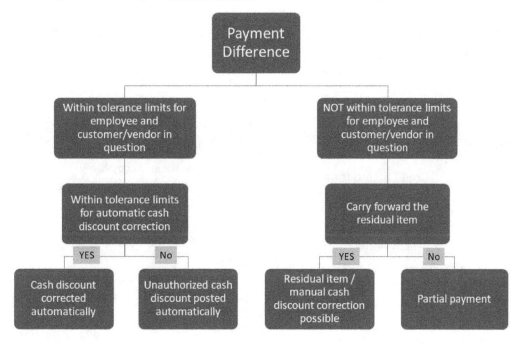

Figure 9.43 Payment Difference Processing during Clearing

You will also encounter payment differences arising out of clearing transaction due to, for example, a customer's underpayment / overpayment, or the customer has made an unauthorized deduction for cash discount. If the difference is immaterial, you usually clear the receivable and post the difference. You can configure the system as how to handle the payment differences (Figure 9.43). The options are:

- If the payment differences are well within the tolerance limits, the system automatically adjusts the cash discount or posts the difference to a separate gain or loss G/L account.
- If the payment difference exceeds the tolerance limits, you can, then, process the payment as a partial payment or enter a residual item for the difference:
  - When you enter a partial payment, the system does not clear the original receivable, but posts the payment with an invoice reference.
  - When you create a residual item, the system clears the original receivable and posts the outstanding difference as residual item to the customer account.

You can only clear open items that are posted to accounts which are managed on an open-item basis. You should define while configuring the system, beforehand, as to which accounts can be cleared automatically. You will not be able to clear certain open items if they trigger another posting in the system, for example, exchange rate difference. You cannot also clear Special G/L transactions using SAP G/L Accounting clearing programs; you need to use the special functions for that purpose.

You can clear open item either manually or automatically using the clearing program. You can use the functions specified in Table 9.2:

Posting transaction	Business transaction details	You need to use (SAP Easy Access):
Incoming payment	Credit memo for a check deposited at the bank	SAP Menu > Financial Accounting > General Ledger > Document Entry > Incoming Payments
Outgoing payment	Debit memo for an issued check	SAP Menu > Financial Accounting > General Ledger > Document Entry > Outgoing Payments
Post with clearing	Clearing the GR/IR clearing account	SAP Menu > Financial Accounting > General Ledger > Document Entry > Post with clearing
Outgoing payment	Debit memo for an issued check	SAP Menu > Financial Accounting > General Ledger > Document Entry > Outgoing Payments

Table 9:2 Functions for Open Item Clearing

You will use manual clearing (a) for bank subaccounts and clearing accounts, (b) where you have agreed a debit memo procedure and (c) if your vendor is making a refund. During manual clearing, you manually select open items that balance to zero from an account. The system, then, marks the items selected as 'cleared' and enters a clearing document number and the clearing date in the document items. The clearing date can be the current date or a date that you enter manually. The clearing document number is the number of the most recent document involved in the clearing transaction.

The clearing functionality in SAP G/L Accounts supports, besides the above, posting reversals / returns (during reversal /returns, all the items that were cleared earlier becomes open items again) and resetting of clearing (helps you to overcome accidental clearing transactions by resetting to the original status).

To configure the system for open item clearing you need to complete the following tasks:

- Define Posting Keys for Clearing
- Define Accounts for Exchange Rate Differences
- Define Clearing Rules
- Assign Clearing Rules to Account Types
- Prepare Automatic Clearing
- Define Tolerance Groups for G/L Accounts
- Create Accounts for Clearing Differences

Let us start with the first task of defining the posting keys for open item clearing.

Project Dolphin

The Dolphin Project team has recommended, to the BESTM management, that there is no need to define any new clearing procedures as the standard ones are sufficient. They also recommended not to change any of the default posting keys for these procedures, as tinkering with the standard posting keys may result in system-wide unforeseen difficulties and discrepancies.

9.4.3.1   Define Posting Keys for Clearing

Use this configuration task, to define the posting keys the system uses to create line items, automatically, during clearing transactions. The payment program also uses these posting keys. For each of the clearing transactions (or procedures) namely AUSGZAHL (outgoing payment), EINGZAHL (incoming payment), GUTSCHRI (credit memo), JVACLEAR (JVA clearing) and UMBUCHNG (transfer posting with clearing), you will see that there are posting keys already defined in the standard system that you can use without making any change.

However, if you want to make a change or define your own (normally, not recommended), you may use the menu path: SAP Customizing Implementation Guide > Financial Accounting > General Ledger Accounting > Master Data > G/L Accounts > Business Transactions > Open Item Clearing > Open Item Processing > Define Posting Keys for Clearing. You may also use Transaction OBXH.

On the 'Maintain Accounting Configuration: Clearing Procedures – List' screen, you will see a list of pre-defined standard clearing procedures like AUSGZAHL, EINGZAHL etc. You may double-click on a row, to look at the details of default posting keys for that clearing procedure on the next screen (Figure 9.44).

We are neither changing any of the standard posting keys nor defining any new key, for BESTM.

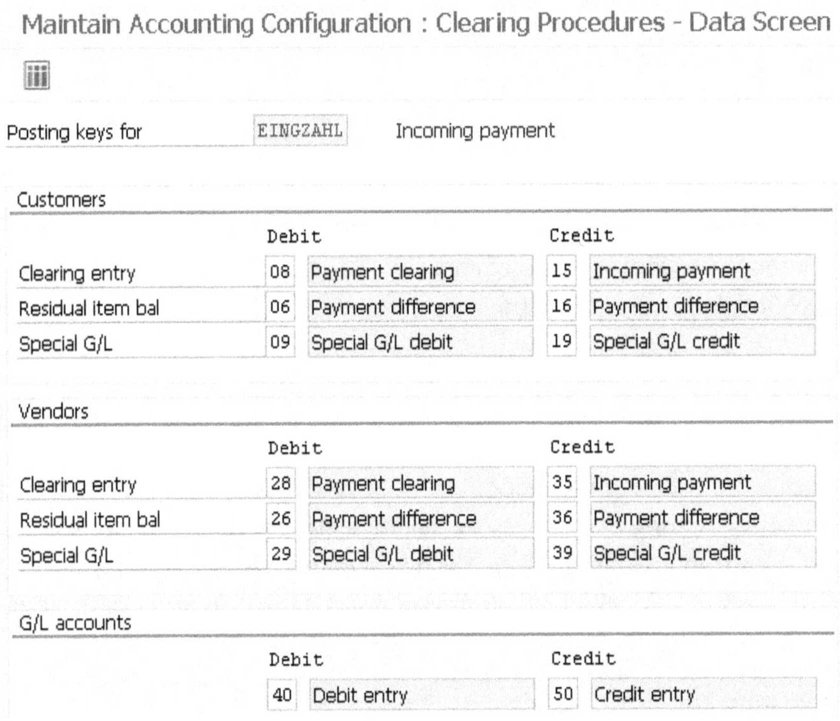

Maintain Accounting Configuration : Clearing Procedures - Data Screen

Posting keys for   EINGZAHL   Incoming payment

Customers

	Debit		Credit	
Clearing entry	08	Payment clearing	15	Incoming payment
Residual item bal	06	Payment difference	16	Payment difference
Special G/L	09	Special G/L debit	19	Special G/L credit

Vendors

	Debit		Credit	
Clearing entry	28	Payment clearing	35	Incoming payment
Residual item bal	26	Payment difference	36	Payment difference
Special G/L	29	Special G/L debit	39	Special G/L credit

G/L accounts

Debit		Credit	
40	Debit entry	50	Credit entry

Figure 9.44 Standard Posting Keys for the Clearing Procedure 'Incoming Payment'

Let us, now, move on to the second configuration task of defining the G/L accounts for exchange rate differences.

9.4.3.2   Define Accounts for Exchange Rate Differences

Here, you will define G/L account numbers to which you want the system to automatically post exchange rate differences (gain or loss) realized, when clearing G/L open items. To enable posting of exchange rate differences, when clearing open items of customers / vendors, you have to specify the reconciliation G/L accounts for customers / vendors in the 'G/L account' field in the respective master records. To automatically post exchange rate differences, when clearing bank sub-accounts, enter the bank sub-account number in the 'G/L account' field. Using this task, you can also define the accounts for valuating open items. You can define separate accounts, for each type of currency, to post the exchange rate differences per currency. Once you make the first valuation run, you should not change your accounts for valuation postings; else, you will not be able to reverse valuation postings.

Project Dolphin

The project team has recommended to use a single set of accounts to take care of automatic posting of the exchange rate differences realized while clearing open items: for loss it will be 72010000, and for the gains it will be 72510000. For valuation adjustments, the loss will be posted to 72040000 and the gains to 72540000; the B/S adjustments will go to the G/L account 11001099.

To make the required settings:

  i.   Use the menu path: SAP Customizing Implementation Guide > Financial Accounting > General Ledger Accounting > Master Data > G/L Accounts > Business Transactions > Open Item Clearing > Open Item Processing > Define Accounts for Exchange Rate Differences. You may also use Transaction OB09.
  ii.   Enter the 'Chart of Accounts' on the pop-up screen. Press 'Continue'.
  iii. The system brings up the G/L accounts, on the next screen, for which you need to maintain the account(s) for automatic posting of exchange rate differences.
  iv.   Select a row (G/L account), click on 'New Entries' and maintain the details, on the next screen (Figure 9.45):
        • Leave the 'Currency' and 'Currency Type' field as blank so that the G/L accounts entered here will be used for all the currencies / currency types. If you decide to define individual accounts for separate currencies / currency types, then, maintain the 'Currency' and 'Currency Type'.
        • Enter the appropriate G/L account for 'Loss' and 'Gain' under the 'Exchange rate difference realized' block. Similarly, enter the G/L accounts for valuation loss / gain in the 'Valuation' block.
  v.   'Save' when completed (Figure 9.45), and repeat the steps to define the G/L accounts, for posting the gain / loss, for both exchange rate differences and valuation, for other G/L accounts by using the 'Next Entry' button.

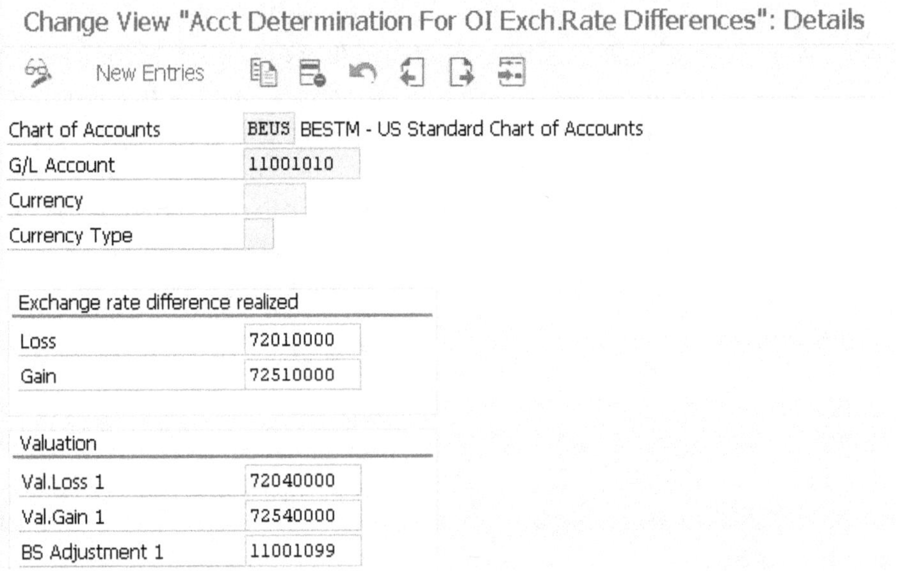

Figure 9.45 *G/L Accounts for Posting Exchange Rate Differences during OI Clearing*

The third task in configuring the settings for open item clearing is to define the clearing rules.

9.4.3.3 Define Clearing Rules

The *'clearing rules'*, defined here, lets you separate and assign clearing entries to accounts. The entries can be separated by various criteria such as the allocation, reference number, or contract number, and at the same time they can be transferred to the appropriate account assignment in the cleared items. For each rule, select the fields you require as criteria for classifying the clearing entries. As you can assign the clearing rules, at the client level and account type level, you can define differing classifications for customer, vendor, and G/L accounts.

Project Dolphin

The Dolphin Project team has recommended not to go for any additional clearing grouping criteria.

As BESTM does not want to have any additional criteria to be defined for grouping clearing items, we are not configuring this task. However, should you want to define a new grouping criterion, create a new clearing rule by using the menu path: SAP Customizing Implementation Guide > Financial Accounting > General Ledger Accounting > Master Data > G/L Accounts > Business Transactions > Open Item Clearing > Open Item Processing > Define Clearing Rules. You may also use Transaction OBIA. Create a new clearing rule with a 2-character ID, then, assign the clearing rules fields to that rule.

The next task will be to assign the clearing rule(s) the account types.

9.4.3.4 Assign Clearing Rules to Account Types

Use the menu path: SAP Customizing Implementation Guide > Financial Accounting > General Ledger Accounting > Master Data > G/L Accounts > Business Transactions > Open Item Clearing > Open Item Processing > Assign Clearing Rules to Account Types. You may also use Transaction OBIB. Assign the clearing rule defined in the previous step to the appropriate account type like customer, vendor and G/L accounts. We are not configuring this task as well for BESTM, as we have not defined any new clearing rule, but decided to go with the standard settings in the system.

With this, we are now ready to configure system for automatic clearing.

9.4.3.5 Prepare Automatic Clearing

The *'automatic clearing program'* also uses the clearing transactions that are provided for manual clearing. This includes, for example, automatic posting of exchange rate differences, or automatic generation of transfer postings if items from different business areas / trading partners are involved in clearing. Also, the program can clear journal entries that were posted using the 'net method' and journal entries that contain parallel currencies.

Here, using this task, you need to specify the criteria for grouping open items, belonging to an account, for automatic clearing. Besides the two standard criteria (account type and account number or number interval), you can enter fiver more user-criteria. You, also, need to specify a clearing date. The program clears the open items that are grouped together, if their total balance equals zero in local and foreign currency.

> **i** There are five user-criteria and a variety of fields you can choose from. Ensure that you specify fields that have an internal length of up to 20 places only. You can enter separate criteria for each account type, and use an account number interval to determine the accounts to which the criteria should apply. If you want the system to continue to group open items by business area or trading partner for automatic clearing, you have to maintain these as user-criteria in the configuration settings.

Project Dolphin

The BESTM management, after some discussion with the project team, requested to configure four more user-criteria for grouping clearing items for automatic clearing, for more flexibility: 'Assignment Number', 'Business Area', 'Trading Partner' and 'Contract Number' for customer and vendor, and 'Segment' (in the place of contract number) for G/L accounts.

To make the required settings:

i. Use the menu path: SAP Customizing Implementation Guide > Financial Accounting > General Ledger Accounting > Master Data > G/L Accounts > Business Transactions > Open Item Clearing > Open Item Processing > Prepare Automatic Clearing. You may also use Transaction OB74.

ii. On the 'Change View "Additional Rules for Automatic Clearing": Overview' screen, you will see the standard settings (for clearing grouping) that includes the account type ('AccTy') and number interval ('From Account' and 'To Account'). In the case of account types D and K, adding both numeric and alpha-numeric number intervals will give all the flexibility. If you leave the chart of accounts field as blank, then, the settings you make here will be valid for all the charts in the system.

iii. You can include five more fields as user-criteria in the fields 'Criterion 1' to 'Criterion 5'. As per BESTM management's requirements, we need to include 'Assignment Number' (ZUONR), 'Business Area' (GSBER), 'Trading Partner' (VBUND) and 'Contract Number' (VERTN) as the additional user-criteria for the chart of accounts BEUS, for the account types D & K. For the account type S (G/L), instead of the contract number, we need to include 'Segment' (SEGMENT). Click on 'New Entries', maintain the user-criteria on the next screen, and 'Save' the settings (Figure 9.46).

iv. Maintain similar settings for the chart of accounts BEIN as well.

Change View "Additional Rules For Automatic Clearing": Overview of Sel

🔍   New Entries   🗐 🗟 🔙 📑 📑 📑 📑

Cht...	AccTy	From Acct	To Account	Criterion 1	Criterion 2	Criterion 3	Criterion 4	Criterion
BEUS	D	1	9999999999	ZUONR	VBUND	GSBER	VERTN	
BEUS	D	A	Z	ZUONR	VBUND	GSBER	VERTN	
BEUS	K	0	9999999999	ZUONR	VBUND	GSBER	VERTN	
BEUS	K	A	Z	ZUONR	VBUND	GSBER	VERTN	
BEUS	S	0	9999999999	ZUONR	VBUND	GSBER	SEGMENT	

Figure 9.46 Criteria for grouping Clearing Items in Automatic Clearing

To execute the clearing program, for G/L accounts, use SAP Easy Access menu path: SAP Menu > Accounting > Financial Accounting > General Ledger > Periodic Processing > Automatic Clearing. You have three options here:

(a) Without Specification of Clearing Currency (Transaction F.13)
(b) With Specification of Clearing Currency (Transaction F13E)
(c) G/L Accounts - Specific to Ledger Groups (Transaction F13L)

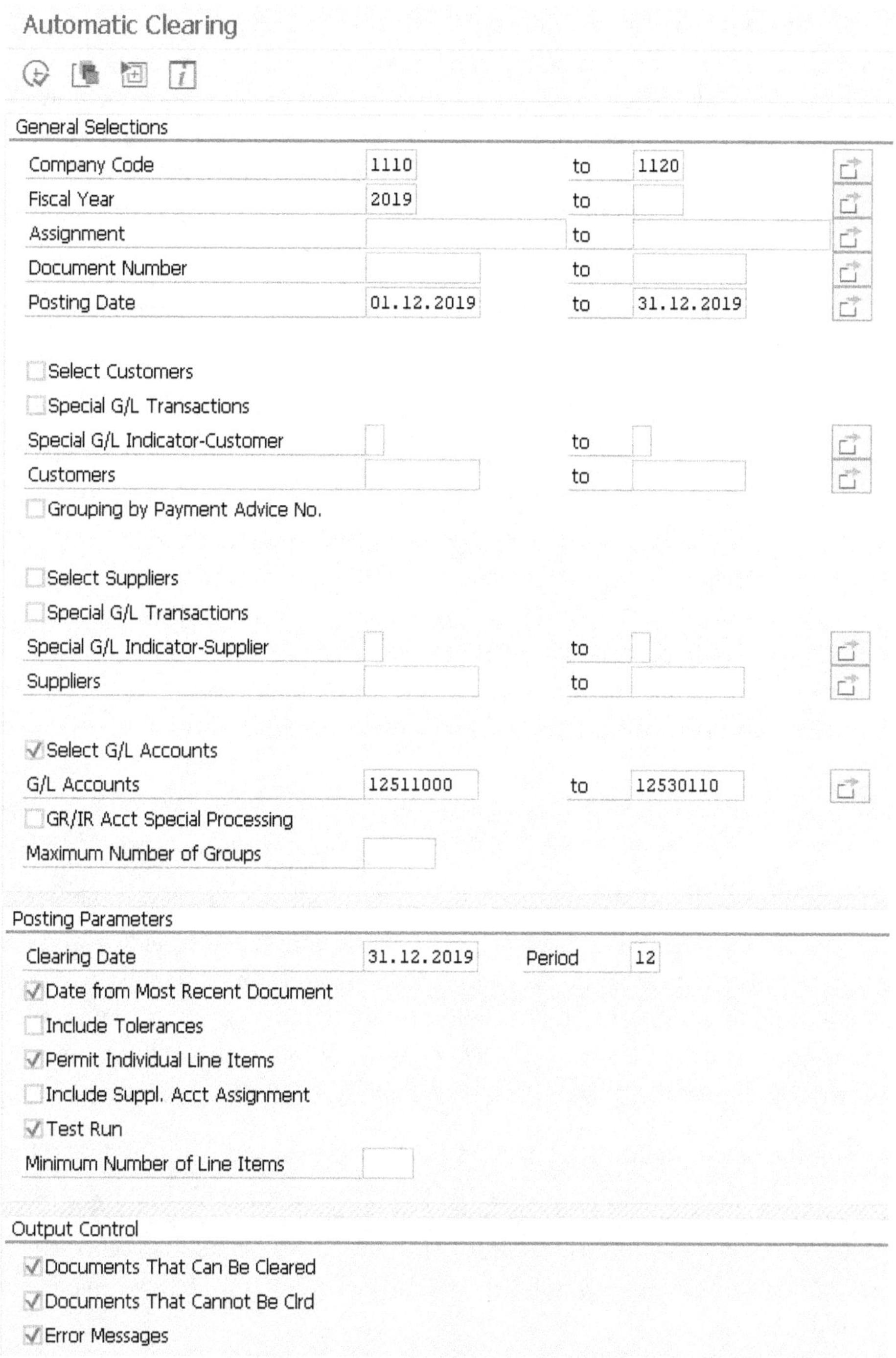

Automatic Clearing

General Selections

Company Code	1110	to	1120
Fiscal Year	2019	to	
Assignment		to	
Document Number		to	
Posting Date	01.12.2019	to	31.12.2019

☐ Select Customers
☐ Special G/L Transactions

Special G/L Indicator-Customer		to	
Customers		to	

☐ Grouping by Payment Advice No.

☐ Select Suppliers
☐ Special G/L Transactions

Special G/L Indicator-Supplier		to	
Suppliers		to	

☑ Select G/L Accounts

G/L Accounts	12511000	to	12530110

☐ GR/IR Acct Special Processing

Maximum Number of Groups	

Posting Parameters

Clearing Date	31.12.2019	Period	12

☑ Date from Most Recent Document
☐ Include Tolerances
☑ Permit Individual Line Items
☐ Include Suppl. Acct Assignment
☑ Test Run

Minimum Number of Line Items	

Output Control

☑ Documents That Can Be Cleared
☑ Documents That Cannot Be Clrd
☑ Error Messages

Figure 9.47 Automatic Clearing Program (Transaction F.13)

When you enter the Transaction (Figure 9.47), specify the 'General Selections' (company code, fiscal year, assignment, document number, posting date, flags to select suppliers /

customers / G/L accounts, maximum number of groups etc), 'Posting Parameters' (clearing date, period, flags for various settings including tolerances, individual line items, test run etc) and 'Output Control' details. The system carries out the actual clearing when 'Test Run' check-box is not selected. The output will contain (a) a line item list, which can be output in either short form or detailed form and (b) an additional log with information about the line items that were not selected, and any system messages about the account types for which no items were selected.

With this we are, now, ready to configure the system to handle the clearing differences through tolerances.

9.4.3.6   Define Tolerance Groups for G/L Accounts

We have already discussed the employee tolerance groups in Section 7.1.10 of Chapter 7. On the similar lines, we need to define, here, the required tolerance groups for SAP G/L Accounting. As in the case of employee tolerance group, we can have two tolerance groups: the null group with strict tolerance terms and a specific group, per company code, with relatively liberal terms. For G/L account clearing, the tolerance groups define the limits within which differences are accepted (that is, tolerated) and automatically posted to predefined accounts. You can enter the tolerance groups defined here in the G/L account master record; if you do not enter a group, then the null tolerance groups come into effect.

Project Dolphin

The project team has been advised by the BESTM management to configure the G/L tolerance groups in the following way:

(a) Null Tolerance Group: The null tolerance group will be applicable for all the employees, and will be the default tolerance group for all the company codes of BESTM, both in USA and India. This will have a tolerance of USD 1 (in absolute terms), with 0.5% as the limit for US-based company codes. In the case of India-based company codes, the null tolerance group will have an absolute limit of INR 10 and the percentage limit will be the same at 0.5%.

Besides the null tolerance group, there will be two more tolerance groups defined in the system: one for US-based company codes and the other for India-based company codes:

(b) BGLU: This will be for the selected employees of all the US-based company codes allowing a tolerance of USD 10, in absolute terms, both for debit and credit transactions; in percentage terms the limit will be 1%.

(c) BGLI: This will be for the India-based company codes - the percentage will be the same at 1%, but the absolute amounts in INR will be 100.

In all the cases, lower of the absolute amount or percentage will apply as the tolerance.

Let us configure the G/L tolerance groups:

i.   Use the menu path: SAP Customizing Implementation Guide > Financial Accounting > General Ledger Accounting > Master Data > G/L Accounts > Business Transactions > Open Item Clearing > Clearing Differences > Define Tolerance Groups for G/L Accounts. You may also use Transaction OBA0.

ii. On the 'Change View "Tolerances for Groups of G/L Accounts in Local Currency": Overview' screen, click on 'New Entries'.

iii. On the next screen, enter the 'Company Code', leave the 'Tolerance Group' as blank as this will be the null tolerance group, add a description for the tolerance group, and maintain the tolerance values both in absolute and percentage terms for both 'Debit Posting' and 'Credit Posting' (Figure 9.48). 'Save' the settings. You have created and assigned the null tolerance group for G/L account processing for company code 1110.

Figure 9.48 Null G/L Tolerance Group for Company Code 1110

> **i** If you are maintaining both an absolute amount and a percentage, the system considers the lowest limit of the two while processing the clearing. You can also configure only absolute amount or only percentage. When assigned to the company code(s), the lowest of either G/L account tolerance or employee tolerance applies.

iv. Copy this to all the US-based company codes of BESTM.

v.   Repeat the steps to create another null tolerance group for India-based company codes.

vi. Repeat the steps, again, to create the specific tolerance groups (BGLU and BGLI) with the absolute amount and the percentages as required by BESTM management for the various company codes (Figure 9.49).

Change View "Tolerances for Groups of G/L Accounts in Local Currency":

New Entries

Tolerances for Groups of G/L Accounts in Local Currency

CoCd	Tol.group	Name	
1110		Null Tol Group for BESTM -US	⌃
1110	BGLU	Spl Tol Grp US for BESTM	⌄
1120		Null Tol Group for BESTM -US	
1120	BGLU	Spl Tol Grp US for BESTM	

Figure 9.49 G/L Tolerance Groups for BESTM

The next step is to define the G/L accounts to post the clearing differences.

9.4.3.7   Create Accounts for Clearing Differences

You can configure the system in two ways: defining (a) a single account to post the clearing difference for both credits (revenue) and debits (expense), or (b) two different accounts, one for debits and the other for credits:

Project Dolphin

The project team has suggested to configure two separate G/L accounts to enable posting of clearing differences. Accordingly, the G/L account 52080000 will be configured for debits and 52580000 for credits.

i.   Use the menu path: SAP Customizing Implementation Guide > Financial Accounting > General Ledger Accounting > Master Data > G/L Accounts > Business Transactions > Open Item Clearing > Clearing Differences > Create Accounts for Clearing Differences. You may also use Transaction OBXZ.

ii.   On the ensuing pop-up screen, enter the chart of accounts (BEUS), and on the next screen, enter the appropriate G/L accounts in 'Debit' and 'Credit' fields, and 'Save' (Figure 9.50).

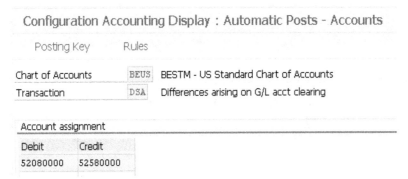

Figure 9.50 G/L Accounts for Posting Clearing Differences

iii.   Repeat and enter the G/L accounts for the India chart of accounts, BEIN, and 'Save' the details.

iv.   Do not change the default 'Posting Keys'; 40 for 'Debit' and 50 for 'Credit'.

v.   Click on the 'Rules' and you will see that the default setting is that the accounts are determined based on 'Debit/ Credit'. Do not make any changes here also.

This completes our discussion on open item clearing. Let us move on to discuss the balance interest calculation.

9.4.4   Bank Account Interest Calculation

You can use the *'bank account interest calculation'* functionality, in SAP FI, to calculate interest on the balance of G/L accounts that are managed on open item basis. Also known as *'balance interest calculation'*, you may use this, for example, to double-check the interest calculation made by the bank on your accounts. Besides the G/L accounts, you can also use this in A/R and A/P to calculate, for example, the interest on the staff loan accounts.

During the interest calculation on the G/L accounts, the system produces a graduated list. You can also have system log the balance interest calculation run which will be, especially, useful if the run does not produce the result you expected. You can, then, check the log and identify the reasons for discrepancy; say, as to why interest was not calculated for a specific account. You will use the following specifications to control the interest calculation program in the system:

- The data from the G/L account master record (for example, the *interest indicator*) which the program uses and the data used for determining the interest calculation period for the account.
- The specifications stored in the interest indicator (including the *interest rates* that need to be used).
- The specifications (like the selection criteria which limits the accounts that are included) that are made for the interest calculation run.

Let us, now, discuss the fields in a G/L account master record which are relevant for balance interest calculation, how the interest indicator works, how the interest calculation period is determined, how to carry out a balance interest calculation run and how you can control this procedure.

Let us start with the fields that are relevant for bank account interest calculation.

9.4.4.1 Fields Relevant for Bank Account Interest Calculation

The following fields (Figure 9.51), in a G/L account master record, are relevant for the balance interest calculation:

- *Interest indicator*: To calculate interest on G/L account balances, the 'interest calculation report' references the interest indicator from the account master record. The most important specifications (such as, the rules used for interest calculation and the interest rate) for interest calculation are stored in this indicator. The interest indicator must belong to the interest calculation type 'balance interest calculation'. All accounts that you want to be included in the automatic interest calculation run must have an entry in this field in their respective master records; if you want to block an account from interest calculation, remove the interest indicator entry from this field.

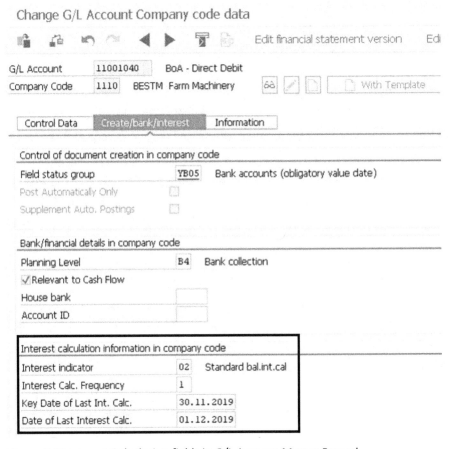

Figure 9.51 Interest Calculation fields in G/L Account Master Record

- *Interest Calc. Frequency*: Here, in this field, you enter the interval (in number of months), which determines how often the account balance interest calculation program is to be run. The system adds this 'interest calculation frequency' to the date of the last interest calculation. You make an entry in this field only if you want the system to determine the interest calculation period automatically. The interest calculation period always refers to the field *'Key Date of Last Int. Calc.'*. You can also define an interest calculation frequency under an interest indicator; then, the entry in the G/L account master record has a higher priority.
- *Key Date of Last Int. Calc.*: The date in this field displays the last time when the interest calculation program processed this account. This is generally the upper limit of the last interest run. After the interest calculation program has been run in the background, the system enters the upper limit of the interest calculation period in this field. This date is, then, used by the system to automatically determine the interest calculation period for an account.

> **i** Generally, this date (*Key Date of Last Int. Calc.*) is automatically maintained by the batch input program. You should make a manual entry, here, only if an error has occurred.

- *Date of Last Interest Calc.*: The interest calculation report enters the CPU date of the last balance interest calculation run, in this field, as the date of last interest calculation. This is necessary to determine whether interest must be calculated for items, with a value date in the past. These are items which are posted to a period for which interest has already been calculated.

> **i** This field is only used for calculating interest on account balances; it does not affect calculations for *'interest on arrears'*. Hence, the date is generally maintained automatically by the program through the batch input. As in the case of *'Key Date of Last Int. Calc.'* field, you should make a manual entry in this field only in the case of an error.

Let us move on to understand the interest indicator.

9.4.4.2 Interest Indicator

The *'interest indicator'* controls the interest calculation in the system. It stores (a) the calendar type (say: bank, French, Japanese or Gregorian) that is used for defining the days due for interest (b) interest rates and the conditions, and (c) the 'Form' for the lists. You can also specify, under the interest indicator, if you want the program to use an interest calculation numerator to calculate the interest; else, the program calculates the interest directly.

No interest is calculated for an account, (a) if you have specified a maximum amount under the interest indicator, but the interest amount calculated is less than that, (b) if you have specified (in the interest indicator) that no credit interest payments should be made, then the system calculates the interest only if the account is in debit and (c) if you have not specified the account for interest calculation in the interest calculation period or if the system has not determined the account, automatically, for inclusion in the interest run.

With this, let us discuss the interest calculation period.

9.4.4.3   Interest Calculation Period

The '*interest calculation period*' is demarcated by an upper and a lower limit (of dates). The days in between these two dates are those for which interest is calculated. SAP uses two methods for determining the interest calculation period in the system:

1) *Manual determination of interest calculation period*: Here, you must manually enter the period, for every interest calculation run. You do not need to enter any additional data; most importantly, you should not make an entry in *Key Date of Last Int. Calc.'* field. You can use this method if you always calculate interest on accounts for periods of the same length, say, once per month.

> **i** In the case of manual determination of interest calculation period, note that the system does not recognize overlaps, if any, with previous balance interest calculation runs. Hence, you need to be doubly sure that you are entering a period for which interest has not been calculated already in the system.

2) *Automatic determination of interest calculation period*: Here, the system determines the period according to rules that you have specified either per account or per interest indicator. You can resort to this automatic determination of interest calculation period to ensure that interest calculation periods do not overlap. This is, especially, useful if you want to charge interest on accounts at irregular intervals; the interest calculation program, then, determines which accounts should be included in the respective calculation run.

To ensure automatic determination of interest calculation period:

- You must enter the interest calculation period which the program uses to determine whether an account is to be included in this current interest calculation run or not.
- The 'Key Date of Last Int. Calc.' field in the account master record must have an entry. You can either have the system, through batch input, make the

entry in this field using the upper limit of the last interest calculation run or enter it manually.

- You should have an *interest calculation frequency* ('Interest Calc. Frequency') specified in the master record, if this has to be determined per account. Alternatively, you can define this frequency under the interest indicator; as already indicated, the entry in the master record has higher priority.
- You must have entered an 'interest calculation day' under the interest indicator. If you always want to run the interest calculation program on, for example, the 20th of the month, then you need to enter 20. However, if you want the run to be on the last day of every month, enter 31 (not 30).

The system uses the above data to determine the upper / lower limits of the interest calculation period. The program adds one day to the data in the 'Key Date of Last Int. Calc.' field and uses the result as the *lower limit* for the interest calculation period. The *upper limit* is determined in two steps: (a) the program determines the *month* by adding the 'Interest Calc. Frequency', which you have defined in the system, to the month of the above-mentioned 'Key Date of Last Int. Calc.', and (b) the program determines the *day* by using the interest calculation date defined in the system.

> **i** Consider the example wherein you have defined the 'Key Date of Last Int. Calc.' as 6/30/2019, the 'Interest Calc. Frequency' as 2 months, and the interest calculation day as 31. With this, the system determines a lower limit as 7/1/2019 and the upper limit as 8/31/2019. As the system has determined 8/31/2019 as the upper limit for this account, if you are calculating interest for the period 7/1/2019 to 8/15/2019, the account is ignored; however, if your calculation is for the period 7/1/2019 to 9/1/2019, the account is included. An account is only included in the interest calculation run, if the upper limit you specify in the program is not later than the upper limit specified for interest calculation. You can, thus, carry out the interest calculation independently of the specified frequency with which interest is calculated on the accounts.

Let us move on to the interest rate definition, next.

9.4.4.4 Interest Rate Definition

Before calculating the bank account interest, you may need to update the *interest rates* defined under the interest indicator. You can define the interest rates in various ways:

- Entering a fixed interest rate for each interest indicator and currency, and for one validity date.

- Entering an amount-dependent interest rate for each interest indicator and currency, and for one validity date.
- *Using reference interest rates*: For this, you need to enter a key for the interest indicator under which the relevant rates are stored; you can also enter the reference interest rate dependent on a validity date.

With this, we are now ready to discuss the interest calculation program.

9.4.4.5   Interest Calculation Program

You start and run the *interest calculation program* from the SAP Easy Access menu: SAP Menu > Financial Accounting > General Ledger > Periodic Processing > Interest Calculation > Balances. You may also use Transaction F.52 (Figure 9.52):

i.   You can limit the G/L accounts that can be included in the interest calculation run using the fields ('Chart of Accounts', 'G/L account' and 'Company code') under 'G/L Account Selection'. You, now, know that only those accounts (a) which have an interest indicator for balance interest calculation in the master record, and (b) that are managed with line item display, are included in the calculation.

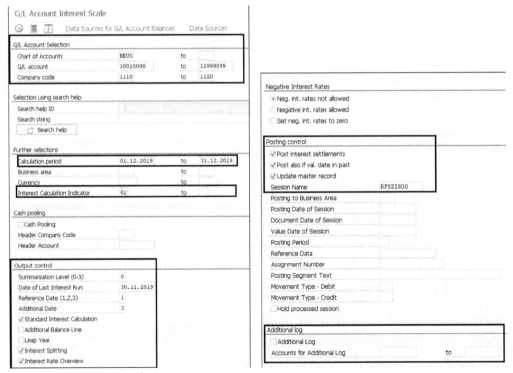

Figure 9.52 Interest Calculation Run - Parameters

ii. Under 'Further selections', you can enter the 'Calculation period'. If the field 'Key Date of Last Int. Calc.' in the master record is filled, the system determines the interest calculation period automatically.

iii. Under 'Output Control':

- Enter the 'Summarization Level (0-3)' to control the output; select the appropriate one from the four options to decide how detailed the interest scale should be.

- Enter the 'Date of Last Interest Run' if you have not entered this date in the master record. The date is used to decide whether items (that are posted to a period for which interest has already been calculated) should be treated as value dates in the past.

- Enter the 'Reference Date (1,2,3)' that lets you determine whether the program takes the value date (1), posting date (2) or document date (3) as the reference date for interest calculation. For balance interest calculation for customer / vendor accounts, the report uses the 'baseline date for payment' as the reference date.

- Select the 'Leap Year' check-box, to calculate interest for 366 days.

- If you select the 'Standard Interest Calculation' check-box, the interest calculation period is put back by one day; this means that the system also calculates interest on the carry forward balance. The items for which interest would usually be calculated up to the period's upper limit are not included in the run.

- If you do not select the 'Interest Splitting' check-box, then, the program clears the debit and the credit interest against each other, and displays and posts only the interest difference for each account. Otherwise, the program splits the interest; if no value dates in the past were to be included, the interest amounts from the calculation period are output separately according to debit and credit interest.

- If you select 'Interest Rate Overview' check-box, then, the program prints an interest rate overview separated according to debit and credit interest at the end of every settlement. This is printed after the interest calculation run.

iv. You also need to maintain the 'Posting Control':

- Select the 'Post interest settlements' check-box, if interest is to be posted. For the balance interest calculation, the data for the interest posting is placed in the batch input session. The posting is carried out when you run the batch input session. Even if you have set the indicator, the system will not post the interest, if there are value dates in the past, and if you have not selected the 'Post also if val. date is in past' check-box.

- The interest calculation data in the G/L account master records is only updated if you select the 'Update master record' check-box.
- You have to enter a 'Session Name' for the background batch input run.

v.   Use the 'Additional Log' block, to decide if you want to have the system to log the details of the run. However, you may need to restrict the G/L accounts using the 'Accounts for Additional Log' fields, as you cannot have the detailed log for all the accounts that are included in the interest run.

vi. Press 'Execute' to run the balance interest calculation program.

This completes our discussion on the requirements and mechanics of bank account interest calculation. Let us proceed to look at the configuration settings for the same. We shall start with the global settings for the interest calculation.

9.4.4.6   Interest Calculation Global Settings

Here, you will make the general specifications for interest indicators, separated by interest calculation type. The two tasks that are included in the global settings are:

- Define Interest Calculation Types
- Prepare Account Balance Interest Calculation

Let us start with the first task of defining the interest calculation types.

9.4.4.6.1   Define Interest Calculation Types

We have already discussed the interest indicators in Section 9.4.4.1 and 9.4.4.2 of this Chapter. Using this configuration activity, you can create your interest indicators with the specification that they are to be used for account balance interest calculation. You will, then, enter this indicator in the G/L account master record of the relevant G/L accounts, enabling the system to select these accounts automatically during interest calculation.

Project Dolphin

BESTM has decided to use two different interest indicators, apart from the standard ones available in SAP. The new interest indicators will be used for calculating the account balance interest on staff loan accounts, one indicator for US-based company codes and the other for India-based company codes.

To define new interest indicators:

i.   Use the menu path: SAP Customizing Implementation Guide > Financial Accounting > General Ledger Accounting > Business Transactions > Bank Account Interest Calculation > Interest Calculation Global Settings > Define Interest Calculation Types. You may also use Transaction OB46.

ii.   On the 'Change View "Interest Settlement (Calculation Type)": Overview' screen, select the row containing the standard balance calculation interest indicator (02) and click on 'Copy As'.

iii.   On the next screen:

- Enter the identifier for the new interest indicator (say, 2U), and enter a suitable 'Name'. This will be used by US-based company codes of BESTM. The standard interest indicators supplied by SAP are denoted as 01 (item interest calculation) and 02 (balance interest calculation) by SAP.

- The account number as interest calculation indicator ('Acct. no. as IntClcInd') check-box, determines whether the account number is to be used as an *extended interest indicator* in the interest terms. You can set only the numeric G/L account numbers as the extended interest indicator; if so, you need to maintain the length of the G/L account number at 10 digits by padding the account number with zeros from the left. As we will not use this, we will not select this check-box.

- Select the appropriate interest calculation type ('Int Calc. Type') from the drop-down list; select 'S' for *balance interest calculation* ('P' will be for item or *arrears interest calculation*).

iv.   'Save' the settings and create the other balance interest indicator for India (2I).

v.   Also create the required item (or arrears) interest indicators for BESTM (1I for India and IU for USA). You have now defined the required new interest indicators for BESTM (Figure 9.53).

Change View "Interest Settlement (Calculation Type)": Overview

New Entries

Interest indicator	Name	Acct no.as IntClcInd	Int Calc. Type	Name of Interest Calculation Type
1I	Arr. Int. BESTM IN	☐	P	Item Interest Calculation
1U	Arr. Int. BESTM US	☐	P	Item Interest Calculation
2I	Bal. Int. BESTM IN	☐	S	Balance Interest Calculation
2U	Bal. Int. BESTM US	☐	S	Balance Interest Calculation

Figure 9.53 Interest Indictors

Let us move on to discuss the next activity in the global settings for interest calculation.

9.4.4.6.2   Prepare Account Balance Interest Calculation

Define the general interest calculation specifications per interest indicator, in this step. The specifications include the period determination, the interest determination, the interest processing, the output controls, and the payment terms.

Project Dolphin

BESTM management wants the project team to configure the two new interest indicators with the details as under:

The interest calculation frequency is to be set at six months for the staff loans, for both India and USA, in the interest indicators. The Gregorian calendar needs to be used for interest calculations. The interest settlement should be configured to be on the last day of the month. The interest needs to be charged on a graduated scale for all the staff loan accounts, for US-based company codes, at 2% interest up to $10,000; 3% up to $25,000; and 4% in excess of $25,000; for India, the corresponding figures will be: 8% for loans up to INR 200,000, 9% up to INR 500,000 and 10.5% for above INR 500,000. The interest will have to be settled when the interest amount calculated is in excess of $10 and INR 100 respectively for US and India-based company codes. The interest needs to be paid within 10 days of interest posting to the respective accounts. The interest posting is to be made to the appropriate G/L accounts, one for interest paid (71100000) and another for interest received (70100000). The system should use the document type SA for interest posting.

To configure the global interest calculation specifications for the two new interest indicators (2I and 2U) that we have created earlier:

i.   Use the menu path: SAP Customizing Implementation Guide > Financial Accounting > General Ledger Accounting > Business Transactions > Bank Account Interest Calculation > Interest Calculation Global Settings > Prepare Account Balance Interest Calculation. You may also use Transaction OBAA.

ii.   On the resulting screen, click on 'New Entries' and maintain the details (Figure 9.54):
   - Enter the 'Interest Indicator'.
   - In the 'Period determination block', enter the interest calculation frequency ('Interest calc. freq.'). This will be 6 for BESTM. As already outlined in Section 9.4.4.1, an entry in this field determines the interval (in months) for interest calculation for the accounts. The system adds the interest calculation frequency entered here, to the date of the last interest calculation to arrive at the upper limit for selecting the accounts for the interest run. You can maintain the interest calculation frequency, either here in the interest indicator or in the G/L account master record. The entry in the master record has the precedence.

   > **i** For example, if you enter 06 (as in our case) here in the interest indicator, with the last interest calculation date being 6/30, the system arrives at the upper limit as 12/31 for the next interest calculation. Also

consider the other example wherein you have specified the interest calculation date (say, 15/12/2019) as a report parameter to determine whether an account is included in a particular interest run. Then, the system compares this new upper limit with the upper limit already calculated (using the interest calculation frequency and last interest calculation date); if the calculated upper limit (say, 12/31/2019) is after the new calculation period based on the date entered in the report parameter (15/12/31), then, that account is not included in the current interest run.

- Along with the interest calculation frequency and the key date of the last interest calculation, the 'Settlement day' determines the upper limit of the interest calculation period to be included in a program run. You can specify a value between 01 and 31.

> **i** Consider the example where in the last interest calculation was on 6/30/2019, and the interest calculation frequency at 3 months. The system, now, calculates the upper limit month as 9 from the upper limit date 9/31/2019. If the settlement day is mentioned as 25, then the upper limit is arrived to be 9/25. In case this calculation results in an invalid date such as 6/31, for example, then the system sets this as to the end of that month, that is 6/30. It also takes care of the year issues by automatically registering a change to the next year when the month of the key date (say, 09) plus interest calculation frequency (say, 06) exceeds 12; the upper limit will, then, be arrived at 03.

- determines how many days per month and year are to be used as the basis for calculating interest. The number of days in the year is used as the divisor for the interest rate to calculate the daily interest rate from the annual interest rate. You have the options like, bank calendar (B) which is 30/360 (30 days in a month and 360 days in a year), French calendar (F) which is made up of calendar months (30,28, 31 days) but 360 days in a year, Gregorian calendar (G) which is the regular calendar (28, 30, 31/365) and Japanese calendar (30 days in a month and 365 days in a year). Select G for 2U.
- Together with the calendar type B or J, this 'Month-end indicator' decides how, for example, February 28 or July 31 needs to be treated. When this is selected and the calendar type is set to be B, then, the month-end is considered to be 30 (not 28 or 31). The system, then, will arrive at the number of days, for example, between January 31 and February 28, as not 28 but 30.

You should not select this check-box for the interest indicator 2U as we will be using the calendar type G.

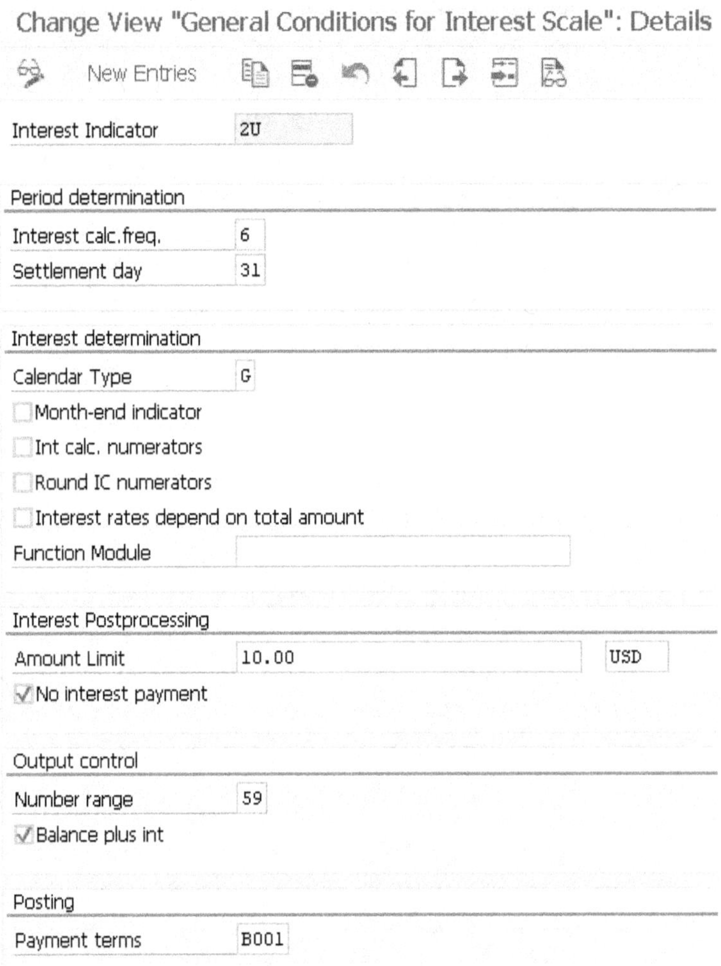

Change View "General Conditions for Interest Scale": Details

    New Entries

Interest Indicator   2U

Period determination

Interest calc.freq.	6
Settlement day	31

Interest determination

Calendar Type	G
☐ Month-end indicator	
☐ Int calc. numerators	
☐ Round IC numerators	
☐ Interest rates depend on total amount	
Function Module	

Interest Postprocessing

Amount Limit	10.00	USD
☑ No interest payment		

Output control

Number range	59
☑ Balance plus int	

Posting

Payment terms	B001

Figure 9.54 Configuring Interest Indictor

- Under 'Interest determination' block, select the 'Calendar Type'. It
- If you select 'Int calc. numerators' check-box, then, the program calculates interest using numerators; else, the interest is calculated directly.
- The 'Round IC numerators' is used along with the 'Int calc. numerators' flag. When this is selected, it rounds off the numerators.
- Select 'Interest rate depend on total amount' check-box if you want to use the graduated (amount-dependent) interest rates for the total amount. When unselected, the interest rates refer to each difference between the amount (slabs) for which interest is calculated and the amount from which the interest rate is valid.

> **i** Consider an example where the outstanding in the account is $15,000. The interest rate is to be calculated as: 0% of amounts up to $5,000, 6% for amounts up to $10,000, 10% on amounts above $10,000. when 'Interest rate depend on total amount' check-box is selected: the interest is calculated at the total outstanding of $15,000 @ 10% which will be $1,500 (=15000*0.10). When 'Interest rate depend on total amount' check-box is not selected: the interest is calculated for the first slab of $10,000 @ 6% and for the next $5,000 @10%, and the interest will be $1,100 (=600+500).

- If you want the interest rate to be determined through a function module instead of the standard method (via, transaction and business types), enter the name of the function module here in this 'Function Module' field.
- Under 'Interest processing', enter the 'Amount Limit' beyond which only the system will create an interest settlement; that is, if the calculated interest is less than the amount entered here, then, there will be no interest settlement made. This way, you can avoid interest settlements being created for small amounts that will be meaningless if, for example, the cost of settling/delivering that interest is higher than the interest amount calculated. Along with the amount limit, you can also maintain the currency here.
- If you select 'No interest payment' flag, then, the system will not make an interest payment even if there is an interest settlement.
- Under 'Output control', enter a 'Number range' to enable numbering of the interest forms; when you post an interest document, then, the system uses a number from this number range and stores the form number in the 'Reference' field. You may enter a range that has not been used earlier, but, in that case you need to create that number range using Transaction FBN1.
- If you select 'Balance plus int' flag, then the system prints the balance plus interest.
- Under 'Posting' select the appropriate 'Payment terms', if required.

iii. 'Save' the details. This completes the settings required for the interest indicator 2U.

iv. You may copy this and make the necessary changes to create the other indicator, 2I.

With this, we are now ready to move to next configuration activity namely, interest calculation.

9.4.4.7   Interest calculation

There are four tasks under this that you need to configure in the system. They are:

- Define Reference Interest Rates
- Define Time-Dependent Terms
- Enter Interest Values
- Specify Function Module for Interest Rate Determination

Let us start with the first task of defining the reference interest rates.

9.4.4.7.1   *Define Reference Interest Rates*

Here, in this ask, you will enter a key and a meaningful name for new reference interest rates. These names classify the type of interest calculation, either debit or credit, with reference to currency and start date.

To configure this:

i.   Use the menu path: SAP Customizing Implementation Guide > Financial Accounting > General Ledger Accounting > Business Transactions > Bank Account Interest Calculation > Interest Calculation > Define Reference Interest Rates. You may also use Transaction OBAC.

ii.   On the resulting screen (Figure 9.55), click on 'New Entries' and define the required identifiers for both 2I and 2U. You will need three such entries, corresponding to the three slabs of amounts for applying the varying interest rates for BESTM, for each of the interest indicators, 2I and 2U.

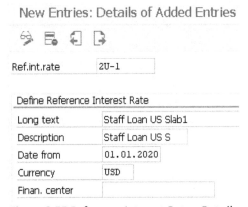

Figure 9.55 Reference Interest Rate - Details

iii.   You may maintain the finance center details ('Finan. Center') if you are using SAP Treasury Management functionality.

iv.   When completed, 'Save' your settings (Figure 9.56).

Change View "Define Reference Interest Rate": Overview

New Entries

Define Reference Interest Rate

Reference	Long txt	Fin.center
2I-1	Staff Loan IN Slab 1	
2I-2	Staff Loan IN Slab 2	
2I-3	Staff Loan IN Slab 3	
2U-1	Staff Loan US Slab1	
2U-2	Staff Loan US Slab2	
2U-3	Staff Loan US Slab3	

Figure 9.56 Reference Interest Rates for BESTM

With this, let us define the time-dependent terms, next.

9.4.4.7.2   Define Time-Dependent Terms

Here, in this step, you can specify how the interest rate is to be determined, per interest indicator. You can make this specification dependent on currency and a validity date. For each of the entries, specify a condition that determines which the type of interest (debit or credit). You can also specify which interest rates are to be used. For configuring the time-dependent terms:

   i.   Use the menu path: SAP Customizing Implementation Guide > Financial Accounting > General Ledger Accounting > Business Transactions > Bank Account Interest Calculation > Interest Calculation > Define Time-Dependent Terms. You may also use Transaction OB81.

   ii. On the resulting screen, click on 'New Entries' (Figure 9.57):

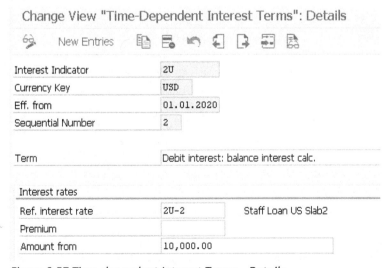

Change View "Time-Dependent Interest Terms": Details

New Entries

Interest Indicator	2U
Currency Key	USD
Eff. from	01.01.2020
Sequential Number	2

| Term | Debit interest: balance interest calc. |

Interest rates

Ref. interest rate	2U-2	Staff Loan US Slab2
Premium		
Amount from	10,000.00	

Figure 9.57 Time-dependent Interest Terms – Details

- Enter the 'Interest Indicator', 'Currency Key', effective from date ('Eff.from') and a 'Sequential Number'.
- Select the appropriate 'Term' from the drop-down list.
- Under 'Interest rates', enter the reference interest rate ('Ref. interest rate') that you have defined in the previous step.
- Enter 'Premium', if required. If you want the system to use the rate entered in the 'Premium' field, then, you should leave ('Ref. interest rate') field as blank. If you enter both the 'Ref. interest rate' and the 'Premium', the effective rate, then, is the sum of these two.

> **i** The value in the 'Premium' field can actually represent either premium or discount. If you have not maintained any value in the 'Ref. interest rate' field but have entered a positive value in the 'Premium' field, then, the system uses this positive value (=premium) as the interest rate for the calculation. The value entered in the 'Premium' field can even be negative, implying that it is actually a discount.

- Enter the 'Amount from'. It will always be zero for the 1st sequence.

iii.   Maintain the details for all the sequential numbers for specific interest indicator. 'Save' the settings.

iv.   Repeat the steps to have the settings defined for the other interest indicator (2I) as well (Figure 9.58).

Change View "Time-Dependent Interest Terms": Overview

🔍 ⬛   New Entries   📋 🗐 ↰ 📑 📑 📑 📖

Int.Ind.	Currency	Eff. from	Seq....	Trans. Type	Amount from
2I	INR	01.01.2020	1	Debit interest: balance interest calc.	0.00
2I	INR	01.01.2020	2	Debit interest: balance interest calc.	200,000.00
2I	INR	01.01.2020	3	Debit interest: balance interest calc.	500,000.00
2U	USD	01.01.2020	1	Debit interest: balance interest calc.	0.00
2U	USD	01.01.2020	2	Debit interest: balance interest calc.	10,000.00
2U	USD	01.01.2020	3	Debit interest: balance interest calc.	25,000.00

Figure 9.58 Time-dependent Interest Terms for BESTM – Overview

The third step of configuring the settings for interest calculation is to maintain the interest values. Let us do that, now.

9.4.4.7.3 Enter Interest Values

Using this activity, you can specify the required interest rates, dependent on the date, for the *reference interest rates.* The interest rates defined here are used, for example, when determining a variable interest rate that is linked to the reference interest rate.

To enter the interest values, use the menu path: SAP Customizing Implementation Guide > Financial Accounting > General Ledger Accounting > Business Transactions > Bank Account Interest Calculation > Interest Calculation > Enter Interest Values. You may also use Transaction OB83. On the resulting screen, click on 'New Entries' and maintain the values as required per reference interest rate. Repeat the steps for all the reference interest rate, and 'Save' the details (Figure 9.59).

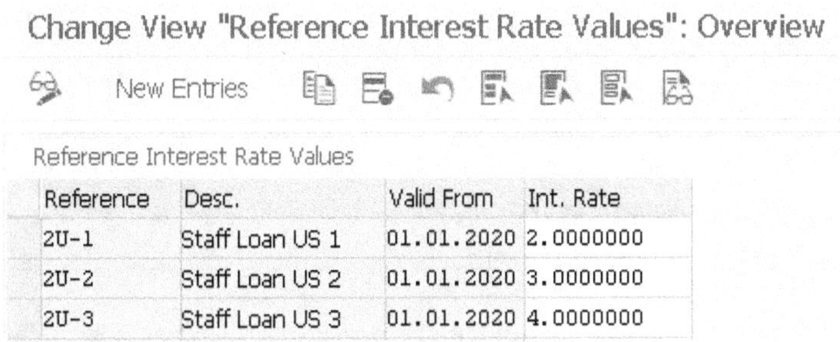

Change View "Reference Interest Rate Values": Overview

   New Entries

Reference Interest Rate Values

Reference	Desc.	Valid From	Int. Rate
2U-1	Staff Loan US 1	01.01.2020	2.0000000
2U-2	Staff Loan US 2	01.01.2020	3.0000000
2U-3	Staff Loan US 3	01.01.2020	4.0000000

Figure 9.59 Interest Rate Values

> **i** Never delete an interest value entry that is already in use in the system. If you want to have new rates defined, you can create them with the new 'Valid From' date.

Let us move on to the final step of configuring the settings required for interest calculation namely, specifying the function module for interest rate determination (if required).

9.4.4.7.4 Specify Function Module for Interest Rate Determination

SAP uses its own standard function modules to calculate the interest in the system. There are four such function modules: two (one for debit and another for credit) for each of the interest calculation types namely, the item (or arrears) interest calculation and account balance interest calculation as outlined in Table 9.3.

Interest calculation type	Debit / Credit	Transaction type	Function module
Balance interest	Debit	D_SAL	INT_RATE_DETERMINE
Balance interest	Credit	C_SAL	INT_RATE_DETERMINE
Arrears interest	Debit	DEBIR	DEBIT_INT_RATE_DETERMINE
Arrears interest	Credit	CREIR	CREDIT_INT_RATE_DETERMINE

Table 9:3 SAP Standard Function Modules for Interest Calculation

You may not, normally, require to define a new function module. However, if you want to define your own function module, then, you can do that by following the menu path: SAP Customizing Implementation Guide > Financial Accounting > General Ledger Accounting > Business Transactions > Bank Account Interest Calculation > Interest Calculation > Specify Function Module for Interest Rate Determination. You may also use Transaction OB85. It is recommended to copy an existing entry (Figure 9.60) to create the new one.

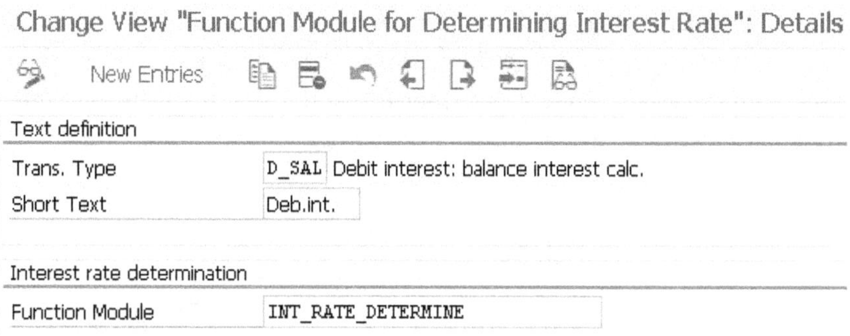

Change View "Function Module for Determining Interest Rate": Details

   New Entries

Text definition

Trans. Type	D_SAL Debit interest: balance interest calc.
Short Text	Deb.int.

Interest rate determination

Function Module	INT_RATE_DETERMINE

Figure 9.60 Function Module for Interest Calculation – Details

> **ⓘ** Note that you will not be able to create a new function module using this Transaction OB85. You use this activity to maintain the newly defined function module to specify other parameters like, transaction type ('Trans. Type'). To define a new function module, however, you should use the Function Builder (Transaction SE37).

This completes our discussion on configuring the system for interest calculation. Let us move on to discuss the settings associated with posting of interest.

9.4.4.8 Interest Posting

You need to make certain specifications for posting the interest calculated, to the respective accounts. The system, via these specifications, determines which posting keys are to be used and which G/L accounts are posted to. The specifications include:

1) *Account determination keys and posting details*: The possible 'account determination keys' are business transaction, company code, interest indicator, and business area. You have to determine account determination keys that are to be used. Based on the account determination keys used, you, then, specify the posting keys and the 'account symbols' (posting details). With the account symbols determining which accounts are to be posted to, you can use them to differentiate between the G/L accounts; you can also use just one account symbol for all the G/L accounts.

2) *G/L accounts*: Per account symbol, define the G/L accounts for interest-earned posting or interest-paid posting. You can differentiate the G/L accounts by currencies, if required.

3) *Document type*: To post the interest, you need to have a document type defined. The standard settings in the system use document type SA.

> **i** The *posting interface* (account determination) establishes a 'posting method' that is dependent on different account determination keys, in which account symbols are named instead of G/L accounts, and the system replaces these account symbols by the actual G/L accounts (to be posted to), dependent on different modification keys.
>
> A *posting method* consists of the specifications of posting key and 'account symbol' for one or two line items (debit/credit entry). You can mask the individual account determination keys (which indicate a posting method) by entering '+'. The entries, masked in this way, are then always valid, if no other qualified entry could be found. You will use the freely definable *account symbols* for grouping similar business transactions leading to different accounts based on a pre-defined differentiation. You can also mask the modification keys by entering '+'.
>
> You can enter the G/L account which is to be posted to, either to fully qualify the account (as in the case of an entry '0000222100' which is always pointing to the G/L account 0000222100) or masking the account partially {as in the case of '++++++++03' leading to the G/L account 0000222103, wherein the masked parts are replaced by the respective G/L account (0000222100) and the non-masked parts (03) remaining as they are}. By this, you will have enough flexibility to use account determination for systematically created interim accounts.

Let us complete the settings required for preparing the system for posting the account balance interest.

9.4.4.8.1 Prepare G/L Account Balance Interest Calculation

Here, using this configuration activity, you will define the specifications that are required for posting interest calculated on G/L account balances. The system determines the accounts using the *posting interface* in application 0004 (account interest scale). As a part of configuration, you will specify the (a) account determination keys along with the posting specifications, (b) G/L accounts and (c) document type:

- For the application 004, create at least one set of posting details for the interest earned posting and the interest paid posting respectively, per business transaction (like, 1000 - Interest received posting and 2000 - Interest paid posting). If you are using interest splitting, enter at least one set of posting details for business transactions: 1010 - Minus debit interest - past value date, 2010 - Minus credit interest - past value date, 1020 - Debit interest - value date in the past, 2020 - Credit interest - value date in the past, 1030 - Interest calculation - period debit interest, and 2030 - Interest calculation period - credit interest.

- In the case of G/L accounts, assign accounts in full to the account symbols for the respective interest earned posting or interest paid posting. For the balance sheet account posting, you may make a generic entry.

- In the case of document type for posting the interest, it is recommended to use the document type SA, though you may define a different one.

> **i** Recommended not to make any changes to the default standard posting specifications of the posting interface 004, provided by SAP; else, you may cause irreparable damages to the functionality, if not done correctly.

Let us configure the settings, now:

i.   Use the menu path: SAP Customizing Implementation Guide > Financial Accounting > General Ledger Accounting > Business Transactions > Bank Account Interest Calculation > Interest Posting > Prepare G/L Account Balance Interest Calculation. You may also use Transaction OBV2.

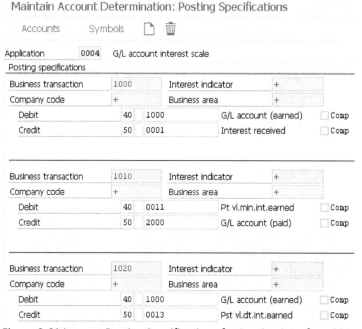

Figure 9.61 Interest Posting Specifications for Posting Interface 004

ii.   On the resulting 'Maintain Account Determination: Posting Specifications' screen (Figure 9.61), you will see the details of posting specifications, per business transaction (1000, 1010, 1020 etc) for the default posting interface 004. You will see the account symbols, for example 0001 for interest received, 0002 for interest paid and so on. You will also see the associated posting keys for each of the account symbols. A '+' in 'Company code', 'Interest indicator' and 'Business area' fields indicate that these posting specifications are valid for all the company codes / business areas / interest indicators.

iii. Select 'Comp' check-box, to compresses line items automatically, before posting.

iv.   You may also enter a special G/L indicator (say, A-down payment, B-bill of exchange receivable, F, G etc) in the field adjacent to the posting keys. When entered, the special G/L indicator determines which account is to be selected, for all line items in customer / vendor accounts that are updated to an alternative reconciliation account.

v.   Click on 'Accounts', and enter the chart of accounts (BEUS). On the next screen (Figure 9.62), maintain the G/L accounts, for each of the account symbols. A '+' entry in the 'Currency' field indicates that the specifications are valid for all the currencies.

Maintain Account Determination: Accounts

Posting specs   Symbols   🗑

| Application | 0004 | G/L account interest scale |
| Chart of Accts | BEUS | BESTM - US Standard Chart of Accounts |

Account assignment

Account Symbol	Currency	G/L Acct
0001	+	70100000
0002	+	71100000
0011	+	70100000
0012	+	71100000
0013	+	70100000
0014	+	71100000
0015	+	70100000
0016	+	71100000
1000	+	+++++++++
2000	+	+++++++++

Figure 9.62 G/L Account Assignment for the Posting Interface 004

ℹ For account symbols 1000 (interest earned) and 2000 (interest paid), make a generic specification, by entering the mask +++++++, in the 'G/L Acct' field as this will be valid for all the relevant G/L accounts.

vi.   Click on 'Symbols' to view the account symbols used in the posting specifications (Figure 9.63).

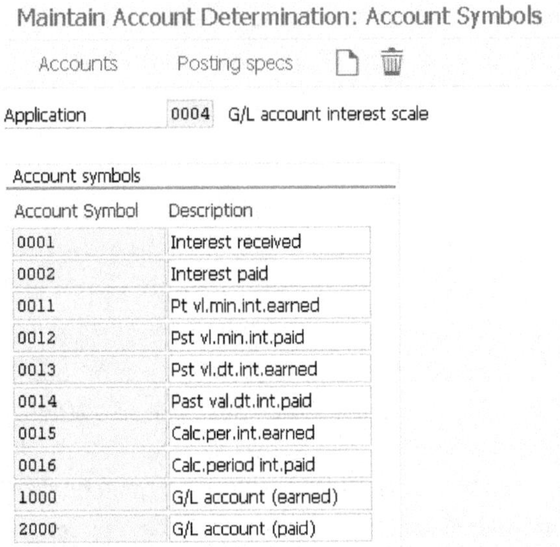

Maintain Account Determination: Account Symbols

Accounts   Posting specs   🗋 🗑

Application   0004   G/L account interest scale

Account Symbol	Description
0001	Interest received
0002	Interest paid
0011	Pt vl.min.int.earned
0012	Pst vl.min.int.paid
0013	Pst vl.dt.int.earned
0014	Past val.dt.int.paid
0015	Calc.per.int.earned
0016	Calc.period int.paid
1000	G/L account (earned)
2000	G/L account (paid)

Figure 9.63 Account Symbols for Posting Specifications

This completes our discussion on preparing the system for posting the account balance interest calculated, and also completes the discussion on bank account interest calculation.

Let us, now, move on to discuss the configuration settings required for the next business transaction, adjustment posting / reversal.

9.4.5 Adjustment Posting/Reversal

SAP allows you to reverse a document that was entered incorrectly; the system clears the open items as well. You can reverse a document only when (a) it contains no cleared items, (b) it contains only customer, vendor, and G/L account items, (c) it was posted with SAP FI, and (d) all the earlier entered values (such as business area, cost center, and tax code) are still valid. You, normally, post the *reversal document* in the same posting period as that of the corresponding original document. However, if the posting period of the original document has been closed already, then, you may enter a date of an open posting period (say, the current period) in the 'Posting date' field.

> **ℹ** If a line item from a source document has been cleared, you can make a reversal only after the clearing is reset. You can reverse the documents from SD with a credit memo, and the documents from MM with functions in that component, because the FI reversal function does not reverse all the values required.

When reversing a transaction, the system updates the transaction figures in two ways: (a) the document and the reverse document increases the account's transaction debit and credit figures by the same amount or (b) after a document has been reversed, the balance of the affected account is shown unchanged as if the document had never been posted to which is also called as 'negative posting' ('true reversal').

You need to complete the following two tasks, to configure the system for adjustment or reversal postings:

- Permit Negative Posting
- Define Reasons for Reversal

Let us complete the settings for negative postings, first.

9.4.5.1 Permit Negative Posting

When you mark the reversal and adjustment posting as 'negative posting', the system reduces the transaction figures in customer, vendor and G/L Accounts. By this, the transaction figures (after the reversal) remain unchanged at the original status, as if you had not posted the reversed document and its subsequent reversal. Such negative postings result in changes in reconciliation between documents and transaction figures: a debit (Dr) item marked as a negative posting reduces the Credit (Cr) transaction figures and vice versa.

We have already discussed the negative posting when we maintained the company code global parameters in Section 6.8.1 of Chapter 6, and enabled this by selecting the 'Negative Postings Allowed' check-box (Transaction OBY6) for the required company codes.

However, you can maintain the same, here as well, using the menu path: SAP Customizing Implementation Guide > Financial Accounting > General Ledger Accounting > Business Transactions > Adjustment Posting/Reversal > Permit Negative Posting. You may also use Transaction S_ALR_87004651. On the resulting screen, select the 'Negative Postings Allowed' check-box and 'Save' the settings.

Let us now go and define the reasons for reversals.

9.4.5.2 Define Reasons for Reversal

When performing a reversal, you must specify the 'reason for reversal' for the system to display that in the reversed document's header. You can define several reversal reasons in the system: it could be an incorrect posting in the current period, an incorrect posting in a closed period, a failed bill of exchange and so on. Specify, for each *reversal reason*, whether (a) negative posting is to be created in the reversal document and (b) the reversal date can differ from the posting date of the document that is to be reversed.

Project Dolphin

In addition to allowing negative postings in all the company codes of BESTM, the project team has been asked to configure suitable document reversal reasons in the system to handle the reversal transactions. It has been clarified to the team that:

- If the reversal is happening in the current period, then, the system should allow negative posting, but not allow to change the posting date (of the document to be reversed).
- If the reversal is to happen in a closed period, then, the following conditions should be met:
  - Negative postings can be allowed but without altering the posting date (of the document to be reversed).
  - Negative postings cannot be allowed but the posting date (of the document to be reversed) can be altered.

Let us configure this:

i.   Use the menu path: SAP Customizing Implementation Guide > Financial Accounting > General Ledger Accounting > Business Transactions > Adjustment Posting/Reversal > Define Reasons for Reversal. You may also use Transaction S_ALR_87004660.

ii.   Click on 'New Entries' on the resulting 'Change View "Reasons for Reverse Posting": Overview' screen.

iii. On the next screen, maintain the required settings:
  - Enter a reason code in the 'Reason' field and provide an explanation in the 'Text' field.
  - Select 'Neg. Pstg' check-box to allow negative posting to be created in the reversal document.
  - Select 'Alt.Pos.Dt' check-box to allow an alternate posting date than that of the document to be reversed.

iv.   'Save' the stings (Figure 9.64).

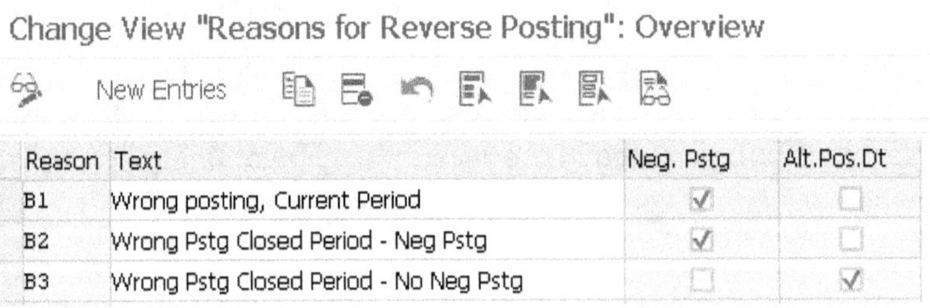

Change View "Reasons for Reverse Posting": Overview

Reason	Text	Neg. Pstg	Alt.Pos.Dt
B1	Wrong posting, Current Period	✓	☐
B2	Wrong Pstg Closed Period - Neg Pstg	✓	☐
B3	Wrong Pstg Closed Period - No Neg Pstg	☐	✓

Figure 9.64 Reversal Reasons

> **i** The system will ignore the 'negative posting allowed' settings made here, if you have not configured the company code to permit negative postings.

This completes our discussion on adjustment posting/reversal. Let us move on to discuss periodic processing, next.

9.5   Periodic Processing

In SAP G/L Accounting, you perform the following functions periodically:

- Integrated Business Planning
- Closing Operations
- Balance Interest Calculation

We have already discussed the balance (bank account) interest calculation, in detail, in Section 9.4.4 of this Chapter. Let us discuss the integrated business planning first; then, we can move on to discuss the closing operations in SAP G/L Accounting.

9.5.1   *Integrated Business Planning*

Also termed as 'SAP Business Planning & Consolidation for SAP S/4HANA', the *integrated business planning* provides a consistent view of the planning process. You can, now, access all planning applications by a Microsoft Excel front-end which provides a homogeneous look and feel. You no longer will encounter silos for the planning data since all planning data is contained in a real-time info cube of the local SAP Business Warehouse (BW), which is optimized for SAP S/4HANA. You can access actual data and master data directly in real-time, without any replication that would otherwise be necessary in a standalone BW.

> **i** You need to set up SAP BPC (Business Planning & Consolidation) for SAP S/4HANA, before start using integrated business planning. With the setting up of SAP BPC for S/4HANA, which uses the SAP BW system (part of the SAP NetWeaver), you do not need a standalone system. Besides, with SAP BPC for S/4HANA, there is no need to replicate data between the S/4HANA system and SAP BPC; you can perform real-time analysis on plan and actual data. By using the 'Planning Application Kit '(PAK), you can, now, run the planning functions (such as, disaggregation) completely in-memory and directly on SAP HANA without any ABAP processing. Besides providing for much faster performance (when you have a lot of planning data), it makes simulations and predictions possible quite easier than ever.

With SAP BPC for S/4HANA, you can use various features that enable building different types of planning processes (Planning - a la Carte). The features include:

- *Standard BI Content on the Model Level*
  This facilitates (a) a virtual 'InfoProvider' accessing the ACDOCA table, (b) a real-time InfoProvider (with almost the same fields as the ACDOCA table), and ACDOCP table for plan data (with almost the same fields as the ACDOCA table) and a virtual InfoProvider to access it, so as to store your plan data and (c) a 'MultiProvider' combining actual and plan data.

- *Standard BI Content on the Business Level*
  With this, you can (a) perform analytics in a web browser or run queries with Microsoft Excel, and (b) plan with Microsoft Excel as a desktop tool. SAP provides standard planning workbooks for planning on years / periods, for cost centers, internal orders, projects, functional areas, market segments, profit centers, the P&L statement, and the balance sheet.

  The standard BI content on business level also provides for aggregation levels, planning filters, planning functions, planning sequences, and variables, which supplement the other standard planning content objects.

With SAP BPC for S/4HANA, you can:

- Copy actual to plan.
- Delete plan.
- Distribute year values across periods with self-reference / equal distribution.
- Allocate (a) planned overhead based on allocation factors, (b) costs of planned services / activities based on planned services and cost rates and (c) consumption of planned costs from a sending cost center to a receiving cost center.
- Calculate planned sales revenue based on planned sales quantities / sales prices.

---

i Since it is beyond the scope of this book, we will not be discussing anything on the 'how to' part of planning for SAP G/L Accounting using SAP BPC for S/4HANA.

Let us move on to discuss the closing operations in SAP G/L Accounting, in the next Section.

9.5.2 Closing Operations

The closing operations, in SAP G/L Accounting, is made up of processes and functions that you will perform at the end of every fiscal year. It is possible, in closing operations, to process data from other SAP application components and external systems.

SAP supports the following closing operations in G/L Accounting:

- Check/Count
- Valuate
- Reclassify / Regroup
- Allocation
- Carry Forward

Let us start with check/count.

9.5.2.1 Check/Count

The program 'Reconciliation of Receivables/Payables in Group (Cross-System)' helps you to reconcile customer documents and vendor documents of the affiliated companies in the group. It reads the open items of selected companies for the key date specified, thereby helping you to identify documents that cause a difference. The overall process is as shown in Figure 9.65.

The intercompany reconciliation program supports the following processes:

- Process 001 (Reconciliation of Open Items in G/L Accounts)
- Process 002 (Reconciliation of G/L Account Line Items)
- Process 003 (Reconciliation of Open Items in A/R and A/P)

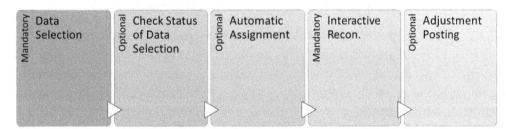

Figure 9.65 Reconciliation of Group Receivables / Payables – Process Flow

The processes 001 and 003 usually relate to the reconciliation of group payables / receivables. You can process 001 and 003 separately or integrate the open items of one process into the other and process the same simultaneously; SAP supports both the options as variants. You can use process 002 to reconcile accounts that are not managed on an open-item basis; usually, postings to revenue and expense accounts are reconciled in this process.

The pre-requisites are:

- On the master record side, ensure that (a) you have defined the number of the trading partner in the customer / vendor master data, and (b) a trading partner was assigned for relevant G/L items during posting, or the number of the trading partner is stored in the G/L accounts.
- On the configuration side, ensure that you have made the required settings under 'Cross-System Intercompany Reconciliation' in the IMG.

There are several configuration settings that you need to make under 'Cross-System Intercompany Reconciliation' for preparing the sender as well as the reconciliation systems. They important ones are:

- Check Assignment of Company Codes to Companies
- Check Assignment of Operational Chart of Accounts to Group Chart
- Assign Operational Accounts to Group Accounts (Automatic / Manual)
- Check Assignment of Operational Accounts to Group Accounts

Let us start with the settings required for preparing the sender system.

9.5.2.1.1   Check Assignment of Company Codes to Companies
We have already completed the assignment company codes to companies while configuring the enterprise structure, in Section 5.4.1 of Chapter 5. However, you can make use of this step to verify those assignments, and make the suitable assignments, if necessary.

Use the menu path: SAP Customizing Implementation Guide > Financial Accounting > General Ledger Accounting > Periodic Processing > Check/Count > Cross-System Intercompany Reconciliation > Preparations in the Sender System > General Settings > Check Assignment of Company Codes to Companies. You may also use Transaction OX16.

9.5.2.1.2   Check Assignment of Operational Chart of Accounts to Group Chart
We have, already, completed assigning the operational chart of accounts (BEUS / BEIN) to the group chart of accounts (BEGR) when (a) we defined the chart of accounts while discussing the company code global parameters, in Section 6.8.1 of Chapter 6, and (b) when we revised the details towards preparations for G/L account master data, in Section 9.3.1.

You can use the menu path: SAP Customizing Implementation Guide > Financial Accounting > General Ledger Accounting > Periodic Processing > Check/Count > Cross-System Intercompany Reconciliation > Preparations in the Sender System > General Settings > Check Assignment of Operational Chart of Accounts to Group Chart, to check and ensure that the operational charts of accounts (say, BEIN and BEUS for BESTM) are indeed assigned to the group chart of accounts (BEGR) as shown in Figure 9.66. You may also use Transaction OB13.

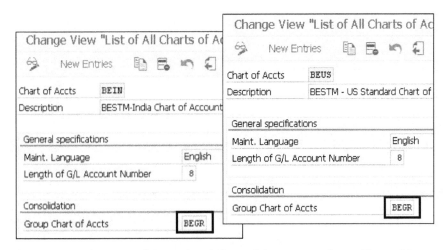

Figure 9.66 Assignment of Operational Chart of Accounts to Group Chart of Accounts

The next step is to assign operational accounts to group accounts.

9.5.2.1.3   Assign Operational Accounts to Group Accounts (Automatic / Manual)

You can accomplish this either automatically or manually. In some circumstances, for example, if the account length is the same in both the charts and the account grouping is almost the same between the two charts, it is possible to automatically assign group account numbers to operational accounts. However, if you cannot automatically assign the group accounts to the operational accounts, you can manually assign the relevant group account to each operational account in this step.

Use the menu path: SAP Customizing Implementation Guide > Financial Accounting > General Ledger Accounting > Periodic Processing > Check/Count > Cross-System Intercompany Reconciliation > Preparations in the Sender System > General Settings > Automatically Assign Operational Accounts to Group Accounts, to take the route of automatic assignment of operational accounts to the group accounts. You may also use Transaction FBIC002.

On the resulting screen, enter the 'Financial statement version' and 'FS item' details. Under 'Generate postings', select either online (Figure 9.67) or background processing, and select the 'Log' check-box to look at the log after the program execution.

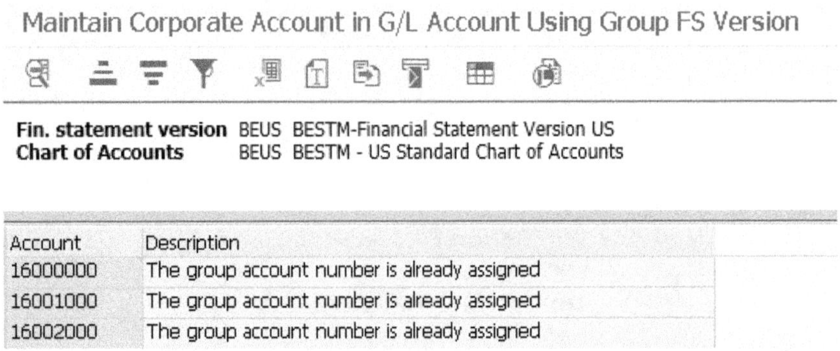

Maintain Corporate Account in G/L Account Using Group FS Version

Fin. statement version BEUS BESTM-Financial Statement Version US
Chart of Accounts BEUS BESTM - US Standard Chart of Accounts

Account	Description
16000000	The group account number is already assigned
16001000	The group account number is already assigned
16002000	The group account number is already assigned

Figure 9.67 Automatic Assignment of Operational Accounts to Group Accounts

As already outlined, if you are unable to make automatic assignment, take the manual route.

Figure 9.68 Manual Assignment of Operational Accounts to Group Accounts

Use the menu path: SAP Customizing Implementation Guide > Financial Accounting > General Ledger Accounting > Periodic Processing > Check/Count > Cross-System Intercompany Reconciliation > Preparations in the Sender System > General Settings > Manually Assign Operational Accounts to Group Accounts. As you would have noticed, this is nothing but the manual maintenance of G/L account master record, centrally, for both chart of accounts and company code areas (Figure 9.68). You may also use Transaction FS00.

Let us move on to the next step.

9.5.2.1.4 Check Assignment of Operational Accounts to Group Accounts

Now, you can check the assignment of operational accounts to group accounts to ensure that all the operational accounts have been properly assigned to the group accounts.

Use the menu path: SAP Customizing Implementation Guide > Financial Accounting > General Ledger Accounting > Periodic Processing > Check/Count > Cross-System Intercompany Reconciliation > Preparations in the Sender System > General Settings > Check Assignment of Operational Accounts to Group Accounts, to check the assignments. You may also use Transaction FBIC001. On the resulting screen, enter the operational chart of accounts and press 'Execute'. On the next screen, you will see a pop-up showing missing assignments, if any, like the one displayed in Figure 9.69.

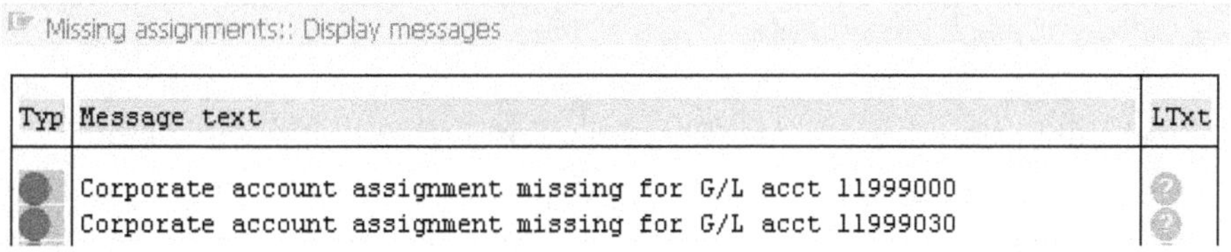

Figure 9.69 Missing Corporate Account Assignment

Correct the missing assignments using 'Manually Assign Operational Accounts to Group Accounts' step of the configuration or by simply using Transaction FS00. When done, run the 'Check Assignment of Operational Accounts to Group Accounts' again. If there are no missing assignments, you will see the pop-up screen as shown in Figure 9.70 indicating that you have, now, completed assigning all the operational G/L accounts to the corporate account number.

> **Information**
>
> ⓘ All G/L accounts have been assigned to a corporate
> account number

Figure 9.70 Successful Assignment of G/L Accounts to Corporate Accounts

Let us, now, see the settings required for the preparations in the reconciliation system.

9.5.2.1.5 Generate Default Customizing

When you execute this step, the program generates default settings for most of the activities under the IMG node 'Preparations in the Reconciliation System'. It will produce a log listing out what has been completed. It generates the settings for all companies, for which you have already maintained the master data when setting up the FI enterprise structure. You just need to review the generated settings and adjust them, if required.

Before executing the program, however, you need to decide which reconciliation processes (001 and 003, or 002) you want use for your company.

- *Reconciliation Processes 001 and 003*
  Typically used to reconcile payables and receivables within the corporate group, both the processes are for reconciling the open items.

  - o Though originally designed to support reconciliation of documents posted to G/L accounts, you can include customer / vendor open items as well in the 'Reconciliation Process 001'. Use the process 001 if most of your intercompany documents are posted to G/L accounts or if you need to reconcile G/L intercompany documents separately from customer / vendor intercompany documents.

  - o Though meant for reconciling documents posted to customer / vendor accounts, you can use the 'Reconciliation Process 003' to include G/L open items as well. Use the process 003 if most of your intercompany documents are posted to customer / vendor accounts or if you want reconciliation of customer / vendor intercompany documents separately from G/L open items.

- *Reconciliation Process 002*
  This process supports reconciliation of accounts without open item management, and is typically used to reconcile revenues and expenses resulting from business transactions within the corporate group.

> **i** Due to large volume of data relevant for reconciliation, you may need to create a Special Purpose Ledger in operative SAP systems from which data is supposed to be extracted for reconciliation.

Project Dolphin

BESTM Corporate wants to reconcile the payables and receivables within the corporate group. Accordingly, the project team has suggested to configure the system appropriately. Though most of the intercompany documents are posted to customer and vendor accounts, BESTM also wants to include reconciliation of G/L open items.

To generate the default setting for most of the activities under the IMG node 'Preparations in the Reconciliation System':

i.   Use the menu path: SAP Customizing Implementation Guide > Financial Accounting > General Ledger Accounting > Periodic Processing > Check/Count > Cross-System Intercompany Reconciliation > Preparations in the Reconciliation System > Generate Default Customizing. You may also use Transaction FBICC.

ii.   On the resulting 'Intercompany Reconciliation: Create Default Customizing' screen, maintain the required details (Figure 9.71):

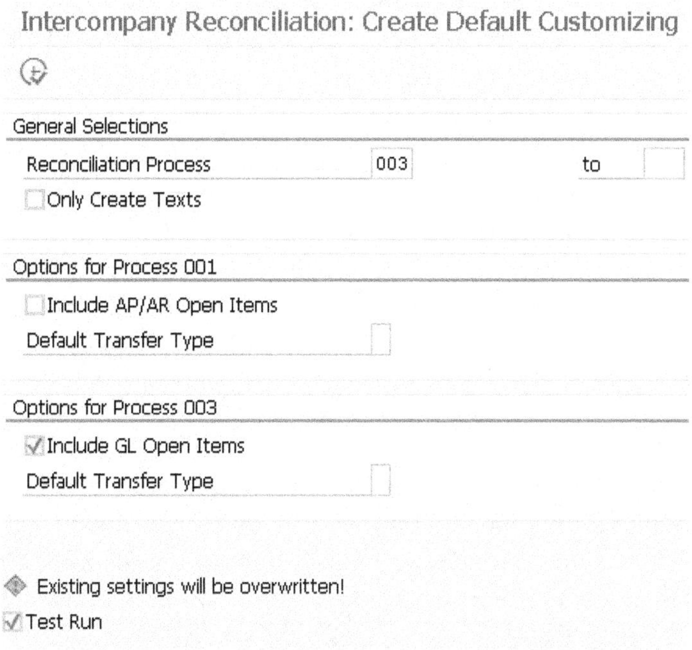

Intercompany Reconciliation: Create Default Customizing

General Selections

Reconciliation Process	003	to

☐ Only Create Texts

Options for Process 001

☐ Include AP/AR Open Items

Default Transfer Type

Options for Process 003

☑ Include GL Open Items

Default Transfer Type

◈ Existing settings will be overwritten!

☑ Test Run

Figure 9.71 Parameters for Generating Default Customizing for Intercompany Reconciliation

- Under 'General Selection', enter the value for the 'Reconciliation Process' field. Since BESTM primarily wants to reconcile customer / vendor open items but also wants to include G/L account open items, enter 003 here in this field.
- Under 'Options for Process 003' select 'Include GL Open Items' check-box; select a suitable 'Default Transfer Type' for data selection. Leave this as blank to activate the default data transfer type ('Asynchronous via Direct RFC Connection').

> **i** The data transfer type *'Asynchronous via Direct RFC Connection'* is the default transfer type for data selection. Though it enables a maximum parallelization within the data selection process, it requires direct RFC connections to the individual sender systems. Also, this type gives you the option of scheduling data selections and automatic assignments as two steps of the same job, which makes sense in an organization with a central approach where data selection and automatic assignment are run centrally, and the users only perform the manual reconciliation themselves.

The other data transfer type '*Synchronous via XI*' was developed to enable data selection using XI, while keeping the control with the data selection program. This data transfer type uses transactional RFCs because asynchronous RFCs are not possible through XI. In order to allow for some parallelization, the data selection program will start several tasks within the reconciliation system, each of which then performs a transactional RFC to the sender system through XI. All of the data is collected and processed further by the data selection program. Therefore, all information regarding the data transfer is available in the log of the data selection program. This data transfer type also gives you the option of scheduling data selections and automatic assignments as two steps of the same job.

The third data transfer type '*Asynchronous Triggered from Reconciliation System*' enables a maximum of parallelization, whether you use direct RFC connections or XI. However, you will not know when the data transfer is actually finished, and hence this transfer type is intended to be used only if you can determine the appropriate start time for automatic assignment and schedule a separate job accordingly, or if the users start automatic assignment by themselves.

- Select the 'Test Run' check-box, and 'Execute' the program.

iii.   The program brings out the default customizing settings that will be carried out eventually, during the production run.

iv.   View the details, and when satisfied that all the required default settings will be created by the program for intercompany reconciliation for process 003, go back to the previous screen, de-select the 'Test Run' check-box, and 'Execute' again.

v.   The program generates the default customizing settings as shown in Figure 9.72. Pay attention to the messages with a Yellow triangle:

- As you can see, the system lets you know that though the default settings were created, you need to review them to make sure that the settings are correct.

- There are couple of activities like 'Create Additional Fields' and 'Define Ledger' for which the program has not generated the settings, and you may need to manually complete that, if required.

- Also, it notifies that you can take up 'Enhancements', if required.

- And, when you check and complete the left out customizing activities, you are informed to 'Activate the Process' and 'Activate Transaction Data Tables'.

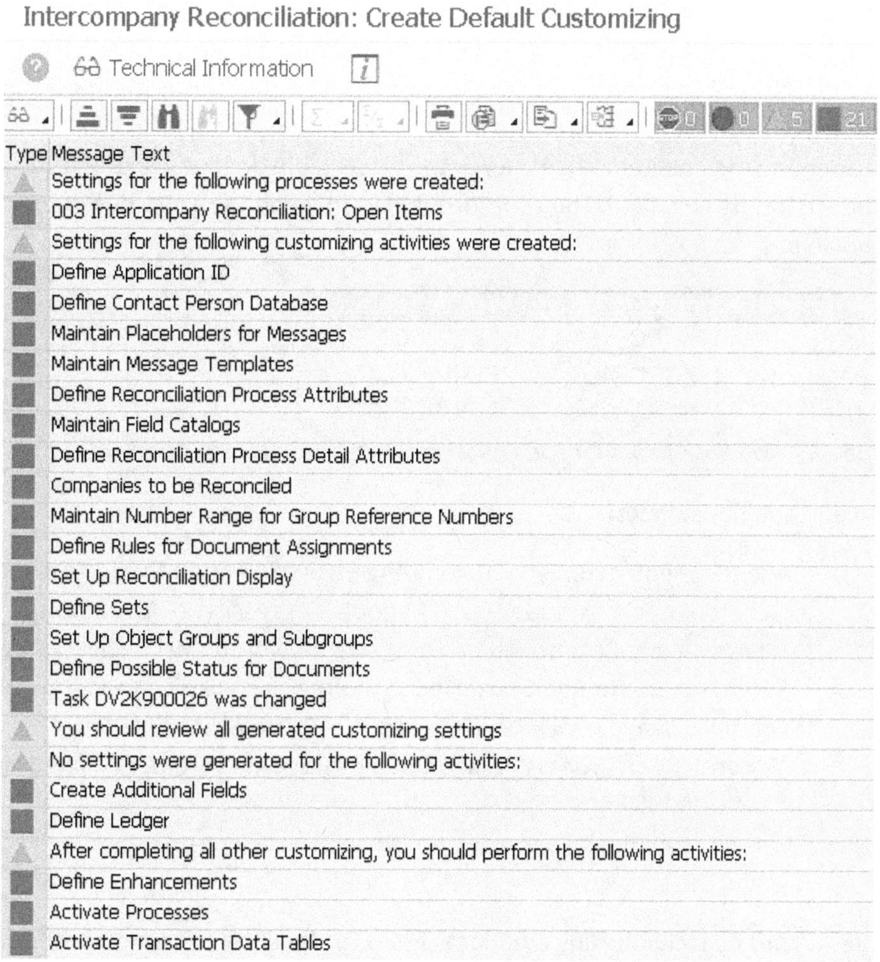

Intercompany Reconciliation: Create Default Customizing

⚙ 6ə Technical Information   ℹ

Type Message Text

⚠ Settings for the following processes were created:
▪ 003 Intercompany Reconciliation: Open Items
⚠ Settings for the following customizing activities were created:
▪ Define Application ID
▪ Define Contact Person Database
▪ Maintain Placeholders for Messages
▪ Maintain Message Templates
▪ Define Reconciliation Process Attributes
▪ Maintain Field Catalogs
▪ Define Reconciliation Process Detail Attributes
▪ Companies to be Reconciled
▪ Maintain Number Range for Group Reference Numbers
▪ Define Rules for Document Assignments
▪ Set Up Reconciliation Display
▪ Define Sets
▪ Set Up Object Groups and Subgroups
▪ Define Possible Status for Documents
▪ Task DV2K900026 was changed
⚠ You should review all generated customizing settings
⚠ No settings were generated for the following activities:
▪ Create Additional Fields
▪ Define Ledger
⚠ After completing all other customizing, you should perform the following activities:
▪ Define Enhancements
▪ Activate Processes
▪ Activate Transaction Data Tables

Figure 9.72 Generate Default Customizing for Intercompany Reconciliation - Results

Now that we have completed generating the default Customizing settings for intercompany reconciliation in the sender system, let us proceed to configure the left out settings as shown in Figure 9.72:

- Create Additional Fields
- Define Ledger
- Define Enhancements
- Activate Processes
- Activate Transaction Data Tables

Let us start with the creation of additional fields.

9.5.2.1.6   Create Additional Fields

You may add the desired additional fields (up to 13) to the tables for the intercompany reconciliation of G/L accounts. You can use these fields for displaying additional document information, definition of object groups, or as secondary organizational units. Whether a field is added to the line item table and/or the totals table depends on the level of availability you choose for the new field. The additional fields are generated into different database tables as shown in Table 9.4.

Process ID	Line Item Table	Totals Table
001	FBICRC001A	FBICRC001T
002	FBICRC002A	FBICRC002T
003	FBICRC003A	FBICRC003T

Table 9:4 Database Tables for Additional Fields in Intercompany Reconciliation

To add additional fields:

i.   Use the menu path: SAP Customizing Implementation Guide > Financial Accounting > General Ledger Accounting > Periodic Processing > Check/Count > Cross-System Intercompany Reconciliation > Preparations in the Reconciliation System > General Settings > Create Additional Fields. You may also use Transaction FBIC006.

ii.   On the 'Display View "Reconciliation Processes": Overview' screen, select the 'Reconciliation Process' ID and double-click on 'Customer Defined Fields' on the left-hand side 'Dialog Structure'.

iii.   On the resulting screen, click on 'New Entries' and maintain the required fields, and 'Save' the settings.

We will not be including any additional fields for the intercompany reconciliation for BESTM. Let us move on to define the (Special Purpose) ledger required.

9.5.2.1.7   Define Ledger

The 'intercompany reconciliation' uses Special Purpose Ledger functionality for storing data that is to be reconciled. Though, from a technical point of view, it is not necessary to actually create a Special Purpose Ledger only for data storage, specify a ledger name to make use of the additional functions of Special Purpose Ledger (like, reporting or extraction of data to BW), at a later point in time.

You can create and maintain a Special Purpose Ledger for facilitating inter-company reconciliation in the system by following the menu path: SAP Customizing Implementation Guide > Financial Accounting > General Ledger Accounting > Periodic Processing > Check/Count > Cross-System Intercompany Reconciliation > Preparations in the Reconciliation System > Data Selection and Storage > Open Item Reconciliation / G/L Account Reconciliation > Define Ledger.

On the 'Select Activity' pop-up screen, double-click on 'Create Ledger' and maintain the required details, and 'Save' when completed. The ledger must have the property settings as in Table 9.5. All other configuration switches should be set to 'No'.

Property	Value
Summary table	FBICRC001T
Ledger postings allowed	Yes
Write lines items	Yes
Transaction currency	Yes

Table 9:5 Properties for Special Purpose Ledger used in Intercompany Reconciliation

> **i** Do not assign any companies / activities to this ledger.

The next task is to define enhancements, if required.

9.5.2.1.8   Define Enhancements

Here, using this step, you can implement the BAdI, 'Business Process Reconciliation: Reconcile documents from different business partners'. This BAdI provides for (a) changing data records after one assignment rule has been run or (b) changing data records after all assignment rules have been run in data assignment.

Use the menu path: SAP Customizing Implementation Guide > Financial Accounting > General Ledger Accounting > Periodic Processing > Check/Count > Cross-System Intercompany Reconciliation > Preparations in the Reconciliation System > Data Assignment > Define Enhancements.

On entering the Transaction, you will see a pop-up for activating the BAdi. Click 'Activate' to activate the inactive BAdi 'FB_RC_Assignment'. Click 'Yes' on the subsequent pop-up screen. The system confirms, through a message, that the BAdi has now been activated (Figure 9.73).

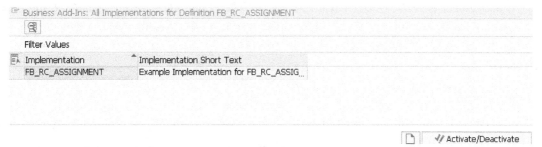

Figure 9.73 Enhancement for Intercompany Reconciliation

Let us, now, move on to activate the reconciliation processes.

9.5.2.1.9   Activate Processes

Using this configuration step, you can activate the individual reconciliation processes. It is important that you have created the Special Purpose Ledger in the system.

For intercompany reconciliation processes 001 and 003, you need to activate tables FBICRC001A and FBICRC003A respectively, depending on which processes you are using. This step is only mandatory in the reconciliation system for these processes.

Use the menu path: SAP Customizing Implementation Guide > Financial Accounting > General Ledger Accounting > Periodic Processing > Check/Count > Cross-System Intercompany Reconciliation > Preparations in the Reconciliation System > General Settings > Activate Processes, or Transaction FBIC031, to make the required changes in the reconciliation system, if it has not been done earlier. If the processes are already active, as shown in Figure 9.74, you do not need to do anything.

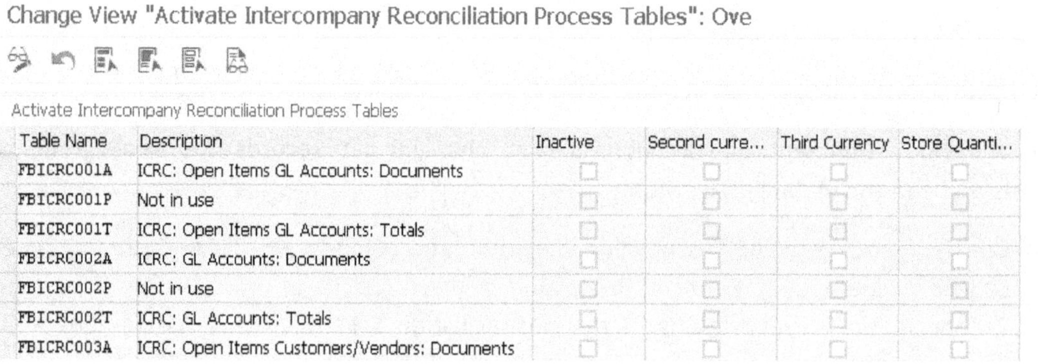

Change View "Activate Intercompany Reconciliation Process Tables": Ove

Activate Intercompany Reconciliation Process Tables

Table Name	Description	Inactive	Second curre...	Third Currency	Store Quanti...
FBICRC001A	ICRC: Open Items GL Accounts: Documents	☐	☐	☐	☐
FBICRC001P	Not in use	☐	☐	☐	☐
FBICRC001T	ICRC: Open Items GL Accounts: Totals	☐	☐	☐	☐
FBICRC002A	ICRC: GL Accounts: Documents	☐	☐	☐	☐
FBICRC002P	Not in use	☐	☐	☐	☐
FBICRC002T	ICRC: GL Accounts: Totals	☐	☐	☐	☐
FBICRC003A	ICRC: Open Items Customers/Vendors: Documents	☐	☐	☐	☐

Figure 9.74 Activating Processes for Intercompany Reconciliation

The last step is activating the transaction data tables.

9.5.2.1.10   Activate Transaction Data Tables

Finally, you need to activate the transaction data tables and generate the posting modules to enable the intercompany reconciliation programs to post data. If you have created any additional fields, they are not visible in the 'Field Catalog' until you have performed this activity.

To activate:

i.   Use the menu path: SAP Customizing Implementation Guide > Financial Accounting > General Ledger Accounting > Periodic Processing > Check/Count > Cross-System Intercompany Reconciliation > Preparations in the Reconciliation System > General Settings > Activate Transaction Data Tables, or Transaction FBIC004.

ii.   On the resulting 'Activate Transaction Data Tables' screen, select the 'Test Run' check-box and 'Execute' to see the results of this activation on the next screen (Figure 9.75).

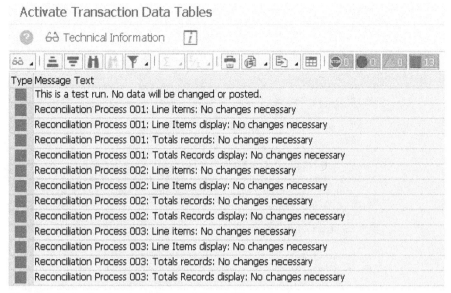

Figure 9.75 Activating Data Transaction Tables – Test Run

iii.   If everything is Green, go back to the previous screen, deselect the 'Test Run' check-box and 'Execute' again. The system brings up, on the next screen, the 'Log' with details of changes made. You will notice that everything has been generated successfully (Figure 9.76).

> **i** You should execute this function while no postings are being made in any client of the system.

Log Display

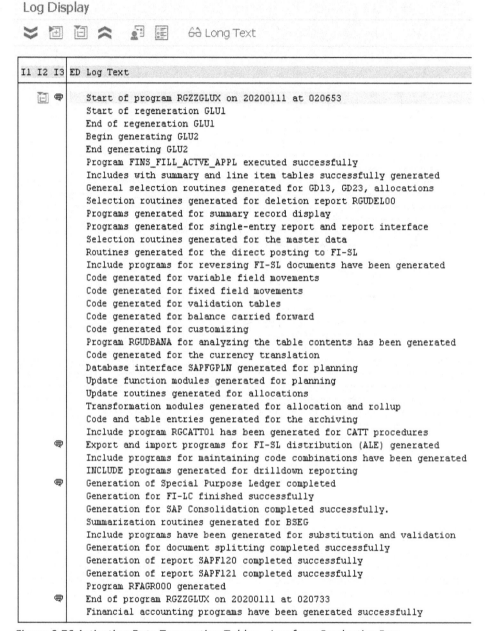

Figure 9.76 Activating Data Transaction Tables – Log from Productive Run

This completes our discussion on configuring intercompany reconciliation (check/count) as a part of closing. Let us, now, look at the settings required for foreign currency valuation.

9.5.2.2 Valuate

To complete creation of financial statements, you need to perform foreign currency valuation. For valuating in foreign currency, you have the option of (a) valuating in local currency (company code currency) or a parallel currency (say, group currency), (b) using different valuation methods like 'lowest value principle' and (c) automatic currency translation (in accordance with FASB 52 of US GAAP) when translating additional currencies from local currency.

---

i The Financial Accounting Standards Board (FASB) issued Statement 52, Foreign Currency Solution, in December 1981. Also known as Accounting Standard Codification 830, FAS 52 provides guidance on handling transactions and reporting that involves foreign currencies. FAS 52 covers a lot of ground, including guidance on implementing currency rates under ambiguous conditions.

More specifically, this Statement replaces FASB Statement No. 8 ('Accounting for the Translation of Foreign Currency Transactions and Foreign Currency Financial Statements'), and revises the existing accounting and reporting requirements for translation of foreign currency transactions and foreign currency financial statements. It presents standards for foreign currency translation that are designed to (1) provide information that is generally compatible with the expected economic effects of a rate change on an enterprise's cash flows and equity and (2) reflect in consolidated statements of the financial results and relationships, as measured in the primary currency in which each entity conducts its business.

The standard SAP supports the following functions towards foreign currency valuation (program FAGL_FCV):

1) *Valuating Foreign Currency Balance Sheet Accounts*: The foreign currency B/S accounts are the G/L accounts that you manage in foreign currency. The balances of G/L accounts that are not managed on an open item basis are valuated in foreign currency.

2) *Valuation of Open Items in Foreign Currencies*: The items that are open on a key date are valuated in foreign currency.

3) Saving the exchange rate differences determined from the valuation per document.

4) *Posting account assignments in valuation documents*: In case you are using document splitting functionality in SAP G/L Accounting, then, the valuation documents are posted with the account assignments that you have defined as the document splitting characteristics. In the case of balance valuation, you can define additional account assignment characteristics which get always updated (even if you do not use document splitting). You can define the additional account assignment characteristics, for foreign currency valuation, using the menu path SAP Customizing

Implementation Guide > Financial Accounting > General Ledger Accounting > Periodic Processing > Valuate > Foreign Currency Valuation > Activate Additional Fields for Foreign Currency Valuation or Transaction FINS_FCT. Refer Section 9.5.2.2.7, for more details.

5) Performing the required adjustment postings.

You need to carry out the following configuration activities for performing foreign currency valuation:

- Define Valuation Methods
- Define Valuation Areas
- Check Assignment of Accounting Principle to Ledger Group
- Assign Valuation Areas and Accounting Principles
- Activate Delta Logic
- Prepare Automatic Postings for Foreign Currency Valuation
- Activate Additional Fields for Foreign Currency Valuation
- Define Account Determination for Currency Translation

Project Dolphin

BESTM Corporate wants to have a single valuation method that will be used worldwide. However, there needs to be different valuation areas to take care of the different valuation needs and requirements of each of the accounting principles. Besides, the corporate also wants to make use of the 'delta logic' functionality in foreign currency valuation to ensure that the system does not execute any reversal postings for the valuation postings in the subsequent period. Besides the default account assignment fields for foreign currency valuation, BESTM wants to include 'Functional Area' and 'Cost Center' as the additional account assignments to have more flexibility.

Let us start with the definition of valuation methods.

9.5.2.2.1   Define Valuation Methods

The 'valuation method' determines how foreign currency valuation is performed, grouping specifications that you need for the balance valuation and line item valuation, during closing. You will be able to use the valuation method across multiple charts of accounts.

Per valuation method, you specify (a) the valuation procedure to be used (for example, *lowest value principle*), (b) how the exchange rate differences determined should be posted (for example, which document type should be used) and (c) the basis on which the exchange rate should be determined (for example, which exchange rate type should be used).

To define a valuation method:

i.   Use the menu path SAP Customizing Implementation Guide > Financial Accounting > General Ledger Accounting > Periodic Processing > Valuate > Define Valuation Methods.

ii. On the resulting screen, click on 'New Entries' to define a new valuation method (Figure 9.77):

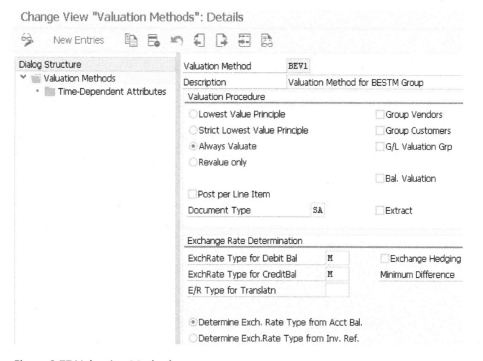

Figure 9.77 Valuation Method

- Enter an identifier for the new valuation method (say, BEV1).
- Under the 'Valuation Procedure', select the appropriate valuation principle (say, 'Always Valuate').
- Usually, the valuation results are posted in a summarized form. However, select 'Post per Line Item' check-box, if required, to generate a line item for each valuated item in the valuation posting as well as in the adjustment account, such as the expense or revenue account.
- To evaluate a group of accounts, you need to select the appropriate check-boxes. This has the effect that balances are created for several accounts. Customer and vendor accounts are balanced and grouped according to the group to which they belong. G/L accounts are balanced according to the

valuation group. During further processing, the group is then viewed as a whole; for example, during foreign currency valuation the group balance is used to determine the exchange rate type. You need to enter the group key in the respective master record under 'Group'.

- If you select 'Extract' check-box, then, you need provide a file name for the valuation run. The system stores a series of information in this file for every valuated line item. The format is determined by the F100FILE structure. You can use this extract for downstream non-SAP applications.
- Enter a 'Document Type'.
- Under 'Exchange Rate Determination', maintain the exchange rate type (say, M) for both debit and credit balance, and select 'Determine Exch. Rate Type from Acct Bal.' radio-button.

iii.   'Save' the settings and maintain the 'Time-Dependent Attributes' for the newly created valuation method BEV1 (Figure 9.77).

With the definition of valuation method completed, the next step is to define the valuation areas.

9.5.2.2.2   Valuation Areas

You can use the 'valuation areas' to report different valuation approaches and post to different accounts. You can save the valuation result, separately for each document item and use it for other closing operations (such as sorted lists).

To define valuation areas for your closing operations:

i.   Use the menu path SAP Customizing Implementation Guide > Financial Accounting > General Ledger Accounting > Periodic Processing > Valuate > Define Valuation Areas.

ii.   On the resulting screen, click on 'New Entries', and:

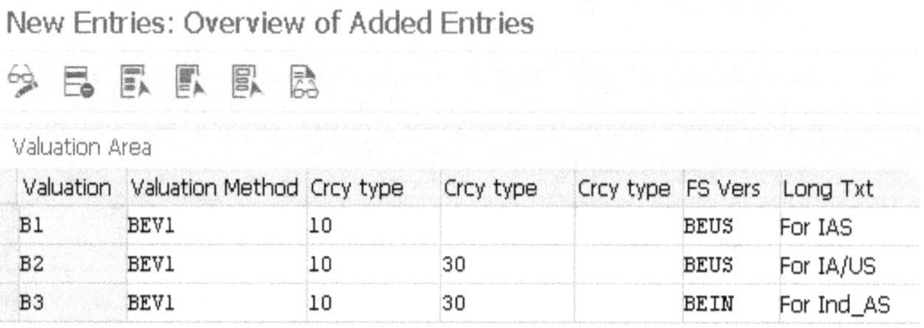

New Entries: Overview of Added Entries

Valuation Area

Valuation	Valuation Method	Crcy type	Crcy type	Crcy type	FS Vers	Long Txt
B1	BEV1	10			BEUS	For IAS
B2	BEV1	10	30		BEUS	For IA/US
B3	BEV1	10	30		BEIN	For Ind_AS

Figure 9.78 Valuation Areas

- Enter a 2-character identifier for the new valuation area in the 'Valuation' field (say, B1)
- Enter the 'Valuation Method' (BEV1).

- You can select up to three currency types in the 'Crcy type' fields.
- Enter the appropriate financial statement version ('FS vers') and enter a suitable explanation in the 'Long Txt'.
- 'Save', when completed

iii. Repeat the steps and define all the other valuation areas for BESTM group (Figure 9.78).

The next step is to check the assignment of accounting principle to ledger group.

9.5.2.2.3   Check Assignment of Accounting Principle to Ledger Group

Using this step, you can check the assignment of accounting principle to ledger group which you have already completed, in Section 6.5.2 of Chapter 6. If the assignment was not done earlier, you can use this step to completed the assignment, now.

Use the menu path SAP Customizing Implementation Guide > Financial Accounting > General Ledger Accounting > Periodic Processing > Valuate > Check Assignment of Accounting Principle to Ledger Group to check or define the assignments.

Let us move on to assign the valuation areas to the accounting principles, in the next step.

9.5.2.2.4   Assign Valuation Areas and Accounting Principles

Assign the desired accounting principles to your valuation areas. As you can use the valuation area for the reclassification or sorted list of payables and receivables and for foreign currency valuation, you can use the valuation area to apply in these reports for the different valuation requirements of the accounting principles.

Use the menu path SAP Customizing Implementation Guide > Financial Accounting > General Ledger Accounting > Periodic Processing > Valuate > Assign Valuation Areas and Accounting Principles. On the resulting screen, make the required assignments (Figure 9.79).

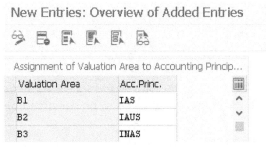

Figure 9.79 Assigning Valuation Areas to Accounting Principle

The next step is to activate the delta logic.

9.5.2.2.5   Activate Delta Logic

The '*delta logic*' ensures that the system does not execute any reversal postings, for the valuation postings in the following (or subsequent) period. You can activate the delta logic separately, per valuation area. When activating, you can determine whether you want to use the clearing date as the date for the reversal, by setting that indicator in the configuration. Use the menu path SAP Customizing Implementation Guide > Financial Accounting > General Ledger Accounting > Periodic Processing > Valuate > Activate Delta Logic (Figure 9.80):

Change View "Delta Posting Logic": Overview

Delta Posting Logic

Valuation	Long Txt	Delta Logic	Reversal After Settlement Date	Monthly reversal
B1	For IAS	☑	☐	☐
B2	For IA/US	☑	☐	☐
B3	For Ind_AS	☑	☐	☐

Figure 9.80 Activating Delta Logic for Valuation Areas

- Select 'Delta Logic' check-box to make sure that the system does not execute any reversal postings for the valuation postings in the following period.

> **i** The '*delta logic*' is a posting logic for consolidation group-dependent entries. In the business consolidation, all documents and totals records that are posted at a lower level in the hierarchy of consolidation groups also apply to the higher levels of the hierarchy. At the higher levels, the system merely posts delta entries. The 'delta' is the difference between (a) the (hypothetical) total document that would normally be posted for the given consolidation group, if no lower-level groups existed, and (b) the (actual) documents posted for the lower-level groups.

- If you select 'Reversal Date After Settlement Date' check-box, the system uses the clearing date of the valuated item for the reversal postings. This may, at time, pose problems since the program cannot ensure that the period is open. If the period is closed, an error message will be output and the posting will not be made; it will be stored in a batch-input session, which will, then, need to be to be corrected before you can make the postings again.
- When you select the 'Monthly reversal' check-box, you will be able to specify whether the reversal of valuation postings is possible in the 'Foreign Currency Valuation' report in conjunction with the delta logic.

With this, we are now ready to prepare the system for automatic postings of foreign currency valuation.

9.5.2.2.6 *Prepare Automatic Postings for Foreign Currency Valuation*

Here, in this step, you define the G/L accounts to which you want the system to automatically post the exchange rate differences, when valuating open items and foreign currency balances. You can use the *currency type* to control account determination during open item valuation and exchange rate difference posting. You can, for example, post gains in local currency and gains in group currency, to separate accounts. When valuating open items, the system posts to a B/S adjustment account and to an account for exchange rate differences (gain/loss) that occur during the valuation. Do not change the SAP-defined posting keys for the automatic postings.

> **i** The valuation of foreign currency balances requires a special key that is assigned to the gain and loss G/L accounts for posting any exchange rate differences that occur during valuation. You can freely define this key. You then enter that in the master records of the accounts that you want to valuate. To post the differences that are determined from a group of G/L accounts to the same gain or loss accounts, enter the same key for all these G/L accounts.

To configure the settings for automatic postings:

i.   Use the menu path SAP Customizing Implementation Guide > Financial Accounting > General Ledger Accounting > Periodic Processing > Valuate > Foreign Currency Valuation > Prepare Automatic Postings for Foreign Currency Valuation. You may also use Transaction OBA1.

ii. You will see a list of automatic posting procedures for posting exchange rate differences, on the resulting screen. We have already defined the required G/L accounts to take care of exchange rate differences arising out of open item clearing (procedure KDF), in an earlier Section 9.4.3.2. Let us, now, configure the accounts for the other required procedures (like KDB and KDW).

iii. Double-click the appropriate row (say, KDB); maintain the chart of accounts (say, BEUS), and 'Continue'.

iv. Enter the appropriate G/L accounts in 'Expense account' and 'E/R gains acct'. The 'Expense account' is for posting the exchange rate losses; any loss resulting from changes in exchange rates is posted to this account. Similarly, 'E/R gains acct' will be used to record the gains from changes in exchange rates.

v.   For the valuation of foreign currency balances, the system uses the 'Exchange rate difference key' to find the accounts for gains and losses from the valuation. You specify which G/L accounts are to be posted to under which exchange rate difference key in the system. If you do not want to differentiate the accounts per key, leave the 'Exchange rate difference key' field as blank (Figure 9.81).

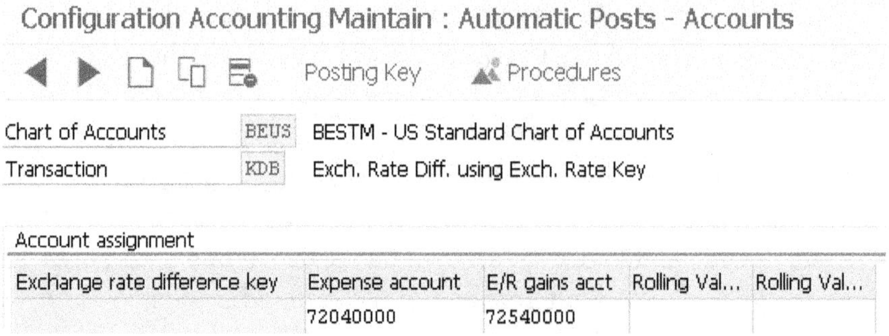

Configuration Accounting Maintain : Automatic Posts - Accounts

◀ ▶ 🗋 🗗 🖹   Posting Key   ⚔ Procedures

Chart of Accounts	BEUS	BESTM - US Standard Chart of Accounts
Transaction	KDB	Exch. Rate Diff. using Exch. Rate Key

Account assignment

Exchange rate difference key	Expense account	E/R gains acct	Rolling Val...	Rolling Val...
	72040000	72540000		

Figure 9.81 Accounts for Automatic Postings of Foreign Currency Revaluation

vi.   To view the associated posting keys, click on 'Posting Key'; the standard keys are, 40 for debit and 50 for credit; and, do not change these default keys.

vii. Repeat defining the G/L accounts for the other procedures (or transactions) as well, and 'Save' the settings when completed.

Let us, now, look at activating the additional field for foreign currency valuation.

9.5.2.2.7   *Activate Additional Fields for Foreign Currency Valuation*

Using this configuration step, you can deactivate some of the existing account assignment fields or activate additional account assignment fields that you want the system to include into the foreign currency valuation. The additional fields that you activate will be included, in all the advanced closing activities and will also be posted to. In the case of deactivation, you cannot deactivate all the active fields as some of them are needed for internal valuation.

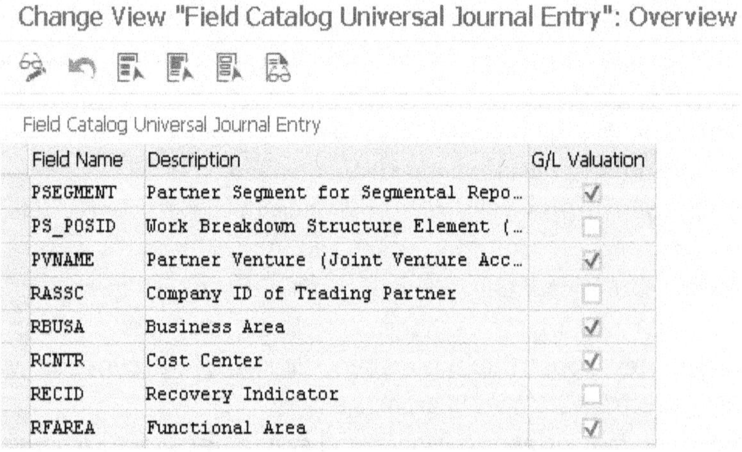

Change View "Field Catalog Universal Journal Entry": Overview

🔍 ↺ 🖹 🖹 🖹 🖳

Field Catalog Universal Journal Entry

Field Name	Description	G/L Valuation
PSEGMENT	Partner Segment for Segmental Repo…	✓
PS_POSID	Work Breakdown Structure Element (…	☐
PVNAME	Partner Venture (Joint Venture Acc…	✓
RASSC	Company ID of Trading Partner	☐
RBUSA	Business Area	✓
RCNTR	Cost Center	✓
RECID	Recovery Indicator	☐
RFAREA	Functional Area	✓

Figure 9.82 Activating Additional Fields for Foreign Currency Valuation

Use the menu path SAP Customizing Implementation Guide > Financial Accounting > General Ledger Accounting > Periodic Processing > Valuate > Foreign Currency Valuation > Activate Additional Fields for Foreign Currency Valuation. You may also use Transaction FINS_FCT. On the ensuing screen, change 'Display' to 'Change' and select 'Functional Area' and 'Cost Center' as additional account assignments for BESTM (Figure 9.82).

> **i** A high number of activated fields may negatively impact the speed of (currency valuation) processes in the system.

The next step is to define G/L accounts for currency translation.

9.5.2.2.8   Define Account Determination for Currency Translation

Per financial statement version and valuation area, you can define appropriate account determination for currency translation for the various financial statement items, in this step.

Use the menu path SAP Customizing Implementation Guide > Financial Accounting > General Ledger Accounting > Periodic Processing > Valuate > Foreign Currency Valuation > Define Account Determination for Currency Translation.

Enter the chart of accounts, valuation area and financial statement version on the pop-up screen, when you enter the Transaction. On continuing, on the next screen, click on 'New Entries' and maintain the financial statement item, (say, 09) in 'FS item field, enter the exchange rate type (say, M) for debit/credit exchange rate type, enter the B/S adjustment account and G/L accounts for value loss and value gain in the appropriate fields, and 'Save' the details.

With this, we have completed configuring the system for foreign currency valuation. Let us, now, move on to discuss the settings required for reclassification of GR/IR accounts.

9.5.2.3   Reclassify

The system makes use of the GR / IR clearing account to make required postings, whenever you receive goods that are yet to be invoiced or invoices for goods that are yet to be delivered. The system needs G/L account numbers for such adjustments and the target accounts. The system makes use of the 'Reclassify' program in analysing the GR/IR clearing account and thereby making the required adjustments, by posting any outstanding amounts to an adjustment account. In the process, the system creates an offsetting entry to the account for (a) goods received but not invoiced (adjustment account) or (b) goods invoiced but not delivered (target account).

Let us define the adjustment accounts for GR/IR clearing for BESTM company codes.

9.5.2.3.1   Define Adjustment Accounts for GR/IR Clearing

Using this activity, you can define the G/L account numbers of the adjustment and target accounts for the automatic postings for the GR/IR clearing account.

i.   Use the menu path SAP Customizing Implementation Guide > Financial Accounting > General Ledger Accounting > Periodic Processing > Reclassify > Define Adjustment Accounts for GR/IR Clearing or Transaction OBYP.

ii.   On the ensuing screen, you will see the two procedures, BNG and GNB, for which you need to maintain the required accounts (Figure 9.83).

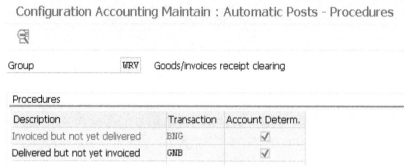

Figure 9.83 Automatic Posting Procedures for GR/IR

iii. Double-click on a procedure, enter the chart of accounts and maintain the required 'Adjustment Account' and 'Targ.acct.' for each of the reconciliation accounts (Figure 9.84).

iv.   Repeat for the other procedure, GNB. You can look at the posting keys, by clicking on 'Posting Key' (do not change the default settings for posting keys).

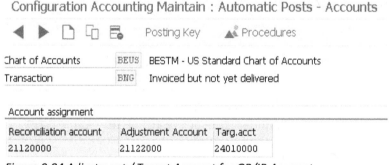

Figure 9.84 Adjustment / Target Account for GR/IR Account

You may also define accounts for subsequent adjustments, if required.

Project Dolphin

BESTM management has indicated to the project team that they want to set up appropriate adjustment accounts to post the results of P&L and B/S adjustments, so as to assign line items to specific account assignment objects like 'Business Area', 'Profit Center' etc. This is to avoid posting the adjustment line items to the original accounts.

9.5.2.3.2   Define Accounts for Subsequent Adjustment

Though setting up of separate adjustment accounts is optional, use this configuration step to define the G/L account numbers to which the system posts the results of P&L and B/S adjustments, if the business wants to set up such separate accounts as in the case of BESTM. Here, you can also maintain G/L accounts for clearing reconciliation postings made in CO, for allocations across business area / functional areas, in the transaction key GAO. Use transaction key GA5, only if you want a user exit for processing the B/S adjustment accounts which are not processed in the standard system.

> **i** An adjustment, retroactively, assigns line items to particular account assignment objects (business areas, cost center, profit center, etc). The system, automatically, generates clearing entries and adjustment postings while assigning these line items. If you do not set up an adjustment account, the system posts the items to the original account. To separate the adjustment postings from other postings, you should create separate adjustment accounts in this activity and have the system post the items to them.
>
> You have to set up a clearing account for the adjustment process so that the postings made, per business area, do not affect the balances. You also have to set up adjustment accounts for reconciliation accounts, tax accounts and any other accounts which cannot be directly posted to. Note that you cannot make these adjustment accounts as relevant to tax; do not enter a 'Tax category' in the G/L account master record for these accounts, and you should select the 'Posting without tax allowed' check-box for all these accounts.

To configure the G/L accounts for subsequent adjustment:

i.   Use the menu path SAP Customizing Implementation Guide > Financial Accounting > General Ledger Accounting > Periodic Processing > Reclassify > Define Adjustment Accounts for GR/IR Clearing or Transaction OBXM.

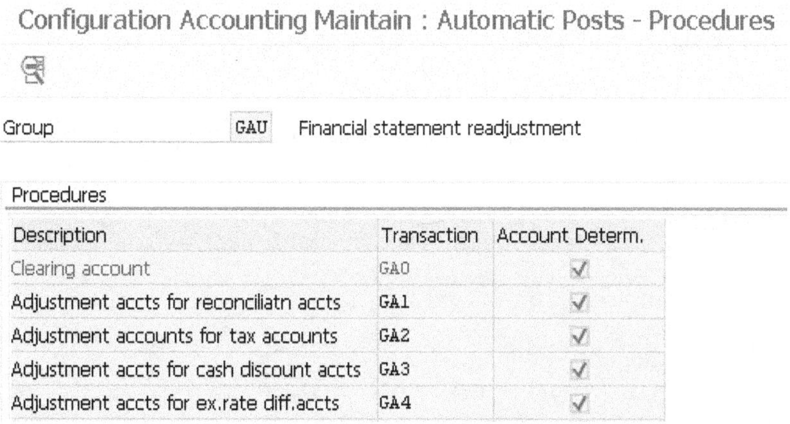

Configuration Accounting Maintain : Automatic Posts - Procedures

Group   GAU   Financial statement readjustment

Procedures

Description	Transaction	Account Determ.
Clearing account	GA0	✓
Adjustment accts for reconciliatn accts	GA1	✓
Adjustment accounts for tax accounts	GA2	✓
Adjustment accts for cash discount accts	GA3	✓
Adjustment accts for ex.rate diff.accts	GA4	✓

Figure 9.85 Procedures for defining G/L Accounts for Subsequent Adjustments

ii.   On the resulting screen, you will see all the procedures (GA0 to GA5) relating to financial statement readjustments (Figure 9.85)

iii.   Double-click on each of the procedures, and define the appropriate G/L accounts on the next screen to define the accounts for subsequent adjustments.

With this, we are, now, ready to discuss the settings that are required for transferring / sorting receivables and payables in the system, as a part of closing process.

Project Dolphin

In closing, for regrouping receivables and payables, BESM wants the configuration team to stick to the SAP's standard sort method. The team has been tasked to assign the suitable G/L accounts, as adjustment accounts, for this default sort method.

There are a couple of configuration steps in making the system ready to transfer / sort receivables and payables during closing. The first activity is to define a sort method and then assigning suitable adjustment accounts for regrouping.

9.5.2.3.3   Define Sort Method and Adjustment Accts for Regrouping Receivables/Payables

To define the sort method and adjustment accounts for regrouping receivables and payables:

i.   Use the menu path SAP Customizing Implementation Guide > Financial Accounting > General Ledger Accounting > Periodic Processing > Reclassify > Transfer and Sort Receivables and Payables > Define Sort Method and Adjustment Accts for Regrouping Receivables/Payables or Transaction OBBU.

ii.   On the resulting screen (Figure 9.86), you will see the default sort method (named as SAP).

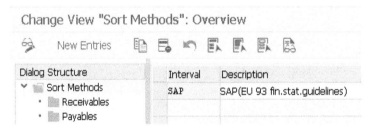

Figure 9.86 Overview Screen for Sort Methods and their Associated Settings

iii.   Select that row, and double-click on 'Receivables' on the left-hand side 'Dialog Structure', and make the required classifications (like, less than 1year, more than 1 year etc) on the next screen (Figure 9.87).

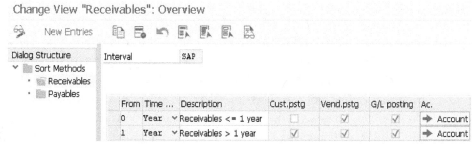

Figure 9.87 Classification Intervals for Sorting

iv.   Click on 'Account' on a row, and maintain the required G/L accounts, for adjustment and target for each of the reconciliation accounts on the next screen (Figure 9.88).

Figure 9.88 Adjustment Accounts for Receivables Regrouping

v.   Repeat assigning the accounts for other intervals say, 'Receivables > 1 year'.

vi.   Repeat the steps for 'Payables' and 'Save' the configuration settings.

The next step is to define the G/L accounts for the adjustment postings for sorting receivables / payables according to their maturity (remaining term).

9.5.2.3.4 Define Adjustment Accounts for Receivables/Payables by Maturity

Here, you define the G/L account numbers required for the adjustment postings that sort the receivables / payables according to their maturity (remaining term). The system makes postings to these accounts to sort the open items which is necessary so that receivables / payables can be displayed according to the legal requirements for creating balance sheets. The customers (with a credit balance) and vendors (with a debit balance) are included in the account determination for sorting.

For setting up the required G/L accounts:

i. Use the menu path SAP Customizing Implementation Guide > Financial Accounting > General Ledger Accounting > Periodic Processing > Reclassify > Transfer and Sort Receivables and Payables > Define Adjustment Accounts for Receivables/Payables by Maturity, for each of the charts of accounts. You may also use Transaction OBBV.

ii. On the resulting screen, you will see the various procedures that group the receivables and payables like, V01 – Receivables > 1 year, V04 – Liabilities >5 years and so on. For each of the procedures, per chart of accounts, maintain the required G/L accounts (adjustment and target) on the next screen (Figure 9.89).

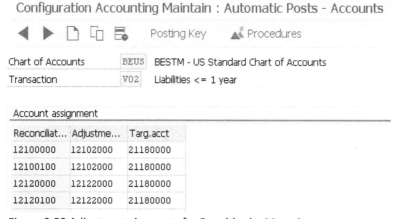

Figure 9.89 Adjustment Accounts for Payables by Maturity

Similar to the above, you can define the adjustment accounts, for changed reconciliation accounts as well as for investment accounts, as detailed below in Table 9.6:

IMG Activity	IMG Menu Path	Transaction
Define Adjustment Accounts for Changed Reconciliation Accounts	SAP Customizing Implementation Guide > Financial Accounting > General Ledger Accounting > Periodic Processing > Reclassify > Transfer and Sort Receivables and Payables > Define Adjustment Accounts for Changed Reconciliation Accounts	OBBW
Define Adjustment Accounts for Investments	SAP Customizing Implementation Guide > Financial Accounting > General Ledger Accounting > Periodic Processing > Reclassify > Transfer and Sort Receivables and Payables > Define Adjustment Accounts for Investments	OBBX

Table 9:6 Adjustment Accounts for Changed Reconciliation Accounts and Investment Accounts

This completes our discussion on configuring reclassification. Let us, now, move on to discuss allocation in SAP G/L Accounting.

9.5.2.4 Allocation

You can use *'allocation'* (by 'assessment' or 'distribution' through the allocation cycle function), to allocate both plan and actual data. The *allocation rules* help you to determine how amounts and quantities should be allocated from the sender (object) to the receiver (object). Just by using the default fields and settings, you can use the allocation functionality, during closing, for the required assessments and distributions for various characteristics including segment and profit center.

The configuration steps include:

- Define Field Usage for Distribution
- Define Field Usage for Assessment
- Define Account Determination for Allocation

Let us start with the first activity of defining field usage for distribution.

9.5.2.4.1 *Define Field Usage for Distribution*

Here, you can define which fields of ACDOCA table are used as sender or receiver fields for the distribution, besides defining whether single values, intervals of values, or sets can be entered in the relevant field. When you are in the Transaction, (a) select a field for processing, (b) specify if and where this field should appear in the distribution definition, (c) specify on what level (cycle, sender tracing factor, sender, receiver, receiver tracing factor) this field should be active and (d) how values are to be entered for this field.

> **i** You should always enter the company code as a single value, at the cycle level, so that the allocation is processed without any problems. Do not try a cross-company code distribution which is not possible, as the allocation must always take place within a company code.

    i.   Use the menu path SAP Customizing Implementation Guide > Financial Accounting > General Ledger Accounting > Periodic Processing > Allocate > Define Field Usage for Distribution. You may also use Transaction GLGCA6.

   ii.   On the resulting screen, you will see a listing of table fields from ACDOCA for 'Distribution' as the 'Allocation Type' for both actual and plan under 'Actual/Plan'. These are all the standard fields that are used for distribution. If required, you may add a new field by clicking on 'New Entries'.

  iii.   You can, then, double-click on any row (say, 'Company Code') and maintain the required field usage settings for that field, on the next screen (Figure 9.90):

        - To display the table field selected, you need to select the 'Display' check-box.

- Used only used in FI-SL allocation, do not select 'Transfer' check-box. The system, normally, carries out summarization automatically, via a field that is not called in the segment. When selected, the sender values (of this field) are always received in the receiver values, even if this field is not defined in the segment definition.
- Under 'Field usage in allocation', enter a '+' in 'Control' field indicating that you should always make an entry for this field.
- Select 'Single value' check-box for field like 'Company Code'.
- When the field 'Control' is blank for 'Sender', then the system does not allow you to process the field during allocation when defining the sender.

iv. Repeat the steps for other table fields as well, and also for both plan and actual processing.

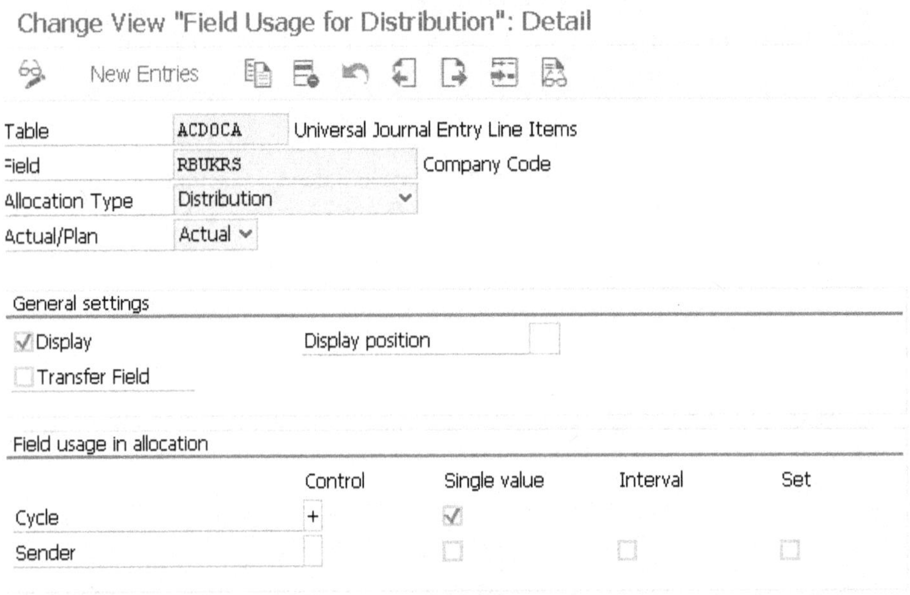

Change View "Field Usage for Distribution": Detail

   New Entries

Table	ACDOCA	Universal Journal Entry Line Items
Field	RBUKRS	Company Code
Allocation Type	Distribution	
Actual/Plan	Actual	

General settings

☑ Display   Display position
☐ Transfer Field

Field usage in allocation

	Control	Single value	Interval	Set
Cycle	+	☑		
Sender		☐	☐	☐

Figure 9.90 Defining Field Usage for Distribution

Similar to the field usage definition for distribution, you need to make the settings for assessment. Let us do that as described below.

9.5.2.4.2 Define Field Usage for Assessment

Similar to the field usage definition for distribution, use this configuration step to define, amongst other things, which table fields are used as sender or receiver fields for the assessment. Also define whether single values, intervals of values, or sets can be entered in the relevant field. As in the previous case, you need to enter the 'Company Code' as a single value at the cycle level, as cross-company code assessment is not possible. The allocation always takes place within a company code.

Use the menu path: SAP Customizing Implementation Guide > Financial Accounting > General Ledger Accounting > Periodic Processing > Allocate > Define Field Usage for Assessment. You may also use Transaction GLGCA1. Maintain the field usage for the required table fields of ACDOCA as indicated, for example, 'Account Number'. As you can see from Figure 9.91, for the 'Sender' and 'Receiver tracing factor', you can set single or multiple values or in a 'set'. The configuration is such that you should always make an entry in this table field as a 'Sender'. Make all the required settings for both actual and plan for assessment as the allocation type.

> **i** Recommended, not to alter the standard settings for the default fields while defining the field usage both for assessment and distribution. Also, recommended, to copy an existing setting when making settings for a new table field.

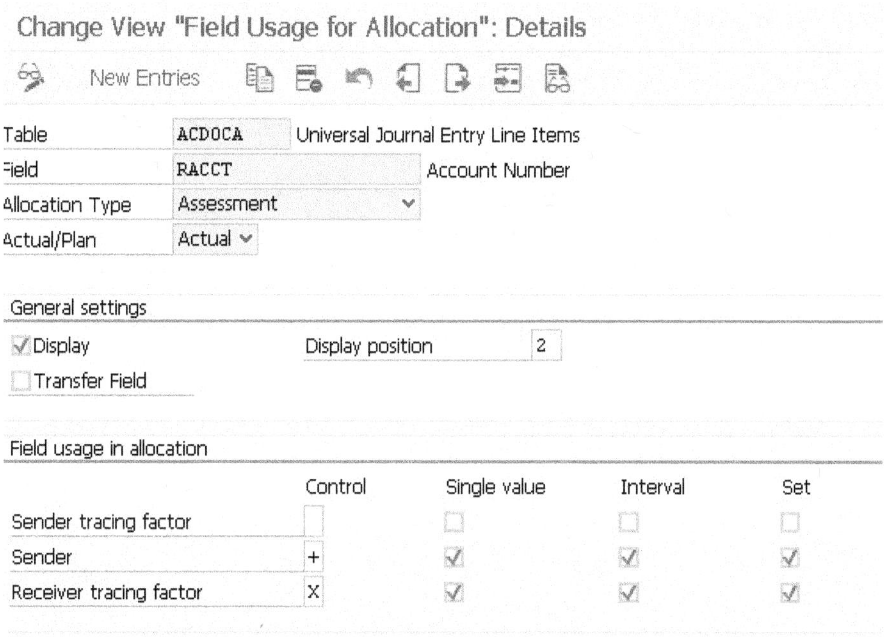

Change View "Field Usage for Allocation": Details

New Entries

Table	ACDOCA	Universal Journal Entry Line Items
Field	RACCT	Account Number
Allocation Type	Assessment	
Actual/Plan	Actual	

General settings

☑ Display   Display position   2

☐ Transfer Field

Field usage in allocation

	Control	Single value	Interval	Set
Sender tracing factor		☐	☐	☐
Sender	+	☑	☑	☑
Receiver tracing factor	X	☑	☑	☑

Figure 9.91 Defining Field Usage for Assessment

The next step is to define the account determination for allocation.

9.5.2.4.3 Define Account Determination for Allocation

Here, you define a clearing account for allocation in SAP G/L Accounting. If more than 1000 items are created during an allocation, the system splits up the FI document with the balance of the document being posted to the clearing account. The settings made here apply only for document splitting during allocation. If you are not using document splitting functionality, you do not need to define this G/L account.

Use the menu path: SAP Customizing Implementation Guide > Financial Accounting > General Ledger Accounting > Periodic Processing > Allocate > Define Account Determination for Allocation. You may also use Transaction OBX2. For the specific chart of accounts, say BEUS, enter the G/L account in 'Account' field for the automatic account determination for the transaction SPL (clearing account for document splitting).

Now that we have made the required settings for allocation as a part of closing operations for SAP G/L Accounting, we need to ensure that the settings are correct. Use the following activity to check the settings.

9.5.2.4.4   Check Settings for Allocation

Use this configuration step and check (and correct, automatically) allocation settings for the summary table of the G/L. During the execution of the program in this Transaction, the system checks whether the settings for field usage, field groups, and data fields are defined correctly.

i.   Use the menu path: SAP Customizing Implementation Guide > Financial Accounting > General Ledger Accounting > Periodic Processing > Allocate > Check Settings for Allocation. You may also use Transaction GCA9.

ii. On the resulting screen, enter the 'Table' name (ACDOCA).

iii. Select 'Assessment' radio-button under 'Allocation Type' and select the 'Record Type' as 'Actual' (Figure 9.92).

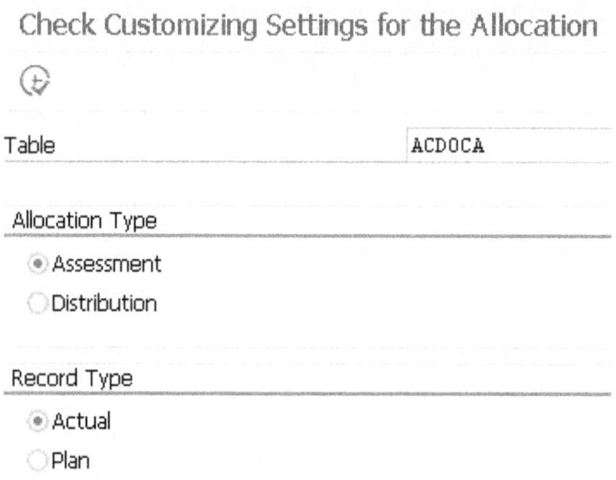

Figure 9.92 Checking Customizing for Allocation

iv. Now, 'Execute' the program. If there are no errors, you will see a message as in Figure 9.93.

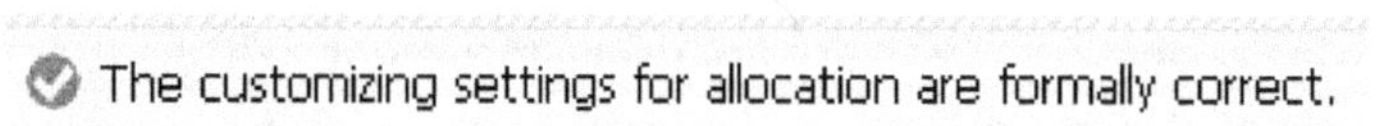

Figure 9.93 Results of Customizing Check for Allocation

v.   If there are errors, you may correct them manually or you may let the system to correct them automatically.

vi.   Now, repeat executing the program for other set of selection: 'Distribution' radio-button under 'Allocation Type' and select the 'Record Type' as 'Plan'

This completes our discussion on allocation.

Let us, now, move on to discuss how to configure the carry forward functionality in the system.

9.5.2.5   Carry Forward

The '*balance carry forward*' or simply the '*carry forward*' (or '*carryforward*') activity involves carrying forward the account balances into the new fiscal year. The balance display of the account shows the amount that has to be carried forward. To carry forward the account balances, you will use two separate programs; for G/L accounts (program SAPFGVTR) and customer / vendor accounts (program SAPF010).

In the case of *G/L accounts*, you have to perform balance carry forward for the new fiscal year at least once; after that, the system automatically updates the balance carried forward whenever postings are made to the old fiscal year.

To perform 'balance carry forward' for all G/L accounts of the specified ledger, you need to follow the SAP Easy Access menu path: SAP Menu > Accounting > Financial Accounting > General Ledger > Periodic Processing > Closing > Carrying Forward > Balance Carryforward; you may also use Transaction FAGLGVTR.

The 'balance carry forward' program creates line items for each G/L account and account assignment. If you perform the balance carry forward very early on in the closing process and then proceed to make a very large number of postings to the previous fiscal year, the system automatically creates a large number of line items to correct the balance carry forward. To reduce the large number of line items in this case, you can perform a 'repeat run' of the balance carry forward program. When you select 'Reset Central Balance Carryfwd' (Figure 9.94), the balance carryforward line items that were already created for the specified fiscal year, are deleted. The intention of this reset is to reduce data volume: the program first deletes all line items that have already been created for the specified fiscal year, and then, the 'balance carry forward' is automatically run again, as an initial run.

When you execute balance carry forward, all currencies of the ledger are automatically carried forward. After balance carry forward, you can display results lists for the B/S accounts and retained earnings accounts for which the balances were carried forward.

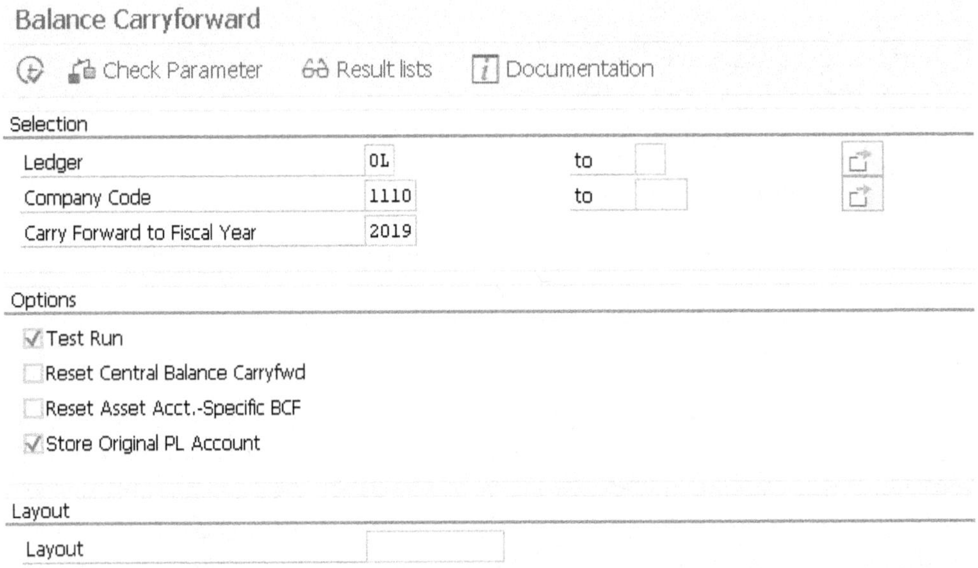

Balance Carryforward

⟳   🔒 Check Parameter   6ð Result lists   ⓘ Documentation

Selection

Ledger	OL	to	↱
Company Code	1110	to	↱
Carry Forward to Fiscal Year	2019		

Options

☑ Test Run
☐ Reset Central Balance Carryfwd
☐ Reset Asset Acct.-Specific BCF
☑ Store Original PL Account

Layout

Layout	

Figure 9.94 G/L Account Balance Carry Forward

> **ⓘ** If, in the new fiscal year, you find that some of the G/L accounts were mistakenly set up as a P&L statement accounts in the previous fiscal year, instead of as a B/S accounts (and/or vice versa), you need to adjust the master data of the affected account records and then repeat the balance carry forward activity.

In case of *customer / vendor accounts*, when the system performs balance carry forward for the G/L accounts of the leading ledger, it automatically performs balance carry forward for these accounts as well. However, you can also perform balance carry forward separately for vendor and customer accounts.

Follow (optional, of course) the SAP Easy Access menu path: SAP Menu > Accounting > Financial Accounting > Accounts Receivable/Accounts Payable > Periodic Processing > Closing > Carrying Forward > Balance Carry forward or you may also use Transaction F.07 (Figure 9.95), to carry forward customer / vendor accounts.

For Special G/L accounts, the SAP Easy Access menu path will be: SAP Menu > Accounting > Financial Accounting > Special Purpose Ledger > Periodic Processing > Balance Carryforward. Or, you may also use Transaction GVTR.

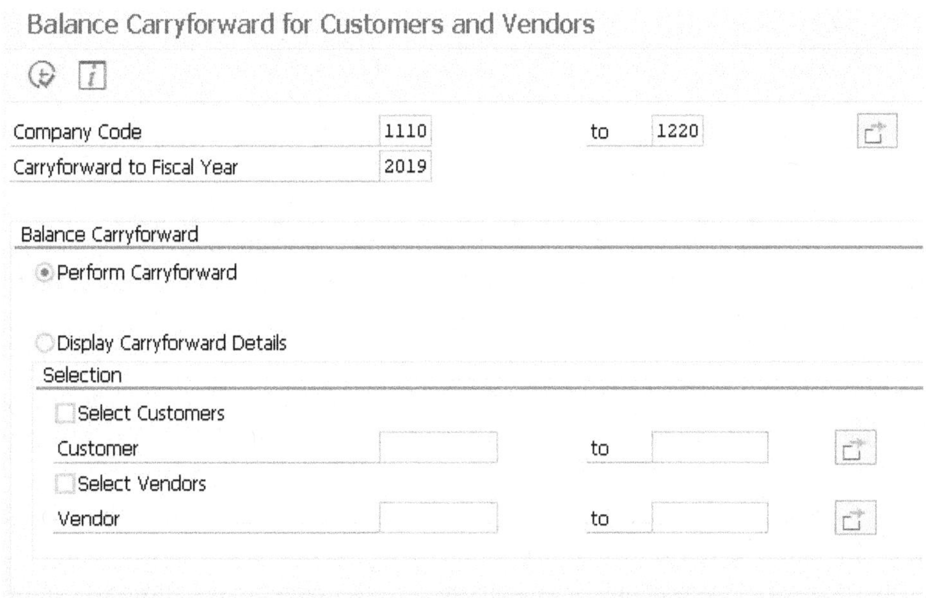

Figure 9.95 Customer / Vendor Account Balance Carry forward

> **i** The system does not perform the balance carry forward automatically, even if you have already made postings to the new fiscal year; you have to perform the balance carry forward program manually.

9.5.2.5.1   Pre-Requisites to Carry Forward B/S Accounts

The following are the pre-requisites for carrying forward the balances of B/S accounts:

- You should have selected the account as the balance sheet (B/S) account in the G/L master record data in the chart of accounts. Refer Section 9.3 for more details G/L account master data.
- For P&L accounts, (a) you have defined the account, in the G/L master record, as a P&L account and also identified that as (i) non-operating expense / income or (ii) primary costs / revenue or (iii) secondary costs, (b) you have specified the retained earnings accounts in Customizing and (c) if you want to perform balance carry forward with account assignments, ensure that you have specified these additional account assignments (Refer Section 9.5.2.5.5 and 9.5.2.5.6). All the required account assignments are selected automatically; you can, of course, add other account assignments.

9.5.2.5.2   Pre-Requisites to Carry Forward Customer / Vendor Accounts

There are no prerequisites for carrying forward the balances for customer and vendor accounts.

9.5.2.5.3   Carry Forward Process

The process of carry forward, in the system, can be summarised as under:

1) The balances on the B/S accounts are carried forward to the same accounts, and the system applies all the configured account assignments.

2) The P&L accounts are carried forward to one or more retained earnings accounts, and the system applies the additional account assignments, if any, defined in Customizing. With the standard settings, balances are carried forward in summarized form to the relevant retained earnings accounts. When balance carry forward is performed, the balance of the profit and loss account is set to 0.

3) The balances on the customer / vendor accounts are carried forward to the same accounts. With the standard settings, the system applies all account assignments for this as well.

4) In the case of Special Purpose Ledgers, if you want to carry forward additional account assignments such as profit centers or functional areas to the new fiscal year, or if you want to summarize account data using additional account assignments, you must assign field movements for balance sheet accounts and P&L accounts to your ledger using the menu path: SAP Customizing Implementation Guide > Financial Accounting > Special Purpose Ledger > Periodic Processing > Balance Carryforward > Assign Field Movements or Transaction GCS5. If you want to use a field movement for (a) B/S accounts, the field movement should contain the dimension 'Account', and (b) P&L accounts, the field movement should not contain the dimension 'Account' unless you want to change the account with the help of a user exit.

The following are the configuration settings that you need to make for using carry forward functionality:

- Define Retained Earnings Account
- FIORI: Define number range used exclusively for preview documents in BCF
- Enter Detail Specifications for Balance Sheet Accounts
- Enter Detail Specifications for P&L Accounts

Project Dolphin

The BESTM management has indicated that they want additional account assignments, in the case of B/S accounts, on 'Order Number' and 'Account Type' besides the standard account assignments in the system. In the case of P&L accounts, BESTM does not want to have any additional account assignments than that of the standard settings.

Let's start with the definition of retaining earnings account.

9.5.2.5.4   Define Retained Earnings Account

You will assign a retained earnings account by specifying a 'P&L statement account type' in the chart of accounts area of each P&L account. At the end of a fiscal year, the system carries forward the balance of the P&L account to the retained earnings account. You can define one or more P&L statement account types per chart of accounts and assign them to retained earnings accounts

> **i** One retained earnings account would, normally, be sufficient to meet your needs, and it is a common practice to define only one retained earnings account. However, by using the P&L statement account type, you can use more than one retained earnings account: this could be useful for international corporations that have to meet various requirements when producing their P&L statement.

Define the retained earnings account using the menu path: SAP Customizing Implementation Guide > Financial Accounting > General Ledger Accounting > Periodic Processing > Carry Forward > Define Retained Earnings Account (or Transaction OB53). We have already defined this, in Section 9.3.1.5 of this Chapter, as a part of G/L account master data preparations, and have assigned the G/L account 33000000 as the retained earnings account.

Let us move on to define the details specifications for B/S accounts.

9.5.2.5.5   Enter Detail Specifications for Balance Sheet Accounts

During balance carry forward (BCF) in the standard system, the balances on B/S accounts along with the default account assignments are forwarded to the same accounts. If you want to carry forward balances with more or a lesser number of account assignments, you need to select or deactivate these account assignments in this configuration activity.

> **i** Note that some account assignments will be always active in the standard SAP system and you will not be able to deactivate them. These assignments are displayed only for information.

Use the menu path: SAP Customizing Implementation Guide > Financial Accounting > General Ledger Accounting > Periodic Processing > Carry Forward > Enter Detail Specifications for Balance Sheet Account (or Transaction FINS_FCT). On the resulting screen (Figure 9.96), you can select or deselect the account assignments as you may want, to suit your closing and reporting. Since BESTM (Project Dolphin) wants to have two more account assignments, on AUFNR (Order Number) and KOART (Account Type), you need to select these two check-boxes and 'Save' the details.

Change View "Field Catalog Universal Journal Entry": Overview

Field Catalog Universal Journal Entry

Field Name	Description	Balance Carry Forward Balance Sheet
ANLGR	Group Asset	☑
ANLGR2	Subnumber of Group Asset	☑
ANLN1	Main Asset Number	☑
ANLN2	Asset Subnumber	☑
AUFNR	Order Number	☑
AWSYS	Logical system of source document	☑
AWTYP	Reference procedure	☐
BLART	Document type	☐

Figure 9.96 Account Assignments for Carry forward in B/S Accounts

We may, now, look at the detail specifications for profit and loss accounts in the next Section.

9.5.2.5.6   Enter Detail Specifications for P&L Accounts

With the standard settings for BCF, P&L statement accounts are carried forward to the retained earnings account (defined already) without any further account assignments. However, if you want to perform the carry forward with some account assignments, you can complete the additional account assignments in this configuration activity.

Use the menu path: SAP Customizing Implementation Guide > Financial Accounting > General Ledger Accounting > Periodic Processing > Carry Forward > Enter Detail Specifications for P&L Accounts (or Transaction FINS_FCT). On the resulting screen (Figure 9.97), select the account assignments as you may want, to suit your closing and reporting. As BESTM does not want to have any additional account assignments for P&L accounts, we are not defining any.

Display View "Field Catalog Universal Journal Entry": Overview

Field Catalog Universal Journal Entry

Field Name	Description	Balance Carry Forward Profit & Loss
ACRITMTYPE	Type of the Item of the Accrual Su…	☐
ACROBJTYPE	Type of the Accrual Object	☐
ACROBJ_ID	Identifier of the Accrual Object	☐
ACRSOBJ_ID	Identifier of the Accrual Subobject	☐
AUFNR	Order Number	☐
AWSYS	Logical system of source document	☐

Figure 9.97 Account Assignments for Carry forward in P&L Accounts

The next step is to define the number ranges, for BCF documents for preview in SAP FIORI.

9.5.2.5.7   FIORI: Define number range used exclusively for preview documents in BCF

Use the menu path: SAP Customizing Implementation Guide > Financial Accounting > General Ledger Accounting > Periodic Processing > Carry Forward > FIORI: Define number range used exclusively for preview documents in BCF (or Transaction SNRO_BCF). On the resulting screen, use the 'Change Interval' button and assign a suitable number range (Figure 9.98).

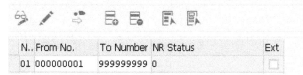

Edit Intervals: BCF preview Docs, Object FGLPRE

N..	From No.	To Number	NR Status		Ext
01	000000001	999999999	0		☐

Figure 9.98 Number Range for BCF Preview Documents (FIORI)

This completes our discussion on (balance) carry forward, and also the closing operations for SAP G/L Accounting.

Let us now, look at the preparation required for a productive start.

9.6   Preparation for Productive Start

Your preparation for productive start of SAP G/L Accounting, depends on whether you are about to 'go-live' on a new system implementation or migrating from classic G/L Accounting to (new) SAP G/L Accounting.

9.6.1   New SAP Implementation

In the case of a new implementation, the preparation for a productive start is relatively simple as there is no complex G/L migration activity. In a new implementation, you will essentially perform the following three steps, before going 'live':

1) Do a data transfer, if required. You may need to do this if you have your G/L accounts in a non-SAP system and want to transfer them to the new SAP installation. Use the menu path: SAP Customizing Implementation Guide > Financial Accounting > General Ledger Accounting > Preparation for Productive Start > New Installation > Data Transfer Workbench. You may also use Transaction SXDA.

> ℹ️ SXDA, is central Transaction for automatic transfer of data from a legacy system. The data transfer workbench provides the tools required for the initial and subsequent data transfer, if any. You will be able to transfer data following a step-by-step process, which also provides you with a description of object-specific features that you need take into account during the transfer process.

2) During the implementation process, you would have created several G/L test data (master as well as transaction) that need to be deleted to remove all the unwanted junk from the system. You may use Table 9.7, as a guidance for deleting the G/L test data.

To Remove	SAP Menu Path	Transaction	Remarks
G/L Master Data (Test)	SAP Customizing Implementation Guide > Financial Accounting > General Ledger Accounting > Preparation for Productive Start > New Installation > Delete Test Data > Delete Master Data > Delete G/L Account.	OBR2	Deletes only master records of accounts that do not contain any transaction data. You can delete the G/L account master records in company code area or chart of accounts area or both. You cannot use this Transaction to delete the chart of accounts section of a G/L account, if the account is also a primary cost element in CO; delete cost elements using program RKSCUS03. You can also use this deletion program to delete customers / vendors.
Chart of Accounts	SAP Customizing Implementation Guide > Financial Accounting > General Ledger Accounting > Preparation for Productive Start > New Installation > Delete Test Data > Delete Master Data > Delete Chart of Accounts.	OBY8	Deletes a chart of accounts with all accounts and definitions made for the chart of accounts. However, if SAP SD, CO, FI-AA etc., refer to the chart of accounts, then it will not be deleted.
G/L Transaction (Test)	SAP Customizing Implementation Guide > Financial Accounting > General Ledger Accounting > Preparation for Productive Start > New Installation > Delete Test Data >	OBR1	Also known as 'resetting' of transaction data in company code, this deletes the transaction data, for individual company codes. Recommended to delete the data of G/L Accounting together with the data of FI-AA to avoid inconsistencies.

	Delete Transaction Data > Delete Company Code Data.	You require authorization F_002 for object S_PROGRAM to use this deletion program (SAPF020). You can also select not to reset the planning data and credit limit. Use this only in the test phase.

Table 9:7 Transaction / Menu Path to delete G/L Test Data

3) After you have deleted all the test data, and after making sure that you have the required data in the system, you can, then, flag the company codes as 'productive'. Use the menu path: SAP Customizing Implementation Guide > Financial Accounting > General Ledger Accounting > Preparation for Productive Start > New Installation > Set Company Code to Productive. Upon executing the Transaction, select the 'Productive' check-box for all the company codes that you want to be productive.

> **i** Once you set a company code as 'Productive', then the system prevents data within the company code from being deleted by the programs for deleting test data.

This completes our discussion of preparation for production in new SAP implementations.

9.6.2 Existing SAP Implementation

In the case of migration of classic G/L Accounting from existing non-HANA SAP system to SAP S/4HANA, follow the steps in the 'Conversion of Accounting to SAP S/4HANA' configuration task.

With this we are now ready to discuss the final topic in SAP G/L Accounting, namely the information system.

9.7 Information System

Use the following configuration steps to specify the parameters or settings, for different reports under SAP G/L Accounting.

9.7.1 Define Balance Display

Here, in this step, you specify which characteristics are available as selection characteristics, for your ledgers, when displaying balances of G/L accounts. You can specify up to five characteristics, as interactive characteristics, per ledger. Use the menu path: SAP Customizing Implementation Guide > Financial Accounting > General Ledger Accounting > Information System > Define Balance Display. On the resulting screen, click on 'New Entries' and maintain the report-selection characteristics ('Characteristic 1' to 'Characteristic 5') for the various ledgers like 0L, BU etc (Figure 9.99).

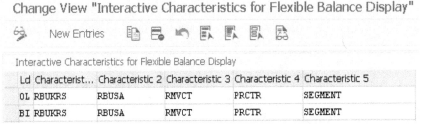

Figure 9.99 Interactive Characteristics for Flexible Balance Display

9.7.2   Define Offsetting Account Determination Type

Using this activity, you define how the system calculates the offsetting account in all applications. This activity is a pre-requisite for the configuration step 'Fill the Offsetting Account in FI Documents' and you have to carry out this activity before you perform any migration activities that affect the offsetting account.

> **i**   During data migration, you transfer FI documents to SAP G/L Accounting in SAP S/4HANA. As part of this process you use this 'Fill the Offsetting Account in FI Documents' Customizing activity to fill the offsetting account in FI documents. This step on HANA-Upgrade fills the new offsetting account fields in the FI line items. This report fills, offsetting Account Number (Field GKONT), offsetting Account Type (Field GKART) and G/L Account of Offsetting Acct in G/L Accounting (Field GHKON) in tables BSEG and BSEG_ADD. You need to execute this step in all clients, including clients that have no transactional data, so that the migration program can set the status of this client to 'Finished.'

Use the menu path: SAP Customizing Implementation Guide > Financial Accounting > General Ledger Accounting > Information System > Define Offsetting Account Determination Type. On the resulting screen, go to 'Edit' and choose 'New Entries'. Then select, as in line with the SAP recommendation, 'Always display offsetting account (highest amount all lines)' option for 'Offsetting Acct Determination' and 'Save' the settings (Figure 9.100).

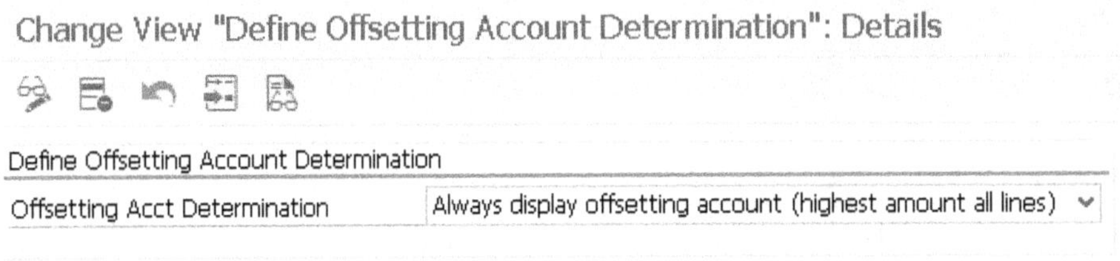

Change View "Define Offsetting Account Determination": Details

Define Offsetting Account Determination

| Offsetting Acct Determination | Always display offsetting account (highest amount all lines) ∨ |

Figure 9.100 Defining Offsetting Account Determination Type

9.7.3 Drilldown Reports (G/L Accounts)

Most of the reports, under 'General Ledger Reports' under the SAP Easy Access menu path: SAP Menu > Accounting > Financial Accounting > General Ledger > Information System > General Ledger Reports, are interactive drilldown reports. The reports are grouped under various categories like financial statement/cash flow, account balances, reports from profit center accounting, reports from segment reporting, line items, document and master data. You can access the reports 'as such' or you can make new/additional settings using the menu path: SAP Customizing Implementation Guide > Financial Accounting > General Ledger Accounting > Information System > Drilldown Reports (G/L Accounts) to create new or enhance the existing reports. While on this, you have to access the appropriate configuration steps to define forms, create reports, define constants, specify global variables, transport reports etc to define the required settings for drilldown reports.

You may also use report writer / report painter functionalities to create reports.

9.7.3.1 Report Writer/Report Painter Reports

You use the '*Report Painter*' to create reports from data in the Special Purpose Ledger (FI-SL) application component and other SAP application components to meet your specific reporting requirements. Through this, you can control the layout of reports directly, define them easily, flexibly, and without using sets. Though similar to the '*Report Writer*', the Report Painter is easier to use. Many of the Report Writer functions are available in the Report Painter, but you do not need to be familiar with Report Writer concepts (such as 'sets') to be able to use the Report Painter. To facilitate report definition, you can use many of the standard reporting objects provided by SAP (such as libraries, row/column models, and standard layouts) in your own specific reports. When you create a Report Painter report, you can use groups (sets), and you can also enter characteristic values directly.

You define Report Painter reports using a graphical report structure, which forms the basis for the report definition. This graphical structure displays the report rows and columns as they will appear in the final report, when the report data is output. When you execute a Report Painter report, the system automatically converts the Report Painter report into Report Writer format. You can also convert a Report Painter report into a Report Writer report so that you can use the complete range of functions provided by the Report Writer. For this, you need to follow the procedure for creating a new Report Writer report, using the Report Painter report as a basis. The Report Painter report is copied and made available as a Report Writer report; the system generates the required sets automatically.

Besides the Report Painter, you can use the '*Report Writer*' to define reports. As in the case of the Report Painter, you can use the Report Writer to create reports from data in the Special Purpose Ledger (FI-SL) application component and other SAP application components to meet your specific reporting requirements. The Report Writer uses reporting building blocks, such as 'sets', which can be used in any report. Though the Report Writer fulfils a similar function to the Report Painter, it is more complex and requires a certain amount of familiarization. To facilitate report definition, in the Report Writer, besides using the standard reporting objects provided by SAP (such as libraries, row/column models, and standard layouts) in your own specific reports, you can also use the additional functions like sets, key figures and variables.

---

i A '*set*' is a system structure that you can use to link together specific values or ranges of values under a name. These values exist within one characteristic of a coding block. A '*characteristic*' is a single field or column of a database table; the 'Account', 'Cost Center', 'Business Area' etc., are all examples of characteristics. Within these characteristics, you can store specific characteristic 'values' under a set name.

Since the Report Writer report definition is based on sets, the look of the report is determined by the set construction. There are a number of ways you can use these sets in the rows, columns and general selection data. Using sets, you define which data is used in your report, and how the data appears in report rows and columns.

As the Report Writer is a multidimensional reporting tool, when you use the Report Writer, you can easily re-arrange the characteristics within a report. For example, the characteristics Cost Center and Account can make up the rows of a report, with Local and Group Currency becoming the columns of the report. Changing the order of characteristics used in this report involves only a small change in the set used in the report; no need to change the whole report. You can easily report on any combination of characteristics' without having to maintain complicated user tables in the background.

Use the menu path SAP Customizing Implementation Guide > Financial Accounting > General Ledger Accounting > Information System > Report Writer/Report Painter Reports, to make the required configuration settings for facilitating defining of reports using the Report Painter / Report Writer.

Once you have completed the configuration settings for G/L information system, you can access the various reports under the SAP Menu in SAP Easy Access. SAP provides you with a host of standard reports, that you can access using the SAP Easy Access menu path: SAP Menu > Accounting > Financial Accounting > General Ledger > Information System > General Ledger Reports.

This completes our discussion on G/L information system, and thereby completing the discussion on SAP G/L Accounting.

9.8 Conclusion

Here, in this Chapter, we started our discussion with the General Ledger (G/L). You understood that G/L is the backbone of any accounting system holding the financial data of an organization. You, then, understood what is SAP G/L Accounting, its purpose and functions. You also understood, in detail, about the various features and functionalities (like extensibility, ledger concept, document splitting, parallel accounting, segment reporting etc) of SAP G/L Accounting. You, also, learned about the pre-requisites for configuring SAP G/L Accounting, to meet your exact business needs.

You, then, moved on to learn G/L account master data: the preparations that you need to create the master data, how to create, and the options you have in creating them. While looking at the preparations, you learned about revising / editing the chart of accounts, assigning company codes to chart of accounts, creating account groups and so on. You, also, learned to create sample accounts that would enable creation of G/L account master records quickly. In G/L account master records, you learned about creating the records in company code area, chart of accounts area, and also in both the areas in a single step. You learned to create the G/L accounts using different methods including the reference method. You saw how to create / edit the master records either individually or collectively for several accounts. You, then, learned about the financial statement structures, with the definition and assignment of financial statement versions.

Later, you moved on to learn about the configuration settings required to set up various business transactions including document splitting, cross-company code transactions, open item clearing, bank interest calculation and adjustment posting including reversals. You learned how to use the 'Document Splitting Wizard' to configure document splitting functionality in the system. While discussing the open item clearing, you learned that an 'open item' is an uncleared transaction that can be cleared and closed by posting an offsetting amount to that account; you learned to define the clearing rules, accounts for exchange rate differences, automatic clearing settings, tolerance groups for G/L accounts etc. In bank account interest calculation, you learned that you can use the functionality, in SAP FI, to calculate interest on the balance of the G/L accounts that are managed on open item basis. During the configuration of bank interest calculation, you came across with the fields that are relevant for this interest calculation; you learned about interest indicator (that controls interest calculation), interest calculation period and interest rate definition; you, also, learned about the settings required for interest calculation and posting. While discussing adjustment postings/reversal, you learned that SAP allows you to reverse a document that was entered incorrectly; understood the difference between a regular reversal and a negative posting (also known as 'true reversal'): you learned that in the case of a negative posting, the system reduces the transaction figures in customer, vendor and G/L Accounts, thereby keeping the transaction figures (after the reversal) unchanged at the original status, as if you had not posted the reversed document and its subsequent reversal.

In periodic processing, you were introduced to the integrated business planning using SAP BPC for SAP S/4HANA. You, in closing operations, learned about the intercompany reconciliation and the settings required to set that up for reconciliation of group receivables/payables (cross-system). You, then, learned that to complete creation of financial statements, you need to perform foreign currency valuation; in the process, you learned about valuation methods, valuation areas and the associated settings including how to activate delta logic, besides making the settings for automatic posting of foreign currency valuation. You, further, learned that the system makes use of the 'reclassify' program, in closing operations, in analysing the GR/IR clearing account and thereby making the required adjustments. In 'allocation', you understood that the allocation rules help you to determine how amounts and quantities should be allocated from the sender (object) to the receiver (object); you, then, made the required configuration settings to make use of allocation in closing operations in SAP G/L Accounting. Finally, in closing operations, you learned about the balance carry forward functionality which involves carrying forward the account balances into the new fiscal year; you learned that to carry forward the account balances, you will use two separate programs: for G/L accounts, you will use program SAPFGVTR and for the customer / vendor accounts, you will use the program SAPF010.

You, then, saw what needs to be done to prepare the system to become 'productive' with SAP G/L Accounting; you saw, in detail, the settings required in new SAP implementations as well as existing SAP installations from which you will migrate to new SAP S/4HANA system.

Finally, in information system, you learned about the settings that you can make to enhance the existing reports (both conventional as well as drilldown reports), besides creating your own reports. You also learned about the Report Painter / Report Writer reports.

***

In this book:

You learned about SAP HANA, SAP S/4HANA and SAP S/4HANA Finance, before actually learning configuring SAP Financial Accounting. While at it, you understood the fundamentals of SAP HANA, its evolution from SAP ERP to the current SAP HANA 2.0. You also understood the HANA architecture and how it helps in processing large volume of data in-memory. You, then, understood the key benefits of SAP S/4HANA and SAP S/4HANA Finance, besides looking at the various options to deploy: on-premise and in-cloud. You, also, understood the capabilities of SAP S/4HANA Finance.

You, then, moved on to the case studies which formed the basis for the various configuration requirements in SAP Financial Accounting. You got an idea of the business requirements that you would be configuring, in the subsequent Chapters, for setting up the system for SAP FI for the different companies covered in the two case studies.

You learned about the various organizational units (forming the enterprise structure) that you would need to create in the SAP system, to configure SAP FI and, to some extent, SAP CO; you understood the organizational units that need to be mandatorily defined and what could be optional to define. You, also, learned about defining the important organizational units like, company, company code, credit control area, business area, FM (financial management) area, segment, controlling area and profit center. You learned about assigning the various organizational units among themselves, to bring out the functional relationship that will enable process and data flow in SAP.

You learned about SAP FI global settings, in detail. You learned about fields and field status variants. You learned about ledgers: the ledger types including the leading ledgers, non-leading ledgers, standard and extension ledgers. You learned about the settings that you need to make for ledgers and currency. You also learned about the universal journal. You, then, learned about fiscal year, posting periods, special periods, fiscal year variants, posting period variants, and how to open / close periods for posting. You learned how to set up the system for parallel accounting. You, also, learned about SAP FI's integration with Controlling. You, then, learned about documents, in detail including document types, number ranges, rules for changing documents, tolerance groups, summarization, sample & recurring documents, document parking and archiving. You also learned the details of inflation accounting and when you should use inflation accounting. You learned about the correspondence functionality in SAP, and how to tailor that to suit your business requirements. You, also, learned how to set up the system for handling taxes including extended withholding tax.

In SAP G/L Accounting, you learned about its features and functions, master data, business transactions etc. You understood how to enable document splitting, cross-company code transactions, open item clearing, balance interest calculation etc. You, also, understood the various configuration that you need to make towards periodic processing in SAP G/L Accounting. You understood how to prepare the system for 'going live', besides understanding the SAP G/L information system for your reporting requirements.

Configuring SAP Financial Accounting (SAP S/4HANA Finance) – Vol. II

The Volume II, of this book, covers the rest of the important areas of in SAP Financial Accounting. The coverage includes the following:

- Case Study
- Accounts Receivable and Accounts Payable
- Contract Accounts Receivable and Payable
- Bank Accounting
- Asset Accounting

The detailed coverage will be as under:

About the Author

Narayanan Veeriah is a Chartered Financial Analyst (CFA), a PMP (from Project Management Institute), and IBM Certified Executive Project Management Professional, having more than 35 years of work experience, in finance, project management and information technology (IT), including 20+ years of experience in SAP implementation and consulting. A member of Certified Associate of Indian Institute of Bankers (CAIIB), he brings along with him a strong domain expertise in Banking and Finance with core competencies in retail banking and credit management, along with SAP.

Narayanan has worked with several multi-national clients for consulting, implementing and supporting SAP, across industries including automotive, banking & finance, electronics, manufacturing, multimedia, pharmaceuticals etc. He has worked with several versions of SAP right from SAP R/3 3.1H to the latest SAP S/4HANA, in new implementations, upgrades and support.

Till recently, he was leading SAP practice, for a couple of industry verticals in a leading multinational IT consulting company. He has authored several books on SAP Finance, besides being a regular guest faculty at management institutions for ERP, SAP, banking & finance and project management.

He is currently a freelance SAP consultant.

You can reach him at vdotn@yahoo.com.

Index

List of Figures

List of Tables

Latest Book by the Author

Configuring SAP Asset Accounting
(SAP S/4HANA Finance)
(1st Edition)

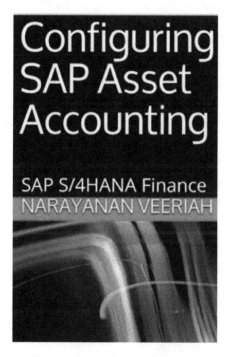

Configuring SAP Asset Accounting, based on the latest version of SAP S/4HANA Finance, is a complete guide to comprehend and configure SAP Asset Accounting (FI-AA). This book follows a case-study approach to make your learning easy. Efforts have been taken, throughout the book, to guide you step-by-step in understanding how to configure your SAP system, to meet your exact business needs in FI-AA. Each configuration activity has been discussed with appropriate screen shots and illustrations, to help you 'see' what is being discussed in that activity / step. You will see a lot of context-based additional information across Chapters, for better assimilation of concepts / configuration settings. The entire content of the book has been presented as in SAP Implementation Guide with appropriate menu paths and Transactions.

324 pages, 1st edition 2020
Formats: Kindle & Paperback
ISBN: 979-865383115

https://www.amazon.com/Configuring-SAP-Asset-Accounting-Finance/dp/B08B333BY6/ref=tmm_pap_swatch_0?_encoding=UTF8&qid=&sr=

Latest Book by the Author

Configuring Financial Accounting in SAP ® ERP
(3rd Edition)

This is your comprehensive guide to configuring Financial Accounting in SAP ERP! Brush up on the old standbys—Accounts Payable, Account Receivable, SAP General Ledger, and Asset Accounting—and then dive in to Contract Accounts Receivable and Payable, Consolidation, Lease Accounting, Travel Management, SAP Fiori, and much more. You'll learn to set up your enterprise structure, use maintenance tools, and ensure your implementation works for your unique business.

916 pages, 3rd, updated edition 2018
E-book formats: EPUB, MOBI, PDF, online
ISBN 978-1-4932-1723-6

https://www.sap-press.com/configuring-financial-accounting-in-sap-erp_4674/

Other Books by the Author

Title: SAP ERP: Quick Reference Guide
Edition: 2
Publisher: Mercury Learning & Information, 2020
ISBN: 1683920961, 9781683920960
Length: 500 pages

Title: SAP FI: Financial Accounting ERP ECC6, R/3 4.70
Edition: 2
Publisher: Mercury Learning & Information, 2017
ISBN: 1683921003, 9781683921004
Length: 350 pages

Title: SAP CO: Controlling
Edition: 2
Publisher: Mercury Learning & Information, 2017
ISBN: 168392102X, 9781683921028
Length: 350 pages

Title: Configuring Financial Accounting in SAP
Edition 2, illustrated
Publisher: Galileo Press, 2014 (SAP Press)
ISBN: 1493210424, 9781493210428
Length: 907 pages

Title: Implementing SAP ERP Financials: A Configuration Guide
Edition: 2
Publisher: Tata McGraw Hill Publishing Co Ltd, 2013
ISBN-13: 978-0-0701-4297-8
Length: 965 pages

Title: SAP FI Financial Accounting: SAP ERP ECC 6.0, SAP R/3 4.70
Author V. Narayanan
Edition: 1, illustrated, reprint
Publisher: Mercury Learning & Information, 2013
ISBN   1937585646, 9781937585648
Length   338 pages

Title: Customizing Financial Accounting in SAP
Edition: 1, illustrated
Publisher: Galileo Press, 2011 (SAP Press)
ISBN   1592293778, 9781592293773
Length 792 pages

Title: Mastering SAP CO: Controlling
Edition: 1, illustrated
Publisher: BPB Publications, 2007
ISBN: 9788183333344
Length: 297 pages

Title: SAP FI
Edition: 1, illustrated
Publisher: BPB Publications, 2010
ISBN: 9788183333238
Length: 302 pages

Title: SAP FI/CO Demystified
Edition: 1, illustrated
Publisher: BPB Publications, 2008
ISBN: 8183332315, 9788183332316
Length: 370 pages

Title: SAP® R/3® FI Transactions
Edition: 1, illustrated
Publisher: Jones & Bartlett Learning, 2007
ISBN: 1934015016, 9781934015018
Length: 530 pages

Title: Mastering SAP R/3 FI: Transaction Made Easy
Edition: 1, illustrated
Publisher: BPB Publications, 2007
ISBN: 8183331319, 9788183331319
Length: 472 pages